Night Hunters

Number 145

Williams-Ford Texas A&M University

Military History Series

Night Hunters

The AC-130s and Their Role in US Airpower

WILLIAM P. HEAD

TEXAS A&M UNIVERSITY PRESS

College Station

First edition
This paper meets the requirements of ANSI/NISO Z39.48-1992
(Permanence of Paper).
Binding materials have been chosen for durability.
♾

Cover: AC-130 painting by James Balletto.
Unless otherwise indicated, all photographs courtesy
78 Air Base Wing, History Office Archives.

Library of Congress Cataloging-in-Publication Data

Head, William P., 1949–
Night hunters : the AC-130s and their role in US airpower /
William P. Head.—First edition.
pages cm — (Williams-Ford Texas A&M University military
history series ; no. 145)
Includes bibliographical references and index.
ISBN 978-1-62349-118-5 (cloth : alk. paper)
ISBN 978-1-62349-119-2 (pbk. : alk. paper)
ISBN 978-1-62349-150-5 (e-book)
1. Spectre (Gunship)—History. 2. Air power—United States—
History—20th century. 3. Air power—United States—History—
21st century. 4. Vietnam War, 1961–1975—Aerial operations, American.
I. Title. II. Series: Williams-Ford Texas A&M University military history
series ; no. 145.
UG1242.G85H426 2014
358.4'283—dc23

2013040102

FROM WHENCE COMETH THE HUNTERS THAT FLY BY NIGHT?

And the enemy gathered among the trees and thickets hiding from our eyes.
They waited for what was to come as the sun set and darkness enveloped the world.
They looked to the heavens hoping to see a glimpse, but nothing could they foretell.
All around them the silence of the night, and then it struck and all was wreckage.
Where had it come from? What had it been? Was this a bolt from heaven or fire from hell?
As the chief gathered the survivors, he looked into their eyes and spotted only terror,
And, so, cried out, "From whence cometh the hunters that fly by night?"
Once more the phantom spit fire, and at last there was nothing, only the silence of the night.

—Bill Head, July 2011

Contents

Illustrations

Preface

Over the past decade I have written three accounts of fixed-wing gunships. The first, on the AC-47, appeared as an article in a scholarly military history journal. The second, on the AC-119G/Ks, was published in 2007 by Texas A&M University Press. Both were long, exhausting projects that left me ready to move on to something besides gunships. Then, in January 2008, I was honored to be invited by the 4th and 16th Special Operations Squadrons (4th SOS and 16th SOS), then both stationed at Hurlburt Field, Florida, to fly training missions with them. Although severe weather prevented or shortened the three missions I was scheduled to fly, I got to know the excellent young people who operate Air Force Special Operations Command's (AFSOC's) AC-130Hs and Us. It was following this enriching experience, and some initial research undertaken at Herb Mason's AFSOC History Office and Archives at Hurlburt Field, that I felt compelled, by respect for all those who have flown or continue to fly gunships, to complete the trilogy of the major US fixed-wing gunship models built by this nation since 1965.

I should mention that some information on the AC-47 and AC-119 gunships has been essentially repeated from my previous works and placed in the early chapters of this book. I did this in an effort to introduce the AC-130s and to make this text capable of standing alone as a general study of all American gunships. In this way readers will not have to have read my previous works in order to know how I got to this point. This seems only logical, since the AC-130U are currently the last reality of a long progression of new concepts and ideas begun by remarkable airmen such as Ron Terry beginning in the early 1960s.

No one completes a study of this magnitude without a lot of support, and I am no exception. Among the many who I need to thank are Herb Mason and Randy Bergeron of the AFSOC History Office; Lt. Gen. Tom Owen (then WR-ALC commander), who arranged my trip to Hurlburt Field; Maj. Gen. Clay T. McCutchan, USAF Reserve retired, chief of the Air Armament Center History Office (AAC HO); and Gen. Mike Wilson, who provided me with an extensive interview about the history of the AC-130s. These men are not only experts on the aircraft and how to use them, but General McCutchan is also a historian for the USAF. Of equal importance, he provided valuable editing and sage advice.

Among those who spent hours editing this beast were my long-suffering wife Randee and General McCutchan's colleague at AAC HO, Michael A. Klausutis, who spent weeks working on the manuscript to be sure it was factually correct. If I got it right, it was because of Mike. As always, Randee has done great work. Others who provided important edits and advice included my friend Dave Mets, my longtime colleague and associate Diane Truluck, and my friend Dennis Mills.

The cover painting was executed by renowned military aviation artist James Balletto, who was gracious enough to provide it to the author specifically for this book on the AC-130. It is an interpretation of a photograph of an AC-130 firing 25mm rounds at night targets during Operation Iraqi Freedom. Working from Blue Heron Studios in Warner Robins, Georgia, Jim has for many years produced important works of military aviation art and numerous other forms of artistic expression. I am honored by his willingness to produce such a stunning painting for this work.

Last, but not least, I want to thank SSgt. Keith Dormar, SMSgt. John O'Dell, and all the other men and women of the 16th SOS and 4th SOS who spent precious hours taking me around to see what I needed to see and explaining to me the important parts and functions of their unit and its weapon systems. Hats off to all of you and to anyone I forgot to mention.

Introduction

During the Vietnam War the US military found itself confronted by various enemy tactics, diverse geographic features, a difficult climate, and constantly wavering political and diplomatic circumstances. In an effort to circumvent these roadblocks to victory, it developed new tactics and weapon systems. The US Air Force developed new aircraft, munitions, and targeting and radar systems specifically for the challenges it faced. Some of these systems would later become part of the military technical revolution of the 1990s. Among them were laser-guided bombs (LGBs), better known today as precision-guided munitions (PGMs), forward-looking infrared (FLIR) imaging systems, and low-level light televisions (LLLTVs). Most important to this study was the development of fixed-wing gunships, specifically the AC-130. While other airframes and other kinds of close air support (CAS) and interdiction weapon systems preceded or flew with the AC-130s, this four-engine cargo airframe proved to be not only the longest-serving fixed-wing gunship, but also by far the most effective.

The AC-130's ability to transport heavier payloads at higher altitudes across longer distances made it the logical choice to be the final Vietnam-era fixed-wing gunship and the only one that continues to fly in the twenty-first century. It employed many of the most advanced weapons, sensors, targeting devices, and fire control systems of the 1970s or of any era. Experts eventually transformed a total of forty-seven C-130 or JC-130A airframes into gunships, the first one being the AC-130A prototype, which became the test bed for the Gunship II program. With the success of the prototype, engineers and technicians modified the seven remaining JC-130A space and missile recovery aircraft into what became known as Plain Janes. One special C-130A was modified into the Surprise Package, while ten other C-130As were converted under Project Pave Pronto, and eleven C-130Es were reconfigured into gunships during Project Pave Spectre. In the post-Vietnam era, ten of the eleven AC-130Es were modified to be AC-130Hs during Pave Spectre II. Between 1987 and 2004, seventeen AC-130Us or "U-Boats" were built from the ground up, making them the only gunships ever constructed from scratch and not melded onto an existing airframe. AC-130J/Ws are currently being built and deployed.

There is no way to understand why the US built gunships without first comprehending the nature of the Vietnam War and the history of the fixed-wing gunship. The United States Air Force (USAF) entered the Second Indochina

War as an organization in transition. After World War II, aviation technology entered into the jet age. On September 18, 1947, a separate US Air Force was born. By the 1950s, it was replete with a magnificent array of jets such as the F-86 Sabre and the F-100 Super Sabre. By the 1960s, other modern jet aircraft, such as the F-104 Starfighter, F-105 Thunderchief, and F-4 Phantom, were also in the active inventory. The Air Force also had new strategic jet bombers such as the B-47 Stratojet and B-52 Stratofortress, designed primarily to counter Soviet nuclear threats under the Single Integrated Operations Plan (SIOP) strategic strike capability. In the early 1960s, this policy of investing large amounts of money in strategic aerial weapons such as higher- and faster-flying supersonic jets and bigger and swifter long-range bombers began to change in earnest. As brushfire or guerilla wars erupted throughout the developing former colonial world, an increasing number of airmen began to examine methods of controlling these wars of national liberation and preventing the nations that emerged from falling into the arms of the Soviet Union. Within the Kennedy administration this was particularly true in the wake of the Cuban missile crisis of 1962, which nearly destroyed the world because both sides lacked the ability to initiate a measured response. Hoping to stem such potential nuclear confrontations in the future, policy makers began to move toward a more limited response to the spread of communism. However, within the Air Force many senior leaders believed that tactical fighters, most of which flew at supersonic speeds, would become the weapons of choice in these new-style wars. This was a vision that would evaporate as the circumstances of the Vietnam War evolved during the late 1960s.[1]

When the Air Force joined the war in Southeast Asia in the mid-1960s, airmen concluded that strategic bombers were not the decisive weapon their World War II predecessors believed they would become. Many wanted to prove the ultimate virtues of fast-moving fighters and fighter-bombers, while a few realized counterinsurgency battles could be best fought by slow-moving aircraft flying at lower altitudes and bristling with powerful rapid-fire guns. Their original weapons of choice were the A-1 Skyraider and the first fixed-wing gunship, the AC-47. The first air campaigns in Vietnam revolved around the White House–directed attacks on North Vietnam known as Rolling Thunder, which began on March 2, 1965 and lasted until March 1968, when President Lyndon B. Johnson, buffeted by domestic political setbacks and the embarrassment of the Tet Offensive, announced he would not run for reelection. Ironically, during that period, while the bulk of Allied air assets were committed to Rolling Thunder, the most successful air campaigns revolved around close air support by AC-47 gunships of US and Army of the Republic of Vietnam (ARVN) antiguerilla ground operations.[2]

Based on President Johnson and Secretary of Defense Robert McNamara's tactic of gradually escalating the military "quotient of pain" on enemy forces in both North and South Vietnam, Rolling Thunder evolved into a series of air attacks by jet fighters and fighter-bombers such as the F-105 and F-4. The operation was closely regulated by senior officials in the White House to the extent that pilots could attack only targets specifically approved by the president. Flying from bases in Thailand and supported by carrier-based aircraft from the Navy's Task Force 77, they flew sorties into thick concentrations of antiaircraft artillery (AAA), SA-2 surface-to-air missiles (SAMs), and MiG-17 and MiG-21 interceptors first in southern North Vietnam and later around the capital of Hanoi.[3]

For much of the campaign, high-value targets such as petroleum storage plants and power generators were off limits. At first, strikes were restricted to targets in southern North Vietnam just above the Demilitarized Zone (DMZ). In spite of Johnson's efforts to avoid controversy by limiting targets, by late 1966 some news articles went so far as to accuse the United States of deliberately attacking civilians. While those stories were untrue, normal collateral civilian casualties harmed the president's political reputation. Gradually, with pressure from senior military leaders, Johnson expanded the target area to include the capital city of Hanoi and Haiphong, North Vietnam's largest port.

Operations reached a peak in late 1967 when LBJ ordered strikes against the petroleum and power facilities. Years after the war, some observers argued that Rolling Thunder came very close to destroying the North's war economy in late 1967. Conversely, others still believe that the campaign never coordinated with any other operations on the ground or in the air in either the North or the South. They argued that because it took so long—specifically, six phases—to unfold and was delayed by seven bombing halts, the results were inconclusive.

Following Johnson's poor showing in the New Hampshire primaries and the shock of the enemy's Tet Offensive throughout South Vietnam in early 1968, on March 31 the president announced on national television he would not seek reelection. After several more months of less intense raids, Rolling Thunder officially came to an end on October 31, 1968. This was not, as time would prove, the end of the air war. Between 1968 and 1973, air power covered the American withdrawal from Southeast Asia. Operations Commando Hunt I–VII sought to prevent communist troops and supplies from crossing the border into South Vietnam. Operation Linebacker I countered the effects of the North Vietnamese Army's (NVA's) Easter Offensive of March 1972, and Linebacker II, or the Christmas Bombings of December 1972, helped convince the Hanoi regime to sign the Paris Peace Accords of January 27, 1973.[4]

As for the fixed-wing gunship, its role in the air war blossomed at the very moment the US war effort was moving from tactical air assets flying strategic missions in the North to more low and slow aircraft to support US and ARVN ground forces attempting to solidify and secure the government of South Vietnam. While the AC-47 had been in Vietnam since the US escalation of its participation in the war, its follow-on cousins, the AC-119s and AC-130s, were supposed to augment and ultimately replace the AC-47s prior to any major enemy ground attacks such as the one that became known as the Tet Offensive. However, internal service politics delayed the appearance of the larger gunships and eventually, instead of being part of a pre-1968 offensive against enemy insurgents, as had been the original intention, the fixed-wing gunships became a key component in covering the United States' withdrawal from Vietnam.

While there are significant books and articles already published regarding all three of the major fixed-wing gunship iterations, including two of my own, and while it is not my intention to reintroduce material from those works, it is necessary to start from the beginning in order to provide a thorough and complete history of the AC-130. I could be arrogant enough to refer the reader to my own publications on the AC-47 and AC-119 and cover only the history of the AC-130, but if this work is to stand alone, as I think it should, then I believe it should begin with the history of fixed-wing gunships and the Vietnam War and review the history of the earlier gunships before we wade full torso into the history of the AC-130s. It is from this perspective that the remainder of this book intends to unfold.

1 The Origins of the US Fixed-Wing Gunships in Vietnam

Experts disagree as to the origins of fixed-wing gunships. Some argue that the concept originated with mail or supply deliveries in the Australian Outback or Amazon jungles, where remote settlers or missionaries were delivered their mail and provisions by small, usually open-cockpit, aircraft. Rather than land and take off dozens of times a day or risk remote landings, pilots buzzed the home or settlement to make sure someone was there, by rope lowered a mail sack or bucket with supplies to near the ground, then initiated a shallow orbit overhead. If the flyer could affect a perfect orbit, the sack or bucket would stay still in the center of the orbit for those on the ground to safely approach it, remove their letters or supplies, and insert their outgoing mail or requests for more provisions.[1]

The first real application of the notion of a military side-firing, fixed-wing gunship surfaced in the Royal Air Force (RAF) in early 1926. Other European nations soon followed suit. The first American venture into this new kind of aircraft came later in the same year, when 1st Lt. Fred Nelson conducted experiments with a de Havilland DH-4 at Brooks Field, Texas. He mounted a .30-caliber Lewis gun on the wing and flew pylon turns, constantly focusing his line of fire on a single ground target. While the tests were successful, and more tests were conducted, the overall program remained experimental throughout the 1930s and 1940s.[2] As Ron Terry, who would become America's primary gunship expert, notes, "Most combat planners felt that 'military aircraft should dive at the ground, drop bombs and shoot guns. They don't fly in circles.'" And so the concept remained in hibernation in the United States.[3]

In the meantime, during the summer of 1932, French Air

Service designers installed a side-firing Schneider P.D. 12.75mm cannon on a Bordelaise A.B. 22 four-engine bomber for use in their far-flung colonies of Southeast Asia and Africa. As Col. Walter Boyne writes in one of his articles on gunships, "One [of these colonies], ironically enough, would become the venue for US gunships—Indochina."[4]

It is also important to recall that the technical views that held dominance at the time believed that bigger bombers that could carry more bombs and wipe out whole cities were the wave of the future. In the late 1920s and early 1930s most bombers were, in fact, as fast as, if not faster than, open-cockpit fighters. It was the German, Italian, Japanese, and British aircraft manufacturers who, by the mid-1930s, began to change this relationship. The advent of the Me-109, Spitfire, and Mitsubishi Zero meant that fighters could fly at 350 to 400 mph and fight in sharp turns and fast dives that made bombers such as the B-17 appear to be standing still.[5]

Within the languishing US military of the 1930s there was a growing intra- and interservice rivalry between its ground officers and its air officers and between the Army and the Navy air arms for single control of the air component. With US military leaders squabbling among themselves and military airmen having a much different vision of air combat, the concept of orbiting gun platforms was anathema to them. It simply did not fit into their plans, and it did not advance the aviators' vision of separating themselves from their ground brethren. Indeed, the airmen believed gunships would be primarily a ground support function that might very well help keep them under the traditional Army structure and prevent the evolution to a separate service.

Ten years later, US airmen resurrected the concept to deal with German submarines lurking off the US coast. In April 1942, 1st Lt. Gilmour Craig MacDonald of the 95th Coast Artillery advocated fixing a side-firing machine gun to a Piper Cub for use in antisubmarine operations. While senior officers embraced the idea, it soon faded away as the Allies used other weapons, such as blimps and long-range bombers, to win the Battle of the North Atlantic. However, MacDonald clung to his belief in the gunship, and as a lieutenant colonel in the 1960s he and others would revive the concept.[6]

Why Use the C-47 Airframe?

While later versions of the fixed-wing gunship played a major role in US air war, the original version introduced in 1965 was the AC-47D. In many respects no group of aircraft is more representative of the Vietnam War than the gunships. They bear out the old adage that necessity is the mother of invention. This was particularly true of the early days when the AC-47s were used in a counterinsurgency role. This first gunship model was built on the pre–World War II C-47 Skytrain, Dakota, or "Gooney Bird" airframe. Designed and manufactured by Douglas Aircraft Company in the mid-1930s, the C-47 or DC-3 cargo transport was the successor of Douglas's first all-metal commercial aircraft, the DC-2. Following a series of upgrades to the DC-2, the resulting DC-3 became one of the most prolific and successful aircraft of its type. The C-47D was the last and most successful of the military models of the DC-3. During the World War II production run that ended in 1946, workers in Santa Monica and Long Beach, California, and Oklahoma City, Oklahoma, produced 10,926 of these aircraft.[7]

By 1965, as US troop commitments increased in Vietnam, more than one hundred C-47s still remained in the Air Force inventory, making it, at the time, the oldest operational aircraft still flying for the service. With a maximum air speed of 160 miles per hour, cargo capacity of 31,000 pounds, range of 1,600 miles, and service ceiling of 24,000 feet, the C-47 seemed to be obsolete. However, when ground commanders began to look for some kind of CAS weapon that could fly low and slow, several bright airmen like MacDonald and Terry hit on the idea of modifying the old bird to fly the CAS mission required to find and destroy enemy insurgents in the three-canopy jungles of Vietnam.[8]

This was especially true since early in the Vietnam War the Viet Cong (VC) guerillas were the main enemy, and the Allies faced little or no AAA fire or enemy aircraft south of the DMZ. This meant that the AC-47s could cover the movements of enemy ground troops in South Vietnam with impunity. As the communists introduced more and better AAA, the lethality of the battlefield environment increased, forcing a modification in US tactics regarding the use of fixed-wing gunships.

The US Fixed-Wing Side-Firing Gunship as a Concept

Before there was a fixed-wing side-firing gunship, there had to be a reason to create one and a concept of what it would be and do. Col. Ron Terry, USAF (Ret.), who became America's fixed-wing gunship godfather, said, in looking back at the creation of the gunship, that "the gunships have been one of the most 'effective things the United States has had for engagements in Panama, Grenada and Afghanistan.'" One could add "Desert Storm," Haiti, and Iraq to that list. Clearly, the first really successful gunship airframe was the C-47.[9]

While the first C-47s deployed to Vietnam in March 1963 for troop transport, cargo airlift, and medical evacuation, it was not long until the Air Force began to focus on the idea of a fixed-wing gunship for the brushfire war in Southeast Asia. Ultimately, fifty-three of the C-47s were converted into gunships, each featuring three side-firing rotating 7.62mm Gatling guns. Allied forces employed what they eventually called Spooky, or "Puff the Magic Dragon" to suppress enemy attacks against US Army Special Forces (Green Berets) outposts or firebases. Circling slowly in a banked turn, the AC-47 covered the ground with deadly, rapid, saturating fire. Employing at first flare capabilities and later night sensors, Puffs also proved effective against night targets.[10]

When the US Air Force began to reinvestigate the virtues of side-firing gunships in the early 1960s, they realized that the planes had advantages beyond those first envisioned. The slow-flying aircraft could execute a protracted pylon-turn that allowed the guns on the side of the plane to be aimed at a ground target for a long period of time while the airplane maintained a constant altitude, slant angle, and range. This provided the aircraft with a high degree of aiming accuracy due to the extended slant ranges and allowed crews ample time to operate sensors and remain focused on the target. It afforded crews the ability to put a saturating fire on the target area and reduce aircraft exposure to enemy small arms and automatic weapon fire, since targets could be identified and attacked without descending to lower altitudes where enemy weapons were more effective. It also reduced the chance of over-flying the target. One unintended benefit proved to be the high angle of the bullet trajectory, which increased the accuracy, lethality, and reliability of the guns. From an operational and developmental standpoint, the fixed-wing, side-firing gunship proved to be a triumph of good old Yankee know-how.[11]Lieutenant Colonel MacDonald submitted the basic design to a Tactical Air Command (TAC) panel of experts on September 14, 1961, in a paper entitled, "Transverse Firing of Rockets and Guns." Almost concurrently, and totally separately, Maj. Ralph Flexman of the Air Force Reserve, assistant chief engineer with the Bell Aerosystems Company, was developing a similar theory based on stories he had heard about the South American missionary Nate Saint. As noted earlier, Saint delivered mail and supplies to remote villages by lowering a bucket tied to the end of a rope from his slow-flying aircraft. As the plane circled in a steep pylon turn, the bucket remained in one spot over the ground. Flexman conceived of a line of fire instead of the rope. To this end, he believed he could employ side-firing guns in a transport aircraft that could be aimed by the pilot at a ground target as long as the plane orbited in a steep bank. Like MacDonald, Flexman submitted his plans and drawings for the conversion of a C-47, but nothing happened for several months.[12]

In late 1961, Flexman met MacDonald at Eglin AFB, Florida, and after comparing notes, Flexman submitted a formal proposal to Dr. Gordon A. Eckstrand of the Behavioral Sciences Laboratory, Wright-Patterson AFB, Ohio.

In 1962, one of the doctor's colleagues, Capt John C. Simons, Aeronautical Systems Division (ASD), Air Force Systems Command (AFSC), forwarded the plan to the Aerospace Medical Research Laboratory and the counterinsurgency unit, Wright-Patterson AFB, as part of Project Tailchaser. While some officials in both the Air Force and Army expressed interest in the concept, when it came to senior Air Force leadership, the whole idea of fixed-wing gunships seemed to be swimming upstream against a very strong current of institutional bias that favored supersonic aircraft. As Colonel Boyne notes, "Many people believed that a side-firing aircraft, particularly the C-47, would be too vulnerable to enemy fire. There was also doctrinal concern that use of a fixed-wing gunship was playing into the hands of the Army, which was becoming dependent upon the helicopter gunship."[13]

The increasing US involvement in the Vietnam conflict changed things. In addition, the involvement of then captain Ronald W. Terry made all the difference in the history of the gunship. Terry, working with 1st Lt. Edwin Sazaki, demonstrated the potential of the gunship and literally resurrected it from its in-basket purgatory. According to Boyne, "Terry brought a unique combination of skills to the program. He had great common sense; while using existing technology, he kept his eye on the latest developments to improve the system." Further, "Terry was able to work the bureaucracy to his advantage, finding those who could say yes to his program and avoiding those who might say no." Ultimately, he was one of the few developers who created a new weapon system "and tested it in combat himself."[14]

As Terry worked on the gunships back home, Air Force leaders in Vietnam were supporting strategic hamlets against the VC using jet fighters that flew at speeds of up to 864 mph for the F-100 and 1,372 mph for the F-105. For close air support, aircraft needed to fly at much slower speeds between 250 to 550 knots (288 and 633 mph). The F-100 and F-105 were never designed to perform best at low altitudes and slow speeds. A combination of difficult terrain features and munitions much less accurate than those to be developed in the 1980s and 1990s made it necessary for these jets to fly at greatly reduced speeds, for which they were not designed. The result was that they missed far more targets than they hit. This had tragic consequences in several early ground engagements such as the Ia Drang Valley, when F-100s accidently bombed their own forces, in some cases with napalm. Not only was speed an issue, but also these jets were designed to fly at higher altitudes, making location of mobile targets under the jungle canopy nearly impossible. Compounding the problem was the fact that there were too many hamlets and not enough fighter aircraft, most of which did not have night or bad-weather capabilities.[15]

In late 1963, Terry, by now assigned to the Flight Test Section, ASD, AFSC, visited Southeast Asia as part of a Systems Command team studying requirements for a limited war operations plan. In evaluating the CAS problem, he reviewed Flexman's study on lateral sighting and firing. This became the basis for follow-on studies that led to the development of the side-firing gun system. In the meantime, Captain Simons pushed through a modest test program that verified the possibility of a pilot tracking a target during a pylon turn. He flew unofficial sorties in a T-28 without guns or sights, using a grease pencil to mark the canopy and validate the flying pattern. In August 1964 Capts. J. D. Boren and J. A. Bert accompanied more sophisticated missions on a Convair C-131/T-29 Samaritan flown by Capt. Edwin J. Hatzenbuehler. At first they used cameras instead of guns and fixed the target with a gunsight built by SSgt. Estell P. Bunch. Later, flying over the Gulf of Mexico and using a 7.62mm Gatling gun, the aircraft exceeded all targeting expectations.[16]

In spite of a lack of funds, Terry and his colleagues continued on with their work in the facilities at Wright-Patterson AFB. That summer events began to break in their favor. Terry spoke to an AFSC team that had spent considerable time researching the tactics of the VC when they attacked Green Berets outposts and Vietnamese hamlets. One aspect that caught his attention was the effective use of C-47 and C-123 flare ships in lighting the nighttime jungle floor and directing accurate fire support.[17]

In September 1964, ASD's Flight Test Section recommended Flexman's basic gunship concept to the Air Force deputy for limited war. War planners embraced the system and soon began tests at Edwards AFB, California, with Terry piloting the modified aircraft, C-47D, tail number (T/N) 44-8462, known as *Terry and the Pirates*. The final test configuration included three side-firing 7.62mm miniguns, each capable of firing six thousand rounds per minute. Test personnel now made plans to present the results to the Air Staff.[18]

With his plans and drawings complete, Terry decided to seek an audience with the chief of staff of the Air Force (CSAF), Gen. Curtis E. LeMay. As Terry recalled, the briefing was set up, and he was directed to "talk about how effective the system would be in attacking VC forces in the open before they got away." Ironically, the briefing just before Terry's was about how successful the VC sapper and mortar attack had been on Air Force assets at Ton Son Nhut AB in South Vietnam. According to Terry, that briefing had caused the general to chew through three cigars. Still, it proved a perfect introduction. Terry opened by saying, "I am here to brief you on a new concept for air base defense in Vietnam." That got LeMay's attention. "He listened and asked the three-stars next to him what they thought—none of them liked it, except one general who said, 'General, this may revolutionize air warfare.'" LeMay asked how many miniguns were available. We told him there were prototypes, and he said, "'Okay, take them to Vietnam and try it out.' We were on our way."[19]

Terry and his team shipped three conversion kits to Bien Hoa AB, where in-theater mechanics modified two C-47 aircraft into "fighter cargo" FC-47 gunships. The two C-47Ds were T/Ns 43-48578 and 43-48579, even then known as Puff the Magic Dragon, or just "Puff." Each prototype had three General Electric miniguns; a Mark 20 Mod 4 sight from an A-1E Skyraider; VHF/UHF/FM radios; tactical air navigation (TACAN) sensors; identification friend or foe (IFF) sensors; forty-five flares, each with 200,000 candlepower; and twenty-four thousand rounds of ammunition.

On November 2, 1964, Terry presented a gunship progress report to General LeMay. The general was so impressed that he ordered the prototype FC-47 in Vietnam to undergo more extensive combat tests. Terry and his group returned to Vietnam on December 1, and on December 15 the aircraft flew its first daytime mission, with Capt. Jack Harvey as aircraft commander. The crew soon demonstrated that the FC-47 was all they had said it was. The Systems Division crews flew over fifty-two combat missions, reporting that the aircraft combined endurance with an exceptionally high rate of fire that proved particularly valuable in dispersing enemy night attacks.[20]

Throughout this process, the major opponents of fixed-wing gunship development were Army leaders who embraced the helicopter gunship and resented Air Force "intrusions" into their area of military aviation. Even so, Terry and his colleagues received another shot in the arm from the Air Force vice chief of staff, soon to be chief of staff, Gen. John P. McConnell, who told his Army counterparts, "We cannot overlook or deny any weapon which will enhance our capability in this area of operations . . . [and] it is certainly in the Air Force's interests to run the program rather than sit on the sideline commenting!"[21]

On December 23–24, 1964, during the FC-47s' first night sorties in the Mekong Delta, they destroyed a massed VC attack on an ARVN and US Army Special Forces firebase. The gunships provided the crews a firing platform that passed slowly over the targets and, at the same time, had the capacity to carry enough ordnance to blunt the attack of a large force. Even the earliest test results had been impressive enough to convince the Air Staff to approve the full-scale production program on December 11, 1964. In retrospect, MacDonald had been the originator of the fixed-wing gunship, while Flexman had been the catalyst, Simons the tester, and Terry the seller.[22]

Not long after the FC-47 began flying missions, officials changed the designation to AC-47, which had much to do with internal Air Force sensibilities. When members of the Air Force fighter world discovered that the old Gooney

Bird had been designated the FC-47, they went nuts. To avert a fraternal controversy, leaders redesignated the C-47 gunship an attack aircraft; thus, A replaced F.[23]

The AC-47 Gunships Evolve

Throughout these early stages the gunships continued to evolve. Sensor technology lagged behind, so the first FC-47s and first production AC-47s did not have very good low-light or low-visibility capability. Most night raids depended on dropping parachute flares and identifying enemy targets visually. This method was fraught with danger for both the low-flying aircraft and friendly ground troops who might easily be mistaken by crews as enemy infantry. As one former gunship commander noted, "Dense foliage and camouflage made target detection difficult in the daytime and afforded the enemy the advantage of tracking and firing at the large, slow gunship. This he did with disconcerting frequency and accuracy." As a result, officials shifted AC-47 operations to the night, which made visual target acquisition even more difficult. It was at this point that AC-47 crews first began to employ parachute flares. Later gunships, such as the AC-119 and AC-130, incorporated better sensors and illuminating devices, which improved targeting. The larger gunships also were able to carry more sensors and operators as well as loiter over the target longer.[24]

During that period designers and crews constantly worked on targeting and illumination issues. They ultimately solved these problems in later gunship models by installing fire-control systems involving computers that provided aiming and guidance information to the pilot. The onboard computer interpreted data inputs from each sensor and created a line of sight to a designated point. It also analyzed wind factors and actual airspeed and altitude and then compared the line of sight with the corrected gun line. This afforded the pilot with the best position and altitude guidance information through an instrument landing system indicator and a gun sight. In many ways the AC-47 became not only a combat weapon but also a test bed for later gunships, which were larger and faster, had greater range, and possessed more firepower and sophisticated avionics but could still land and launch from small airfields.[25]

Initially, aircrews employed the AC-47 in a CAS role during search and destroy operations, which focused on killing enemy ground personnel. This role expanded with the introduction of later gunship models. Some deemed it the perfect close air support weapon. In a 1970 *Air University Review* article, Lt. Col. Ross Hamlin wrote that in Vietnam the gunship "had achieved a reputation for its responsiveness, fire support, battlefield illumination and surveillance, convoy escort, airmobile operations and search and rescue operations." Hamlin and others believed that gunship roles could be expanded to include forward air control (FAC) and interdiction missions, to include destruction of railroads, highways, bridges, ferries, harbor facilities, marshaling yards, truck parks, supply depots, petroleum, oil, and lubricant (POL) sources, vehicle repair shops, and other hard points as well as night and daylight destruction of individual transport vehicles, boats, troops, and tracked vehicles.[26]

Even as the AC-47 progressed from prototype to the operational phase, there were Air Force leaders who opposed putting it into production. On March 20, 1965, the commander-in-chief, Pacific Air Forces (CINCPACAF) asked the Air Staff to approve the use of sixteen C-131/T-29 transport aircraft fitted with GAU-2B/A 7.62mm side-firing miniguns. Air Staff members considered the request, but on May 12, 1965, after reading the FC-47 combat test results, they selected the C-47 airframe as the single gunship airframe for production. However, they did adopt the PACAF recommendation to install three GAU-2B/A trackless automatic miniguns in each of the twenty aircraft initially chosen for modification. They assigned Air Force Logistics Command (AFLC) and ASD personnel to perform a feasibility study to determine the time, nature and cost of the reconfiguration process. On May 17, AFLC officials delegated overall project management to the Warner Robins Air Materiel Area (WRAMA) located at Robins AFB, Georgia. Most of the C-47 airframes were obtained from the Air Force "boneyard" at Davis-Monthan AFB, Arizona.[27]

The Modification Process Begins

On June 18, 1965, workers completed the modification of four AC-47s, using interim .30-caliber machine guns, for immediate action with the 2nd Air Division in Vietnam. Concurrently, PACAF officials notified the Air Staff that the new aircraft would require seventy-nine additional officers and 250 enlisted personnel. Experts also proposed that once there were enough GAU-2B/A miniguns on hand, they be installed on all new production AC-47s and retrofitted on the four original aircraft. A month later, on July 17, Air Force officials approved procurement modification requirement (M/R) 1445 (FS-1729/C-47) directing that twenty-six C-47 aircraft be modified by November 7, 1965. This was an increase of six from the original quantity. Of this number, sixteen were to be sent to PACAF units and six to TAC, and four were to be used for command support and advanced attrition. Each aircraft was eventually to be equipped with the GAU-2B/A 7.62mm miniguns.[28]

On July 19 the WRAMA Directorate of Procurement and Production received modification work order WOP6C-14, designated Operation Big Shoot, from AFLC. On July 27, WRAMA awarded contract AF09 (603)60452 to Air International Inc., Miami, Florida, to reconfigure the twenty-six C-47s. Under the provisions of the contract, initial delivery was scheduled to begin on August 29, with the delivery of one aircraft every two days thereafter until completion on October 15, 1965. Additional requirements agreed on during production delayed the delivery of the first aircraft by ten days. By the completion of the eighth aircraft, however, the program was back on schedule, and it concluded on time.[29]

Between April 1966 and February 1967, amendments were made to the contract which called for the modification of fourteen more aircraft as well as camouflage paint and red eyebrow instrument lights for all AC-47s deployed to Vietnam. This essentially ended the first phase of the contract at a total cost of $5,669,100. The second phase began on June 16, 1967, when Air Force officials approved a Pacific Air Forces (PACAF) request for five more AC-47s. These aircraft, designated for advanced attrition in Vietnam, were also modified by Air International.[30]

The program cost $6.7 million and was officially completed when the fifty-third AC-47 rolled off the assembly line on January 5, 1968. In its final form, the AC-47 had two Pratt and Whitney R-1830-90-D piston engines, each producing twelve hundred horsepower; a wingspan of 95 feet, length of 64 feet 4 inches, and height of 16 feet 10 inches; a maximum speed of 230 mph, ceiling of 24,000 feet, range of 2,125 miles, and load capacity of 7,500 pounds; and three GAU-2B/A 7.62mm miniguns as part of the side-firing MXU-470/A gun module that was capable of firing three thousand to six thousand rounds per minute. It flew with a standard crew of seven and had a maximum gross take-off weight of 33,000 pounds. The enemy called this lethal new weapon "the death dragon that flies at night." To the Allies it was exactly the CAS weapon they had been looking for—that is, as long as the enemy had nothing that could shoot it down. In 1965, they did not.[31]

AC-47 Operations

On July 9, 1965, the Joint Chiefs of Staff (JCS) ordered the deployment of an operational AC-47 unit no later than November 7. Three days later, TAC formed the 4th Air Commando Squadron (ACS), whose primary mission was to direct fire against enemy ground forces in support of Allied ground operations, provide flare ship support, and assist any other assigned mission. Officials activated the 4th ACS on August 5, 1965, and four days later, with the arrival of the first sixteen AC-47s, the crews began training at Forbes AFB, Kansas. They departed for Tan Son Nhut AB, Republic of Vietnam, on November 14. Upon arrival, they were assigned to the 2nd Air Division (later the Seventh Air Force) and placed under the 6250th Combat Support Group. Spooky began operations on January 24, 1966, in support of the 1st Air Cavalry Division and US Marine units carrying out search and destroy operations in Binh Dinh and Quang Ngai Provinces. Flying one hundred mostly night missions until March 10, 1966, they inflicted heavy casualties on main-force VC and People's Army of Vietnam (PAVN) regulars.[32]

Air Force personnel flew thousands of AC-47 sorties over the next three years, especially during the Tet Offensive of 1968, the siege of Khe Sanh, and even in support of early Commando Hunt operations designed to cut off enemy supplies entering South Vietnam. By the time the Air Force transferred the AC-47s to the Vietnamese Air Force (VNAF) on December 1, 1969, they had lost twelve of the forty-seven gunships deployed to Southeast Asia. They had flown five thousand combat missions inflicting seventy-five thousand enemy casualties and destroying hundreds of vehicles and thousands of tons of supplies. However, the experiences of the AC-47 highlighted its limitations as well. It lacked firepower, range, loiter time, and the ability to destroy increasing numbers of trucks pouring down the Ho Chi Minh Trail. As a result, Air Force officials looked for new kinds of airframes upon which to build a new, more lethal gunship that would meet the ever-changing needs of the Allied forces in Vietnam.[33]

2 The AC-119G/K Gunship Program
An Overview

Although not originally intended, the second major production model gunship deployed to Vietnam was the AC-119G, followed by the AC-119K. Air Force leaders never meant for Shadow and Spectre to replace Spooky, but airframe availability and Washington politics made it so. The AC-130 was initially designated to replace Puff, and the AC-130A prototype did fly several dozen combat test missions in 1967, long before the AC-119s deployed. But numerous internal disagreements among senior Defense Department officials caused the AC-130 program to be delayed. As a result, the AC-119 evolved into a spur-of-the-moment solution that leaders such as Secretary of the Air Force (SECAF) Harold Brown believed would rapidly augment the AC-47s. Thus, while the C-119 was the third major airframe designated for conversion into a gunship, it became the second one to go into full-scale production.

Like the C-47, the C-119 was a vintage cargo/transport aircraft. Originally built in the 1950s by Fairchild-Hiller Aircraft Inc., Saint Augustine, Florida, it had a checkered career as a transport. In 1967 it was dragged out of reserve duty to augment the AC-47 and prototype AC-130A as well as act as a bridge between the AC-47's retirement and the activation of the production AC-130As. In the end, Fairchild-Hiller reconfigured fifty-two, making it the most numerous replacement gunship model ever built. Plans called for the AC-119 to assume convoy escort, hamlet defense, and CAS duties from Spooky. It did these jobs well. While it never could kill trucks as effectively as the AC-130 models could, and, the G model proved in some ways only a minor improvement over the AC-47s, the K models were truly lethal interdiction weapons. The K model added increased engine power with two J-85 jet engines that supplemented its two propeller engines. It also had greater firepower with the addition of two 20mm Gatling guns to the G model's four 7.62mm miniguns, an improved fire control system, and a forward-looking infrared (FLIR) system. The AC-119G proved a worthy successor to the AC-47 for missions in South Vietnam, while the K models not only complemented the AC-130's interdiction efforts but more than held their own along the Ho Chi Minh Trail.[1]

Leaders designated the modification program Project Combat Hornet. Fairchild-Hiller converted twenty-six C-119Gs to AC-119Gs at their plant in Saint Augustine, incorporating four 7.62mm SUU-11A/1A minigun pods, later replaced by General Electric MXU-470 minigun modules. They also fitted the G models with high-tech equipment that included the AVQ-8 twenty kilowatt xenon light, night observation systems (NOSs), LAU-74A flare launchers, armor, and electronic countermeasure (ECM) equipment. Given the call sign Shadow, the Gs were initially assigned to the 71st Air Commando Squadron (later in 1969 the 71st SOS) and later the 17th SOS, which was part of the 14th Special Operations Wing (14th SOW). Fairchild also reconfigured twenty-six C-119s into AC-119Ks by attaching J-85-GE-17 jet engines under the aircraft's wings. The Ks incorporated even better high-tech radars, avionics, and electronic countermeasures as well as two M61A1 20mm Gatling guns. The first AC-119Ks were delivered on November 3, 1969 to the 18th SOS, also part of the 14th SOW. Its call sign was Stinger.[2]

A Brief Background of the AC-119

Fairchild-Hiller designed and produced the C-119 Flying Boxcar as a substantial upgrade and modification of its C-82 Packet. The first C-119 flight was on November 1, 1947, and, by the time the last of ten versions rolled off the assembly line in October 1955, eleven hundred of them had been produced. The C-119 aircraft were particularly distinctive because of their twin tail booms, which came forward alongside the fuselage and attached to the wings where the engines continued in front of the wing. The aircraft became TAC's primary in-theater troop transport, its main paratroop drop aircraft, and its number one aerial resupply aircraft during the Korean War. In spite of its remarkable service, by the end of the war the Air Force was looking for a replacement. Among those companies vying to build this upgrade was Lockheed, which had already begun the development of the C-130. As ever-growing numbers of C-130s rolled off the assembly line, the C-119s slowly migrated to the Air Force Reserve troop carrier wings.[3]

While a fascinating story, the modification of the C-119s into gunships has been covered in detail in other major works. However, it is worth repeating that the AC-119 was seen as a stopgap measure designed to take as little time as possible to reconfigure. For this and other reasons, such as internal expertise, Fairchild-Hiller's choice to modify the C-119 and make it an AC-119G or K seemed to be logical. Another key factor to selecting the airframe was SECAF Brown's support for the AC-119 and his desire to fill the need for more gunships as quickly as possible. There also proved to be another reason why officials selected the C-119. Hundreds of C-119s were available in storage and not being used. At the same time, the C-130 was the key component of the Air Force's tactical airlift function, and it did not want to spare any of its aircraft for reconfiguration into anything, especially a fixed-wing gunship. Many Air Force officers, trained in the world of heavy bombers and fast jets, opposed the entire notion of using the C-130 or any other "trash hauler" to make an attack aircraft.[4]

After a protracted debate within the upper levels of the Air Force and Department of Defense (DOD), the AC-119 program began. On June 8, 1967, Harold Brown officially selected the C-119 airframe as the gunship to immediately follow the AC-47. He directed that the more numerous G models be immediately modified, but if production or testing indicated a need for K models, they be added to the reconfiguration program as soon as practical. In turn, on August 10, Secretary of Defense Robert McNamara approved the transfer of forty-six Air Force Reserve C-119G aircraft and equivalent crews to active duty for the purpose of converting the aircraft to gunships and then deploying them to Southeast Asia.[5]

As one expert noted, "Though approved in 1967, the AC-119 gunship program progressed at a snail's pace. Modification scheduling slipped due to major funding problems. Mr. McNamara's hesitant approval to release C-119 airframes, and changes in plans for equipment [meant that] all hope for an early AC-119 deployment rapidly vanished."[6] Among the reasons for the delay was the insistence of some senior Air Force officials that they focus gunship funds on the AC-130, which had begun prior to the AC-119 program with the construction of a single AC-130A. While originally opposed to converting C-130s into gunships, by August 1967 both Seventh Air Force commander Gen. William W. "Spike" Momyer and CINCPACAF Gen. John D. Ryan had changed their minds, since the C-130 aircraft then being proposed for conversion were JC-130s, which had already been altered for space vehicle rescue and recovery and were not being used for airlift.[7]

On November 7, 1967, Brown agreed to authorize the modification of two JC-130As. In turn, leaders such as Ryan, Momyer, and CSAF John P. McConnell seized on this opportunity to get Brown's approval to modify the remaining five JC-130s. The earlier success of the AC-130 prototype tests provided

McConnell with compelling evidence to argue decisively in favor of filling out the AC-130 fleet under the Shed Light program. He also supported the continuation of the AC-119 project, but with the immediate addition of the K model being held in reserve.[8]

While everyone involved in this senior-level wrestling match argued their point with the best interest of the nation at heart, it only served to delay the vital stopgap AC-119 program. However, it is important to remember that these generals served during a time when the Air Force was still a new service and was in a constant struggle for resources with the Army and Navy. With their experiences in the immediate post–World War II and Korean War time frame, jets seemed to be the wave of the future. Vietnam presented them with a unique tactical situation, and while there were still some aerial dogfights, and some were even historic, they were not on the scale of either Korea or World War II. Especially early in the war, the most pressing need for Allied air power was to attack ground targets in South Vietnam. Once Rolling Thunder began, air power took on a more conventional role. This was not even its major role, and, once that bombing campaign ended, it was another three years before conventional roles returned in terms of tactical and strategic combat missions. Jet fighters and fighter-bombers often struggled in operations over North Vietnam, and they were not even as effective in the South. It was left to a handful of fixed-wing gunships built on airframes of aged cargo aircraft to do the job that was needed in the place where the war would ultimately be won or lost.[9]

As 1967 came to a close, the success of the AC-130A combat test convinced Secretary Brown to create a mixed gunship force, with AC-119s supplementing AC-47s until the AC-130s could be deployed. To this end, on December 20, 1967, Brown formally approved the modification of the remaining five JC-130As. He declared that the AC-130s would provide a proactive aerial interdiction force having improved night and all-weather capabilities as well as increased survivability in high-threat environments. He also announced his support for the AC-119 program. In this way, Brown aimed to please all of his senior officers and, at the same time, quickly fill the need for more gunships in South Vietnam. He also hoped to remove the last hurdle from the initiation of both the Gunship II and Gunship III programs. On January 26, 1968, ASD delivered a report to Brown that provided test data supporting a mixed gunship force comprised of thirty-two AC-119s for combat operations, twenty AC-119s for training and attrition, and, eventually, the prototype AC-130A and the seven modified JC-130As. The report concluded that AC-119 reconfiguration should begin immediately in order to have a positive impact on the war in Vietnam as soon as possible.[10]

Based on the report, the SECAF planned to deploy the thirty-two AC-119s in two squadrons and place them under the 14th Air Commando Wing (14th ACW). He envisioned stationing them at six bases—Nha Trang, DaNang, Phu Cat, Pleiku, Phan Rang, Bien Hoa, and Binh Thuy—so they could be on twenty-four-hour alert. They would also be under Seventh Air Force command support and operational control. At this point, officials predicted that production G models would cost $16.2 million and K models $68.7 million.[11]

Building the G Models

Late in September 1967, work began on modifying a single C-119G aircraft into a prototype gunship. With growing support among senior Air Force officers for the AC-130, most AFLC leaders did not believe the Gunship III program would last beyond the construction of this prototype. Since Brown seemed to be the only DOD policy maker who favored what by the end of 1967 had become a dual replacement program, AFLC sought to save money by executing the prototype project, named Combat Hornet, as slowly as possible. For that reason they never acknowledged the informational messages from Air Force headquarters seeking a replacement for the AC-47. Neither did they believe that Brown, pressured as he was, would stand by his initial decision to modify the C-119G. By August 1967, Secretary McNamara had approved Brown's request to transfer forty-six Air Force Reserve C-119s to the active inventory for gunship modification.[12]

Just after Thanksgiving 1967, following Brown's formal approval for the expansion of the AC-130 project, Shed Light, Gen. Bruce Holloway, Air Force vice chief of staff, publicly announced that the AC-47 would be retired in favor of the new AC-119s and AC-130s. Holloway also predicted that the bigger gunships would begin phasing in during early 1968. This announcement appeared in major news media throughout the United States and seemed to confirm, once and for all, the SECAF's determination to implement a dual replacement program.[13]

Since most managers at Warner Robins had not been privy to the high-level debate, they were caught off-guard. In spite of that, their workforce moved ahead with the Gunship III project, and on October 20, 1967, officials in the Air Force Directorate of Maintenance Engineering (USAF/MAE) formally issued a modification program management directive (PMD) to install Phase I equipment in all C-119G aircraft. Demonstrating the significance Secretary Brown placed on this program, his office assigned the modification program a precedence rating of 1–9, which meant that if production bottlenecks developed, production managers were authorized to use Battle Directive Secretary of the Air Force (BDSAF) 138 Priority Precedence, Defense Material and Priority System precepts to facilitate the completion of any portion of the project, but especially the prototype phase.[14]

Once Warner Robins officials had completed the acquisition of the prototype components and the assembly of the modification kits, they focused their attention on establishing a prototype production schedule. As 1967 came to a close, leaders at both AFLC and ASD decided to complete the prototype work and testing through a contract with Fairchild-Hiller. In hindsight, Air Force officials' directives for the prototype were all but etched in stone, with the delivery date of March 15, 1968, for the prototype aircraft. They established the deadline, and as they did, decisions in Washington were made to begin full-scale production even before the prototype was completed.[15]

In spite of continued efforts by some in the Pentagon to scuttle the AC-119 program, on January 5, 1968, Brown and the Air Staff issued a plan to deploy six AC-130s and thirty-two AC-119s to support thirty-two AC-47s still operating in Southeast Asia. A month later, on February 2, Brown sent a message to the CSAF specifying that he wanted sixteen AC-119Gs and sixteen AC-119Ks to comprise the AC-119 deployment, with ten more for backups in case of aircraft losses and for training crews. He determined there should be six G models in-theater by July and four K models by November. He designated that Phase I of crew training should be conducted at Clinton County AFB, Ohio, and Phase II at England AFB, Louisiana. He also recommended that a new illuminator, a night observation device, and a fire control system be added to the G-model conversion.[16]

With this directive on their plate, Air Staff members urged the secretary to provide additional resources for acquiring and modifying the C-119Ks. On February 8, 1968, Brown, with Air Staff support, formally requested that the Defense Department approve the dispatch of thirty-two Air Force Reserve C-119K aircraft to appropriate locations for modification. He wrote to McNamara, "I see a clear distinction between the more localized support and protective role of the AC-119 aircraft and the predominantly search-and-destroy concept envisioned for the AC-130." He further stated that he had decided to "proceed with the AC-119G in the interim, while working at full speed on the AC-119K as well." However, his vision of the numbers of aircraft had changed to thirty-two, not sixteen, Gs; thirty-two, not sixteen, Ks; thirty-two AC-47s; and six AC-130s. Sixteen days later, Deputy Secretary of Defense Paul H. Nitze formally granted all Brown's gunship requests.[17]

From the standpoint of the WRAMA workforce, as March dawned in 1968, it mattered little if those in Washington were still debating the final gunship numbers. By that point, full-scale development of the AC-119 had been initiated, and their job was clear—produce and deploy a production AC-119 by

July 1, 1968. During that spring, as they toiled, the squabbles over gunships continued in Washington. It was this posturing that eventually pushed the first production completion date back from April 23, 1968, to May 21, 1968, and deployment from July to November.[18]

In spite of the struggles within the national government and problems with the contractor, on May 21, 1968, WRAMA commander Maj. Gen. Francis C. Gideon accepted the first AC-119G aircraft from David W. Pertschuk, Fairchild-Hiller vice-president and the Aircraft Service Division's general manager. In a low-key plant ceremony at Fairchild's Saint Augustine facility, the first AC-119G rolled off the modification production line. In accordance with AFLC instructions, only the news media in the north Florida area covered the event. The Air Force did not want to stir up further antiwar sentiments at home or arouse possible enemy interest in Vietnam.[19]

On June 9, 1968, TAC officials took possession of the first AC-119G and began testing at Eglin AFB, Florida. The testing lasted until June 30 and was comprised of firing, flare, sensor, and smoke egress system analysis. They flew twenty-five test sorties covering fifty-three flying hours. In the meantime, Fairchild workers completed the remaining G models on October 11, 1968, and the Air Force took possession of all twenty-six aircraft. Throughout that period, the contractor and Warner Robins gunship workforce eased into a productive routine that facilitated the program's completion. Even when General Gideon left to become a lieutenant general and commander of the Thirteenth Air Force on July 22, 1968, his replacement, Maj. Gen. A. J. Beck, slipped right into the leadership role, and the program never skipped a beat. On September 21, Beck accepted the first AC-119K gunship for the Air Force, again from David Pertschuk. Over the next eight months the K-model reconfiguration also progressed smoothly, and by May 20, 1969, all twenty-six Stingers were completed. Officials at WRAMA now disbanded the Program Office and reassigned management responsibility to WRAMA's Materiel Management, System Management Division, to assure routine depot sustainment of the new weapon system.[20]

Once the AC-119s began rolling off the modification lines in quantity, the responsibility of Warner Robins and AFLC shifted from managing the reconfiguration to parts supply and system sustainment. In the meantime, in order to commit the AC-119s to combat quickly, the Air Staff decided to recall Air Force reservists familiar with flying the C-119 cargo versions of the airframe. Air Force leaders reasoned that such a process would eliminate delays caused by retraining and transitioning active-duty personnel to AC-119 gunships. This was complicated, since each G model flew with a pilot, copilot, two navigators, one illuminator operator, one flight mechanic, and two weapon mechanics. Later K models would have even more crew personnel.[21] Reservist training consisted of learning how to use the new weapons and avionics systems in the AC-119s. Air Force officials decided that as aircrew replacements were required as a result of rotation, trained active-duty crew members would be available through new Air Training Command (ATC) classes being formed specifically for gunship training.[22]

On May 13, 1968, HQ Air Force issued orders that mobilized the 930th Tactical Airlift Group (930th TAG), Air Force Reserve, Bakalar AFB, Indiana, for a twenty-four-month active-duty tour. On June 1, 1968, the unit transferred to Lockbourne AFB, Ohio, becoming TAC's 71st SOS with all of the 930th TAG's personnel except for one additional officer and one airman assigned to the new unit. At Lockbourne AFB, members of the 4413th Combat Crew Training Squadron (CCTS) began the process of training the reservists. Once instructors completed this training process, they began a routine of training active-duty personnel in order to maintain a sufficient number of aircrew personnel to supplement and/or replace AC-119 gunship crews as needed. Much of the initial training actually was conducted by Reserve instructors from the 302nd Tactical Airlift Wing (302nd TAW), Clinton County AFB, Ohio, on loan to and supervised by 4413th CCTS lead instructors.[23]

On September 4, 1968, TAC officials convened a conference among the affected units. From this meeting came a new proposal to deploy the 71st ACS (later 71st SOS) between November 1968 and January 1969, if aircraft were available. It also recommended that three K models deploy in April 1969, seven in May, and eight in June to form the squadron of sixteen combat aircraft previously planned for. Two additional aircraft would be forward-deployed to compensate for attrition.[24]

The Air Staff opposed the immediate disposition of the AC-47 fleet, instead restating their plans to continue to use them until mid- or late 1969 and then turning them over to the VNAF. Gen. George S. Brown, the Seventh Air Force commander, sent a message supporting AFSEC Brown's original plan to have a full fleet of fifty-two AC-119G/K aircraft supplemented by the AC-47s until the full transition was complete. He also proposed moving airborne battlefield central command and control (ABCCC) operations headquarters to Thailand, which he believed would not only move the AC-119s closer to their mission areas and reduce flight time to their targets but also alleviate much of the headroom problem for the incoming AC-119 crews.[25]

On September 25, 1968, CINCPACAF, Gen. Joseph J. Nazzaro told CSAF Gen. Joseph McConnell that the enemy had stepped up attacks on populated areas in South Vietnam and that the AC-119 squadron was urgently needed. Since the base facilities were completed, Nazzaro suggested sending the gunships as soon as they could travel, even though headroom problems might keep most of the 71st SOS in the continental United States (CONUS). Finally, in October the DOD, with presidential approval, increased the headroom limit to accommodate both the G and K model crew members and support personnel. The debate culminated when Deputy Secretary Nitze officially approved the dispatch of the 71st on November 27.[26]

After a long, hot summer and fall of training and waiting, in mid-November 1968 the instructor staff pronounced the original AC-119G crews ready. The Air Staff ordered the 71st SOS to Nha Trang AB, Republic of Vietnam, between January and March 1969. There they would become part of the 14th SOW. The deployment, like the entire program, fell behind schedule for most of the same reasons the overall program had.[27]

The AC-119s Arrive and Begin the Fight

On November 4, transport and program officials conferred at WRAMA to discuss how best to ferry the AC-119Gs to Southeast Asia. They decided to remove the four gun pods and mounts, which together weighed nearly ten thousand pounds, and temporarily install a five-hundred-gallon Benson rubberized fuel bladder on each aircraft to extend its flying range. Plans called for the aircraft to fly in pairs from the contractor's plant in Saint Augustine to Lockborne AFB, Ohio; to McClellan AFB, California; to McChord AFB, Washington; to two stops in Alaska; to the Aleutians; to Midway, Guam, and then Wake Island in the Pacific; to Kadena AB, Okinawa, Japan; to Clark AB, the Philippines; and, finally, to Nha Trang AB.[28]

The first two gunships departed on December 5 and arrived on December 27, 1968. Eventually, six G models were forward deployed at Phan Rang AB and five at Tan Son Nhut AB, from where they began a two-month combat evaluation program that lasted from January 5, to March 8, 1969. Five other aircraft had to stop along the route for significant repairs but eventually made it to their in-theater forward operating locations (FOLs). By mid-March 1969, with combat evaluation completed, the Gs were ready for operations.[29]

From the beginning there were disagreements on how best to employ the AC-119Gs. Those in Seventh Air Force wanted to use them for close air support, base and hamlet defense, and search and rescue, while those in the 14th SOW, by then deeply involved with Operation Commando Hunt, wanted to use them to stem the flow of enemy supplies and troops along the Ho Chi Minh Trail. Following the January–March combat evaluation tests using the first G to arrive, the evaluators reported they had done "as expected." While they performed their CAS and base/hamlet defense roles well, they were "slow and hard to maneuver and vulnerable to even small arms fire." They did

AC-119G.

not perform well in fog or bad weather, since they did not have the array of radar the K models did. All this limited their missions to restricted duties in South Vietnam along the lines proposed by the Seventh Air Force.[30]

If the crews did not squirm enough at these restrictions, the thing they hated the most was their new call sign: Creep. They lobbied against it. About the time the last crews and aircraft bedded down and began routine combat operations, leadership gave in. Instead of Creep, they would be Shadow. At first this, too, seemed insulting to some, but soon the men of the 71st began to warm to the new call sign. Harkening back to the 1930s radio show "The Shadow," they embraced all the implications the nickname held and accepted it. Declaring "only the Shadow knows," they created a unit slogan that rang true: "Deny him the night!" The AC-119Gs performed so well that the enemy in the South, after three months of facing the 71st SOS and two years of facing their successor, the 17th SOS, came to fear the Shadow as much as any American aircraft in Vietnam.[31]

Early in 1969, AC-119Gs normally operated within predetermined patrol boxes guided by TACAN ground navigation radar stations. Over one-third of their sorties were flown at night using MK-6 flares to mark potential targets. Crews flew attack runs at three thousand to thirty-five hundred feet (maximum range for their 7.62mm miniguns) on a left orbit turn, firing only one or two guns at a time and at a slow rate of about three thousand rounds per minute. It was based on these flights that the evaluation report noted, "The close air support role is the most effective for the AC-119G." The report pointed out that the G models had a decent, if not spectacular, 78.8 percent combat readiness rate. During these early missions, the AC-119Gs had received ground fire eighty-six times but had been hit only once, and that on a wingtip. A major part of this excellent battle damage record was due to the fighter escorts that effectively suppressed any and all enemy antiaircraft artillery fire. By March 10 the remaining five combat gunships and the two attrition ships had arrived. The next day, the 71st SOS commander, Lt. Col. James E. Pyle, declared the 71st SOS combat-ready. Soon, routine combat operations began to unfold, and many an Allied ground soldier came to thank God for the effectiveness of the Shadows against enemy ground units. Still, many in the 14th SOW realized they had room for an even more powerful gunship to meet increasing enemy infiltration. Thus, they anxiously awaited the arrival of the more lethal K models and their AC-130 cousins.[32]

The K Models Arrive and the 18th SOS Stands Up

On September 24, 1968, the first AC-119K rolled off the Fairchild-Hiller assembly line, even as plans were going forward to deploy the 71st SOS to Southeast Asia. In turn, the Air Staff activated the 18th SOS in late January 1969 and sent its personnel to Lockborne AFB, where they began training to fly the AC-119Ks or, as they became known, Stingers. Unlike the 71st SOS crews, who had to wait for the completion of modifications to their aircraft, the 18th SOS was activated after workers finished the K models at the contractor's plant. At the AC-119K deployment conference held on December 18, 1968, an agreement was reached with TAC officials for K models nine through thirteen to be stored at the Fairchild-Hiller plant until the 18th SOS was formally activated. Leaders at TAC, concerned that this scheduled activation of the 18th SOS might be adversely affected by a lack of manpower, had the contractor's personnel maintain the final five aircraft until well into the spring of 1969, when sufficient personnel were trained and available for deployment.[33]

Senior leaders originally considered sending the Ks on the same route used by the Gs while deploying. However, after some lengthy discussion, they decided to replace the stopover at McClellan AFB with a stop at Malstrom AFB, Montana, since it was a more direct flight path from there to Washington and then to Alaska. As with the AC-119G deployment, personnel attached Benson fuel tanks to each aircraft and removed the guns and flare components to accommodate the additional fuel. This reduced the weight by nearly 20 percent and facilitated takeoffs and landings.[34]

The first six AC-119Ks departed Lockborne AFB on October 21, 1969. Lt. Col. Ernest E. Johnson, 18th SOS commander, and an advance team had already arrived at their FOL in Phan Rang AB on October 11. Eventually, 125 officers and 441 enlisted airmen followed. The first aircraft arrived on No-

AC-119K in flight.

vember 3. The last K model left its home base on December 27 as part of a melancholy send-off only two days after Christmas. The final gunship arrived on January 25, 1970, following several misadventures during the ferrying process. Seventh Air Force confirmed that the 18th SOS was C-1 combat ready on February 4, 1970.[35]

With the final AC-119 deployed, Project Combat Hornet officially came to an end. It had been two and one-half years since Secretary Brown had selected the C-119 airframe to be an interim augmentation for the AC-47 gunship. Cost overruns gave the program a bad name in Washington congressional parlors even though most legislative leaders knew or cared little about the project or gunships in general.[36]

However, it did catch the eye of muckraking Connecticut Democratic senator William Proxmire, later famous for his golden pork barrel awards for government waste. Then chair of the Subcommittee on Economy in Government, Proxmire, during hearings on February 3, directed a scathing attack at Assistant Secretary of the Air Force for Installations and Logistics Philip N. Whittaker, most of it focused on "why 26 planes went from $50 million to $158 million." The very inaccuracy of his numbers alone bears witness to the misconceptions about the program festering inside the Washington beltway and mirrors the haphazard method of forming defense policy formulated by members of Congress. This should come as no surprise to anyone, since, throughout the Vietnam conflict, far too many Washington leaders acted in such a publicly divisive manner even with the safety of young soldiers, sailors, airmen, and marines hanging in the balance.[37]

In his reply, Whitaker pointed out that "52 aircraft had increased from $81.2 million to $141.4 million," an increase of $60 million, not the $100 million alleged by Proxmire. Further, the secretary noted that this increase had included modification of numerous state-of-the-art components, several design changes required to assure crew survival, equipment and component alterations, and fixes as well as spare parts needed for a one-of-a-kind weapon system. Indeed, $20.9 million of the increases came from the new sensors, such as the FLIR imaging system, which enhanced not only safety but also the gunship's lethality. Problems with the contractor also increased costs and delays. These included defining contracts, unexpected overtime costs, and inflation in the nation's overall economy. Besides, as Whitaker intimated, at least half of the delay had come from mostly arbitrary headroom numbers established by those in charge in Washington—this after they had originally declared that the program was urgent to assure victory. By the end of the war many, even some of those who had at first opposed the AC-119, came to believe that the program was well worth the $141.4 million price tag. If the combat record is any determinant, it probably was.[38]

Even as the AC-119s entered combat and the AC-47s were transferred to the VNAF, the Air Force continued to work on the Gunship II program, for which many senior leaders had high hopes. To most officials, the AC-130 was a long-term commitment, not an interim program like the AC-119s. From the date of February 26, 1967, when Maj. Ron Terry selected the 1953-era C-130A airframe to be the prototype for the next level of fixed-wing gunships, those involved were convinced it would provide a superior platform for an enhanced array of weapons and sensors. This was not mere speculation but, rather, a logical conclusion, since Terry and his colleagues had first demonstrated the effectiveness of the AC-47 in 1964–65 and then the AC-130A in 1967–68. Their experience alone provided a unique insight into how to proceed with the larger and faster C-130 airframe once they had received the okay to build the first prototype AC-130A and, later, the first production four-engine AC-130 gunships. Thus, in the mid-1960s the evolution of fixed-wing gunship technology progressed from the original AC-47 to the interim AC-119 and finally the AC-130, which is the main topic of this work.

3 A Wondrous Variety
Moving Towards the Spectre

While the most famous fixed-wing gunships proved to be the AC-47, AC-119, and AC-130, the Air Force did initiate other experimental projects to bolster the gunship fleets and even replace the AC-47s. During Project Tailchaser in August 1964, experts at Eglin AFB converted a Convair C-131B, serial number 53-7820, by arming it with a General Electric 7.62mm SUU-11A/A Gatling minigun. Other modified aircraft included the AC-123K and NC-123K, which were all part of Project Black Spot. In the mid-1960s Fairchild-Hiller reconfigured 183 C-123Bs into C-123Ks by attaching two J85-GE-17 jet engines pods under the wings. In early 1966 they extended the nose to house an X-band forward-looking radar. Just aft of the new radome was a turret with a FLIR imaging system, LLLTV, and laser rangefinder and illuminator. They also installed a low-level Doppler navigation radar and weapons release computer. The aircraft were equipped with twelve chute dispensers in a container in the aft cargo compartment. Each chute carried three cluster bomb units (CBUs) that, depending on the type of CBU, loaded twenty-six hundred to sixty-three hundred one-pound miniature bombs.[1]

By February 1968, Fairchild had incorporated the AN/ASD-5 Black Crow direction finder set and engine ignition sensor on two C-123Ks. Known as Black Spot aircraft, they were designated as AC-123K or NC-123K. They flew twenty-eight operational missions between August 19 and October 23, 1968, over the South Korean Sea. From November 14, 1968, to May 11, 1969, the aircraft flew night missions over the Ho Chi Minh Trail. They launched 186 missions, destroyed 415 trucks, and damaged 273 more. They also attacked boats in the Mekong Delta. Subsequently, the

Black Spots were assigned to the 16th SOS at Udorn Royal Thai Air Force Base, and from December 1969 until June 1970 they continued to operate against enemy infiltration efforts until both aircraft were reconstituted as standard C-123Ks at Davis-Monthan AFB, Arizona, and continued to serve as normal transports. Several other C-123Bs were painted black on the underside and standard three-tone camouflage on top and employed as flare ships by the 14th SOW using the call sign Candle.[2]

While the C, AC, and NC-123s performed numerous missions in several configurations, they proved to be a utility infielder to the star shortstop—the AC-130. The role of the C-123–based gunship, while important, was secondary to that of the original gunship, the AC-47D, and even the interim replacement, the AC-119G/K. The AC-130 would become the star of the US fixed-wing gunship fleet in Vietnam and would be the only one to remain in the active inventory after the war was over.

A Prologue to Spectre: A Gunship II Background

On November 1, 1966, Air Force leaders initiated the Gunship II program by selecting the C-130 airframe to replace the AC-47D. With four powerful turboprop engines, it possessed greater range and higher performance capabilities than its aging cousin. Even the initial A-model AC-130, with four 7.62mm and four 20mm Gatling guns, carried greater firepower than did Puff, with three 7.62mm guns. Eventually it would mount an array of sensors and radars the likes of which had not been witnessed in such a fixed-wing cargo-type aircraft.[3]

In February 1967, key personnel at ASC, led by then major Ron Terry, selected the very first C-130A to be modified into a gunship. Originally built by Lockheed in 1954, tail number 54–1626, Vulcan Express, or Super Spooky, was quickly reconfigured by an organic workforce for combat testing in Vietnam. On September 15, 1967, Terry returned to Southeast Asia, this time with the next generation of gunship—the AC-130A. The resulting test report declared that the new Spectre was a "threefold improvement over its predecessor, the AC-47." Many in TAC and PACAF went so far as to declare it "the most cost-effective close-support and interdiction weapon in the Air Force inventory." The Air Force deployed four AC-130s to Southeast Asia in November 1968. Soon thereafter another AC-130 arrived in-theater. Together, the five Spectre gunships proved the most lethal interdiction weapons of the Vietnam conflict. Between January 1968 and April 1969, AC-130s flew fewer than 4 percent of all Air Force combat sorties, but they claimed over 29 percent of all enemy vehicles destroyed. With a track record like that, it is little

First Lady crew in Vietnam.

wonder they were the favorite of every Air Force and Army commander in Southeast Asia.[4]

As with the AC-119s, domestic political and geopolitical concerns as well as rivalries and conflicts within the DOD delayed the production of the AC-130s to the point that some leaders, such as Secretary Brown, began to consider alternative airframes to augment the AC-130s. As activity of enemy AAA and surface-to-air missiles (SAMs) increased in Laos and South Vietnam, concerns about the vulnerability of all gunships grew. Air Force experts decided the immediate solution was the addition of heavier armaments that would do more damage to communist air defenses and targets.

To this end, Terry recommended, and leadership approved, incorporating two 40mm and two 20mm guns on the AC-130s as standard weaponry. He and his team suggested the addition of better avionics, such as LLLTV, an improved infrared sensor, replacement of the analog computer with a digital computer, and the addition of a laser designator. This overall component group, known as Surprise Package, was approved by senior officials in September 1969. Following CONUS tests, the new Spectres deployed to Thailand, arriving on December 5. During combat appraisals that lasted until January 18, 1970, test personnel described the new model as "twice as effective as the existing AC-130s," which later proved so valuable during Commando Hunt V. Later, experts made further efforts to increase the killing power of the AC-130 by adding a 105mm howitzer to the gunships' arsenal of weapons. This process took very little time, and the new gunship configuration was ready for the final Commando Hunt VII operation and the first Linebacker operation, which lasted from the fall of 1971 to the fall of 1972. Of all the trucks destroyed in Commando Hunt VII, nearly two-thirds were claimed by the AC-130s, and of the tanks destroyed during Linebacker I, 55 percent were claimed by the Spectre aircraft.[5]

Despite the effectiveness of the AC-130, it took a long time to modify and deploy. Months went by from the initial combat tests to their full involvement in the war. As noted in the previous chapter, anxious to augment the aging AC-47s, many leaders in Washington sought an interim weapon system until the AC-130 came on-line. That system was, of course, the AC-119G/K and was deployed to Vietnam from late 1968 to late 1969. While Shadow and Stinger were a superior close air support weapon, they had limits when it came to dealing with vehicular traffic along the Ho Chi Minh Trail. As a result, experts such as Terry continued to work with the AC-130 airframe in an effort to rescue it from Washington civil and military politics and delays. It was this effort that led to the construction of the AC-130H and AC-130U fleet that still serves America's national defense today halfway around the world.[6]

The AC-130A Comes Full Circle

On September 10, 1995, the AC-130A gunship known as *First Lady* retired from active duty after forty years of service. In some ways it had gone full circle. In 1953 the original airframe, T/N 53–3129, became the original C-130 Hercules prototype to roll off the Lockheed Aircraft Company's production line at Marietta, Georgia. Fourteen years later, it became the first of five production-model AC-130As modified by Lockheed for the Vietnam War. After forty years and 13,600 hours, *First Lady* retired from the 919th Air Force Reserve SOW at Duke Field, Florida, to permanent display at the Air Armament Center Museum at Eglin AFB, Florida. Many other A models were also placed on permanent display, while the remainder were sent to the Aerospace Maintenance and Regeneration Center at Davis-Monthan AFB, Arizona. It was the end of an era. The AC-130A prototype and production models had flown countless combat sorties first in Vietnam, then in Panama, and then the Persian Gulf during Operation Desert Storm. On that day in 1995 the Air Force formally retired the AC-130As because the latest gunships, the AC-130Us, the first and only airframe specifically built to be a gunship, had come on-line. Bristling with a 25mm Gatling gun, a 40mm Bofors cannon, and a 105mm artillery piece as well as the latest radars, radios, and high-tech detection devices, the U model was the most awesome gunship ever built. It was a far cry

AC-130 prototype.

from the original A model, but in many respects it was one more in a long line of AC-130s first flown in 1967.[7]

The first C-130A airframe given to technicians to modify into a gunship was 97 feet 9 inches long and 38 feet 3 inches tall and had a wingspan of 132 feet 7 inches and a wing area of 1,745 square feet. Initially, this C-130 had a maximum speed of 384 mph and an unrefueled range of 2,450 miles with a maximum payload. Of course, with aerial refueling, the range for the later-model gunships was only limited by crew endurance. The C-130's high-wing design and its large capacity made it particularly well suited to be a gunship. Engineers armed the first AC-130As with 7.62mm and 20mm weapons. Later the AC-130Es, which became the AC-130Hs, flew with 20mm, 40mm and 105mm guns. When the AC-130s deployed to Afghanistan in 2003, they remained one of the most lethal CAS and interdiction weapons in the US military arsenal. As they had thirty-six year earlier in Vietnam, they proved to be the most potent truck killers ever built and a weapon that struck fear into the heart of the enemies of the United States. How did it grow from the mind of a remarkable engineer like Col. Ron Terry into such a dynamic and resilient Air Force weapon?

The Birth of Spectre

The story of the AC-130 began with the success of the AC-47. No sooner had Terry, the godfather of America's fixed-wing gunships, concluded deployment of the AC-47 than he, and others, began considering how to improve the design. These gunship experts realized that the AC-47 lacked load capacity, range, and firing range because of its wing position. They believed that a four-engine aircraft could carry not only more ordnance but also more powerful weapons.

On June 1, 1966, the Air Force initiated Operation Little Brother, and on June 21, Terry and Capt. James Wolverton presented a briefing on fixed-wing gunships to the Limited War Study Group (LWSG), a task force from AFSC headquartered at Andrews AFB, Maryland. While Terry believed the obvious choice for an upgrade was the C-130 Hercules airframe, the LWSG members recommended, on July 1, that the Air Force transition its gunship fleet to a Cessna Super Skymaster, model 337. The 337 was a high-wing twin-engine aircraft capable of carrying a two-thousand-pound payload. The decision proved to be a grave disappointment to Terry and his colleagues. To them the logic of reconfiguring the C-130 seemed obvious, and yet it had seemed to elude everyone else. Still, plans went forward, and engineers armed the Skymaster with semirecoilless 40mm and 42mm guns capable of firing five hundred rounds per minute. They housed the guns in an MXU-470/A minigun module primarily because that was the cheapest and most available component. While the load capacity was not what experts had envisioned, the fact that the proposed gunship could land and take off from unimproved runways, operate during the night or day, and fly for ten unrefueled hours provided it with some notable advantages.[8]

The main concern proved to be fitting an advanced fire control system on this rudimentary airframe. Experts at the Air Force Avionics Laboratory (AFAL) at Wright-Patterson AFB, Ohio, developed the fire control system from an earlier design fabricated by RAF wing commander Thomas C. Pinkerton. Once the lab technicians at ASD, also located at Wright-Patterson, completed the modification, they initiated flight testing. This proved so successful that engineers began planning to construct an even better gunship model that could be fitted into a four-engine aircraft, likely the C-130. The success of the Cessna tests led experts to lobby even harder for adapting the basic concepts to the more powerful airframe.[9]

In spite of initial success with Operation Little Brother, the reality that the Cessna was simply not adequate for the changing combat needs in Southeast Asia eventually led to cancellation of the project in November 1968. By that time, Air Force designers were convinced, as Terry and his team had been from the outset, that they needed a larger four-engine airframe. Even before the gunship issue arose, the ability of the VC to use the night and bad weather to elude US air attacks compelled Air Force officials to focus much of their attention on seeking ways to provide night and bad-weather capabilities for all their assets. Whatever new airframe they used, the gunship would need to have these advantages, or it would be increasingly useless.[10]

Between the late summer of 1964 and late spring of 1965, the military aircraft panel of President Lyndon B. Johnson's Scientific Advisory Committee began research on night operations. Panel members urged the president's special assistant for science and technology, Donald F. Hornig, to convince those in power to support night vision development. On June 3, 1965, Hornig contacted Harold Brown, then the director of Defense Research and Engineering, Office of the Secretary of Defense (OSD), asserting the need to speed up night vision tests to get such capabilities into the field as soon as possible. In turn, Brown placed high priority on the addition of night capabilities to "helicopters and slow- and high-speed fixed-wing gunships."[11]

In subsequent communication between President Johnson and Secretary of Defense Cyrus R. Vance, the latter explained that night vision tests in Vietnam were scheduled for both helicopters and A-1E Skyraider propeller aircraft throughout 1966. He also told the president that night capability flight testing on "transport aircraft's reconnaissance-strike systems primarily designed for interdiction missions, would be evaluated in Vietnam in January 1967." On June 3, 1966, following the initial helicopter tests, Hornig told Johnson that the pace of night vision development needed to be accelerated even if it meant increasing funding.[12]

This piqued President Johnson's interest, and he decided to convene several conferences on the subject of night visions systems. Among those attending were Dr. Vincent V. McRae, technical assistant to Hornig; Richard S. Garwin, director of the Scientific Advisory Committee; Gen. Bernard A. Shriever, commander of AFSC; and Lt. Gen. James Ferguson, Air Force deputy chief of staff (DCS) for research and development. From these meetings was born Operation Shed Light. In turn, in February 1966 the Air Force formed a team of experts to recommend the future direction for this evolving night vision technology. A month later, the team members made twenty-nine recommendations that, among other things, suggested that Air Force scientists should develop a self-contained night attack capability in low-threat environments for targets of opportunity and enemy lines of communications. They also suggested the creation of a battlefield illumination airborne system to support ground units and focused nearly every appropriate Air Force unit on developing fields of navigation, illumination, target marking, and sensors for target detection and acquisition in every environmental condition.[13]

On March 18, 1966, Air Force leaders formally began the Shed Light program. Five days later, they instructed AFSC to formulate cost estimates for the twenty-nine recommendations. Subsequently, ASD constructed a plan to integrate sensors and weapons. In turn, AFSC put together an overall program plan that was approved by the Air Force chief of staff on July 15, 1966.[14] Even as the night vision issues moved into high gear, the Air Force began a new program to incorporate Major Terry's concept of "a bigger, meaner AC-47." This program, designated Project Gunboat, proposed picking a more robust airframe than the existing AC-47D or the Cessna Model 337, since they had never satisfied the concept of the fixed-wing gunship. By August the project had been placed in the hands of the Air Force director of development, DCS for research and design. The first planning meeting took place on September 2, 1966, at Wright-Patterson AFB. Based on discussions at that meeting, experts from AFSC and ASD determined to test the use of high-caliber weapons in four-engine airframes.[15]

Personnel at ASD created the prototype and performed the tests. On November 16, 1966, as part of the Gunship II program, they tentatively selected a C-130 airframe for the Gunboat aircraft to be tested. The Air Staff told them they had to move quickly and decisively. Experts decided to test 7.62mm miniguns, 20mm cannons, and .50-caliber machine guns. Plans called for test personnel to perform in-house tests for six months to ascertain which guns performed best at altitudes varying from six thousand to ten thousand feet and whether the new starlight intensifier optical viewer and the latest fire control system could be integrated into the airframe.[16]

On February 26, 1967, upon completion of the tests, officials selected a C-130A airframe, specifically T/N 54-1626, to become the AC-130 prototype, originally designated the Vulcan Express. Many of those in the test group were less than secure about the aircraft, as it had experienced three major accidents during its operational history. Some crew members cynically dubbed it "sick-two-six" and wondered out loud whether the short-nosed JC-130A was the right choice.[17]

Considering the lack of interest in the program by most senior airmen, the fact that they got any aircraft at all was a major step forward. Still, the C-130 airframe had many advantages over its AC-47 predecessor. It had much greater compartment space, which afforded a larger load capacity and allowed it to carry four 7.62mm General Electric (GE) MXU-470/A miniguns and four 20mm GE M-61 Vulcan Gatling-style cannons capable of firing twenty-five hundred high-explosive incendiary rounds per minute. Personnel at Systems Division began the prototype modification process on April 1, 1967, at Wright-Patterson AFB. At first known as the Super Spooky, a reference to the AC-47 Spooky, the prototype, besides powerful new weapon arrays, had several important sensor features. These included a starlight scope night observation device or system (NOD or NOS), which intensified images illuminated by ambient moon- and starlight. It also employed side-looking radar, FLIR, a Bell optical-sight steerable illuminator with a 20 kw xenon arc lamp searchlight that provided ultraviolet and infrared light, a semiautomatic flare dispenser, inert fuel tanks, Doppler navigation radar, direction-finding homing instruments, and an FM radio transceiver. Originally, it was painted in the standard grey and white scheme of the time. Just before deployment, however, this was changed to jungle camouflage. One of its biggest assets was its ability to fly all-weather missions.[18]

Testing began on June 6, 1967, at the Air Proving Ground Center (as of October 1998 the Air Armament Center) at Eglin AFB. Leadership changed the project designation from Gunboat to Gunship II and focused the new weapon system on replacing the AC-47. Officials at AFLC dubbed the modification project Loggy Stinger and gave it a 1–7 precedence code. After testing the sensor, fire, and gunsight systems, test personnel transferred the final tests to Wright-Patterson AFB for the last forty-five days. It was there they installed the FLIR, side-looking radar, and NOD. During that phase the new gunship attacked targets at the Eglin range, destroying twenty-nine of thirty. The tests proved so successful that officials began planning to transfer the AC-130A to Nha Trang AB in South Vietnam in September 1967.[19]

Concurrently, Terry and his compatriots at ASD began to discuss the number of crew members they would need to operate the AC-130A prototype. They decided they required twelve: aircraft commander, pilot, fire direction officer, navigator, night observation device operator, sensor operator, flight engineer, loadmaster, master armorer, scanner, armorer for the 7.62mm guns, and armorer for the 20mm cannons. Initially, half the crew came from AFSC and half from TAC units. Early on, most of the sensor and special systems operators were AFSC/ASD expert technicians or scientists such as master navigation officer Lt. Col. James R. Krause, formerly an engineer in the Air Force Avionics Laboratory and an ASD infrared expert. In order to formulate tactics for the new gunship, Terry and Wolverton led nearly every sortie, later writing the new tactical doctrine in their reports. From that point they developed the regulations that following crews would use in later AC-130 versions.[20]

After a routine deployment, the Vulcan Express arrived at Nha Trang AB on September 21, 1967, for a sixty- to ninety-day combat test. Maj. Jack L. Kalow acted as the evaluation team commander. The team immediately planned to fly close air support in South Vietnam's Delta region, IV Corps Tactical Zone (CTZ), around Binh Thuy, which had the fewest terrain issues and least threat from enemy ground fire. During phase two of testing, they planned to focus on cutting enemy lines of communication and infiltration routes in a region of Laos designated Tiger Hound. The last phase involved armed reconnaissance and ground support for Allied units operating in the II CTZ in the Central Highlands.[21]

They flew their first sortie on September 24 and their last one on December 1, 1967. Officially, the test flights ended on December 8. During that period the prototype sighted ninety-four trucks and destroyed thirty-eight. Of special note was an armed reconnaissance mission piloted by Terry on November 11, on which they spotted a large communist convoy on one of the infiltration roads of the Ho Chi Minh Trail. Following several attacks, they confirmed one truck totally destroyed and eight more severely damaged. For pressing such a successful attack, Terry won the Distinguished Flying Cross (DFC).[22]

Maj. Gen. William G. Moore, Air Force DCS for research and development, declared that Super Spooky had "far exceeded fighter type kill ratios on enemy trucks and other equipment." All totaled, the AC-130A had flown one to three missions a day, had fired 87,720 rounds of 20mm ammunition and 222,800 rounds of 7.62mm ammunition, and had dropped 310 flares. Its kill ratio was remarkable not only in terms of sorties but also in ordnance expended. This proved to be a vital point to the technocrats who were running the military aspects of the Vietnam War.[23]

Original plans called for the AC-130A to return to the United States for seven months to be thoroughly overhauled and upgraded. Instead, the commander of Military Assistance Command, Vietnam (MACV), Gen. William C. Westmoreland, facing increased enemy activity, insisted that Seventh Air Force commander Lt. Gen. Spike Momyer return Super Spooky to the States for only minimum maintenance and have it back by early February 1968. Even though Momyer initially loathed the idea of low and slow old cargo aircraft flying combat missions, he had grown to appreciate the success of Vulcan Express. As a result, he willingly complied with Westmoreland's request like a proud new papa. Ultimately, T/N 1626 returned on February 12, and, while the original TAC/AFSC crew continued to fly until the end of its temporary duty (TDY) assignment, in late March plans had already begun to replace them with a permanent crew.[24]

Once the AC-130A completed its brief maintenance stint in the States, it returned to in-theater operations based at Ubon RTAFB, Thailand, was assigned interdiction missions along the Ho Chi Minh Trail, and was placed under Detachment 2, commanded by Lt. Col. Ross E. Hamlin. It flew its next combat mission on February 27. On its third sortie, Super Spooky's crew destroyed nine trucks and left two storage areas in smoldering ruins. Over the remainder of 1968, while the prototype continued its interdiction role, it also spent time in South Vietnam with the 14th ACW, flying CAS in support of several Allied ground operations, including those fending off the enemy's Tet Offensive of 1968. Results proved to be spectacular. Early in 1968, the AC-130A crew spotted more than 1,000 trucks, destroying 228 and damaging 133. They also destroyed nine of thirty-two sampans and damaged eight. Momyer and all US leaders were impressed and delighted. As the United States made preparation to face the third phase of the Tet Offensive, they assigned the AC-130A to the area around Saigon. While Super Spooky continued to fly throughout South Vietnam, from the DMZ to the southernmost tip, 151 of its 246 sorties supported Allied ground troops. The crew confirmed 248 kills of NVA and VC forces. If the truth be told, they probably got a lot more.[25]

As the number of sorties increased, so did concerns over maintenance. Increasingly, sensor and equipment malfunctions beset the prototype's ground crews. They flew their last mission on November 18, 1968, eventually arriving back at Wright-Patterson AFB on November 26. Even as the prototype completed its operations, discussion had begun about when to send production models to Vietnam. One of the most compelling reasons to move forward with an expanded AC-130 program proved to be the efficiency of the aircraft. In an analysis by the Air Force director of development, experts reported that AC-130 development costs had totaled $357,399 for spares and servicing. Concurrently, Super Spooky participated in 749 major combat events and averaged $5,676 per confirmed kill, making the prototype one of the most cost-effective weapon systems in the Air Force at that time—for that matter, at any time.[26]

Building the Production Model

With such positive data flowing to the Air Staff, there is little wonder that the Air Force eventually chose to modify the seven JC-130As previously mentioned. Even so, CSAF, General McConnell, had originally formed a study group in May 1967 that had recommended that "the C-130 and C-123" both be "seriously considered for the role because they [C-130s] were needed for airlift." At that point leadership was considering the C-121, C-119, C-54, C-118, P-2E, and C-97. This process led Dr. Brown to select the AC-119G/K as the interim fixed-wing gunship on June 8, 1967. The Gunship III program led to the deployment of the AC-119G/Ks in 1968 and 1969 to Vietnam. With ground commanders pushing for the AC-130A, the AC-119 deployment would not be the last gunship to visit Vietnam. General Momyer was particularly outspoken in his preference, decrying the selection of the AC-119 in a June 30, 1967, message to CINCPACAF General Ryan. He wrote that the AC-119 was "yet another obsolete system" that was a "mere substitution, and possibly a regression rather than an advance." He recommended the Air Force charge ahead with the AC-130 program, since it was more cost effective, was based on a better airframe, and actually had little impact on airlift. Ryan agreed, as did TAC officials. In the summer of 1967, prototype tests continued to bolster the reputation of the AC-130s and led them closer to full-scale production.[27]

Late that summer, the Air Staff finally recommended that the Vulcan Express not be the only AC-130A produced. In a report to Brown, they recommended that at least seven of the eleven JC-130s being used for telemetry acquisition on the Eastern Test Range (ETR) be modified into gunships. Subsequently, on September 27–28, 1967, twelve generals from HQ Air Force, TAC, PACAF and Seventh Air Force gathered to review the Shed Light program. In early October, they reiterated their plea that seven JC-130s be reconfigured into Gunship II aircraft and four into near-real-time reconnaissance and intelligence aircraft. Brown approved the latter but reduced the production run to two in order to continue testing and stay within their research and development budget. On November 1, 1967, he also agreed to modify the other five as funding allowed. To those who believed in the AC-130A, this was a foot in the door. As the positive data continued to roll in from the prototype test in late 1967, Brown's promise soon became as good as a guarantee that seven production models would be built.[28]

The seven JC-130As selected for immediate modification included T/Ns 53-3129, 54-1623, 54-1625, 54-1627, 54-1628, 54-1629, and 54-1630. T/N 3129, better known as *First Lady,* was, as previously mentioned, the first production model C-130A completed at the Lockheed assembly plant in Marietta, Georgia, on March 10, 1955. Even as the reconfiguration work began on these seven gunships, no one could have known that five would remain in the Air Force inventory for more than twenty-five years. While T/Ns 1625 and 1629 were lost in combat, *First Lady* did not retire until 1995. *Ghost Rider,* T/N 1623, is displayed at Dobbins AFB, Georgia, and the prototype is at the Air Force Museum at Wright-Patterson AFB.[29]

In November 1967, officials decided that the AC-130A production run would be a joint ASD and WRAMA project. Concurrently, they assigned program management responsibility for the conversion to ASD. This meant that personnel at ASD had overall engineering responsibility for the development of the modified C-130 airframe during its development, testing, and evaluation phases. They received this role since Lockheed and ASD experts had already developed and field-tested the similarly designed prototype aircraft. WRAMA depot experts were assigned the responsibility of acting as AFLC's systems support manager following the conclusion of the development, test, and evaluation phases, with the C-130 Support Management Branch (WRNH-4) of WRAMA's Directorate of Materiel Management (WRAMA/WRN, or DMM), headed by Col. Irving B. Schoenberg, acting as the program support manager. In short, they would manage the follow-on aircraft production schedule to begin prior to July 1969.[30]

Between 1956, when Lockheed completed the production run, and 1969, when the first AC-130A production models were built, the Air Force procured a total of 771 C-130 aircraft, with the other services purchasing 87 more and foreign governments 130, for a total of 988. Of this number, 231 were A models; 230, B models; 464, E models; and 63, HC-130 H/Ps, used primarily for search and rescue and aerial refueling. By 1969, attrition losses had reduced the number in the Air Force inventory to 702. Among the special-service C-130s were the eleven JC-130B/E/Hs used for telemetry and air-to-air recovery/refueling. As full-scale production began, these were the airframes designated for reconfiguration.[31]

With the airframes selected, Air Force contracting personnel put the actual conversion contract up for bid. On December 15, 1967, they concluded negotiations and signed a letter contract with Ling-Temco-Vought Electrosystems (LTVE), Greenville, Texas, to begin the modification process for the first two planes. Since these aircraft were scheduled to be operated by TAC personnel and with units in PACAF, both commands had representatives engaged in the modification process. Since WRAMA for AFLC and ASD for AFSC were managing the project, they also played a major role in the program.[32]

At first, one of the most daunting issues facing the program proved to be the fact that the AC-130A gunship modification program ran simultaneously with the reconfiguration of the C-119 Flying Boxcars into sixteen AC-119G Shadows and sixteen AC-119K jet-assisted Stingers. While actual construction of the AC-119s took place at the Fairchild-Hiller plant in Saint Augustine, Florida, a special gunship office in Warner Robins's DMM acted as the project manager. At the same time, Lockheed-Georgia, the prime contractor for the C-130, also became the prime airframe contractor for the AC-130 program. Modifying two different gunship models using two different prime contractors, both with different program managers, created many problems. In addition, both programs needed many of the same component parts and relied on many of the same subcontractors. While this had the advantage of parts commonality, it also led to competition for those parts and delays in both programs while priorities were established.[33]

From the outset, officials designated the AC-130A project the Gunship II program, now known as Project Pacer Stinger, and, as mentioned earlier, they assigned ASD to be the project manager. The WRAMA DMM acted as AFLC's project manager for the AC-119 modification, also known as the Gunship III program, or Project Combat Hornet. While WRAMA had a representative on the Configuration Control Board for the AC-130 project, ASD had ten, and TAC and ATC also had one each. Even so, WRAMA was the only organization that had a direct hand in the actual construction work for both projects, and plans also called for Warner Robins ultimately to assume sustainment management responsibility for both programs and both aircraft.[34]

In December 1967, when General McConnell sent Secretary Brown an interim report on the performance of the prototype in Vietnam, he attached a cover memo declaring, "It justifies the conversion of the remaining five JC-130A aircraft made available for the 'Shed Light' program from the ETR resources." McConnell recommended that the Air Force continue the AC-119 Gunship III program and modify all seven JC-130As, since, in his opinion, the AC-130s were "the most effective 'break through' we have experienced in tactical aviation."[35] Near the end of the month, Brown approved the reconfiguration of all seven JC-130As and directed that experts continue to work to improve the night and all-weather capabilities of the newest gunships. In turn, he advocated keeping the AC-47s in-theater for base/hamlet defense duties until all the AC-119s had arrived and were in a position to replace them.[36]

On January 5, 1968, in a memo to the Air Staff, Brown reiterated his vision for the gunship forces in Vietnam as he requested their support for a fleet of sixteen AC-119Gs, sixteen AC-119Ks, seven AC-130A production aircraft, and the refurbished prototype AC-130A. This was to be a mixed fleet, not just a replacement of the AC-47Ds. On the other hand, many senior Air Force officers favored using only the AC-130As and ending the AC-119 program in order to put the funds into expanding the more flexible and powerful AC-130As. To this end, Momyer had suggested to PACAF officials that thirty-two Super Spooky aircraft be built and deployed as quickly as possible. The commander-in-chief PACAF agreed completely and asked TAC to provide a concept of operations, deployment plan, units of assignment, personnel requirements, support concepts, and manpower ceilings.[37]

On December 31, 1967, seven Air Force senior officials recommended to CINCPACAF that the initial seven production AC-130s and the prototype be stationed in Thailand. They also assured him that they could accommodate as many more AC-130s, which would be built and sent to South Vietnam. This, they argued, would increase the number of personnel by only 1,402 over the number of AC-47 personnel. They maintained that this would fit existing headroom requirements if some other programs, such as Blind Bat, could be canceled. The USAF had already canceled the AP-2H self-contained night attack program.[38]

On February 12, 1968, after considering all viewpoints of those in Southeast Asia, General Ryan expressed his formal opinions in the final report on the AC-130A prototype combat tests. He recommended against making a one-for-one exchange of AC-130s for AC-47s, which seemed to underscore Secretary Brown's January pronouncement of a mixed force of eight AC-130As and, by now, thirty-two AC-119s. He had declared that these gunships would share duties such as hamlet defense, close air support, convoy escort, and interdiction. He advocated they fly most sorties from six orbit points located in South Vietnam. He suggested that AC-47 and AC-119 bases be located in Nha Trang, DaNang, Phu Cat, Pleiku, Phan Rang, Bien Hoa, and Binh Thuy. He also agreed with Brown, who eventually wanted the AC-47s to turn over all their duties to the AC-119s. Concurrently, he advocated that the AC-130s be based in Thailand and act primarily as truck killers along the infiltration routes in Laos and South Vietnam.[39]

Secretary Brown anticipated that the first production AC-130A would be completed by June and the seventh by October 1968. He called for the first AC-130, now called Spectre, to be deployed to Vietnam in December after the crews had received adequate training. At roughly the same time, the secretary of defense scheduled the AC-119s to begin deployment on July 1, 1968. All the while, many members of the Air Staff continued to lobby against the AC-119Gs, which appeared to them to be only a slight improvement over the antiquated AC-47Ds.[40]

On February 8, the secretary of defense had asked his own experts to provide him facts in support of a mixed-fleet force. They did, and on February 24, Paul Nitze approved the proposal directing the SECAF to continue to examine the need to retain the AC-47s. As the month ended, it seemed all the planets had begun to align for the early deployment of the AC-130s. TAC officials facing the Tet Offensive wanted the eight Spectre aircraft in-theater as soon as possible. While PACAF leaders recognized the need, they suggested that the AC-130s remain in America for thorough evaluation and crew training. Enemy pressure in South Vietnam finally convinced all those involved that deployment of all gunship assets needed to happen as quickly as possible. Anticipating communist attacks during the northeast monsoon season as the Tet attacks sputtered along throughout Vietnam, all in-theater commanders and Air Staff officers concurred that they needed all their gunships on station by the spring of 1969 to blunt another potential enemy assault.[41]

The Tet Offensive also affected Brown's thinking on the number of AC-130s. This, along with the success of the AC-130A prototype during the enemy's Tet attacks, led Brown, on March 29, 1968, to order the Air Force to examine the possibility of increasing the gunship fleet threefold. He gave top priority to investigating what kind of aircraft should be modified, how they should be configured, and what the price would be. The initial proposal called for eighteen AC-130s, twenty-six AC-119Gs, twenty-six AC-119Ks, and fourteen AC-97s. The most popular and ambitious plan aimed at adding forty-four AC-47s, doubling the AC-119Ks, adding fourteen AC-130s to the mix, and totally eliminating the AC-97s. While AFLC officials believed the AC-97 was a good choice, due to its availability and solid airframe, Brown ultimately rejected it because of its high sustainment costs, its need for long runways, and its protracted modification lead time.[42]

As the spring unfolded, new proposals continued to roll into SECAF's office. On April 12 the Air Staff recommended deploying twenty-six AC-119Gs, fifty-two AC-119Ks, and thirty-two AC-130As. They believed this was the most cost effective arrangement. The secretary concurred with this suggestion but determined that the Air Force only needed eighteen AC-130As. Air Staff members pointed out that even as the final decision was being made, the cost of the AC-119 program had gone up $7,630,000, and deployment had been delayed by four months. This was not the end of it. On April 29, Air Force leaders shocked Washington by changing their gunship fleet request to fifty-five AC-47s, twenty-six AC-119Gs, twenty-six AC-119Ks, and sixteen AC-130s. Air Force commanders in Southeast Asia were dumbfounded. Several key officers replied that the fifty-five AC-47s were simply a waste of precious funds and let Washington know they wanted only the AC-119s and AC-130s. They, rightfully, argued that such a large force would compromise manpower ceilings, and that while JCS and CSAF pressure had led them to accept the AC-119s, this proposal was simply too much to bear. Momyer, Ryan, and others let it be known, in no uncertain terms, that the AC-130s should replace the AC-47s as soon as possible.[43]

Often circumstances overtake events, and this discussion over numbers of gunships soon became mostly irrelevant. In July, OSD officials rejected the construction of more Spectres, opting to stick with the original plan to deploy seven production AC-130As and the refurbished prototype. This decision arrived at nearly the same moment reports from the Vulcan Express 1967 combat tests were beginning to circulate through the upper echelons of the Washington defense community. The data decisively proved that the AC-130 could be modified, operated, and maintained at a low cost. They also indicated, without question, that it not only performed its close air support role better than any other aircraft available, but was far more effective than A-26s and F-105s at flying interdiction missions. The cost per enemy vehicle destroyed for the AC-130 was $5,100; it was $5,900 for the A-26 and $118,000 for the F-105. It seemed like a no-brainer.[44]

Bolstered with this new information, Air Force leaders decided to reopen the issue of AC-130s with the new secretary of defense, Clark M. Clifford.

What they apparently failed to grasp was the fact that the entire course of the war had changed. Although US and ARVN forces had beaten back the pressure of the communist Tet Offensive, the public relations losses for President Johnson's Vietnam commitment had been devastating. In late March, on national television, he declared he would not run for reelection in the 1968 presidential campaign. He halted the bombing of North Vietnam in an effort to initiate meaningful negotiations with Hanoi. While this change was more obvious, just beneath the surface Tet had sown the seeds for a new US policy designed to extricate its forces from the conflict in Southeast Asia. As South Vietnamese ambassador Bui Diem later wrote, "The South Vietnamese, in fact, failed to understand the real nature of the US intervention, making erroneous assumptions about the staying power of America and, in the process, abdicated their own role in the war. This resignation, which in retrospect appears to be one of the fatal mistakes made by my countrymen, was somewhat facilitated by their partners, the Americans, who either out of impatience or overconfidence, tried to do everything themselves."[45]

When Bui Diem met with President Johnson on March 18, 1968, as he put it, "I went into the Oval Office, where I saw a man . . . completely lost!" Instead of greeting his visitor jovially, as he he normally would do, the president seemed down. While LBJ promised he would resupply the South Vietnamese and maintain the US commitment, Diem noted, "His gray and melancholy appearance made it clear to me that Tet had meant the beginning of the end of American commitment to South Vietnam."[46]

By the time Clifford became secretary of defense, the Vietnam War was already evolving into a covering action for a US withdrawal. In the meantime, in Vietnam, the reality of conflict remained intense both in the air and on the ground. People were dying, and any new weapon system that could reduce those casualties was welcomed by theater commanders. As the AC-119s began to arrive, Seventh Air Force and PACAF commanders decided to swap out the AC-47s. The new MACV commander, Gen. Creighton W. Abrams, agreed with that plan, even though Air Force leaders in Washington sought to keep both gunships in the inventory.[47]

In December 1968 an Air Force advisory group recommended transferring the AC-47s to the VNAF. With this plan on the table, the need to speed up completion of the seven AC-130As became urgent. To that end, the workforce at ASD, WRAMA, Lockheed, and LTVE put on a full-court press to complete the AC-130 reconfiguration. PACAF officials worried aloud that having two different managers for the two different gunship programs would delay them both at a very critical time. Officials at Warner Robins reassured them, explaining, "Due to the magnitude and urgency of this mod USAF assigned

ASD total responsibility. AFLC (WRAMA/SM) assumes management of entire C-130 series airframe and MAC [Military Airlift Command] coded items assigned to WRAMA for support of modifications. Until such time WRAMA receives transfer of engineering responsibility of the Gunship modification from ASD, responsibility lies with ASD."[48]

While debates swirled in Washington and policy makers decided who had responsibility for what and whom, government and contractor personnel back at the plant continued to work on the complex modification, parts, and management aspects of the overall gunship programs. For example, ATC established parameters for both crew and ground support orientation and training with Lockheed and LTVE. As a result, LTVE held courses at Lockborne AFB, Ohio, in May and June 1968 for AC-130 airmen, while Fairchild-Hiller held sessions for AC-119 personnel at the same location from April 15 to June 3, 1968. At the same time, courses on parts and equipment familiarity, flight characteristics, and unique maintenance responsibilities were also held at Ellington AFB, Texas, and Clinton County AFB, Ohio.[49]

Both Gunship II and III programs had extensive relationships with subcontractors. Among the most prominent were Motorola Inc., Scottsdale, Arizona, which produced and furnished the AN/APQ-133 side-looking and AN/APQ-136 forward-looking radar sets. Electro-Optical Systems, Inc., of Pomona, California, dealt with the NOS/NOD eyeglass and the high-beam illuminator. Texas Instruments Corporation of Dallas, Texas, worked with infrared receiving systems such as the terrain avoidance system and the FLIR system. Their technical experts also collaborated with Motorola on the AN/APQ-136 radar system. TRW Inc. Systems Division of Redondo Beach, California, produced the fire control display and fire control computer. Chicago Aerial Industries, with facilities in Barrington, Illinois, and Inglewood, California, developed the gun sight. Last, but not least, General Precision Corporation, Kearfott Division, Glendale, California, developed the principal fire control computer system. Each subcontractor had representatives at the offices of the prime contractors and at Robins AFB, Georgia. They also had "technical representatives of these companies serve, to some extent, at the stateside training center at Lockbourne and at the operational activities in Southeast Asia to meet contracted support requirements."[50]

During the first year of the developmental stage, plans called for LTVE to support the AC-130 by providing contractor-furnished equipment (CFE) unique to the Gunship II configuration. Experts anticipated that WRAMA would assume organic follow-on support as soon as the contract ran out. However, Air Staff officials wanted to anticipate as many issues that might arise during the project as possible. For example, they believed that senior

DOD leaders might well decide to increase the number of AC-130s, since Secretary Brown had consistently wavered on the number of AC-119s to be built as well as the total gunship force he envisioned. Besides, the dynamics of the debate among the senior generals and Defense Department leadership continued to affect these potential numbers. The use of common modification components and operational training sites for both projects meant that any shortages in parts or even a minor delay in delivery or completion of training could cause the scheduled milestones of production to be slipped. Air Staff leaders pressed ATC officials to be sure that maintenance personnel would be trained before deployment of the aircraft to Southeast Asia. Nearly everyone involved had some question about the basic configuration of the airframe and the project scheduling as a whole. WRAMA officials alerted their AFLC counterparts that in their opinion, as things stood in the spring of 1968, "first year organic support [was] 'out of the question.'"[51]

Even before the DOD approved the AC-130 full-scale production program, Air Force officials decided to conduct a joint program review of the Gunship II program. They determined that if they needed a contractor logistics support (CLS) plan, AFLC should fund the program, while TAC and PACAF would fund the portion of the CLS plan dealing with field maintenance. They also expected AFLC to fund the depot repair costs under this plan.[52]

Financial experts projected that the Gunship II program would cost $38.5 million once Air Force officials approved the final project plan. In turn, Air Staff leaders directed their counterparts in AFSC not to make any alterations in the program without their approval, since "the present Gunship II operation in SEA [was] producing significant data which could lead to recommended changes to production of follow-on gunship aircraft." This directive caused a debate between TAC and PACAF officials over the form the CLS plan should take. Members of PACAF worried that the proposed support plan would make them dependent on the contractor for the supply of limited assets and possibly delay the arrival of important parts and equipment. They promoted relying on WRAMA for this support.[53]

TAC opposed a dual support plan, assuring the Air Staff that "within this command, the AC-130 and AC-119 Maintenance activity will be the same; therefore, this headquarters does not desire dual contractual supply support for the Gunship Program. Highly recommend that all gunship peculiar system support be by one manufacturer." On the other hand, Air Force–level experts continued to develop a support plan that assigned CLS to the prime contractors of both Gunship II and III programs, specifically LTVE and Fairchild-Hiller.[54]

In the meantime, ASD leaders, frustrated by this apparent lack of focus, acted to gather specific direction from senior Air Force officials in Washington. This plan had allowed for contractor support of spares, aerospace ground equipment, depot repair, and technical support from June 1, 1968, to June 30, 1969. After having initiated the technical services aspects of the approved CLS plan, the Air Staff had halted their work on the new reconfigured design and development of the AC-130s. To ASD, this was not fair to the contractors, who had already spent so much money on the project. Nor, in their opinion, was it an efficient way for the Air Force to spend its own dollars on this important modification program. In a message to WRAMA officials, ASD leaders declared that the Air Force was "obligated for first-year contractor support; that LTVE had proceeded to order spare parts and train technical representatives and that termination action would be 'unthinkable.'"[55]

AFLC officials countered that WRAMA had no money to pay for logistics support during the initial stages of the modification program, and CLS was the only alternative. They also reminded all the parties that under Air Force Regulation (AFR) 67-17, "Field Maintenance and Supply Support," and Air Force Manual (AFM) 66-18, *Contract Field Services,* it was not reasonable to expect WRAMA to undertake field-level maintenance, which was supposed to fall to the using commands. Thus, command leaders directed Warner Robins personnel to examine its support policies toward both gunship programs with a view toward combining the resources for the two projects at the earliest possible date.[56]

The Air Force response directed TAC and PACAF to fund all "organizational and field maintenance performed by contract within their commands." They also requested assurance from AFLC officials that all "the depot level maintenance and supply portion of the contract services" would be funded by AFLC. They also directed AFLC to place the logistics support program under contract for review at higher headquarters and address provisions for normal Air Force support capability at the earliest date, keeping in mind that AFR 66-17 did not provide contract training for active-duty personnel. They also requested an educated projection as to how many months an interim support agreement would be required. They told all parties they expected them to be flexible in their support of both gunship programs in the forward operating areas (FOAs) and zone of the interior (ZI). Last, but not least, they requested a "time phased plan to guarantee availability of standard Federal Stock Numbers (FSNs) and stock listings well in advance of the conclusion of contractor services."[57]

One of the major concerns both AFLC and WRAMA experts had, pursuant to the AC-130 program, was WRAMA's ability to support the prototype AC-130A already deployed to Southeast Asia. They argued that since ASD had developed the aircraft and had several contracts with various vendors to provide various levels of support for every aspect of the aircraft, it made no sense to switch horses in midstream. AFLC officials emphasized that the new AC-130s were not configured exactly the same and that LTVE was not going to be the same prime contractor. They believed it would be much easier for ASD to extend the contracts from August 15, 1968, to May 1, 1969, to support the prototype, which would, at some point, be back in the field with the production models. They concluded that all indications were that the prototype would not be modified to resemble the planes in the Gunship II Program but, rather, be returned to Vietnam for further research and development analysis. This is exactly what did happen.[58]

Throughout the Gunship II program, funding was always a problem. On May 27, 1968, experts from WRAMA/WRN reported to their counterparts at AFLC that they needed $2.225 million in P431 funds for fiscal year 1969 (FY69) in order to assure depot-level maintenance for AC-130 components in the Gunship II program. They insisted that they had to have these dollars by July 1, 1968, because they could not provide logistics support with the resources available in the initial phase. They believed the contractor should assume depot supply responsibilities for CFE and modified government-furnished equipment (GFE). In addition, they believed that supply services should include all actions affecting the "acquisition, receipt, binning, warehousing, issuing, re-issuing, repair and return, servicing, delivering, and status reporting pertinent to the effective management of equipment and materiel for this program." Warner Robins also advised AFLC that contract services for the Gunship II program would be needed from June 1, 1968, to June 30, 1969.[59]

On June 11–12, 1968, WRAMA representatives hosted a planning meeting that included experts from Air Force, ASD, AFLC, TAC, and PACAF. After a vigorous discussion, the attendees agreed that the prime contractors should provide support for the gunships until it became available through normal Air Force supply and maintenance channels. From this, a single management policy evolved, with supply and maintenance being provided under a contract with LTVE for the AC-130s and Fairchild-Hiller for the AC-119s. Stakeholders at the meeting further agreed to keep contractor-operated base supply and Air Force base supply completely separated. In turn, the contractors would control turn-in, issued, return of peculiar and modified GFE parts to base personnel, in-country personnel, and the ZI or contractor-operated supply and maintenance facility, including three sites in the United States, two overseas, and one in the ZI. As for depot-level contractor supply, the contractors would serve as item manager for issue and receipt of peculiar and modified government furnished parts (GFP), with one site each at Greenville, Texas, and Saint Augustine, Florida. They also agreed to move all unique and modified reparable GFPs to the prime contractor, which meant LTVE for the AC-130s and Fairchild-Hiller for the AC-119s.[60]

On June 27, 1968, officials at HQ Air Force also sent a message to leaders at AFSC and AFLC outlining the support parameters for AC-130 test-bed aircraft. As alluded to earlier, they concluded that since ASD had handled management and support of nonstandard items on the test-bed plane in FY68, they should continue this process in FY69 and that AFLC should provide funds to ASD to help with the effort. They also specified that AFLC funding, based on prior-year data, would require $200,000 every six months from August 1968 to May 1969. Under this final contract, LTVE became responsible for logistics support for unique CFE and modified GFE. This included inspection, repair, and overhaul of all these unique systems and maintenance of depot supply services at the contractor's facilities and base supply services at the ZI and at one main operating base in Southeast Asia. To fund this plan, WRAMA experts estimated $975,000 and $554,000 would be needed for all supply support services.[61]

Throughout the Gunship II program, each aircraft underwent a formal review that included a safety inspection and a first-article configuration inspection (FACI). The FACIs took place at LTVE's facility in Greenville, Texas. The inspection focused on verifying the aircraft's product configuration baseline and completion of the formal acceptance test processes.[62]

In late July 1968, Air Force officials also concluded a memorandum of agreement with the main contractors that established a contractor-operated supply facility at Lockbourne AFB, Ohio, to support both the AC-119s and the AC-130s. It provided a supply center for unique equipment used by Fairchild-Hiller and LTVE, respectively. Both supply operations functioned twenty-four hours a day, seven days a week and were supported by Warner Robins supply experts, who made sure the supplies were warehoused correctly and the appropriate parts were in stock.[63]

Concurrently, WRAMA technicians acted to help the operating commands and contractors create contract-operated supply functions for contractor furnished equipment (CFE) and GFP at main support bases in Southeast Asia. WRAMA requested eighteen military personnel to man those facilities, but PACAF could not provide the personnel. Officials at WRAMA solved this manpower problem by temporarily deploying two of their own rapid area supply support (RASS) teams comprised of civilian technicians to support the main support base supply facilities in Southeast Asia. Plans called for them to supply the operational units with unique equipment and spare parts for six to nine months until normal Air Force supply and maintenance channels could accommodate these new gunship units.[64] Experts established the primary AC-130 support base at Ubon RTAFB, Thailand, in July, and soon after, RASS team members arrived to commence full operations. Original plans called for team members to remain on temporary duty until April 30, 1969, but unforeseen issues delayed their return until June 30. With all these necessary components in place, modification moved more quickly. By December 1968, four AC-130As had arrived in Southeast Asia, and three more had arrived at Lockbourne AFB for crew and maintenance training.[65]

In January 1969, as the Gunship II program continued to unfold, WRAMA personnel began preparations for assumption of systems responsibility for the AC-130As. Plans called for LTVE to relinquish this function on July 1, 1969. This included inventory management and specialized repair activities. Delays in transition forced WRAMA officials to extend the LTVE contract by ninety days. By October 1969 the specialized repair functions were staffed and equipped, allowing specific Warner Robins units to take over both inventory management and specialized repair activities operations. WRAMA handled GAU-2 miniguns, M-61 Vulcan cannons, and LAU-74 flare launchers, while their comrades in WRAMA's DMM serviced AAD-4 infrared devices, AN/APQ-133 radar, the AVG-2 NOS for the AC-130s and AVG-3 NOS for the AC-119s, AWG-13 fire controls, AVQ-8 and AVQ-16 illuminators, as well as ARQ-25 interrogation devices. Other units in WRAMA's DMM worked on AN/APQ-136 radars.[66]

Why Is the Damn Thing Taking So Long? A Focus on Development and Deployment

To completely understand why it took so long to build and deploy both the AC-119 and AC-130, one must dig deeply into the inner workings of what was then AFSC and AFLC. AFSC, specifically ASD, acted as the program manager for the AC-130, and AFLC, specifically WRAMA, did the same for the AC-119. Since the two modification programs evolved at the about the same time, both pulled in opposite directions to acquire the limited specialized equipment and unique parts and armament. In early 1968, as the programs began, the Air Force chief of staff suggested that the two major commands create a joint program office to coordinate both projects. Officials at AFLC believed that the existing channel of communications between AFSC and AFLC was adequate. The chief of staff relented but called for a meeting in late January 1968 at LTVE's Greenville facility to make sure everyone agreed.[67]

Representatives from LTVE, ASD, TAC, AFLC, and WRAMA attended the Greenville meeting in order to define the responsibilities each would assume. They decided that LTVE would provide special support items, such as aeronautical ground equipment (AGE), spares, contractor field support, and depot maintenance for the AC-130. They also agreed to train AC-130 maintenance personnel and flight crews at Lockborne AFB, Ohio, and Ubon RTAFB, Thailand. In turn, Warner Robins was to furnish common support items through normal channels, but they warned that program urgency might require alteration to this arrangement and even limit time for training. From the outset, AFLC had anticipated and planned for support. In addition, they recommended that since the test-bed AC-130A, T/N 1626, had returned for repairs, it be reworked into a "contractor-modified Gunship II configuration." This would later become an issue, since ground commanders in Vietnam were urging the return of the Vulcan Express, and this recommendation was never carried out.[68]

As noted earlier, on February 12 ASD, with AFLC approval, arranged with LTVE to organize a sixteen-person unit to go to Southeast Asia in August to support the AC-130 fire control system (computer, gun sight, and safety display) as well as the FLIR, airborne-illuminator xenon lights, NOD/NOS, beacon-tracking radar set, Mark 24 flare dispensing system, and UHF homing and ranging system. This action soon caused a disagreement among the stakeholders. On April 23–24, 1968, during a joint AC-130/AC-119 logistics support conference held at Robins AFB, Air Staff attendees questioned the efficiency of such an arrangement. PACAF officials agreed with the Air Staff and expressed concern that this setup might affect the AC-119 program, which was just getting started with the production of the G models. Conversely, AFLC, Warner Robins, and ASD experts argued that as there was not an existing AC-130 organic depot-level maintenance capability, there might be time delays, since there were so many separate contracts with so many vendors. As a result, they believed that the only workable arrangement was to have contract and field maintenance for the high-priority AC-130 modification components. This seemed logical, since initial operational support would come from the contractor production line and their vendors. The two sides could not come to an agreement by the end of the meeting and were left to finalize the debate long-distance. Ultimately, ASD constructed a compromise that called for a one-year contractor support arrangement that would evolve into Air Force support with a large contractor role. Looking back, is there any wonder that both programs took many extra months to complete?[69]

By July 1968 the standard work pattern was in place. ASD continued as the AC-130 program manager, focusing on engineering, reconfiguration, and modification of the seven aircraft as well as initial testing. Warner Robins acted as AC-130 system manager, and LTVE performed the actual airframe reconfiguration, management of the unique component supply system, and operation of the repair depot. ATC began crew training for the TAC and PACAF personnel who would fly the newly reshaped weapon systems. In late August, the stakeholders met at the LTVE main plant to discuss issues involving technical orders (TOs), requisitions, and shipment of spares and AGE. Two of the gunships were already in crew training, and officials expected final acquisition of spares to be completed on September 15, 1968, with TO completion by November 1, 1968.[70]

Throughout this period LTVE struggled to stay on schedule. They never had much time with the Vulcan Express test-bed aircraft, since it returned to the United States from initial combat tests in December 1967 and then went back to Vietnam in February 1968. Original plans had called for the prototype to spend time in the LTVE factory for analysis and evaluation. However, the AC-130A's unique attributes were needed in Vietnam to help quell the enemy's Tet attacks, so the depot maintenance work was accelerated so T/N 1626 could return as soon as possible. Air Force leaders decided to use the first two production models for crew training, which meant that they never received later modifications, and it was not until the third production model was completed that they could send an AC-130A to Vietnam. Many Air Force officers also believed that LTVE used its time poorly, and this, coupled with normal delays, put the program behind the curve. One big problem this situation led to was the different equipment used in the first two and last five production AC-130As.[71]

On March 5, 1968, after the first two AC-130As were already in crew training, HQ Air Force decided to have LTVE install enhanced radar systems at a cost of $2,553,225 on the last five gunships, increasing the total program cost to nearly $22 million and delaying the production run by several weeks. They also installed upgraded FLIR. This is not to say that the additions were not a good thing, but it did expose the mistake of sending the first two aircraft into crew training before the others had been completed. Not only did this mean that the first two had to be retrofitted at a later date, but it also meant that crew training had been compromised, since the training gunships and the deployed aircraft were not the same. This, along with sensor and integration issues, pushed back the project completion date to late summer of 1968. Additional crew training issues again delayed completion to February 1969.[72]

Chapter Conclusion

With the AC-119s in operation and the AC-130As either in-theater or soon to be, in August 1969 WRAMA officials acted on a request from their counterparts at PACAF to establish the Weapon Systems Support Logistics Office

(WSSLO) at Ubon RTAFB for both gunship programs. The WSSLO replaced the departing RASS teams and assumed contractor responsibilities for overall AC-130A systems support at all the main support bases. It was at this point that the AC-130s were on the verge of going into combat. In retrospect, one has to wonder why it had taken so long to deploy the Gunship II fleet, which was actually near completion in late 1968. It is a question worth further examination.[73]

4 Final Production and Deployment; Operations in Vietnam

When the AC-130A test-bed aircraft first deployed to Vietnam in 1967, officials placed it under the 14th Air Commando Wing. In July 1968, CINCPACAF created the 16th Air Commando Squadron and placed it under the 8th Tactical Fighter Wing. This arrangement did not last long, for on August 1, 1968, the 16th ACS was redesignated the 16th SOS, and the 14th ACW was redesignated the 14th SOW. They stationed the prototype at Ubon RTAFB so it could be colocated with its parent wing. It also made it easier to resupply the 16th SOS and also allowed the Seventh Air Force to keep direct control over the unit. Original plans called for the unit also to be activated on August 1, but the Air Force delayed the formal standup until October 31 while it worked to receive government permission to bring more US forces into Vietnam. Eventually, this took place, and the aircraft and personnel were placed, as planned, under the 16th SOS.[1]

Under Special Orders 543-69, the gunships were to provide both offensive and defensive combat support for US forces in Southeast Asia. The AC-130As flew night interdiction and armed reconnaissance missions against vehicular and water infiltration traffic, close air support for US and allied ground forces, missions in support of outposts and strategic towns and cities, search and rescue missions, and daylight armed escort. The night missions allowed them to take advantage of their new sensors. The production models flew their earliest sorties in support of outposts southeast of Ban Than Teng in south central Laos near a major north-south enemy supply route. On one such mission, the prototype flew for four straight nights, firing 16,200 rounds of 20mm shells and 16,500 rounds of 7.62mm ammunition to repel an attack by communist forces. They killed 240 of the enemy and completely broke the back of the attack. This inspired the interest of US officials. With Hanoi increasing the pace of troops and supplies pouring into the South, the Laotian panhandle became a key target area for the AC-130As and their unique abilities to stem that tide.[2]

By early 1969 the enemy infiltration routes, best known as the Ho Chi Minh Trail, had grown into an extensive and redundant network of roads, trails, and footpaths. Supplies were moved by thousands of trucks, bicycles, and porters on foot. Winding their way through dense double-canopy jungles and across steep mountains, the communists moved mostly at night along seventeen hundred miles of twisting roads with dozens of detours and alternate routes. They stored and stockpiled supplies in numerous caves and dedicated 150,000 mostly young people to sustain and repair the roads and truck stops throughout the maze. As the sixties faded into the seventies, the enemy added AAA and SAM batteries all along the trail to defend these precious commodities so essential to winning the war. It became a North Vietnamese obsession.[3]

One key issue that American airpower faced in Vietnam was the unique terrain. Maj. Louis Seig, in his historic 1970 Air Force Contemporary Historical Examination of Current Operations (CHECO) report on geography and its effect on air operations in Vietnam, wrote; "It must be pointed out that due to terrain, forest canopy, etc., we quite often get only one shot at a target before we lose his precise location." This was a theme repeated in many reports by both airmen and ground officers, then and now.[4]

While terrain was important, the linchpin to the entire infiltration process proved to be the weather, since the monsoon season created alternating periods of very good or very bad weather. US officials planned Operation Commando Hunt to take advantage of weather conditions during air attacks against enemy supply and troop targets. Indeed, between May and November, when the southwest monsoons hit, air operations over Laos proved difficult for American aircraft, most of which lacked all-weather capabilities. At first, this did not concern air operations officials, since they assumed trucks were no more capable of driving down the Ho Chi Minh Trail in this extreme weather than their aircraft could fly over it. In retrospect, this proved to be a false assumption, since the rains that clogged the muddy roads facilitated the passage of PAVN barge and boat traffic down the multitude of streams and rivers in Laos and Vietnam. The communists soon realized the rainy season meant fewer air sorties, and those few fit into an utterly predictable pattern. Of course, during the northwest monsoon season, which lasted from November to May, things dried out, and the PAVN picked up their pace, as did the American air attacks. US aircrews called it "hunting season."[5]

Ultimately, the AC-130s, with their ever-improving sensors, proved highly effective against the flow of communist troops and supplies. As they gained experience during operations, they created better tactics and developed better equipment. Indigenous agents captured enemy prisoners, watched roads, and reported on the main routes being employed by the enemy to push materials into South Vietnam. They also used aerial reconnaissance flights and later acoustic sensors planted in the jungles to gather additional data to support gunship missions. As a result, the Americans focused on two primary areas in Laos. One was Barrel Roll in Northern Laos, and the second was Steel Tiger in the Panhandle. The PAVN used the Mu Gia and Ban Karai passes to enter Laos and the Ban Raving and Nape passes to leave Laos and enter South Vietnam. In an effort to generate targets, provide strike control, and provide damage assessment, the Air Force also began Operations Tiger Hound and Cricket. Besides AC-130As designed for night interdiction, the Air Force employed many and varied aircraft, including propeller-driven A-1s for close air support and aerial interdiction and B-52s to create mudslides on the mountains and close the passes. Despite all this effort, the flow of supplies and troops was only partly and temporarily stopped.[6]

Commando Hunt Operations

In order to understand the role of AC-130s once they deployed to Vietnam, it is important to have a basic understanding of what kind of war it was they were about to enter. During the period from 1969 to early 1972, the most significant air campaigns and all-out interdiction campaigns waged by the United States were the seven numbered air operations known as Commando Hunt. Their target was the Ho Chi Minh Trail and the resources the enemy brought down that network of roads.

In the early 1950s, as the Viet Minh struggled to dislodge the French from Indochina, they built a rudimentary network of infiltration roads to supply their units in the South. After the French left and Vietnam was divided at the seventeenth parallel, the new leadership in Hanoi formed contacts with the antigovernment southern factions for the purpose of reunifying Vietnam under a communist regime. In 1957, communist guerilla units, supported by the NVA, were established, and over the last two years of the decade the National Liberation Front came into being to act as the political arm of this antigovernment movement in South Vietnam. Concurrently, Hanoi created the 559th Transportation Group (established in May 1959 or the fifth month, thus, 559) to furnish the southern partisans with materials from the North. The 559th's routes became the origin of the Ho Chi Minh Trail.[7]

Responding to American aid to the South, between April and December 1964 more than ten thousand NVA, including the first tactical units, journeyed into South Vietnam to support the indigenous communist forces there. Northern engineers, led by Col. Dong Si Nguyen, began to upgrade the road network through Laos. In spite of the inhospitable terrain in the Laotian panhandle, or Steel Tiger, the North Vietnamese carved roads through the mountain passes from North Vietnam into Laos, across the limestone cliffs, and through the mountains as high as five thousand feet. They pushed through the jungles and bamboo forests and forded raging rivers.[8]

By 1971 the 559th Transportation Group, by then the 559th Military Region, had expanded the Ho Chi Minh Trail from "a fragile net of jungle footpaths" into thousands of miles of "well-tended motor roads." Hanoi subdivided southern Laos into fifteen semiautonomous military districts, or *binh tram*s, each with a commander responsible for all functions. Transportation battalions moved supplies through each district, engineer battalions built and repaired roads and moved supplies if needed, liaison battalions managed the infiltration of personnel along trails separate from those used for supplies, while support groups provided food, shelter, medical services, and other staff functions.[9]

Even though US leaders had planned to close these routes by aerial interdiction, it was not until November 1968 that enough air assets were available, following the cessation of Rolling Thunder, to begin such operations. Until the end of Tet 1968, most US efforts were used in support of southern ground operations, in which ground forces attempted to destroy northern units and supplies once they had reached South Vietnam. This is not to say Laos wasn't bombed, but the full brunt of Allied air power would not fall on the Laotian panhandle until after Tet revealed the full importance of the trail.[10]

On November 15, 1968, only two weeks after Rolling Thunder ended, Commando Hunt I became the first of seven such operations, each lasting roughly six months and alternating from the winter-spring dry season to the summer-fall monsoon wet season. Using mainly bombers to attack the road network, as well as fighter-bombers and lower and slower aircraft that would eventually include AC-119Ks and the AC-130s in later Commando Hunt operations, attacks concentrated on four primary kinds of targets: trucks traveling on the trail; the road network itself, including truck parks, rest areas, and the like; terrain such as passes, river fords, and jungles; and AAA and SAM sites that the enemy placed along the route. The USAF employed laser-guided bombs, usually delivered by fighters, on the later targets, including bridges.[11]

The communists often traveled at night, when the vast majority of US aircraft, lacking night or all-weather capabilities, did not fly. Beginning in 1969 and continuing through early 1973, the Air Force overcame this disadvantage by using AC-119K and AC-130A/E fixed-wing gunships. The AC-119K Stingers

Early AC-130 cockpit, pilot's position.

used their four 7.62mm Gatling guns, two 20mm cannon, and infrared sensors to run up remarkable kill numbers. The Vulcan Express prototype and the later production AC-130As, with two 40mm cannon and two 20mm cannon, also wreaked havoc on the enemy. Later models were fitted with one 105mm cannon, which replaced one of the 40mm cannons and was made all the more the effective by the wide range of ever improving sensors the gunships carried.[12]

According to official counts, by the end of the war the eighteen AC-130s that were ultimately deployed claimed 7,335 truck kills, compared to 461 by B-57s and 1,873 by fighter-bombers. Sensors made the AC-130s particularly deadly at night, but they were blinded by daylight and heat, especially at dawn and at dusk. The B-52s, affectionately known as Buffs, were particularly effective against the passes and stationary targets such as trucks congregated at choke points. Employing standard bombing doctrine, the Seventh Air Force's aircraft bombed using one-square-mile boxes, labeled A, B, C, and D, covering the Ban Karai, Mu Gia, Ban Raving, and Nape passes. An average of 27 B-52 sorties per day attacked those passes. However, by the time Commando Hunt V began in late 1970, tactical aircraft had begun to fly the lion's share of sorties, averaging 125 a day. In December 1967, even before the first Commando Hunt mission, the Americans had established the Igloo White sensor system, which was operated by Task Force Alpha at Nakhon Phanom Royal Thai Air Force Base and designed to guide the airborne attacks.[13]

By the time Commando Hunt I began in late 1968, the entire process had begun to run like a well-oiled machine reminiscent of a large American corporation. While this seemed like a good idea, eventually Air Force sortie scheduling became so thoroughly routine in nature that it also became predictable, and the ever resourceful enemy soon adapted. Generally, the hours that the enemy used the trail were from 4:00 a.m. to 8:00 a.m. and 4:00 p.m. to 8:00 p.m., which "coincided with shift changes at American bases and with changes in the deployment of aircraft. Fighter-bombers usually arrived on station after dawn, at around 8:00 a.m. Pilots preferred to bomb after the sun had fully risen to avoid visual misperceptions more common in the half-light of dawn or dusk." Besides, it was better to be shot down early in the day so you had a better chance of rescue and would not have to risk spending the night in the jungle.[14]

Initially, Commando Hunt operations were confined to a seventeen-hundred-square-mile sector of Laos that bordered South Vietnam. Commando Hunt I employed 40 percent of its sorties to cut the narrow roads along the trail, while 35 percent attacked trucks and storage areas and 10 percent attacked antiaircraft sites. The campaign began in November 1968 and ended on April 30, 1969. By that time the newer gunships in-theater were being employed in increasing numbers against those targets. It was at that point that analysts decided they had inflicted enough damage to force the enemy to use "water routes including the Cambodian port of Kompong Som." At first, they planned to focus their next efforts against those water routes. However, at least one report did not paint such a rosy picture and even concluded, "Notwithstanding their rising material losses, the Communists doggedly continue to send a substantial flow of supplies through Laos into South Vietnam."[15]

At the outset of the southwest monsoon season in May 1969, Commando Hunt II began with B-52s dropping 500- and 750-pound bombs that caused mud slides along the wet mountain passes and helped the rains close the roads. The PAVN used frequent bad-weather bombing pauses to rebuild the roads and to stage troops, trucks, and supplies along their border. Supported by the Soviet Union and Eastern Bloc, they also imported more and better trucks; built a petroleum, oil, and lubricant pipeline; and set up air defenses all along the trail. Besides, with bombing of the North curtailed, as Seventh Air Force commander Gen. George S. Brown put it, "The enemy had a 'free ride' to the border of Laos and South Vietnam."[16]

With the next dry season, the third campaign witnessed the employment of seismic and acoustic sensors to detect truck movements. These sensors were unaffected by darkness and allowed spur-of-the-moment gunship attacks to catch the enemy exposed. From November 1969 to April 1970, B-52s supported Commando Hunt III, and during April and May, they also supported ground operations in both Laos and Cambodia. However, "during Commando Hunt III the tempo of air operations declined gradually." In early 1970, intelligence estimates indicated that infiltration was down over 50 percent. With growing domestic dissent and the ever-draining expense of what seemed to be a never-ending war facing him, Nixon cut the sortie ceiling on February 26, 1970.[17]

What most US analysts apparently failed to understand was that the enemy was rebuilding. In this war, the enemy required almost no logistics lines, since their troops lived off the land, the people, and foreign resupply of vital materials.[18]

As Commando Hunt operations unfolded for the fourth time, B-52s were diverted to Barrel Roll in northern Laos to support General Vang Pao and his operative forces, the Hmong, in their ever-widening struggles with the Pathet Lao and the PAVN. In late 1970, as Commando Hunt V began, intelligence discovered vast stockpiles of supplies around Tchepone at the upper end of the trail—a supply hub for forces headed south. US leaders, fearing this was the buildup for an attack on South Vietnam, moved to eliminate the depot using ARVN ground troops and US aircraft.[19]

Phase I of the Laotian invasion, code-named Lam Son 719, commenced on October 30, 1970, as US aircraft cleared Quang Tri and US troops set up a logistics base on the Laotian border near the Khe Sanh and Vandegrift Marine bases. The Air Force airlifted twenty thousand tons of supplies and over twelve thousand ARVN soldiers. Phase II began on February 8, 1971, and by February 23 more than seventeen thousand ARVN troops had entered Laos, supported by gunships, tactical aircraft, and 399 B-52 sorties. On February 25, twenty-four thousand PAVN combat troops counterattacked. This larger-than-anticipated force was supported by 120 tanks and artillery. The ARVN offensive ground to a halt on March 3, and a week later another enemy counterstroke forced the ARVN ground commander, Lt. Gen. Hoang Xuan Lam, to order a withdrawal. The retreat soon turned into a rout. Aided by US helicopters, which airlifted survivors, and B-52 strikes that covered the withdrawal, most of the ARVN were extracted by March 24.[20]

The cost was high, with 107 helicopters lost and 601 damaged. The United States lost 176 killed and 1,042 wounded. By the time the operation officially ended on April 6, 1971, the enemy had lost 14,000 killed, 4,800 wounded, 20,000 tons of food and ammunition, 156,000 gallons of fuel, 1,530 trucks, 74 tanks, and 6,000 individual weapons, mostly due to air strikes. The ARVN lost 1,519 killed, 5,423 wounded, 651 missing, 75 tanks, dozens of personnel carriers, 198 crew-served weapons, and 3,000 individual weapons.[21]

Commando Hunt VI lasted from May to October 1971 as a diminished operation. At the same time, the enemy flow of traffic down the trail grew markedly. The PAVN added 140 miles of new roads, and by October they had over 2,170 miles of single-lane roads, multilane roads, parallel routes, bypasses, and spur roads in Laos. They also added 344 AAA batteries and dozens of SA-2 SAM sites, most along the Laos–North Vietnam border, as well as new MiG bases in southern North Vietnam. One estimate placed ninety-six thousand NVA in Laos, sixty-three thousand in Cambodia, and two hundred thousand in South Vietnam. Thus, concerned US leaders planned one final massive campaign.[22]

Plans for Commando Hunt VII called for US air forces to bottle up the northern transport system within Laos, employing B-52s to close the passes leading from North Vietnam into Laos and subsequently from Laos into Cambodia and South Vietnam. Planners hoped to force communist vehicles to congregate in truck parks, where they would be attacked and destroyed. Concurrently, Buffs would bomb other roads to divert traffic to specific routes, where gunships and tactical bombers could attack exposed vehicles with "predictable success."[23]

The PAVN used several simple techniques to counter US airpower. They added 310 miles of uncharted main roads as well as hundreds of miles of small back road cutoffs and bypasses. In the early years, the enemy built roads along "the paths of least resistance," usually near rivers or in valleys, but this made the roads vulnerable to flooding and mud slides. As the PAVN engineers gained experience and received better equipment, they built roads at higher altitudes. Most were twelve to fifteen feet wide and surfaced with gravel, logs, or bamboo where drainage was poor, and while this network could not sustain heavy traffic during the rainy season, some traffic always got through.[24]

When Laotian roads were unusable during the rainy season, the Communists partially compensated by using rivers as alternative means of transportation, since the same rains that made the roads impassable provided the rivers with powerful currents that carried supply containers over long distances. The PAVN often used the Kong and Banhiang Rivers, whose tributaries flowed across the DMZ into Laos, and they located transshipment points several miles apart, where supplies were unloaded using nets and booms and stored for transport by trucks or porters.[25]

The communists also constructed pipelines. Three ran into Laos from the North Vietnamese panhandle, near facilities where Communist Bloc tankers docked, through the Mu Gia Pass to points along the northern parts of the Ho Chi Minh Trail, where they serviced truck parks. Another ran "through the

Ban Raving Pass to a distribution point near Tchepone." From there, other pipelines stretched to the Lao Bao Pass and the A Shau Valley, both of which were entrances into South Vietnam. They were made of Soviet-imported plastic pipes and were connected with metal couplings. Soviet-made pumps propelled motor oil, gasoline, diesel fuel, and kerosene.[26]

Commando Hunt VII began on November 1, 1971, and employed the latest airborne technology and weaponry available. OV-10 FAC aircraft directed laser-guided bombs dropped by fighters. Target-detection had been upgraded on most US aircraft, especially the AC-119s, AC-130s, and B-57Gs, including LLLTV, illuminators, beacon-tracking radar, and infrared sensors. Newly modified F-4 fighter aircraft, equipped with long-range electronic navigation (LORAN) position-fixing bombing systems, provided all-weather bombing capabilities.[27]

Commando Hunt VII unfolded in three phases, with initial operations centered in the Steel Tiger areas of Laos. Phase I began when Buffs struck the Mu Gia and Ban Karai Passes. Concurrently, fighter-bombers with laser-guided bombs attacked earth-moving equipment repairing roads. As the roads dried, the B-52s struck the southern routes at the Ban Raving Pass and in the western DMZ to detour traffic through the northern Mu Gia and Ban Karai Passes.[28] During the first three weeks, tactical aircraft and B-52s dropped 14,400 instantaneously fused 500-pound bombs and 17,100 750-pound bombs, as well as hundreds of 2,000-pound laser-guided bombs, Mk-36 magnetic-influence mines, and CBU antipersonnel mines. The initial appraisal determined that "enemy traffic had been slowed some of the time in some places." But by November 4 intelligence indicated that the Mu Gia Pass roads were already being repaired and that the flow was nearly normal.[29]

During Phase II, US aircraft struck enemy units as they moved south. Roads were cut by B-52s, which left large craters and created choke points and blocking belts. As enemy truck traffic backed up, Air Force fighters attacked with laser-guided bombs. During Commando Hunt VII, the Air Force created three major blocking belts.[30] They also seeded the area with air-dropped mines. As enemy units attempted to clear the mines or repair the roads, further attacks caught them exposed.[31]

The final phase began in early 1972 and shifted attacks to exit points from Laos into South Vietnam. Official reports claimed that large numbers of enemy vehicles were destroyed or damaged, with thousands of NVA killed and tens of thousands of tons of supplies destroyed. US officials declared the operations a success. However, on March 31, 1972, Commando Hunt came to a halt a day after PAVN Sr. Gen. Vo Nguyen Giap launched the Easter Offensive into South Vietnam. Even as 200,000 PAVN attacked key positions in the Republic of Viet Nam, Seventh Air Force officials proudly announced that Commando Hunt VII had destroyed 4,727 trucks and allowed only 5,024 of the 30,947 tons of supplies sent into Laos to reached South Vietnam. The irony of this report was not lost on Gen. Alton D. Slay, who had directed the final Commando Hunt operation. In his reply to this final Commando Hunt VII love note, he pointed out that the report of his deputy, Brig. Gen. Richard G. Cross, concluded, "This interdiction effort failed to prevent the enemy from positioning sufficient supplies to initiate an all-out offensive against South Vietnam."[32] It left the big question: If you destroyed so much, how can the enemy launch a 200,000-man attack supported by two hundred tanks?

For all its efforts, Commando Hunt left many questions about its value. It probably helped buy the United States time to withdraw its ground forces and begin Vietnamization, but as Earl Tilford points out in his book *Crosswinds:* "The strongest evidence against the reputed success of "Commando Hunt" was North Vietnam's launching of a major invasion against South Vietnam in late March 1972." There are those who have argued that the supplies and troops used in 1972 "had been carefully husbanded and stored in Laos over a period of four years." There is no question that many enemy soldiers and tons of supplies came south between the end of Tet and the start of Commando Hunt VII, but this means if Commando Hunt VII was a success, then the other operations were not.[33]

The greatest controversy is over the vast claims of trucks destroyed, since if one follows the official indices for success, then it should have been impossible for the PAVN to launch any kind of offensive. After Commando Hunt V, MACV officials created a flurry of controversy when they estimated that 16,266 trucks had been destroyed and 4,700 damaged. The Central Intelligence Agency (CIA) pointed out that such a number "more than doubled the total number estimated in all of North Vietnam and Laos."[34]

Later, Seventh Air Force officials claimed they had destroyed 11,009 trucks and damaged 8,208, well above the 4,727 destroyed and 5,882 damaged in Commando Hunt VII. In both cases the criteria for truck damage claims were haphazard. If a truck was seen to be hit and stopped, it was claimed. This proved nothing, since most truck drivers, when attacked, abandoned their vehicles to seek shelter. Most trucks hit by gunships might have holes in them, but they still might be usable. Later tests by US vehicle units proved that unless a truck blew up or burned, it was hard to put out of action. The communists had many repair facilities along the trail, and trucks were quickly repaired.[35]

It is worth noting that the North was importing trucks from the Soviet Bloc at a rate of between 4,500 a year in 1968 to around 10,000 in 1972, and "even if the US Air Force destroyed 4,727 trucks during Commando Hunt VII, such losses were probably insufficient to disrupt the logistical operations of the North Vietnamese for extended periods, if at all." The Seventh Air Force estimated that at the beginning of Commando Hunt there were 2,000–3,000 trucks in service along the trail. This was an estimate probably based on how many trucks it would normally take to operate the infiltration routes. But it ignores the fact that others such as Task Force Alpha, using photographic reconnaissance, indicated that the communists had "about 9,850 trucks in storage." Eduard Mark, in his definitive book *Aerial Interdiction,* argues that "even if it be assumed that the 3,000 initially in "Steel Tiger" were destroyed twice over (which was not claimed), the North Vietnamese would still have been able to replace the trucks destroyed with those in reserve at the beginning of the dry season, to say nothing of those subsequently received from the Soviet Union and other Communist countries."[36]

The number of trucks getting through was important mainly in regard to how much materiel got through. US analysts multiplied each truck by three tons in the wet season and by four tons, or the maximum payload of the communist trucks, when the country was under drought conditions and the roads were completely dry. The estimated total number of trucks was multiplied to predict the amount of materiel starting out. These figures were then reduced by the number of trucks destroyed. Three tons were subtracted for each southbound truck hit, while 1.5 tons were subtracted for each truck in a truck park. An additional ton was subtracted if the truck was moving, but only 0.5 ton if it were stopped. If the direction of the truck could not be determined, the subtraction level was divided by two. An additional 0.2 tons was subtracted for observed fires at storage areas and 0.5 ton for an explosion.[37]

This process was generally denounced by intelligence officials, who dubbed it the "numbers game." Based on their own sources—usually agents inside the enemy forces—the CIA concluded that "Communist forces in South Vietnam were only occasionally inconvenienced by interdiction." The assumption of great material loss when a truck was disabled or damaged is doubtful, not only because trucks were easily repaired, but also because of the simple, but effective, precautions the enemy took to save resources, such as covering southbound supplies with bags of rice. If the trucks were hit with bullets or shrapnel, the bags absorbed them. As long as the truck did not burn, even if it was inoperable the supplies got through.[38]

Thousands of young men and women lived in work camps near the trail and quickly repaired it at night and during bad weather, extending the road network into small auxiliary roads through the dense jungle and underbrush, diversifying it, and actually improving it. The road system became too redundant and too easily repaired to be a good target. The communists also built an entire route system in western Laos that was almost uncharted and nearly devoid of sensor coverage. The years of bombing so defoliated the landscape that it "probably made it easier for the North Vietnamese to keep the passes open." Since B-52 bomb patterns were so evenly distributed, few bombs actually struck the narrow roads. Where they did, the PAVN built temporary bypasses where the soil, "tilled by thousands of bombs, had become easier to work."[39]

The communists also used waterways and coastal water routes not often attacked by US aircraft. They floated barrels and plastic bags of supplies that barely broached the surface and were difficult to detect from the air. Dams and channeling walls were hard to hit and easy to repair, as after bombings the enemy collected the scattered dam stones and piled them back.[40]

The sensors, though effective at first, were soon discovered by the NVA forces, who devised dozens of ways to fool them. Sensors had a short 60- to 160-day lifespan under normal conditions. The first strings were seeded on September 8, 1971, but Commando Hunt VII did not begin until November, and many of the first sensors were not functioning. To add to the predicament, Commando Hunt VII was competing for sensors with Operation Island Tree, which was attempting to detect the infiltration of enemy soldiers. The PAVN soon came to realize that seeding aircraft dove differently than bombing aircraft, and they could fix the general location of many of the sensors. Some were neutralized, but more often they opted to deceive rather than disable the sensors. To fool the Black Crow ignition and exhaust detection sensors, enemy personnel wrapped their ignition systems with aluminum foil to suppress electromagnetic emanations. To counter infrared sensors, they placed layers of banana leaves and bamboo over hot spots on vehicles.[41]

The air-dropped magnetic-influenced mines proved to be just as ineffective, since they had been designed to work against steel-hulled ships and had limited effect on wooden boats. The NVA most often cleared mines that formed the blocking belts by throwing rocks tied to ropes or cords into the mine field. As they retracted the ropes they caught the trip wires on the wide-area antipersonnel mines, causing them to explode. They usually cleared blocking points in fewer than twelve hours.[42]

During Commando Hunt VII, enemy air defenses were far more vexing than during previous campaigns. The PAVN had six hundred to seven hundred guns by the end of Commando Hunt V and fifteen hundred at the height of Commando Hunt VII. A total of eighteen aircraft were shot down over southern Laos. SAMs were also a problem. During Commando Hunt V there had been 49 SAM firings, while during Commando Hunt VII there were

153. On November 9, Air Force intelligence sources detected SAMs, and the B-52s stood down until the threat could be assessed. Tactical air assets could not keep the route package closed, and enemy traffic surged south as the roads dried and the passes opened. The B-52s returned to bombing on November 20 but once again were called off because one MiG-17 fired a single missile at the vulnerable old Buffs. B-52s returned again on November 21–22 for the final days of Phase I, but by then many enemy convoys had escaped.[43]

The SAM danger was demonstrated on December 12, 1971, over the Mu Gia Pass when an F-105 was destroyed by a Soviet-built SA-2. Not only did the B-52s have to be cautious, but so did the AC-130s. On January 13, 1972, with SAMs located near Tchepone, the lumbering gunships were withdrawn from the vital central Steel Tiger region. Only after intensive January 11–15 fighter-bomber attacks reduced the threat could the AC-130s return. On March 29, 1972, ten miles north of Tchepone an SA-2 shot down an AC-130, killing the crew of fourteen. Three other AC-130s and three AC-119s were damaged by AAA.[44]

At first there was hope that at least some of the crew might have survived, and search and rescue efforts began in earnest, but with heavy enemy activity in the area, they had to be suspended. In 1986 a joint US–Laotian team excavated the crash site and recovered remains and artifacts that identified nine of the AC-130 crew members. It was not until 2006 that further surveys of the site recovered enough effects and equipment to allow forensic experts to identify Lt. Col Henry P. Brauner, Maj. Barclay B. Young, SMSgt. James Caniford, and the two other crew members (families withheld their names) not previously identified. Caniford was buried at Arlington National Cemetery on May 28, 2008. Thus came to closure one of the most traumatic events in the history of the AC-130 gunship world.[45]

Of equal importance in 1972 was Air Force's expenditure of 4,066 fighter-bomber sorties attempting to suppress enemy AAA and SAM air defenses. Since fighter-bombers flew 4,209 sorties against vehicular targets, this meant that nearly half of all fighter-bomber sorties were diverted from their primary interdiction missions. While MiG-17s posed a lesser threat, their mere presence forced the Air Force to plan for potential attacks, again diverting attention from the primary task.[46]

In addition, the US bombing efforts were never well coordinated, since each group of attackers—fixed-wing gunships, night raiders such as B-57Gs and A-26s, tactical air support, B-52s, and Task Force Alpha—all pulled in opposite directions. During that time of withdrawal from Vietnam, each unit sought to justify its own existence and funding. Perhaps most damaging of all was the bombing halt over North Vietnam, which gave the PAVN a head start and provided staging areas from whence they fanned out throughout the bypass roads of Laos.[47]

The Legacy of Aerial Interdiction

As French officers and authors had emphatically suggested in the mid-1950s and US authors declared in later years, aerial interdiction, especially in the jungles of Vietnam, was a very difficult task. Commando Hunt consistently experienced many of these frustrations and never was really able to stem the flow of enemy supplies. The fact that General Giap was able to stage vast quantities of supplies, tens of thousands of troops, and two hundred tanks in preparation for launching the Easter Offensive of March 30, 1972, indicates that even the two most ambitious operations, Commando Hunts V and VII, were not totally successful.[48]

Spotting well-disguised PAVN movements in the dense jungles, fog-shrouded mountains, and vast, sparsely populated regions of Laos and Vietnam proved a very difficult task for American pilots. The torrents of the monsoon season also meant that the North had periodic relief from bombing raids. Maintaining blocking belts and choke points and destroying trucks proved difficult. The massive resupply of trucks from the Eastern Bloc, as well as the growing sophistication of the enemy's massive POL pipeline complex throughout North Vietnam and Laos, made it next to impossible to cut off communist movements into South Vietnam totally. Aerial interdiction had been difficult enough in World War II and Korea; it was even more so in Viet Nam.[49]

From a public relations standpoint the worst part of Commando Hunt was that it ended as the Nguyen Hue or Easter Invasion began. This was the very thing it was designed to prevent. And yet some fourteen divisions of PAVN drove deep into the Republic of Viet Nam in the largest invasion of one country by another since Operation Overlord, the Normandy invasion of June 6, 1944.[50]

Ultimately, in spite of all of its problems and those inherent with aerial interdiction, Commando Hunt was significant for two reasons. First, although not a stated goal, it covered US withdrawal, since it bought the United States almost four years to carry out Vietnamization. In fact, no Tet-style attacks meant that ARVN forces could take over the vast majority of roles once reserved for US ground forces. Gen. Bruce Palmer concluded: "The North Vietnamese defeats were the accomplishments of the South Vietnamese infantry, tactical close air support, and the B-52s."[51]

Second, it is probable that by the time Commando Hunt began, the seeds for the Allied defeat had already been sown. Thus, with victory in the classic sense unattainable, US leaders and officers sought methods to measure success and deflect the inevitable criticism that would come as defeat became more apparent. Statistical ethos allowed US managers to measure results achieved versus resources expended. As a result, there evolved sortie counts, aircraft and systems operational figures, bomb tonnage numbers, bomb damage assessments, and, most notably, the infamous truck counts. Ultimately, these numbers proved no substitute for strategy and, for all its apparent achievement, Commando Hunt instead created an illusion of victory that fooled leaders into thinking that such a campaign was strategically viable.[52]

Of course, in early 1972 the reality of this situation was not so clear. Besides, the PAVN invasion had once again changed both ground and air wars. This time the ARVN, not the Americans, would face the brunt of communist attacks. This time the PAVN were on the offensive in a classic conventional ground operation. With the need to resupply two hundred thousand combat troops, two hundred tanks, and hundreds of mortars, artillery pieces, and so on, they employed long logistics networks that soon experienced the full fury of US airpower. Linebacker I and Arc Light raids, mostly in South Vietnam and Laos, would be, as noted by General Palmer, the deciding factors in preventing the fall of the South in 1972. Moreover, the failure of the PAVN's offensive would also, along with Linebacker II in December, lead to a peace settlement on January 27, 1973. The Republic of Vietnam had been saved, or so it seemed. Within twenty-seven months, it fell to another invasion. By that time, not only had the United States removed its military forces, but President Richard M. Nixon, who had driven Commando Hunt and benefited from the peace, also was gone.

AC-130 Deployment and Operations during Commando Hunt

While the ultimate results of Commando Hunt or the outcome of the war itself were not clear during the modification deployment and employment of the AC-130, to American airmen, performing their duty and returning home was a clear focus. As it evolved, Commando Hunt's dependence on night raids meant that the AC-130's role became increasingly significant. The A models finally arrived and, based on combat experience, were constantly upgraded. Soon, ten more AC-130As would be reconfigured and join the fight that had become an effort to cover America's withdrawal.

When AC-130 operations began, the NVA held several advantages over the aircraft the United States had been using. The enemy moved most of their supplies at night, and initially most US aircraft operated poorly at night or in bad weather. The communists were dedicated to sustainment of the infiltration routes, and bombing often plowed up the hard soil, making it easier to repair and extend infiltration roads. US intelligence, in spite of great efforts, was often incomplete or inaccurate. Attack planners frequently lacked information on road capacity, the time needed to traverse each route, how many trucks the enemy had, as well as the length of and the number of roads. Of equal importance, the United States did not have the right combination of aircraft to get the job done. Officials spent too much time and effort arguing whether they needed more jets or more propeller aircraft. This tended to fragment overall efforts and often left several concurrent air operations competing for the same scarce resources. Command issues and setups usually left air operations decisions in the hands of senior ground or naval officers and not in the hands of a single air commander. This resulted in a lack of an overall strategy or even an interdiction strategy.[53]

One key Air Force conundrum resulted from its determination to conduct initial interdiction strikes close to areas of utilization. Commanders sent deep strike sorties against supply sources, troop training areas, and staging sites. What alarmed Air Force leaders in Vietnam was the fact that while initial reports determined that the propeller aircraft were nine times more effective against trucks and watercraft, they had a significantly higher loss rate. The question was how to sustain or even increase the kill rate and reduce their losses.[54]

The Shed Light Program and the prototype combat test data bore out the tactical virtues of the AC-130 and its state-of-the-art systems. The evolution of NOD systems as well as targeting and radar sensors increased the possibility of better interdiction capabilities during combat operations in the early 1970s. As Col. Philip Meilinger argues so convincingly in his classic pamphlet *Ten Propositions Regarding Air Power:* "In essence, Air Power is targeting, targeting is intelligence, and intelligence is analyzing the effects of air operations."[55]

In 1966, when aircraft primarily spotted targets visually, only twenty trucks were sighted and eight destroyed over a three-month period in the dry season. Even though the numbers of trucks would increase over the next three years, it is significant to note that in 1967, when the AC-130A test bed first arrived, the combat tests revealed that its NOS/NOD and sensor systems spotted 597 vehicles. Merely spotting these targets was significant enough, but in this case it also destroyed 83 vehicles and guided other aircraft to those targets with great success.[56]

Throughout 1968, the evolution of the LLLTV and other AC-130 sensors improved the gunship's ability to locate and attack high-value moving targets. The tests conducted on these subsystems also proved vital, since many of the new electronic systems were incorporated into other aircraft, such as the B-57

Canberra night bomber and the A-1 Skyraider propeller-driven aircraft. The B-57's night sensor tests, designated Tropic Moon, further verified the significance of all of this new technology.[57]

Soon the Air Force tied their newest weapon subsystems in with the Igloo White set of airborne-deployed sensor fields monitored by Task Force Alpha twenty-four hours a day, seven days a week by wing-level personnel at their surveillance center in Nakhon Phanom, Thailand. With the deployment of the seismic and acoustic sensors, an all-weather, day-night surveillance network that would target all enemy traffic now seemed possible. In Secretary Brown's mind the key element was the AC-130, which had the capacity to wreak havoc on the enemy supply net. By mid-1968, it appeared the Air Force was on the verge of combining the right aircraft with the proper night tactics to impede the flow of NVA men and materiel. In retrospect, the psychological blow of Tet may have already made this impossible.[58]

In July 1968 the new secretary of defense, Clark Clifford, after discussions with Deputy Secretary of Defense Paul Nitze and other senior DOD and White House officials, contacted the new MACV commander, Gen. Creighton Abrams. expressing his concerns over potential increases in enemy infiltration as the United States ended Operation Rolling Thunder and prepared for negotiations with Hanoi. It was at that point that preparations began for Operation Commando Hunt I, which commenced in November 1968 and lasted until May 1969. The previous August, General Nazzaro, Seventh Air Force commander, briefed Abrams on aerial interdiction plans. Plans called for reconnaissance flights to select priority targets such as roads, passes, vehicles, and rest areas for attack. As mentioned above, they planned to use aerial photographs and Igloo White sensors to find predictable targets and create choke points, blocking belts, and traffic control points where it would be difficult for the NVA to detour trucks. They decided initially to attack in daylight with precision bombs and, subsequently, in late afternoon with delayed-action bombs, air-delivered mines, and area denial munitions. As night fell and repair forces attempted to repair the damage, the AC-130As would arrive over the area supported by strike aircraft, suppression of enemy air defenses (SEAD) or flak suppression aircraft, and flare ships. The gunships were to attack vehicular targets slowed by the choke points, truck parks/supply centers, and AAA sites.[59]

Seventh Air Force initiated aerial interdiction missions in the late summer of 1968, even before Commando Hunt began and long before the AC-130s arrived. While the interdiction package launched five hundred sorties a day and clearly slowed NVA traffic into Laos, initial reports also suggested that Hanoi, resupplied with trucks from the Eastern Bloc, had increased the vehicular traffic down the diversified Ho Chi Minh Trail. While this meant more targets and, eventually, more kills for the AC-130s, it also meant that tens of thousands of tons of supplies were getting into South Vietnam to bolster communist forces bloodied by the Allies' counterstrokes during the Tet Offensive.[60]

The first AC-130 sorties (at first by Vulcan Express and later by the production models) were armed reconnaissance missions into southern Laos in the Steel Tiger region. As the crews gained experience, they moved north into Barrel Roll. Part of the education process involved understanding command and control policies as well as the unique theater rules of engagement. Battlefield directions came from the Seventh Air Force tactical air control center through ABCCC aircraft and sensor data from Task Force Alpha. There were tactical restrictions approved by the Laotian government, and some targets could only be attacked after the Air Force received the okay from the US ambassador in Vientiane. Most of the ABCCC work was performed by OV-2 FAC pilots and crews, but later both the AC-130A pilot and copilot received FAC training and performed some of these duties in lieu of the ABCCC aircraft.[61]

While none of the later 1968 sorties were exactly the same, some patterns did develop. In his book on gunships, Jack Ballard recounts, from a mission report by AC-130A T/N 54-1629, *The Arbitrator,* on December 30, 1968, a specific mission. It was the first time a preplanned fighter escort accompanied a gunship. Loaded with flares and six thousand rounds of 20mm ammunition, *The Arbitrator* departed about dusk at 5:05 p.m. The crew checked their equipment over Ubon RTAFB, and in only ten minutes they had "crossed the fence"—the Mekong River. At that point they contacted Moon Beam, the orbiting ABCCC over southern Laos. The ABCCC assigned them an area of operations, and the navigator plotted the course to the position. Known by their call sign Spectre 1, a common name for all AC-130s, they arrived on station at 5:20 p.m. There they had fifty-five minutes to work with F-4 Phantoms providing fighter cover against AAA sites. At 6:15 p.m. the sensor operators began probing infiltration route 922, continually checking fifteen-mile segments waiting for a target to appear.[62]

At 6:40 p.m. they detected four "eastbound movers," and the sensor data was fed into the fire-control computer to line up the pilot's gun sights. The pilot began a left orbit at forty-five hundred feet above ground level (AGL) to target the lead truck in order to stall traffic. He fired one thousand 20mm rounds in a four-minute burst and severely damaged the truck. Further down the road, they spotted three more vehicles in a truck park. In spite of receiving 37mm AAA fire, the pilot fired another thousand rounds at the parked trucks and the AAA location. This was followed by a large explosion and fire

AC-130A, tail number 54-1629, in 1969.

at the AAA site that illuminated the entire night sky. They soon located two more trucks and damaged them both, while their two support F-4s attacked and destroyed two more AAA sites. They departed the area at 10:35 p.m. after spending three hours and fifteen minutes over the area and expending all six thousand of their 20mm rounds as well as fifteen Mk-6 flares. Even though visual results proved difficult to confirm, they reported four trucks damaged, one 37mm AAA site destroyed, and another "silenced." They touched down at Ubon RTAFB at 11:15 p.m. after a four-hour and ten-minute mission.[63]

While the first three production model gunships, T/Ns 53-3129, 54-1623, and 54-1625, had been used for crew training and were being retrofitted, T/Ns 54-1627, 54-1628, 54-1629, and 54-1630 were flying these initial combat missions. The prototype T/N 54-1626 was at Wright-Patterson AFB undergoing repairs and enhancements. Even with only four AC-130As on station, at 28 percent of truck kills they were still the most lethal interdiction weapon in Southeast Asia. By April 1969, while the 16th SOS flew only 3.7 percent of the sorties over the trail, they had 44 percent of the kills.[64]

Some AC-130 missions at the time were nothing short of spectacular. On April 7, 1969, T/N 54-1627 destroyed two vehicles on Route 917 and was then sent by ABCCC to route 911 just south of the Mu Gia pass. Loitering northwest to southeast at two thousand feet above the rolling jungles and karst mountains, the crew used their NOD and FLIR systems to spot twenty-three trucks. They attacked immediately and later reported twenty-seven huge secondary explosions and fires that turned the night into day. Later reconnaissance confirmed that they had destroyed all twenty-three trucks, making it twenty-five for twenty-five on that single night alone.[65]

Not every night was as good. A week later, on the same Route 911, the same crew hit only two of thirty-seven trucks because of erratic gun and fire control system function. On May 8, 1969, T/N 1629 attacked more than a dozen trucks in only twenty minutes, destroying them all. The reality was that these were dangerous missions, especially as AAA fire increased. On May 24, 1969, the same T/N 1629 was damaged during a routine mission and crashed and burned as it tried to land at Ubon RTAFB. No combat weapon, no matter how good it is, can be successful every time. In this case, kill results were mixed with tragedy, and only through the lessons learned from these disasters was the 16th SOS able to create new tactics to prevent such losses in the future.[66]

If the prototype tests had proved anything, it was that survivability was already becoming more difficult for the gunships. During their fifty-seven sorties in late 1968, they had received AAA fire on fifty-six occasions. Even so, AAA had not been as prolific as the enemy defenses would become. By May 1970, one report determined that the enemy had increased its AAA by 400 percent. Many of these were larger than the old 37mm guns and included 57mm and 105mm AAA. This meant that many road networks were off limits to the gunships without escorts. To counter the growing threat, the gunships waited for the moving targets to arrive at less well defended areas or called in fighter strikes to clear AAA before they attacked the trucks.[67]

The first planned fighter escort missions took place on December 30, 1968. By the next February the success of these new tactics led to F-4s on alert to fly armed escort and flak suppression for the Spectres at all times. The F-4s orbited, waiting for a gunship's call. Periodically they needed to be refueled by the Spectre Shuttle aircraft orbiting over Thailand. When the AC-130s called regarding enemy AAA fire, the F-4s attacked from different directions, dropping single CBUs through the gunship's orbit. This required precision and knowing the gunship's exact location at all times. Concurrently, the AC-130As acted as FACs, dropping flares to illuminate AAA sites for the F-4s. Together, the combination soon became a lethal team.[68]

Between January and April 1969 the F-4/AC-130A package destroyed sixty-three 37mm guns and heavily damaged fifty-nine. They reported 1,026 secondary explosions, 1,152 large fires, and twenty-six trucks destroyed. As Maj. Gen. Robert L. Petit, Seventh Air Force deputy commander noted, "The enemy pays a hell of a price to go after a 'Spectre.'"[69] Soon after the United States changed its tactics, the NVA began to change its AAA tactics. First, the communists moved the AAA sites and then replaced the 37mm AAA with Soviet-built, radar-guided 57mm AAA guns with a 13,100-foot slant range and 19,700-foot optical range. To counter this, the Air Force added new electronic countermeasures systems to the AC-130As, and in later models they replaced one of the smaller guns with guns as large as 105 mm so the gunships could fly at higher altitudes.[70]

The contest began to reach a fever pitch in early 1969. On March 3 an AC-130 was hit by a 37mm AAA round, receiving minor damage. As mentioned earlier, on May 24 T/N 1629 was also hit by several rounds of 37mm AAA. Late in the mission, four explosions erupted on either side of *The Arbitrator,* with one hitting the tail section and one the rear fuselage. SSgt. Jack W. Troglen, the illuminator operator (IO) who had first seen the flak, was grievously wounded. The hydraulic system was lost, as were the rudder, elevator, trim, and autopilot. The pilot, Lt. Col. William Schwehm, and copilot, Maj. Gerald H. Piell, used the aileron trim and the engine power to bring the crippled Spectre near their base at Ubon. Schwehm ordered nonessential crew members to bail out while Piell and flight engineer SSgt. Cecil F. Taylor manually lowered the landing gear. They tried to land at a lower speed, but the nose bounced on the runway, and they could not reverse engines. About two thousand feet down the runway the gunship veered right, and in spite of a desperate effort to regain control of the aircraft, its right wing sheared off and the plane exploded. As the plane came to an abrupt stop, the pilot and copilot made a dash for the opening in the nose and escaped. Troglen, who had already died, and Taylor were engulfed in the flames. Later that evening search and rescue helicopters located the remainder of the crew, and they were rescued.[71]

This disaster left only three AC-130As in-theater. Sensitive to the need to replace the lost aircraft, officials in the States sped up the retrofit of the remaining three production models. As the United States prepared for Commando Hunt III, the gunships were sent to Thailand, bolstering the 16th SOS to six aircraft. In spite of the loss of T/N 1629, leaders in Southeast Asia believed that the AC-130As had done a remarkable job. US embassy officials in Laos sent a message to the State Department in Washington declaring that the gunships had been an "unqualified success" and urging that "additional C-130s be configured as gunships; ASAP!"[72]

The official 1969 gunship report claimed 3,941 trucks sighted, 1,573 destroyed, and 542 damaged. With the potential effective impact on the air war that these numbers portended, the Air Force pushed the remaining production models through the LTVE assembly line as quickly as they could. By the summer of 1969, T/Ns 53-3129, 54-1623, and 54-1625 had arrived in Thailand, which meant that all the production models were in-theater and ready for combat. They also worked to return the retrofitted prototype. Soon experts began to believe that six or seven AC-130s were not enough.[73]

Gen. George S. Brown, who had replaced Momyer as Seventh Air Force commander in August 1968, declared on June 9, 1969, following Commando Hunt III, that the operation had been "so effective . . . that of each five tons of supplies the enemy started southward through Laos only one entered the Republic of Vietnam."[74]

While many analysts disagreed with the overall assessment of Commando Hunt operations (then and now), most also believed that the gunships, in general, and the AC-130s, specifically, were the most effective truck killers they had. Amidst all this apparent success, the obvious question that should have arisen was, if Commando Hunt was working, why was there a need to conduct such extensive ground operations looking for growing numbers of well-supplied NVA troops? Official examinations of enemy activities in I and II Corps areas noted increased enemy movements during 1969. Since these same reports claimed that only one in five tons of supplies that left North Vietnam reached South Vietnam, critics asked how the NVA could increase operations with only one-fifth the supplies they were supposed to receive. American intelligence sources such as the CIA estimated that, in spite of the hard work of the AC-130 crews, thirty-six hundred tons of supplies were getting through each month, even as the number of troops also increased.[75]

One of the problems that faced the United States was the diversion of supplies to other operations. As noted earlier in this chapter, by the summer of 1969 the United States, albeit covertly, were heavily committed to the ever-expanding conflict between the American-backed forces of Gen. Vang Pao and the NVA in the northern Laotian area called the Plain of Jars. As a result, while the Air Force tried to concentrate on each of the Commando Hunt operations in Steel Tiger, their attention was frequently shifted to Barrel Roll. Beginning in November 1968 and continuing into the spring of 1969, AC-130s supplemented AC-47 missions into Barrel Roll to provide close air support for Hmong forces engaged in heavy fighting with the communists. The AC-130s also flew night missions against PAVN and Pathet Lao forces that were making night attacks against Lima radar and observation sites.[76]

On June 25–28, 1969, AC-130s flew several sorties each night in an effort to save Lima Site 108 at Muong Soui from NVA rocket and mortar attacks. On June 27 the gunships even spotted enemy tanks. The AC-130 air support proved essential to the site's survival, since on the fourth night, when extreme bad weather prevented the AC-130s from launching, the enemy overran the position.[77] Perhaps it is not surprising that the early reports on the Gunship II aircraft were all completely positive. The author of the 8th TFW history, writing in April–June 1969, declared, "Its sensors, fire-control system and better armament, had proved more effective than hoped!"[78]

Please Sir, May I Have Some More? A Move to Increase the Fleet

By the end of 1969 there were only four AC-130s in-theater as well as sixteen AC-119Ks. It was an effective force, but it was overused and wearing out at a fast rate. To those who cared to think about it, there needed to be more to get the job done. While effective, the new weapon was not altogether invulnerable, and experience had caused crews and engineers to seek further improvements to achieve greater success. Besides, since the AC-130s were the most effective gunships, they were always in demand, and their missions soon became overstretched. Those who understood their role and potential began to advocate more and better gunships that could sweep the jungles free of enemy night movers and supply trucks.[79]

Of course, by 1969 the war itself had also changed, and it was evolving into a withdrawal that included a marked reduction in US ground forces. In January 1969, Republican Richard M. Nixon was sworn in as president of the United States. He had run his campaign promising to seek an honorable peace and to end America's participation in the war. In May 1969, Nixon's new SECAF, Robert C. Seamans Jr., convinced of the value of the AC-130s but concerned about their vulnerability, commissioned a study to make recommendations for improving the AC-130 platform. In July 1969, James A. Reamer, director of technology, deputy for tactical warfare, met with Maj. Ron Terry, by this time chief of the AFLC AC-130 Gunship Program Office, and engineers Lt. Col. James R. Krause and Maj. James Wolverton, both experts on gunship design. They gathered for a "vigorous discussion about the design of a new AC-130." It was from this meeting that several new models of gunships were eventually derived, gunships that would prove even more lethal than their predecessors and aircraft that would serve well into the future.[80]

This aspect of the AC-130s' story would unfold in the early 1970s and would have a great deal of impact on both the role on the AC-130s in Vietnam and the future deployment and sustainment of the Spectre within the regular and reserve Air Force aircraft inventory.

5 Expansion of the AC-130 Fleet
It Really Was a Surprise Package

The Terry, Krause, and Wolverton meeting was highly significant. Terry had played a vital role in the birth of both the AC-47 and the AC-130A, and the others had major supporting roles. So it is not surprising that they made such an important impact on the future of the AC-130 fleet. The direct result of their meeting was an agreement to reconfigure another JC-130, specifically T/N 56–0490, into the Surprise Package or Night Stalker. Constructed under a program known as Pave Pronto, the new gunship was, in fact, the eighth production model AC-130A. Ultimately, Pave Pronto would also lead to the reconfiguration of ten more A models nicknamed Plain Jane. While some called all of these eleven planes Surprise Package, the original aircraft was unique enough that it was in reality the only Surprise Package.[1]

The aircraft the group conceived had increased standoff range, better night targeting equipment, two 20mm Gatling guns, two 40mm Bofors antiaircraft-type guns to replace the 7.62mm miniguns, improved LLLTV and infrared radar, a more powerful 2-killowatt illuminator to pinpoint tactical targets, and the new Pave Way I laser designator. Officials designated an eighth JC-130A for this upgrade, and rather than award a contract to a private company, Reamer recommended to AFSC commander Gen. James Ferguson that Surprise Package be built in the ASD shops as a high-priority project. Ferguson approved the proposal, as did the Air Staff and PACAF and TAC commanders. So popular was the proposal that the CINCPACAF asked that the aircraft be available by November 15, 1969. On September 2, 1969, Air Force Chief of Staff General Ryan directed Ferguson to begin the program. He declared: “Your engineers are to be

Surprise Package.

commended for evolving an inventive and unique proposal to counter a potentially serious threat to our gunship operations."[2] Concurrently, Ryan also expressed his concern over enemy AAA threats and declared that he favored the addition of the 40mm Bofors to the AC-130s so they could fire from higher altitudes. Ultimately, officials projected the program cost at $1.5 million. Most believed it was a bargain at any price.[3]

Throughout the life of the program, making and keeping to deadlines proved much more difficult than anyone expected. Considering past tardiness with regard to all but the first gunship conversion program, perhaps no one should have been surprised at future delays. In the end, ASD personnel worked day and night shifts to keep the project as close to schedule as possible. Wolverton had daily meetings with subcontractors; Krause spearheaded the integration of the infrared radar, LLLTV, and other high-tech components, while Terry directed the engineers and ASD shop personnel regarding all the subsystems.[4]

One of the thorniest issues proved to be the installation of the 40mm guns. Originally built as naval AAA prior to World War II, they had never been designed to fire downward or in an airplane flying at four thousand to twelve thousand feet. Engineers had to completely redesign gun mounts from ones that had held 20mm Gatling guns to ones that would hold the much heavier 40mm cannons. Once that was accomplished, they took the aircraft to Eglin

AFB, Florida, for initial testing. The firing tests on the ground caused a crack to form under the left wing. Eventually experts discovered this only occurred on the ground, and once airborne, the problem did not replicate itself. This proved to be a great relief, especially for designers and schedulers.[5]

By October 27, 1969, the aircraft was ready for systems testing, which was scheduled to last from October 28 to November 15, 1969. It was delayed by severe bad weather at Eglin AFB and slow equipment deliveries. Once testing began, the results were better than expected, and General Ferguson recommended to General Ryan that Surprise Package be deployed as soon as a crew could be gathered. On November 17, Ryan directed that the new AC-130 be sent to Southeast Asia for combat evaluation. In the end, the modification program was an overall success, producing an extremely lethal weapon system. For his part Major Terry received the Dr. Harold Brown Award of 1969 for "professional leadership, skill, and energy which played such an important part in making the deployment possible."[6]

On November 25, 1969, Surprise Package, the AC-130A prototype in the upgrade program or project now officially designated Coronet Surprise by TAC, left for Thailand. Following an engine change in Guam, it arrived at Ubon RTAFB on December 5, 1969. The crew, headed by Maj. R. C. Binduim, had arrived on November 27. The members of the aircrew were from PACAF and TAC, while Terry led a group of engineers and technical personnel from ASD to support Surprise Package. The combat evaluation test was based on TAC Operations Plan (OPLAN) 132, dated October 17, 1969. The maiden mission was against NVA truck traffic on December 12, 1969.[7]

The first six missions took place between December 12 and 19. They proved more successful than anticipated. Surprise Package confirmed the destruction of 11 and severe damage of 9 of 24 trucks spotted. Between December 19 and 30 it destroyed 19 and damaged 8 of 30 trucks targeted. It also attacked fourteen storage centers, which resulted in six explosions and seven large fires. The final evaluation mission took place on January 18, 1970. The evaluation team concluded that it had been a "very satisfactory" performance during the thirty-eight days of testing. All together they had targeted 333 trucks, destroyed 178, and damaged 63. They had faced 3,475 23mm and 37mm AAA rounds and had survived intact. The only negative aspect of the tests proved to be the malfunction of some of the basic equipment. However, this proved a minor annoyance, and after Secretary Seaman visited Southeast Asia from January 10 through 21, 1970, support for all the gunships not only improved in-theater, but their approval among Air Force leaders in Washington became unanimous.[8]

Surprise! We're Here!

Following the test phase for AC-130 Coronet Surprise, the crew and aircraft transitioned into full combat mode with the other six gunships on-station in support of Commando Hunt III, which lasted until April 30, 1970. The aircraft that many nicknamed "Super Chicken" destroyed 604 trucks and damaged 218. One Seventh Air Force report called Surprise Package the "single most successful truck killer in Southeast Asia during Commando Hunt III."[9]

One of the most effective operations came against a new road and bridge being used by NVA vehicles to bypass the main Laotian infiltration route. It had been cut through dense jungle and was hard to spot. The enemy had a mobile bridge, which they set up at different locations each night. Once the bridge was erected, they quickly sent thirty trucks across. The only sensors able to target the bridge and traffic were on Surprise Package. For five straight nights command and control vectored the new AC-130 to attack the bridge. Not only did they destroy most of the enemy trucks using it, but they marked the bridge so that fighter aircraft could attack it with precision-guided munitions. On the second attack it buckled and went down.[10]

On January 7, 1970, Task Force Alpha located a pipeline and relayed the target information to the 16th SOS. Surprise Package attacked it on January 9. The aircraft's 40mm cannon caused two fires at one of the pumping stations and also destroyed sixteen trucks pumping fuel. The next two nights the gunship again sortied against the same target, this time supported by F-4 fighters. They destroyed fifty-five trucks and two large fuel tanks. Two days after that, Task Force Alpha spotted a storage point and truck park near a Laotian karst mountain covered by dense jungle. Surprise Package, three F-4 Phantom escorts, one LORAN F-4, and six fighter-bombers directed by ABCC attacked several vehicles, a radar site, and AAA sites. The AC-130's LLLTV verified the targets, and ultimately Surprise Package destroyed twelve trucks, while the F-4s damaged the AAA site and subsequently destroyed the radar site using laser-guided bombs.[11]

On the night of February 14, 1970, Coronet Surprise had forty-three kills and damaged two more on just one mission. Much of its success was derived from the new targeting, radar, and infrared devices that it alone had. Its enhanced sensors came from many sources. For example, the LLTV came from Tropic Moon, a B-57 project, and the 40mm guns and Black Crow engine ignition sensor came from the Navy. In a sense, Surprise Package was a flying laboratory to test and develop better equipment in the field. The LLLTV was comprised of a search camera with a wide area of view and a narrow-field camera for precise targeting, both projecting from the left side of the aircraft.

It worked in light ranging from bright sunlight to moonlight. While the early LLLTV versions had problems with their vacuum tubes, as engineers replaced them with printed circuits the system proved much more effective. No equipment worked all the time, but with quick fixes and field and depot modifications all the new sensors evolved into cutting-edge military components.[12]

Over the succeeding years, all the AC-130As received component modifications such as Black Crow, infrared radars, and LLLTV. They also were enhanced with air-to-ground moving and long-range target indicator processor supplemental parts. Ultimately, all the AC-130As also received upgraded FLIRs, and of course the modified 40mm Bofors cannons, which made their missions safer at higher altitudes. During Commando Hunt, enemy AAA nicked the AC-130 Surprise Package far less often than it had previous AC-130As and caused far less damage.[13]

In spite of the excellent kill numbers by the prototype, in December 1967 then MACV commander Gen. William Westmoreland asked exactly how the crews were able to confirm their impressive numbers. Now there was the rub. This was and has always been a major problem for recording aerial kills against other aircraft and targets on the ground. To this end, General Momyer responded by changing the rules for recording damage to, and destruction of, enemy vehicles. In turn, on March 31, 1968, Detachment 2 (Det 2) of the 14th ACW (later 14th SOW) conducted firing tests on moving vehicles and stationary containers at the Ubon RTAFB firing range. On many occasions what seemed like a destructive hit proved less than totally lethal and fell into the "no-visible-damage" results category. While crews argued that their numbers erred on the side of conservatism, Momyer decided to alter confirmation methods by having the NOD operator or one of the two sensor operators confirm claims of "destroyed" by the pilots.[14]

At the same time, the Seventh Air Force sought mechanized means of conformation. One plan had RF-4C reconnaissance aircraft take photos of the areas early the next morning. Unfortunately, the fast-moving jets had problems spotting the previous night's targets. Since crews were certain they were doing better than reconnaissance flights indicated, officials decided to use the 432nd Tactical Reconnaissance Wing at Udorn RTAFB to fly night missions and take night photographs of the confirmed kills. This, too, proved frustrating, as it was hard to distinguish definitively between destroyed and damaged trucks. Besides, taking the time to count their kills in detail slowed target acquisition and reduced the number of attack runs the gunships could make. It diverted too many support aircraft, such as the vital F-4 fighter escorts, as well. Finally, PACAF approved the incorporation of kinescope-type battle damage assessment (BDA) recorders on both AC-130As and AC-119Ks.

In the BDA system, infrared imaging data was input through film sensors, and photos were recorded and later developed for careful examination. To guarantee fixing the targets, officials at AFSC also believed they needed to have better navigational equipment and began the process of coming up with the necessary systems.[15]

It all sounded like a great idea, but it proved to be more complicated than expected. Thus, plans to use the NOD for filming kills were eventually scrapped because the NOD could not be steadied sufficiently to take an accurate photograph. Instead, experts decided to place a 16mm camera in the second NOD station forward and left of the paratroop doors and behind the 20mm guns. They bore-sighted the second NOD with the weapons and used a video recorder camera placed in that NOD location. Record and playback controls were located in the cargo booth. Surprise Package had the camera and video-audio recorder tied to the infrared sensors, not the NOD. This new arrangement eventually gave a high-quality validation of strikes, and in March 1970, Seventh Air Force officials approved the new system. What the confirmation process proved was not only that the crews were more accurate on their kill claims than many critics thought, but that enemy trucks were much more difficult to destroy than to target and damage.[16]

Another issue facing not only the Surprise Package but all the other AC-130As as well was the inconsistent performance of the fire control system. Directional data from the system were often incorrect, and manual corrections were hard to implement. Seventh Air Force officials suspended use of the fire control system early in August 1969. Lt. Col. Bradford W. Parkinson of ASD remedied the problem by installing a dual-axis gyro and a complete solution computer, which significantly reduced system errors. Leaders at TAC verified the modification, and Air Force officials approved the new fire control system for both the AC-130As and AC-119Ks on August 30, 1969.[17]

The low-altitude radar guidance system known as LORAN performed so well on Surprise Package that it was retrofitted onto all the AC-130As and even F-4Ds. The LORAN reduced collateral targets and cross-checked inertial navigation and the targeting systems. Another initial problem for the gunships was the lack of computer generators, which caused electrical troubles that led to computer errors, uncertain target storage, incorrect azimuth, wandering sensor input, and memory wipeouts. In addition, the platform for LLLTV was inadequate. Experts at AFAL upgraded all these systems by the end of Commando Hunt III. They also reworked the 40mm floor mountings to prevent floor bolts from being loosened by firing. Many important components, such as the FLIR and LLLTV, were a big step forward in military technology and improved gunship performance.[18]

As a result of the component and sensor improvements, an electronic warfare crew member was added to the AC-130A standard crew, bringing the total to fourteen by the summer of 1970. The new crew consisted of a pilot, copilot, flight engineer, fire control officer, table navigator, LLLTV operator, FLIR operator, electronic warfare (EW) officer, IO/NOD officer, and five gunners. Like the original prototype tail number 1626, Surprise Package was a test bed that in many respects was jury-rigged together with components that engineers and crews would only understand after they had been tested together in the field. While it had several maintenance problems, these were usually easily repaired. Its performance had been exceptional and led many in the gunship world and in Vietnam to call for more AC-130A Coronet Surprises and for all previous A models to be retrofitted in this manner. However, Seventh Air Force officials rejected this idea since they needed operational aircraft, not planes on production or repair lines.[19]

On May 1, 1970, ASD suggested that Surprise Package be sent back to Wright-Patterson AFB for refurbishment at a cost of $3.4 million and returned to Thailand for the fall 1970–spring 1971 dry season campaign. Seventh Air Force approved the request on May 6, and PACAF concurred on May 20. Surprise Package returned to Wright-Patterson AFB on June 4, 1970, amid a swirl of discussion by the technical experts and senior officials in the defense world over the value of gunships and the numbers needed for the war. Secretary Seamans, following his January 1970 trip to Vietnam, had become an advocate of the AC-130 Surprise Package. He had been in Ubon RTAFB on January 18, 1970, the day the Coronet Surprise combat evaluation had ended. He saw the report and was deeply impressed. Upon his return, he told Under Secretary of the Air Force John L. McLucas that all the Spectres should be configured like the Surprise Package.[20]

While Seamans subsequently directed Seventh Air Force field teams to install Surprise Package components on the original six A models in the field, General Brown was also pushing for Air Staff approval of a plan to convert C-130Es as fast as possible into AC-130Es. TAC and Air Force officials concurred. The JCS wanted a measured A-model modification program along with a high-tempo conversion of E models. In turn, the secretaries of the Air Force and Defense both favored full conversion of all the A models into a Surprise Package configuration. The most critical issue facing everyone was the availability of the specific airframes, support components, spare parts, and contract dollars to complete either program. As far as TAC was concerned, AC-130s had a low priority in their budget, and initially the 1971 budget had no line in it for the procurement of any more C-130Es. This left the Air Force in a position of having to choose between assuring adequate in-theater airlift and risking a shortage in this area to convert a workable number of E models into gunships. To that end, TAC officials queried the Air Staff, asking for a clarification on the future of the fixed-wing gunship.[21]

The Future of the AC-130

Even before Seamans trip to Southeast Asia in January 1970, other key advisers were pressing the defense establishment for more AC-130s. Members of the Scientific Advisory Committee, led by President Richard Nixon's science adviser, Dr. Lee A. DuBridge, had suggested to Secretary of Defense Melvin Laird that he should "get more effective weapons into the Vietnam Theater." He advocated modifying eleven more AC-130s and ten more AC-119Ks to up the total to eighteen and twenty-six, respectively. He believed such a force used properly on a daily basis could destroy 150–200 trucks a day. This, argued DuBridge, was the number (200) that US intelligence was estimating the communists were sending into Laos and back each day and night. Since field reports announced that the current gunship force was getting twenty to thirty kills per night and that the enemy had a standing inventory of 1,300 to 1,500 trucks, they were currently achieving nothing. He wrote Laird that he could not understand the delays to a program worth every penny and strongly supported by the president. He expressed frustration over cost studies and internal haggling that delayed "a program of such imagination and potential for helping the war effort."[22]

As a result of DuBridge's powerful letter, Laird wrote to Seamans to ask how many gunships were in Southeast Asia, how many were scheduled to be there, and whether Seamans had considered an increase in those numbers. Seamans replied that there were seven AC-130s, thirty-two AC-119s, and two AC-123s on-station. Soon after, General Ryan, by then the Air Force vice chief of staff, reported to Seamans that end-of-the-year plans called for these numbers to remain constant and that he had no plans to expand the AC-130 fleet, since they had just deployed sixteen AC-119Ks, the three remaining AC-130A production models, and two Black Spot AC-123Ks, a 300 percent increase in truck killers. Besides, he argued, the value of the gunships was in question, since their vulnerability meant they could fly only in areas where flak was not plentiful. Last, he noted that budget cuts made it more advisable to invest in retrofitting the existing AC-130As with self-contained night attack systems to increase survivability than to build a lot more different models of gunships.[23]

At that point, in late August 1969, Seamans chose to back his senior officer in the Pentagon. However, in December, Deputy Secretary of Defense David Packard witnessed a firing demonstration at Lockborne AFB. He was so impressed that he directed the Air Force to "formulate an R&D [research and development] program for improved GUNSHIPS . . ." for future deployment into their inventory. While Packard and others in the DOD hoped to reconfigure more C-130s into deadly killing machines for Southeast Asia, they also realized that the president intended to reduce the US military presence in Vietnam as his Vietnamization program swung into full force. Still, officials believed there would be a US military presence of significance after the US pulled out of Vietnam and one very likely to face future brushfire wars like the one they were currently in. As a result, they continued to plan for new and better gunships to serve in the US Air Force of the 1970s and 1980s.[24]

By the time Seamans returned from Vietnam in January 1970, he had become a gunship convert, and he was soon employing every bit of his power and influence to have the six AC-130A production models upgraded into Surprise Packages. He also directed AFAL engineers to provide even more enhancements by adding such components as beacon tracking, depleted uranium ordnance for the 20mm guns, and Pave Aegis laser sensors. In short, the secretary wanted the biggest bad boy to evolve into seven even bigger, badder boys.[25]

On January 21, 1970, the same day Seamans returned from Asia, ASD specialists briefed the Air Staff on the cost of modifying AC-130As into "Surprise Packages." The next day, the Air Force directed AFSC and AFLC personnel to modify five of the A models with a limited Surprise Package upgrade in the field at a cost of $1.5 million. Eventually, this proved impractical, and the retrofit was moved to CONUS, where the AC-130As also went through an inspect or repair as necessary overhaul as required by regulation, since it had been two years since the original reconfiguration.[26]

Even as the program unfolded, TAC commander Gen. William Momyer voiced his concerns over continuing to use the old A model. He called on the SECAF to use E models, since they would require less maintenance and expense because of their newer airframe. With the Air Force already converting C-130Bs into C-130Es with more powerful and efficient engines and carrying capacity, the potential AC-130E would provide thirty thousand pounds more carrying weight, and even the C-130B model airframes could carry ten thousand pounds more weight than the As. The large C-130E engines and fuel capacity also meant that this gunship version could extend its loitering and mission time by one to two hours. Ultimately, this was the point of making the gunship in the first place. The E models could have more armor added to increase survivability of the crews. With the A models all over fifteen years old, PACAF officials recommended that the Air Force contract for two Es by late 1971 and seven more by late 1972.[27]

AC-130, tail number 69-6569.

Seamans was left to ponder his options. He could procure five to twelve new AC-130s by modifying new production C-130Es as they rolled off the assembly line (which he preferred to do), he could have C-130Bs reconfigured into C-130Es and then made into gunships, or he could take C-130As or C-130Es out of the operational inventory, which would reduce tactical airlift capability. He decided to attack this problem logically and study his options carefully. Between February and March 1970 the Air Force conducted a study based on cost and force structure analysis. In March and April, Seamans met on several occasions with leading gunship engineers and experts to discuss his options and seek their opinion on which was the best solution. In late April the Gunship System Program Office recommended that the Air Force use two brand new E models from the Lockheed-Georgia C-130E production line to be reconfigured as gunships to act as AC-130E test-bed aircraft. On April 28 the chief of staff approved this proposal, mainly because the Air Force contract with Lockheed-Georgia to build C-130Es ran out in early 1971, and to delay might mean there would be no new E-model airframes to reconfigure if they decided to modify more than two.[28]

Ultimately, officials decided to have WRAMA alter two cargo Es into AC-130E prototypes at a cost of $17.3 million. Plans called for them to be deployed to Southeast Asia between October and December 1971. This bought Seamans time to consider whether he should or would build additional (probably seven) AC-130Es. The program was fielded on May 7, 1970, and designated Pave Spectre. They began work under AFSC Program Directive 0000-1-70-300, dated June 17, 1970.[29]

Even as the E-model program began, DuBridge contacted Seamans and expressed his belief that in addition to the AC-130Es, twenty new Surprise Packages should be built. He insisted that this had been the original intention in 1967 when then Air Force secretary Harold Brown had organized the original gunship fleet. Seamans, still stinging from coming down on the wrong side of the earlier Laird-DuBridge gunship debate, expressed his general support for the enlarged gunship force. At the same time, Air Force Director of Operations Maj. Gen. Joseph J. Kruzel told DuBridge that circumstances were limiting the construction of more AC-130s and that the need for in-theater airlift was more important. He said that for the immediate future they would have to continue with the air assault package they had. This included OV-10 reconnaissance aircraft used for nighttime forward air control, F-4s with lasers, F-4s with LORAN, gunships (possibly with LORAN), and the eventual addition of B-57G night bombers.[30]

On May 14, Seamans received word that delays in the E-model program were already being projected because of a shortage of personnel. Both he and McLucas expressed their frustration to Gen. John C. Meyer, arguing that if the prototype program was going to be late anyway, why should they not just expand it into one larger program to reconfigure nine to eleven AC-130Es? Meyer replied that the prototypes were only the first phase in the AC-130E project and that, following reports on the upcoming Air Staff study, a decision could be made on how many more AC-130Es needed to be procured. Clearly, for those involved in this discussion, all of whom knew that President Nixon and his foreign policy adviser, Henry Kissinger, were working for a peace settlement to end US involvement in Vietnam, the ultimate consideration about the gunship fleet was how it would be configured and used after the war.[31]

On May 20, 1970, Secretary Laird moved the debate back to more pressing and immediate issues specifically aimed at the future of Commando Hunt operations, by now being used to cover America's withdrawal, and how the gunships would be used in upcoming interdiction campaigns. Although it was not an original idea, Laird embraced the notion of using B-52s to bomb Laotian mountain passes and key points along the Ho Chi Minh Trail to create choke points so the AC-130s could attack these less mobile targets with impunity. The reports from Commando Hunt III seemed to bolster this idea. Seventh Air Force reported that during Commando Hunt III, jet and attack aircraft accounted for 3,900 kills, or 39 percent, while gunships destroyed

48 percent while flying only 8 percent of the sorties. In turn, the report noted that the most effective of the gunships was Surprise Package. It went on to say that the AC-130 Surprise Package damaged or destroyed 822 vehicles during 112 sorties, while the AC-130A production aircraft had destroyed or damaged 2,552 vehicles during 591 sorties. By comparison, AC-123Ks had 440 kills on 141 sorties, AC-119Ks 987 on 435, A-6s 977 during 1,486, A-1s 1,271 during 2,332, A-7s 959 on 3,147, F-4s 1,576 on 6,310, and A-4s 245 on 1,223, for a total of 9,839 destroyed or damaged on 15,777 sorties.[32]

Of course there were and are many who question the actual number of kills, as noted in chapter 4. Still, even if the actual numbers proved hard to confirm or the enemy's ability to repair or restore vehicles was greater than observers or analysts realized, what is clear is that the gunships were more effective. Ironically, in the midst of this rush toward building more AC-130s, the chairman of the JCS, Adm. Thomas H. Moorer, weighed in by cautioning everyone that while the gunship numbers were impressive, they were still vulnerable and siphoned off other important fighter assets to escort them during missions, especially in highly defended areas. The main reason for building more and better gunships was to slow the communist traffic of men and materiel into South Vietnam, and the E-model program seemed to be dragging along with this important mission staring everyone in the face. Some key executive advisers wondered whether the Air Force would keep the AC-130s in the inventory after the war or, as with the AC-47s, turn them over to the VNAF. From the Air Staff point of view this was a waste of time, since there was not, nor had there ever been, a presidential directive to turn over AC-130s to anyone. Besides, they reckoned there would be likely future conflicts for which the AC-130s would be needed and in which they would perform effectively. For this reason alone they pushed for more AC-130s. Still, others argued that if this were so, then what was the need to rush toward the reconfiguration of the additional AC-130s? They argued that it was better to have a well-considered product than to quickly deploy a less adequate weapon system.[33]

Under Secretary McLucas agreed that the United States would continue to use the AC-130s after the war, but he warned that total withdrawal would take a long time, and even then US airpower would remain to support ARVN forces. He went on to say that the newer AC-130s were also less vulnerable, and besides, "at about $5 million per gunship I don't see how we can go wrong in converting a dozen or so." With so much pressure to act, the Air Force decided to increase the size of the gunship fleet by December 1970 or January 1971. They determined to modify three or four more gunships for $6.7 million per aircraft through a sole-source contract with LTVE. They gave WRAMA and ASD unlimited authority and funding. In spite of this approach, other issues soon threw up roadblocks such as a lack of the proper yokes in which to mount NOD, a shortage of management personnel, a lack of computer and gun assets, and a concern over LTVE's reliability. After all, LTVE had fumbled the ball during the original AC-130A production run. To take total control of the program and wrench it back on schedule, Warner Robins and ASD experts quickly drew up plans for the program and briefed General Meyer on June 22, 1970. A day later they met with Seamans, and a week after with General Ryan. The result was a contract to modify six additional AC-130As with a ninety-day option to reconfigure three more. These A models, later known as Plain Janes, would be added to the two E models under construction and increase the gunship fleet by eleven.[34]

WRAMA had been at the forefront of the modification of all the Air Force gunships and continued to perform depot maintenance on all those that had previously been deployed. Indeed, the same could be said in 2009. This meant that with these technicians, engineers, and managers in charge of this aspect of the gunship program, everyone had reasons to be optimistic that this latest addition to the fleet would be a success. On July 2, 1970, the WRAMA commander, Maj. Gen. A. J. Beck, directed his workforce to commence planning while Washington continued to discuss the final numbers. Ironically, Beck had recommended against more A models, since the Es had a larger payload, provided more loiter time, were newer and more reliable, and had more spare parts available. Beck, frustrated by the growing political delays, called for leaders to make a final decision on how many aircraft they would modify and pick one model and reconfigure them to be the same. His obvious concerns were for future support and sustainability issues that his folks at WRAMA would have to deal with. As noted, leadership did not listen to General Beck and opted for a mixed-model fleet.[35]

It was later that summer that the Air Force made the decision to modify six more AC-130As for a total of $45.3 million through a contract with LTVE to be completed by January 1971. If this went smoothly, they planned to build three more for $6.7 million. The reconfiguration would follow the Surprise Package pattern by adding 40mm Bofors cannons, special sensors, digital fire control computers, and inertial navigation systems. Funding was derived from the special activities portion of the 1970 Air Force missile procurement and research development/test and evaluation budget. Seamans ordered ASD, WRAMA, and LTVE to pursue an all-out effort using three shifts seven days a week, twenty-four hours a day. This led the Air Force in the direction of a more survivable, self-contained night and all-weather attack platform with maximum lethality.[36]

On July 3, 1970, Packard gave verbal approval to Seamans's plan, and a week later the defense secretary told Packard that procurement had begun involving LTVE, Lockheed-Georgia, Fairchild-Hiller, and Hayes International, Kokomo, Indiana. Packard gave final formal approval on July 11, 1970, and it took LTVE eleven months to build the first of the new Surprise Packages. Once under way, however, the process moved quickly, and it took only four more months to complete the final five.[37]

On July 14, 1970, the Air Force chief of staff announced the approval for the six additional gunships and the acquisition of equipment and parts for three more at a cost of $46,659,000. The modification components included flare launchers, 20-kw illuminators, moving target radar indicators, damage assessment systems, laser target designators, LLLTVs, the latest model fire-control systems, two-axis gyros, two each 7.62mm miniguns, two each 20mm Gatling guns, two each 40mm Bofors cannons, electronic countermeasures gear, LORAN low-altitude night radar, sensor-light angle display systems, beacon-tracking radars, form-in fuel tanks and armor packages, ac/dc distribution modification systems, sensor operator consoles, FLIRs, and mission command consoles.[38]

Between July 22 and 25, 1970, ASD officials hosted a meeting at Wright-Patterson AFB to discuss the program's progress and scheduling. Pursuant to DOD directives, plans called for three new AC-130As to deploy to Southeast Asia by January 1, 1971, and three more a month later. In preparation, minor changes had to made in the facilities at Ubon RTAFB to accommodate the six additional aircraft. Officials decided to keep two AC-130As and two AC-119Ks at Lockborne AFB for training for what they believed would be eleven new AC-130s.[39]

At that point the Air Force had no less than five gunship programs working at the same time. They had invested over $4 million to upgrade the original AC-130A production models, more than $3 million on the Surprise Package Second Season, $4 million to add the Black Crow engine ignition sensor and the laser targeting devices built into the LLLTV platform, $46.7 million on the six new AC-130As, and $17.3 million on the two AC-130E prototypes being modified by LTVE. All totaled, they had committed more than $72 million to prepare for a maximum gunship effort during Commando Hunt V, scheduled for the 1970–71 dry season. As preparations progressed, Packard made it clear that he and other senior leaders wanted the gunship's tactics changed to include increased AC-119K and AC-130 sortie rates against the infiltration routes. He also pushed for attack packages that included B-52s creating choke points, F-4s using laser-guided bombs, and increased night sorties by more aircraft, including B-57s.[40]

Ryan worried that the increase in enemy air defenses along the Ho Chi

The emblem of the 16th Special Operations Squadron.

Minh Trail endangered the lumbering gunships. Admiral Moorer expressed similar concerns to Secretary Laird. As a result, the Air Force continued to add as many better sensors and components to as many of the AC-130 versions as they could fit on the airframes without having them fall off. By November 1970, Hayes International Inc., during the IRAN process, had also installed video recorder systems for battle damage assessment on five of the AC-130As, and Lockheed-Georgia had put Black Crow systems in four of the AC-130As. Concurrently, TAC, PACAF, and ASD developed tactics for their B-52, F-4, and gunship attack packages and commenced training and testing at Eglin on September 8. This testing lasted until September 28.[41]

Modification efforts reached a climactic point in late 1970. On September 15, Secretary Seamans visited the LTVE plant to view the AC-130E modification line. That evening he took a flight on a Surprise Package test flight. Two weeks later, on October 1, 1970, he sent a memo to Secretary Packard to inform him that the Air Force planned to amend the LTVE contract to modify the last nine AC-130Es by March 1, 1971. He raised the total AC-130 funding to $80 million and ordered Air Force personnel in Southeast Asia to prepare to house the entire gunship fleet, which now figured to total as many as eighteen AC-130s.[42]

Chapter Conclusion: Where Do We Go from Here?

Ultimately, the various gunship versions and their crews deployed to Thailand to become the focal point for the remaining Commando Hunt operations, especially Command Hunt V and VII. Much rested on this effort, as noted earlier, and the United States, in particular the Air Force, believed they had the weapons finally to blunt the north's constant flow of men and materiel into South Vietnam. However, the process of getting the gunships and other aircraft to the place where they could do the most good continued to be a frustrating and complicated effort compounded by the fact that while on the surface it seemed all AC-130s were generally the same, in fact different models were very different, most notably at the core of their sensors, weapons, and airframe. In addition, the politics of the modification process and the reality that America was continuing to pull out of the war only added a murky quality to this ever-growing conundrum.

6 Development and Deployment of the New AC-130s

Before the story of the AC-130s moves on to the final years of the war and the important air operations that made up those days, it is critical to examine in detail the production of the AC-130As and Es. This is particularly true since, unlike the AC-47s and AC-119s, the AC-130s would continue to serve the national defense for many years after the end of the Vietnam War in 1973. Thus, the following pages focus on the actual work done on the Surprise Package, Pave Pronto, Plain Jane, and other unique AC-130 designs that followed.

The original production run of AC-130As had produced six aircraft—a total of seven with the original prototype. The loss of T/N 1629 left six. Surprise Package returned that number to seven and led to the approval to begin the production of six and later nine more Surprise Package aircraft under the Pave Pronto program. Having allowed the first one of these aircraft to be modified organically, in early 1971 the Air Force contracted with LTVE to reconfigure the last five as Pave Pronto gunships. Ultimately, LTVE and ASD modified eighteen C-130 airframes into AC-130As and Es between 1967 and 1971. Ultimately, two aircraft were lost in combat, and the original prototype was placed in a limited war test-bed category and taken out of combat for both research and public relations reasons.

Originally officials considered calling the aircraft from this second run of AC-130As Surprise Package after the prototype; however, by the time they reached Southeast Asia their paint scheme had changed from that of Surprise Package and was deep black and dark green, which distinguished it from other gunships. The original AC-130A production models were also retrofitted to assume this same appearance and carry most of the same equipment. As a result, they became known more often than not as Plain Jane, or, by the 16th SOS's call sign for all the AC-130s, Spectre. Thus was the situation with the AC-130 fleet when the Air Force refocused on the Pave Spectre program that involved the conversion of C-130Es into gunships.[1]

Introduction of the AC-130E/H

It is important to realize that between late 1969 and early 1971 the gunship world made a major advance in both technology and airframe quality. As we have seen briefly in the previous chapter, the A models were not in the same ballpark as the E model C-130s. The As' gross weight limit was 124,200 pounds, and even upgrading their sensors and weapon systems only provided a limited enhancement of the gunship fleet. Thus, not much more could be done with the A-model airframe, and officials decided to build an E-model gunship with a gross weight of 155,000 pounds that allowed it to carry more equipment, more fuel, and more ammunition. All together, eleven C-130Es were converted, featuring the same equipment and armament as those of the Pave Pronto AC-130A, and become known as the Pave Spectre AC-130E. The first aircraft arrived at Ubon RTAFB on October 25, 1971.[2]

The first two E models converted into gunships were T/Ns 69-6566, which served until February 2003 before being sent to the Aerospace Maintenance and Regeneration Center, and 69-6567, later upgraded to an H model, named *Ghost Rider,* and lost with all aboard over Kuwait during Desert Storm on January 31, 1991. The remaining three are still in the Air Force inventory and include T/Ns 69-6568, *Bad Company;* 69-6569, *Fatal Attraction;* and 69-6570, *Hussie,* all of which have been converted to H models. Tail number 69-6571 was converted to AC-130E, designated Spectre 22. It was damaged by AAA on March 30, 1972, near An Loc, Vietnam, and the pilot flew the aircraft back over friendly territory, where the crew parachuted to safety. Although the aircraft was severely damaged, all those on board survived and were rescued. Tail numbers 69-6572, *Gravedigger;* 69-6573, *Nightstalker;* 69-6574, *Iron Maiden;* and 69-6575, *Wicked Wanda,* were later enhanced to be H models and are still serving with the 16th SOS. Tail number 69-6576, *Hell Raiser,* was also upgraded to an H model, but it crashed in Kenya on March 14, 1994, as a result of the accidental explosion of ammunition on board. Of the fourteen crew members, eight died. Tail number 69-6577, *Death Angel,* was also upgraded to an H model, and the final E model converted to an AC-130H was T/N 69-6578, which crashed at Little Rock AFB in 1971 even before it reached Vietnam.[3]

The first production E model, like the next seven, had a digital tactical computer system that interfaced the heads-up display (HUD), the information management system, and the sensors. The computer positioned symbols

An AC-130H's big gun lights up the night sky with bad intentions.

on the HUD allowing the guns to be pointed at the target even if the aircraft were not in perfect geometry—that is, bank angle, airspeed, and altitude. Sensor equipment consisted of an LLLTV with gated laser illuminator and laser target ranger/designator, an improved FLIR, beacon tracking radar, and Black Crow. The aircraft carried two 20mm Vulcan Gatling guns, two 7.62mm miniguns, and two 40mm Bofors, all mounted to the airframe.[4]

By early 1972 the aft 40mm was replaced by a fixed 105mm howitzer. Later in 1972, the 105mm fixed mount was replaced by a computer-controlled hydraulically operated trainable mount. With this addition, the 105mm could be pointed at a target by maneuvering the aircraft within a 12-degree by 12-degree box centered on the nominal condition. By the end of 1973, the fixed 40mm mount was also replaced by a trainable mount, and soon three more E-model gunships were built for a total of eleven aircraft. On these last three aircraft, the T56-7 engines were replaced with the more powerful T56-15 engines and were redesignated AC-130H models. This was necessary for survivability with two engines out. As T56-15 engines became available, the original E models were retrofitted with them and redesignated as H models.[5]

While all of this seems simple enough, it was not. As for all the other gunship programs, the actual work was arduous and protracted, and it would be wrong to breeze over the numbers and ignore the work that ASD, WRAMA,

11.

The various sizes of ordnance used aboard fixed-wing gunships. *Left to right:* 7.62mm NATO, 20mm, 25mm, 40mm Bofors, and 105mm howitzer.

---

and the contractors did to bring this next generation of gunship into the Air Force inventory. In September 1969, Deputy Defense Secretary David Packard went to Lockbourne AFB, Ohio, for a routine visit. While he was there he participated in a practice mission on an AC-130A. As noted in the previous chapter, he was so impressed by its combat potential that when he returned to Washington he sent a memo to Secretary of the Air Force Robert Channing Seamans Jr. advocating the continuation of the AC-130 program and the modification of additional C-130s. This led to the decision to build the original two prototype AC-130Es.[6]

Packard was not the only gunship supporter. In early 1970, during the dry season or "hunting" season in Vietnam, members of the Presidential Scientific Advisory Board visited Southeast Asia and observed the war first-hand. They reported back to Henry Kissinger on what they believed to be the primary needs for the war effort. One of the key programs identified proved to be the AC-130 program. In turn, Kissinger sent a memo to Melvin Laird that eventually filtered down to SECAF. Based on this exchange, the Air Force determined to reconfigure nine AC-130As under the Pave Pronto program as Plain Jane A models. The program began in July 1970 and was completed by LTVE in March 1971.[7]

This was only step one. With the old A models limited by their airframe capacity and age, officials soon decided to build the previously mentioned AC-130Es. Experts held a meeting at ASD in January 1970 to plan what the AC-130 permanent force structure would look like for 1970–80. ASD and WRAMA engineers and technicians were present to consider whether the next generation of gunships would be A-, B-, or E-model C-130s. Key points, not yet mentioned, in favor of the C-130E airframe were that Lockheed-Georgia was the only company producing C-130Es and their parts, and far more E models had been produced since the early 1960s than any other model under consideration.[8]

In a subsequent interview, WRAMA experts from the Directorate of Materiel Management's Tactical Aircraft Systems Management Division (MMH), Thomas Knight and Howard Wright, believed that the key factors for selecting the E model were "(a) gross weight, (b) ferry range, (c) sortie duration, (d) maintenance of the airframe, and (e) reliability of the airframe." In turn, the official Air Force Research and Development Division report declared that the Es had been selected because "the larger gross weight capacity of the AC-130E provides increased armament loads, longer time on target and increased survivability provisions which were not possible on the AC-130A." The report went on to say, "The larger payload capacity of the AC-130E also provides a growth capability." They concluded that "the newer airframes, improved systems and more advanced manufacturing techniques provide increased maintainability and reliability." Yet another study concluded that "installation of PAVE SPECTRE equipment will provide an improved AC-130 side-firing gunship capability. This modification will enhance PACAF's gunship capability, provide attrition replacement aircraft and form the basis for a 1970–1980 gunship force." Last, the AC-130Es had heavier flaps that made them steadier and more able to withstand the blast effects of the 40mm cannons they would carry.[9]

On May 7, 1970, once the chief of staff of the Air Force approved the reconfiguration of the AC-130Es, the planning process began. WRAMA commander Maj. Gen. A. J. Beck directed leaders in MMH to initiate a feasibility study to examine the benefits of WRAMA's producing the prototype and production AC-130E gunships. Soon they also received funding approval, and Warner Robins officials took steps to begin work immediately. However, like all the other gunship programs, this one was also delayed because the Pave Pronto program was already underway and it diverted many of the important engineering and production personnel as well as the key parts, equipment, and production facilities necessary to move ahead with the AC-130Es.[10]

The Air Staff immediately decided to make two prototypes and wait to determine how many production models to make until after the prototypes finished flight testing in July or August 1971. However, as Ted Lynch of the Gunship Program Office noted, "Due to the importance of the weapon system to the efforts in Southeast Asia, the decision was accelerated and moved to March." He went on to say that doing things this way caused a lot of confusion about what to do with the engineering personnel and data. "We were then in a position of building production airplanes, modifying production airplanes concurrent with the prototyping." Most members of the Gunship Program Office were frustrated, since they were "undertaking three different kinds of processes on two widely different models of the same airframe."[11]

If the turmoil were not bad enough, at first ASD assumed they would perform the prototype work at Wright-Patterson AFB as they had done on aircraft previously. Even before they received the formal approval in May 1970, ASD briefed officials at both HQ Air Force and ASC on their capacity to build the prototypes. After much deliberation, experts decided that in-house "cost risks" were lower than contracting out. However, as they looked at the in-house option, they realized that WRAMA had the better manpower, expertise, and facilities to execute the project. With General Beck ready and willing to undertake the program, Warner Robins seemed the logical selection for both the prototype and the production AC-130Es. That summer, WRAMA representatives accompanied Lynch and Lt. Col. Ron Terry to the Pentagon to make the pitch for the in-house E program.[12]

Their efforts proved successful, and with the Air Staff's approval in hand for the modification of the first two C-130Es, they returned to Robins AFB to begin the process. Plans called for the prototype reconfiguration to take place at WRAMA with ASD providing on-site engineering. The reorganization of the new Gunship Program Office began even as ASD began initial engineering design work, which was scheduled for completion in March–April 1971. Once Pave Pronto began, much of that work was delayed, but work on the hydraulics, armor, and survivability components continued piecemeal until the Gunship Program Office formally opened in October 1970.[13]

Based on the feasibility study that General Beck had ordered in May, experts at Warner Robins and ASD pieced together a series of milestones for the prototype workload. Initially, planners determined to modify T/Ns 69-6566 and 6567, but when 6566 proved difficult to obtain, they changed the schedule, planning on inducting T/Ns 69-6567 and 6568 instead. They decided to start the first aircraft on October 15 and the second by October 30, 1970. Depending on the engineering work, they scheduled both to be completed in the spring of 1971 and testing to begin in July 1971. Deployment was to take place in the fall of 1971 or the dry or hunting season.[14]

As prototype planning unfolded, members of the WRAMA Systems Management Division (MMHO-4) of the Directorate of Materiel Management, led by Howard Wright, using data and directives gathered from the feasibility study and the gunship meeting held in Washington on May 12–13, 1970, worked to determine the advisability of providing fabrication and installation work required for the two E models. Concurrently, they put together additional planning information derived from experts at ASD. ASD projected that the overall project would last from October 1970 to June 1971. The WRAMA study determined that the program would take 50,000 production man-hours per aircraft, including 10,000 hours for sheet metal work, 10,000 hours for electrical work, 2,500 hours of plastic work, and 2,500 hours of machining, all from the Directorate of Maintenance's Manufacture and Repair (M&R) Division. In addition, the Aircraft Division of the Directorate of Maintenance was expected to provide 10,000 hours of electrical work, 7,500 hours of sheet metal work, and 7,500 hours of general work. Finally, WRAMA planners also concluded that in addition to these 100,000 hours for the two prototypes, they would have to contract for five standard C-130E IRANs—required before deployment—at 50,000 hours each. WRAMA determined that the Aircraft Division could absorb 50,000 of these hours and the M&R Division could manage 4,500 hours. That left 44,500 hours they believed could be handled by "unprogrammed depot level maintenance" funds and personnel.[15]

Brig. Gen. Ralph Holland, WRAMA's vice commander, notified AFLC on May 28, 1970, that, given the scheduled FY71 projected unit costs, the inspection of the five E models would cost $640,000. He further noted that at the May 12–13, 1970, meeting the chief of staff had predicted that the alternative contracted process would cost over $800,000 and that Warner Robins was willing and able to take this project on. He told AFLC leadership, "We have control and flexibility which in my opinion will allow accomplishment within a minimum down time."[16]

Even as the project to construct the two AC-130Es began, discussions in Washington and among Air Force leaders in Southeast Asia led WRAMA project leaders to wonder if the overall program might be altered so that there would be a mixture of older and newer E models or, worse, E models and more A models. Regarding the A models, WRAMA experts told their AFLC counterparts that "we are not as concerned with systems reliability as we are with the basic airframe." Their major concern was that mixing the newer E models they had with older Es would require more sustainment work and delay deployment, and while newer Es could stay in the field longer, the older ones would have to rotate frequently. As they said, "Disregarding the calendar age of the 1963–1964 aircraft, our records indicate that only five 1963–1964 aircraft have less than 3,000 flying hours. Excluding the 1968–1969 models, the C-130E fleet average is about 6,800 hours per aircraft."[17]

If that plan was a poor idea, then WRAMA logisticians argued that mixing additional A models with the ones they already had was even worse. To quote one study: "While there might be some logistic support impact in mixing 1969 model E's with the PACAF early E's, this is minimal compared to mixing E's" of any model with "A's as we understand will be done upon completion of the two prototypes in the fall of CY1971." Supported by PACAF officials, they also contended that if the program went on beyond two E models, they believed all the AC-130s should be standardized as much as possible.[18]

Throughout the summer and early fall of 1970, leaders at WRAMA and AFLC went so far as to explore the possibility of assuming engineering management from ASD for the overall project in order to speed things up. General Beck argued that Warner Robins should manage the total package "as a result of know-how from prototype involvement." On June 16, 1970, ASD leaders, in a message to the Air Staff, reemphasized their belief that they should retain engineering responsibilities and retain overall management of the program. Indeed, they went on to state that they should also oversee the "installation of all equipment in the two aircraft" and "perform all major contracting efforts for subsystems and . . . be responsible for overall financial control."[19]

Throughout the remainder of that summer, the chief of staff continued to reserve his decision on whether ASD or Warner Robins would take over total responsibilities. In the original May 1970 arrangement, AFSC became the program manager, and AFLC assisted when needed. Indeed, AFSC was directed to use the "installation contractor" approach to execute the modification work; however, in July 1970 WRAMA became the "installation contractor." While at first this arrangement continued on as the date for production of the first aircraft drew closer, ultimately WRAMA won its point and became the lead dog. Undoubtedly the significance of this project and all the other AC-130 programs proved more important than who had what role in the project. As far as the Air Staff was concerned, the lead dog was Warner Robins.[20]

The AC-130E prototype construction was not the only project underway in 1970–71. Three other programs were also operating. These were the AC-130A IRAN upgrade and overhaul of Coronet Surprise or Surprise Package and the modification of nine Pave Pronto A-model aircraft with a higher 1-3 precedence designed to make them ready for the 1970–71 interdiction campaign. The key point was that ASD asserted that the engineering data used on these three programs could also be used on Pave Spectre, thus keeping that program on schedule. Soon the Air Staff invigorated the importance of the program by assigning priority precedence 1-6/DX industrial rating to the program. This was the same high priority the original AC-130A program had. Leadership directed that the program be completed in seventeen months, thus providing initial operational capability (IOC) by November 1, 1971. The schedule also called for all testing and evaluation to be completed before the end of calendar year 1971. Senior management believed this would be better than the original AC-130A program that was rushed to deployment. To make the end product even better, they made sure that they adhered to the letter of the approved project agreements that called for the incorporation of state-of-the-art sensors and fire control systems that would make it part of the permanent force.[21]

To facilitate the process, officials sent a number of WRAMA specialists to ASD between July and October 1970 to observe work on the Surprise Package in order to use this knowledge to modify the E models. By September, Warner Robins began to collect personnel from various skill areas to commence production on the two prototypes. On September 17, WRAMA Special Order A-1240 assigned seventeen individuals from the Maintenance Directorate's Maintenance Production Control, Production, Industrial Engineering, Quality Control, and Technical Engineering Divisions, as well as the Base Support Division of the Directorate of Distribution, to a preplanning team. Management in DMM also assigned liaisons to the group to represent Service Engineering and C-130 System Management. Each C-130 System Management branch had a monitor.[22]

Aircraft T/N 69-6567 arrived on October 6, 1970. It already had 840 flying hours. As soon as it was in the hangar, Warner Robins workers stripped it of its nonessential components. In turn, ASD began engineering work. Structural design drawings had already arrived, with all changes made on the spot by ASD engineers in coordination with WRAMA maintenance professionals. Being a joint ASD and WRAMA effort, they had to schedule assignments to avoid duplication of effort and to assure each work crew had plenty to do on the project. In an effort to maintain complete and accurate documentation, ASD contracted with Systems Research Laboratories (SRL), Dayton, Ohio, who sent a representative to Robins AFB on October 15, 1970. ASD also footed the bill to complete a contract for technical manuals. While WRAMA authorities believed the engineering process would be the pacing factor, no one else did.[23]

Hal Cotton, deputy director of materiel management, sent a memo to Col. John Beck on October 20 stating: "We have noted much enthusiasm on the part of involved WRAMA personnel. The ASD and SRL on-site personnel appear to be well qualified and dedicated individuals. In a joint effort of this nature cooperation and understanding are of the utmost importance. Be assured that our people within DMM will exert every effort to make PAVE SPECTRE a successful program."[24]

Thus began the Pave Spectre program, which was classified as Class V Modification Project Number 2572. It was also designated by its numerical identity number 434. Later, the number was changed to 498. The assignment of Pave Spectre to WRAMA was unique to AFLC and eventually won them a great deal of praise from Air Force leaders for the superior job they were doing and would do. The program was set up with ASD engineers manning the system program office at Robins AFB and WRAMA doing the dirty work. It was work that the folks at Warner Robins not only were used to but also excelled at.[25]

As noted earlier, at first the Gunship Program Office wanted to build the E-model prototypes at ASD facilities just as they had done with the A model. However, by the fall of 1970 an Air Staff directive to increase the number of AC-130Es and to speed up the reconfiguration tempo for the overall gunship production program jolted everyone involved in a new direction. Since flight testing could not be performed any faster, nor could additional personnel be trained overnight to facilitate the completion of Pave Spectre, the Air Staff concluded that putting all the Pave Spectre work at the same location would make things move along more smoothly and quickly. To this end they directed Warner Robins IRAN and prototype personnel to assume the role of directing the overall project. Even so, the WRAMA and ASD management and workforce personnel still had to work on two variations of the AC-130 gunship at the same time and in the same place. Since the A model work had precedence, it delayed work on the Es. However, the delay was less than it might have been.[26]

Although the first C-130E arrived for modification at the Robins AFB facilities on October 6, 1970, the second aircraft, T/N 69-6568, did not arrive until January 6, 1971. Since plans called for the first prototype to be completed by June 15, 1971, and the second on July 15, 1971, ASD and Warner Robins employees worked closely together to increase the work tempo. Led by Col. Bradford W. Parkinson, experts from WRAMA and Air Force laboratories adapted superior A-7D aircraft fire control systems into the new sensors in the C-130E airframe. They also upgraded the ordnance itself by converting the 20mm rounds into high-density rounds and fitted 40mm rounds with a misch metal liner made with a lightweight pyrophoric metal. Developed by specialists at the Naval Weapons Labs and flight tested at Eglin AFB, these incendiary rounds could set trucks on fire with a near miss. Eventually the overall program grew to include reconfiguring four and later five more aircraft and proved to be one of the largest organic in-house projects ever executed by Air Force Logistics Command. Best of all, both prototypes rolled out on time at a total cost of $14,859,525, well below the project price.[27]

Following the rollouts, planners scheduled a ninety-day flight test program with the IOC to take place on November 1, 1971. Last, but not least, Category I and II testing were to be conducted in the CONUS, and following this procedure the aircraft would be ferried to Ubon RTAFB under the command of PACAF.[28]

On August 6, 1970, the CSAF notified AFLC that P1600 and P4921 funding requirements for Pave Spectre Group A components totaled $1,670 and $15,030, respectively, and the P1600 and P4921 costs for Group B parts were $1,706,400 and $189,600. The AGE P1600 and P4921 costs were $297,473 and $33,052, respectively, while data fees totaled $177,000 under P1600 funding requirements. The total P1600 funding costs were $2,182,543, and the total P4921 costs, $237,682. The Air Force also planned to use $2,476,800 in P1100 funds for an overall cost of $3,633,800.[29]

Plans called for subsystem deliveries to be completed between November 1970 and April 1971 and on-site engineering to take place between October 1970 and June 1971. Experts expected the Group A fabrication release to be completed between September 1970 and January 1971. As noted, with these milestones met, the first modification construction would begin in early October 1970 and end in June 1971, and the second was to begin in late October 1970 and end in early July 1971. Category I and II testing were to begin in early June and end in late September 1971. IOC was to occur on November 1, 1971. In spite of beginning behind the curve, WRAMA employees met every deadline. In January 1971, Air Force leaders announced that they had approved $14,859,525 for the total cost of the project. They noted, "This amount reflects a reduction of $2,476,800 as a result of the decision to have the equipment installed by WRAMA instead of by a contractor." At the same time, Air Force administrators had already notified WRAMA item managers (IMs) and materiel services executives that they would allot $2.4 million for the purchase of spare parts. Equipment to be installed included: LAU-74A flare launcher, FLIR, APN-59 radar, LLLTV, fire control system with digital computer, and inertial navigation system and gun sight/fire control display, two-axis gyros, two 7.62mm miniguns, two 20mm cannons, two 40mm cannons, ECM, numerous communications systems, ARN-92 LORAN C/D, S-band Black Crow, 20-kw illuminator system, and several other high-tech radar systems. The FLIR, Black Crow, fire control system, and several other packages that had been part of the Surprise Package aircraft had to be tested to be sure that the engineering specifications would be functional on the E models.[30]

Most of the sensor qualification work was part of the larger Provost Sensor program under Operation Shed Light. This work was given Force Activity Designator I. Many of the parts and components being used in the Pave Spectre program were also being used in the Pave Pronto project and were available to both, so WRAMA materiel management officials were not as concerned about Class B items as others.[31]

When the Air Force chief of logistics, Lt. Gen. Hank Goldsworthy, visited Robins AFB on September 29, 1970, WRAMA commander Maj. Gen. A. J. Beck assured him: "We'll categorically beat schedule on Pave Spectre." On October 13, 1970, one week after the first E model arrived, ASD opened the System Program Office as an extension of the Gunship Program Office at Building 12, Area B, Wright-Patterson AFB. This aircraft had been assigned to the 64th TAW at Little Rock, Arkansas, since August 1969 and had 840 flying hours. The second E model, which arrived on January 6, 1971, had also been flying with the 64th since August 1969, having logged 921.5 flying hours.[32]

None of those involved let the grass grow under their feet. The first management meeting was held at the system program offices on January 13 in Building 155 at Robins AFB. Attended by twenty-four project officers from ASD and WRAMA, it was presided over by Gene Bryant, the overall ASD project officer. ASD promised to provide updated technical data as it became available as well as armor plating, guns, gun mounts, black boxes, and other such related equipment. Warner Robins management agreed to manufacture structure changes, racks, booths, ducting, and all Group A component-related equipment. They also agreed to furnish all Federal Supply Classification materials and hardware.[33]

On December 3–4, 1970, ASD and WRAMA experts met at Robins AFB for a technical data review that eventually produced the Pave Spectre technical manual. The actual process was contracted out to SRL. All future meetings were based on this technical manual. While the early pace of the program seemed to indicate that Pave Spectre would be ahead of schedule, ASD's AC-130A modification of nine more A models contracted to LTVE had higher priority. Even though they shared some parts, this potentially meant a sixty-day delay in Pave Spectre and endangered the June 15 and July 15 completion dates. Through extended workdays and yeoman efforts by all involved, the WRAMA/ASD team still made the deadline, and in early April 1971 the Air Staff, pleased by the success, assigned WRAMA the follow-on task of producing six more AC-130Es. At first some officials in the Air Force considered twelve more, but they eventually settled on six. These additional six planes extended the overall program to the end of 1971. In fact, it also meant the WRAMA/ASD team would have to produce six aircraft in the same time they did the first two.[34]

Even as the funding, airframe and sensor components, and scheduling issues were being worked out, logistics issues such as spare parts and depot-level repair were also being dealt with. Officials in ASD purchased unique AGE items and spares from subsystem vendors. Since there was no prime contractor, WRAMA went directly to the vendors to purchase or to other commands to obtain common AGE items from "excesses." As for depot-level repair, WRAMA asked, and ASD agreed, to add a depot-level repair provision to the production contract. Thus, Warner Robins would begin repair work on July 1, 1971, as the prototype production contract phased out. In addition, the responsibility for Pave Pronto logistics support was also transferred from ASD to WRAMA on the same date.[35]

While there were no specific directions on logistics support from AFLC or AFSC in the ASD-WRAMA joint agreement, there was guidance that allowed for a jointly developed logistics support plan. They created a plan that covered both the test phase and the deployment phase of the aircraft life cycle in the ASD-WRAMA Joint Agreement for the AC-130E Modification and Development Program Plan. With this in place, the actual production of the prototypes began in December 1970 when Warner Robins obtained production jigs, fixtures, and templates from LTVE and completed preproduction tooling and preparations. All the tooling finally arrived on February 2, 1971. The delay was due to A-model priorities for the same equipment.[36]

Delays and Solutions

Between January and March 1971 there was much uncertainty about the Pave Spectre program. As time seemed to fly by, the program moved at a snail's pace. In addition, it was not until April that an official decision was made as to how many production models would be made, and that, too, delayed work on the prototypes. To add to the conundrum, ASD was mired in the process of working on both the A- and E-model programs. Indeed, five A models were scheduled to return to the United States and be overhauled in the Pave Pronto program, while Plain Jane modifications were also underway. At the same time, the ASD managed Surprise Package, which in March 1971 was due for an IRAN enhancement scheduled to be completed by WRAMA at facilities at Robins AFB. Like relieving sinus congestion with one squirt of a fast-acting nasal spray, the March 1971 Air Force announcement that six E models would be built eased the stress and got everyone back on track with the E program.[37]

While other issues, such as Group A and Group B parts availability, would cause additional minor delays, the main bottleneck was the fire control system. Functional and flight testing had to be delayed from May to June since the fire control system did not arrive for installation until June 7, 1971. To be sure to meet the scheduled deadlines, "functional check flights would have to be performed prior to complete availability of black boxes and flight test checks for the entire fire control system."[38]

Some very bright people had been planning while the bureaucrats in Washington pondered the numbers of AC-130Es they wanted. From the very beginning of the program, Pentagon officials had pressured the Gunship Program Office to "use . . . an existing fire control system." This was not as easy as it may seem, since there were few such systems in the inventory and there was a heavy demand from the other programs as well. To deal with the problem, Warner Robins employed the skills of a dozen experts from the Air Force Academy who had PhDs in engineering. One of the key players was Lt. Col. Bradford Parkinson. The engineers searched the entire inventory to see if there was a fire control system not yet designated for other weapons systems. They wanted to make sure that whatever they used "was supportable in the current Air Force inventory." While this slowed things down, it also led WRAMA and E model officials to schedule two meetings to search for ways to speed up the program and restore it to its original timetable.[39]

The first meeting convened on March 30 and lasted until April 2, 1971, at Wright-Patterson AFB. Since WRAMA was the main manager for the C-130 and was managing all C-130–related work, this conference had the potential to affect the very heart of WRAMA's overall workload. Naturally, Warner Robins needed and wanted definitive answers to parts availability, specific management authorities for all portions of the various gunship programs, and clear Air Force directions. Conferees agreed that support kits should be assembled at and by WRAMA. They also agreed that separate A-model and E-model kits had to be prepared, since AC-130As were scheduled to deploy on September 15, 1971, and AC-130Es exactly a month later. At long last there was to be a clear-cut set of guidelines on who got what parts and when. This spirit of cooperation relaxed the situation and pushed all the AC-130 programs closer to their scheduled milestones.[40]

The second meeting, held on April 27, made additional progress, this time in resolving IM responsibilities for the A-7 fire control system for the AC-130E. This proved essential, since the structure of the E model and its difference from the A model meant that the fire control system of each was unique. In May the stakeholders decided on the A-7D fire control system for all the AC-130s. To accelerate the process, Oklahoma City Air Materiel Area remained the manager for this particular fire control system, since their expertise reduced the production time. WRAMA was concerned because the completed components would then have to be shipped to Robins AFB for installation. In the end, both groups worked tirelessly and completed this important aspect of the program on time.[41]

Finally, ASD hosted a follow-up meeting on May 5–6, 1971, in an effort to reduce the cost of AGE in the A-7D avionics, specifically the fire control system and navigation system. Cost reduction proved fairly easy, since it affected only eight aircraft, and most were still not in the production system. All parties had to review all the Tech Order manuals because of discrepancies between TOs and A-7D provisioning allocations. The AGE options facing them were, first, full contractor maintenance for the first year in Southeast Asia; second, diversion of A-7D mobility aeronautical ground equipment kits to Pave Spectre until their AGE could be supplied from the long lead-time production process; and third, any AGE options that would meet scheduled Pave Spectre costs and maintenance. After some discussion, the representatives agreed that ASD changes in the digital fire control system for Pave Spectre had created a cost-effective relationship with the Pave Pronto analog fire control system. This melding of options ultimately led to a solution in the final aspects of the fire control system issues and restored continuity to the program. Indeed, the team spirit of the management team proved essential to solving all the major problems that arose during Pave Spectre. Because of that, it is important that we view this management group before we complete a detailed review of the program.[42]

Pave Spectre Management Team

As mentioned, the Air Force assigned WRAMA the job of producing six more AC-130Es on March 23, 1971. They also instructed WRAMA to complete the IRAN modification on the remaining five Plain Janes and the Surprise Package, which were supported by LTVE. AFLC also increased the Warner Robins depot maintenance manpower ceiling by 311 civilian slots, to last from April 1, 1971, to March 31, 1972, and allowed them to hire temporary employees to keep the project on schedule. To make all this work required a management team of the highest quality. The upper echelon of the team included Lt. Gen. James Stewart, ASD commander; Maj. Gen. A. J. Beck, WRAMA commander; ASD Deputy Director for Systems Management Col. C. J. Clemence; WRAMA Director of Maintenance Col. W. R. Kelso; WRAMA Director of Materiel Management Col. Irving B. Schoenberg; Col. Nelton R. Wilson, WRAMA chief of the Tactical Aircraft Systems Management Division; Col. A. S. Hess, chief, WRAMA Maintenance Directorate, Aircraft and Engine

Division; and Lt. Col. Ronald W. Terry, chief, and M. E. Bryant, deputy chief, ASD Gunship Program Office, located at Robins AFB.[43]

At the outset of the project the ASD Gunship Program Office was located in Building 155 at Robins AFB, but early in the process it moved to the third floor of Building 125, one of the massive hangar buildings originally built in 1942 and one of only a few facilities in AFLC large enough to house the Pave Spectre work that was being done. In turn, the Warner Robins Project Management Office was on the first floor of the same building. In both cases the management team was as close to the actual work as they could realistically be and not be on site.[44]

As Maj. Ken B. Richardson, a key member of the WRAMA management office later recalled, "As the program progressed into the August [1971] timeframe . . . it had fallen considerably behind the desired production schedule on the first aircraft, and a WRAMA management office was set up in the Maintenance area immediately adjacent to the work site, and was staffed by members of the Materiel Management, Maintenance and Distribution directorates to provide real time on-the-spot support to the construction or modification project."[45]

Within the WRAMA Management Office were several key personnel, including Ron Blackwell, the program manager; the maintenance project officer, Col. John D. Walker; and the Distribution Directorate's project officer, Capt. Walter L. Monroe. All three proved to be essential to making the project run as smoothly as possible. Many of those who joined that office had worked with the AC-119 project and had a great deal of experience and expertise that made them particularly qualified for the AC-130E program. All totaled, at one time or another throughout the program, this group consisted of 22–25 people, all of whom worked sixteen-hour shifts that often extended to twenty-hour days to make sure the program met its deadlines. Of course Richardson was one of the key people.[46]

Not only did the management team work extended hours to make up for the Air Force–level delay in the decision to produce the follow-on AC-130Es at WRAMA, but also the Maintenance Directorate, Aircraft Modification Group, of the Aircraft and Engine Division literally "moved down on the floor and rebuilt the first plane, and then put the technical or engineering draftsmen on the [next] airplane." Management put the engineers, electricians, and sheet metal personnel in small groups together on the floor to build the prototypes.[47]

To anticipate the possible decision of March 23, 1971, the engineering work began before the on-site office opened. Subsequently, this ability to lean forward and spend extra hours at work proved significant. Ultimately, Warner

Robins Program Manager Capt. L. E. "Gene" Faggard convinced senior management at WRAMA and ASD to formalize the on-site overtime work. He was not asking anyone else to do what he was not willing to do. Beginning on August 14, 1971, he and a handful of other engineers worked with line workers. What had once been an ad hoc overtime process became the actual business practice. It markedly sped up the prototype process. Senior management's support of this special management team and the periodic visits by the Warner Robins commander and vice commander demonstrated to everyone the importance of what they were doing.[48]

By late August these extreme measures had put the program back on schedule, and the flight test program on the first prototype was able to commence. It lasted more than two weeks, culminating in early September. The second flight test for the second aircraft followed soon after. Concurrently, the full-scale production effort had also begun, and unlike the prototype, it began on schedule and, in fact, stayed ahead of schedule. By that time one of key reasons the project was able to pick up the pace was the cooperation between both WRAMA and ASD leadership and personnel. However, this excellence had not been attained without effort. Originally, experts had expected to spend about fifty thousand man-hours on the two prototypes but wound up using sixty-five thousand. Still, the lessons learned from the prototype facilitated and improved the production run, since it required only forty thousand man-hours to produce those six. To quote Ted Lynch, "They simply got better and more experienced. The cost of the prototypes made this possible."[49]

In echoing these sentiments, Robert F. Willingham of the WRAMA Maintenance Directorate's Aircraft and Engine Division declared, "You really have to admire these people—they have been working seven days a week, 10 hours a day. . . . They know what we've got to do and how important it is."[50]

One Down and Two to Go

By the fall, the Pave Spectre program had increased its pace while the Pave Pronto program reached its final stages. Now the Air Force shifted several LTVE and Air Force engineers and logisticians from Texas to Warner Robins. This began slowly but eventually focused almost all the AC-130 attention on the E models. As noted, by May the first prototype was nearing completion, but management realized it could not be released by its scheduled June 15 deadline with all the equipment installed. To make ends meet, they decided to leave off the side wall armor until later. With the delivery complete on June 15, testing began at Eglin AFB, Florida, and continued during the summer and fall of 1971. The Category I and II tests took place from June 20 to July 31, 1971.

Test personnel conducted thirty-five flights, with thirty involving live firing. Acceptance testing took place between August and December 1971.[51]

Ideally, the production should not have started until after the prototypes had been completed. However, as Lynch recalled, "in view of the tactical requirement to provide Southeast Asia with the AC-130E aircraft as outlined in System Management Directive 1-464-400G(5), 17 June 1971, the 'fly before buy' methodology of R&D completion prior to production could not be followed." Management decided to make a "drastic deviation from normal management and procuring techniques with WRAMA." They believed this "might, with some refinement, prove useful in future programs of this nature."[52]

One late potential roadblock proved to be the lack of design data. Even though LTVE had been working on AC-130As for a long time, they provided WRAMA with very little data and few drawings that could be used to work on the AC-130Es. The author of the WRAMA official history of the program noted that "WRAMA personnel felt that ASD should have documented and retained drawing revisions to the Ling-Temco-Vought engineering drawings in the AC-130A, while ASD claimed the WRAMA individuals who assisted them were instructed to retain such data." It would seem that ASD was slow in delivering revised drawings throughout. This had more to do with ASD serving two programs and less to do with lack of effort. The intense effort by all parties made these potential problems less difficult to remedy in the long run.[53]

In spite of all these difficulties, the WRAMA workforce pressed ahead with supreme dedication to meet and even exceed their deadlines. In late October 1971, Gen. Jack G. Merrell, AFLC commander, just "popped up" to check on the program. He and General Beck toured the production area. Beck told Merrell, "We are going to meet or beat our schedules on these six production airplanes." No one else was that confident. However, Beck knew his "airmen," and ultimately he proved to be correct. The production schedule called for the delivery of T/N 69-6569 on October 15, 69-6571 on November 5, 69-6572 on November 15, 69-6573 on November 26, 69-6570 on December 6, and 69-6574 on December 16, 1971.[54]

On the same day the final E-model production aircraft rolled out of the WRAMA production line, Secretary Seamans held a press conference at the Pentagon to explain the E model's role. He explained that the Spectres would fly CAS, interdiction of enemy supplies and troops moving into South Vietnam, and support for the ARVN as they built their forces. Seamans concluded with great praise for the workforce that had built the new gunships and the AC-130s themselves, saying that "the twelve in SEA had played a major role in the destruction of large quantities of enemy supplies during 1971." He claimed that only ninety-five hundred tons out of sixty-eight thousand tons actually got through to South Vietnam and declared that the future of the war looked better with the Spectres on station.[55]

Chapter Conclusion

This was not the end of AC-130E development. Soon a new program unfolded, designated Pave Aegis, in which all AC-130Es would have one gun position replaced with a 105mm howitzer. This would be followed by Pave Spectre II, which would exchange E-model engines, making them the AC-130Hs that bristled with two 20mm M61 Vulcan cannons, one 40mm L60 Bofors cannon, and one 105mm M102 howitzer. In retrospect, the AC-130Es, like their ancestor AC-130As, were products of the Vietnam War and built to deal with the unique problems US airpower faced during that conflict. At the same time, they were also transition gunships, since the models that fly today were only being introduced to the inventory in 1972. By the 1980s and 1990s the current versions, specifically the AC-130H and AC-130U, would be on line, and yet it was not until the 1990s that the Air Force Reserve would finally retire the AC-130As.[56]

The vision that Seamans had for the new gunships proved in error. As the apparently successful Command Hunt V wound down in 1971, negotiations and diplomatic maneuvering to end the US involvement in Vietnam continued to gain pace. There were still eighteen months of fighting before US combat forces could come home for good. Most of that fighting would be done by US air personnel, many flying gunships. The AC-130s would fly their last Vietnam mission in 1973. For the forty years after Vietnam until operations in the Persian Gulf and Central Asia, the AC-130s and their crews would fly many more sorties and face many more dangers.

7 The War Grinds On

Just because the Americans were busy upgrading and modifying their AC-130s did not mean the war had stopped or even taken a break. Throughout Richard Nixon's first term, the enemy continually redefined the strategic and tactical rules of the engagement, and it fell to the Allies to respond to each communist transformation. While production work on the new Pave Pronto and Plain Jane AC-130As came to an end in October 1970, as we have seen in the previous chapter, the E-model work was just getting underway. The A models began their deployment to Southeast Asia on October 25, 1970, sixteen days ahead of schedule. The first combat sorties took place on November 17, forty-five days ahead of schedule. While this was excellent news, the performance of the new gunships was disappointing. During the first two weeks only 37 of 202 vehicle targets spotted were damaged or destroyed. Initial response to this was to assume something was wrong with the new sensors or weapon systems.[1]

To examine this problem first-hand, ASD dispatched their most renowned expert, Col. Ron Terry, and a crew of seven. They arrived in Ubon RTAFB on December 1 and flew several missions between December 1 and 22, 1970. They damaged or destroyed 361 of 532 vehicles they spotted. In his final report, Terry concluded that the main problem was not the new technology but the lack of experience of the aircrews. In short, training had been lacking, and as experienced crews rotated home, the gunship squadrons experienced a huge drop in performance.[2]

By the end of 1970 it had become clear to all senior Air Force officials that crew training had become critical to the overall success of the gunship program. To fly productive sorties required well-trained crews. However, most of the

AC-130 night fire.

original crews had completed their one-year tours of duty, and they had been almost totally replaced by new crews for dry-season missions. Instead of rotating crews in a staggered manner so that some experienced or trained crew members, or at least leadership, remained, they rotated entire units, which meant that the institutional memory of the squadrons was limited. In addition, Air Force officials had decided to deploy more AC-130s in-theater and keep fewer at Lockborne AFB for training. As many as five of the trainees' orientation flights took place on AC-119Ks before they were able to transition to AC-130s. While the Stinger was a fine aircraft, it was not the same as the AC-130A, especially with regards to the power of the engines and weight of the airframe. With the introduction of newer and more technically advanced versions of the AC-130A, such as Surprise Package and Pave Pronto, or later, Pave Aegis, the experience gap grew even greater.[3]

Even so, in late December 1970, Secretary Seamans could report that the overall gunship force was larger and better than ever and that three of the new A models could be designated for crew training to correct training issues. Best of all, Seamans informed the secretary of defense that the program was ahead of schedule and well under budgeted cost. In an era marked by gross cost overruns, the AC-130 programs had been able to return dollars.[4]

In spite of the passionate initial debates over the gunship project, once agreements were reached, the overall program experienced a great deal of cooperation and progress. The primary success came from the specialists and managers involved—many at the ASD Gunship Program Office and at the Warner Robins Directorate of Materiel Management. With strong support from officials at higher levels and a great deal of latitude to use letter- or sole-source contracts, the program moved smoothly once it began. Of equal significance was the total commitment to the AC-130s by officers such as Terry, Krause, Wolverton, Hubbard, Pickerton, Lt. Col. Charles R. Gentzel, and Lt. Col. Charles F. Spicka. Most were not just excellent engineers but also first-class crew members who flew on both the AC-47 and AC-130 prototypes. They had flown in combat and had firsthand knowledge of what other crews faced. Most often they had been the ones who developed the tactics used by future pilots and crews. Ultimately, no one knew gunships as did Colonel Terry, whose theoretical and practical expertise literally brought the Air Force fixed-wing gunship into existence. Terry flew 56 AC-47 and 140 AC-130 combat missions, and it was upon his shoulders that the future brilliance of the AC-130s would be based. For their efforts the members of the Gunship Program Office received the Air Force Organizational Excellence Award from the SECAF at a January 28, 1972, ceremony in the Pentagon.[5]

Why Were 1970 and 1971 So Important to the AC-130s?

At the risk of being redundant, it is worth recalling some of the specific engagements and roles that the AC-130s, especially the new A models and E models, played in the major air engagements of 1970, 1971, and 1972. To this end I propose to look back at that period from late 1970 to the late spring of 1972 to focus on the gunships' role.

As Commando Hunt V began on October 10, 1970, Allied aircraft attacked four main interdiction boxes along the Laotian routes leaving North Vietnam. As previously noted, B-52s and fighter-bombers created blocking belts at the passes, while other tactical aircraft and B-57G night bombers attacked vehicle traffic leaving Laos and passing into South Vietnam. In turn, FACs and Igloo White directed gunships against enemy trucks, most of which were Russian-built ZIL 157 six-wheel-drive, five-ton trucks that traveled at forty miles per hour along the dirt and paved roads of the Ho Chi Minh Trail. Intelligence personnel in MACV estimated that at the beginning of the operation North Vietnam had 2,400 trucks, with 72 percent operating in the Steel Tiger area at an average of 450 trucks on the infiltration routes each night. Most of the drivers were veterans of the trail and knew each inch of it intimately. Most experts later were convinced that MACV's estimates of the number of trucks were far short of what the North Vietnamese really had. Later appraisals placed the available trucks at two to three times this number.[6]

During Commando Hunt V the biggest issue facing the communists was the depletion of supplies. Fortunately for them, they had an easy alternative to trucking supplies down the trail. At the peak of operations, they used small boats and barrels to float supplies down the many rivers and streams in the area. In addition, the Soviets were helping the North Vietnamese extend an ever-growing network of pipelines used to transport petroleum, oil, and lubricants to key points in support of vehicle traffic along the trail. As one analyst put it, the enemy's network was "all business." It moved the stuff of war, such as guns, ammunition, rice, fuel, and medical supplies, into the South like a raging torrent. Concurrently, the Americans moved even more of the same things to their forces but added such things as components for swimming pools, disinfectants, movies, beer and liquor, sports equipment, televisions, air conditioners, ice cream, and most important, condoms.[7]

The gunships had a poor start, as bad weather kept them grounded for several days. However, as the weather cleared, truck traffic dramatically increased, and so did the AC-130 sortie rate. On January 14, 1971, Spectres from the 16th SOS spotted 78 trucks, destroyed 58, and damaged 7. Over the next three months they reported locating 9,601 vehicles and claimed to have destroyed 6,576 and damaged 1,659, a more than 85 percent kill rate. The squadron's gunships averaged thirteen sorties a night to rack up those numbers. Of course, as previously alluded to, analysts' later review of the numbers brought into question not only the integrity of the crews but also the ability of any aircraft to totally destroy an enemy truck. Not only was the way kills were counted or confirmed flawed, but later tests at Eglin AFB proved that it was extremely difficult to damage trucks to the point that they could not be repaired with relative ease. This is not to say that the crews or the new battle damage assessment sensors were blind or deluded; rather, it proved that it was simply hard to tell from high altitude when a truck was actually hit and whether it was disabled or destroyed. In fact, trucks proved resilient and easily repaired.[8]

What one can say for sure is that the AC-130s were the most effective truck killers in-theater. They also intimidated the communists even if they did not destroy as many trucks as they claimed. With the wet season beginning in June, sortie rates dropped to 57 per night, and actual damage reported to 118 trucks per night. When Commando Hunt V ended on June 30, 1971, officials reported that their final count of 13,809 vehicles damaged or destroyed meant a threefold increase over the numbers of the previous dry season. In March alone the AC-130s had accounted for more than 70 percent of all trucks reported destroyed or damaged. The final report also noted that while in Commando Hunt III in 1970 they had destroyed or damaged only 44.2 percent of the trucks spotted, all aircraft had increased that ratio to 72.4 percent in 1971.[9]

This also meant that the numbers for F-4 fighter aircraft also increased, in large measure because of their employment of the new pod-mounted Pave Sword laser-guided bomb (LGB) first used on February 3, 1971. On one occasion Phantoms escorting Spectre 12 totally destroyed a large 37mm AAA emplacement with an LGB that caused a forty-foot plume of fire and smoke Several days later they used more LGBs to destroy two trucks with the same kind of spectacular results. Of course, destroying trucks meant destroying the supplies they contained, and in the same Command Hunt V report, experts estimated that only 2,088 tons of the 14,560 tons of supplies that left North Vietnam arrived in South Vietnam.[10]

Not So Fast, My Friend: Interpreting the Reports

However, everyone's enthusiasm soon was dampened by the onslaught of torrential monsoon rains that seemed worse and more concentrated than usual. Summer reconnaissance flights estimated seeing more than eight thousand trucks moving through the intricate network of roads and paths from the North to the South. A subsequent investigation determined that communist nations were sending four hundred new trucks a month to the North Vietnamese, which more than made up for any previously destroyed. They also received word that the enemy had been spending significant efforts on improving, expanding, and diversifying the road system to make it more difficult for aircraft to locate the new trucks under the triple-canopy jungles of Laos and Vietnam. Last, but not least, river traffic had increased as the monsoons did, and this proved an essential means of providing material aid to communist forces operating in the South.[11]

During a briefing held for Lt. Gen. Donald Bennett, director of the Defense Intelligence Agency, on April 7, 1971, the issue of the accuracy of the truck kill number arose. While General Bennett did not question the official numbers, he pointed out that others in Washington's policy making hierarchy did. His own investigation determined that the crews' reports had been as honest and accurate as humanly possible. Nearly everyone acknowledged the integrity of the airmen, but it was a simple fact that they had claimed more than thirteen thousand trucks destroyed or damaged, and solid intelligence proved that the enemy still had thousands more that were delivering thousands of tons of supplies to their forces. Leadership decided to tighten reporting standards even more than they already had to make sure kills were really kills. On May 1, 1971, crews were ordered to identify and verify all hits to determine if there were secondary explosions and/or sustained fires. Only if they could prove without question that a truck was hit and was burning intensely could they count it as a confirmed kill. A direct hit alone was no longer counted as a kill. One test, held on May 12, 1971, at Bien Hoa AB, demonstrated that even direct hits by numerous 40mm rounds did not always destroy a truck—in this case a Ford truck. It proved trucks could absorb a lot of punishment, especially when the enemy covered them with bags of rice or palm branches on vulnerable parts such as the hood or cab of the truck. In their final report, test personnel asserted that it was "harder to kill trucks than previously believed."[12]

Another problem AC-130s faced during Commando Hunt V was that they were not flying only in the Barrel Roll area of Laos, but they had also been diverted to Cambodia to support the withdrawal of ARVN forces at the end of the disastrous Lam Son 719 operation. To that end they had flown 1,108 sorties in Cambodia during the first six months of 1971. In addition, AC-130s and AC-119Ks flew 239 sorties in support of the ARVN ground operation between Khe Sanh and Tchepone during the first three months of 1971. They flew more than 60 sorties during the final five days of Lam Son 719, destroying twenty-four tanks in thirty-nine attacks and saving hundreds of ARVN soldiers from certain death. Of the tanks sighted, fourteen were Soviet-built PT-76 light tanks that had initially ripped through South Vietnamese lines of retreat. One AC-130 circled Objective 31 for three consecutive nights. When it attacked, it completely annihilated an entire NVA armored and infantry column taking refuge for the evening, thereby saving the ARVN battalion the column was pursuing.[13]

Operational Preparations for Late 1971 and Early 1972

While a second AC-130A was lost on April 22, 1970, none were lost during Commando Hunt V. However, they had been very lucky, since enemy AAA fire had increased markedly, and the communists had introduced a deadly new weapon, surface-to-air missiles (SAMs), which previously had been restricted to areas around Hanoi and Haiphong harbor in North Vietnam. While improved electronic countermeasures and flying at higher attack altitudes partially remedied the effect of this new threat, the thought that this very creative adversary was about to increase the lethal nature of the combat environment proved sobering to all the aircrews involved.[14]

In the meantime, the Air Staff requested that AFSC and AFLC send appropriate data so they could decide whether to modify all twelve AC-130Es and deploy the five remaining Plain Janes back to the States for a complete upgrade. On February 26 the Air Staff recommended modifying six instead of twelve E models in addition to the two prototypes already in production. The Air Force chief of staff and the SECAF both approved this plan and schedule to retrofit and modify the latest gunships. Final plans dictated that eleven AC-130As would enter the new production modification line no later than July 1, 1971. This called for them to undergo a full Surprise Package and

IRAN enhancement and be sent back by October 1, 1971. In turn, the six new AC-130Es would be modified and deployed no later than January 1, 1972. In fact, Warner Robins employees exceeded this deadline. The original two prototypes initially remained in the United States for crew training. As mentioned in chapter 6, WRAMA authorities had already procured twelve sets of the latest gunship components and subsystems in anticipation of modifying twelve AC-130Es. The original funding plan made on March 23, 1971, put the modification costs at $56.2 million, which required congressional approval. However, with budget constraints in place, to assure approval the Air Staff cut the number of AC-130Es in half. This was, at least in part, a result of the fact that Secretary of Defense Melvin Laird, in a report to President Nixon, recommended not only more AC-130Es but also twenty-seven new Cobra helicopter gunships for deployment to Southeast Asia.[15]

Back in Southeast Asia, PACAF and Seventh Air Force leaders were not too thrilled about pulling any gunships off the line and returning them anywhere for very long. Finally, they had an effective close air support weapon and a pretty doggone good truck killer that they believed, if provided in the right numbers, could tip the balance of the war in their favor. They had already had to send one AC-130A back for maintenance, and by June they would send a second. The Seventh Air Force commander urged officials in Washington to send the three training AC-130s to act as replacements at least until the other could return. General Ryan sent two. In a desperate effort to stay ahead of the flow of enemy supplies, the Air Force used the summer rainy season to send five AC-130 Plain Janes back to LTVE for a rapid and total upgrade in preparation for the November 1971–May 1972 dry season hunting operation, better known as Commando Hunt VII.[16]

While LTVE personnel worked around the clock on the AC-130As, production work on the E models also sped up. As the workforce continued with the original work plans, they added improvements to the production E models. Technicians added a digital fire control system for faster target acquisition. They increased fuel capacity, which increased loiter time and allowed the aircraft to carry larger ordnance payloads. They installed new electronic countermeasure systems and one thousand Mk-24 flares in canisters with chaff to confuse radar-guided SAMs. At that point ASD engineers became like mad scientists, considering every possible change that might make the AC-130s the most awesome aerial battleship thus far created.[17]

Ultimately, the most important change proved to be the addition of a 105mm howitzer to replace one of the 40mm Bofors guns. The howitzer fired a projectile weighing roughly forty-eight pounds, with a 5.6-pound high-explosive charge. By comparison, the total weight of the 40mm shell was

6.5 pounds. The 105mm round could also be delivered at a higher and safer altitude. Air Force tests had already determined that the C-130 airframe could easily stand the stress of the 105mm recoil, and August–September 1971 feasibility tests convinced Air Force leaders that installation of the howitzer was a truly brilliant plan. On November 18, 1971, the CSAF approved the new addition to be added under project Pave Aegis.[18]

In December 1971, ASD hosted a conference to plan the addition of the 105mm gun. Attendees decided to place it aft of the 40mm gun and APQ-150 beacon-tracking radar. This new gun arrangement gave the Es one 40mm, the 105mm gun, and two 20mm Gatling guns. New anti-SAM tactics were also conceived. With the full array of scanners, including the new Black Crow system, on the constant lookout for missiles, the crew would know if they had been targeted, and if a SAM were spotted, the pilot could wait until the projectile was close and then dive so the SAM would pass overhead. Of course, one negative aspect of this system was that it brought them that much closer to AAA fire. Still, the SAM became the greater threat and survival priority number one. A direct hit from AAA was something an AC-130 could survive, while the odds of surviving a hit by a telephone pole–sized missile were slim.[19]

By the end of 1971, the US involvement in the Vietnam War was about to enter its final phase. Moreover, the AC-130s that had played such a vital role in this protracted initial draw-down of US forces were hardly the same weapon system that had originally arrived in 1967 as the AC-130 T/N 1626. The E models were at least one, if not two, generations advanced and soon proved to be the perfect weapon for this final act in the tragic history of America's involvement in Southeast Asia. As the new weapon systems returned to the area of responsibility (AOR), preparations were already underway for what turned out to be the last great hunting season. Commando Hunt VII was the fourth major fall–winter (November 1971–May 1972) campaign designed to disrupt communist resupply efforts along the Laotian infiltration routes. All seven operations, but especially numbers five and seven, were also supposed to provide South Vietnam enough time to make President Nixon's Vietnamization policy a success.[20]

While it would be redundant to rehash the events of Commando Hunt VII previously developed in earlier chapters, an examination of the detailed role of the AC-130s in this campaign is vital to understanding how its performance and the circumstances of 1972 led it to remain part of the Air Force's active-duty inventory after the war was over. Commando Hunt VII focused almost entirely on the use of Allied airpower. With an ever decreasing number of US ground forces in Vietnam, this meant that whatever ground component Allied dry-season operations would have would be comprised almost entirely of ARVN troops. At the same time, planners seeking to involve VNAF pilots and maintenance crews in the war undertook a conceptual plan called Creditable Chase to involve them in both close air support and interdiction efforts. The South Vietnamese were stretched thin, and even plans to fund new minigunships and to turn over AC-119s to the VNAF crept along too slowly because of competing demands for money and resources from the AC-130 programs.[21]

With Commando Hunt VII scheduled to start in November 1971, almost everything else took a back seat, with only gunships and their supporting aircraft receiving attention. By November 1 the North had added four hundred miles to their Laotian infiltration roads, and the Ho Chi Minh Trail now totaled more than twenty-seven hundred miles. Graveled, paved, or covered with logs, most roads were capable of supporting heavy traffic during nearly all kinds of weather, allowing them nearly unimpeded travel during the wet season and the ability to cache massive supplies in Cambodia and South Vietnam in preparation for the right moment to strike.[22]

Reports at the end of Commando Hunt V estimated that the number of enemy 23mm, 37mm, 57mm, and 100mm antiaircraft guns had reached 655. Experts predicted that by the time Commando Hunt VII began, that number had increased at least 20 percent. As mentioned earlier, the B-52s began operations escorted by F-105s and EB-66s bombing the wet passes, causing mud slides and choke points. Air-dropped mines were seeded on the trails to prevent repairs and force trucks to travel longer routes over more exposed roads. Phase II used the blocking belts, air-dropped sensors, FACs, and Task Force Alpha monitoring to vector aircraft to attack traffic jams along the trail. The third phase repeated the attacks of the first phase, except this time it was against vehicles exiting Laos and entering South Vietnam. As for the enemy, the United States expected them to move large quantities of materiel only in the dry season through the mountain passes and then store them along the central route area, where shuttle teams directed them toward southern Laos then into Cambodia and finally into South Vietnam. Air Force officials expected this process to peak in March and April 1972. They determined to use both VNAF and Seventh Air Force weapon systems and personnel to increase the number of aircraft capable of attacking the enemy and to train the VNAF crews so they could take over the war someday.[23]

AC-130 Operations from November 1971 to May 1972

It is worth noting that American aircraft in-theater had decreased from 1,584 in October 1970 to 833 on December 31, 1971. Indeed, the number of strike aircraft had shrunk from 911 in Commando Hunt V to 535 for Commando Hunt VII. This also meant a drop-off in sortie rates. The gunships were authorized seven hundred sorties a month, and tactical aircraft, ten thousand. This was a decrease from the previous year of three hundred and four thousand, respectively. Many Air Force leaders believed at first, based on initial weather forecasts, that the weather would clear sooner than usual, but three large storms (one a major typhoon) soaked everything on mainland Southeast Asia and meant that the operation did not begin at the pace they had hoped.[24]

The AC-130s, based at Ubon RTAFB, Thailand, played a major role in the campaign, flying in the Barrel Roll and Steel Tiger areas of Laos, in Cambodia, and even in South Vietnam. The majority of sorties were in central and southern Steel Tiger. The panhandle was divided into nine parts, which the gunships attacked on a regular basis. However, in March 1972 two gunships were shot down, and AC-130 activities were cut back to sectors six through nine. Concurrently, the AC-119Ks operated out of DaNang, South Vietnam, and Nakhon Phanom, Thailand, mostly against Barrel Roll targets. Initially, the crews employed the same old tried-and-true tactics of the past. However, with fewer fighters in-theater, escorts were cut from three to two for AC-130s and then only in high-threat areas. The AC-119Ks continued to have three escorts because of their vulnerability. However, all that changed when the two Spectres were shot down. From that point they again had three escorts.[25]

In an interview conducted by Lt. Col. Robert G. Zimmerman in 1975 with Squadron Fire Control Officer Lt. Col. Stephen J. Opitz, the latter described what dodging AAA was like and how crew members dealt with the threat. He noted that the AAA fire was always substantial along the infiltration routes, but "we thought we were fairly impervious to being hit by AAA because the IO, who used to drop flares, would hang out the back of the aircraft, actually hang with his chest out, look underneath the bird while we flew orbit and acquired a target." When the IO saw the muzzle flashes from the 37mm and 57mm AAA, he knew it took about six seconds to reach their altitude. He would say, "AAA, 6 o'clock, coming up." Then he would say, "break right," or "break left." The pilot would turn the aircraft out of orbit, and normally the flak would miss them. Still, as Optiz recalled, the shells would explode, and "you could hear them and smell the cordite."[26]

Usually the AC-130s avoided the shells. Sometimes they got hit by shrapnel bits, but the damage was minor. In November 1971, during one night mission that was part of Commando Hunt VII, Opitz's aircraft took a 57mm hit directly in its belly. According to Opitz, it "blew a hole in the bottom of the aircraft just aft of the wheel well, right in the booth." Opitz noted that "you could stand four people in it." Capt. Gary Chandler, their infrared (IR) sensor operator, was sitting in the forward position in the crew booth, and the shell exploded under and aft of him. He had just sat down when it went off. Luckily, under each seat engineers had placed a piece of ceramic armor for just such an occasion. His chair was blown out, and "his feet were sticking over the side" and out of the aircraft. According to Opitz he "fell in the hole." Luckily, Capts. DeRosa and Bush, the electronic warfare officer "pulled him out." As Opitz recalled: "I flew the next night with my crew and it was interesting to watch them—the whole squadron was uptight and everybody was wondering now who's going to be the next one to get it."[27]

Finding targets also became an issue, since the enemy improved their tactics, too. Specifically, the North Vietnamese began to space their trucks further apart to reduce the Americans' ability to spot large convoys. They also camouflaged the vehicles better, and even though US fire control computers operated better, the communists moved the vast majority of their trucks at dusk and dawn, which was a vulnerable period for the gunships and their essential fighter escorts. Indeed, sensors simply did not operate well at those times of the day. During that time the enemy also began to make great use of the rivers and streams to float boats, barrels, and barges down the Mekong and its tributaries into South Vietnam. On some missions crews spotted 150–200 vessels; however, over the entire operation they would only claim 223 water vessels destroyed and 142 damaged.[28]

While problems of targeting were annoying, the biggest concern soon became the increase in the number of SAMs. One AC-130A, *Prometheus,* T/N 55–0044, piloted by Maj. Irving B. Ramsower, was shot down near Tchepone on March 28, 1972, by a Soviet-built SA-2. As mentioned earlier, only hours later AC-130E T/N 69–6571 was hit over the Ho Chi MInh Trail and crashed near An Loc. No one was killed, as they all bailed out. In thinking back, Lieutenant Colonel Opitz remembered that he had switched places with another officer named Hank Bower on the night of March 28. According to Opitz, "He was flying with my crew then. I traded crews; he took my crew; I took his crew, and we traded airplanes. They took our missions; we took theirs; they got shot down . . . , my crew got shot. I feel kind of weird when I think back. Oh, it's just one of those kinds of things you think about how close you come to getting it."[29]

All this would prove ironic later, since it would be the AC-130s that would fly in some of the most lethal air combat environments of the war later when they supported ARVN ground forces during the PAVN's Easter Offensive. During Commando Hunt VII, though, SAMs became worse as they became more mobile, especially when the PAVN introduced shoulder-fired, infrared-seeking SA-7 Strela missiles on May 5, 1972. Only days later, another AC-130A was hit by this new SA-7 weapon, but it was able to land safely at Tan Son Nhut AB. The introduction of this new missile system was a big surprise and left crews with no applicable defensive tactic to avoid the lethal new threat.[30]

Colonel Opitz recalled that the AC-130s had been flying some daylight missions near An Loc, since the enemy in that area did not have heavy AAA or SA-2s. As he put it, "We weren't sweating small arms too much and they launched this thing" at the AC-130A. On the gunships there were two lighting modes, one overt and the other covert. The visible light provided illumination for the LLLTV. According to Opitz, "A Strela followed that beam of light up because it hit right underneath the light which is just over the cargo doors in the back." It hit right next to the IO's head, ripped the back doors off, and knocked his flak helmet off, causing a severe wound that required fourteen stitches. While they landed safely, when they did "the torque stopping the bird and the stress bent the tail over about seven degrees. It just wiped out the airplane as far as being able to use it again."[31]

Although such shoulder-fired weapons were terrifying, the gunship crews took steps to counter their effectiveness. After some trial and error, they came up with a tactic that began when the IO first saw the Strela. He would "take the flare gun which was put in a Velcro holster right alongside of him or tied to his wrist, but it had to be readily accessible, grabbed the flare gun, and pointed down at the Strela, and shot it." As Opitz recalled, "That seemed to work because we had one launched; the IO called, and he shot, and it whistled on by us." Still, the Strelas continued to be a threat throughout the remainder of the war. Opitz remembered that "in May or in June," another AC-130 took a hit in its right wing but recovered at a "couple thousand feet." At that point a piece of the wing came off, and the plane cartwheeled, throwing the fire control officer out of the aircraft. He found himself "in space a couple of thousand feet up, popped the chute," and survived. As the colonel noted, while the AFSC people back home were quickly developing "a heat shield for the bird, the Strelas limited our capability and they became a high threat."[32]

The significant increase in AAA and SAMs also meant that truck kills decreased. One of the most straightforward solutions to air defense proliferation was a B-52 Arc Light raid that saturated areas of the trail with five-hundred-pound iron bombs. However, many of the AAA guns were mounted on tracked vehicles, and many of the SAMs were also mobile. With adequate warning this meant they could bug out before any aerial strike took place. Thus, hitting those weapons was not easy, so aircraft battle damage increased throughout Commando Hunt VII, with dubious kill results. Even so, the gunships were critical to the interdiction effort and the choke point strategy, and their lethality eventually did have the desired effect. However, the enemy's need to send trucks down the trail also continued to diminish as their pipeline network expanded. Still, the night hunting was good for the Spectres.[33]

On the night of January 26, 1972, Spectres 12 and 18 destroyed fifteen trucks and damaged thirty-seven. On the evening of March 1, 1972, AC-130E Pave Aegis racked up twelve kills in only fifteen minutes. Air Force leaders were ecstatic over the numbers being claimed. Nonetheless, this success was frequently tempered by the realization that the enemy's air defenses had sharp teeth as well. On November 14, 1971, Spectre 21, piloted by Capt. Charles E. Baertel, came under heavy AAA fire while tracking a vehicle and was hit by a round near engines three and four. The bursts were from the communists' larger AAA and probably radar-guided. As soon as the shell shook the aircraft, the plane plummeted twenty-five hundred feet before Baertel could regain control. Once he leveled out, the captain ordered that the crew assess the damage. They had experienced a severe hit and were unable to sustain a constant altitude. Baertel ordered that they jettison all nonessential equipment and lighten the load. In the next few minutes they dumped more than seven thousand pounds of ammunition and materials overboard. With this completed, Captain Baertel used the control surfaces and flaps to nurse the wounded gunship back to Ubon RTAFB. Even though he had to come in almost sideways, they landed safely and lived to tell their hair-raising story.[34]

A similar event took place on March 30, 1972, during a nighttime armed reconnaissance mission when Spectre 22, piloted by Capt. Waylon O. Fulk, was targeting a convoy along one of the Laotian infiltration roads. They had just destroyed three trucks in three spectacular fireballs and were looking for more when they were hit on the right wing and fuselage by a 57mm AAA shell. Fuel began to leak from the pylon tank, and as the cockpit crew worked to feather the engines and employ the fire suppression systems, the wing burst into flames that covered the entire right side of the aircraft. Fulk guided the wounded plane away from the AAA fire and prepared the other crew members for a bailout. Another plane came alongside and told Fulk that the damage was severe. Constantly flying toward friendly positions and radioing their positions to rescue personnel, the captain ordered the crew to abandon ship. With the rest in the silk, Fulk put the Spectre on autopilot, and he and the IO jumped out of the rear cargo ramp. As they jumped, the gunship ordnance and fuel exploded. After several hours of hiding from enemy patrols, the next morning all fifteen crew members were rescued in what became the largest single rescue in US history.[35]

When Commando Hunt VII was finally halted on March 30, 1972, US aircraft had claimed 10,609 trucks damaged or destroyed, with the AC-130s accounting for 2,782 kills, or more than half of the overall 4,727 vehicles destroyed. All of this was accomplished during 1,806 sorties in the Steel Tiger region. The gunships had flown missions every night but two and had experienced good hunting nearly every night. Official analysis, using the same dubious methods as discussed in chapter 4, determined that of the 31,000 tons of supplies Hanoi had sent down the Ho Chi Minh Trail, only 16 percent, or 5,000 tons, had reached its destination in South Vietnam.[36]

Those were spectacular results, to say the least, yet even as the interdiction campaign came to an end, PAVN Sr. Gen. Vo Nguyen Giap launched the massive communist conventional Easter Offensive. What many experts, then and now, realized is that the number of truck kills claimed had probably been too high. They also discovered later that while the Air Force was bombing the trail, the communists were sending masses of equipment and supplies directly across the DMZ through extensive pipeline systems and down the numerous waterways that crisscrossed Vietnam. Add this to the previously mentioned difficulty in destroying trucks and the fact that the enemy used the infiltration routes more extensively than first believed during the bad weather of the wet season, and one can understand why they could launch a large ground offensive. Even though the AC-130s had performed heroically, the communists had gotten much more materiel to their forces already in the South than anyone counted on.[37]

Colonel Opitz, who was on location, reminds us how difficult it was for even the greatest truck killers in history to completely destroy a truck. Opitz said that "if trucks were movers, they would usually stop" when AC-130s began their attacks. "Rarely would you get a guy that would just floor it and try to outrun it. He usually ran off the road or he would go around the corner and run into another dead truck or you would lay one right on him and hit him and kill him and kill the truck. Or you would put a couple on the road and he would get out and then you get the truck." Targeting the vehicles wasn't all that easy, either. On one occasion Opitz and his gunship were tracking what they believed to be a really large truck and two jeeps. As they did, the vehicles ran into very thick undergrowth. Opitz called out: "Well, gee, that's kind of thick terrain for doing that." After some time examining the situation, it finally dawned on Opitz that "they were elephants and they were probably a mother, and a father, and the one that was panic stricken was the baby running around, because we fired and the three of them would just circle around." Opitz told them to cease fire before they accidentally killed the elephants.[38]

To Opitz the AC-130s never got enough credit for all they did in the Commando Hunt campaigns, especially not in the media. He pointed out that his flight alone claimed 169 kills one evening and that the reports he saw credited the gunships with more than 80 percent of all the truck kills. He also noted that at first counting kills was a haphazard process that depended on the honesty and eyesight of the crew members. However, by the time Opitz began flying, the gunships had a "TV tape recorder which was hooked into the IR set and the TV set. The fire control officer's job was to punch that set on record when you were shooting a truck. At the end of each mission, and you would fly usually 4 or 4 ½ hours, the whole crew took the tape and went to the debriefing at Intel and then they played the tape on the monitor and you had an Intel officer there and you all agreed." As he pointed out, "I believe in 1970 and 1971 we were getting a lot of credit for dead trucks, and then you would go out for photo reconnaissance for an authentication and the truck would be gone.[39]

Opitz was right when he recalled that "they did some analysis and set some [US] trucks up and found out that they weren't destroyed when you would hit them—the truck would be tough." Furthermore, even if the gunship "chewed a hole through the bed or blew all the tires, the Cong would come the next day and put new tires on it and haul the thing away." As a result, officials changed the criteria for counting kills: "It had to burn or explode before you got a kill. And if it did not burn or explode, it was damaged. But we had quite a few."[40]

During one night mission in early March 1972, Opitz's gunship came across a huge truck convoy on the northern rim of the Mekong Delta paralleling an enemy barge floating down the Mekong River. They attacked the barge and caused an explosion that lit up the night. As Opitz put it, "it was a field day." They were operating at 13,000 feet, and some of the crew were suffering from hypoxia, but no one complained. At one point they hit a truck that erupted all over the road, blocking all the others. From there they "just started walking up," progressing from truck to truck up the line. When the last of the trucks exploded, Opitz recalled, "The columns of flame came up about 7,000–8,000 feet." The only reason they had to pull out was that they had destroyed so many trucks that the fires were illuminating them, and the AAA gunners began to shoot at them. Opitz remembers that on that mission they "got 78 trucks, and I think that particular night—we all got the DFC for it, mainly I guess for hanging in there and wiping out the convoy."[41]

Summing Up the AC-130 Role and Defending the South

The gunship personnel, like those flying with Colonel Opitz, throughout operations from 1970 to 1972, especially Commando Hunt VII, risked everything on a nightly basis. Night after night they flew over some of the most vital targets of the Vietnam War and into some of the thickest and deadliest flak since World War II. As Jack Ballard notes in his seminal work on gunships,

"Some survived combat, some did not. All joined those countless men down through the ages who braved the battle."[42]

However, as the PAVN poured into South Vietnam in March–April 1972, no gunship crew member was worrying about kill numbers; they were preparing to defend South Vietnam against the largest invasion of one nation by another since the Second World War. In January 1972, general plans for the Easter Offensive had fallen into the hands of American intelligence. While the details were vague, it was clear that Hanoi was planning another Tet Offensive on an even larger scale than in 1968. Some analysts feared another Dien Bien Phu. As early as December 1971, aerial reconnaissance revealed considerable evidence that the NVA was stockpiling an enormous cache of supplies along the DMZ. Even Soviet-built tanks had been spotted in jungle groves and clearings. As the Spring Offensive unfolded, and with Henry Kissinger's Paris peace talks stalled, President Nixon ordered the Air Force to take action to prevent South Vietnam from being overrun.[43]

It is worth remembering that by late 1971 President Nixon's Vietnamization policy had reduced US Air Force strike aircraft from a high of 737 in 1968 to 277 and personnel from 54,434 to 28,791. Even before the Nguyen Hue Offensive began, as US air operations decreased, enemy infiltration increased, with the North stockpiling weapons and troops in South Vietnam. To halt this buildup, Nixon approved a five-day bombing campaign code-named Operation Proud Deep Alpha. Between December 26 and December 30, 1971, Air Force B-52s and fighter aircraft as well as naval aircraft from the carrier *Constellation* launched 1,025 preplanned sorties against North Vietnam. Concentrated on Route Package I, just south of the twentieth parallel, the campaign had two main goals. The first was tactical and focused on the destruction of increasingly effective SAM sites. The second objective was strategic and sought to destroy enough enemy supplies and troops to discourage them from launching a major offensive. In the largest US bombing campaign since Operation Rolling Thunder (1965–68), US aircraft attacked SAM sites, enemy road construction along the DMZ, and POL storage facilities. Since sorties were flown in southern North Vietnam, Hanoi continued its troop and supply buildup in the North, and the missions had little effect on enemy plans for an invasion. The Air Force and Navy lost five aircraft and seven airmen.[44]

While leadership thought that this campaign would solve their immediate problem of a potential invasion, by February 1972 concerns over an enemy offensive persisted. As a result, the Air Force began a redeployment known as Operation Bullet Shot. It evolved into Strategic Air Command's five-phase dispatch of units back to Vietnam that lasted from February 5 to May 23, 1972. Leaders hoped this further dispatch of B-52s would increase air operations and discourage the continued buildup of enemy forces and materials. Once the PAVN began their invasion, these units were used to attack the NVA units moving into South Vietnam.[45]

On February 5, Strategic Air Command (SAC) initiated Bullet Shot, eventually sending 124 B-52s to Andersen AB, Guam, and U-Tapao Royal Thai Navy Airfield, Thailand. Ultimately, this brought the number of B-52s in Guam to 150, making it the largest B-52 unit in the Air Force. The total in-theater B-52s ultimately reached 209. To support the bombers, between February 8 and May 21, 1972, SAC also deployed twenty-four KC-135 aerial refueling aircraft to Kadena AB, Japan, and seven to U-Tapao. By the time Bullet Shot ended, B-52s were capable of 3,150 sorties a month. They were also able to expand their bombing missions throughout Vietnam, even attacking north of the DMZ. It should be noted that between May and October 1972, these bombers played a key role in Operation Linebacker I, and later, during Linebacker II (December 18–29, 1972), they helped to force the enemy to complete negotiations and sign the January 1973 Paris Peace Accords.[46]

Also during this same period, PACAF planners developed Operations Plan C-101 designed to augment the in-theater Seventh Air Force F-4 Phantom fighter force. In one of many redeployment operations undertaken in late 1971 and early 1972, Operation Commando Flash sent F-4 fighter jet aircraft from the Philippines to Thailand. That operation began on December 29, 1971, when 6 F-4s left Clark AB, the Philippines, and relocated to Korat RTAFB. On February 8, 1972, 12 more departed Clark AB, with 6 going to Ubon RTAFB and 6 to Udorn RTAFB. As the Easter Invasion began, PACAF developed a second plan, known as Operation Plan C-103 or Operation Commando Fly. It began on April 3, 1972, only five days after the PAVN launched their attacks and sent 8 F-4s to Ubon RTAFB and Da Nang AB, South Vietnam. Once the magnitude of the invasion became clear, more fighters were sent, eventually totaling 144 more F-4s and 12 F-105s during what was designated as Operation Constant Guard. These aircraft were used during Operation Linebacker I and helped blunt the enemy invasion. All totaled, between late 1971 and mid-1972 the US increased the number of US Air Force and Navy aircraft from 375 to 900.[47]

And Where Do We Go from Here?

Even as these initial buildups progressed, it became clear that the enemy was up to something big. In spite of preparations made in February, the invasion took nearly everyone by surprise, especially with regard to its size and intensity. The deluge of troops into the South soon became alarming and dangerous to the very survival of the Republic of Vietnam. To facilitate American air operations, what had been confusing and debilitating rules of engagement changed when Nixon allowed the Air Force to create a set of preapproved target areas near the Central Highlands in Military Regions I and II. What was most encouraging to Air Force planners was the fact that it was a conventional assault in the classic World War II form and required long, often exposed logistics columns and advancing lines of infantry and tanks. Since PAVN had learned their primary tactics from Soviet advisers, their tactics had significant Soviet components, including lots of artillery support. This frequently meant fixed targets. This battlefield environment was perfect for the Air Force gunships, and while tactical air assets and B-52s spent most of the spring returning to Southeast Asia, the AC-130s had never left. They were ready to chew up the advancing enemy. Indeed, the whole Air Force was salivating over this enemy offer of battle in terms they had long been trained for.

8 Linebacker I and II
America's Involvement Winds Down

In order to grasp the significance of the role of the AC-130s at the end of the Vietnam War, one needs to understand how the Nguyen Hue or Easter Offensive unfolded and how US airpower responded. The enemy invasion officially lasted from March 30 to September 16, 1972.[1] Communist goals were to erode flagging US public war support during an election year, to counter South Vietnamese successes in rural areas since 1969, and to win the war before Nixon's détente policy affected Soviet and Chinese material support of Hanoi.[2] What communist leaders failed to grasp was that the audacity of the attack "provided Nixon with the public support necessary to retaliate."[3]

US forces were mostly caught off guard, having scheduled reductions in American troops from two hundred thousand to sixty-nine thousand in May and aircraft from 500 to 375. However, in the spring of 1971 the CIA had warned of a potential election-year invasion, but they believed the enemy could not "launch a nationwide military offensive on anything approaching the scale of Tet 1968."[4] At least two hundred NVA tanks were deployed undetected to various staging areas in 1971–72, and, as one analyst later noted, "This stealthy deployment, together with the persistent perception that the enemy's logistical system was less efficient than it was, deflected American intelligence analysts from a correct understanding of Communist plans."[5]

The initial assaults came from Laos by 40,000–50,000 troops against Quang Tri Province in Military Region (MR) I. The next day, 160 miles south of the DMZ, in the Central Highlands in MR II, 28,000 more NVA struck Kontum Province. The enemy opened a third front with 31,000 men attacking 375 miles south of the DMZ and 60 miles west of Saigon. Of the 200,000 communist troops eventually involved, 120,000 were NVA regulars, 50,000 were VC main force troops, and 30,000 were VC irregulars. Supported by tanks and artillery and protected by low-lying clouds, NVA units in MR I pushed ARVN units out of Quang Tri City by May 1, 1972. The new ARVN commander, Gen. Ngo Quang Troung, withdrew south in good order and established a tenuous defensive line on the south bank of the My Chanh River. By May 14, enemy units in MR II had overrun Dak To and put Kontum City under siege, while in MR III the NVA had destroyed an ARVN division, taken Loc Ninh, and surrounded An Loc by April 13.[6]

At An Loc the PAVN 5th, 7th, and 9th Divisions surrounded the outnumbered and outgunned ARVN 5th Division and 3rd Ranger Group and some Binh Long provincial forces. Throughout the battle, gunships flew numerous close air support missions, in one case killing ninety-eight enemy soldiers near the Dak Pek Ranger Camp. Gen. Spike Momyer believed that the savior of An Loc as elsewhere was American airpower. According to the general, An Loc "would have been lost without the day and night support flown by fighters and the AC-130 and AC-119 gunships."[7]

At Kontum City on May 11, with the eastern part of the city under attack from NVA regulars, one enemy POW later recalled that the B-52s and gunships struck at about 5:00 a.m., pounding the city's eastern approaches every hour on the hour for twenty-five continuous hours, bombing or strafing several targets more than once. Entire NVA units were wiped out. When Buffs were not overhead, gunships circled like great birds of prey, cutting exposed enemy columns to pieces. Five days later, a PAVN unit, supported by twenty tanks, attacked an ARVN force just south of Kontum City on Route 14. Three cells of B-52s, later supplemented by dozens of gunship sorties, targeted each enemy column and "obliterated" them "utterly." On May 26 the communists made one last assault on Kontum City that failed in a hail of lead and raging explosions set off by a tenacious ARVN defense, American gunships, and B-52 sorties. Between May 14 and June 6, 1972, US gunships, especially AC-130s, killed 5,688 enemy troops and destroyed 38 tanks and dozens of artillery pieces.[8]

As mentioned earlier, in December 1971, even before the invasion, Nixon, concerned by intelligence reports, had responded with Operation Proud Deep Alpha, in which Air Force fighters flew over one thousand sorties against enemy staging areas just south of the twentieth parallel. Additional attacks took place in February 1972 but were limited during the president's trip to China. Simultaneously, the number of American aircraft in Southeast Asia increased with the dispatch of 207 F-4s from late December to May 13, 1972, bringing the total in-theater to 375.[9]

Operation Constant Guard was one of several operations designed to redeploy US aircraft to Southeast Asia in 1972, initially to prevent an NVA invasion and later in response to it. The operation consisted of four phases. Constant Guard I–III was the buildup of TAC fighters and fighter-bombers, while Constant Guard IV focused on augmenting tactical airlift capabilities. On April 1, 1972, with the initiation of Constant Guard I, TAC sent thirty-six F-4Es from Seymour Johnson AFB, North Carolina, to Ubon RTAFB and four EB-66s, equipped with electronic warfare systems, from Shaw AFB, South Carolina, to Korat RTAFB. They also sent twelve F-105G Wild Weasels from Seymour Johnson to Korat. The F-105s were equipped with enemy air defense suppression (SEAD) systems designed to disable enemy radar, SAMs, and AAA sites with antiradiation missiles by using the site's own radar signal to guide the missiles.[10]

By April 15 the first deployment was complete, and the next day, Constant Guard II began with the dispatch of two squadrons of 18 F-4s, one from Eglin AFB, Florida, and the other from Homestead AFB, Florida. Both restationed at Udorn RTAFB. Constant Guard III, the final deployment of fighters, began on May 3, 1972, when 72 F-4s from Holloman AFB, New Mexico, reopened Takhli RTAFB, which had been closed in 1970 as part of Nixon's downsizing plan. This redeployment ended on May 13, 1972. All totaled, the Air Force sent 144 F-4s and twelve F-105s first to the Republic of Korea and then to various bases in Thailand. These aircraft all played a key role in Linebacker I, flying their last mission on October 23, 1972.[11]

During the return of all these aircraft, the one constant had been the AC-130s and AC-119Ks. On a daily basis, Spectres flown by the 16th SOS and Stingers flown by the 18th SOS, as well as Shadows and AC-47s now flown by the 89th Attack Squadron of the VNAF, made sure that enemy troops could not gain the final victory they so desperately sought. More than any other weapon, they shattered communist troop formations, accounting for more than 30 percent of the enemy casualties from May to September 1972.[12]

At the same time, by April 20, 1972, Marine leadership had deployed 40 F-4s to Da Nang and two squadrons of A-1s to Bien Hoa. Nixon sent the USS *Kitty Hawk* and USS *Constellation* to join the *Coral Sea* and *Hancock* in the Gulf of Tonkin. At the end of the month, the *Midway* had also arrived, followed on June 27 by the *Oriskany* and on July 3 by the *America,* which replaced the *Constellation.* At that point, three and one-half months after the offensive began, the United States had six carriers on station, each with 60 strike aircraft, a total of more than 350 naval planes. American strike aircraft in-theater now totaled 1,380, up from 495 present in March.[13]

As Nixon himself declared, he was now ready "to go for broke and bring the enemy to his knees."[14] He was determined to resume bombing North Vietnam and mining Haiphong harbor. Having negotiated closer ties with both Moscow and Beijing, he believed he could afford to be bolder with Hanoi. Gen. John W. Vogt Jr., on his way to assume command of the Seventh Air Force, met with the president and later described him as "wild-eyed."[15]

Soon Nixon authorized air strikes against AAA and SAM sites and logistics targets 25 nautical miles north of the DMZ. Initially, poor weather hampered operations. On April 5, 1972, US fighters attacked supply and logistics targets south of the eighteenth parallel, 60 miles north of the DMZ, as part of Operation Freedom Train. The results were disappointing, since the major flow of enemy supplies and troops remained unimpeded. As a result, Nixon expanded the area of operations to the twentieth parallel, about 250 miles north. On April 16, using B-52s for the first time since the invasion began, Nixon sent eighteen Buffs, stationed at the airfield at U-Tapao, to attack oil storage facilities near Haiphong. Four more April B-52 raids followed with impressive results.[16]

As Nixon prepared to send Kissinger back to Paris to negotiate with North Vietnamese representative, Le Duc Tho, on May 2, he considered a three-day series of B-52 raids against Hanoi, beginning on May 5. However, Kissinger, fearing domestic reactions, and Gen. Creighton Abrams, MACV commander, declaring his need for the B-52s in South Vietnam to support gunship attacks in an effort to curb the enemy offensive, convinced the president to hold off. Instead, Nixon opted for a plan from Kissinger's military assistant, Maj. Gen. Alexander Haig, which called for sustained bombing by tactical bombers and mining of Haiphong and other enemy harbors. Similar in design to Operation Rolling Thunder, its main force was to be tactical aircraft from the carriers of Task Force 77 and from the Seventh Air Force. Only a handful of gunships and B-52s were to be used, mostly in the South. The operation, called Linebacker, began on May 10 and officially ended on October 15, 1972.[17]

Planners developed Linebacker in four phases. The first focused attacks against railroad bridges and rolling stock in and around Hanoi and then northeast toward the People's Republic of China (PRC). The second phase targeted primary storage areas and marshaling yards near the North Vietnamese capital. Phase three was aimed at storage and transshipment points created to cope with the results of phases one and two. Attack planners envisioned these targets being hit at the discretion of local commanders as often as necessary to impede the shipment of supplies into South Vietnam. The final phase targeted associated enemy defenses such as ground control intercept radar sites, command and control, MiG airfields, SAM and AAA sites, and their logistics depots and support facilities.[18]

Part two of the overall operation, code-named Operation Pocket Money, involved aerial mining of northern ports. On May 9, at 8:00 a.m. Saigon time,

Nixon announced, on national television, that US planes would begin mining ports and harbors one hour later and that the mines would be activated on May 11, 1972, at 6:00 p.m. Saigon time. At first glance the mining seemed to achieve its goal. As one report noted, "From the day the mines came alive through September, no vessels are known to have entered or to have left North Vietnam's ports." However, the communists overcame this problem by anchoring ships twelve miles from port and off-loading six thousand tons per month. Soon the Americans got wind of this tactic, and US fighters attacked the freighters as they lay at anchor. To counter this switch in US tactics, the North Vietnamese simply waited until night to conduct the off-loading process. While this game of cat and mouse did not stop the flow of supplies, the fact is that the flow was restricted to the point that it began to cause the enemy a great deal of suffering.[19]

The risks of Linebacker were great, since Nixon was scheduled to meet with Soviet leaders in late May, and many advisers feared negative public reaction as well. However, Nixon's instincts told him that the public would accept a Soviet failure over the fall of Saigon. As was often the case in the president's long career, his political nose had picked up the right scent. Ultimately, the summit was a success, and South Vietnam, in large measure due to the bombing campaign, did not fall just yet.[20]

During Operation Freedom Train, a component of Linebacker I flown from April to June 1972, US forces flew 27,745 attack-and-support sorties, 1,000 of which were flown by B-52s and more than 2,000 of which by gunships. The Americans lost fifty-two planes—seventeen to SAMs, eleven to AAA, three to small arms, fourteen to MiGs, and seven to unknown causes. The enemy fired 777 SAMs in April, 429 in May, and 366 in June. Initially, they used ripple firing tactics—one high, one low, and one in the middle—for complete coverage. Early enemy successes were later offset by US countermeasures, including the use of chaff, especially by the B-52s. The US also utilized Iron Hand anti-SAM tactics employing F-105 Wild Weasels, which used communist SAM radar rebound signals to guide AGM-78 standard antiradiation missiles (STARMS) or AGM-45 Shrike missiles to the target. The US also used killer-hunter formations that called for Wild Weasels to spot targets and F-4s to drop high-explosives and cluster bombs on them.[21]

The enemy was well armed with four thousand 23mm to 100mm AAA weapons, half of them around Hanoi and Haiphong. Air Force analysts determined that these defenses were less dangerous than those faced during Rolling Thunder because LGBs "were dropped at a much higher, and therefore safer, altitude than unguided munitions."[22] Hanoi also had over two hundred MiG fighter aircraft, including seventy modern MiG-21s. The rest were older

MiG-17s and MiG-19s. They flew fewer sorties and used fewer aircraft than they did during Rolling Thunder, concentrating their efforts around Hanoi and Haiphong. Only one US aircraft was lost to MiGs over North Vietnam during Freedom Train, while the Americans downed nine enemy fighters. The numbers were not as good for the overall Linebacker operations.[23]

As the larger Linebacker campaign unfolded, the NVA revised their tactics again, using ground control radar to direct MiG-21s onto the tail of an American formation heavy with fuel and munitions. They fired air-to-air missiles as vulnerable US planes maneuvered on their bomb runs at lower speeds. MiG-21s also attacked from the rear to force formations to take evasive action while a second wave of MiG-19s struck from the front. By July, enemy fighters had downed twenty-six US aircraft while losing thirty-two of their own. The American reaction was the employment of the Teaball weapons control center in Thailand, which coordinated data from airborne radars over Laos and the Gulf of Tonkin to warn US aircraft of enemy aircraft locations. From August 1 to October 15, MiG losses totaled nineteen, while US losses dropped to five.[24]

In early June, PACAF reported that "the enemy has 'shown no signs of response to the interdiction . . . ; therefore it is estimated that only a small amount of material is entering NVN via the highway system.'"[25] As tactical aircraft struck the North, Allied gunships and most B-52s continued to support ground operations in the South. The Seventh Air Force, still responsible for support of defenders facing Route Package (RP) I in southern North Vietnam and the DMZ, concentrated B-52 raids against communist storage areas, supply transportation choke points, and enemy staging areas. As the offensive slowed, it revised its role to attacks on bridges, ferries, and fords in MR I or northern South Vietnam, moving up to RP I in phase two. In phase three Seventh Air Force created choke points around Dong Hai in RP I by destroying bridges on Highways 101 and 1A. On average, B-52s flew thirty daily sorties, most against RP I bridges. Concurrently, AC-130s and AC-119Ks continued to attack what few enemy soldiers and vehicles still dared to move during daylight. For gunships, it became an around-the-clock operation, since it was at night that the communists most felt the sting of all the Allied gunships.[26]

Officials also revised campaign priorities, placing at the apex of their attack list North Vietnamese rail lines branching out of China, rail and road links between China and Hanoi and Haiphong moving south to the DMZ, oil and gas storage areas, power stations, and rolling stock and equipment and supply storage depots. By late June, northern industry, mine clearing forces, and inland waterways were added to the priority list. In spite of this emphasis on North Vietnamese high-value targets, 86.8 percent of the missions flown were aimed at road, rail, and storage targets in the South. They were forced to set these priorities because even with the buildup there were too few aircraft to cover ARVN defenses in the South and attack all the targets in the North. Once ground fighting began to taper off in September, attacks moved north of RP I.[27]

At the beginning of Linebacker air leaders were pleased by promises to lift Rolling Thunder restrictions. However, while political limitations, caused by fears of direct Soviet or Chinese intervention, had been reduced by détente, the Americans still had no desire to incite a rash act. Nixon understood that Vietnam, while important, was only part of a much larger chess match, and that better relations with the USSR and PRC benefited US interests more than anything short of what seemed to be an unlikely total victory in Vietnam. While Linebacker I generally had fewer restrictions than Rolling Thunder, it still faced strict guidelines. Linebacker limitations included a no-bombing area on the Sino-Vietnamese border as well as no bombing of Northern dams, dikes, civilian watercraft, civilian population centers, and non-Vietnamese seaborne shipping. All attacks were approved by the JCS. Restrictions were especially tight from May 21 to June 5, 1972, during Nixon's trip to Moscow.[28]

The most effective attacks against bridges and railroads employed GBU-10 LGBs, which composed more than 90 percent of the precision-guided munitions (PGMs) used in the Southeast Asia war. They were two-thousand-pound general purpose bombs with a laser-seeking head, a small computer, a tail assembly, and canard control surfaces. One other less effective electro-guided bomb was the Walleye launch-and-leave glide bomb, directed by a computer and a television camera. Often fooled by camouflage, clouds, and/or smoke, it was used only in daylight. Its very low six-thousand-foot release point also proved to be a major drawback.[29]

In May and June, F-4s, using GBU-10s, destroyed the main bridges on the Sino-Vietnamese border, including the Thanh Hoa Bridge over the Song Me River. The primary rail and road lines in the northwest remained interdicted through the end of June, while the northeastern passages were less effectively blocked. Nothing seemed to be very effective against less sophisticated targets, such as inland water traffic. One JCS report determined that it "was the most difficult system to attack." Even mining inland streams and rivers with Mk-36 mines had little effect. Only armed reconnaissance or naval gunfire had any impact. This was because these routes had no real choke points, and loading and unloading small vessels required only "a firm bank and a few planks."[30]

While mining northern harbors seemed to deter enemy seaborne shipping, the pipelines out of China were so widely dispersed that PACAF analysts concluded they were virtually immune to serious disruption, since they were "too hard to find, too hard to hit, and too easy to repair." Linebacker also failed to cut highways totally; they also proved difficult targets to destroy. These well-defended targets required large, fully escorted formations that drained US resources. Night attacks were limited because of technology gaps, and there were never enough gunships to fly armed reconnaissance. On June 28, PACAF admitted that the "tonnage involved in shipments from China to North Vietnam could easily equate to the amounts received via Northern ports prior to US mining operations."[31]

The inability of Commando Hunt operations to interdict NVA supplies totally allowed the communists to pre-position caches of supplies and personnel in South Vietnam. Thus, they had plenty of material support during the spring and early summer of 1972. As a result, the most important air operations were carried out in the South in support of ARVN defenders, and many of the battles between ARVN and PAVN troops were so intense that gunships, often AC-130s, flew hundreds of sorties each day and night while B-52s bombed within one thousand feet of the defenders. In April and May, B-52s flew 1,682 sorties in MR II, with 727 sorties flown in support of the defenders at An Loc. In the South, enemy air defense threats were less than in the North, even though one hand-held SA-7 did shoot down the first AC-130 gunship lost in South Vietnam. The reduced-threat environment allowed the Allies to use fixed-wing gunships, helicopter gunships, and other propeller-driven aircraft, including those of the VNAF, which flew nearly three thousand close air support sorties between April and October. Flying lower and slower, at five hundred feet, these prop aircraft, including the AC-119Ks, proved very effective. For those who had doubted the efficacy of the old Hercules and Boxcar, this period of the Vietnam War changed many minds and helped them decide that at least some of those gunships should transition into the postwar Air Force.[32]

While the fixed-wing gunships of the Seventh Air Force were busy cutting up enemy troops and tanks in the South, F-4s destroyed forty-five bridges along the DMZ, and F4s and AC-130s together killed eleven of twenty-three PT-76 Soviet-built light tanks trying to outflank ARVN units at the My Chanh defense line near the South Vietnamese coastline. Gunships and B-52s returned to RP I in July, with the Buffs flying 1,308 sorties by September and destroying 109 supply depots, truck parks, and fuel storage sites. The AC-130s and AC-119Ks doubled those sortie numbers, soon crippling the enemy's logistics lines that had come out into the open to support their conventional invasion. During Linebacker I operations, American aircraft of all kinds flew over 6,000 sorties in RP I, making it the most heavily bombed region during the spring and summer of 1972.[33]

Crewing the 105mm gun.

In late May the NVA offensive began to slow, and by late June it had ground to a complete halt. The last big assault took place on May 25 against the My Chanh line. It was thoroughly blunted by ARVN ground units supported by VNAF and American air components, especially gunships such as the AC-130s and AC-119Ks, each flying sortie after sortie, often twenty-four hours a day. Those on the ground were deeply appreciative for the unflinching dedication of the weary aircrews. On June 8, ARVN units began a counteroffensive, again supported by American airpower (especially gunships), that eventually retook Quang Tri City on September 16, 1972. Among the key elements in the NVA's failure was their inability to use their tanks fully because of the constant Allied close air support operations—most notably fixed-wing gunships. Indeed, it is worth reemphasizing that in spite of their superior speed and power, the fighters did no better than the AC-119s and AC-130s in saving the Republic of Vietnam from being overrun. In looking back, the enemy suffered heavy casualties in taking Quang Tri City, and this delayed their original timetable and prevented them from moving on Hue as they had in the Tet Offensive four years earlier. The AC-130 raids played a decisive role in cutting communist supply lines and creating high casualty numbers. Their constant assaults on enemy logistics and communications lines delayed the communist advance at least two or three weeks, forcing the enemy to expend far more of their pre-positioned materials than they had planned or hoped to do.[34]

Linebacker I and collateral air operations (April 5–October 23, 1972) dropped 155,548 tons of bombs on North Vietnam, or about 25 percent of what Rolling Thunder had expended. General Vogt declared, "More damage was done to the North Vietnamese lines of communications during 'Linebacker' than during all our previous efforts." He claimed that US aircraft destroyed almost all fixed oil storage facilities and 70 percent of the electric power generating capacity in North Vietnam, meaning that nearly all of Hanoi's portable generated power had to go to military use. In addition, the psychological effect was great, since 20 to 40 percent of Hanoi's residents had to be evacuated.[35] It is worth reiterating Gen. Bruce Palmer's conclusion, "The North Vietnamese appear to have had in South Vietnam and adjacent areas of Laos supplies sufficient to see them through their defeats, which were the accomplishments of the South Vietnamese infantry, tactical close air support [gunships], and the B-52s.[36]

In spite of their losses, the NVA still held much of the South Vietnamese countryside and were still dictating the tempo of the war. The communists had not been defeated strategically, only delayed by a tactical setback. They slowed the offensive to preserve their remaining southern forces, which they planned to rebuild during another series of negotiations with the United States. Without question, American airpower played a major role in preserving the Republic of Vietnam in 1972. The initial phases of the invasion had moved forward supplied by pre-positioned materials until late May and early June. But, unable to resupply their forces through the normal network of trails and waterways, the enemy were forced to curtail their offensive. In short, Allied airpower had been the reason the invasion stagnated. Even so, the North Vietnamese had cached some significant amounts of supplies. During the ARVN offensive to retake Quang Tri City, six PAVN divisions, albeit undermanned, were well equipped, especially with artillery shells, often an excellent indicator of logistics strength. The communist defenders expended three thousand rounds each day against the three attacking ARVN divisions. As one analyst put it, "It is not likely the NVA in MR I were ever effectively interdicted."[37]

America's prodigious Linebacker effort meant that the Laotian interdiction ceased almost completely, since Allied air forces, even after the spring buildup, were not sufficient to continue simultaneous operations against the Ho Chi Minh Trail and the Easter Offensive on the level necessary to thwart the enemy completely. After all, if B-52s and gunships had been the primary weapon of aerial interdiction, and they were busy defending South

Vietnamese ground positions against the enemy's spring assaults, who was attacking the infiltration routes? They tried to do both, but it was a matter of priorities. The trail was slow death, and the invasion was immediate. The CIA and Defense Intelligence Agency reported that the enemy still had fourteen thousand trucks available during the Easter Offensive and that from fifty-five thousand to seventy-five thousand tons of supplies were being successfully shipped south each month. All this countered harbor mining and the limited effects of Commando Hunt. With their extensive pipeline network, plentiful waterways and vast numbers of trucks, heavily defended by air defenses and hidden at night, the communists could, and did, weather Linebacker to wait for a better day.[38]

American air forces could not afford even modest attrition rates, which meant that the Seventh Air Force was reluctant to conduct armed reconnaissance missions in the northern route packages, not only because the enemy's AAA and SAMs were so effective, but also because to do so meant risking or diverting resources and weapon systems from other critical missions. The United States tried to compensate by using PGMs, which proved effective against bridges, structural features, and industrial targets, but with supplies pouring in unimpeded from the Soviet Union and China, Hanoi was not totally dependent on such things.[39]

Chapter Conclusion

There was one last great air operation during the Vietnam War, and that was Linebacker II. However, it was a thoroughly strategic campaign mainly built around B-52 raids on the North. Throughout the remainder of 1972 and into 1973, gunships continued their primary missions. They returned to their routine of CAS, base support, armed reconnaissance, convoy escort, and interdiction at a reduced level. On January 1, 1973, the 18th SOS transferred its AC-119Ks and operational responsibilities to the VNAF. Enemy activities slackened, even though they were still there, lurking just out of sight in South Vietnam or just across the border in Cambodia or Laos. They were still sustained by supplies and reinforcements traveling down the various infiltration routes into the South.

The next time the North Vietnamese initiated conventional attacks, the Americans were gone, and with the advent of the Paris Peace Accords of January 27, 1973, no salvation was available for South Vietnam, and communist victory would be assured. After all the death and destruction they had wrought upon the NVA and VC forces, neither the US gunships nor any other Allied weapons could overcome the determination of the enemy's will or the willingness of northern leaders to sacrifice the lives of thousands and millions of their own people to gain ultimate victory and unification of Vietnam. Nor could they overcome the geopolitical sweep of world events that far too often led to political restrictions being placed on them by their own leaders—some perceived and some necessary and some not.

For their price in blood, the crews of the AC-130s and other gunships won the honor of having done their duty as best they could. During Command Hunt VII alone, the AC-130s had claimed more than seven thousand trucks destroyed or damaged. While many intelligence experts have suggested that the numbers may have been inflated or the impact of these kills on the enemy overemphasized, the attacks did slow down the NVA buildup. In addition, their CAS missions during the Easter Offensive helped blunt the invasion and left the enemy assault forces in a shambles. Even if official numbers were too high, those who flew the sorties and those on the ground who saw or even touched the burned-out hulks of trucks and tanks in Laos and South Vietnam bore witness to the fact that those gunships were lethal weapons in the Air Force inventory.

One must wonder, had it not been for the massive resupply of vehicles and supplies from the Soviet Union, Eastern Bloc, and, to a lesser extent, China, what might have been possible? In many ways it seems clear that expecting, at their height, less than seventy-five gunships (only eighteen AC-130s) to destroy enough trucks or supplies or kill enough enemy troops was, in hindsight, a pipe dream. In World War II it had taken thousands of bombers and fighters to attain anything approaching a decisive effect against a conventional enemy. By comparison, this was more like trying to win by poking a finger in their eye—an eye that was nearly impossible to find. The fact that American airmen did as well as they did is amazing, especially given the restrictions placed on them from Washington and the environment in which they fought. Vietnam was undoubtedly the worst theater of war in which the US Air Force has ever had to fight and be expected to win.[40]

Since that time, with the application of modern technology, the maturation and application of better theory and doctrine, US airpower in general and gunships specifically have become the cornerstone of victory in every US contingency since Vietnam. So, while the AC-130's role in Vietnam was over by 1973, unlike their AC-47 and AC-119 cousins, their role in the Air Force was not. Indeed, 1973 and 1974 witnessed not only their return to the United States but also the continued upgrade of the aircraft into yet another generation of AC-130s that would continue to serve America's national defense to this very day.

9 "Goodbye Vietnam!" The AC-130s Transition

The AC-130 sorties during Linebacker I involved some of the most intense missions of the Vietnam interdiction campaign. Beginning in April 1972, crews implemented new tactics to more successfully attack columns of enemy vehicles. The AC-130s approached potential targets using their infrared sensors to identify the heat signature emanating from the motors of the enemy's trucks or their antiaircraft artillery guns. This made it easier to locate these high-value targets. Once they were located, the AC-130s went into their attack orbit while the gunners prepared the Pave Aegis 105mm howitzer and/or their 40mm Bofors gun. If the target was large or significant enough, they also had the option of calling in F-4 fighters armed with LGBs. Initially, they had also planned to vector B-52 raids, but the Buffs were diverted to operations in the North, so it fell to the gunships to fly those sorties. The AC-130s spent 55 percent of their time flying sorties against NVA forces attacking ARVN defensive positions in the South.

The AC-130s performed well, destroying hundreds of AAA sites, dozens of tanks, and thousands of tons of supplies and killing thousands of troops. Allied ground forces often became dependent on gunships and were always heartened by their appearance over the battlefield. Between May and September 1972, the gunship flyboys mostly supported South Vietnamese troops in struggles for control of several key cities, such as Quang Tri City and Kontum. Of particular significance was the work of the new AC-130E aircraft with their howitzers. They proved notably effective against tanks, accounting for 55 percent of all the tracked vehicles damaged or destroyed over the five months they were in action in this campaign.[1]

To be sure, in April and May the battle for Quang Tri City had gone in favor of the Allies, and as summer began, the crucial struggles in Military Region II also began to turn in favor of the US and ARVN forces. The struggle for Kontum City lasted from May 4 to June 8, 1972, when the city itself was completely cleared of enemy forces. During those early dark days of the invasion, the AC-130s proved critical in preventing the complete collapse of the South Vietnamese forces. Flying dozens of sorties each week in support of the ARVN, the AC-130Es (especially Pave Aegis) and AC-130As accounted for 5,688 enemy killed and thirty-eight tanks destroyed. One report described one battlefield as "a landscape of burning wreckage."[2]

An Loc: The Death Struggle

The third prong of the enemy offensive struck in Military Region III and focused on Loc Ninh and the regional capital of Binh Long Province, An Loc. The ultimate goal of the communists was the capture of Saigon, which lay only a few dozen miles south. The main route into Binh Long Province was Highway 13. When the attacks began in early April, some enemy troops feigned a move toward Tay Ninh while the main units struck the minimal defenses at Loc Ninh, planning to capture the town and push on toward An Loc and then Saigon. The campaign began well enough for the enemy, and soon An Loc was cut off from ground resupply. Only American aircraft, particularly with tactical airlift airdrops and AC-130 attacks, prevented the fall of the city itself. At that point the NVA began the siege of An Loc, which lasted until June.[3]

As the invasion enveloped the entire province, around-the-clock American air sorties commenced in an effort to stem the enemy advance. As the communists pressed their attacks, AC-130s began to operate continuously, coordinating with ground commanders whenever possible. Frequently, ground units requested strikes within a few yards of their own troops. Throughout April, May, and June, the struggle ground on, with the AC-130s assaulting NVA troops, tanks, and artillery with lethal and pinpoint accuracy. They also acted as forward observers, guiding other aircraft to targets of opportunity. In turn, they used their illumination devices to mark drop zones for C-123s, C-130s, and C-9s bringing in critical supplies for the ARVN ground forces. This process went so smoothly that the enemy never captured a single parcel dropped to Allied forces squeezed into their defenses in An Loc.[4]

A particularly dangerous addition to the combat was the enemy's introduction of Strela shoulder-fired missiles to the struggle. Early in the campaign the gunships were introduced to these lethal new weapons when one AC-130 was severely damaged but made it back to base. In spite of the missile threat, tanks and artillery were relatively easy targets for the Spectres, since they often were caught in the open or spotted by personnel responding to their report. By late May the NVA offensive was at a complete standstill, and the hunter had now become the hunted. On June 12, 1972, AC-130s spearheaded the injection of sixteen hundred reinforcements flown in by US helicopters. Now able to take the offensive, the ARVN slowly expanded their perimeter, and two weeks later a South Vietnamese relief column broke through to the city's defenders. An Loc had been saved. While many factors such as bomber and fighter-bomber sorties had been important, as well as ARVN determination and heroic forward air control pilots, most observers, including Gen. Creighton Abrams, MACV commander, believed that the AC-130s had played the major role in first saving the ARVN and then defeating the PAVN.[5]

As one observer later noted, during the Easter Offensive the gunships had come full circle. The AC-47s had first come to Vietnam to fly CAS for American units, particularly during search-and-destroy operations or to defend armed hamlets or Special Forces bases. By the time the AC-119s arrived, they were a key element in the interdiction campaign covering America's withdrawal. By 1972 the AC-130s were again flying CAS, this time for the ARVN. The difference was that in 1965, AC-47s faced low-intensity counterinsurgency forces with little or no air defense capability, while by the 1970s the AC-119s and AC-130s were flying in high-intensity conventional combat environments against highly sophisticated AAA and SAM sites often employing radar guidance capabilities. By August 1972 the enemy had pulled back to preserve their forces and supplies, and thus the gunships flew fewer CAS sorties. Leaders also began planning for another dry-season interdiction campaign. However, gunship forces had been reduced by that time, with six AC-130As back in the United States for maintenance and the AC-47s and AC-119s now being flown by the VNAF. This left the 16th SOS with only five AC-130Es and three AC-130As in-theater. The rotation of gunship crews meant that there was also a shortage of trained and experienced ground and crew personnel. As early as June 30, 1972, they were 212 billets short. Technical experts also began efforts to find means to counter the threats from the SA-7 Strelas. On September 25, ASD personnel began installing SUU-25C/A flare launchers on the AC-130 wings to divert the SA-7s. Other survivability solutions included radar detectors, radiation intelligence detectors, infrared transmitters, and even changes in the paint scheme to make the aircraft darker and greener and harder to detect on enemy radar.[6]

As the planning for another Commando Hunt campaign that would never take place went forward, actual operations moved into Cambodia. Throughout the last weeks of 1972 and into early 1973, with increasing communist pressure on pro-American president Lon Nol's government, AC-130s flew cover for boats, ships, and barges bringing food and supplies down the Mekong River to Phnom Penh. That proved to be a great success and contributed to saving the Cambodian government—at least for the time being. The AC-130's last major mission in Southeast Asia was to fly patrol for troops in Saigon's Capital Military District; that continued until the Paris Peace Accords were signed on January 27, 1973.[7]

Later, "the threats to the gunship had increased even with resulting change in gunship technology and tactics." As noted, one of the most effective tactical developments proved to be teaming fighter escorts with the gunships. As the war in Vietnam proper wound down, the Spectre–fighter escort package had become a lethal partnership, since the new modus operandi increased the range of the operating environment of the gunship. The gunships drew AAA fire, allowing the fighter escorts to destroy the guns, which in turn allowed the AC-130s to operate in a safer area containing an abundance of higher-value targets and survive. In 1973 these tactics continued to evolve as the 16th SOS and its AC-130s joined missions in Laos and Cambodia as a result of the Vietnam peace accords, which went into effect on January 28 and curtailed AC-130 operations over South Vietnam. On February 22, 1973, operations also ended over Laos but continued in Cambodia. During the period the overall paint scheme of the AC-130s started to change gradually from a primarily green and black scheme to gunship gray, or "gray ghost." Once repainted, most of the AC-130s maintained the gunship gray scheme into the 1990s.[8]

AC-130 Losses

The success the AC-130s experienced during the war was not without a price. The first production model, T/N 53-3129, *First Lady,* did not go unscathed. On March 25, 1971, it was hit in the nose by a 37mm AAA round that damaged the aircraft just below the crew deck. Fortunately, the plane made it back to base and landed safely without any casualties. As chronicled earlier, *Arbitrator,* T/N 54-1629, was not so lucky. It was hit by a 57mm round over southern Laos on May 24, 1969. Twelve of the crew members bailed out and were rescued, but the pilot and navigator were killed during their attempted emergency landing. Another loss was T/N 54-1625, *Warlord.* On April 22, 1970, it was hit by a 37mm round along the southern end of the Ho Chi Minh Trail and crashed. The only survivor was SSgt. Earl Fields. During the Spring Offensive, four were hit by enemy fire. On March 28, 1972, while attacking truck traffic along the trail, AC-130A T/N 55-0044, *Prometheus,* piloted by Maj. Irving B. Ramsower, became the first Spectre to be hit by a SAM. It crashed, killing the entire crew. Also, as mentioned before, two days later E-model T/N 69-6571, also hunting along the infiltration routes, was hit by a

57mm AAA shell not long after confirming three truck kills. It crashed near An Loc, but not before the crew bailed out safely. They were rescued after one of the largest search and rescue operations in Air Force history.[9]

On June 18, 1972, AC-130A T/N 55-0043 was shot down by an SA-7 twenty-five miles southwest of Hue. The Strela ripped off the number three engine and most of the wing. Three crew members parachuted to safety, but the rest died in the ensuing explosion. The final AC-130 loss came on December 21, 1972, even as Linebacker II B-52 operations over Hanoi and Haiphong were underway. The AC-130A T/N 56-0490, *Thor,* was struck by a 37mm round, and the aircraft exploded, killing all except two crew members who parachuted to safety. All totaled, of the eighteen AC-130s that had been in Indochina at any time, seven had been damaged severely and six destroyed. All of them had all suffered some kind of minor damage. Worst, of the crew members in the aircraft damaged or destroyed, fifty-two lost their lives. While the AC-119s suffered fewer casualties, they also flew in generally less hazardous combat areas. In fact, all those who flew gunships were at great risk of never making it home. In the end, however, most did, and while most of the older-model gunships would not, the AC-130As and Es did come home to a whole new set of circumstances and challenges.[10]

The Gunships Come Home

To quote Air Force historian and former AC-130 pilot Maj. Gen. Clay T. McCutchan, "The twenty years between 1973 and 1993 were very active years for the United States Air Force gunship fleet."[11] In 1973, as the US withdrew, there were no longer many gunships still in the Air Force's active inventory. Over the next three decades they would be in continuous use around the world. Initially, they served primarily as training platforms, but later they also served in critical real-world missions. Beginning in 1973, the future of the side-firing gunship rested mainly with "the AC-130 'Spectre' gunship and two squadrons."[12]

By 1973 the AC-47 Puffs and Spookies, AC-119G Shadows, and AC-119K Stingers had been turned over to South Vietnamese air forces. From then on, with few exceptions, "the AC-130 provided most of the Air Force gunship muscle." For the next two decades, the gunships were flown by the active-duty 16th SOS, which by 1975 was "ably backed up by the Air Force Reserve's 711 SOS." The 16th SOS crew members flew AC-130As and Es in the Southeast Asian war. When the gunships returned to Hurlburt Field, Florida, the A models went to the Air Force Reserve's 711th SOS of the 919th SOG (later, 919th SOW) at Duke Field, not far from Hurlburt Field.[13]

As the withdrawal continued in early 1973, the Air Force initiated Project Pave Spectre II, which by May 18, 1973, had upgraded the ten remaining

AC-130 commencing attack orbit.

AC-130Es (T/Ns 69-6567–6577) to H models with the installation of the more powerful -15 version of the T-56 turboprop engines. The 16th SOS continued to fly the H model throughout the remainder of the twentieth century and to the date of this publication. Among the other most important enhancements were the addition of two AN/ALQ-87 ECM pods mounted one on each wing between the engines. Sustainment experts also added state-of-the-art flare dispensers to counter heat-seeking missiles and chaff dispensers to deceive radar-guided missiles. As the spring passed into the summer, the AC-130Hs returned to Thailand, and the final AC-130 combat mission in Southeast Asia was flown on August 15, 1973, over Cambodia.[14]

Between July 19 and 22, 1974, the 16th SOS moved from Ubon RTAFB and joined the 388th TFW at Korat RTAFB. The 16th's main focus at Korat continued to be intensive peacetime combat training. However, real world events soon put them back in the saddle. In April 1975, in rapid succession both Cambodia and South Vietnam fell to communist forces. On April 12, 1975, 16th SOS gunships participated in operation Eagle Pull, covering the evacuation of US and Allied personnel from Phnom Penh as Khmer Rouge insurgents seized Cambodia. To assure safety on the ground for the evacuees, the AC-130s flew continuously to provide close air support throughout the evacuation. Soon after, North Vietnamese forces overran South Vietnam, and the Spectres circled overhead during Operation Frequent Wind on April 29,

1975, as American and South Vietnamese personnel and family members were evacuated from Saigon. The gunships orbited high over the capital city or Tan Son Nhut airport and observed the evacuation helicopters. The rules of engagement did not allow them to fire on enemy positions despite taking heavy AAA fire. The last Spectre over South Vietnam escorted the last helicopters out of Saigon on April 30, 1975.[15]

Mayaguez

Even as the gunship crews planned a return home, world events drew them back into combat in Southeast Asia as the communist Khmer Rouge in Cambodia began what officially became the last battle of the US involvement in the Vietnam War. The incident began on May 12, 1975, when Cambodian communist naval forces, operating former US Navy Swift Boats, seized the American container ship SS *Mayaguez* in international waters and subjected the crew to "intense" interrogation (torture). Surveillance aircraft soon discovered the ship had been moved to Koh Tang Island, some fifty miles off the southern coast of Cambodia.[16]

News of the hijacking of the ship hit the Ford administration like a bolt out of heaven. Already devastated by the fall of South Vietnam and America's withdrawal from Saigon two weeks earlier, they were confronted by yet another potentially humiliating incident they feared might further damage the nation's international reputation. Having been president for only ten months, and being unelected, President Gerald Ford believed he had to act decisively and with military force. Since the United States had no diplomatic contact with the new Khmer Rouge regime in what they now called Kampuchea, Ford had few other options. Calling the seizure piracy, Ford ordered the American armed forces to retake the ship and its forty-man crew. The first step came when the aircraft carrier USS *Coral Sea* was redirected to the waters near Cambodia. In addition, several hundred Marines were repositioned from Okinawa and the Philippines to U-Tapao Royal Thai Navy Airfield, Thailand, on May 14, 1975, without the express permission of the Thai government. The previous day, sixteen Air Force CH-53 Sea Stallion and HH-53 Super Jolly Green Giant helicopters of the 40th Air Rescue and Recovery Squadron and the 21st SOS in Thailand had been designated for the rescue operation. In turn, officials directed the Seventh Air Force to keep an eye on the *Mayaguez* to prevent the Khmer Rouge from moving the crew to the port of Kampong Som.[17]

Early on May 14, F-111A fighter-bombers from the 347th Tactical Fighter Wing, based at Korat RTAFB, located the *Mayaguez,* being moved, with four enemy gunboats escorting it. AC-130s were ordered to shadow these four enemy gunboats and fire across their bows to prevent them from reaching the coast. The Spectres' 40mm cannon and 105mm howitzer forced three of the gunboats to turn back. Flights of F-111A, F-4D, and A-7D fighter-bombers attacked in front of the remaining gunboat with two-thousand-pound bombs, 2.75-inch rockets, and riot control gas, but the boat refused to stop, and an A-7D sank it. Soon after, a Thai wooden fishing boat departed Koh Tang Island. US aircrews believed the boat was carrying the crew of the *Mayaguez,* so they did not fire directly on the vessel. During the four hours it took the boat to reach Kampong Som in Cambodia, A-7s and F-4Ds strafed with rockets in front of it in an attempt to make it stop and return to Koh Tang. It turned out that the crew was on the small craft, but since that fact could not be confirmed at the time, for some still unexplained reason military planners proceeded as though the crew were still on the island.[18]

The rescue mission was a very complex plan—probably too complex. A unit of fifty-seven US Marines was sent in three helicopters to the destroyer escort USS *Harold E. Holt* to board the *Mayaguez.* Another force of six hundred Marines, in eight helicopters, was ordered to seize and hold Koh Tang. Two other CH-53s were to act as search-and-rescue helicopters, supported by HC-130 command-and-control aircraft. The flight from U-Tapao to Koh Tang was a four-hour round trip. Planners assigned the guided missile destroyer USS *Henry B. Wilson* to support the Koh Tang operation, and the frigate USS *Schofield* to block the water passages between American troops and the Cambodian mainland to prevent any Khmer reaction forces from reinforcing the enemy troops already on the island. At the same time, aircraft from the USS *Coral Sea* were to attack targets on the Cambodian mainland to prevent interference with the rescue.[19]

At 6:00 a.m. on May 15, phase I of the operation began with the transfer of the Marines to the *Holt.* At 7:20 a.m., the destroyer escort came alongside as an A-7 aircraft poured down tear gas canisters on the *Mayaguez.* Wearing gas masks, the Marines captured the ship after an hour-long fight, only to discover that it was empty. As this was going on, five CH-53 and three HH-53 helicopters attacked Koh Tang Island, encountering unexpectedly intense automatic weapons and rocket-propelled grenade (RPG) fire from the enemy forces. One CH-53 crash-landed, but its twenty Marines and crew of five survived. They quickly established a defensive perimeter but remained isolated for the remainder of the operation.[20]

Soon after the first CH-53 went down, a second was shot down by two RPGs. It crashed just off-shore, where the pilot, five Marines, and two Navy corpsmen were killed. Another Marine drowned swimming from the wreckage, and three Marines were killed by gunfire trying to reach the beach. A tenth Marine died of his wounds while clinging to the burning wreckage. The surviving ten Marines and three Air Force crew members had to swim for four hours before being rescued by the *Wilson.* On the west beach, two other CH-53s arrived about 6:30 a.m., and things went well at first, but while off-loading the Marines they came under heavy fire, and one helicopter lost an engine. After some frantic repair efforts, the chopper was able to take off, covered by suppressing fire from the second CH-53. Smoke billowing from it as it flew out to sea, the first CH-53 was able to ditch a mile off-shore, where all but one crew member were rescued. Soon the enemy damaged the second CH-53 so severely that it turned back with its Marines, including the company commander, and crash-landed on the Thai coast, where all on board were saved. The four helicopters of the two remaining sections of the first wave eventually landed all of their Marines between 6:30 and 9:30 a.m. They were supported by withering fire from an AC-130H gunship of the 16th SOS. The Spectre was able literally to cut a path through the enemy positions and escort the helicopters to their landing area to unload their Marines. All totaled, eighty-one Marines landed on the west beach.[21]

Indeed, air support began to improve as AC-130 Spectre 61, arrived overhead. The pilot identified himself to the pinned-down marines and fired several spotting rounds—one of which hit an enemy bunker. "How was that?" an AC-130 spotter asked. "Right on, but it didn't do much," replied the Marine sergeant. Then the Spectre fired a 105mm round, which demolished the bunker. "Jesus Christ!" the Marine exclaimed. Then he added: "What was that? Have I got targets for you!" The firepower from Spectre 61 and its sister ships enabled two groups of Marines to join forces and helped them live through the ordeal.[22]

As the 130 Marines on the west and east beaches pressed their assaults, they met heavy resistance from a well-entrenched foe. Only fire support from numerous mortars as well as gunship and fighter close air support allowed them to make any progress. Of the eight helicopters assaulting Koh Tang, three had been destroyed and four others had received such bad damage that they could not continue operations. One of the three choppers employed on the *Holt* portion of the operation had also been severely damaged attempting to pick up the platoon isolated on the east beach. This left only three helicopters of the original eleven available to bring in reinforcements. To compensate for these losses, the CH-53s scheduled as the search-and-rescue component of the operation were reassigned to carry troops. These five Jolly Greens airlifted 127 Marines of the second wave from U-Tapao between 9:00 and 10:00 a.m.[23]

The cruel irony was that the crew of the *Mayaguez* had already been removed from Koh Tang Island and released before the Marines began their operation. The crew members were all alive and in good health and were found floating at sea on a fishing boat and subsequently transferred to the *Holt.* With word of the ship's rescue and the crew's release, the JCS decided that further actions were not necessary, and they recalled the second wave. However, Lt. Col. Kenneth Austin, ground commander at Koh Tang, soon made it clear to senior leaders that additional troops were necessary to prevent his forces from being overrun as they departed the theater of operations. The second wave eventually landed 100 Marines and evacuated nine wounded, leaving a total of 202 Marines and five airmen on Koh Tang. Supported by air strikes, some by AC-130s, and mortar fire, the evacuation of these Marines began around noon and continued most of the afternoon under heavy fire.[24]

The process proved agonizingly long. Each time a helicopter picked up a group of Marines, it required AC-130 close air support to escort the thirty to fifty Marines back to the *Coral Sea.* As the troops withdrew, they had to contract their perimeter. They carefully supervised the redeployment of their remnant each time to ensure no one was missing, but during the last airlift three Marines manning a machine gun were accidently left behind on the beach—a fact only discovered afterwards. The last extraction took place at 8:10 p.m. and evolved in pitch-black darkness under heavy mortar fire. Altogether, fourteen Marines were killed or missing, two Navy corpsmen were killed, and two airmen were killed. Later, officials discovered that twenty-three airmen had died during May 13 preoperational sorties. This raised the death toll to forty-one. The Marines had thirty-five wounded, and the Air Force, six. Reconnaissance confirmed that the Khmer Rouge lost sixty to sixty-five killed, while estimates determined they had half that many wounded.[25]

All those killed and wounded, except for the Marine who drowned, were recovered and brought home. As for the three missing Marines, on July 21, 1976, they were reclassified killed in action due to a lack of reliable information to corroborate their survival. Later rumors suggested that they had survived the battle but were executed by the Khmer Rouge, but at the time no hard evidence existed to confirm that fact. In the late 1990s a Joint Task Force–Full Accounting team found bone fragments on the beach that could have belonged to the three Marines, but DNA tests proved inconclusive. Officially, the Marine Corps does not believe that the Marines were alive when the last helicopter departed.[26]

Subsequent controversy also arose since the Thai government had not given the United States approval to use the airfield at U-Tapao for the rescue. Thai officials called it a violation of Thailand's sovereignty. To calm things down, returning Marines were quickly spirited off to the Philippines. Many Thai groups called for the withdrawal of all US forces. In addition, the American military was roundly criticized for its handling of the incident. The apparent failure of intelligence to determine where the *Mayaguez* crew was and that there was a large enemy force on Koh Tang was a source of ridicule. At first, questions over the timing also swirled around Washington until it became clear that combat operations had already been underway before the crew was released. Later, the Marines who participated in the operation were critical of the ad hoc nature of the joint operation and the perceived pressure from the Ford White House for hasty action in order to save face for the loss of Vietnam. While so much of this mission was either poorly planned or poorly executed, the one clear success was the performance of the AC-130s. On constant alert at their bases in Thailand, the 16th SOS crew members acted swiftly and professionally to deal with each emerging crisis during the rescue mission. This convinced many Air Force officials that their decision to keep the AC-130s in their active inventory as America withdrew from Southeast Asia and for the foreseeable future was a good one.[27]

It is worth noting that during this operation 16th SOS crews worked together to meet the urgent situation in which requirements constantly changed. For example, on May 14 and 15, with the intensity of the battle building to a climax, the Spectres began to fly sorties designed to deny Khmer gunboats access to Koh Tang Island and also acted as forward air control for the Air Force and Navy fighter sorties. Once given the okay to fire on the Khmer gunboats, they sank or ran aground several, perhaps as many as a dozen. When the Marines landed on Koh Tang on May 15, the AC-130s provided direct fire with their 20mm, 40mm, and 105mm fire, sometimes firing within fifty feet of the Marine positions. Throughout the operation, the AC-130s provided accurate and continuous suppressive fire and used their sensors to confirm the location of friendly units. In truth, the gunships proved so effective that many in the special operations world wondered, in retrospect, why the gunships had not been used more. To be sure, the *Mayaguez* recovery was an ideal scenario for the AC-130, but its full capabilities were not completely understood by command and control officials, who were mostly Navy personnel who had never worked with a side-firing gunship. While the *Spectres* made a vital contribution to the mission, they could have done more if the full potential of their suppression, precise firepower, and documentation capabilities had been more fully understood and used.[28]

Frustration inside the White House was acute as well. Not long afterward, a chagrinned Henry Kissinger admitted privately, "We entered Indochina to save a country and ended by rescuing a ship."[29]

Of course, Ford is an easy target for criticism, but as he pointed out years later, given the timing of the event, he believed he had no practical choice but to take action, and as quickly as possible. If he had not, he might well have wound up in the same conundrum as Jimmy Carter did in Iran only a few years later. Considering the bruising US pride had suffered with the fall of Vietnam, one sharp punch in the nose seemed to satisfy American governmental leaders and public opinion. Indeed, most polls at the time were very supportive.

The military options also had appeal to the White House, given the lack of any sort of diplomatic relationship with the radical anti-American Cambodian communist regime. Once Ford committed to military action (and the entire cabinet agreed), the chance of some Americans dying was a foregone conclusion, since no rational analyst can deny that military action is not without risk. Many have argued that it was regrettably the only course open. However, having said that, many others still believe that the Ford administration is at least partly culpable for the loss of forty-one American lives and what can at best be described as a flawed rescue operation. Then, and now, conservative analysts have blamed Democratic president Lyndon B. Johnson for constantly interfering with military planning and execution, keeping the US military from winning the larger war. Yet it was President Ford who also micromanaged the *Mayaguez* operation and hesitated on several occasions to carry out aspects of the original plan. Worse, it was a plan with too many moving parts, all of which had to work perfectly to avoid high numbers of casualties. Ultimately, few aspects worked well together, but most were attempted with the wrong weapon systems. In retrospect, with the lack of good intelligence and poor cooperation among the military services, perhaps it is amazing that things did not go much worse. Of course, in hindsight we now know that backdoor diplomacy might very well have solved the problem without bloodshed.[30]

In May 1975 the US military was not prepared to carry out such a rescue, and military leaders hated the operation mostly because of their lack of confidence in the directives coming from the White House. To quote Vice Adm. George P. Steele, the Seventh Fleet commander: "The sad part of the *Mayaguez* is that we had sufficient force coming up with the Seventh Fleet, after it had been turned around from the evacuation of Vietnam stand down, to seize Southern Cambodia. I begged for another day or two, rather than commit forces piecemeal as we did. The idea that we could use US Air Force air police and Air Force helicopters as an assault force appears to me as ridiculous today as it did then."[31]

Then again, leaders make mistakes, and most often the US military tries to learn from their mistakes. Unfortunately, it took several more rescue disasters before definitive steps were taken to create a structure to extricate captured citizens. Carter's failure in Iran; Ronald Reagan's adventure in Grenada, where troops had to purchase maps from service stations; and George

Bush's costly mission in Panama finally led to the creation in the early 1990s of the US Special Operations Command (USSOCOM), which was designed to coordinate military action. Ultimately, *Mayaguez* remains a footnote in the history of the Vietnam War. The desire of the nation to distance itself from the Vietnam debacle had much to do with that. The final paradox is that the *Mayaguez* affair was technically a success, as it did recover the container ship and its crew. It defined the Ford presidency, and until his death in 2006, Ford pointed to the mission as saving America's pride and reputation. But it came at a terrible price, and in the end it was, as many historians have suggested, the last tragedy in a decade-long tragedy in mainland Southeast Asia.

As for the AC-130s, it was time to go home. However, combat was not far away.

Good Night, Folks, It's Time to Leave

For those who paid attention, the AC-130s' performance in Southeast Asia had been remarkable. Aside from the thousands of vehicles they destroyed, they had proved to be the most accurate close air support and interdiction weapon in the Air Force arsenal. While the 16th SOS had lost fifty-two crew members, this loss rate for combat hour flown was less than that of all other major weapon systems employed during the war. As General McCutchan declared years later, "The gunship could work and survive despite undocumented beliefs that it was not survivable. When teamed with fighter escort it was even more effective."[32]

As the Vietnam War and America's role in it petered out, the gunships began to come home. In late May 1975, Air Force leaders deemphasized their role and ordered that the 16th SOS personnel begin planning the redeployment of their AC-130H gunships to Hurlburt Field, Florida. They also ordered the transfer of the AC-130A gunships to the Air Reserve Station at nearby Duke Field (Eglin Auxiliary No. 3), Florida. In addition, they inactivated the 415th SOTS on June 30, 1975, temporarily placing its personnel and two AC-130Hs under the 8th SOS. They reassigned the three AC-130As of the 415th SOTS to the 711th SOS of the 919th Special Operations Group, converting those units from tactical airlift to special operations.[33]

By December 1975 the 16th SOS had redeployed to the United States, and all the gunships had been programmed to receive only Air Force Reserve funding, since there were no future plans for active-duty funding. Soon after, the 16th SOS formally bedded down at Hurlburt Field and had all of their gunship assets returned from the 8th SOS. The squadron of ten AC-130Hs was officially placed under the 1st SOW. Concurrently, 16th SOS AC-130As were transferred to the Reserve's 711th SOS. When all twelve A models eventually arrived at Duke Field, they were in poor condition, many having "serious fuel leaks, extensive corrosion . . . and missing equipment." Two of the AC-130As had such severe corrosion that officials sent them to the Air Force boneyard at Davis-Monthan AFB, Arizona. This left the 711th SOS with ten gunships. Throughout the next twenty years, 711th SOS operated one or two standard C-130 "slick" (no guns) transports for training, administrative, and in-house airlift support. In turn, the 16th SOS used 1st SOW slicks for the same purposes.[34]

As a part of their new routine, the two gunship squadrons began a rigorous training program. As part of the training regimen the 16th SOS sent active-duty advisors to help cross-train the 711th SOS reservists. The prevailing conventional wisdom at the time was that reserve personnel could not perform the gunship mission as well as the active-duty crews. Determined to show everyone they were just as good as their counterparts in the 16th SOS, the 919th SOG and 711th SOS personnel labored long and hard to establish a professional program second to none. The maintenance crews at Duke Field put in protracted and tedious hours to bring the A models up to standards equal to those of the H models. Reservists not only worked their civilian jobs all day but also then traveled many miles to fly the gunships, often most of the same night. In spite of high levels of fatigue and stress, by June 1976 they had four combat-ready aircraft and crews. Within two years the reservists at Duke Field had passed the first peacetime, stateside operational readiness inspection (ORI) of any gunship unit. To culminate this achievement, members of the 16th SOS and 711th SOS staged a "shootout" competition at the Eglin AFB, Florida, practice gun ranges. While the active-duty AC-130Hs won the overall competition, the reserve AC-130As won the individual "top gun" crew award.[35]

To quote General McCutchan, "From what I see the Air Force turned away from SOF [special operations forces], turned away from Gunships and these sort of missions and focused on big blue Strategic Bombardments, Strategic Airlift, and Tactical fighters." Indeed, McCutchan believes that, as in 1973, "in 1975, the plan was to put the A models in reserve (711 SOS) at Duke Field and the E/H models in the active force (16 SOS) at Hurlburt Field." Funding for the E/H models on active duty was in doubt beyond 1980, and senior planners originally considered sending the A models to the boneyard at Davis-Monthan. As a result, the reserve forces were anticipated to pick up the E/H models, thus leaving no gunships on active duty.[36]

For a time the gunships led a quiet, routine existence, but as Maj. Gen. Michael N. Wilson, former AC-130 pilot, points out, "When I came in during 1976 it was just routine, but in 1979 the Iran hostage crisis resurrected the

AC-130 on a training mission.

need for Gunships and changed everything. The Air Force decided to keep the H models around and the A models in the Reserves."[37]

During the last half of the 1970s, the 16th SOS and 711th SOS intensified their training for new crew members in order to be ready for any future contingency. Soon those missions manifested themselves. Most of them involved 16th SOS assets to protect American interests and citizens abroad by evacuating US personnel and their families or protecting US embassies and other property. Often they stood on alert at Hurlburt Field, but sometimes they staged forward and stood ready overseas. The operations tempo was always high. For example, they flew around the clock during the April 1976 Lebanon crisis, the August 1976 Korean crisis, and the July 1979 Nicaraguan emergency. The gunships were also used for security reconnaissance, such as the deployment of the 16th SOS to Kwang Ju, Korea, in July 1978 to support classified peacetime missions. The DOD and National Aeronautical and Space Administration used both the 16th SOS and 711th SOS for missile launch security and downrange safety monitoring during 1970s and 1980s space missions. Most of those operations took place at Vandenberg AFB, California, and Kennedy Space Center in Florida. The 16th SOS also spent a great deal of time in El Salvador, Panama, and other Latin American nations during 1979, searching for terror groups, guerillas, and drug runners and protecting the Panama Canal.[38]

During those days a handful of surviving AC-47/DC-3s, which had been used by former drug runners and seized by the US government, were rebuilt as essentially new AC-47s and employed in counterinsurgency activities in El Salvador and Columbia. One AC-47, nicknamed "Fantasma," in Columbia dealt not only with a guerrilla threat but also was used against drug traffickers. To operate more effectively, culturally sensitive 16th SOS instructors established a successful working relationship with their Salvadoran and Colombian counterparts. Keeping aircrews current on the AC-47 proved difficult, since the Air Force no longer flew AC-47s, and even former AC-47 crew members had been flying AC-130s for many years. Sadly, this time spent in Latin America flying AC-47s, while useful, proved harmful to the careers of many of the crews, since most AC-47 pilots were passed over and retired despite excellent performance records.[39]

Concurrently, members of the 711th SOS began teaching members of the Mexican, Honduran, Colombian, and Peruvian Air Forces how to operate the basic slick C-130A. They quickly established a special relationship with their military counterparts in Central and South America. Many of the field-grade officers who checked out in the C-130A at Duke Field later became general officers in their respective air forces, and they always remembered their comrades in the 711th SOS. This proved to be very important during the 1980s.[40]

Iran Hostage Crisis

A world away in Iran, events unfolded that would once again involve the AC-130s in a rescue mission that proved to be one of the worst failures in US history. After more than twenty-five years of ruling a secular pro-Western nation, the Iranian Shah was overthrown by a fanatical fundamentalist Islamic regime that hated the United States. The new ruler, Ayatollah Khomeini, denounced the US government as the Great Satan and the Enemy of Islam. When the Shah was diagnosed with lymphoma, he requested treatment in the United States. The request was granted, and it so enraged the Iranian radicals that on November 4, 1979, a seething mob of five hundred "students," who called themselves Imam's Disciples, besieged the American embassy in Tehran.[41]

Although six staff members managed to escape with the help of the Canadian embassy, another sixty-six US citizens and diplomats, caught totally off-guard, and completely outnumbered, surrendered and were held hostage. Women and African Americans were soon released, but fifty-one hostages remained imprisoned for 444 days. One very ill hostage was released midway through the ordeal. President Jimmy Carter quickly imposed economic sanctions and used diplomatic pressure to hasten a negotiated settlement. This even included the cancellation of oil imports from Iran, expulsion of Iranians from the United States, and the freezing of eight billion dollars in Iranian assets in America. At first, the fundamentalist government claimed it had had nothing to do with the incident and was powerless.[42]

In February 1980 the new Iranian leaders issued a list of demands for the release of the hostages. Those demands included the return of the Shah for trial and an apology for American interference in Iranian affairs, including the infamous CIA-sponsored coup against the democratic, nonaligned government of Prime Minister Mohammad Mossadegh in 1953. They also demanded a promise of the withdrawal of all American personnel forever. The president decided he could not accept these demands.[43]

In late April, Carter decided to undertake a secret rescue mission, designated Operation Eagle Claw. It was excessively intricate, hastily planned, and, in retrospect, probably doomed to failure before it began. Tehran was surrounded by seven hundred miles of desert and was home to four million people tightly packed into a combination of slum hovels and modern skyscrapers. The embassy was huge and well guarded. Plans called for a two-night process requiring a minimum of six helicopters and about the same number of C-130 cargo transport aircraft. At the last minute, two additional helicopters, neither of which had received proper maintenance, were added to the plan. As planning went forward, the Air Force and Lockheed-Georgia experimented with rocket-assisted takeoff (RATO or RTO) pods attached to the fuselage of the C-130s so they could land in the Tehran soccer stadium and then relaunch with the hostages on board. Designated Credible Sport, the program literally blew up with one of the prototypes.[44]

Even with that ominous beginning the US went ahead with the effort. Once inside Iranian borders, the cumbersome air force advanced under the cover of darkness to a predetermined staging area fifty miles outside the Iranian capital city in the Great Salt Desert. One chopper had to abort with engine problems, and two others broke down in the face of a sandstorm that clogged their engines with dust. Worse, the Iranians soon discovered the attack and sent troops against the Americans. Fearing a total disaster, President Carter ordered a recall of the US forces. As the withdrawal began, the blinding dust storm caused another helicopter to crash into a C-130, killing eight military personnel. The aftermath proved to be a public relations nightmare. The Iranians eventually found the wreckage and paraded pieces of the aircraft in the streets of Tehran to be witnessed on worldwide television. Back in the United States the debacle led to a torrent of investigations and congressional hearings. And, if this was not enough, Secretary of State Cyrus Vance, who had opposed the plan in the first place, resigned in protest.[45]

In July 1980 the death of the Shah in Egypt and the invasion of Iran by Iraq made the Iranians more receptive to resolving the hostage crisis. In America, failure to end the crisis contributed mightily to Ronald Reagan's victory over Carter in the November presidential election. After the election, with the assistance of Algerian diplomats, the two sides began more fruitful negotiations, and on January 20, 1981, the day of Reagan's inauguration, the United States released most of the eight billion dollars in frozen Iranian assets and the hostages were freed. The agreement also gave Iran immunity from lawsuits arising from the incident.[46]

Even though the AC-130s never really got into the fight, it would be wrong to ignore their role, since the 16th SOS was supposed to be involved in the embassy rescue effort. They prepared for the rescue raid, deployed, and were poised to attack in support of it. Indeed, as early as December 1979, in immediate response to the original crisis, the 16th SOS had sent four AC-130Hs nonstop from Hurlburt Field to Anderson AFB, Guam. The nearly thirty-hour flight became the longest for a C-130 airframe aircraft up to that time. After five months waiting to be called into action, they returned in March of 1980 only to redeploy a month later to Egypt to support Eagle Claw. While plans had called for the gunships to play a major role in covering the outward-bound air assets carrying the hostages, the Spectres never engaged because President Carter abruptly called off the final phases of the operation. In many ways the lack of resolve shown by the White House is reflected in its unwillingness to complete the mission or to commit the most effective weapon they had to at least attempt to rescue American citizens.[47]

Grenada Operations

With President Ronald Reagan in the White House, US foreign policy became more aggressive and decisive. This was born out in late 1983 when US forces invaded the tiny Caribbean island of Grenada to rescue US students and expel Cuban military forces. Operation Urgent Fury began in October 1983, when the 16th SOS deployed three AC-130s to forward locations in preparation for the invasion of Grenada. In spite of bad weather and systems failures, the 16th SOS crews suppressed ground fire and provided the only significant Air Force close air support throughout the operation. One crew, led by Maj. Clement W. Twiford, was awarded the 1984 William H. Tunner Award by the Air Force Association as the most outstanding aircrew in the Military Airlift Command for that year. Maj. Twiford's crew made their greatest contributions to the operation at Point Salines Airfield on October 25, 1983.[48]

As discussions for the Grenada operation began, planners quickly realized that the AC-130s needed to be a part of the invasion force. With the Reagan administration focused on the Middle East, in many ways Grenada came out of left field for the American public. The decision to invade the little island was quickly made, and some experts would argue it was planned in overhaste, much like the disaster in Iran. Even those who developed the operations plan worried whether intelligence data was thorough or accurate. Technically, Operation Urgent Fury began on October 25, 1983, but the problems and disagreements that led to the conflict had their sources in the 1970s when Grenada gained its independence from Great Britain.[49]

In 1974, Sir Eric Gairy had led Grenada to independence from Britain and became the new nation's first prime minister, but his tenure began in a highly charged political environment. After two years, Gairy, leader of the Grenada United Labour Party, apparently won the 1976 general election, but the opposition refused to accept the results. Street violence soon erupted between government supporters and gangs organized by the New Jewel Movement (NJM). As the decade wound down, NJM members turned to Cuba and other leftist outside sources for military training in preparation for an uprising designed to overthrow the government. On March 13, 1979, while Gairy was out of the country, the NJM, led by Maurice Bishop, initiated an armed revolt that eventually toppled the elected government. Bishop suspended the constitution and ruled the country by decree until 1983. All opposition parties were banned, and no elections were held. To the consternation of the United States, Bishop aligned himself with Cuba and other communist governments.[50]

With the election of Ronald Reagan, the United States took a hard line against any and all communist regimes in the Western Hemisphere. Events reached a boiling point in 1983 even as Bishop's government began building an international airport with the help of Canada, Mexico, and other nations. That March, Reagan declared that the runway was evidence of "Soviet-Cuban militarization" of Grenada and was a potential threat to the United States. Asserting that the nine-thousand-foot runway and its oil and fuel storage tanks were unnecessary for commercial flights, the president argued that could only mean that the airport was to become a Cuban-Soviet airbase in America's backyard in defiance of the Monroe Doctrine. While this might have been possible, the fact is that the airport had been first proposed by the British government in 1954, when Grenada was still a docile colony. It was to be designed by a Canadian company, underwritten by the British government, and built by a London firm.[51]

As the war of words escalated, the US State Department accused the Grenada government of aiding in a Cuban-Soviet military buildup aimed at the security of the entire hemisphere. Bishop claimed that the airport was being built to accommodate commercial aircraft, since the existing airport was not large enough for big jets to land, and the large mountains surrounding the old facility restricted the number of planes and, therefore, tourists that could visit Grenada. On October 13, 1983, a party faction led by Deputy Prime Minister Bernard Coard staged a successful coup and placed Bishop under house arrest. Popular protests against the coup led to Bishop's release and restoration to power. However, the rebels did not stop there. They soon struck again, and this time Bishop was arrested and murdered along with several members of the government loyal to the former dictator. The army, headed by Hudson Austin, formed a military council to rule the country. They quickly placed the governor-general of Grenada, Paul Scoon, under house arrest and instituted martial law, declaring that anyone seen on the streets would be subject to summary execution.[52]

Alarmed by the chaos in Grenada, the members of the Organization of Eastern Caribbean States (OECS) appealed to the United States, Barbados, and Jamaica to restore order on the tiny Caribbean island. American officials cited the murder of Bishop and general political instability in the country near its own borders as well as the presence of US medical students at Saint George's University on Grenada as reasons for military action. Most historians believe that the United States would have intervened anyway, but now they had the official approval of Grenada's neighbors.[53]

On October 22, 1983, Cuban dictator Fidel Castro cabled Cuban operatives in Grenada, urging them to take no action in case the United States invaded unless they were directly attacked. He told his representatives that if American forces "land on the runway . . . fully refrain from interfering." He told the Grenada military leaders that sending reinforcements was impossible and "unthinkable." The Cuban government repeated this message the next two days, emphasizing that it would be politically impossible and morally wrong to help a government that had assassinated Bishop. In short, Castro made it clear Cubans would only defend Cubans. While the White House publicly declared that it did not trust Cuban or Grenadan promises, Castro's declarations made it clear that he would not interfere with an American military action. With that fact in place, Reagan could declare that the United States would do whatever necessary to protect American lives. In turn, the State Department warned that since the political situation in Grenada was so fluid, and Grenadan government officials could not guarantee the safety of the US medical students, the Americans were prepared to act.[54]

The Allies launched the operation just after midnight on October 25, 1983, from Grantley Adams International Airport on Barbados. The AC-130s arrived around 3:30 a.m., escorting helicopters and C-130 cargo transports carrying about seven thousand US Marines and Army Rangers. The invasion was the first major operation conducted by the United States since the Vietnam War, and a great deal of American military prestige was on the line. In addition to US forces there were three hundred troops from the OECS. They were to be confronted by fifteen hundred Grenadans and roughly seven hundred Cuban "construction workers," who were "highly trained in combat." Besides those opposing forces there were sixty Soviet, North Korean, East German, Bulgarian, and Libyan advisers present in Grenada. Even before the gunships arrived, Navy Sea, Air, and Land (SEAL) teams had landed to undertake reconnaissance of the beaches and landing areas and be sure there were no mines or booby traps where the Americans were to land.[55]

It is worth remembering that it was Maj. Clement Twiford's AC-130H that led the first US forces into Grenada about 3:30 a.m. on October 25. The aircraft had deployed in a nine-hour, thirty-minute flight from Hurlburt to Barbados that had proved both challenging and dangerous, requiring two difficult night aerial refuelings. Once Twiford's aircraft was over Grenada, the airmen, who had slept very little since departing Florida, had to initiate the combat phase of Urgent Fury. When he came in to Point Salines, Twiford noticed obstacles blocking the runway. Even as they received heavy machine gun fire and light AAA fire, he radioed the situation to the mission commander. He spent the next several minutes suppressing the enemy batteries to protect the MC-130Es and C-130s bringing in the Army Rangers. Despite being exposed by the early morning sunlight, the AC-130 took out four Zu-23–2 antiaircraft guns.[56] As General McCutchan wrote, "While they were dropping those Rangers there was a Gunship right there shooting up the Cubans, you know, protecting them."[57]

Employing their LLLTV, night vision gear, and infrared radar systems, all the AC-130s were deployed to support the C-130s landing on the main airfield at Point Salines. As this aspect of the operation unfolded, they soon discovered that the airfield was heavily defended with AAA weapons for aircraft above one thousand feet. In retrospect, one wonders why such a contingency was not considered or why US intelligence did not discover this rather significant fact. Following a rather hurried discussion between Maj. Gen. William J. Mall Jr. of the Twenty-third Air Force (the mission commander) and the Rangers' commander, it was agreed they would conduct a parachute drop from five hundred feet commencing at 5:00 a.m. An MC-130E Combat Talon and EC-130E command and control aircraft led them into the combat drop area. From the outset, the Americans came under heavy fire. Mall ordered the AC-130s to suppress the enemy fire. Specifically, he directed one AC-130H, commanded by Maj. Michael J. Couvillon, to "get the guns!"[58]

With this order ringing in Couvillon's and Twiford's ears, both attacked additional enemy antiaircraft sites. As other gunships arrived, the enemy fire began to wane, but the fight was far from over, and the gunships engaged as many targets as they could find, neutralizing them all in short order. Finally, Twiford's crew ran out of ammunition, and their fuel was extremely low, so they returned to Roosevelt Roads, Puerto Rico, while the other gunships returned to Barbados to refuel and rearm. Ultimately, they spent 30 hours in action, including 16.7 hours in the air.[59]

The Marine helicopters began arriving at about 5:20 a.m. in the midst of a torrential rainstorm at Pearl's Field, which was a 5,200-foot airstrip on the east side of the island. They soon captured twenty-five Cubans who were crew members of a Soviet-built An-26 used to transport the Grenadan junta leaders. Within an hour they had taken the town of Grenville and the rest of eastern Grenada. In the meantime, the Rangers, from Fort Stewart, deployed in three waves from Hunter Army Air Field, near Savannah, Georgia, flying on C-130s. A second group, which had been stationed with the 82nd Airborne at Fort Bragg and had departed out of Pope AFB, North Carolina, arrived about fifteen minutes after that. Their flight was led by the Combat Talon from the 1st SOW, supported in the first wave by three more MC-130Es with terrain-following radar and an AC-130H loaded with radar and sensor arrays. Four C-130s carried the Rangers. Wave number two had two MC-130s and one AC-130H and three C-130s. The third wave consisted of four C-130s from the 317th TAW. The flight time from the United States was eight hours. Original plans called for C-5A Galaxy cargo aircraft of the 436th Military Airlift Wing to fly from Barbados and land on the newly built airport runway to deliver nine Army helicopters and the airlift commander and his staff. This aspect of the plan was eventually canceled, since it was not necessary.[60]

By 5:30 p.m. the 20mm and 40mm Bofors guns of the AC-130Hs had completely silenced the enemy fire at Point Salines. As a result, the parachute drop recommenced around 6:00 a.m. and lasted until 6:20 a.m. The landing operation ended around 8:00 a.m. when the threat level dropped enough to land the C-130s. The Americans captured two hundred Cubans and quickly rescued the 138 students at the Medical School Campus designated "True Blue." Once on the ground, the Americans soon discovered their intelligence had failed to note that there was a second campus at Grand Anse, south of the Grenadan capital of Saint George. They also learned that an additional two hundred US citizens were held on the L'ance aux Epines Peninsula. Since the enemy had not cut the telephone wires, the American troops contacted the students at Grand Anse using a local telephone book to look up the number. To locate the Americans and find a route to them, the Rangers employed local road maps from filling stations, since their own maps proved inaccurate or had not arrived with them. Late on October 25, the students at the second campus were rescued, and three days later the Americans at L'ance aux Epines were also retrieved. Since the Rangers had only small arms, they received constant close air support from six AC-130Hs that rotated shifts so that at least three of the gunships supported the Rangers at all times. Two other gunships remained on alert near the original landing areas, while one other was rotated with these two, going back to Barbados periodically to receive repairs and allow the crew to rest. As soon as it had picked up more fuel and ordnance it returned.[61]

The good news for the gunship crews was that there was no shortage of targets, and after the initial flurry of AAA fire, little, if any, antiaircraft threat. Among the enemy's forces were three armored personnel carriers operating near the landing area. The AC-130Hs attacked from low level, spraying them with a hail of 20mm and 40mm rounds that halted their movement. The gunships then fired four 105mm rounds into the vehicles, leaving the three smoldering hulks. By 2:00 p.m. the runway at Point Salines had been secured enough to allow large planes to land with heavy equipment and supplies. The flightline and the surrounding area soon became crowded with incoming and outgoing personnel and equipment. In addition, resistance proved to be much more intense than expected.[62]

The first day, the US formed secure landing zones across the Island at Point Salines, Grenville, and the medical school campuses. Marines also landed at Grand Mal Bay just north of Saint George's late in the day. The Navy SEALs moved to rescue the governor general, who had been detained in Saint George's. It soon became clear that Castro's public pronouncement that he would not send reinforcements was true, so as Allied forces arrived, operations began to move more rapidly. On the morning of October 26, C-141B Starlifters arrived to begin airlifting the students from True Blue out of Grenada to Charleston, South Carolina. In all, the 315th MAW, from Seymour Johnson AFB, North Carolina, airlifted 688 students, priests, nuns, missionaries, and other foreign nationals to safety in the United States. The C-141s also brought in units of the 82nd Airborne Division to help take Grand Anse and Saint George's. By the end of October 26, 1983, enemy forces were trapped between an ever tightening vice of the Marines in the north, the Army in the south, and the gunships overhead.[63]

On October 27, Army units were flown by Marine helicopters to Grand Anse, where they secured 224 students surrounded by enemy forces. The AC-130s, Navy jets, and offshore destroyer fire provided cover. The gunships cut the Cuban and Grenadan positions and vehicles to ribbons, eventually pushing them into a final stronghold at the Calivigny Barracks. The next day, as the Army forces prepared for a final assault, AC-130Hs made several attacks to suppress any potential mortar or artillery fire. So effective were these attacks that even though three helicopters were damaged and forced to make emergency landings, resistance proved to be minimal, and soon the enemy surrendered. Bernard Coard and Hudson Austin were captured and later convicted of Bishop's murder. US officials declared a formal end to the operation on November 2, 1983. The casualty numbers included eighteen Americans killed in action, with 106 wounded, one of whom died later. A total of twenty-four Cubans and twenty-one Grenadans were killed, as well as twenty-four civilians. The enemy wounded totaled 396, with 673 captured.[64] One of the most controversial aspects of the operation was the less than stellar performance by US intelligence and planning—again. One critic later declared: "We won in Grenada in spite of ourselves."[65]

While the invasion had general popular and congressional support, some critics suggested that the timing of the invasion, two days after the 1983 Beirut barracks bombing, could have been a way to distract the public from the Lebanese disaster. Led by communist and Islamic states, the UN General Assembly roundly denounced the invasion and voted 108 to 9 for Resolution 38/7, which condemned the armed intervention in Grenada since it "constituted a flagrant violation of international law and of the independence, sovereignty and territorial integrity of that State." The Security Council considered a similar resolution that received widespread support but was vetoed by the United States.[66]

Most embarrassing of all for America was the fact that the United Kingdom, Trinidad and Tobago, and Canada all opposed the invasion. British Prime Minister Margaret Thatcher personally opposed the US intervention, and her foreign secretary, Geoffrey Howe, announced to the House of Commons on the day before the invasion that he had no knowledge of any possible US invasion. Indeed, Reagan had assured the British that he was not considering an invasion. According to the president, Thatcher "was very adamant and continued to insist that we cancel our landings on Grenada. I couldn't tell her that it had already begun."[67]

Afterwards, Grenadan governor-general Paul Scoon was reinstated and the constitution restored. A new government was formed, and a few US troops remained behind, including military police, special forces units, and specialized intelligence detachments to guarantee the peaceful transition of the new government. Many experts expressed concerns over the military's lack of competent intelligence about not only the enemy but also the island of Grenada itself. One of the most embarrassing features was the fact that neither planners nor the senior officers knew that the students were actually at two different campuses, which caused a thirty-three-hour delay in rescuing students at the second campus. Also, as alluded to earlier, maps supplied to the soldiers on the ground were so bad that they did not show the contour of the topography and were not marked with crucial positions. The landing strip was drawn by hand. All of this was unnecessary, since the State Department had all of these maps and data on hand if anyone had bothered to ask. Later DOD reports recommended that all branches of the US military needed to improve communications and coordination among themselves. Had the gunships been used more often and more effectively, many casualties might have been prevented. In the long run, these mistakes led in 1987 to the formation of USSOCOM, with an emphasis on joint operations and the improved use of special ops aircraft such as the AC-130s.[68]

Chapter Conclusion

In the first years after the Vietnam War, AC-130 crews trained to be ready for a campaign just like Grenada. In spite of their numbers, the crews had already flown thousands of hours supporting nearly every military evacuation and operation between January 1973 and December 1983. Even as the airframe aged and the aircrews rotated in and out of the 16th SOS and 711th SOS, they maintained their high level of training and professionalism in order to remain prepared for the next call for help. It seemed, however, that most US operations would be small brushfire wars like Grenada. The initial focus in the late 1980s would be another operation in Latin America, specifically Panama. However, this was only the prelude to a major conflict in the Persian Gulf. In both Panama and the Gulf, the crews of the AC-130s would soon write a glorious new chapter in the history of their kind.

10 AC-130s and the Birth of US Special Operations Command

The immediate post-Grenada world of gunships focused on training crews and maintaining aging airframes. Soon, the 711th SOS became one of the main units for training Army, Navy, and Marine conventional or special operations surface forces in all kinds of operations, especially in AC-130 tactics. These reservists also became increasingly involved in foreign internal defense efforts in Central and South America, going so far as to deploy their gunships throughout the area. These foreign internal defense deployments led 711th SOS personnel into counter-drug operations in Latin American. However, while this activity was significant, it soon took a back seat to a much larger alteration of the entire structure of special operations in the US military.[1]

While the 711th SOS worked on their routine, senior officials in the DOD examined the lessons they believed they needed to learn in the aftermath of the Grenada operation. With the progression of post-Vietnam brushfire wars in the 1980s, it soon became apparent that the United States needed a joint unit to deal with these contingencies more effectively. To that end, Congress examined why intelligence, maps, and other specifics of the invasion went wrong. This eventually led to the creation of USSOCOM, which would prove to be important to the AC-130s' future role.[2]

By late 1983 there was a growing notion in Congress that military reforms were needed. As early as June of that year, the Senate Armed Services Committee, chaired by Arizona Republican senator Barry Goldwater, initiated a two-year study of the DOD with special emphasis on SOF. In turn, the Defense Department created the Joint Special Operations Agency on January 1, 1984. While a good idea, the agency had no actual operational or command authority over any SOF units or materials in any service. In fact, it did little to enhance SOF readiness or capabilities. Not only did this disillusion those in the special operations world of gunships, but it caught the attention of powerful and knowledgeable senators such as Goldwater. In turn, Senators Sam Nunn, a Democrat from Georgia, and William Cohen, a Republican from Maine, both colleagues of Goldwater's on the Armed Services Committee, and Virginia representative Dan Daniel, Democratic chair of the House Armed Services Subcommittee on Readiness, led a growing number of congressional members who concluded that the nation's SOF abilities were second-rate. Nunn and Cohen also believed that the DOD was not adequately preparing for future threats and advocated a clearer organizational focus and chain of command for special operations to deal with low-intensity conflicts.[3]

In October 1985 the Senate Armed Services Committee published the results of their review of the military entitled *Defense Organization: The Need for Change.* Its conclusions were so compelling that they led to the passage of the Goldwater-Nichols Defense Reorganization Act of 1986. By the spring of 1986, advocates of special operations forces had introduced reform bills in both houses of Congress to flesh out the larger bill. While the military, in general, opposed the notion of a joint command and joint operations, by the summer both houses had passed reform bills that directed the creation of unified defense organizations. At that point the bills went to conference committees to work out the final details. Ultimately, the combined bill called for the formation of a joint command headed by a four-star general for all special operations, an assistant secretary of defense for special operations and low-intensity conflict, a coordinating board for brushfire wars within the National Security Council (NSC), and a new Major Force Program (MFP-11) for special operations.[4]

The final bill was attached as a rider to the 1987 Defense Authorization Act and was signed by President Ronald Reagan in October 1986, exactly three years after Grenada. It was left to the DOD to implement the law. To make sure this happened, Congress passed two additional bills with specific directions and funding sites. The new program gave what would become USSOCOM the capacity to modernize its weapons and forces and encourage interservice cooperation by having a single commander for all SOF units from all services. The first commander was Gen. James Lindsay.[5]

The evolution of USSOCOM was slow and sometimes difficult. However, by the late 1980s and early 1990s, each service had begun to create its own component special operations command. The first test of this new organization came during Operation Earnest Will, when in September 1987, Navy SEALs, special boat teams (SBTs), and the 160th Special Operations Aviation Group, later known as the 160th Special Operations Regiment (Airborne) or 160th SOAR Night Stalkers, worked together to guarantee that neutral oil tankers and other merchant ships could pass safely through the Persian Gulf during the Iran-Iraq War.[6]

Slowly but surely, each major military branch formed its own special ops units to work together through USSOCOM. Relevant to this story, the Air Force formally established the Air Force Special Operations Command (AFSOC) on May 22, 1990. Headquartered at Hurlburt Field, Florida, at the time it became the ninth major command in the Air Force and the Air Force component for USSOCOM, which was then headquartered at MacDill AFB, Florida. Initially, AFSOC was to "provide the Air Force special operations forces for worldwide deployment and assignment to regional unified commands." The command was comprised, at the time, of the 1st SOW along with the 352nd SOG, 353rd SOG, and 720th Special Tactical Group. Last, but not least, they had responsibility for the USAF Special Operations School. Most important to the gunships was the 1st SOW, which was over the 16th SOS as it had always been.[7]

As for the effects on the gunships and their crews, little changed organizationally except that joint operations now became official and battlefield commanders were not only brothers at arms but actual commanders on the ground or in the air. Even before AFSOC formally stood up, things were getting better for the airmen of the 16th SOS and 711th SOS. The 1980s witnessed the revitalization of American special ops in general, and the gunships benefited from more attention and more funding. This meant much-needed money for systems upgrades and even the development of a new kind of AC-130 gunship. The late 1980s and early 1990s would see not only the creation of the AC-130U gunship, but also important H-model modifications and even specific enhancements for the aging A models.[8]

These changes came none too soon. In December 1989, gunships of the 16th SOS and 711th SOS spearheaded Operation Just Cause, the largest US military action since the Vietnam War. The operation proved to be the perfect environment for AC-130 gunship operations. Ironically, when the operation began, two gunships of the 711th SOS were on standard rotation to the Panama Canal Zone and were the first gunships to join the contingency. As General McCutchan later wrote, "Their success was absolute proof that the USAF's efforts as a total force worked." Ultimately, the 16th SOS crews that flew combat in Just Cause received the 1990 MacKay Trophy for the Air Force's most meritorious flight of the year and the Tunner Award as the most outstanding crew in the Military Airlift Command. One H-model aircraft commander also received the 1990 Jabara Award for superior airmanship over Panama. At the same time, the 711th SOS crews became the first Air Force reservists to enter direct combat without being recalled by an American president. For their efforts one crew received the President's Award from the Air Force Association as the 1990 Outstanding Reserve Crew. Subsequently, the 16th SOS participated in Operation Promote Liberty, the pacification of Panama. This operation lasted, on and off, until the late 1990s and was finally discontinued after seven years.[9]

Operation Just Cause stemmed from events in Panama beginning in the late 1960s. After years of struggling to make democracy work in the small isthmus nation, the elected government was overthrown by Col. Omar Torrijos-Herrera and his notorious henchmen known as the Guardia Nacional. Torrijos ruled Panama with an iron fist until his death in 1981. The US had, since Panama gained its independence in 1903–4, maintained a "quasi-colonial relationship" with the leaders of Panama. This method of ruling Panama proved useful to the United States, since Torrijos became an anticommunist pillar in Central America.[10]

Torrijos's successor was one of his protégés, Manuel Antonio Noriega, who almost immediately established his own dictatorship, cleverly hidden behind the trappings of a newly elected "democratic" regime. Noriega even altered the role of the Guardia, combining it with the Panamanian armed forces to create the Panamanian Defense Force (PDF). In reality, the Guardia still acted as Noriega's personal force and maintained a special position within the military and the government.

At first the United States was reluctant to challenge Noriega's rule, since he was providing intelligence to the CIA on communist activities in El Salvador and Nicaragua.[11] However, by 1984–85 relations had begun to sour, since it was discovered that much of the intelligence he was providing proved to be second-rate or completely fraudulent. Worse, the CIA soon discovered that Noriega was working with the Colombian drug lords to traffic drugs into the United States. They also gathered evidence that indicated he was obtaining aid from Cuba and providing material aid to both sides in the civil wars in El Salvador and Nicaragua. Clearly, he had become nothing more than a thug.[12]

Initially, American diplomats attempted to persuade Noriega to reform his government. When he did not, they began supporting potential opponents. As relations worsened, on June 26, 1987, the US Senate passed a resolution calling for his ouster. In turn, the US embassy was attacked by a mob that was later discovered to be mostly Guardia members. In protest, the United States cut off all aid. Panamanian military units and authorities began harassing US citizens, in particular military personnel. Much of the anti-American activity was designed to deflect attention away from the persecution of Panamanian political opponents and the murder of one opposition leader. One coup attempt failed, and its leaders were brutally punished.[13]

The climactic act began with the election of May 1988. After Guillermo Endara formed a coalition of opposition parties, Noriega stepped in and dissolved the new government by force. His force of thugs, best known as the Dignity Battalion, or "Dig Bats" (American GIs called them "Ding Bats") began to harass and assault US citizens and Panamanian political opponents. They became so brazen that they even beat one political opposition leader in public. These events soon began to appear on American television and in newspapers. Fearing a Panamanian attack on the Canal Zone, the president sent nearly two thousand Army and Marine combat personnel to protect US citizens and property. In turn, vice president and Republican presidential candidate George H. W. Bush called on Noriega to honor the results of the election.[14]

As US units from Southern Command (SOUTHCOM) arrived, they began moving American citizens from Panama to the Canal Zone and many back to the United States. Having begun planning for an invasion many months before, the United States took its first step by sending additional troops to Howard AB, Canal Zone, as part of so-called exercises known as Purple Storm or Sand Fleas. In turn, aircraft from the 24th Tactical Airlift Squadron, 24th Composite Wing, arrived at Howard as part of the "exercises." They used OA-37s to overfly Panamanian military positions to see what reaction they would get. During the night of April 12, 1988, the PDF, probably supported by Cubans, attacked a tank farm near Howard AB. In the ensuing firefight, several attackers were killed. The United States sent an angry protest to Panama City warning Noriega to stop his anti-American activities or face a "stern response." On October 3, 1989, Noriega was confronted by another coup, led by Maj. Moises Giraldi, which focused the dictator's attention on suppressing the insurrection. When President Bush failed to act in support of the rebels, many in the media labeled him a "wimp." Stung by this internal smear of his reputation, the president announced that the United States would not negotiate with a known drug runner and warned Noriega to step down or "face dire consequences."[15]

US intelligence personnel observed the PDF response, especially that of the elite Battalion 2000. Noteworthy data was folded into the ever-expanding operations plan. Since many high-ranking leaders of the PDF took part in the coup attempt, US planners believed the time was fast approaching when not only would Noriega be vulnerable internally, but also US public and congressional support would be strong enough to guarantee success of an invasion.[16]

On December 15, 1989, following the coup attempt, the Panamanian legislature announced that a state of war existed with the United States. For the time being, the United States remained publicly passive and continued secret planning for Noriega's ouster. Originally, the Americans had openly condemned the Panamanian government for the rift, but as early as January 1988 they switched the blame to Noriega, condemning him for drug running. Indeed, in February 1988, two federal grand juries had indicted him for his drug trafficking activities.[17]

In January 1989, not long after Bush was sworn in, planning for an invasion began in earnest. Eventually, the plan they chose was Operation Prayer Book, a four-part plan that opened with Klondike Key, the simple removal of noncombatants, followed by Krystal Ball (later Blind Logic), a vague civil affairs postmilitary action designed to make Panama a democracy. Both were soon shelved while planning on phase three, Elder Statesman (later Post Time), and phase four, Blue Spoon, went forward. Post Time involved the buildup of forces, while Blue Spoon became the combat plan. Most troops selected for the operation would come from the 7th Infantry Division (Light), which would be commanded by Lt. Gen. Maxwell R. Thurman, commander of SOUTHCOM. Final planning was headed by Lt. Gen. Carl Stiner, XVIII Airborne Corps, Fort Bragg, and designated Joint Task Force South.[18]

The overall plan soon evolved into a more straightforward rapid deployment attack against PDF locations, initially by thirteen thousand troops, later to be increased to twenty-five thousand. Many of the twelve thousand backup forces would come from the 82nd Airborne Division and 75th Ranger Regiment, both of Urgent Fury fame. Finally, the operations name was changed to Just Cause, since Blue Spoon seemed to trivialize the operation. As part of the newly formed USSOCOM, Air Force, Army, Navy, and Marine joint special operations personnel took part in Just Cause. Ground units included the Atlantic unit, comprised of two brigades of the 7th Infantry Division, scheduled to attack along the Caribbean side of the Canal Zone; the Semper Fi unit, made up of Marines assigned the job of securing the area around Howard AB; the Bayonet unit, the 193rd Infantry Brigade, which was to secure positions in and around Panama City, especially PDF headquartered at La Comandancia; and the Pacific unit, comprised of two brigades from the 82nd Airborne, which were to follow up an assault by Task Force Red special ops forces and secure Torrijos International Airport and Tucuman Military Airfield to provide a landing area for reinforcements.[19]

Ironically, the United States had been slowly reducing its military presence in the Canal Zone in anticipation of turning over the Canal to the Panamanian government on December 31, 1989. Still, having a base of operations within the Canal Zone made things easier. The 7th Infantry jump-off for the invasion was Fort Howard in the Canal Zone, while Quarry Heights became SOUTHCOM headquarters. In November 1989, US forces began moving the remaining military dependents to safety. Even so, dozens of Americans remained in the area. The JCS approved the final plan, and training intensified. On December 16, 1989, one day after the Panamanian legislature declared a state of war, four US service personnel were stopped by PDF troops. As they tried to drive away, the PDF opened fire, wounding two and killing Marine Lt. Robert Paz. That same day, a Navy lieutenant and his wife were stopped and detained for several hours, during which they were severely beaten and threatened with execution. Although they were released, the incident drove the United States closer to Operation Just Cause. That evening, Gen. Colin Powell and members of the JCS met with Secretary of Defense Dick Cheney and all the service chiefs. Powell and Cheney then went to the White House to brief President Bush, Vice President Dan Quayle, Secretary of State James Baker, and National Security Adviser Brent Scowcroft. After a brief and pointed discussion, the president declared, "Let's do it!"[20]

On December 18, General Stiner left Fort Bragg and traveled to Panama in preparation for H-hour, scheduled for 1:00 a.m. on December 20, 1989. His Joint Task Force, South headquarters was located at Fort Clayton. Gen. Max Thurman located his headquarters at Quarry Heights to oversee overall operations. Just Cause began as scheduled and eventually involved 57,648 US forces and more than three hundred aircraft, including AC-130s. In fact, the Air Force had initiated the operation by finalizing preparations for the ground assault. The day after Paz's death, on December 17, 1989, twelve C-5, seventeen C-141, and two C-130 cargo aircraft had arrived at Howard AB with the last load of troops and equipment. All those involved prayed for a quick victory but realized that the broad nature of the operation and the need not only to suppress enemy forces and capture Noriega (alive if at all possible), but also to protect US lives and property and restore democracy to Panama, might make that goal difficult to achieve. On December 18, amidst a chaotic scene at Pope AFB, North Carolina, C-141s began the process of transporting the 2,176 82nd Airborne troops to Panama to assault Torrijos International Airport and Tucuman Airfield. Twenty of the Starlifters transported the troops, while thirty-three others carried their heavy equipment first to Charleston, South Carolina, then to Panama. On December 19, an ice storm struck the Carolinas. Everyone available urgently pitched in to help with the deicing procedures and the loading process. Even retired Army and Air Force reservists helped out. In addition, deicing machines and chemicals were flown in to facilitate the launching process. In spite of the weather, every aircraft departed on or nearly on schedule. More than fourteen thousand troops were added to the twelve thousand on-site to provide a "decisive advantage" on the ground. Sixty-three C-141s were employed in this phase of the operation.[21]

One problem soon became evident: security. Even before the invasion began, Dan Rather of CBS News reported that "planes were taking off from Ft. Bragg." As a result, the Americans struggled to stay ahead of schedule in order to maintain some kind of secrecy for the operation. The action began with an assault on strategic targets such as the civilian Punta Paitilla Airport in Panama City; a PDF barracks and airstrip at Rio Hato, near one of Noriega's homes; and other key military command and control nodes throughout the nation. One of the most spectacular attacks occurred at the central headquarters of the PDF, more commonly known as La Comandancia. The target of this attack was the capture of Noriega, but he was not present. In fact, he would not be taken until January 3, 1990. US ground forces came under heavy fire as they closed in on La Comandancia. They were supported by two AC-130Hs, which fired several 40mm and 105mm rounds into the various buildings, causing them to catch fire. Soon the fire spread to adjacent buildings, and before long the entire poorer section of the city was ablaze. La Comandancia was finally captured later that afternoon.[22]

One of the more well known gunship stories from Operation Just Cause recounts that on the first night an 82nd Airborne unit was pinned down by enemy fire from a multistory building in Panama City. The unit commander, Capt. Steve Hagan, called for air support. Soon, a voice from an unseen, unheard AC-130H radioed back, asking for the target location. Hagan recalled: "We explained our situation and the guy said, 'Where are you?' and we showed him, and he said, 'Where are the bad guys?' and we showed him that." After a "pregnant pause for a couple of seconds," the voice from above said, "'You need to move back 18 feet.'" About two seconds later, two rounds from the Spectre's 105mm side-mounted cannon went through the building window with explosive results. Hagan waited a few seconds before moving his troops forward, but soon he realized there was no more enemy fire, no more enemy noise, no more enemy anything. He thanked his unseen savior, to which the airman replied, "Roger that . . . glad to be of service!" Years later, Gen. Carl A. Hagan, recounting this story about his son's unit, concluded: "Now that's close air support!"[23]

Fort Amador was secured by members of the 508th Airborne Infantry Company and sappers from the 59th Engineer Company in a night air assault that captured the positions in the early morning hours of December 20. Supported by AC-130s, the attack unfolded with smooth precision. The gunships caught many of the enemy troops scurrying across the golf course and caused total panic. Many of the PDF stripped off their uniforms and made every effort to blend in with the local civilian population. Fort Amador was a vital position, since it was located at the Pacific entrance to the Panama Canal and the Pacific end of the Bridge of Americas that crossed the Canal. It was also near a large oil farm and a key PDF command and control center. In addition, it had a large US housing area, which the Americans secured as quickly as possible to prevent the PDF from capturing US citizens and using them as hostages. Last, but not least, it also guarded the left flank of the US attack on La Comandancia. La Comandancia was located in the El Chorrillos neighborhood and heavily populated with pro-Noriega Dig Bats.[24]

One of the more intense engagements of the conflict occurred at the Pecora River Bridge, east of the airfields along the highway to the enemy's elite Battalion 2000 headquarters at Fort Cimarron. As US ground troops began loading onto helicopters at Albrook Air Station, they came under heavy fire. As other US forces pushed onto the bridge, they soon discovered that they were confronted by a large PDF convoy supported by far more enemy personnel than anticipated. As night fell, the situation became fluid and perilous for the Americans. To avoid catastrophe, ground commanders called in AC-130s to rake the convoy and enemy troops with 20mm, 40mm, and 105mm fire. As one account recalled, the AC-130 close air support "stopped them cold!" Throughout the night the gunships and ground controllers worked together to coordinate attacks on Defense Force movements. They literally finished them off. Ironically, early the next morning a second convoy from Panama City, unaware of the danger, tried to cross the same bridge. Another AC-130 was vectored onto the scene and utterly destroyed the column. The area had been secured once and for all.[25]

Meanwhile, "the largest nighttime airdrop since World War II," was taking place almost simultaneously at the Torrijos International Airport, Tucuman Airfield, and Rio Hato Airfield. Army Rangers and 82nd Airborne units led the attack and landed in a hot LZ. Unbeknownst to the US forces, a Brazilian airliner with 376 passengers was late and trying to make a landing. The Panamanians realized that the civilians on board could be used as hostages. To obviate the danger to ground units and prevent the capture of the airliner, AC-130s and AH-6 attack helicopters were sent in to attack the PDF troops. What few people knew was that Noriega was at Tucuman with one of his many call girls. Noriega barely escaped capture, fleeing into the night in his skivvies.[26]

At 1:03 a.m. twelve C-141s arrived over the drop zone and dropped the Rangers from five hundred feet. Soon after, four C-130s from Hunter Army Air Field, Georgia, dropped their Rangers. Normally, their minimum drop altitude was eight hundred feet, but they came in low to allow for a more precise drop, since they feared parachuting into enemy fire. About an hour later, after the first troops secured a perimeter with the help of gunships, twenty-eight more C-141s arrived to drop more troops and heavy equipment, including Sheridan tanks. The last waves of American cargo aircraft came in between 2:11 and 5:15 a.m. Throughout, gunfire continued from PDF positions. Finally, as the sun rose the Americans were able to begin to extend their positions and the enemy was silenced. At the airport terminal there were several tense moments as some PDF tried to seize a handful of the four hundred civilians (mostly from the Brazilian flight) as hostages. In the end, none of the civilians were hurt, and the Defense Force troops surrendered. By noon on December 20 the entire area was under US control and the runways cleared of debris. By 3:00 p.m. the first C-141s were able to land, bringing the entire 7th Infantry Division. The Americans had had one GI killed and five wounded in the battle. In turn, nineteen had been injured during the low-level night jump. The enemy had lost thirteen killed, twenty wounded, and fifty-four captured. The US forces seized hundreds of small arms, twelve helicopters, and thirteen fixed-wing aircraft. While some drop items had been damaged or lost in the surrounding marshes, nearly every item was eventually recovered and repaired, including eight Sheridan tanks. Overall, these first two parts of the operation had been a great success due in no small measure to the role of the gunships.[27]

A third combat area was Rio Hato, where 637 Rangers were dropped by thirteen C-130s. Two Special Operations Low Level II (SOLLII) C-130s provided electronic warfare and radar jamming support, while two other C-130s parachuted heavy equipment into the area. The AC-130s, AH-6 helicopters, and AH-64 Apache helicopters provided continuous close air support that proved highly effective. Concurrently, Secretary Cheney reluctantly agreed to deploy two FA-117As, which dropped two two-thousand-pound GBU-27 LGBs within two hundred yards of the Defense Force barracks in spite of low-lying cloud cover. Unfortunately, security leaks alerted many of the PDF to the attack, so most had escaped, which gave the FA-117A critics reasons to call into question the effectiveness of the aircraft. Even so, the fact that the Defense Forces had bugged out allowed the Americans to secure the area. Since other enemy positions remained active, AC-130s moved to rake the area, eliminating the enemy's ZPU-4 AAA batteries, barbed wire fences, concrete barricades, walls, and power lines in the LZ. The battle itself was brief but violent. Twenty-six Americans were wounded during the drop, while four were killed and eighteen wounded during the actual fighting. The PDF had thirty-four killed and 362 captured.[28]

By dawn on December 21, the invasion was over except for small pockets of individual resistance. As Air Force historian Bernard Nalty notes, "Most of the defenders preferred to surrender, especially after watching the AC-130s supporting these forays put on accurate displays of their frightening fire power."[29] One unexpected consequence was the evaporation of basic law and order. Soon civil order began to break down. To prevent chaos, US forces took over police activities. Fortunately, since the vast majority of Panamanians were happy to see the Americans, they remained passive and proved to be very supportive of the troops. Noriega stayed on the run until Christmas Eve, when he was cornered in the Nunciature Vatican Embassy in Panama City, where he had received temporary asylum. There ensued a ten-day standoff, during which General Thurman had US troops encircle the embassy and psychological operations units blast the complex with loud and raucous rock-and-roll music playing on huge speakers. Noriega finally surrendered on January 3, 1990, following assurances he would not be harmed. No sooner was he in custody than he was spirited back to Miami, Florida.[30]

Upon his arrival in the United States, Noriega was held in custody until April 1992, when he was tried on eight counts of drug trafficking, racketeering, and money laundering. He was convicted and sentenced to prison for forty years. Noriega was imprisoned in a unique individual cell in Miami, where he served twenty-five years. When he was released in September 2007, he faced extradition to both Panama and France for convictions in absentia in 1995 for murder and in 1999 for money laundering. France was granted its extradition request in April 2010. Noriega arrived in Paris on April 27, 2010. After a retrial, he was found guilty and sentenced to seven years in jail in July 2010.[31] A humorous note was the fact that when the former dictator was brought to the United States to await trial, one of the charges brought against him had to be dropped when what had been widely reported as fifty kilograms of cocaine in his possession was found to be tamales.[32]

As General McCutchan says, "It was a busy little war and it was tougher than many expected."[33] Official US figures reported 23 US personnel killed in action and 325 wounded, while the Panamanians lost 205 killed and more than 700 captured. Civilian casualty numbers continue to be a matter of controversy, since the Pentagon reported 200 killed and about 2,500 displaced. Some human rights groups initially estimated that as many as 4,000 died and 15,000 were displaced, most by the fires in downtown Panama City. These same groups claim that the PDF suffered more than 1,000 casualties and that many of them were shot after they were captured. In the twenty-plus years that have passed, most experts believe, based on hard evidence, that the Panamanian numbers were much closer to the Pentagon's estimates and that US troops conducted themselves in a thoroughly professional manner, especially with regard to prisoners of war. One compelling fact is that US military and civilian aid groups provided housing, food, clothing, and medicine for about three thousand people, which would decisively contradict the claim of fifteen thousand displaced persons. US aid more than took care of these displaced civilians.[34]

Perhaps the most telling aspect of Operation Just Cause has been the quality of life Panamanians have experienced since January of 1990. While there remain some bitter feelings toward the United States since Noriega fell, democracy has begun to take hold. Each succeeding election has been open and fair. Opposing parties and factions have peacefully, if not always happily, exchanged power on several occasions. Significantly, immediately following the invasion, President Endara abolished the PDF and replaced it with the Panamanian Public Forces. In addition, in 1994 a new, more democratic constitution went into effect, and throughout the 1990s the Panamanian economy recovered. While it is not an industrial power, it is at least a stable economy. In short, Panama in the twenty-first century is freer and more prosperous than it was when the AC-130s covered the US invasion of December 1989.[35]

While an examination of Operation Just Cause highlights the vital role of the AC-130s, some of the details magnify the awesome lethality of these aircraft and the valor of their crew members. Capt. Charles G. McMillan and his crew won the MacKay Trophy, making them the second gunship crew to do so, during Just Cause. McMillan and his crew were part of a two-gunship formation that flew out of Howard AB to attack the PDF headquarters compound at La Comandancia in Panama City. Their AC-130H's accurate firepower saved the lives of many US ground troops and facilitated the occupation of several strategic enemy military positions. In some cases they provided close air support within twenty yards of friendly ground forces in order to root out hidden enemy snipers and other forces. Although they launched three hours ahead of schedule and encountered heavy AAA fire, they adapted to the threat environment and after ten intense flying hours completed their mission.[36]

Among the gunship crews who played a key role on December 20, better known as "hit night," was that of the AC-130H flown by Capt. George Gabreski. He and his crew flew sorties that played a pivotal role in securing the Rio Pacora Bridge by supporting Army Ranger forces. They also prevented PDF reinforcements from reaching La Comandancia and Torrijos and Tucuman Airports. Most of the night, Captain Gabreski and his crew repulsed repeated enemy assaults by mechanized infantry on the Rio Pacora Bridge with precise firepower, landing several rounds within twenty yards of their own ground troops without a single friendly-fire casualty.[37]

Maj. Clay T. McCutchan (now major general, retired) and his crew received

AC-130 dispensing flares and chaff to confuse enemy SAMs.

the 1990 President's Award for the top crew in the Air Force Reserve. He and his AC-130A crew had been in Panama for their annual summer camp when Just Cause began. McCutchan and Capt. Mike Wilson's A-model gunships soon joined the action. They were the last gunships to overfly La Comandancia on the night before the commencement of hostilities and by chance the first gunships airborne out of Howard AB on hit night. Their main mission was to provide airfield defense at Howard AB. In that role they had a ringside seat to the 16th SOS's AC-130H precision attacks on December 20. As the operation unfolded, McCutchan's crew suppressed PDF small-arms and mortar fire at Albrook Air Station. Later, they picked snipers off a roof within twenty feet of Army paratroopers en route to the Marriott Hotel, where there was a hostage situation. Not only did they support the resolution of the situation at the hotel, but throughout the night they provided all forms of fire, escort, and visual support for American forces. For all they did that night, McCutchan won a medal for what he did not do.[38]

Late during the first night of the operation, forward air controllers mistakenly vectored McCutchan's aircraft to an area that was being swept by what turned out to be an American ground force of "some kind." While it had initially been an area where the PDF was active, it had long since been cleared, and US forces were now in the kill zone. The crew soon located the ground signatures, and the FAC ordered them to fire on what was not known to anyone at the time to be friendly forces. Realizing that the ground force very well could be Americans, McCutchan took it upon himself to disregard the order and returned to Howard AB. Upon hearing his report, McCutchan's commanding officer remarked, "Either they will court martial you or pin a medal on you." As it turned out, McCutchan's intuition was correct, and he saved the lives of several American servicemen. For his initiative he was awarded the Distinguished Flying Cross.[39]

Captain (later, Major General) Wilson's A model also performed many of the same functions as his friend McCutchan's AC-130A did, and in the end, both of the 711th SOS gunships received great praise for their efforts in Just Cause. Overall, the AC-130As and Hs performed a vital role in the success of the Panamanian invasion. While it would be nearly impossible to determine just how many American ground troops survived as a result of AC-130 close air support or how many enemy were killed or wounded by AC-130s, it is clear that, given the ideal gunship environment and the crying need for close air support, the gunships' role in Just Cause was robust. However, gunship crews had little time to bask in their glory. Events were unfolding or about to unfold as they returned from Panama that would change everything in their world. First was the protracted construction of the AC-130Us. The second was the standup of AFSOC that spring. Last, but certainly not least, was the Iraqi invasion of Kuwait in the summer of 1990 that would eventually lead the gunships back into combat, this time halfway around the world in a totally different kind of combat environment and in by far the largest American military commitment since Vietnam.[40]

11 The Early 1990s
The Persian Gulf to Somalia

In retrospect the history of the AC-130s in the 1980s had been a dress rehearsal for the events of 1990s. No sooner were the H models returned to Hurlburt Field and the AC-130As to Duke Field than the final steps were completed for the standup of AFSOC. This completed the Air Force's initial commitment to the new USSOCOM begun in the previous decade. In May 1990 all the gunships changed commands again, this time transferring to AFSOC. Ironically, forty-two years earlier the fledgling US Air Force had been confronted by the first great test of the Cold War, the Berlin Airlift. In 1990, the newly formed AFSOC would be plunged into the crucible of combat in the Persian Gulf.[1]

The Persian Gulf region of the Middle East, with its oil-rich nations such as Iraq, Saudi Arabia, Kuwait, and Iran, had immediately after World War II been under the thumb of Western oil companies fueling the massive expansion of industrial powers such as the United States, Great Britain, France, and even rebuilding West Germany. Throughout the Cold War Iraq had grown to be a closer ally of the Soviet Union, supplied with Soviet weapons. Tension between the secularist Iraqi regimes and America grew throughout the 1970s and 1980s. Of particular concern to the United States was Iraq's support of Palestinian radical groups fighting America's primary ally, Israel. In 1979 the rise to power of the nonreligious Baathist dictator Saddam Hussein and the fall of the pro-western shah in Iran soon led the new fundamentalist Iranian regime of the Ayatollah Khomeini into an almost decade-long war (1981–88) with Iraq. With Hussein willing to support at least some American policies in the region, the administration of President Ronald Reagan began a process not only of normalizing relations but also of providing material aid to Iraqi forces in their war with their mutual enemy, Iran.[2]

When leaders signed the cease-fire between Iran and Iraq in August 1988, both sides were spent. For all intents and purposes Iraq was bankrupt and owed millions to their Saudi and Kuwaiti neighbors. The next year, Kuwait made matters worse when, contrary to Organization of Petroleum Exporting Countries policy, they raised their oil production by 40 percent. This caused oil prices to collapse and further damaged the Iraqi economy. Saddam Hussein publicly declared the Kuwaiti action to be economic warfare. While Hussein's concerns for Iraq's economy were reasonable, his potential method of solving the problem by invading Kuwait was, as Don Oberdorfer wrote in the *Washington Post,* like the man who decided "to get out of bankruptcy, you rob a bank."[3] Saddam Hussein also condemned Kuwait's method of slant drilling, which he claimed was tapping Iraqi oil reserves from the Ramaila oil field. For this and other reasons, Kuwait and Iraq soon found themselves in a very tense relationship. However, there was more to it than that. They had had a tenuous relationship since Iraqi independence.[4]

In 1899 the al-Sabah family in Kuwait concluded a protectorate agreement with Great Britain, removing Kuwait from the Ottoman Empire. Once the province of Basra in Iraq, Kuwait was now free to handle its own internal affairs, while Great Britain took care of its foreign policy. Following World War I, Britain dominated the entire region. As the 1920s came to an end, the British began granting the states of the Gulf full independence. In the process, the British high commissioner drew the Iraq-Kuwait border in order to restrict Iraqi access to the Persian Gulf sea lanes, thus making sure Iraq would never threaten British domination of the Gulf and the oil trade. From that time forward, Iraq refused to recognize this arrangement.[5]

Operations Desert Shield and Desert Storm

In June 1990, with Iraq's economy in dire straits and Hussein fearful of an internal rebellion, long-standing discussions with Kuwait over a political arrangement more favorable to Iraq began in earnest. However, they soon broke down under Iraqi threats to attack its smaller neighbor if Iraqi demands were not met. In June and July, even as Hussein negotiated, thirty thousand Iraqi troops had already begun massing on the border. The next day, Hussein and US Ambassador to Iraq April Glaspie met to discuss the crisis. In one of the most controversial and disputed diplomatic events in history, there was a clear discrepancy concerning America's attitude toward Iraq's position in the two different transcripts produced by the two nations. This soon became the cornerstone of what would become the Persian Gulf War.[6]

In one version, the United States expressed concerns over the Iraqi buildup. In both, Hussein laid out his grievances against Kuwait and promised that he would not invade Kuwait before one more round of negotiations. However, in the version published by the *New York Times* on September 23, 1990, Glaspie expressed concern over the troop buildup to Saddam Hussein, saying, "We have no opinion on the Arab-Arab conflicts, like your border disagreement with Kuwait." Some experts later interpreted portions of Glaspie's statements as giving an American green light to the invasion. The State Department never confirmed the authenticity of these transcripts, instead claiming that they handled everything by the book. Still, others have argued that Saddam Hussein may have been influenced by the perception that the United States was not interested in the issue and that he may have felt so in part because of US support for the reunification of Germany. It is clear that Hussein underestimated the extent of a US response.[7]

On August 2, 1990, Saddam Hussein sent one hundred thousand troops into Kuwait. After two days of intense combat, most of the Kuwaiti armed forces were either overrun by the Iraqi Republican Guard or escaped into neighboring Saudi Arabia. Within hours of the invasion, Kuwaiti and US delegations in the United Nations requested a meeting of the Security Council to condemn the invasion. Within hours the members of the council passed Resolution 660, condemning the invasion and demanding a withdrawal of Iraqi troops. The next day, members of the Arab League passed their own resolution calling for a solution by the league that warned against foreign intervention. On August 6, UN Resolution 661 placed economic sanctions on Iraq.[8]

President Bush and his advisers were also deeply concerned that Iraq might not stop with Kuwait but invade Saudi Arabia as well. Indeed, the decision by America and its allies to confront the Iraqis had as much to do with preventing an invasion of Saudi Arabia and its oil reserves as it did with the liberation of Kuwait itself. The lightning victory of the Iraqi army left it within easy striking distance of the Hama oil fields. Iraqi control of those resources, Kuwait's and its own reserves, would have given them control of the majority of the world's oil reserves. Iraq certainly had a motive to invade Saudi Arabia, since the Saudis had loaned Hussein $26 billion to fight Iran, and he remained reluctant to repay the loan. The Saudis feared the influence of the mainly Shia Muslims who led Iran's Islamic revolution and their own Shia minority, since most of the Saudi oil fields were in an area populated by Shias. Soon after his conquest of Kuwait, Saddam Hussein began threatening Saudi Arabia, declaring that the US-backed Saudis were an illegitimate guardian of the holy cities of Mecca and Medina.[9]

With these concerns confronting America, President Bush announced that the United States would undertake a "wholly defensive" mission to prevent Iraq from invading Saudi Arabia. The United States launched Operation Desert Shield on August 7, 1990, when F-15s from the 27th and 71st Tactical Fighter Squadrons, 1st Tactical Fighter Wing, Langley AFB, Virginia, left for Saudi Arabia. The previous day, Saudi King Fahd bin Abd Al'Aziz Al Saud formally invited friendly nations to participate in the defense of his country. After flying eight thousand miles nonstop in fifteen hours with seven aerial refuelings, the F-15s arrived at Dhahran. Within hours of their arrival, they were placed on alert. The next day, C-141Bs carrying the US airlift control element arrived in Dhahran along with E-3 airborne warning and control system (AWACS) and KC-10 refueling aircraft.[10]

Also, on August 8 Iraq declared parts of Kuwait to be extensions of the Iraqi province of Basra and the rest to be the nineteenth province of Iraq. The US Navy soon mobilized two naval battle groups under the aircraft carriers USS *Dwight D. Eisenhower* and USS *Independence* and sent them to the area. All totaled, forty-eight US Air Force F-15s from the 1st TFW eventually landed in Saudi Arabia and commenced twenty-four-hour air patrols of the Saudi-Kuwait-Iraq border areas to prevent further Iraqi advances. During Desert Shield they flew 4,207 sorties. The United States also sent the battleships USS *Missouri* and USS *Wisconsin* to the region. The military buildup continued from there, ultimately reaching 543,000 troops, twice the number used later in the 2003 US invasion of Iraq. While much of the material was airlifted, other items were carried to staging areas on fast sealift ships known as "Ro-Ro" (roll-on, roll-off) ships, allowing a quick massing of troops and equipment.[11]

Planning the Air War While the Gunships Deploy

Overall commander of the operation was Gen. H. Norman Schwarzkopf, Central Command (CENTCOM), while the overall air commander was Lt. Gen. Charles Horner. They both arrived in Saudi Arabia on August 6, 1990, and worked closely with JCS chair Gen. Colin Powell. The next day, while Horner remained to plan the air defenses, Schwarzkopf returned to Washington to brief the president. On the day US aircraft began to arrive, Schwarzkopf discussed with Lt. Gen. Mike Loh, Air Force vice chief of staff, the process of having Air Force planners begin drawing up a strategic air campaign. This commenced the famous Desert Storm planning process under Operations Plan 1002–90V, also known as the Air-Land Battle Plan. Loh assigned Col. John Warden and Checkmate, the Air Staff planning group, Directorate of Plans, to create an offensive plan to destroy Iraqi air defenses, centers of industrial production, ground forces, and centers of command and control. Among those in the Iraq Target Planning Cell was Col. David A. Deptula, who

Later model AC-130 cockpit.

was the Joint Force Air Component commander's director of campaign plans. He played a key role not only in developing the original air war plan but also in target selection throughout the operation.[12]

On August 10, the DOD officially named the contingency Operation Desert Storm. Over the next several weeks, coalition forces continued to pour into Saudi Arabia. On August 17, 1990, intelligence indicated that the Iraqis had begun to build massive defensive bunkers all along the Saudi border and the Persian Gulf seashore. On August 18, F-117A stealth fighters, F-4G Wild Weasels, KC-135 refueling aircraft, A-10 attack aircraft, and C-130s deployed. In addition, President Bush activated the Civil Reserve Air Fleet. On August 22, the president issued Executive Order 12727 to call up two hundred thousand reservists. Finally on September 6, 1990, the 16th SOS began deploying to the Gulf. The first AC-130Hs arrived on September 8, with the A models making it to the Gulf four days later. The primary responsibility for all the gunships was to provide close air support for coalition ground forces and interdict Iraqi logistics and supply lines. Most of the Desert Shield phase of the Gulf War saw the gunships bedding down and learning their role in the air and ground combat operations soon to come.[13]

While the 16th SOS deployed to the Gulf, the 711th SOS stayed in the

United States, continuing its training by working with Army ground forces and flying missions in Panama, some on the one-year anniversary of Operation Just Cause. They also covered deployments to Colombia, flying against drug cartel members. Finally, in late January they were recalled to active duty and were sent to the Persian Gulf to bolster the AC-130H forces. In the meantime, President Bush and Secretary of State James Baker continued to build a thirty-four-country coalition that included several Arab nations. While the German Federal Republic and Japan did not officially join the coalition, Germany contributed ten million dollars and Japan six billion dollars. On November 29, the United Nations passed Resolution 678, which presented Iraq with a January 15, 1991, deadline to withdraw from Kuwait. Resolution 678 also declared that the coalition could use any means to uphold Resolution 660 and restore Kuwaiti independence.[14]

Both the United States and the United Nations made many public justifications for involvement in the Gulf. The two most compelling reasons were the Iraqi violation of Kuwaiti national sovereignty and the defense of Saudi Arabia. What went unsaid was Saudi Arabian importance in the region as the key supplier of oil to many nations in the west. In this regard, the Allies had little room to back down. Indeed, while they wanted the crisis to end short of war, it came down to Iraq having to withdraw from Kuwait if peace was going to be preserved. Throughout the remainder of 1990, several peace proposals were floated but none concluded. On each occasion the Americans consistently insisted that the only terms for peace were Iraq's unconditional withdrawal from Kuwait. Iraq insisted that pulling out of Kuwait must be tied to a simultaneous adherence by its neighbors to similar UN resolutions, such as the withdrawal of Syrian troops from Lebanon and Israeli troops from the West Bank, Gaza Strip, Golan Heights, and southern Lebanon. While Morocco and Jordan bought this proposal, Syria joined the coalition, and Israel remained officially neutral in spite of later Iraqi rocket attacks on its civilian population. American diplomats worked diligently to prevent Israel from getting involved in order to hold the Arab portion of the coalition in place.[15]

After much passionate, often televised, debate, on January 12, 1991, the US Congress authorized the use of military force to drive Iraq out of Kuwait, voting 52–47 in the Senate and 250–183 in the House of Representatives. The following day, UN Secretary General Javier Perez de Cuellar met with Saddam Hussein in one last desperate effort to prevent hostilities. Following the meeting, Perez de Cuellar announced to the world that Hussein remained determined to stay in Kuwait and that the hope for peace seemed remote. This was confirmed on January 15, when the withdrawal deadline passed without any Iraqi movement.[16]

The War Begins

The Persian Gulf War began with an intense and widespread aerial bombing campaign, in which nineteen nations of the coalition flew over 118,661 sorties and dropped 88,550 tons of bombs, utterly destroying the Iraqi military and civilian infrastructure. The first aircraft to launch were seven B-52Gs from the 596th Bomb Squadron, 2nd Bomb Wing, at Barksdale AFB, Louisiana. They carried the newest AN/AGM-86C air-launched cruise missiles, designed to destroy enemy command, control, and communications nodes throughout Baghdad. Most of the aircraft used in the campaign, which officially lasted until February 28, 1991, were launched either from Incirlik AB, Turkey, as part of the 744th Provisional Composite Wing, or from Saudi airfields. At 3:00 a.m. Persian Gulf time on January 17, 7:00 p.m. on the east coast of the United States, the Buffs arrived over their high-value Iraqi targets. Only ten minutes later, Air Force F-15C pilot Capt. John Kelk made the first kill of the war when he shot down an Iraqi MiG-29. On the first day, land-based aircraft flew 750 sorties and Navy aircraft 228 sorties.[17]

On January 17, 1991, eight US AH-64 Apache helicopters and two MH-53 Pave Low helicopters destroyed Iraqi radar sites near the Iraqi-Saudi border. With the Iraqi early warning systems immediately destroyed, two EF-111 Ravens with terrain-following radar were able to lead twenty-two F-15E Strike Eagles against airfields in western Iraq. Minutes later, one of the EF-111 crews, pilot James Denton and his EW officer, Capt. Brent Brandon, destroyed an Iraqi Dassault Mirage by forcing it into the ground. This engagement proved significant, since it was the first and only air-to-air kill credited to an F-111 airframe, and it was accomplished by an unarmed EF-111 "Spark-Vark." In addition, ten Air Force F-117A Nighthawks escorted by three EF-111s, bombed Baghdad, setting off a wild nighttime display of enemy AAA which proved totally ineffectual against the stealth aircraft. The entire scene was captured by western news camera crews in downtown Baghdad and shown on television news in the United States. Even as the Iraqis began to shake off the initial attacks, Navy BGM-109 Tomahawk cruise missiles fired from guided-missile frigates in the Persian Gulf struck targets in Baghdad. Other coalition aircraft attacked targets throughout Iraq, such as government buildings, television and radio stations, Iraqi airfields, and Hussein's various presidential residences. Only five hours into the campaign, Baghdad state radio broadcast a speech by someone identified as Saddam Hussein who declared, "The great duel, the mother of all battles, has begun." Indeed, and the gunships would be there for the final kill.[18]

The Persian Gulf War soon became a high-tech war owing to the widespread use of precision-guided munitions, or smart bombs, and cruise missiles. Ironically, only about 10 percent of the ordnance used was PGMs, while 90 percent was iron or "dumb" bombs. The coalition also employed such awesome ordnance as fifteen-thousand-pound conventional bombs such as the BLU-82 "Daisy Cutters," which were dropped with great affect by MC-130E special operations aircraft. The Air Force also used CBU-87 combined effects munitions, CBU-89 Gator, and Mk-20 Rockeye cluster bombs. Iraq struck back by launching eight Iraqi-modified Scud missiles into Israel on January 18, 1991, and continued similar attacks through the remainder of the six-week war. Initially, the Allied priority was the destruction of the Iraqi Air Force and its AAA facilities using EA-6Bs, EF-111 radar jammers, and F-117As to elude Iraq's extensive SAM and AAA systems. These sorties, launched mostly from Saudi Arabia and from the six coalition aircraft carriers in the Persian Gulf and Red Sea, proved completely effective in destroying Iraqi air defenses. The one Iraqi weapon that proved particularly effective was the shoulder-launched ground-to-air missile, which accounted for 75 percent of Allied aircraft losses, especially among RAF and Navy aircraft, which flew at low altitudes to avoid radar. Iraqi air defenses seldom relied on radar. Instead, to a large extent they employed small-scale weapons that easily targeted low-flying aircraft. The next level of enemy targets proved to be command and communications facilities. Taking out those nodes had a great impact on the Iraqi military, since Saddam Hussein micromanaged the Iraqi forces at even the lowest levels. To that end, coalition planners rightly believed that Iraqi resistance might collapse if it was deprived of command and control lines of communications.[19]

During the first week of the air war, few Iraqi aircraft sortied, but those that did proved to be easy prey, as thirty-eight Iraqi MiGs were destroyed by Allied planes. Not long after, the Iraqi Air Force sent 115 of 140 aircraft to Iran. This mass exodus caught Coalition leaders by surprise, since Iran and Iraq were still bitter enemies, and most experts expected the Iraqis to seek safe haven in Jordan. Indeed, Coalition aircraft were on alert to engage Iraqi aircraft flying across western Iraq. Following this first bugout, the Americans established a cordon of F-15 and F-14 fighters along the Iraq-Iran border. As a result, the Iraqi Air Force never was a factor in the war.[20]

The next and broadest phase of the air campaign targeted nodes throughout Iraq and Kuwait. These included Scud missile launchers, weapons of mass destruction (WMD) production facilities, weapons research facilities, and naval stores. Many command bunkers were destroyed, as well as eleven of twenty power stations, with six heavily damaged. More than one-third of Coalition airpower focused on attacking Scuds, which were on trucks and therefore difficult to locate. Some American and British special forces teams had been covertly inserted into western Iraq to aid in the search for and destruction of these missiles, but the lack of adequate terrain for concealment hindered their operations, and many of them were killed or captured, as in the infamous case of the Bravo Two Zero patrol. In what became known as the Great Scud Hunt, Coalition forces spent a lot of time and energy seeking and destroying those missile systems in a desperate effort to keep Israel out of the war and to protect Allied service personnel in Saudi Arabia. Sadly, one Scud did get through Allied missile defenses on February 25, killing twenty-eight and wounding ninety-eight Army reservists in Dhahran.[21]

Among the television accounts of the techno-war, the AC-130s also played an important role. After a brief lull in air attacks because of bad weather, on January 22, 1991, the air campaign resumed, concentrating around Basra, the main Iraqi supply route from Baghdad into Kuwait. Orbiting E-8A Joint Surveillance and Target Attack Radar System (JSTARS) aircraft, being used for the first time in the war, discovered a massive Iraqi convoy headed into Kuwait. They vectored an AC-130H and two A-10 Thunderbolt IIs into the area. The aircraft struck with devastating effect, totally destroying fifty-eight of the seventy-one vehicles in the convoy and tearing up all the surrounding roads and bridges supporting the convoy's advance.[22]

The Battle for Khafji

As planning went forward for the ground invasion, and the air war continued with crushing success, the Iraqis brought the war to the Allies' front door. On January 29, 1991, in two towns named Khafji and Al Wafrah, just across the Iraq-Saudi border, Iraqi ground forces met Allied forces for the first time, and airpower played a key role. As those who planned the air war no doubt believed, later reports proclaimed that airpower would prove essential to victory. As one specific report on Khafji claimed, "Air superiority is prerequisite for the successful application of maneuver warfare. With air superiority, your ground forces are able to move at will." The report concluded: "Without air superiority, your ground forces are vulnerable to attack in both day and night, and will be unable to move without risking heavy loss, loss of unit cohesion and possibly lead to your ground units' destruction."[23]

This initial battle began late on January 29, when fifty Iraqi tanks and fifteen hundred mobilized infantry troops attacked a Marine screening patrol force and drove them out of Khafji. Unbeknown to the Iraqis, a handful of Marines were still in the town, hiding on the roofs and calling in close air support and artillery fire. For the first time in the war, Coalition ground forces struck back, as elements of the 1st Marine Division counterattacked using antitank weapons and automatic weapons. E-8A JSTARS aircraft reported that two divisions of Iraqi reinforcements were on the way. Officials directed an AC-130H to the area to assault the relief column. The gunship slaughtered the reinforcing troops, forcing the survivors to flee for their lives. The next day, the combat continued, with the Americans threatening to overrun the Iraqi positions.[24]

The battle would ultimately last until January 31. Throughout the conflict, the AC-130s flew cover against the enemy vehicular traffic in and around Khafji. Early on the last day, Saudi and Qatari forces arrived to support the Marines. They made a frontal attack on the town, supported by two AC-130Hs. With such a display of lethal and accurate firepower, the Iraqis withdrew, and the Marines soon retook the town. Coalition forces lost three armored vehicles while destroying twenty-four enemy tanks and thirteen other armored vehicles. During the three days of combat, the Allied airpower remained constantly overhead ready to spring into action against any and all targets at a moment's notice. All totaled, the gunships and other close air support aircraft left more than three hundred Iraqi vehicles smoldering wrecks between Khafji and Kuwait. As Gen. Charles Horner, the Central Air Forces (CENTAF) commander noted: "Systems that were especially effective were the AC-130 gunship patrolling the coast road by being just offshore of the coast in southern Kuwait." The stunning victory did not come without a price. In the darkness of early morning, one A-10 mistakenly fired on a Marine light armored vehicle, killing seven Marines.[25]

Each night the gunships licked their chops at the prospect of plentiful targets, minimum antiaircraft defense, and no enemy aircraft. They feasted on the enemy columns during each of the three nights. However, as the dawn light began to break through, the AC-130Hs were ordered out of the area for fear they would become easy targets for shoulder-fired SAMs. On the night of January 30, gunship T/N 69-6567, call sign Spirit 03, nicknamed *Ghost Rider,* was busy on station. With so many high-value targets under their guns, the crew was reluctant to withdraw with their mission incomplete. However, this night their luck ran out when suddenly, without warning, an enemy shoulder-fired SAM, probably an SA-14 or SA-16, struck the AC-130H. The ensuing explosion hurled the gunship to the ground, killing all fourteen crew members on board. It was the worst single loss of the air war.[26] As Generals McCutchan and Wilson recalled many years later, "It was a tragic loss that affected every single member of the gunship community." Indeed, it was an event that no one who flies gunships has forgotten to this day.[27]

The air campaign continued for four more weeks before the land invasion began. Throughout, a variety of aircraft performed a myriad of tasks, from B-52s stationed at Diego Garcia carpet bombing dug-in Iraqi positions,

Ghost Rider undergoing field maintenance.

to fighter-bombers using PGMs to shut off oil leaks and extinguish oil fires purposely started by the Iraqis. Ultimately, the air campaign devastated entire Iraqi brigades deployed in the open desert in combat formation and prevented effective Iraqi resupply to forward deployed units engaged in the actual fighting. It also stopped hundreds of thousands of Iraqi troops from concentrating for the upcoming land battle.[28]

While the air war seemed to presuppose victory, American leaders grew concerned that it had not yet caused Hussein to give in on any points. Of course there were those who suggested that, given enough time, the air campaign would bring about the results the US wanted and with less loss of life. Then and now there certainly seemed to be good evidence that this was true. However, anxious area commander General Schwarzkopf pushed for planning to move forward with a ground assault. Throughout the planning phase, many senior officers, including the general himself, feared that even if the Coalition won, it might do so only with heavy casualties.[29]

Maj. Gen. Richard Larson, Schwarzkopf's senior in-theater Army supply and logistics officer, recounted a story to this author that on one especially dark desert night, not long before the ground campaign began, an agitated General Schwarzkopf gathered several of his senior officers together, put them in Humvees, and drove them to a spot near the front lines where they could observe the enemy defenses through high-resolution night-vision binoculars. After everyone had had a turn to peer at the impressive Iraqi walls of sand, he turned to them and declared, "Do you see those fortifications . . . that barbed wire . . . those tank traps? Two, three, four, ten thousand maybe more of our boys could die taking those positions! I'll be responsible! How can I face their mothers and fathers? How can I face the American people?" Everyone stood dumbfounded. After a tense moment the general loaded everybody up and returned to headquarters. No one ever spoke of the incident again. Still, it indicated that even in the minds of the American leaders, the subsequent battles were not something they took for granted.[30]

In retrospect, however, those involved should have seen the results coming, since the Iraqis had been trained and supplied by the Soviet Union, and American and European forces had been preparing for a Soviet mechanized land invasion in Western Europe for forty-five years. Simply stated, the Iraqis were a light beer version of their Soviet instructors. The Coalition ground forces also had the significant advantage of being able to operate under the protection of Allied airpower achieved in the first hours and days of the war. They also had two important technological advantages, since their main battle tanks proved to be much better than the Iraqis.' The American M-1 Abrams, British Challenger 1, and Kuwaiti M-84AB were superior to the export version of the Soviet-built T-72 tanks used by the Iraqis. Besides, Coalition crews were better trained and had properly developed armored doctrine. They also employed global positioning satellite system (GPS) technology, which made it possible to navigate without reference to roads or other fixed landmarks. As a result, they could fight a battle of maneuver rather than one of encounter. They knew where they were and where the enemy was, so they could attack specific targets at a safe distance rather than wandering all over the desert and shooting at whatever forces they happened upon.[31]

Throughout early and mid-February 1991, Coalition aircraft continued to pound Iraqi targets, and Allied reconnaissance units continually probed Iraqi defenses. On February 22, Iraqi Foreign Minister Tariq Aziz agreed to a Soviet-brokered ceasefire that called for Iraq to withdraw their forces from Kuwait within twenty-four hours. However, the ceasefire soon fell apart without Iraqi troops withdrawing from Kuwait. On February 24, the American VII Corps launched an armored attack into Iraq just to the west of Kuwait, taking Iraqi forces completely off-guard. Concurrently, the US XVIII Airborne Corps began a sweeping left-end run across a mostly undefended portion of desert in southern Iraq. The assault was spearheaded by the 3rd Armored Cavalry Regiment and the 24th Infantry Division. The left flank of the invasion was protected by the French 6th Light Armored Division, including units of the

French Foreign Legion and elements of the US 82nd Airborne Division. This swiftly moving force soon rolled over the Iraqi 45th Infantry Division, suffering only a handful of casualties. Once through the initial enemy line, they took up blocking positions to prevent any enemy troops from enfilading the Coalition flank. The right flank of the assaulting forces was guarded by the British 1st Armored Division. Once they were deep into Iraqi territory, they turned eastward, initiating an attack against the Republican Guard's right flank. Soon, elements of the US 101st Airborne Division had reached the south bank of the Euphrates River and stood astride Iraqi Highway 8, a primary supply route into Kuwait, poised for the final movement into Kuwait itself.[32]

Rather than the protracted bloodbath many had feared, the battle became a rout. Many thousand Iraqi conscripts began to surrender as soon as the shooting began. Some even surrendered to TV camera crews and news reporters, stripping off their uniforms to show everyone they were wearing American clothes underneath. One conscript wearing a Chicago Bears T-shirt stared into a television camera and in perfect English exclaimed, "God bless America." Indeed, the advance was much swifter than most Allied generals had expected, and by February 25, Iraqi commanders began planning a withdrawal out of Kuwait. As the advance units filtered out, they set fire to Kuwaiti oil fields. Soon a long line of trucks and vehicles formed, preparing to use the main highway out of Kuwait. With so many troops and vehicles in one location, soon a major target of opportunity presented itself as the Coalition got wind of Iraqi plans.[33]

On the night of February 25, one particular stretch of highway out of Kuwait received specific attention from an E-8A JSTARS. Coalition intelligence had alerted their leadership that the Iraqis might try to evacuate Kuwait City. Soon the E-8 radars lit up like Broadway on opening night. In what some reporters described as the "mother of all retreats," thousands of military and civilian vehicles, laden with looted goods, began to leave, clogging the four-lane highway like rush-hour traffic on I-285 in Atlanta. Little did the Iraqis realize that they had been spotted and targeted. The CENTAF command center quickly organized an assault force that included F-15E Strike Eagles with the Low Altitude Navigation and Targeting Infrared for Night System (LANTIRN) leading a dozen other Allied aircraft such as gunship helicopters and fixed-wing gunships. They struck without warning, first hitting targets near Mutla Ridge, cutting off the escape route, and then turning on the tail end of the retreating Iraqis as they left Kuwait City so they could not move in either direction. Using F-15Es and A-10s in daylight and helicopter and fixed-wing gunships at night, Allied airpower decimated the enemy column. In what became known as the Highway of Death, more than fourteen hundred vehicles, including fourteen tanks, were destroyed, and three hundred Iraqi soldiers were killed, since most had the good sense to abandon their vehicles and flee into the desert.[34] As General McCutchan recalls, "Richard S. Haddad [today major general] got the most kills for the 711 SOS over the 'Highway of Death' and for all of Desert Storm reserve gunship participation."[35]

As the second and third days' momentum continued to grow, Allied ground forces encountered more trouble from the mud created by unexpected rain showers than from enemy resistance. The Coalition air assets were also slowed by the bad weather, but whenever they could get into the air, they continued to inflict terrible destruction on the Iraqi columns. The AC-130s and other CAS aircraft flew three thousand sorties on February 27, 1991. With enemy AAA and SAM sites totally eliminated by A-10 "Warthogs" and F-15E Strike Eagles, the night skies became the perfect hunting ground for the gunship predators. Indeed, on February 25, two A-10s destroyed twenty-three tanks and damaged ten. The AC-130 night action reaped a similar harvest, destroying more than two dozen tracked vehicles. These attacks became so successful that with the Coalition ground forces facing so little opposition, 61 percent of the air sorties were converted from close air support to interdiction attacks featuring gunships and attack aircraft.[36]

Some enemy units did escape Mutla Ridge, only to be trapped by another choke point at the Hawr al Hammar Causeway (Hammar Lake) and along the nearby marshes just north of Basra. There, F-111s led another wave of air attacks, which destroyed six hundred more enemy trucks on February 26 and 27. Concurrently, Allied ground forces pressed their assault, and on the afternoon of February 26, 1991, the 2nd Armored Cavalry Regiment encountered the Republican Guard's Tawakalna Division. In just six minutes they annihilated the enemy units. Early the next day, the 24th Infantry Division took the Tallil and Jalibah airfields, and soon after, Coaliton forces, led by Arab forces, marched into Kuwait City itself. While US Marines had actually entered the city the previous night, the honor of the capture went to the Arab members of the Coalition. The Marines did get credit for taking Al Jaber Airbase and Kuwait International Airport. In the midst of the euphoria surrounding the liberation of Kuwait City, the war continued as both sides made a mad dash for the Iraqi border, where the war would be decided once and for all. On February 27, at Medina Ridge, the 1st Armored Division encountered the Medina Armored Division of the Republican Guard, which was not prepared to give up just yet. Many experts described the battle as the largest tank engagement since the 1943 Battle of Kursk on World War II's Eastern Front. It proved to be a mismatch. In only two hours the Americans destroyed three hundred enemy armored vehicles and killed dozens of Iraqis. The United States lost one killed.[37]

That afternoon, after consulting with General Powell and wishing not to appear to be piling on, President Bush announced that the United States would end hostilities at 8:00 a.m. local time on February 28. Coalition troops were ordered not to fire unless attacked. The time was selected since it was exactly one hundred hours since the ground campaign began. That same day, Aziz notified the United Nations that Iraq would accept a ceasefire and all twelve UN resolutions. Even so, sporadic fighting continued, with the most intense coming on March 2, when the 24th Infantry Division, continuing its eastward movement, encountered the Republican Guard's elite Hammurabi Division. Up to that point they had been all but untouched during the conflict. They were spread out along the road leading to the partially destroyed Hawr al Hammar Causeway. With the Americans arrayed to the west of their chaotic retreat, the frightened Iraqis opened fire. For the next few hours, US armor and Apache helicopter gunships ravaged the Iraqis. When the smoke and dust cleared, 185 armored vehicles, including sixty tanks, four hundred trucks, and thirty-four artillery pieces, lay in smoldering ruin. Dozens of Iraqis died, and hundreds more became prisoners. Sadly, one of the biggest battles of the war came after the initial cease-fire and need not have happened had the Iraqi leaders done their job of telling their troops to surrender. Finally, on the morning of March 3, at Safwan, Iraq, General Schwarzkopf and Saudi Lt. Gen. Khalid bin Sultan, commander of the Arab Coalition forces, met with eight Iraqi senior officers for about one hour. The Iraqis had little choice but to accept UN terms and end the war. On April 1, 1991, at 10:00 a.m. Eastern Standard Time, Iraq formally accepted the ceasefire resolution, and the Persian Gulf War came to an end.[38]

The Result of the War and Its Effects on Airpower

Clearly, US airpower had proved to be the dominating factor in the war. Throughout the conflict Air Force, Navy, and Coalition aircraft roamed the skies over Iraq with impunity. According to the *Gulf War Airpower Survey* (*GWAPS*) Coalition aircraft flew 118,661 sorties during the 44 days of Operation Desert Storm and 147,375 during the 163 days of Operation Desert Shield. During Desert Storm the Air Force flew 60 percent of the sorties, the Navy 15 percent, the Marines 9 percent, and Coalition air forces 26 percent. Coalition air forces during Desert Shield lost twenty-four aircraft, including seven Air Force aircraft, and during Desert Shield, thirty-eight, with fourteen being Air Force. In addition, thirty-four airmen died in the war and eight were captured. While they were returned to freedom after the ceasefire, the POWs had suffered terrible treatment while in captivity. Numbers aside, as *GWAPS* authors noted: "It was not the number of tanks or artillery pieces destroyed, or the number of Iraqi soldiers killed that mattered. It was the effectiveness of the air campaign in breaking apart the organizational structure and cohesion of enemy military force and in reaching the 'mind of the Iraqi soldiers' that counted."[39]

Of the thirty-four airmen who perished in the Persian Gulf War, fourteen were the crew members of Spirit 03. As General Horner later remarked, "The AC-130 problem was it is vulnerable to ground fire, and of course, we lost Spectre 03 with the people on board." However, he also noted: "On the other hand, its ability to find targets at night and strike them with precise fire, through primarily its 105 howitzer, was critical to stopping the establishment of particularly air defenses as the Iraqi forces came forward. It was blowing them away before they could get set up." Later, in the official report of the Battle of Khafji, he went on to say, "There is no getting around the effectiveness of AC-130s' 105 howitzer firing into vehicles coming down that coastal road. I think those were probably our most effective munitions during the battle of Khafji."[40]

Although they did not make the headlines or video clips as the PGMs or F-117As did, the AC-130s played a significant role in chewing up Iraqi vehicular and infantry targets. Many Marines and soldiers survived the war because of AC-130 close air support. By the time the last gunships returned to Hurlburt Field on May 27, 1991, the United States had turned its attention to maintaining the peace in Iraq, protecting the Kurds, and reconstituting the forces it had used to win the victory in the Gulf. The 16th SOS and 711th SOS were part of that process.[41]

When Desert Storm began, the 16th SOS was not at full strength, since many of its H models were undergoing SOF improvement modifications. In fact, by the end of the war combat losses and damage left only two H models in Iraq and Kuwait airworthy. During the conflict the 16th SOS's AC-130Hs flew armed reconnaissance, interdiction, CAS, airbase ground defense, and ground and airborne alert missions. The most successful missions were preplanned interdiction sorties, which included several deep penetration missions into enemy territory to destroy early warning radar or known or suspected Soviet Scud missile sites. Like so many young airmen during the war, the 16th SOS crews spent several hours behind Iraqi lines in the heart of the most lethal threat environment of the war, searching for targets of opportunity. While they were frequently successful in destroying many high-value targets, on several occasions they were attacked by infrared and radar-guided missiles and intense AAA. While they managed to survive by taking extreme evasive maneuvers, the process began to place stress on both the crews and the aging airframes. Two of the aircraft were worn beyond their airframe air-time limits and had to be returned home for routine inspections and maintenance as well as extra work brought on by flying more than they should.[42]

As the Gulf War air campaign evolved, preplanned interdiction assignments were reduced and armed reconnaissance increased. One of the main reasons for this was the in-flight diversions needed to fly the preplanned missions. Frequently crews had to make time-sensitive decisions about viability of the operations while airborne and lacked current, accurate intelligence and threat information. The best example of the kind of potential danger this caused was the destruction of Spirit 03 during the battle of Khafji. This proved to be the first time in the war that the 16th SOS flew a direct ground support operation providing specific CAS for embattled Marines. In their after-action reports the Marines had high praise for the Spectres.[43]

However, the gunship crews' zealousness also created a dangerous situation. As noted earlier, on January 31 the dedication to the mission of Maj. Paul Weaver and his crew caused them to remain over their targets too long. They had been the third gunship over the targets and had destroyed several enemy targets that threatened the Marines on the ground. As the dawn broke, they were ordered home. However, the rules of engagement left it to the crew to decide whether to continue the mission. Concerned for the safety of their comrades on the ground, and aware of the numerous high-value targets still under their guns, they stayed to take out one last target: a FROG (free rocket over ground) missile system. As Clay McCutchan notes so well in his survey of the AC-130s; "A nighttime weapon system caught in the early morning light is not good!" This time their luck ran out, and they were shot down by a shoulder-fired SAM. This was the single greatest air loss during the Gulf War, and as General McCutchan recalls, it was an event that "cast a pall over gunship operations for the rest of the conflict."[44] And, I might add, it is still in the back of every gunship crew member's mind when he or she launches on a combat mission.

Capt. Phil Lebrun commanded one of the 16th SOS gunships that flew over Iraq. During the nighttime hours of January 21–22, 1991, officials ordered his AC-130H to attack a reported Scud site and other high-value targets. They soon flew into an area of heavy 23mm and 37mm AAA fire. Even so, they were able to strike several enemy facilities, such as two missile launchers and an early warning radar command and control building. Vectored to additional targets, they registered an SA-8 SAM launch and had to execute an acute defensive maneuver. Even as they seemed to avert this danger and leveled out, they found themselves bracketed in by more Iraqi AAA and SAM fire. Eventually, LeBrun and his crew dodged every round and returned to base.[45]

On another occasion, Capt. Bill Preaskorn and his crew flew into a similar situation when they were directed to find and destroy a Scud missile storage facility and early warning radars. They arrived over the target to discover that the threat environment was much worse than anticipated. Almost immediately, an SA-6 crew locked on and fired. The AC-130H quickly undertook several defensive turns and procedures to evade the missiles. No sooner had they leveled off than an SA-8 SAM radar got a fix on them, which forced them toward the fire from several antiaircraft batteries. Only some of the most skillful defensive flying maneuvers possible allowed them to escape. While the flak shrapnel had left holes in the wings and fuselage, none of the damage was catastrophic, and Preaskorn was able to return to base safely. Throughout the Gulf War, while the fixed-wing gunships proved, as they had in Vietnam and elsewhere, that they were one of the most effective air weapons available, the defensive weapons they faced reminded everyone involved that they were after all made from vulnerable cargo airframes and were flying in some of the most lethal areas of the war.[46]

Ultimately, airpower became the key to victory in the first Gulf War. Maj. Gen. Thomas Olsen, CENTAF deputy commander during Operation Desert Storm, spent most of his time up close and personal during the air operation missions. He declared in a 1996 interview: "Air power was the key here. The ability to be flexible and to move the impact of air power was a key to the success of this battle. When we figured out where they were and where they stopped, then they became fixed targets." He went on to say: "We had a lot of air power going into Kuwait. We had aircraft going into the northern, western, southern Kuwait, attacking the in-place forces, attacking the air defenses, the air bases, whatever was necessary in Kuwait." As for the gunships he concluded, as did so many others who were on scene, that "once we knew the enemy's location it was easy to shift some of those forces immediately over to that target area. We did that with the A-10 and some Marine AV-8s and other aircraft like the AC-130. Indeed, it was this vectoring of resources such as the AC-130s that allowed Air Power in the Gulf to not only operate as a strategic force that destroyed the enemy's command, control and communications nodes but as a tactical support military component that was the primary weapon that chewed up enemy ground forces so effectively."[47]

General Olsen, like General Horner, had nothing but the highest praise for the gunships. As he put it:

> The AC-130 had a long time proven capability, because it had been with us since the Vietnam War. All we've done in those years since the Vietnam War is to improve the capabilities of the AC-130. The only problem with the AC-130 is you can't put it into a heavily defended area. It has to go into an area where it can survive. When it was employed that 105mm cannon along with its 20mm Gatling guns, it's a very devastating weapon. You cannot hide from it! If you're on the ground you'll be found, because it has infrared sensors. It has radar sensors and all these sensors locate the targets very, very well.[48]

So, as the Gulf War wound down, it became clear that not only had the effectiveness of new airpower weapons and technology been at the core of the victory over Saddam Hussein's forces in Kuwait and Iraq, but so had older weapon systems such as the AC-130s and B-52s. It had been the gunships that had played such a lethal role in the devastation of Iraqi ground forces and in bringing to a conclusion the final phase of the ground war. They had once again done their job well, and so as the spring of 1991 unfolded, plans were made to redeploy the AC-130s back home to the panhandle of Florida.

As was often the case throughout the lifespan of the AC-130s, combat not only won victories but also taught the Air Force lessons. In this particular case, following their return home the AC-130Hs were slowly but surely rotated through their ground depot station either with their Lockheed contractor or Warner Robins Air Logistics Center (WR-ALC) to have the Sundstrand Mark VII Ground Proximity Warning System installed. At the same time, the AC-130As were fitted with Night Vision Imaging System (NVIS) compatible lighting. Both new systems would soon play an important role in the success of both AC-130 models in later combat scenarios.[49]

Operation Provide Comfort, No-Fly Zones, and the March toward Somalia

As the victorious Allied forces returned from the Gulf, Saddam Hussein turned on the ethnic minority in northern Iraq known as the Kurds. Soon a civil conflict broke out in which the Iraqis used helicopters to drop napalm and chemical warfare agents on the Kurdish rebels and their villages. Unwilling to intervene for second time in Iraq, this time in Iraq's internal affairs, the Coalition powers decided to keep most of their forces on the sidelines. However, the brutish nature of Hussein's attacks caused President Bush to set up a safe zone in northern Iraq along the Turkish border. On April 5, 1991, the president authorized a massive relief effort, known as Operation Provide Comfort. Soon some 350,000 individuals were squeezed into the safe area, being supplied and protected by the 7440th Composite Wing flying out of Incirlik AB, Turkey. What was supposed to last 90–120 days continued throughout the 1990s, and by 1996 one estimate placed the number of refugees at 1.3 million. Soon, the Shiite minority in southern Iraq also rebelled, and the 4404th Composite Wing was created to fly the same sort of missions for them.[50]

The United States created a no-fly zone in both northern and southern Iraq to keep Iraqi military aircraft out of the refugee zones. At first the Iraqi pilots were not very aggressive, but on December 27, 1992, two Iraqi MiG-25s attempted to intercept two F-16Ds of the 33rd Fighter Squadron patrolling the no-fly zone. One enemy pilot fired an air-to-air missile at one of the F-16s as they crossed the 32nd parallel. The Iraqi pilot's missile missed. The two-seat F-16D, piloted by Lt. Col. Gary North, responded by firing an AIM-120A and downing the MiG-25. During the next several weeks, the Iraqis continued to be increasingly brazen. They even set up missile batteries along the Kuwaiti border. On the night of January 13, 1993, 104 US, British, and French aircraft, including F-15Cs, F-15Es, F-16Cs, F-16Ds, and F-117As, all guided by AWACS E-3s, attacked several missile sites near Kut and Basra. While bad weather frustrated their initial attack, the operation continued for several days and destroyed most of the sites. On January 17 an F-16C downed an Iraqi MiG-29, and later that day, Navy ships attacked the Zafaraniyah nuclear fabrication facility southwest of Baghdad with Tomahawk missiles, causing catastrophic damage. Unfortunately, one missile strayed and struck the Al Rashid Hotel, causing severe damage and several civilian casualties.[51]

Throughout the remainder of the decade, the two sides continued the game of cat and mouse, highlighted by an Iraqi plot to assassinate former president Bush as he visited Kuwait in April 1993. President Bill Clinton responded by authorizing the launch of thirty-three Tomahawk missiles against the Iraqi secret police buildings in Baghdad on June 26, 1993.

These events did not take place without tragedy. One of the worst friendly fire tragedies in history occurred on April 15, 1994, when an F-15C accidently fired on two US Army helicopters, killing all twenty-six on board. It was a sobering reminder that Operation Desert Storm might be over, but the conflict with Saddam Hussein was not.[52]

Somalia and More Jobs for the AC-130s

As the Persian Gulf continued to be a major focus for the US defense world throughout the 1990s, commitments to other parts of the world also became a concern for American interests. Eventually, the 16th SOS and its AC-130H crews would be engaged in combat again. Once more, in spite of their overall success, tragedy would strike the small band of brothers.

Along the horn of Africa lay the destitute nation of Somalia and its fractured political situation. For many years the country had suffered from famine, disease, and civil war. The struggle among the ruling warlords had left thousands dead, homeless, and struggling to survive. UN Secretary-General Boutros Boutros-Ghali begged his member states to provide aid, and on August 4, 1992, President Bush approved a humanitarian effort named Operation Provide Relief. It airlifted thousands of tons of supplies to Africa through the efforts of the newly organized Air Mobility Command.[53]

The humanitarian flights began on August 17, 1992, as supplies arrived at Moi International Airport, Mombasa, Kenya, aboard C-130 and C-141 aircraft. On August 21, C-130s of the 314th Airlift Wing began arriving at airfields and airstrips along the Somali border. A week later, C-130s commenced flying into Somalia itself, landing on dirt or worn-out runways. In total they flew 1,598 sorties and off-loaded 13,404 tons of relief supplies. Unfortunately, because of the fractured political system, much of those supplies failed to reach those in the greatest need. To protect the supplies the United Nations sent one thousand Pakistani soldiers and their equipment on C-141s and C-5s to Mogadishu, the Somali capital. While the stores were now safe, the force was too small to protect key routes into the interior of the nation, where the famine was worst. Ships soon began to arrive with additional provisions, only to be shelled along with the harbor storehouses. The secretary-general called for US help to prevent a massive famine.

On November 26, 1992, President Bush ordered forty thousand troops to Somalia to support the relief effort. One week later, the UN Security Council passed Resolution 794 sanctioning the use of American troops to secure Operation Provide Relief. While France, Italy, Belgium, Canada, Australia, Pakistan, and smaller forces from twenty other nations joined the US contingent, the vast majority of troops were Americans.[54]

President Bush formally assigned Gen. Joseph P. Hoar and CENTCOM the task of carrying out the Somali mission. In turn, Hoar designated Lt. Gen. Robert Johnston (USMC) as commander of Joint Task Force Somalia, later renamed the United Task Force, or UTF. Units of the Marine 1st Expeditionary Force and the Army's 10th Mountain Division, as well as Air Force and Navy elements, were at the focal point of what was now named Operation Restore Hope. As the military component gathered, the relief mission continued. The operation officially began on December 9, 1992, when airlifters from McGuire AFB, New Jersey, landed in Mogadishu carrying the first Marine units. This was just the beginning of one of the most complex airlift operations in Air Force history, involving cargo and refueling aircraft landing at airfields throughout Africa and the Middle East. Mogadishu Airport remained the focal point of the initial phase of the operation. On December 22, Air Mobility Command delivered 923 tons of cargo, the most of any single day of the mission. On December 31, 1,470 troops arrived, the largest number of troops on any single day. On January 24, 1993, 450 fixed-wing and helicopter aircraft landed or took off, making it the single busiest day. While it was not the Berlin Airlift, flying the Hump, or even the Gulf War airlift, it was still a major undertaking. It was an operation that would also soon involve gunships of the 16th SOS.[55]

The initial amphibious and airborne landings became an unexpected media circus, with news cameras filming Navy SEALs as they emerged from the surf and thirteen hundred Marines landing via helicopter at Mogadishu Airport. Fortunately, there was no resistance to them, and within two weeks the Coalition forces had established a secure zone from which to expand their operations. On December 20, 1992, Allied troops pushed out to open roads for relief convoys. They secured airfields at Baidoa and Baledogle and the second largest city in Somalia, Kismayu, and its port. Kismayu had the longest runway in the country, and C-141s and C-5s were able to use it to ferrying in elements of the 10th Mountain Division to secure that part of the nation. On December 31, phase II began as UTF forces expanded security operations into central Somalia. Phase III finally secured southern Somalia in January, and the situation appeared stabilized enough for General Johnston to turn over the operation to a UN peacekeeping force. By May 4, 1993, officials declared Restore Hope completed. During the 147 days of the mission the Air Force had deployed or redeployed forty-eight thousand personnel and delivered thirty-two thousand tons of supplies.[56]

While four thousand American forces remained in Somalia, most of the UN force was from eight other nations, which soon discovered that it was one thing to supply starving Somalis but quite another to end the clan wars that had plagued Somalia for far too many years. On June 5, 1993, the forces of Mohammed Farah Aideed, strongman in Mogadishu, ambushed Pakistani troops, killing twenty-four. It was then that the AC-130Hs entered the conflict.[57]

On June 11, US special operations forces moved to quell the growing civil violence and restore order in the capital city. The ground operations were supported by three AC-130Hs from the 16th SOS. That same unit had provided CAS during the initial contingency landings and operations nearly seven months earlier. This time they led the ground forces into Mogadishu. First, they cut Aideed's communications centers, destroyed radio towers used to broadcast his propaganda messages, and demolished the clan's nearby compound, which housed dozens of military vehicles and senior clan leaders. The gunship's 105mm and 40mm cannons bent the seemingly indestructible radio towers into twisted metal wreckage. The mission proved so successful that five days later, on June 16, the AC-130Hs were back over Mogadishu, this time utterly destroying Aideed's headquarters facilities. The gunships returned with devastating precision twice more in June and July. Still, Aideed survived, and without sufficient ground forces or overall Allied resolve to press the initiative, he was able to hide and reconstitute after each attack. As a result, he could order attacks on relief convoys and steal provisions meant for famine victims.[58]

Throughout the summer, things grew worse. Concerned about the safety of US military and civilian personnel in Somalia, President Clinton directed Secretary of Defense Les Aspin to deploy a joint special operations task force to respond to enemy attacks on UN forces and relief personnel. Designated Task Force Ranger, its assignment was to capture Aideed, who had gone into deep underground hiding following the highly effective AC-130 attacks. There existed a confusing chain of command that often separated UN and American command structures. Even so, by August 28, 1993, these new units were in place and were carrying out numerous tactically successful raids. One on September 21 captured Osman Atto, one of Aideed's primary deputies. In spite of the overall success of that raid, an ominous trend began. For the first time in the conflict, US personnel took fire from RPGs. The Pakistanis lost an armored personnel carrier and two killed during one sortie into the city. On the one hand, while Aideed was pinned down in hiding, he was also still free and giving orders. As a result, the level of violence increased. It soon reached a terrible climax.[59]

The first indication of Aideed's resolve came on September 8, 1993, when US and Pakistani troops, attempting to clear roadblocks near the so-called Cigarette Factory were fired on by 106mm recoilless rifles, RPGs, and small arms. Only an intense response by Allied forces quelled the violence. Later that day, militia forces supported by a mob of more than a thousand attacked the same unit. Several other similar engagements occurred throughout the remainder of the month. On September 25, things became extremely tense. On a sweep of the most active area, a US Army MH-60 Black Hawk helicopter was shot down, and two soldiers of the 101st Airborne and one from the 25th Aviation Regiment were killed. American and Pakistani troops secured the area under heavy fire and recovered the bodies. The most alarming aspect of this attack was that a single RPG had brought down the helicopter. Just a week later a full-fledged battle would occur that would cause many more casualties.[60]

Things in Somalia soon went from bad to worse for the US peacekeepers. In the mid-afternoon of October 3, 1993, Task Force Ranger (Delta Force and Army Rangers) initiated its seventh mission. It focused on Aideed's stronghold in the Black Sea slum area near the Bakara Market. The aim was to capture Aideed's two top subordinates. The attack area was a maze of narrow streets and tightly packed buildings unfamiliar to the Americans. The lead elements of the assault were helicopters, mostly Army MH-60 Black Hawks. As they took up a hover position to disembark their troops, they came under heavy fire, as did the advancing ground troops. Even though the blocking force soon established a perimeter and captured twenty-four Somalis to be transported back on the convoy trucks, things soon went very wrong. A Black Hawk was hit by an RPG and crashed three blocks from the target area. Immediately, a six-man team from the blocking force, an MH-6 assault helicopter, and a modified MH-60 Black Hawk with a fifteen-man combat search and rescue (CSAR) unit convoyed to the crash site to rescue the survivors. Among those heavily engaged were Air Force combat controller SSgt. Jeffery Bray and pararescue personnel MSgt. Scott C. Fales and TSgt. Tim Wilkinson. They remained on-site for more than eighteen hours, and, even though wounded themselves, they attended to other wounded comrades. When they arrived on-site, Fales and Wilkinson were the last two members of the CSAR team to depart their MH-60 helicopter. As they descended the lowering cable and touched the ground, an RPG hit their chopper. The pilot steadied the aircraft long enough for the team to reach safety and finally returned safely to base. Soon, two more MH-60s were hit, and one crashed less than a mile southwest of the first crash site. A mob overran this second site, killing MSgt. Gary Gordon and Sfc. Randall Shughart and capturing the wounded pilot. Gordon and Shughart were posthumously awarded the Congressional Medal of Honor.[61]

In the meantime, ground units secured the first crash site around 7:00 a.m. on October 4. Eventually, a full-sized armor support ground force arrived on-scene to support the withdrawal of wounded Somali prisoners and the first dead pilot's body. In spite of an intense mortar attack on October 6, the fighting soon petered out, but not without a high price. While casualty counts vary, in fact, between October 3 and 6, 1993, the Americans lost eighteen killed and eighty-four wounded, and the Somalis suffered between five hundred and eight hundred casualties. The bloody nose caused the Clinton administration to reconsider the value of the US presence in Somalia. With the United Nations unwilling to provide additional troops, the president decided to withdraw. Sending in additional troops and aircraft, including AC-130s, the president ordered theater commanders to prepare for a complete withdrawal. On October 9, US Ambassador Robert B. Oakley began negotiations to broker the release of the wounded MH-60 pilot, CW2 Michael Durant. He finally succeeded in getting Durant's release, along with that of a captured Nigerian soldier, on October 14.[62]

Within days the US announced its intention to pull out by March 31, 1994. Secretary of Defense Aspin resigned, taking partial responsibility for the failure. In fact, by March 25, 1994, all US military forces were gone except for three thousand Marines offshore to support about one thousand US civilian aid workers who were still trying to provide at least some food supplies to those starving in the countryside. A year later, with the civil war still gripping the nation, UN leaders gave up and ordered everyone out. Unfortunately, the casualty toll had risen on March 14, 1994. During a final training mission before departing the Somali theater of operations, AC-130H, T/N 69-6576, *Predator* (previously named *Bad Company, Wicked Wanda,* and *Widow Maker*), had its 105mm accidentally misfire and explode inside the fuselage. The ensuing fires spread to the wings and the engines, and the aircraft had to ditch. When it hit the water, it broke in half, and in spite of a heroic rescue effort by CSAR personnel, eight crew members died. It was one more reminder that flying in combat or even during training exercises can be a dangerous way to make a living.[63]

The Gunships Return Home Again

As the AC-130 gunships returned home in the spring of 1994, the decade was not yet half over, and they had been in the middle of two major US military deployments and combat operations. Two of their aircraft had been lost, and the sting of the memory of fallen comrades weighed heavy on the hearts of the crews. However, a new generation of gunships was about to join the AC-130Hs of the 16th SOS. In November 1994, the next generation AC-130Us would come on-line, to be operated by the 4th SOS stationed at Hurlburt Field, Florida. Eventually known as Spooky II, in honor of their older AC-47 cousins, they would ultimately replace the A models flown by the Air Force Reserve. They would soon see combat alongside their sister H models. With turmoil in Haiti and the former nation of Yugoslavia, the decade would require more US contingencies and more AC-130 deployments.

12 The Late 1990s
Repair, Upgrade, and a New Model

Throughout the 1980s and early 1990s, the AC-130As and Hs had flown long, grueling hours in lethal combat environments. With the birth of AFSOC, those involved with the fixed-wing gunships believed now was the time to build a more modern version of the AC-130. As early as August 22, 1985, funding was in place for this new gunship. Assistant Secretary of Defense for Acquisition and Logistics James P. Wade sent a memo to Secretary of the Air Force Verne Orr approving the construction of a new gunship, thus officially launching the AC-130U production program. Most officials expected Lockheed Aircraft Service Company (LASC) of Ontario, California, at that point the AFSOC's expert on the C-130 airframe, to receive the contract not to modify an old C-130 airframe but to build an AC-130 from the ground up.[1]

For many years Air Force and industry sustainment experts had been working on the AC-130A and AC-130H models to make them the most up-to-date gunships possible. In early 1972, the professionals at ASD had modified the E models with the addition of the M137A1 manually fed 105mm howitzer at position number six. This became standard equipment when the Es became Hs, and it would be included on the AC-130Us as well. All the AC-130Hs carried one hundred 105mm rounds and had three gunners to work the gun, which could fire six to ten thirty-four-pound high-explosive, armor-piercing incendiary shells per minute. As told in a previous chapter, late in 1972 the AC-130Es had their engines replaced with more powerful and efficient Allison T-56A-15 turboprop jet engines, a change so significant that the Air Force redesignated the E models as H models. Ironically, the AC-130Hs returned to action in the Vietnam War at Ubon RTAFB in March 1973 just in time for

AC-130 on final approach.

the US drawdown to enter its final phase. By the fall of 1975, all ten surviving AC-130As and all ten surviving AC-130Hs had returned to the United States, flying under the 711th SOS of the 919th SOG and the 16th SOS of the 1st SOW, respectively.[2]

In the late 1970s all special operations aircraft, including the AC-130Hs, MC-130s, EC-130s, and airborne command, control, and communications (ABCCC) aircraft, were modified with in-flight aerial refueling capabilities. To prove the worth of this modification, two AC-130Hs set a world record for C-130 airframes by flying nonstop from Hurlburt Field to Anderson AB, Guam, in 29.7 hours with four aerial refuelings.[3]

The AC-130As were not ignored. On July 19, 1982, Air Force officials issued Program Management Directive (PMD) L-Y2136 (1), T116218, directing personnel at the WR-ALC, which managed all DOD C-130 airframes, to replace all A-model Allison three-blade propellers with Hamilton-Standard four-blade propellers to extend the life expectancy of the aging AC-130A fleet. Ultimately, this project was completed by the WR-ALC at Robins AFB, Georgia, and by contract personnel at Hamilton-Standard's main plant in Schenectady, New York. Over the ensuing two years, not only were the propellers replaced, but an enhanced joint information distribution system for jam-resistant voice communications and the AN/ARC-164 Have Quick secure ultra-high frequency (UHF) antijam communications system were also installed.[4]

In December 1986, LASC concluded a contract to install precision navigation systems, dual redundant fire control computers, improved infrared targeting sensors, enhanced electronic warfare systems, and improved communications systems. It was a package that upgraded all the AC-130s in operation and extended their life for many years.[5]

Even so, the Air Force conceived an aircraft that would make a generational advance in fixed-wing gunships. On July 2, 1987, to the surprise of many senior Air Force leaders, the SECAF awarded a contract not to Lockheed, but instead to Rockwell International of El Segundo, California, to create a highly advanced AC-130H prototype. After some discussion, Rockwell experts decided to build this gunship version from the ground up and not modify an existing airframe. The result was the AC-130U. In May 1988, Rockwell concluded the preliminary design review, and they delivered the prototype AC-130U in October 1988. On September 1, 1989, they completed the critical design review. These successful milestones led to two full-scale development contracts for AC-130Us—one in October 1989 and the second in April 1990. The first flight of a production-model AC-130U lasted three hours and went from the Rockwell plant in Palmdale, California, to Edwards AFB, California.[6]

Including the prototype, the initial development effort produced twelve U models. The prototype was T/N 87-0128, *Big Daddy*. Production run number one included T/N 89-0509, *Total Carnage;* T/N 89-0510, *Gunslinger;* T/N 89-0511, *Predator;* T/N 89-0512, *Dead On;* T/N 89-0513, *Killer Instincts;* and T/N 89-0514, *Maximum Carnage*. Production run number two was comprised of T/Ns 90-0163, *Bad Omen;* 90-0164, *Bad Intentions;* T/N 90-0165, originally *Midnight Medusa* and later *Thumper;* T/N 90-0166, *Hell Raiser;* and T/N 90-0167, *Terminator*. In November 1992 a third and final contract provided for the construction of a thirteenth and, for the time being, final U model, T/N 92-0253, *Eight Ball,* to replace *Ghost Rider,* the H model lost in the Persian Gulf War.[7]

Flight testing for the AC-130Us began at Edwards AFB in February 1991 with combined AFSOC, Air Force Flight Test Center, and Rockwell flight crews. These tests generally went well, and in August they fired the 40mm and 105mm guns to see how they affected the airframe. The outcome of these tests was successful; one observer exclaimed, "This dog can hunt!" This was an important part of the testing phase, since the success of the U model's performance was predicated on its array of new targeting sensors and communications systems. Of significance was the fact that unlike the A and H models, the U models had pressurized cabins that had to be depressurized prior to firing the guns. In addition, the 20mm guns had been replaced by the GAU-12 25mm automatic Gatling gun. Capable of firing 1,800 rounds per minute from an automatically fed 3,000-round magazine, the GAU-12 normally fired short bursts of 150 to 350 rounds of half-pound high-explosive incendiary rounds capable of penetrating the thickest tank armor. The first tests of the new guns took place in December 1991. Final tests were completed two years later, and among the other components examined was the new fire control system, which provided for a dual target attack capability, with two sensors controlling the single 25mm gun to fire at different targets up to one kilometer apart. In the end, the average cost of each aircraft was $72 million.[8]

While the construction of the aircraft proved highly successful, the cost of the program and the relationship between the Air Force and the contractor left much to be desired. The original contract, first agreed upon in July 1987, budgeted for a total price tag of $432.2 million, with $152.8 million for development and $279.4 million for production. However, by the fall of 1991 the development costs had exceeded $300 million, and with production barely begun, the projected cost was more than $290 million. Indeed, the two hundred employees at Rockwell's North American Aircraft Division, Palmdale, California, plant worked around the clock to meet their deadlines and keep costs down. However, nothing seemed to salvage the situation. To save the company from economic ruin, Rockwell leaders appealed to President George H. W. Bush to recoup some of their expenses. This soon led to a major confrontation with Secretary of Defense Dick Cheney. The dispute would last for over half a decade and all but break Rockwell.[9]

Although the program crept along at an ever increasingly high cost, the company continued to exceed expectations with regard to the quality of the aircraft. While Rockwell completed the first successful test flight on December 20, 1990, it was not until March 30, 1991, that the second successful test flight took place. Once on pace, the production process moved ahead more quickly, with the fourth test flight concluded on September 4, 1992. Throughout this period, private disagreements between the contractor and Secretary Cheney slowly escalated, with Rockwell arguing that they should receive additional funding to compensate them for hundreds of millions of dollars in unintended and unexpected development and production costs.[10]

The AC-130U Becomes Operational

In spite of the increasingly difficult relationship, Rockwell delivered the first production-model AC-130U to the 4th SOS at Hurlburt Field, Florida, on July 1, 1994. Thus, it became the first "gunship to be designed and built by a non-government agency." As mentioned earlier, it was built from the ground up. Specifically, the thirteen airframes were originally intended to be C-130Hs, the most modern cargo airframe from the C-130 production line. Instead, the

U-model gunships were begun like any other C-130H but reconfigured on the assembly line so that they rolled off as gunships and not cargo aircraft.[11]

At 12:30 p.m., on November 14, 1994, during formal ceremonies at Hurlburt Field, John A. McLuckey, president of Rockwell Defense Systems; Lt. Gen. Richard Scofield, ASC commander; and Maj. Gen. James L. Hobson Jr., AFSOC commander, officially transferred the AC-130U fleet to AFSOC. By late 1996, five U models were operating with the 4th SOS. The U model was the most modern, high-tech gunship ever built. As one report noted, "It is the most complex weapon system in the world today." Capable of flying to its target with a pressurized cabin and then depressurizing to fire its ordnance, it had a cruising altitude of thirty thousand feet, an unrefueled range of twenty-two hundred miles, and essentially an unlimited refueled range. It could fight at eight thousand to twenty-five thousand feet, and its mission computer, EW, and avionics and communications systems were operated by more than six hundred thousand lines of software code, providing it with the most modern navigation, communication, and defense systems of not only any other gunship at the time, but also such aircraft as the stealthy B-2 Spirit and F-22 Raptor. Crewed by thirteen highly trained personnel, the aircraft's specific armament included the GE GAU-12/U five-barrel 25mm Gatling gun, with a maximum rate of fire limited to eighteen hundred rounds per minute; one Bofors L60 40mm cannon, with a maximum firing rate of one hundred rounds per minute; and one US Army 105mm M137A1 cannon, with a rate of fire of six to ten rounds per minute. Unique to gunships, the AC-130U incorporated a built-in test feature for its integrated diagnostic and repair system.[12]

One of the improvements on the AC-130U was the design and placement of the venerable 40mm Bofors cannon. The gun had been designed and first built by AB Bofors, Kariskoga, Sweden, in 1933, and the first production model was produced a year later. The US Army soon purchased several of the M42 versions, and not long afterward the Navy discovered that the Mk1 and Mk2 were particularly useful on their surface ships. In 1942 Chrysler Corporation contracted to build the Navy version used throughout World War II, which had a different breech casing and a water-jacketed barrel. The guns were adapted to Air Force gunships in 1967 because they were powerful and abundant, since they could be salvaged from ships being scrapped. While this made them cheap to buy, the lack of interchangeable spare parts made sustainment more expensive. The H models used M2A1-model Bofors, while the AC-130Us used modified RH models.[13]

With a gross takeoff weight of 155,000 pounds, the AC-130U carried more ordnance than any previous gunship. The thirteen crew members included five officers: the pilot, copilot, navigator, fire-control officer, and EW officer. The remaining eight crew members were NCOs: the flight engineer, the all-level light television (ALLTV) operator, the infrared detection set operator, four airborne gunners, and the loadmaster. Even with all this, the AC-130U's mission remained the same as that of its older cousins: CAS, air interdiction, and combat search and rescue support.[14]

Not All Is Well in the Gunship World

Once the U models began to come on line, the Air Force began considering what to do with the older gunships. To this end, they phased out the ten remaining Air Force Reserve AC-130As, some going to displays at places such as the Air Force Museum while others went to the Air Force boneyard at Davis-Monthan AFB, and they converted the 919th SOW into a unit flying MC-130E Combat Talons and MC-130P Combat Shadows. Ultimately, Rockwell produced thirteen AC-130Us, and by late 1997 the Air Force had two fleets of active-duty operational gunship units: the 16th SOS, which flew nine AC-130Hs, and the 4th SOS, which flew the thirteen AC-130Us. Rockwell was still bitter over the costs of the project and the Air Force's resistance to providing additional funding to make up for the cost overruns. Faced with near financial disaster, on June 26, 1995, even with the U-model production line still operating, Rockwell filed a complaint in the US Federal Court of Claims for $547 million plus interest.[15]

To be sure, Rockwell had done its job in creating a shiny new gunship, the like of which no one had ever seen. However, while they could also report a net income of $149.5 million for the first quarter of 1994, their aerospace earnings had dipped 5 percent, due to an $11 million cost adjustment on the AC-130U gunship program. Rockwell leadership believed this general pattern of cost overruns, which began from the outset of the gunship program in 1987, was due in large measure to the Air Force's constant insistence on upgrades and design changes that caused delays and costly changes in the prototype and initial production run.[16]

Not unexpectedly, Air Force leaders disagreed, arguing that the changes had not only been reasonable and necessary but were brought on by the company's methods of development and production. While both sides agreed that the aircraft itself was a marvel of modern aviation design and engineering, the disagreement over the money destroyed Rockwell's relationship with the Air Force, and as it did so, it also destroyed the solvency of its Aerospace Division. Even before the arrival of the first production model in June 1994, Rockwell had warned the Air Force not to expect early delivery of any of the remaining production models, since they had "no incentive" to do so. Soon after Rockwell filed their formal legal complaint the following year, the Air Force responded by threatening to withhold payments because of "aircraft deficiencies." ASC commander Lt. Gen. James A. Fain Jr., sent a letter to Assistant Secretary of the Air Force for Acquisitions Darleen Druyun recommending that plans go forward by the Air Force to stop payments until the Air Force completed final plans on how to respond formally to Rockwell's intransigent position.[17]

With these legal matters delaying the production line, the second AC-130U was not delivered until April 1996. According to Rockwell, the government refused to step up progress on payments, and thus put them more than $400 million behind the eight-ball. Even the Air Force admitted that Rockwell had invested $750 million at that point—a number that would ultimately reach as much as $800 million by the end of the production program.[18]

As the conflict progressed, Rockwell finally decided to escalate their claims into a formal lawsuit, designated Court of Federal Claims No. 95-425C, "Rockwell International Corporation v. United States." Since the Air Force had been sued as part of the US government, it fell to the US Justice Department to organize the case for the government. On March 5, 1996, in a letter to Maj. Gen. Hobson, James Kinsella, assistant director of the Commercial Litigation Branch, Department of Justice, formally reiterated that "Rockwell seeks $547 million plus interest for alleged contract violation by the government on the AC-130U gunship program." He went on to request Air Force assistance in gathering all related documents, which he estimated could "involve as many as 10–20 million pages." The disagreement had reached the point of no return, and in the end neither side would benefit as things existed. However, that was about to change.[19]

With such rancor spewing forth, no one really knew what would happen to the remaining AC-130U production models. While aircraft continued to arrive, the program dragged along at a snail's pace. Then, in a supremely ironic twist, on December 5, 1996, Boeing Aircraft Company announced that they were acquiring "Rockwell's aerospace and defense units in a transaction valued at approximately $3.1 billion following approval by Rockwell's shareholders." The actual signing ceremonies took place the next day. The new division of Boeing was designated Boeing North American, Inc., and was headquartered in Kent, Washington. It operated as a subsidiary of the parent Boeing Company. Boeing not only acquired thirty-four thousand highly skilled new employees and dozens of new contracts and clients, but also took over the lawsuit. One might wonder why any company would want to inherit such a conundrum as the Rockwell lawsuit. The answer is that Boeing had also obtained several very promising new contracts, such as that for the F-35 joint strike fighter, as well as several new facilities. Indeed, no sooner had Boeing taken over the AC-130U contract than aircraft began to arrive ahead of schedule. By July 1996, two more U models were delivered, and in less than two years all thirteen were at Hurlburt Field. In addition, the two sides concluded a sustainment contract, and Boeing hired eighty-seven new personnel to perform these duties.[20]

As the days passed, the legal maneuvering slacked off and the bitterness subsided. This was partly because of the passage of time, but it was also due in large measure to the fact that Boeing officials had no personal feelings invested and were looking for a solution that would bring the disagreement and the overall program to a conclusion in a peaceful and cost-effective way. Besides, with other profitable contracts moving ahead, Boeing in 1999 was much more tractable than Rockwell had been in 1995. So with both sides willing to settle things, in the spring of 1999 Air Force, Justice Department, and Boeing executives initiated a mediated settlement. All the parties agreed to resolve each and every pending claim and dispute. After twelve tempestuous years they embraced a structured process that worked toward a mutually beneficial settlement. By doing so, they were able to isolate the singular items under dispute. To this end, the government proposed, and Boeing agreed, to employ something called alternative dispute resolution, a program begun by the DOD for personnel issues in the mid-1990s. This process allowed both sides to express their point of view to an impartial mediator accepted and agreed upon by both sides. Assisted by third-party mediator Judge Martin Harty of the Armed Services Board of Contract Appeals, over a six-month period in 1999 the parties reached an agreement that settled what had become a $785 million claim. Of note were the efforts of the Air Force representative, Brig. Gen. Frank Anderson, whose friendly and positive demeanor went a long way toward melting the icy situation. Ultimately, the process succeeded because both sides realized it was in everyone's best interest, especially that of the American people.[21]

In the summer of 1997, even as the lawsuit began to work its way toward a solution, members of AFSOC leadership began inquiries with their senior historian, Herb Mason, requesting a change of the designated name of the U model from Spectre to Spooky. Crew members of the AC-130Us reasonably asserted that they wished to have their own identity separate and distinct from the AC-130Hs, which were known as Spectres. After some discussion, Mason pointed out that the AC-47 had been designated Spooky, and that while it would be a great honor to the AC-47 crews to change the U model name, perhaps it would be more proper to alter the name in some small way. Indeed, the AC-47 was no longer in the Air Force's active inventory, but some were still on display at various museums, and a few were even flying with private groups. Therefore, Mason recommended calling the AC-130U Spooky II. He wrote to the AFSOC commander: "The AC-47 was named 'Spooky,' so the AC-130Us official name cannot also be 'Spooky.'" In a responding staff summary sheet dated August 19, 1997, the AFSOC commander officially proposed naming the AC-130U "'Spooky II,' differentiating it from the Vietnam-era gunships but also honoring that aircraft by using its name." Thus, the AC-130U became the Spooky II on September 1, 1997.[22]

The 4th Special Operations Squadron

Originally, when the first U models arrived at Hurlburt Field in 1994, they were assigned briefly to the 16th SOS, but soon they were transferred to the 4th SOS. The 4th had begun operations in April 1942 as the Air Corps Ferrying Squadron. Over the next twenty-seven years it operated under numerous designations until it became the 4th SOS in August 1969. Not only did it fly attack missions in Southeast Asia, but also reconnaissance, FAC, search and rescue, and equipment testing sorties. The 4th flew C-47s, AC-47s, FC-47s, and HC-47s. It was inactivated in December 1969 when the original Spookys were turned over to the VNAF, but after several more iterations the current 4th SOS was activated on May 4, 1995. As the final twelve production-model AC-130Us left the assembly line and later their flight testing phase at Edwards AFB, they came to Hurlburt Field and were officially placed in the hands of the newly formed crews of the 4th SOS. Not long after, in October 1995, the crews and gunships flew their first missions during Exercise Foal Eagle in South Korea. The following September they made their first operational deployment to Brindisi, Italy, in support of Operation Joint Endeavor—peacekeeping operations in Bosnia-Herzegovina. That mission proved to be prophetic, since by the end of the century southeastern Europe would be the site of the next great deployment of US air forces, and the AC-130s would again be in the middle of conflict.[23]

Modifications, Maintenance, and Sustainment in the 1980s and 1990s

Both the AC-130Hs and AC-130Us remained active during the remainder of the century. Both participated in numerous contingencies, and both, especially the H model, underwent upgrades and modifications. In April 1996, operational AC-130s deployed in support of Operation Assured Response, which evacuated twenty-one hundred noncombatants from Monrovia, Liberia, which had erupted in civil violence. Not only did the AC-130s provide air cover for ground and evacuation operations, but they also guided rescue aircraft through heavy ground fire to find isolated individuals. No sooner did the H models return to the United States than they were sent through depot maintenance at Robins AFB that included the installation of the AN/ALQ-172 low-band jamming capability, through Engineering Change Proposal 93, to increase memory and flight line reprogramming capabilities. The workforce at the WR-ALC Maintenance Directorate was supported by contract employees from International Telephone and Telegraph under a sole-source, fixed-price contract that was completed late in 1996.[24]

However, this was not the only maintenance work done on the AC-130s during that period. With the gunship's services in high demand throughout the 1980s and 1990s, Air Force leadership directed the WR-ALC, by then manager of all SOF aircraft, to redouble their efforts to perform routine and special maintenance more quickly to keep the AC-130s airworthy and ready for combat. As early as August 1985, Maintenance, Materiel, Management, and Distribution Directorate personnel at WR-ALC began examining ways to reduce the flow time for programmed depot maintenance (PDM) for AC-130As and Hs, MC-130s, EC-130s and HH-53 SOF aircraft. It took several months to convince Air Force and AFLC leadership that a substantial reduction in flow time would allow for adequate and thorough standard repair work to be completed. However, with improved technology and significant dedication by the workforce, Warner Robins ALC experts convinced those above to move forward with a reduction in the flow time.[25]

In the spring of 1989, Warner Robins leaders from Materiel Management's Production Management Branch and from Maintenance's Engineering and Planning Branches created a Productivity Enhancement Working Group (Tiger Team) that determined to cut PDM on the AC-130Hs by 50 percent and on the AC-130As by 25 percent. This meant the H-model PDM went from 180 days to 90 days, and the A-model PDM from 180 days to 120 days. By the fall of 1989, one AC-130A (T/N 53-3129) and one AC-130H (T/N 69-6572) had completed PDM, the A model 49 days ahead of the new schedule and the H model 22 days ahead of the 90-day schedule. The program proved an enormous success, and the process continued to be repeated throughout the next two decades on all gunships and other SOF aircraft, keeping these aircraft ready to deploy anywhere that American interests were threatened.[26]

In late 1989, with one A model and one H model now shining with fresh paint and new parts, plans went forward to push two of each model through WR-ALC each quarter and continually rotate all the SOF aircraft through the depot as time permitted as often as possible to be sure they had the latest technology to keep the crews as safe as possible in the highly lethal combat environments in which gunships typically flew. Among the new components that each gunship got were a cutting-edge fire control system with a state-of-the-art HUD system; a new defensive system that included the most current AN/AAQ-17 FLIR; a cutting-edge navigation system that included, among other things, the APN-232 combined altitude radar altimeter system; and a new communication system with the latest secure intercommunications and brand new radios. The gunships were also fitted with newer, stronger, and more resilient 40mm and 105mm gun mounts.[27]

Throughout Desert Shield and Desert Storm the WR-ALC worked on numerous quick repair projects for the gunship fleet. For example, in March 1991 the C-130 directorate "expedited the repair of a rainbow fitting on an AC-130." The repair was on AC-130H T/N 69–6569. Its fitting was twenty-two years old, and the crack near the fitting was discovered during PDM. In fact, the problem would grow later when it would be discovered that the small cracks were the prelude to larger cracks in the center wing box that connects the two wing sections at the top of the fuselage of the C-130 airframes. The predicament arose as the center rotated the AC-130s through the repair shops just prior to combat operations beginning in the Gulf War in January 1991. In early February 1991, AC-130H 6569's ground crew discovered a very small crack in the center wing box rainbow fitting. The flight crew nursed the aircraft back to Robins AFB and inducted it into the Westside Hangar of Building 110 on February 6, 1991. With air operations already underway and the ground assault ready to begin, repairing the gunship was an urgent matter. Working around the clock, a special C-130 team at Warner Robins completed the repair work by February 15 at a cost of $200,000, and by February 16, 6569 was on its way back to the theater of operations. What would normally have taken fifty to sixty days to complete had been accomplished in nine, a testament to the dedication of the maintenance work force at WR-ALC.[28]

At the same time, Warner Robins personnel continued to work on the Special Operations Forces Improvement (SOFI) Program previously mandated at the Air Staff level. One of the key components of the SOFI proved to be the integration of the integrated navigation system under the rapid aerospace process (RAP). The navigation system included what was at the time the latest GPS. Together, Warner Robins SOF directorate and Lockheed Aeronautical Systems company personnel installed the AN/ARN-15(v)1 on seven AC-130Hs in eight weeks at a cost of $700,000. To supplement the remaining A models, the directorate obtained AN/PSN-9 GPS manpacks for use on the remaining gunships. They purchased twelve manpacks from Texas Instruments, Plano, Texas, at a cost of $400,000. Ten were for the ten A models, and two were for spares. The Warner Robins ALC RAP team traveled to Duke Field to train the Air Force Reserve ground crews on how to install the manpacks. Team members installed one, and the Duke Field personnel completed the other nine. The WR-ALC and Duke repair crews also added the new AN/ALE-40 countermeasure dispenser system (CMDS) to counter the effectiveness of the growing number of SA-7, SA-14, and HN-5A portable heat-seeking SAMs being used by enemy forces in the Gulf and elsewhere.[29]

With the downing of Spirit 03 during the Gulf War, the Air Force began installing as many anti-SAM devices and systems on the gunships as possible. Indeed, the CMDSs were only the beginning. Among the other systems was an infrared suppressor shield that significantly reduced the infrared (IR) signature of the AC-130's engine exhaust to lower the SAMs' ability to lock onto the heat signature of the aircraft's engines. In early 1992, WR-ALC awarded contract F09603–91-C-2017 to Allied-Signal Aerospace Company of Torrance, California, worth $960,867, to build four modified CC-22 prototype IR suppressors for SOF qualification and demonstration testing. The first tests put a prototype suppressor on engine three of AC-130H, T/N 69–6573, and had a select crew from the 2875th Test Flight Squadron, stationed at Robins AFB, use an IR signature measuring device to gather data to be analyzed by experts from Science Applications International Company, Panama City, Florida. Tests were completed in three phases between April and October 1992. The results of the test supported the use of the IR suppressors on the gunships. Over the next two years, this SOFI component was installed on each SOF aircraft as it rotated through the WR-ALC PDM repair depot process. This included the remaining nine H models.[30]

In 1994, Warner Robins officials began the process of installing the latest night vision imaging system (NVIS) on not just the AC-130s but all SOF aircraft. It was designed to permit, "during wartime and contingency operations, . . . certain aircraft to undertake most tactical operations at night with crews who used Night Vision Goggles (NVG)."[31] Warner Robins also completed the first phase of a project begun when the rainbow fitting exposed cracks in the center wing box of all C-130 SOF airframes. Through three and one-half years LASC, headquartered in Marietta, Georgia, and WR-ALC mechanics labored to replace the center wing box on these aircraft. The program cost $156.5 million and repaired nine AC-130Hs and forty-two other SOF aircraft. In fact, it took until 1999 to complete all aspects of the repair work, which took place during standard PDM at Robins AFB. By the end of the program it was as if there was an entirely new SOF fleet. Of course, the 16th SOS had lost another H model, and by 1995 the A models were no longer in the inventory and the U models were on-line.[32]

In 1995 yet another minor aircraft modification made on the AC-130Hs was the addition of a liquid oxygen (LOX) system ordered by Secretary of the Air

Force Sheila Widnall. With the gunships supporting Operations Deny Flight and Provide Promise in Iraq on a high operational tempo, the need to provide crews more oxygen increased. Moreover, in Vietnam the maximum operating altitude was twenty thousand feet, and most sorties were flown at eight to twelve thousand feet. In turn, crews often dropped to two to four thousand feet during attack orbits. Owing to increased threats from mobile and shoulder-launched SAMs and more accurate radar-guided AAA, the AC-130s were forced to higher altitudes of as high as forty thousand feet above sea level. To this end, Air Force leaders decided to provide a second source of oxygen for all fourteen crew members. The first modification took place on T/N 69-0574, which arrived at Robins AFB for PDM on February 4, 1995. The first installation took place in thirty-nine days, twenty-one fewer than the sixty allotted. To speed up the process, a fifteen-person team from the 653rd Combat Logistics Support Squadron traveled to Hurlburt Field to install the remaining twenty-five-liter LOX components on the remaining AC-130Hs. Work began on March 22, 1995, on T/N 69-6569, and it was completed on the eighth and final gunship, T/N 69-6577, on April 21, 1995, four days ahead of schedule. The program proved to be a complete success.[33]

In 1997 the Air Staff issued Programmed Management Directive (PMD) 2318(2)PE 1160 404BB, which directed the experts at WR-ALC to install the AN/ALQ-172(v)3 ECM jammer on the AC-130Hs. The most recent jamming system for larger aircraft available at the time, it embodied low-band frequency improvements that upgraded version one software on all SOF aircraft. The new system provided high- and low-band transmitters, antennas, and antenna control units, front and aft, and common display and control units. The Group B component kits were contracted with International Telephone and Telegraph Avionics of Atlanta, Georgia, to integrate low-band frequencies into the overall system. Group A kits were contracted with Raytheon E-Systems, Waco, Texas, to install government-furnished equipment into the AC-130H's structural mountings. These included aircraft wiring, cooling systems, pressurized systems, a blanking interface unit (BIU), and a forward transmission component for radome attachments. The project began in March 1997, and due to several problems with the BIU, it was not completed until late 1998. The jammer would prove very useful in future conflicts.[34]

One of the last major sustainment programs for the AC-130s during the 1990s began in January 1998, when the first AC-130U, T/N 90-0166, arrived for its first PDM at Robins AFB. It was the first U model to be inducted at the WR-ALC facilities. Representatives from AFSOC, 16th SOS, ASC, WR-ALC, MacAudry-Brown Inc., Shalamar, Florida, and Boeing, Inc., Fort Walton Beach, Florida, had been working toward this day since September 1997. They created an AC-130U PDM working group that met weekly from September through December in 1997 to prepare for the January arrival of the first aircraft. Things operated smoothly as the remaining aircraft arrived and departed over the next several months for their routine maintenance.[35]

By the spring of 1999, the AC-130Hs and AC-130Us were on the cutting edge of gunship technology and effectiveness. It proved to be just in time, too, as President Bill Clinton, fed up with the brutality and cruelty of Serbian dictator Slobodan Milosovic toward the minority groups in Southeastern Europe, reluctantly engaged US forces, along with North Atlantic Treaty Organization (NATO) and UN forces, in another foreign conflict, this time in the former nation of Yugoslavia. This contingency, better known as Operation Allied Force, became a testing ground for the latest advances in airpower. Even if they would not steal the headlines, the gunships would play a role in a decisive US Air Force/Allied airpower victory.

13 AC-130s on the Fringes
Kosovo and Operation Allied Force

On June 6, 1999, the preeminent military historian John Keegan, in an editorial in the *Daily Telegraph,* wrote: "There are certain dates in the history of warfare that mark real turning points. . . . Now there is a new turning point to fix on the calendar: June 3, 1999, when the capitulation of President Milosevic proved that war can be won by air power alone."[1] It was a victory that AC-130s would be part of, if only marginally.

Since the only NATO or UN forces employed during Operation Allied Force (OAF) were aircraft, and it was not until after armed conflict that NATO ground forces were introduced as peacekeepers troops, it is hard not to agree with Keegan. In many ways OAF was the full flowering of the aerospace technological revolution begun during the Persian Gulf War. The possibility of such a victory had been strongly suggested in Bosnia when NATO airpower had forced a peace settlement among the warring parties, but it had been such a small display few felt it significant.[2]

The religious and ethnic problems that existed in the late 1990s originated at the Battle of Kosovo Polje in 1389, when a Christian army of Serbs, Hungarians, Bosnians, Poles, Albanians, and Vlachs was defeated by Ottoman Turkish forces led by Sultan Murad I. This battle became a patriotic event in Serbian history. One Serbian proverb declared, "Wherever Serbian blood has been shed, there lies Serbia."[3] More than five hundred years later, in 1948, Josip Broz Tito led the creation of an independent communist Yugoslavian regime that in 1974 made Kosovo an autonomous province within Serbia. However, in the 1980s the death of Tito, the dissolution of Yugoslavia, and the growth of Serbian nationalism eventually altered this relationship.[4]

In the spring of 1987, Slobodan Milosevic, a lesser-known protégé of Marxist Serbian president Ivan Stambolic, was swept to the forefront of Serbian politics on an enormous wave of often violent pronationalist Serbian antigovernment protests. By the fall, Milosevic had led the overthrow of Stambolic, and by 1989 he had become president of Serbia. Soon after his ascension to power, he revoked Kosovo's autonomy. Milosevic's apparent goal was the resurrection of a Yugoslavian state dominated by Serbia and Milosevic. This goal soon began to crumble as communism waned in Eastern Europe. In spite of his support of violent excesses in Bosnia and Croatia, the dream of a unified Yugoslavia ended with the creation of new states such as Croatia. Instead, all Milosevic gained was the epithet, the Butcher of the Balkans.[5]

By 1992, Kosovar separatists had proclaimed a republic and elected Ibrahim Rugova president. Rugova, an advocate of peaceful methods to gain independence, soon received recognition from Albania. However, continued repression by Serbian forces led other Kosovar Albanians to form the Kosovar Liberation Army (KLA) in 1996. KLA bombings and the death of two Serbian policemen on February 28, 1998, led to Serbian-sponsored ethnic cleansing—the murder of thousands of civilians and the displacement of hundreds of thousands more.[6]

On March 5, 1998, KLA and Yugoslav forces clashed during a battle for the village of Prekaz, where two Serb police and twenty ethnic Albanians died. Other reports indicated that more than fifty other Albanian Kosovars were massacred by Serb police. Two weeks later, Kosovo voted for a new president and parliament. Serbian authorities declared the elections illegal. Following five more months of violence, on September 24, NATO representatives issued an ultimatum to Milosevic to end the conflict or face air strikes against military targets.[7]

With more than three hundred thousand displaced Kosovars facing starvation as winter set in, on January 29, 1999, the six-nation Contact Group (major NATO/UN powers) called for a peace conference between the parties to be held in Rambouillet, near Paris. However, these talks remained deadlocked over Milosevic's refusal to allow international peacekeepers into Kosovo.[8]

On March 18, Kosovar Albanian representatives signed the international peace agreement in Paris. Yugoslav representatives boycotted the meeting, as did the Russians. The next day the Contact Group adjourned the talks. Four days later, US envoy Richard Holbrooke traveled to Belgrade for one last, desperate effort to convince Milosevic to modify his position—he would not. At 7:00 p.m. GMT on March 24, 1999, NATO forces initiated air attacks over the Federal Republic of Yugoslavia (FRY).[9] Over the next three and one-half months, these operations would escalate and witness the introduction of new weapons and aircraft never before used in combat. By June, Milosevic capitulated and withdrew all Serbian forces, Kosovo was occupied by NATO/UN peacekeeping forces, and the process of rebuilding the broken land began. By most interpretations, airpower was a decisive factor.[10]

The Air War, March 24–June 20, 1999

On January 19, 1999, Gen. Wesley Clark was appointed NATO commander. He and his staff drew up plans, approved by NATO, that called for a three-phased attack. Phase I was aimed at enemy air defense systems and command centers in Kosovo. Phase II targeted military targets below the forty-fourth parallel south of Belgrade. The final phase committed NATO aircraft to attacks against military targets in and around Belgrade. The Allies' ultimate goal was to restore peace to the war-torn province and guarantee Kosovan autonomy.[11] Even as more than four hundred NATO aircraft prepared to strike Yugoslav military targets, including the forty thousand army and police forces in and around Kosovo, President Clinton declared, "In dealing with aggressors in the Balkans hesitation is a license to kill. But action and resolve can stop armies and save lives."[12]

The Serbian integrated air defense system (IADS) was no laughing matter. Their SAMs and interconnected radar directing systems were placed carefully in a mountainous area full of hidden and connected valleys as well as low-lying clouds and constant fog. Unlike the vast flat and open expanses of the Persian Gulf theater of operations, Serbia and Kosovo were slightly larger than Maine and full of mountains and valleys.[13]

The FRY's "substantial and redundant" IADS included fifty to sixty SAM battery sites, each with dozens of Russian-made radar-guided SA-2s, SA-3s, and mobile SA-6s. They sported about two thousand mostly mobile AAA guns and thousands of shoulder-fired missiles. They also had 240 combat aircraft, of which only about 80 were of much operational consequence. These included 15 MiG-29s and 60 MiG-21s. While most of the IADS was at least fifteen years old, the FRY operators were well trained.[14]

Allied planners respected the FRY IADS enough to predict the loss of ten aircraft during initial strikes. The most ominous aspect of the plan was how much the plan's goal smacked of Vietnam. Instead of an all-out series of well-coordinated attacks aimed at key military and infrastructure targets, as was the case in Iraq, the goal, albeit implied, was to cause enough pain and suffering to convince Milosevic to return to negotiations—much as Lyndon Johnson had tried to increase the "quotient of pain" on North Vietnam. Some leaders and experts believed that the mere show of force would compel Milosevic to acquiesce.[15]

The Gunships' Role

While the gunships would not play the major role, ultimately they did deploy. This time the U models would be part of combat for a second time in Southeastern Europe. The deployment was a protracted mission, but one specifically suited for the U models. The AC-130U gunships had set a new record for the longest sustained flight by any C-130 airframe. They had been active in Southeastern Europe in 1998. In August of that year elements of the 4th SOS had participated in operations in the Bosnia-Herzegovina area of operations. The gunships proved to be extremely effective against Serbian ground forces, since they never had to fear enemy aircraft. AC-130U Spooky gunships flew 237 sorties, providing CAS, interdiction, and reconnaissance for Allied troops implementing the Dayton Peace Accords. No sooner than matters began to settle down in Europe, than they were sent to the Persian Gulf as part of the buildup of US forces attempting to compel Saddam Hussein to comply with UN weapons inspections.[16]

Throughout late 1998, AFSOC maintained a constant CSAR alert posture as part of Operation Joint Guard, with aircraft and personnel rotating from Hurlburt Field to San Vito, Italy, on a regular basis. With planning for OAF underway in early 1999, this role increased significantly, and in March 1999 the 4th SOS flew into the Southeast European Theater of Operations to prepare for their role in OAF. In April 1999, the AC-130Us conducted their first combat operations over Kosovo. Their primary role was to seek and destroy night vehicular and troop movements by Serbian and FRY ground elements. They flew at higher altitudes than ever before for fear of the lethality of enemy missiles and AAA. AFSOC's aircraft played an important role in bringing the conflict in Kosovo to an end. Among other things, during the NATO air campaign, SOF aircraft conducted two successful CSAR operations to rescue one downed US F-117A pilot on March 27, 1999, and one F-16 pilot on May 2.[17]

During OAF the Air Force had to be ever mindful of its duties to the western Pacific. To that end, Secretary of Defense William S. Cohen ordered one F-15E fighter squadron, a carrier battle group, B-52s and EA-6Bs to remain poised in the United States, ready to deploy on short notice. In addition, two Air Force AC-130H gunships, deployed to Korea, remained on station, while the 13 AC-130Us deployed to Aviano AB, Italy.[18]

The Conflict Begins

At about 2:00 p.m. EST, General Clark informed NATO Secretary-General Javier Solana that OAF had commenced. Soon, reports of massive explosions and blinding flashes of light came rolling in from various news sources in the region.[19] At the same time, President Clinton announced that the campaign had three goals: "to demonstrate NATO's opposition to aggression and its support for peace; to impose a price on Milosevic if he continues or escalates attacks on helpless civilians; and to diminish his military ability to wage war in Kosovo in the future."[20]

The first strikes came from four US ships, two US submarines, one British submarine, and six B-52s. They fired Tomahawk land attack (cruise) missiles (TLAMs) while the Buffs launched AN/AGM-86C conventional air-launched cruise missiles at military utility and communication grids. These were followed by continuous night attacks by NATO fighter-bombers on FRY air defenses, specifically SAM sites, radar, and military communications targets in Kosovo and in southern Serbia near Podgorica, the capital of Montenegro. The pilots flew above fifteen thousand feet, even though this often reduced bombing accuracy.[21]

Ironically, FRY gunners didn't fire a single SAM on the first night. Instead, a dozen FRY fighters tried to intercept the NATO aircraft. The Yugoslav pilots proved to be no match for NATO airmen, and two MiG-29s were shot down by an Air Force F-15C and one by a Dutch F-16.[22] Clark soon told reporters, "We're going to systematically and progressively attack, disrupt, degrade, devastate, and ultimately, unless President Milosevic complies with demands . . . , we're going to destroy these forces and their facilities and support."[23] However, initially, leadership seemed reluctant to press the attacks, and thus Milosevic continued to kill or expel as many Kosovar Albanians as possible.

Early in the conflict two B-2 Stealth bombers of the 509th Bomb Wing, Whiteman AFB, Missouri, dropped two satellite-guided one-thousand-pound joint standoff weapons (JSOWs), obliterating targets inside Serbia. Each mission was thirty hours long nonstop against heavily defended targets. The success of the $2.1 billion aircraft, while spectacular, had greater ramifications for the future of airpower than to the outcome in Kosovo. As one analyst declared, "In its first combat test, the B-2 bomber defeated not only the Serbian air defense system but also the critics who for years had insisted it would not work as advertised or would never be risked in real war."[24]

On March 27, yet another kind of American aircraft made the headlines when a USAF F-117A was shot down by an Isayev S-125 (SA-3) near Belgrade. It was the kind of news every NATO leader feared, especially Clinton. After several hours of gripping television coverage, the pilot was rescued unharmed by a mission conspicuously supported by AC-130 gunships. With the potential of casualties staring at the American public, the tepid support for the president's policy, emanating from Washington and the nation, came bubbling to the surface. While Congress officially supported Clinton, many, such as Senator John S. McCain (R-Arizona), a former Vietnam-era Navy pilot and one of America's most famous former POWs, led some respected critics to wonder how the current trickle of bombs would ever get Serb leadership to cease its cruelty. Recalling the timid policies of Vietnam, McCain called for NATO to crank it up or get out. There were even private and guarded criticisms of the operation within the Air Force.[25]

With these words echoing in his ears, Clark asked for and received North Atlantic Council permission to intensify the offensive. Soon there were more than 250 aircraft and 7,300 US personnel committed to OAF. Cohen also suggested that the Army's highly publicized AH-64 Apache attack helicopters should be deployed. This remained a controversial subject, since many in NATO, Washington, and the administration feared that the Apaches would send a signal to a squeamish public that a potentially bloody ground war was in the offing. Many military experts worried privately about the survivability of the AH-64s in such a missile- and AAA-laden environment. Indeed, the AC-130s had as yet not been fully committed for that very reason.[26]

The air war dragged on with only an average of 50–70 daily sorties. This was a "far cry from the 800–1,200 during the Gulf War air campaign." Bad weather and orders not to risk bombing civilian and nonmilitary targets meant that dozens of sorties returned without dropping their ordnance. This left Milosevic to continue the mass expatriation of Albanian Kosovars.[27]

In spite of UN relief efforts, which created sprawling border tent towns mostly on the Albanian border, it soon became clear that the neighboring countries and provinces of Albania, Macedonia, and Montenegro could not fully accommodate the hundreds of thousands of displaced people. The United Nations and dozens of international aid agencies began discussing airlifting thousands to other countries to avert a humanitarian catastrophe.[28]

In early April 1999, Milosevic's attitude grew even more defiant when the United States suffered the humiliation of having three noncombatant soldiers abducted and beaten while patrolling on the border of the former Yugoslav Republic of Macedonia. NATO leaders put a brave face on, but they all realized the gravity of the incident. Clark declared, "We've all seen their pictures. . . . We don't like the way they are treated." British foreign minister Robin Cook condemned the entire affair, saying, "There is no justification for using soldiers who have been captured for propaganda purposes."[29] In the United States the media played up the story, wondering if the lives of any Americans were worth involvement in a strictly European affair. With public support for the president already shaken by earlier impeachment proceedings at home and the general isolationist sentiment of US citizens, this and other incidents placed not only OAF in jeopardy but also the future of NATO as a viable institution. While the three soldiers eventually would be released through the ex officio efforts of the Reverend Jesse Jackson, the weeks of captivity undermined what was, so far, a reluctant effort on behalf of OAF.[30]

On April 2, Cohen directed the deployment of twelve more F-117A Stealth fighters from Holloman AFB, New Mexico, to join NATO forces. This addition brought to twenty-four the number of F-117As in the theater and to 210 the number of strike aircraft.[31] In addition, during early April the DOD airlifted five hundred thousand humanitarian ration units, including food, large tents, cots, clothes, and blankets on C-17s, C-5 Galaxies, and even civilian contracted Boeing 747s.[32]

As the Allied air campaign entered its third week, the overall focus shifted from attacks on IADS to destroying FRY/Serb supply lines and lines of communications. In a classic aerial interdiction scenario, NATO not only targeted logistics and communication, but also sought to create choke points to force vehicle concentrations that its gunship aircraft could attack. In addition, they targeted storage and marshaling areas. The entire process proved to be very difficult.[33]

This was made more difficult by bad weather, dense foliage, mountainous terrain, and a dedicated and determined enemy. Enemy dispersion tactics were extremely effective, as were their greater than expected theater air defenses. Successful aerial interdiction requires a robust ground presence and an intense and redundant air campaign. It is the essence of joint operations and at the core of air land battle doctrine. The AC-130s should have been in this engagement; instead, the restricting factors kept them mostly inactive during this period of indecision.[34]

By the second week of April, it seemed all the elements of defeat were in place in Kosovo. The air campaign muddled on in a less than decisive fashion, the weather was horrible, the terrain was often impossible, and the Serbs seemed as determined as ever. Worst of all, there was no threat of NATO ground action. The NATO leaders had emphasized this omission from the outset, fearing a lack of public support to accept even minimal battlefield casualties. This was a concern enhanced by the initial response to the F-117 downing and the seizure and mistreatment of the three American soldiers. One Pentagon spokesman exclaimed, "We miscalculated. We thought when the bombing started Milosevic would play the victim, not turn into Adolf Hitler, Jr." Even DOD spokesman Ken Bacon in a briefing admitted, "I think right now it is difficult to say that we have prevented one act of brutality at this stage."[35]

Some senior US military leaders privately (sometimes not so privately) expressed fears that, as currently arranged, the air campaign would fail. One general described the air campaign as "operation constant drizzle." Most airmen agreed, especially those SOF crews stuck in place. Even NATO civilian leaders, albeit slowly, came to realize nothing short of an intensive and massive campaign would work—with at least some threat of ground operations.[36]

Cohen soon announced that the USS *Theodore Roosevelt* carrier battle group would stay in the Mediterranean and redeploy to a position capable of launching air strikes into Kosovo. Two days later, Clinton approved an increase in air operations. In addition, twenty-four Army Apache attack helicopters, multiple launch rocket system (MLRS) artillery, two thousand US ground troops, and fourteen Bradley fighting vehicles were deployed to Albania. This at least planted the possibility of ground operations in the minds of FRY leaders. Weather improvements also meant that NATO planes, including AC-130s, which performed armed reconnaissance and forward air control missions, were finally able to get at the well-hidden Serbian forces.[37]

NATO Finally Gets Serious

On April 10, Pentagon officials announced the dispatch of 82 more US aircraft, publicly blaming the weather for the poor showing until then and stating that the new additions would increase their "deep-strike capability and help increase the intensity of round-the-clock air strikes in Yugoslavia."[38] A week later, the total of NATO aircraft had reached 988, more than doubling the number the US and its allies had started with.[39]

President Clinton, at least in part, hesitated to acknowledge publicly a state of war for fear that he might be confronted by an already hostile Republican Congress over the War Powers Act.[40] Perhaps of equal embarrassment, and certainly of greater tragedy, was the fact that interdiction campaigns often lead to attacks against friendly forces or innocent noncombatants. On April 15, Secretary Cohen acknowledged NATO responsibility for an accidental bombing of a refugee convoy in which sixty-four Albanian Kosovars had died. One of the biggest problems facing Allied pilots throughout April and May was the difficulty in identifying enemy and refugee convoys. This was particularly true since most of the assets used were fast-moving jets instead of the much preferred low and slow gunships.[41]

While Secretary Cohen publicly reiterated the administration's resolve not to introduce ground forces into combat areas, Secretary of State Madeleine Albright wondered out loud to the media whether, from a strategic point of view, ground forces might have to be sent in at some later date. Even Gen. Michael J. Ryan, chief of staff, US Air Force, declared in the *New York Times,* "I don't know if we can do it without ground troops."[42]

Still, those around the president, as well as those in the Air Force, held out hope that the air campaign might work. Air Force leaders were convinced that a focused, intensive, and dedicated series of attacks against meaningful enemy targets would prove decisive. By mid-April, Clark's insistence had forced a consensus among NATO leaders, led by Prime Minister Blair, that the ground option had to at least be a possibility.[43]

To demonstrate his resolve, President Clinton asked Congress for $6 billion to finance OAF and humanitarian aid to the Balkans. About $5.5 billion was earmarked for air operations, replenishment of cruise missile stocks, precision-guided munitions, and refugee relief. Air Force leaders now prepared for attacks against targets around Belgrade.[44] This included key industrial and infrastructure targets within Serbia. These four pillars, as they became known, were Milosevic's political power centers, the tightly controlled Serbian electronic and published news media, his security forces and their facilities, and Serbia's economy, especially its oil refineries, electrical grids, and lines of communication. Other targets included roads and bridges over the Danube River; petroleum depots and oil refineries; railroad lines and military rolling stock; military headquarters buildings, communication lines and sites, and facilities; as well as factories producing weapons, munitions, and spares.[45]

On April 21 the new strikes began when three cruise missiles hit the central Belgrade radio/television complex, temporarily shutting down all service. The attack brought the war home to the Serbian people and opened up the threat of further attacks against Serbian business and finance centers run by friends or relatives of Slobodan Milosevic. Indeed, no sooner had the first wave of missiles struck than another wave hit the headquarters of Milosevic's Serbian Nationalist Party.[46] This was followed quickly by raids on Milosevic's family dwellings. The highlight was a GBU-28 4,700-pound bunker-buster dropped on the FRY national command center, which was a multistory underground facility located over one hundred feet below ground level. A planned safe haven for Milosevic and his family, it had extensive communications nets, food supplies for more than a month, and living space and medical supplies/facilities for the main FRY civilian and military defense leadership.[47]

On April 23, 1999, NATO leaders convened a summit meeting in Washington. The meeting, which lasted until April 25, not only briefly paid homage to the fiftieth anniversary of NATO, but also solidified the resolve of the alliance to bring Milosevic to heel. After three days of talks, NATO leaders restated their original demands: "a verifiable stop to Serbian military action in Kosovo; withdrawal of all Serbian forces; an international military force in Kosovo; refugee return; and acceptance of a political framework based on Rambouillet."[48]

On April 27, Clinton signed a selected reserve call-up authorizing 33,102 reserve component members to be called to active duty for OAF. The call-up covered a 270-day period, and its initial action focused on 2,046 airmen and forty-seven aircraft in eight Air National Guard and Air Force Reserve Command (AFRC) units. They were sent to Budapest, Hungary.[49]

Two days later, during a Pentagon news briefing, Gen. Henry Shelton (USA), chair of the JCS, announced the deployment of thirteen more US aircraft, including ten B-52Hs. Shelton emphasized that the air campaign was finally having an effect and reminded reporters that "we faced three formidable challenges in the area. First was the integrated air defense system; second was the terrain; third was the weather." Shelton assured the gathering that in spite of the problems, NATO aircraft would soon move into the "'domination phase' of the operation where NATO aircraft will aim at decimating Yugoslav field forces." Both he and Secretary Cohen reiterated NATO resolve and openly chortled at what they called Milosevic's "underestimation of the will of the alliance." Decimating field forces was something the AC-130H/Us were experts in—a fact they would prove again.[50]

On the night of May 3, Air Force F-117As attacked five major electrical transformer facilities in and around Belgrade, employing CBU-94s. The significance of this single attack cannot be overstated, since 70 percent of the electricity in Yugoslavia was cut off for several hours. The CBU-94s proved to be a diabolically effective weapon. As the canisters dropped, they released numerous BLU-114B submunitions, which unwound as huge numbers of electrically conductive filaments. The filaments covered high-tension wires and transformer stations like massive amounts of silver tinsel on a Christmas tree, and once they hit, they shorted out the power. Most of the targets were focused on electric service to the Yugoslav 3rd Army.[51]

On May 6, the foreign ministers of the Group of Eight nations (G8) met in Bonn, Germany, in an initial forum to formulate a framework for the eventual settlement. At Bonn the NATO foreign ministers agreed on the basic principles for resolving the crisis. Communicating through Finnish president Martti Ahtisaari and Russian premier and envoy Viktor Chernomyrdin, Milosevic eventually agreed to terms on June 3. On June 7–8, in Bonn and Cologne, the G8 foreign ministers signed a draft agreement that became UN Security Council Resolution (UNSCR) 1244 on June 10.[52]

By mid-May, some Yugoslav officials began to admit openly that Serbia's economy was suffering from the upgraded assaults. This meant widespread hardship among the people of Serbia. Unemployment soon became a particular hardship, with over one hundred thousand civilians having lost their jobs. One attack on a large munitions plant and car and truck plant in Krujevac left more than twelve thousand employees without work. Without orders for tires, plastics, windshields, etc., collateral industries were forced to shut down or cut back thirty to forty-five thousand jobs. Many other factories suffered the same fate.[53]

Targets still not exploited were the electric power generating systems. What had been an initial target during Desert Storm had received only an early May love tap that temporarily shorted power but destroyed nothing. On May 24, NATO planes attacked, obliterating the entire electrical grid. Yugoslav air defenses, defense and banking computers, and numerous other key national and military institutions utterly dependent on the electrical power source lost power. Belgrade was black. But why had it taken so long? Two months into the war, decisive action was finally approved. As an apparently vindicated General Clark said later, "This was the only air campaign in history in which lovers strolled down river banks in the gathering twilight and ate at outdoor cafes and watched the fireworks." That is, until May 24.[54]

Still, Milosevic had not capitulated, so throughout May the buildup continued, with Secretary Cohen ordering 176 more fighters and refueling aircraft to Europe. The deployment was the culmination of General Clark's April request for 1,000 aircraft.[55]

Beginning of the End

On the battlefront, operations shifted to Kosovo, where finally the AC-130s took on a major role. On May 26, four thousand KLA irregulars advanced into Kosovo at two points along the southwestern border. Their goal was to form a secure corridor in an effort to resupply their beleaguered comrades. The offensive soon slowed, and enemy forces, using effective artillery fire, quickly forced the KLA into a defensive position on 6,523-foot Mount Pastrik, just inside Albania. On the one hand, this seemed a terrible turn of events, since it proved that even after two and one-half months of air attacks, the FRY troops in Kosovo were strong. On the other hand, it drew into the open seven to eight hundred FRY troops and dozens of vehicles and artillery.

According to initial reports, when KLA forces counterattacked, FRY forces had to congregate to defend themselves. Finally, the ground element so critical to successful aerial interdiction was present. Employing E-8C JSTARS aircraft stationed at Robins AFB, Georgia, NATO forces soon spotted groups of FRY troops trying to run for safety. As they did, NATO fighters and gunships tore their columns to pieces. While the destruction was not at the level of that of the Kuwaiti Highway of Death, most of the Serbian mechanized vehicles were destroyed.[56]

In the aftermath several skeptical reports appeared in the media, helped by Serbian propaganda. This prompted a major NATO effort to research the

AC-130 up close and very personal.

battle and get the real picture. The investigation proved the skeptics wrong and showed that the actual numbers were not far short of the original NATO estimates. Still, Serbian ground forces departed Kosovo in good order and with less damage than that suffered by Iraq's army in the Gulf War. Even though it was another devastating example of the power of the AC-130s, the damage to Milosevic's fielded forces was not the only decisive factor in his decision to quit.[57]

On May 6, a terrible public relations catastrophe occurred when NATO aircraft accidentally bombed the Chinese embassy in Belgrade, killing three persons described as journalists and injuring twenty others, six critically. The outcry from China was considerable. On May 8, President Clinton apologized for the bombing and expressed profound condolences to Chinese president Jiang Zemin. In spite of these generous US and NATO apologies, the Chinese seemed inconsolable. In China, thousands of demonstrators hurled rocks and debris at the US and British embassies in Beijing in several days of riotous demonstrations. Even so, China could do very little to change the progress of the conflict. After a time, the furor died down, and the bombing continued.[58]

By early June the Serbs were near the end. The NATO buildup had finally proved effective enough that diplomatic efforts began to bear fruit. On June 2, *Jane's Defence Weekly* reported that the Serbs were near the end of their SAMs because they had wasted many of them often firing blind shotgun-pattern salvos at NATO attack aircraft. Many were lost to NATO SEAD operations spearheaded by USAF F-16CJs carrying AN/AGM-88 high-speed anti-radiation missiles (HARMs). *Jane's* believed the SEAD attacks had been so effective that most subsequent attack sorties were unopposed. One unnamed F-16 squadron commander told a *Jane's* reporter, "We have 80% attrited their SAMs—they have fired off 80% of their SAMs. They can't have an endless supply."[59]

With disaster staring him in the face, Milosevic blinked. On June 2, former Russian prime minister Viktor Chernomyrdin and Finnish president Martti Ahtisaari, representing the European Union, traveled to Belgrade and offered Milosevic a plan to end the war. The next day, Clinton announced that both sides had agreed to a draft proposal that all Serbian and FRY forces would withdraw, all refugees would be allowed to return, self-rule of Albanian Kosovars under Yugoslav sovereignty would be restored, a few hundred Serbian liaison personnel would assist in removing mines, and Allied peacekeeping forces would occupy key positions in Kosovo to assure a peaceful transition. Clinton and Cohen agreed that NATO would provide about fifty thousand peacekeepers and the United States, seven thousand. NATO and now UN forces, such as Russia, were scheduled to participate as part of the peacekeeping force, even though Russia was not a welcome partner.[60]

After some minor squabbles and additional bombing raids delayed the final outcome, on June 9 a final agreement was reached and signed in Macedonia. Following the signing, NATO secretary-general Javier Solana officially suspended NATO air attacks. However, he warned they would resume if Serbia did not follow the letter of every provision of the peace agreement. Plans called for all Serb forces to be out of Kosovo in eleven days. The province was divided into three zones of occupation to be administered by the United States, Great Britain, and France.[61]

On June 10 the UN Security Council voted 14–0, with China abstaining, to approve Resolution 1244. Not only did the resolution put Kosovo under UN international civilian control, but it also reconfirmed previous UN and NATO resolutions calling for Serbian troop withdrawals, Kosovan autonomy, and an international peacekeeping force under UN authority.[62]

The Aftermath

On June 11, 1999, Clinton declared victory in a nationwide speech. The next day, with FRY forces already pulling back, the first peacekeeping forces entered Kosovo, preceded by a Russian advance party that, without prior agreement, took up positions around Pristina Airport. Although an annoyance, the Russian move hardly stopped the UN force deployment. Eventually the Russians were integrated into the overall occupation forces. By June 20, Serbian forces had completely withdrawn, and UN forces had taken up their places on schedule. Overall commander, Lt. Gen. Sir Michael Jackson of the British army, began the difficult task of disarming the KLA within ninety days. With the occupation in place, Secretary General Solana officially terminated the air campaign on June 20. At that point the AC-130s returned to Florida.[63]

Officially, the NATO air campaign lasted from March 24 to June 20, or eighty-nine days. During the last eleven days no actual attacks took place. All totaled, 22,200 Air Force, Army, Navy, and Marine personnel were assigned to US European Command. Not all participated in the conflict. In the seventy-eight days of air attacks, the Allies flew 38,004 sorties, including 10,484 strike sorties. All totaled, 829 aircraft from fourteen countries directly participated in the air campaign. Initial target reports showed that NATO had destroyed eleven railroad bridges, thirty-four highway bridges, 29 percent of all stored ammunition, 57 percent of stored petroleum supplies, all Yugoslav oil reserves, 268 nontracked military vehicles, 1,220 trucks, 203 armored personnel carriers, 314 artillery pieces, 100 aircraft of all kinds, and ten military-capable airfields.[64]

Official NATO sources estimated that FRY and Serb forces suffered nearly ten thousand killed and wounded, while the United States lost two soldiers killed in a helicopter accident and three Chinese diplomats died in the NATO bombing of the Chinese embassy in Belgrade. The UN High Commission for Refugees and the Yugoslav government counted five hundred civilians dead and five thousand wounded during the air raids. The United Nations reported that by the end of OAF, half of all Albanian Kosovars were displaced persons. A total of 200,000–300,000 ethnic Albanians had fled Kosovo prior to the air attacks, while another 68,000 had taken refuge west in Montenegro, 440,000 southwest in Albania, and 240,000 southeast in Macedonia. In all, more than 900,000 of the 1.8 million Albanian Kosovars had left the province.[65]

Nineteen NATO nations contributed to OAF. A total of 31,600 US service personnel participated—18,400 ashore and 13,200 at sea. The United States had committed over 650 aircraft, including a squadron of AC-130s.[66] As Clark remarked when asked if the operation had been a success, "The final standard is: Did it work? Did it provide crucial leverage to diplomacy? I think yes, it did."[67] Kosovo air operations during the first four weeks suggested to many air leaders the essential mistake of allowing political restriction to dictate targeting and limit the offensive capability of airpower. The last six weeks tended to verify the efficacy of basic Air Force aerospace doctrine, since there can be little question that airpower, once provided proper leeway, projected power beyond the battlefront and diminished the enemy's means and will to fight by taking the war to his heartland. During the last days of the conflict, it also performed its battlefield role with equal effectiveness. Former CSAF

Tony McPeak summed it up best by saying: "So many people have predicted that airpower would be ineffective if it's used alone that, now, they have to describe what's happened in this case as some sort of a defeat. Now victory comes in many flavors, and this one will obviously not be to everyone's taste, but the fact of the matter is, airpower carried the day."[68]

Later, many who thought there was more to it than airpower at least granted that it had played a major role. Secretary Cohen was one example. So airpower proponents had ammunition to argue that Kosovo was a victory and a confirmation for airpower theory and doctrine, one that again demonstrates its decisive nature and its potential for the future. Notwithstanding the role of diplomacy and the implied threat of a ground invasion, airpower advocates had additional evidence for the argument that sometimes airpower, including AC-130s, may indeed be able to win alone. Cohen thought so when he declared: "The crews who flew the bombers, fighters, and support aircraft carried out the most precise air campaign in history."[69] And, of course, among those aircraft were the deadly AC-130s, which became the scourge of enemy ground forces in OAF.

14 Operation Enduring Freedom

As the gunships of the 4th SOS and 16th SOS returned from OAF, the world entered the twenty-first century with positive anticipation. After all, the United States had twice in the 1990s formed a mighty coalition of the most prosperous and powerful nations in the world to fight for peoples they believed were being unfairly treated by invaders or by those committing genocide. They had also joined together to discuss the need to spread their wealth and environmental concerns to the developing world. Sadly, in less than two years the dreams of peace were dashed by a single event so dastardly conceived and executed in such a coldblooded manner that it shocked the entire world into a state of tension perhaps not experienced since the bombing of Pearl Harbor and the onset of World War II. Fortunately, the United States, in particular its Air Force, specifically its gunships, was not sitting idly by.

During the 1990s the AC-130U had entered the active inventory and had continued the distinguished combat history of side-firing gunships. Boeing had configured the AC-130U gunship airframe with an armor protection system, high-resolution ALLTV, infrared detection set (IDS), strike radar, cutting-edge avionics and EW systems, a sophisticated software-controlled fire control system, and an armament suite of side-firing, trainable 25mm, 40mm, and 105mm guns. Of singular significance, they had created the first gunship capable of all-weather and night target acquisition and strike. The acquisition program evolved in the mid-1980s from a congressional mandate to reinvigorate SOF forces. The original contract was awarded to Rockwell in July 1987 and the first aircraft flew on December 20, 1990. It was so successful that in 1992 additional funds were provided to build a thirteenth U model to replace the AC-130H lost during Desert Storm. By late 1998 all the AC-130Us had been delivered, and the program had transitioned to the sustainment phase.[1]

While the eight remaining AC-130Hs of the 16th SOS were older and had less range than their new cousins, they continued to be upgraded with similar and, in some cases, identical sensors and weapon systems to keep them capable of executing nearly all the same combat missions as the those of the AC-130Us. Technicians installed new defensive systems, including ECM dispensing systems that released chaff and flares to counter radar and infrared-guided antiaircraft missiles. The H models also had infrared heat shields mounted underneath the engines to disperse and hide engine heat sources from infrared-guided antiaircraft missiles.[2]

New programs also upgraded software and hardware systems in both models. Among those were the combination of all necessary software requirements for the system integration test (SIT) system and hardware and software improvements for the APQ-180 strike radar system; upgrading of the tactical situation map; improvement of core avionics and computers required for the multimission advanced tactical terminal and integrated defense avionics system installation; upgrading of the EW suite; and modification of the software and hardware required to operate the trainable gun mounts. Yet another improvement program involved an upgrade to the AN/AAQ-26 infrared detection set that enhanced the optics on the AN/AAQ-17 IDS originally installed on thirteen AC-130U and eight AC-130H gunship aircraft. The AC-130H/U wiring, operational flight program (OFP), control displays program, track handle, bus multiplier, control panels, and variable slow rate feature were also modified by Raytheon and LASC. The Directional Infrared Countermeasures Program also developed and procured sixty systems for fifty-nine SOF aircraft. It worked in conjunction with other onboard self-protection systems to enhance the aircraft's survivability against existing infrared guided missiles. As it turned out, these upgrades and plans proved fortuitous, since in the fall of 2001 the 4th SOS and 16th SOS would again be called upon to defend the nation, this time from terrorists. Not only would the gunships live up to their past reputation, but they would perform so successfully that Congress would approve the funding for four new AC-130U gunships.[3]

September 11, 2001: Prelude to Enduring Freedom

The airliner terror attacks conducted on September 11, 2001, often referred to as 9/11, were a series of coordinated suicide attacks planned and executed by members or operatives of an Islamic terror cell named al-Qaeda. On the morning of September 11, nineteen al-Qaeda terrorists hijacked four

AC-130 coming on station at twilight.

commercial airliners filled with passengers. Too late, it became clear they intended to use four planes as human-guided suicide bombs to attack key facilities in the United States.[4]

Two groups of hijackers crashed their aircraft into the World Trade Center's (WTC) Twin Towers in New York City, killing everyone on board and many others working in the buildings. Both buildings collapsed within two hours, destroying nearby buildings, damaging others, and killing everyone still inside, including many first responders. Hijackers hurtled a third airliner into the Pentagon in Arlington, Virginia, near downtown Washington, DC. Some of the passengers on the fourth plane rushed the assailants controlling the aircraft, and in the struggle it crashed in a field near Shanksville in rural Pennsylvania. It was later discovered that the target of the fourth aircraft was the White House or Congress. All together, 2,974 innocent victims and the nineteen hijackers died. This included persons from ninety different countries.[5]

Before the end of the day, the Federal Bureau of Investigation (FBI) had determined who the hijackers were. One terrorist's luggage, which had not made it onto American Airlines Flight 11, contained papers revealing in detail the plot and those responsible. The morning of the attacks, both US and German intelligence intercepted communications that indicated that al-Qaeda and radical Saudi national Osama bin Laden were behind the incident. The leader of the hijackers was Mohamed Atta. Three weeks later, the FBI released information about the nineteen hijackers: fifteen of them were from Saudi Arabia, two from the United Arab Emirates (UAE), one from Egypt, and one from Lebanon.[6]

With both the United States and Great Britain convinced that bin Laden and al-Qaeda executed the attacks, both countries began a thorough investigation in an effort to locate the organization and eliminate it and bin Laden. Al-Qaeda had begun in early 1979 when the USSR invaded Afghanistan. Ironically, it was the United States who helped bin Laden to infiltrate Afghanistan in an effort to organize the Arab Mujahideen and Maktab al-Khidamat (MAK) to resist the Soviet troops. Urged on by charismatic US congressman Charles Wilson, Congress covertly supplied the mujahideen with sophisticated shoulder-fired SAMs and other vital weapons for nearly ten years until, nearly bankrupt, Soviet leaders withdrew their forces in 1989. Almost immediately, the MAK transformed itself from anticommunist freedom fighters to a "rapid reaction force" spearheading jihad against any government in the Islamic world that refused to embrace their fundamentalist beliefs.[7]

In 1996 and again in 1998, bin Laden, the son of a wealthy Saudi family, condemned the US presence in Saudi Arabia and US support for Israel, threatening to take harsh steps. It was during this time that the 9/11 plot was hatched by Khalid Sheikh Mohammed. With bin Laden intent on attacking the United States in response to its negative response to the African embassy bombings in 1998, Mohammed soon convinced the al-Qaeda leader of the potential of the plot. While bin Laden changed some of the original targets, such as the US Bank Tower in Los Angeles, California, the plan went forward very much as originally planned.[8]

As the millennium ended, al-Qaeda had returned its headquarters to Afghanistan from the Sudan and was focused on carrying out the attacks on the United States. The nineteen men selected to carry out the deed were not the usual suspects. Instead, they were young adults, they were educated, and they had families. By the spring of 2000 most of them had arrived in the United States, and those who were to fly the aircraft found it easy to enroll in courses in California, Arizona, or Florida to learn basic piloting skills. By June 2001 all was in place for the attacks, and it was at that point that bin Laden's public pronouncements became more pointed. Critics later argued that this and other events should have tipped off the United States that something was afoot. For example, only two days before 9/11, Ahmed Shah Massoud, leader of the anti-Taliban Northern Alliance, was assassinated in a bombing attack. It was the prelude to the worst attack on US soil since Pearl Harbor.[9]

Following the attacks, the president was shuttled around the country in an effort to ensure his safety. By the next morning he was back in Washington and held a meeting of his national security teams. Publicly he declared the attacks an act of war against the United States and Osama bin Laden the leader of the group responsible for the attacks. Two days later, Congress granted the president the power to "use all necessary and appropriate force against those nations, organizations, or persons he determines planned, authorized, committed or aided the terrorist attacks."[10]

On September 16, 2001, bin Laden denied involvement on the Arab world's satellite channel Al Jazeera. On September 19, 2001, President Bush directed military leaders to issue orders to their forces for a general deployment to Afghanistan. The Taliban claimed that bin Laden was not in Afghanistan. The next day, President Bush addressed a joint session of Congress denouncing the acts and resolving to begin a war on terrorism that would root out and totally destroy all the terror cells responsible for the attacks. The president also paid his respects to the 9/11 emergency workers who responded to the scene and died in a desperate attempt to rescue people and fight fires. At the same time, NATO declared that the attacks on the United States were attacks on all NATO members. Ultimately, most nations joined the United States in a call for a war against bin Laden and al-Qaeda as well as their protectors, the Taliban.[11]

Operation Enduring Freedom Begins

The Taliban was the product of a power vacuum created by the withdrawal of Soviet troops in the late 1980s. Following a protracted power struggle among warring factions and tribes, the Taliban took control of the government in 1996. They embraced radical Islamic law banning music, television, sports, and dancing and enforced harsh judicial penalties such as amputation and public executions at the Kabul football stadium. Women's rights were all but nonexistent under the Taliban, and groups throughout the world called for international intervention. At this point, bin Laden moved al-Qaeda to Afghanistan at the invitation of the Northern Alliance leader Abdur Rabb ur Rasool Sayyaf. When the Taliban seized power, bin Laden switched sides, with al-Qaeda's 055 Brigade being integrated into the Taliban army from 1997 to 2001.[12]

On September 20, 2001, President Bush demanded that the Taliban deliver to the United States all of the leaders of al-Qaeda, release all imprisoned foreign nationals, close every terrorist training camp, hand over all terrorists and their supporters to appropriate authorities, and give the United States full access to terrorist training camps for inspection. The next day the Taliban rejected the ultimatum, claiming there was no evidence linking bin Laden to the September 11 attacks. Two days later, the UAE and Saudi Arabia withdrew their recognition of the Taliban government in Afghanistan, leaving neighboring Pakistan as the only remaining country with diplomatic ties.[13]

On October 5, 2001, Operation Enduring Freedom (OEF) was poised to begin America's response to 9/11. Originally designated Operation Infinite Justice, the name was altered out of respect for the Muslim members of the coalition, who viewed the original name as a usurpation of God's sole right to impart ultimate justice. In fact, OEF became one of several operations that were part of the global war on terrorism. Military operations in Afghanistan were actually two operations. OEF was a joint US, British, and Afghan (Northern Alliance/Coalition) campaign, and the other was a parallel venture sponsored by NATO.[14]

On October 6 the president made a last appeal to the Taliban to turn bin Laden over to international authorities, but he reminded them that "time is running out!" The following day, the Taliban proposed to try bin Laden in Afghanistan in an Islamic court, an offer that was promptly rejected. On October 7, 2001, combat operations began with air strikes from land-based B-1B Lancer, B-2 Spirit, and B-52 Stratofortress bombers, carrier-based F-14 Tomcat and F/A-18 Hornet fighters, and Tomahawk cruise missiles launched by American and British surface and submarine vessels. That same day, in a speech to the nation, President Bush reiterated his war aims, first made in his September 20 speech.[15]

In spite of defiant warnings on November 1 by Taliban leaders such as Mullah Omar that the Afghani people would fight to the death, a week later Northern Alliance forces, supported by allied airpower, smashed through Taliban positions at Mazar-i-Sharif in Balkh Province. The battle for Mazar-i-Sharif was the first major offensive of the Afghan war, and it featured the skill of US SOF personnel and the precision of US bombers, fighters, and gunships. For several days prior to the ground assaults by Northern Alliance forces, US CENTCOM leaders believed that the city was too well defended and that even with expert aerial bombardment by US aircraft it might not fall for some months. In a pleasant surprise, the bombing proved so effective that the Northern Alliance troops quickly captured the outlying villages, and rather than face the bombs of the B-1s and B-52s as well as precision ordnance of the F-15Es and AC-130s, the Taliban withdrew from the city. When the city fell, many of those suspected of being Taliban were killed; a total of three hundred bodies were counted. Another five hundred suspects were captured or defected. The capture of this important city soon led to a rapid deterioration of Taliban forces in Northern Afghanistan.[16]

Two days later, the city of Herat fell to the Alliance, and on November 17 the capital of Kabul fell at the start of Ramadan. A week later, the Taliban fled

Kunduz, leaving Kandahar as the only major city in their hands. During this sweep south in November 2001, US forces discovered a videotape on which Osama bin Laden spoke to Khaled al-Harbi and admitted his role in the 9/11 attacks. Subsequently, copies of the tape were turned over to the media and broadcast by many news networks beginning on December 13, 2001. While some argued the tape was a US creation, most believed bin Laden's distorted appearance on the tape can be attributed to tape transfer and that the tape was real. To most Americans it was the final proof that bin Laden and al-Qaeda were responsible for the 9/11 attacks.[17]

On November 25, US Marines landed near Kandahar, and within twenty-four hours they had captured the Taliban's final stronghold. To the north, in an effort to distract US-Coalition attention, Taliban inmates being held at the aging nineteenth-century fort at Mazar-i-Sharif staged an uprising. Poorly guarded and perhaps helped by some of the Afghan guards, they seized key parts of the prison and held it for six days. The Americans finally retook the fort, but only after US air strikes killed 317 of the 400 prisoners. The 83 survivors had escaped death by taking refuge in basements. Among the Americans killed was CIA agent Johnny Michael Spann. In addition, forty-six of the anti-Taliban Uzbeki forces were killed and more than two hundred wounded. At the same time, the US military and its allied forces established their first ground base, Forward Operating Base (FOB) Rhino, located in Afghanistan just southwest of Kandahar.[18]

On December 1, 2001, Mullah Omar declared that his troops still in and around Kandahar would continue to fight until Judgment Day. Within a week, all the Taliban forces in the area had been defeated, including the staunchest defenders around the Kandahar airport. Their final haven in Afghanistan was the Tora Bora Mountains south of Jalalabad, on the Pakistan border. There the enemy had a cave complex built during the fight against the Soviets.[19]

On December 11, anti-Taliban forces advanced through the Jalalabad region, supported by US strike aircraft, including AC-130s. B-52s dropped bunker buster bombs that penetrated deep into the caves before exploding and sucking out the oxygen. Some experts speculated that both Omar and bin Laden might have been killed. Two days into the campaign, the original bin Laden videotape became public, and, soon after, a second tape showed him supposedly hiding in Pakistan. On December 18, organized resistance at the Tora Bora caves ended, and Coalition forces began a mopping up with a search for bin Laden. He was not found.[20]

As if to add symmetry to the conflict, the next day firefighters put out the last smoldering fires at ground zero of the World Trade Center, and three days later Hamad Karzai, leader of the Northern Coalition, formed a new pro-

American provisional government in Afghanistan. On December 27, 2001, the entire second bin Laden video was released. In it he declared, "Terrorism against America deserves to be praised because it was a response to injustice, aimed at forcing America to stop its support for Israel, which kills our people." Ironically, he stopped short of admitting responsibility for the 9/11 attacks. Based on this additional evidence, on January 16, 2002, the UN Security Council unanimously decreed an arms embargo and freezing of assets belonging to bin Laden, al-Qaeda, and the Taliban.[21]

Even though it seemed that the Taliban and al-Qaeda were defeated, and the president had declared "mission accomplished," sporadic fighting continued. On March 2, 2002, only nine weeks after the Coalition overran Tora Bora, US and Allied leaders decided to launch Operation Anaconda in the Shah-i-Kot region, near Gardez in eastern Afghanistan, again supported by US air cover. Designed to destroy al-Qaeda once and for all, the operation was carried out by elements of the US 10th Mountain Division; 101st Airborne Division; US Special Forces Groups Task Force (TF) 11, TF Bowie, and TF Dagger; as well as British Royal Marines and forces from Norway, Canada, Afghanistan, Germany, Australia, and New Zealand—a total of fifteen hundred Allied soldiers.[22]

Reminiscent of the search-and-destroy operations in Vietnam, American fighter-bombers dropped guided bombs during the day, while AC-130s annihilated enemy forces at night. From the outset, resistance proved to be greater than expected, and an additional five hundred troops had to be committed. In one of the fiercest ground engagements in the war, eight US (seven when an RPG downed an MH-47 Chinook helicopter) and three Allied soldiers were killed, while the enemy lost at least 450 killed.[23]

On March 6, three hundred more troops arrived to bolster the campaign. Three weeks later, estimating they had killed eight hundred al-Qaeda and Taliban fighters, officials declared the operation a complete success and withdrew their forces. However, later evidence suggested that while many enemy fighters were killed, many more escaped into Pakistan and survived to fight another day and to recruit more supporters.[24]

This would not be the last sweep of the southeastern mountains. On August 18, Allied forces initiated Operation Mountain Sweep, a weeklong operation aimed at paring back the increased number of enemy that had returned to the area. In an operation styled after Anaconda, huge weapons caches and reams of Taliban documents were captured. With two thousand ground troops and at least five combat air assault missions flown by dozens of strike aircraft, the operation was a conspicuous display of Coalition military power. Again, the SOF units were involved with great success. By the beginning of the next month, Allied leaders had decided to send elite antiterrorist forces to search inside and outside of Afghanistan to see if bin Laden was still alive. While much of the combat would soon die down as preparations for Operation Iraqi Freedom began, the gnawing problem of Afghanistan would not only continue but also grow during the next five years, and by the time Barrack Obama became president in January 2009, the war would have intensified and what by the fall of 2002 seemed a victory would become a problem that would become more troublesome than either of the wars in Iraq.[25]

The Air War

Even before combat operations began in Afghanistan, US planners compiled a target list of all significant targets in the AOR. Once engaged, they acted to control the movement of all warplanes in Afghan airspace from the sophisticated operations center a thousand miles away at Prince Sultan Air Base near Riyadh, Saudi Arabia. Navy jets were flying five hundred miles each way from carriers in the Arabian Sea. Air Force bombers also were flying six-hour round-trip missions from Diego Garcia in the Indian Ocean, and Air Force fighter-bombers were flying from bases in the Persian Gulf, missions that took eight to nine hours.[26]

During Operation Desert Storm, the Allies flew more than three thousand sorties a day. In OEF, they flew two hundred sorties a day. The commander of CENTCOM, Gen. Tommy R. Franks (USA), later reported that the two hundred daily sorties hit about the same number of targets as the three thousand sorties in Operation Desert Storm. In short, it took ten aircraft to take out a single target during the first Gulf War, while a single aircraft in OEF could eliminate two targets on average. In addition, CENTCOM planners prior to operations calculated that it could take from three to five months of intense air strikes before the ground forces of the Northern Alliance could assault the capital of Kabul. It took only twenty days, and within twenty-four hours after the last air raids the capital fell. In OAF the Allies flew forty-seven thousand sorties, but they flew only twenty-three thousand in the initial combat phase of OEF that officially ended at the end of April 2002. The initial air operations were carried out by heavy bombers such as B-1s, B-2s, and B-52s. Most of the aerial attacks during the initial combat phase of OEF, which lasted from October 2001 to April 2002, were performed by B-52s, while approximately 75 percent of all the tactical sorties were flown by carrier-based naval fighter and fighter-bomber aircraft.[27]

On October 12, 2001, the AC-130s arrived after a difficult flight of more than eighteen hours. Three days later they flew their first mission, executing more than half of the ninety-four combat sorties that strike aircraft flew.

Most were against ground targets at night around Kandahar and Kabul. Their primary missions were to support Allied ground forces as they moved south to confront the Taliban, and to interdict enemy vehicles using the roads as they retreated south. On the first night only two gunships flew missions, but by the next night five were airborne, and by October 17, six were flying sorties. On November 21, three more were deployed to Uzbekistan, making a total of nine gunships in all. Throughout these intense early months, all eight AC-130Hs and thirteen AC-130Us not specifically deployed elsewhere (Asia, Persian Gulf, or Latin America) were rotated to bases in Central Asia at one point or another. They alternated missions, with two to six flying each night while those not flying were kept airworthy by ground crews.[28]

The gunships remained in the area until April 2002. While most of the targets were vehicles, others included camps and caves. Specifically, the AC-130s flew in coordinated assaults with F-15Es and other fighter aircraft, including F-16s and A-10s, many using precision-guided munitions. Not only were they capable attack aircraft, but they once again demonstrated their excellence in tracking down and identifying targets for their fighter cousins and even Allied ground forces. With the latest sensors and the ability to loiter for long periods, they proved to be an excellent FAC aircraft. They not only had several hundred confirmed truck and several thousand infantry kills, but they also supported fighter aircraft in destroying key enemy headquarters as well as command, communications, and control centers.[29]

In the aftermath, the AC-130s, including the four new U models built during the late 1990s and early 2000s, rotated in and out of the Afghan Theater of Operations. While their home base was at Hurlburt, they were maintained at Robins AFB, Georgia. The 16th SOS and 4th SOS also flew continuous training missions to remain ever vigilant to new enemy threats and new tactics designed to seek and destroy Taliban and al-Qaeda forces and resources.[30]

A total of 211 Air Force planes used Ukrainian air corridors, flying mainly over the neutral waters of the Black Sea between October 9 and November 7, 2001. With the vast majority of Allied aircraft based by early November, the refueling aircraft, based in Bulgaria, flew six missions a day throughout the combat phase of OEF, which lasted until April 2002. These tankers refueled the strike aircraft, attacking targets in Afghanistan. The base, located on the Black Sea, housed between 200 and 250 Air Force personnel. In addition, twenty sorties a day headed for the AOR crossed through Romanian airspace.[31]

As early as October 23, 2001, B-1, B-2, and B-52 bombers of the 28th Air Expeditionary Wing, Diego Garcia, had expended more than 80 percent of the tonnage dropped on combat missions over Afghanistan during Operation Enduring Freedom. The Air Force had flown more than six hundred sorties, including strike missions against al-Qaeda and Taliban targets in Afghanistan. These targets included early warning radars, ground forces, command and control facilities, al-Qaeda infrastructure, airfields, and aircraft. Senior leadership reported in late November that the Alliance aircraft had dropped or launched ten thousand bombs or missiles, with 60 percent being PGMs. They also announced that the eight B-1s and ten B-52s operating out of Diego Garcia had dropped 72 percent of the forty-seven hundred tons of munitions aimed at enemy targets. They did so with the B-1s flying four sorties per day and the B-52s five each day. Bomber missions, flown mostly across the vast expanse of the Indian Ocean, a roundtrip distance of 5,500 nautical miles, lasted twelve to fifteen hours. Factoring in mission planning, each strike was often a twenty-four-hour trip. Planning took place at night, when the crews studied flight plans and reiterated the bomb runs, which by the third or fourth day most airmen had committed to memory. In the meantime, at Diego Garcia the ground support crews worked around the clock to keep each aircraft airworthy.[32]

By late 2002, while the Air Force had flown only 25 percent of the sorties, they had dropped 79 percent of all the ordnance expended in OEF up to that point. While they employed iron/dumb bombs, between two-thirds and three-fourths of the ordnance were precision-guided munitions. They also employed six hundred cluster bombs that included combined effects munitions bomb units CBU-87s and CBU-103s. Air Force support aircraft, such as UAVs, RC-135s, U-2s, E-3s, and EC-130E/Hs, had flown more than 325 missions. In addition, C-130 and C-17 cargo aircraft had established a nightly air bridge to FOB Rhino south of Kandahar, with the C-130s averaging ten flights each night and the C-17s flying a total of forty-three missions into Camp Rhino.[33]

In mid-January 2002, Vice Adm. John Nathman reported that forty-six hundred of the twelve thousand munitions expended were joint direct attack munitions (JDAMs), many delivered by JSOW aircraft such as the B-2. In this regard, the joint standoff aircraft would release a two-thousand-pound bomb outside the enemy's antiaircraft weapons envelope and guide the JDAM directly to the target employing laser, television, or satellite guidance capabilities on the aircraft. The admiral reported that in addition to the JDAMs, a vast array of other PGMs were being used, and plans called for Allied aircraft to soon employ guided munitions in more than 90 percent of all bombs dropped. In retrospect, this probably was an evaluation of Naval operations and not a generally accurate statement, since the Air Force still used mostly dumb bombs for B-52 carpet bombing raids, and none of the AC-130 raids used PGMs, nor did the auxiliary fighter attacks flying in conjunction with the AC-130s or alone during daylight raids.[34]

In an effort to clarify the situation pursuant to air operations in OEF, on February 7, 2002, CENTCOM commander Gen. Tommy R. Franks testified before a Senate committee that ten thousand of the eighteen thousand bombs, missiles, and other ordnance used to that date were precision-guided munitions. Of the ten thousand precision munitions, about half were laser-guided bombs, and the other half were GPS satellite–guided bombs. He also stated that American air assets had flown twenty thousand sorties up to that point, Navy carrier-based aircraft accounting for 75 percent of the tactical strike sorties and all together just over half of all sorties. In turn, he stated that the Air Force had flown a little less than half of the total sorties, which included tactical and strategic airlift, humanitarian aid, reconnaissance, and medical airlift flights; night attacks by gunships; bomber attacks; and tactical fighter attacks. As noted previously, in the last category the Air Force accounted for only one-fourth of the sorties. He also told committee members that the Tomahawk targeting cycle had been reduced from 101 minutes during OAF to 19 minutes during OEF, with half of the Tomahawks being fired from submarines. He concluded by explaining that between October 7, 2001, and February 6, 2002, refueling aircraft had flown approximately five thousand refueling sorties over Afghanistan, while another five thousand tanker sorties were flown from September 11, 2001, through early February 2002 to refuel aircraft over the continental United States as part of Operation Noble Eagle.[35]

As noted, Operation Anaconda was one of the largest US ground operations of OEF, and it is worth reexamining from an airpower point of view. Allied ground units initiated the campaign on Friday, March 1, 2002. This joint operation began with fifteen hundred troops and eventually totaled more than twenty-two hundred. Throughout the operation, aircraft, which included ten long-range bombers, thirty to forty fighters, and two to six AC-130 gunships, flew daily missions over the battlefield. In this one campaign alone, the Air Force used about half the force they had employed during the five months from October 2001 through February 2002. On the first two days they dropped more than 350 bombs on caves and buildings. Gunships attacked dozens of vehicles trying to use the night lull in bomber attacks to escape into Pakistan. They expended thousands of rounds of 40mm and 105mm rounds destroying 90 percent of all the targets they identified. These attacks intensified as time passed, with Coalition aircraft dropping 190 bombs on Sunday, March 3, 2002, in support of US and Allied forces. The only aircraft that were not effective were Army AH-64 Apache attack helicopters, which were easy targets for enemy shoulder-fired ordnance and were removed from the combat area. This, in fact, forced an increase in AC-130 raids. By late March, American leaders had ended continuous operations.[36]

Even with the cessation of most operations in April 2002, the fighting went on. By mid-August 2002, a total of 38 Americans had been killed in combat and noncombat incidents in Afghanistan, and more than 340 had been wounded. To be sure, the Afghan government had become more stable, but then again, nearly any government would have been an improvement. In addition, the apparatus for free elections and other trappings of democracy, as well as efforts to restart the economy without it being dependent on the sale of opium, had also begun. However, the United States was slowly turning its attention away from Afghanistan and toward planning for a more ambitious campaign against the Iraqi government of dictator Saddam Hussein, who continued to hinder UN arms inspectors and who had led many in the US government to believe he had weapons of mass destruction (WMDs). This issue, of course, has since been hotly debated, as have been President Bush's motives for eventually invading Iraq in 2003. In fact, as it would turn out, this initial phase was just that: an initial phase. Much like a patient with a serious infection who is prescribed an antibiotic by his doctor to kill the bacteria but fails to take all the pills, Afghanistan was never cured, and it remains ill as of this writing.

As for the AC-130s, during their periodic tours in this AOR from 2002 to the present, their primary missions continued to be night patrols for close air support and armed reconnaissance. Still, heavily armed, they were greatly feared by enemy forces. They had also integrated into their array the most current and sophisticated sensors, navigation systems, and fire control systems that provided surgical firepower or area saturation during extended periods at night and in adverse weather. The sensor suite consists of an ALLTV sensor and an infrared sensor. Radar and electronic sensors also give the gunship a method of positively identifying friendly ground forces as well as effective ordnance delivery during adverse weather conditions.[37]

Between October 2001 and January 2009, OEF had cost the United States $150 billion with less than successful results. Perhaps the proof of that is that beginning in November 2002, the United States began to initiate operations to strike down al-Qaeda outside Afghanistan. In that month American aircraft fired a Hellfire missile at a compound in Yemen containing a group of six al-Qaeda suspects. While the attack killed Qaed Salim Sinan al-Harethi, the planner of the October 2000 attack on the USS *Cole,* the fact that the Afghan war had intensified instead of ending and that al-Qaeda now existed outside of the original AOR indicated that much was left to be done and that AC-130s could expect to return to fight.[38]

Of further significance was a tape of Osama bin Laden released the Sunday before the 2004 presidential election. In it he publicly admitted that al-Qaeda had perpetrated the attacks on the United States. He said that the attacks were carried out because "we are free . . . and want to regain freedom for our nation. As you undermine our security we undermine yours." He further declared that he personally directed the nineteen hijackers, saying, "We had agreed with the Commander-General Muhammad Atta, Allah have mercy on him, that all the operations should be carried out within 20 minutes, before Bush and his administration notice." Another video sent to Al Jazeera in September 2006 showed Osama bin Laden with Ramzi Binalshibh and two of the hijackers making plans for the attacks on the American targets.[39]

If the goal of OEF was to prove that bin Laden was the culprit who planned and ordered the 9/11 attacks, then it was a success. If it was, as President Bush stated, to destroy al-Qaeda and the Taliban, then it was not a success until President Obama's introduction of drone bombing, which has damaged al-Qaeda leadership. However, as of the date of this writing, the United States has been in Afghanistan for nearly thirteen years, and US military operations are still underway from places such as Camp Eggers and Camp Phoenix and are focused on enemy pockets in areas such as Kandahar, Bagram, and Kabul. It should be noted that many of these engagements are night operations supported by AC-130s.[40]

Of course, there has been some success in the Alliance's efforts to establish a legitimate regime and create a stable nation. For example, on October 9, 2004, the Afghan people held their first direct elections, and Hamid Karzai was elected president. A little less than a year later, on September 18, 2005, they conducted their first parliamentary elections with relatively minor violence. Since 2002, hundreds of schools, mosques, and other modern buildings have been built, millions of dollars in aid has been distributed, and, at first, events of violence were reduced. While progovernment forces still have to interdict insurgents and maintain security, provincial reconstruction teams have constructed roads, bridges, and lines of communications throughout their nation. They have also worked to provide food and water to refugees while new housing is built for them to move into. Perhaps best of all, many former warlords have agreed to recognize the legitimacy of the new government, surrendering many of their weapons and integrating their former soldiers into the new Afghan National Army, police, and border guards.[41]

However, the Taliban has, recently, made a comeback, preying on the corruption of the Karzai regime and the economic hardships of the Afghan farmers, who had agreed to stop their profitable opium production and find alternate crops. The Taliban still wields strong influence in many regions, especially among the Pashtun tribal areas near the border with Pakistan. Many argue that Karzai is only a warlord himself, and his real power does not extend much beyond Kabul. Whatever the truth, the US military has had to continue to fight the insurgents, and as a result, Coalition military casualties have continued to grow each year. In 2001, the United States lost 12 killed, and in 2002 they suffered 49 killed, while their allies lost 20. As of December 3, 2012, the number of American military killed had reached 2,161. Counting Coalition dead, the number came to 3,221 and 18,071 wounded. Part of the increase was due to the surge of twelve thousand personnel sent by President Obama, which increased the total number of US forces to nearly sixty thousand.[42]

In late 2011, as US forces withdrew from Iraq, the original antiterrorist campaign in Afghanistan seemed hopelessly mired in domestic and Afghan politics. In spite of increasing US troop levels, there are simply not enough ground forces to get the job done, no matter how many sorties American air forces fly. With Pakistan a tenuous ally and most of the Taliban and al-Qaeda well hidden and sheltered among their Pashtun brothers, the chances of US success in the region remained no more feasible than those of British, Russians, or even Alexander the Great's Macedonians generations before. One piece of good news that can be added as of May 2, 2011, was the "execution" of Osama bin Laden. On that night, President Obama and his key advisers received the coded message, "Geronimo-E KIA." It was live confirmation that an elite team of twelve from SEAL Team 6 flew in on stealth Blackhawk helicopters, stormed a walled compound in Abbotabad, Pakistan, killed bin Laden, and seized numerous films and documents exposing al-Qaeda activities. Many believed the raid was vindication for OEF.[43]

As for the history of the AC-130 and its crews, OEF was only a warmup for an even bigger war that would begin in April of 2003. While a larger engagement in every way, it was somewhat less controversial than the war in Afghanistan. While it began later, the second Gulf War, unlike the war in Central Asia, has ended. In this regard, the AC-130s have deployed to both theaters of operation and not only have played a significant role in the combat but also have saved the lives of countless scores of American and Allied ground forces while chewing up enemy vehicles and forces. As has been their tradition since their first flight in Vietnam, they have continued to rule the night.

15 Operation Iraqi Freedom

From the standpoint of the Air Force fixed-wing gunship fleet, as difficult as the war in Afghanistan proved to be, Operations Iraqi Freedom (OIF) increased its operations tempo and the stress level on the crews. While they would never complain, nor would they ever shirk their duties or fail at their mission, the demand for their services from 2003 to 2011 remained consistently high and full of pressures not experienced by American fighting personnel since Vietnam, Korea, and World War II. It was the ninth significant military conflict they had been involved in since the Vietnam War.[1] With this in mind, it is important to recall how the United States became involved in another war in Iraq.

Following the first Persian Gulf War, the United States projected a policy of containment towards Iraq, complete with economic sanctions, UN oversight of arms and military matters in Iraq, and enforcement of no-fly zones in both northern and southern regions of Iraq. Throughout the 1990s Saddam Hussein tested the limits of US patience by periodically refusing to allow weapons inspectors to inspect his weapons development labs. Up to early 2003, Hussein would turn inspectors away defiantly, only to back down after threats of intervention by US and UN officials. Simultaneously, he would also test the limits of the northern no-fly zone designed to protect the Kurds and the no-fly zone in the south designed to protect the Shia minority. Not only did this infuriate Americans, but it concerned them because there seemed to be evidence that Hussein was directing his scientists and technical experts to develop WMDs such as gas, nuclear, and biological weapons that might be delivered by missiles or aircraft as terror weapons, killing masses of people in major population centers from Tel Aviv to Mecca.[2]

In October 1998 the US Congress passed the Iraq Liberation Act, designed specifically to encourage the people of Iraq to topple the existing regime of Saddam Hussein. Provisions of part of the act provided $97 million for Iraqi "democratic opposition organizations" to "establish a program to support a transition to democracy in Iraq."[3] In the meantime, the UN Security Council was primarily concerned with the enforcement of UNSC Resolution 687, which aimed at stopping Iraqi weapons development programs to prevent any potential terror attack on a global scale. In support of this aspect of UN policy, in November 1998 American and British planes initiated an aerial bombardment campaign designated Operation Desert Fox, specifically aimed at destroying Iraq's ability to make chemical, biological, and nuclear weapons.[4]

During the Clinton years, the United States sought to avoid another conflict with the Iraqis, mainly because we did not see the value of such a conflict in terms of the expenditure of money and lives it might cost. Besides, Hussein, as evil as he was, provided a nonsectarian buffer to the radical Muslims in Iran. This policy changed with the election of George W. Bush in 2000. Instead of a diplomatic solution, his administration, even before 9/11, began planning for an invasion of Iraq and a "regime change." His party's platform had called for "full" application of the Iraq Liberation Act, and Bush's key advisors, specifically Vice President Dick Cheney, Secretary of Defense Donald Rumsfeld, and Under Secretary of Defense Paul Wolfowitz had long advocated finishing the job begun in 1991. It is revealing that former Bush secretary of the treasury Paul O'Neill, after leaving the administration, made convincing claims that the attack on Iraq had been planned since the inauguration and that Bush's very first NSC meeting involved a detailed discussion of just such an invasion scenario. As O'Neill told interviewer Leslie Stahl in a *60 Minutes* report, "From the very beginning, there was a conviction, that Saddam Hussein was a bad person and that he needed to go. . . . Going after Saddam was topic "A" 10 days after the inauguration—eight months before Sept. 11." In fairness, it is equally clear that this issue was also a continuation of a policy being considered by the Clinton NSC. Still, Bush's more aggressive policy toward Iraq facilitated a move toward invasion.[5]

These seeds began to sprout soon after the attacks on September 11, 2001. The very day that terrorists attacked the WTC and the Pentagon, Rumsfeld asked his aides for information on whether it was possible to take down Hussein concurrently with Osama bin Laden. This can only be described as conjecture, since no real planning occurred in the immediate aftermath except for the initiation of OEF. It was not until September 12, 2002, that the president focused on Iraq in an address to the UN General Assembly.[6] While Great Britain sided with the United States, France and Germany opposed an invasion of Iraq. Subsequently, America introduced Resolution 1441 to the Security Council, calling for a resumption of weapons inspections and "serious consequences" for refusal to cooperate. After much debate, in which France and Russia argued against a use of force to sustain the resolution, a compromise resolution was approved.[7]

On November 13, 2002, Saddam Hussein accepted the resolution, and weapons inspectors returned. In their February 12, 2003, report the inspectors declared that they had "found no evidence or plausible indication of the revival of a nuclear weapons program in Iraq." They went on to assure the United Nations that some items that could have been used for nuclear enrichment centrifuges, such as aluminum tubes, were actually intended for other uses. Ultimately, while they did find and deactivate some chemical rocket warheads and laboratory quantities of mustard gas, the process of digging deep enough to know for sure whether WMDs or their components did exist promised to take a long time, and neither the United States nor Iraq seemed prepared to provide that time.[8]

In October 2002 the US Congress passed the "Joint Resolution to Authorize the Use of United States Armed Forces against Iraq." While the resolution authorized the president to "use any means necessary," Americans polled in January 2003 widely favored further diplomacy over an invasion. However, the Bush administration operated an elaborate and effective public relations campaign that eventually convinced 85 percent of the American public that Hussein had hidden WMDs from the inspectors and planned to use them. By February 2003, 74 percent of the citizenry believed the United States should take military action to oust Saddam Hussein.[9]

On February 15, 2003, Secretary of State Colin Powell, the most respected statesman in the Bush administration, spoke to the UN General Assembly in an effort to obtain UN support for an invasion. Using many of the same intelligence figures, charts, and photographs he had used to convince Congress to support the invasion in October of the previous year, he argued that the Iraqis were actively producing chemical and biological weapons, and with their close ties to al-Qaeda, the possibility of WMD terror attacks was not only high but imminent. In consequence, the United States and its supporters proposed a UN resolution authorizing the use of force in Iraq. While the United Kingdom, Poland, Italy, Australia, Denmark, Japan, and Spain supported the proposal, NATO members such as Canada, France, and Germany, together with Russia, urged continued diplomacy. The plan had failed, and facing a losing vote, the resolution was withdrawn. Even with this failure in the United Nations, the United States and its supporters decided to invade without UN approval, a fact that triggered international protests by twenty to thirty million people objecting to what they believed to be a flagrant violation of international law. Powell later admitted his data were wrong. He claimed he had been provided bogus intelligence, particularly pursuant to WMDs.[10]

Going to War in Iraq—Again

The actual invasion of Iraq, designated Operation Iraq Freedom (OIF), lasted from March 20 to May 1, 2003, and included 248,000 troops from the United States, 45,000 from Great Britain, 2,000 from Australia, and 194 from Poland. They also received significant support from Kurdish troops in northern Iraq. On February 18, 2003, more than 100,000 US troops assembled in Kuwait. On March 17, 2003, President Bush addressed the nation and publicly demanded that Hussein and his two sons Uday and Qusay leave Iraq within forty-eight hours. While the land invasion was planned for March 20, 2003, in fact, operations began on March 18, when the president approved aerial bombing raids along the southern border of Iraq.[11]

This dampened the spirits of those who had continued to work for a peaceful settlement. The official US line remained that the only reason the Coalition would invade would be if Iraq failed to disarm. All during that time, Bush and his advisers asserted that WMDs were hidden throughout Iraq. At one point they asserted that Hussein had bought yellowcake (partially processed) uranium from Niger. To bolster this claim, on March 7, 2003, the United States submitted intelligence documents to the International Atomic Energy Agency as proof. After much inspection, even by outside experts, these materials proved to be forgeries. American officials responded that any problems with the authenticity of the documents was "more likely due to incompetence not malice."[12]

It did not matter what reality was made of, the Bush administration was determined to go to war with and remove Saddam Hussein. Still, they were not simply going to be able to walk in and take over. They faced a formidable force, at least on paper. While the actual number of soldiers in the Iraqi Army just before the war was uncertain, it is clear that they were not as well equipped as they had been in 1991. The International Institute for Strategic Studies estimated the Iraqi armed forces were comprised of 375,000 in the army, 2,000 in the navy, 20,000 in the air force and 17,000 in the air defense forces. They also had 44,000 in the paramilitary Fedayeen Saddam and 80,000 in the Republican Guard, for a total of 533,000 military personnel. The institute also estimated that the Iraqis had 650,000 unreliable reserves. Another estimate projected that Iraq had thirteen infantry divisions, ten mechanized and armored divisions, and some specialized units.[13]

During the invasion foreign "volunteers," mostly from Syria, went to Iraq to fight, usually under the command of the Fedayeen Saddam. The number of these so-called volunteers is vague, but US intelligence estimated that 50 percent of all Iraqi combatants in central Iraq were foreigners.[14] In northern Iraq the fanatical Islamic terrorist group Ansar al-Islam controlled small areas and operated outside of the control of Saddam Hussein. They had been fighting Kurdish forces since 2001. Led by Jordan-born Abu Musab al-Zarqawi, they had about eight hundred fighters. Their role was short-lived because by late March a joint US-Kurdish force destroyed their havens and expelled the survivors from Iraq during Operation Viking Hammer.[15]

On March 19, 2003, the Coalition forces began what they called a decapitation attack, launching cruise missiles and bombing key military command and control targets inside Iraq. Among those attacks was one planned to eliminate Hussein and fifty-five of his top advisers. Intelligence reported that Hussein was visiting his sons Uday and Qusay and their families at Dora Farms on the outskirts of Baghdad. About 5:30 a.m., two F-117As dropped four two-thousand-pound satellite-guided GBU-27 bunker busters on the compound. In addition, Tomahawk cruise missiles were fired by four ships and two submarines in the Red Sea and Persian Gulf. While the bombs hit their targets, none of cruise missiles hit inside the compound. The damage was considerable but useless, since neither Hussein nor his family nor any members of the government were present. One civilian was killed and fourteen wounded—mostly women and children. Worse, later investigations confirmed that Hussein had not visited the area since 1995.[16]

On the morning of March 20, Coalition forces began to roll into Iraq. These included units of the 3rd Squadron, 7th Cavalry Regiment, the US 3rd Division, and the 1st Marine Expeditionary Force. A British air and ground attack captured Iraq's Al-Faw Peninsula, and US Marines took the port of Umm Qasr. Throughout this phase, both sides launched missiles—the Coalition more than sixty cruise missiles—and several days after the war began the Iraqis began launching Scuds. Operation Iraqi Freedom had begun.[17]

As the ground troops moved into predetermined positions in Iraq, air strikes against key targets in Baghdad began. At 10:15 a.m. EST, President Bush announced that he had ordered an "attack of opportunity" against specific targets in Iraq. In turn, Iraqi national television broadcast a defiant address by Saddam Hussein. Many in the West speculated that Hussein was dead and the broadcast was a phony. As it turned out, he was very much alive. It was at that point that Australian, British, and US Special Forces units began pushing forward to prepare the way for the larger units only now crossing the border.

In the dark morning hours, an ominous opening occurred when a Coalition transport helicopter crashed, killing eight British and four US soldiers. To make matters worse, massive protests erupted in both Britain and Australia.[18]

Initial plans called for opening a second front in the north. The United States dropped three thousand paratroopers from the 173rd Airborne Brigade in northern Iraq to join with fifteen thousand troops of the 4th Mechanized Infantry Division. They expected to join with Kurdish partisans to move south in a pincer movement designed to crush Iraqi troops in between them. However, this action never happened, since America's Turkish NATO allies objected to anything that might increase the prestige of their traditional Kurdish enemies.[19]

Most observers had expected a protracted aerial bombing campaign prior to the ground assault, like the one they had seen during Desert Storm. However, Coalition operational plans in OIF called for simultaneous air and ground assaults to decapitate the Iraqi forces as fast as possible in an effort to avoid large engagements with the Iraqi military. The notion was that superior mobility and coordination of Coalition forces would allow them to attack the heart of the Iraqi command structure and quickly destroy it, thus minimizing civilian casualties and reducing the damage to the infrastructure. With Turkey's decision not to support a northern front, the primary bases for the invasion had to be in Kuwait. As it would turn out, the invasion was a swift strike that did cause a rapid collapse of the Iraqi military and government.[20]

As the first day ended, US forces were moving west along Highway 1 through the center of the country, and British forces were moving northward through the eastern marshlands. Concurrently, Spanish units moved south to the Saudi-Iraqi border, then drove north to join US forces. Polish troops moved with US Marines, and Danish soldiers fought with the British and Australians in southern Iraq. Throughout the next few days, air strikes increased not only in Baghdad but also in Tikrit, the ancestral home of the Iraqi dictator. It was during this time that the gunships returned to action in Iraq. Indeed, many believe that the actual first shots of the war were fired by AC-130Us of the 4th SOS. Ultimately, the gunships would fly more than one thousand combat hours from three separate FOLs along the periphery of Iraq. Flying the usual missions, the AC-130Us and AC-130Hs would remain a cornerstone of the night skies not only during the invasion but also during the occupation period that ended in December 2011.[21]

By March 22, Allied troops had advanced 150 miles into Iraq, and eight thousand personnel of the Iraqi 51st Army Division had surrendered or deserted along the southern border. The Coalition had flown one thousand sorties against numerous Iraqi targets from fighter attacks on command centers in Baghdad to night close air support and interdiction raids by AC-130 gunships. By 10:00 a.m. local time, US troops were on the outskirts of Basra and preparing to take the city. Their British comrades were also making progress toward joining the US forces near Basra.[22]

Not everything went well. On March 23 the US 1st Marine Division swept through the Rumaila oil fields and moved north to Nasiriyah (225 miles from Baghdad), which was a Shiite stronghold. It was important because it was a road junction near the Talil Airfield and near important bridges that crossed the Euphrates River. Pursuant to the rapid-strike tenor of the invasion, the Army's 3rd Infantry Division quickly defeated Iraqi forces entrenched in and around the airfield and bypassed the city to the west. At the same time, the Marines prepared to take the bridges and the city itself. Later that evening, an eighteen-vehicle convoy manned by thirty-one soldiers from the 507th Maintenance Company and two others from the 3rd Forward Support Battalion, 3rd Infantry Division, including female American soldiers Jessica Lynch and Lori Piestewa, made a wrong turn through the heart of the city and were ambushed by Fedayeen troops. Eleven US soldiers were killed, and six, including Lynch and Piestewa, were captured. Not long after her capture, Piestewa died of her wounds. The remaining five prisoners of war, including Lynch, were later rescued.[23]

That night, Marines supported by A-10s and AC-130s entered Nasiriyah in force. Confronted by heavy resistance, they suffered significant casualties, some from friendly fire. In spite of a barrage of RPGs and small-arms fire from the enemy forces, the Marines took the city, leaving a trail of Fedayeen dead strewn through the narrow streets. By the next day US forces began to converge on the city, and soon the Coalition established a forward operating base and logistics center about ten miles outside of Nasiriyah to supply their troops on their way to Baghdad. Concurrently, US and British troops overran the airport outside Basra.[24]

The Battle of Nasiriyah, one of the first major battles of OIF, began during the early morning hours of March 23, 2003, when the supply convoy took the wrong turn into the city. In looking back, the convoy was a disaster waiting to happen. Commanded by Capt. Troy King, a supply officer with no combat training, the group of vehicles got lost almost as soon as it entered the city. Iraqi pickup trucks carrying machine guns mounted in the beds began shadowing the convoy as it crossed the Euphrates River. It was not until the convoy reached the northern outskirts of the city that King realized that he was lost. Instead of forging ahead, he turned around to retrace his route. At 7:00 a.m. the convoy began to take small-arms fire, mortar fire, and even fire from Iraqi tanks. This resulted in the death of the eleven soldiers and the capture of

Lynch and the five others. Ultimately, fifteen of the eighteen vehicles, which included Humvees and heavy expanded mobility tactical trucks (HEMTTs), were destroyed.[25]

The able-bodied troops formed a screen around their wounded and fought off Iraqi counterattacks until finally being rescued by Alpha Company, 8th Tank Battalion of the 2nd Marine Expeditionary Brigade. With these soldiers secured, the 2nd Marine Expeditionary Brigade, under the call sign Task Force Tarawa, attacked north into the city, seizing two major bridges along Ambush Alley. In heavy urban fighting, eighteen Marines were killed, including six Marines who were killed when A-10s from the Pennsylvania Air National Guard mistakenly strafed a group of amphibious assault vehicles of Charlie Company north of the Saddam Canal. The A-10 strike had been approved by the battalion's FAC, who was with Bravo Company on the eastern outskirts of the city and did not have contact with Charlie Company. He was not aware that Marines were so far north. Ultimately, the Iraqis had 431 killed, three hundred wounded, and one thousand captured. The United States lost 29 dead, sixty wounded, and six captured. Out of these losses, twenty-one soldiers died of hostile fire, six from friendly fire, and two drowned.[26]

Over the next several days Coalition forces, supported by thirty Apache helicopters, attacked the Medina Division of the Republican Guard entrenched near Karbala. Even though two helicopters were shot down and their pilots captured, the advance continued. The Chinese sent a secret message to the United States explaining where their embassy was in Baghdad to avoid a repeat of the disaster in Belgrade in 1999. In addition, the Americans accused the Russians of selling arms to the Iraqis. While this was never really resolved, it hurt Russian-American relations. To make matters worse, the Arab League voted twenty-one to one demanding that the Coalition remove its forces immediately.[27]

On March 25, British and American forces began their assault on Basra itself. As they moved into the city, they were soon confronted by a massive counterattack, which they suppressed with the support of air cover, mostly from AC-130s. As Coalition forces moved in for the coup de grâce in the Iraqi capital, an enormous dust storm temporarily halted the advance on March 27–28. Even when it ended, there were still roadblocks, such as the battle for Najaf against the Republican Guards and fleeing civilians who clogged roads out of Basra.[28]

On April 1–2, Coalition forces surrounded Baghdad as other units cleared cities such as Nasiriya and Basra. On April 2, main Coalition units began moving into the city itself. On April 3 they launched an assault on Saddam International Airport just southwest of the capital. The next day, Maj. Gen. Stanley

McChrystal announced that twenty-five hundred Iraqis had surrendered and the airport was in Coalition hands. One US unit located and showed reporters evidence of laboratories in northern Iraq that were making the deadly toxins ricin and botulinum. These were located near training camps used by Ansar al-Islam, which had ties to al-Qaeda. Concurrently, US troops seized the Latifiyah Explosives and Ammunition Plant, south of Baghdad, and discovered thousands of boxes full of vials of a white powdery substance called atropine, which is a nerve agent antidote, as well as Arab-language documents on how to engage in chemical warfare. It seemed as though they had located the smoking gun. However, the International Atomic Energy Agency, which had suspected the plant to be a chemical, biological, and nuclear weapons site, later reported that UN weapons inspectors had visited the plant at least nine times, including as recently as February 18, 2003, and had found nothing like this. Months later, tests on the substances indicated that they were not the chemical WMDs that the United States suspected Hussein had.[29]

Upon securing the airport, US forces moved into downtown Baghdad, with the Army's V Corps pushing up from the south and the 1st Marine Expeditionary Force approaching from the southeast. Over the next four days, the Allies slowly worked their way through the inner city, often fighting hand-to-hand. They also blocked the roads and highways leading out of the city and brought in reinforcements and supplies to support the final assault. On April 6, Basra finally fell to the British. Plans had originally called for a slow move into the city, forcing Iraqi armor to be clogged in pockets in the city. This proved unnecessary, since most Iraqi armor was destroyed on April 5 during an engagement south of the city in which air strikes obliterated most of the enemy's tracked vehicles. While the Iraqis inflicted significant casualties on the American forces near the airport from their defensive positions, they also suffered severe casualties from air strikes by fighters and AC-130 gunships. By April 7 the presidential palace was taken, and controlling television coverage throughout Iraq, US officials now demanded that Iraqi forces within Baghdad surrender or face a full-scale attack. The attack was not necessary, as it soon became clear that Iraqi soldiers and government officials had disappeared. On April 9, 2003, Baghdad was formally occupied, and Saddam Hussein's regime ended. While much of Baghdad remained unsecured, and skirmishes continued both in the city and on its outskirts, the invasion part of OIF was over. Hussein had vanished, and many Iraqis celebrated by destroying portraits and statues of him. The most famous of these incidents was the toppling of a giant statue of the dictator in Baghdad's Fardus Square.[30]

On April 10, 2003, Iraqi forces in Mosul in the north surrendered to elements of the Army's 173rd Airborne Brigade, Kurdish militia, and the 1st Marine Division. Later that same day, Coalition forces confronted Iraqi troops during the Battle of Kani Domlan Ridge just southeast of Kirkuk. In a brief but bloody engagement, the US and Kurdish forces defeated well-entrenched enemy fighters and soon took control of Kirkuk. On April 12, Marine and Army ground forces began a move toward Saddam Hussein's hometown of Tikrit, which was then one of the few major cities or towns still not under Coalition control. The vast majority of towns and cities surrendered peacefully, most, like Kut (forty miles southeast of Baghdad) welcoming the American occupiers with open arms. At this point Coalition officials were more concerned with controlling looting and the destruction of stores, museums, and other important or sacred buildings and facilities in cities such as Baghdad and Basra. With the Iraqi police dispersed, for the most part civil control became a thorny problem for the occupying military forces throughout the nation.[31]

On April 13, Marines of Task Force Tripoli attacked twenty-five hundred Iraqi fighters in Tikrit in what turned out to be a less difficult battle than expected. By the next morning, the city was in Coalition hands, and for the most part the major battles of the invasion were over. Over the next two weeks, so-called mopping up operations went forward along with declarations of success and victory mainly in the United States and Great Britain.[32]

On May 1, 2003, just forty-three days after OIF began, and to the surprise of everyone in the United States except his closest advisers, President Bush landed on the deck of the aircraft carrier USS *Abraham Lincoln* in a Lockheed S-3 Viking to the cheers of all on board. Reveling in nearly total approval back home, the president announced that "major combat operations in Iraq have ended." He declared that ending Hussein's dictatorship was "one victory in a war on terror that began on September 11, 2001, and still goes on." At first the landing seemed a spur-of-the-moment event, but television news clearly showed a professionally made sign behind the president as he spoke that read, "Mission Accomplished." For this reason many critics called his flight to the *Abraham Lincoln* not only a premature statement, but also a risky and expensive publicity stunt. It was at the time criticism that fell mostly on deaf ears. The president concluded his remarks with what would become prophetic words, when he said: "We have difficult work to do in Iraq. We are bringing order to parts of that country that remain dangerous." Over the next six years, the commitment of thousands of more troops, the expenditure of billions of dollars, and countless attacks by insurgents would indicate just how difficult the work would be. As for the gunship crews, they had played their usual role in the operation. It had not been headline news, but it was about to become increasingly important as dozens of ground campaigns would require their support over the next eight years.[33]

On October 21, 2011, President Barrack Obama announced the end of Operation Iraqi Freedom. It had cost America $900 billion, much of that after victory was declared. Official US government reports placed the number of American military killed up to May 1, 2003, at 139. As of December 3, 2012, that number had increased to 4,486 (4,804 Coalition) with 55,216 wounded. Official western press reports place the numbers of Iraqi dead at more than 30,000, with an additional 7,500 Iraqi noncombatants killed up to May 1, 2003. Since that time, estimates say 60,000 to 80,000 civilians have died. In November 2006, Iraqi health minister Ali al-Shemari asserted that at that point 130,000 to 150,000 Iraqis had died at the hands of insurgents, based on the number of individuals treated in public Iraqi hospitals.[34]

The Occupation Phase Begins

In May 2003, Gen. Tommy Franks assumed control of Iraq as the supreme commander of occupation forces. He spent the next few weeks just trying to reestablish law and order in the war-torn nation. One controversy evolved after Franks retired at the end of the month. In an interview, he seemed to affirm the theory that the sudden collapse of Baghdad was part of a deal between Coalition leaders and Ba'ath Party leaders, who were paid to defect. The validity of this *safqua* is still argued today, and it is unclear how many leaders and officers actual did defect. This controversy aside, much of the occupiers' time was absorbed with searching for Saddam Hussein. American officials posted most-wanted Iraqi playing cards throughout Iraq to assist in their search for the top Iraqi and al-Qaeda bad guys. The fifty-five playing cards provided a photograph and information about each individual. The Coalition offered rewards up to $1 million for their death or capture. By late 2005, forty-six of the fifty-five had been killed or arrested.[35]

On July 22, 2003, the intensive search bore fruit when soldiers of the 101st Airborne Division and Task Force 20 surrounded several of Saddam Hussein's family members near Baghdad. Attempts were made to have them surrender, but they refused, and a massive fire-fight ensued in which Saddam's sons Uday and Qusay and one of the dictator's grandsons were killed.[36]

On December 13–14, 2003, during a sweep of potential hiding places known as Operation Red Dawn, elements of the Army's 4th Infantry Division and members of Task Force 121 entered a rundown shack and discovered a trap door, under which they found an unshaven old man whom they later confirmed was Iraqi dictator Saddam Hussein. In an effort to abide by the laws of the interim Iraqi government, Hussein was turned over to the Iraqi courts to be tried for treason and murder. After a protracted investigation and trial, he was convicted and sentenced to death by hanging. While there were

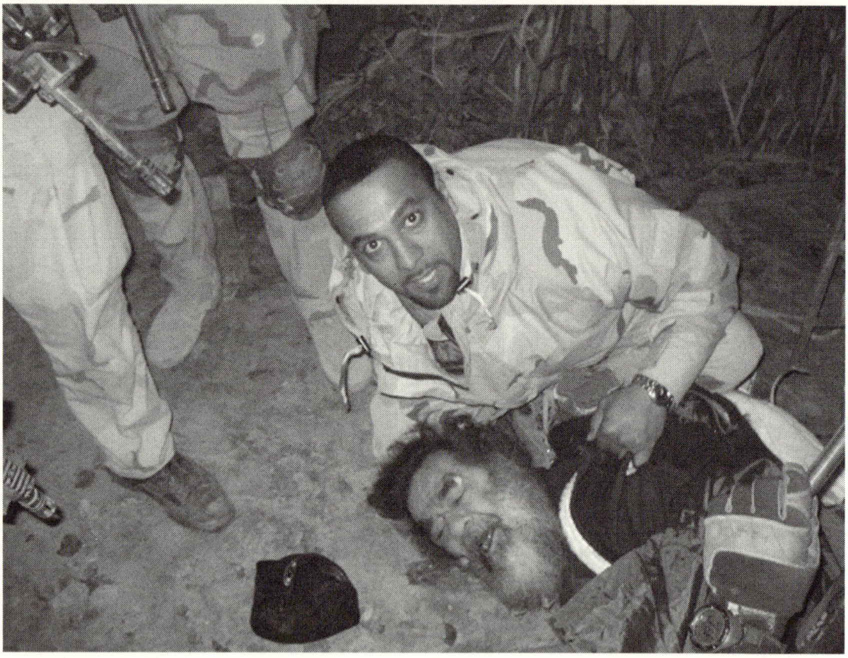

The capture of Saddam Hussein.

many crimes Hussein could have been convicted of, it turned out that he was sentenced for his massacre of a Shiite village in 1982 following an attempt on his life by Shiite radicals. In the early hours of December 30, 2006, the sixty-nine-year-old former strongman was hung. Local and international media were shown the body to confirm that his days had come to an end. He had ruled Iraq with an iron fist since 1979, and now he was dead.[37]

If anyone thought this brought the proceedings to an end, they were sadly mistaken. Throughout the next eight years insurgents of varying kinds continued to attack the occupying forces and Iraqi civilians, especially Iraqi officials, in an effort to undermine the Coalition's efforts to rebuild and bring self-government back to Iraq. No one knew this more than the gunship crews, who even after the May 1, 2003, declaration "mission accomplished" were flying missions against some very bad and dangerous people.

Throughout this protracted period of occupation, the Coalition (mostly the United States) found it necessary to conduct raids in numerous cities and against various enclaves to suppress insurgent activities. Beginning on December 24, AC-130s supported a sweep by the 1st Armored Division in Baghdad itself against fourteen insurgent cells. Flying day and night, the gunships and Air Force fighter aircraft aimed their attacks against tightly hidden targets in the narrow streets of the old part of the city. In one segment of gun-camera footage, a group of US soldiers called for support against approximately forty insurgents. As the gunship slipped into the air space, the pilot asked how he could be of assistance. The ground commander asked him if he could see the enemy swarming into the street near their position. He could and asked command and control for permission to "waste" them. With the go-ahead given, he opened up with his 105mm cannon. In thirty seconds there were only pieces of bodies strewn on the street. The comment of the ground commander summed things up: "Whoa, dude!" During these many years, even to late 2011, gunships were in high demand from ground troops who see them as angels from above. Not only do they decimate enemy vehicle and troop formations, but, unlike other aircraft, they had a track record regarding friendly fire casualties that was tops.[38]

In this particular offensive during the Christmas holidays, the ground troops, artillery, and air cover worked in perfect harmony. Employing intelligence derived from interrogation of high-ranking prisoners, including Saddam Hussein, they rounded up numerous senior and mid-level enemy leaders, including Sunni leader Ghazi Hanash, chief of the al-Ta'ee tribe in the north near Mosul. He, his sons, and his aides were arrested at his apartment in Baghdad. Not only did Hanash have a key role in the Hussein regime, but he also had close ties to Vice President Izzat Ibrahim al-Douri, who was number six on the Americans' fifty-five most wanted list and number one of the thirteen remaining at the end of 2003. Gen. Richard B. Myers, JCS chief, said using information gathered from the capture of Saddam Hussein had allowed this and other similar raids to round up fifty former regime leaders. The raids not only were successful in capturing leaders of the former regime but also had taken place with very few casualties. Many leaders attributed this to the presence of Allied airpower, especially the soldiers' favorite—the fixed-wing gunships.[39]

The Debate of When to Fly AC-130s

In late 2004, Elaine M. Grossman wrote an article on AC-130s and their role in the insurgency phase of the war in Iraq. Published in *Inside the Pentagon,* it not only provided a view of a typical operation for AC-130 gunships, but also examined both the most positive and negative aspects of how the gunships fit into the various operational aspects of the Iraq war.[40]

In November 2004, one of the most significant battles of OIF took place in a town whose name has gone down in US military history along with Khe Sanh, Guadalcanal, Antietam, and Bunker Hill. The fight to gain total control of the city of Fallujah in mid-November has been seen as both infamous and heroic. The bitter resistance faced and the hard-fought victories have made it a name to remember among historians and military personnel. Designated Operation Phantom Fury, it officially lasted from November 7 to December 23, 2004, and was spearheaded by both US Marine elements and British troops of the famous Black Watch battalion of the Royal Highland Regiment. It was the second effort by Coalition forces to take total control of that key city; the first had been in April 2004.[41]

It was a fight that the AC-130s participated in almost totally at night for fear of being attacked by highly accurate SAMs, which the enemy had in great quantity. It was tactical standard operating procedure for the gunships and had been since the Vietnam War. The bitter and bloody fighting in and around the city caused some ground commanders to complain that keeping one of the most powerful ground support weapons out of the fight in daylight was forcing them to fight with one hand tied behind their backs.[42]

Most of the ground commanders around Fallujah at the time, as well as Elaine Grossman in her article, leaned toward the notion that since the ground forces were taking heavy casualties in close combat, the AC-130s should have taken the risk to provide them CAS even during daylight hours. Those critics seem to have forgotten the consequences of even the least amount of daylight to Spirit 03 during operations in Desert Storm in January 1991. It was not that the Army did not like the AC-130s. One Army officer said, "The AC-130—what a great platform. When it's flying, the insurgents are killed by the buckets. However, they will not fly during the day. . . . In Fallujah, we had a better time during periods of darkness, and in the day [we] experienced difficulties because of the absence of the AC-130."[43]

As gunship crews explained to the Marines, the AC-130s have electro-optical and infrared sensors best employed at night. Human targets on the ground stand out on screens inside the specially fitted cargo aircraft, with the shadows and clutter of daytime eliminated. On the other hand, the gunship has a large profile, flies in predictable orbits, and is slow to maneuver out of harm's way. While C-130 cargo aircraft flying tactical supply missions routinely fly daytime missions, they seek to avoid threat areas rather than linger right over them. It should also be noted that CENTCOM deputy commander Lt. Gen. Lance Smith, USAF, also noted, "If the situation absolutely required the AC-130 to operate during daylight hours, then it was used that way." He also assured Inside Washington Publishers that "both the commanders and crews will do whatever is necessary to best support the troops on the ground, given the total complex of systems available." Naturally, the AC-130 crews agreed with that assessment, saying, "Obviously we've surged aircraft in support of current operations. "There's . . . twice as many [in Iraq] as four months ago." This was correct, since by late 2004 there were at any one time as many as twelve gunships in the AOR, as opposed to the six that had originally been deployed. This was true, even with demands for AC-130 services still urgently being sent to Washington by forces in Afghanistan.[44]

From 2003 to 2011, one of the biggest concerns for AC-130s was the threat of man-portable air defense systems, or MANPADs. As these weapons proliferated, the risk to the AC-130s increased at a similar rate. As Smith noted, "To effectively employ its weapons . . . the AC-130 has to fly within the envelope of a number of enemy [MANPADs and antiaircraft artillery], which this enemy has in quantity." He concluded, "Even if it could survive—'a big if,' it would either constantly be moving out of its orbit to avoid threats, or [it would] incur combat damage resulting in the system being unavailable for long periods of time due to repairs." To the ground troops the spectacular results of gunships' 105mm was much appreciated, as was the rapid rate of fire of the AC-130s' 40mm cannon, whose ordnance can pierce thin-skinned vehicles. The U model could engage two targets simultaneously, and with its enhanced survivability, increased stand-off range, armor protection, and electronic countermeasures, it provided nearly all the handful of daytime missions flown in dire emergencies. Most daylight close air support was flown by aircraft such as the A-10 attack aircraft or F-16 fighters, which employed internal guns, bombs, and rockets to attack enemy positions. However, while they were more agile, their inability to loiter over the target limited how long they could support ground forces.[45]

Throughout this period of insurgency, the AC-130 was in very short supply, with only eight H models and thirteen U models—although four more of the advanced Spooky versions were in production and expected by 2006. Of course, one of the main disadvantages was that ground forces wanted the gunships, and not everyone could have them. Senior leadership was not inclined to risk these high-demand/low-density (HD/LD) assets. Some ground commanders criticized such caution. One Army officer at Fallujah complained: "Instead of sticking it out and supporting the Marines [and] soldiers in the day with the best ISR [intelligence, surveillance, and reconnaissance] and air strike platform, they leave the area." As a result, our troops fighting in very complex and difficult terrain are left to less efficient and less agile air platforms." The truth was that AC-130 pilots and crews were always willing to jump in the fight to protect their comrades on the ground. Some even argued that MANPAD threats were relatively low, given the higher altitudes at which they flew. Still, official policy restricted such daytime missions. This caution should not be sneered at, considering that the loss of one gunship would cost fourteen young lives and one of only twenty-one gunships.[46]

Some critics, such as Col. David Hunt, a former Green Beret, declared: "It's not the captains and the majors flying these missions. They're the bravest of the brave! The generals are making a statement: 'We'll tell you how best to use our airplanes.'" He went on to say: "The problem is AFSOC's [standard operating procedures], routine and legacy of not flying during the day. . . . They are frankly ignoring the intelligence and actual capabilities of the insurgent." Others went so far as to declare that most SAMs in Iraq "topped out in a range below the AC-130s normal operating altitude, but 'these insurgents [also] are operating with old, worn-out equipment.'" They concluded: "I've seen these MANPADs, and I have not found one that was in very good working order. All these factors make the risk well within the margins to fly during the day." Hunt continued: "The Air Force is still trying to protect [the gunships] from the rocket-propelled grenades and the SA-7s, [and] the truth is the Air Force will care more about their flying platforms than the infantry and special forces and Marines on the ground. If a guy on the ground says they want the AC-130, they should get it—now."[47]

In response, one senior Air Force leader replied: "These are critical HD/LD assets that are not easily replaced!" However, he went on to say: "But given the other risks we are taking there with folks on the ground, if the AC-130s can provide a unique capability with persistence and precision, why wouldn't we use them?" Even with such bravado noted, the truth was that dozens and later hundreds of Soviet/Russian-made SA-7s, -9s, -14s, and -16s were discovered in caches throughout Iraq where the insurgents were strongest. In retrospect, we now know that the enemy had many more where those came from and were just waiting to deploy them against the slow-flying Spectres and Spookys. As one Air Force officer later pointed out, "You cannot exactly predict what threat will be present." Besides, from the beginning of OEF in 2001 to this very day, SOF aircrews have taken huge risks with the AC-130s in Iraq and Afghanistan, almost always agreeing to come to the aid of their fellow Americans.[48]

As one might expect, this was not the first time this kind of debate had percolated to the surface. The daylight loss of Spirit 03 and its fourteen crew members during the action near Khafji during the 1991 Persian Gulf War caused most Air Force special operators to be uneasy about committing their assets to daytime battles. Some ground personnel privately made it seem the fliers were scared. But the loss of the aircraft and crew was a valid lesson, and there is a great deal of difference between being brave and being foolhardy. It is worth noting that in March 2002 some Army officers had criticized the Air Force for withdrawing an AC-130 from Roberts Ridge during Operation Anaconda in Afghanistan after an overnight battle in which friendly troops

AC-130U in Iraq preparing for takeoff.

were under intense fire. The fact is that the AC-130 was engaged for more than two hours and was running low on fuel. Unfortunately, no backup gunship was sent due to daytime restrictions. As one former AFSOC commander said, "There are certainly times when they can fly in the daytime [however] it's just that when [the threat] catches up with you, it can be disastrous." Besides, as some ground commanders admit and most airmen already realize, it is up to senior commanders to appraise the big picture and use their assets prudently. After all, a threat always seems "most intense to the guys in the foxhole," and soldiers tend to get attached to a particular platform. To quote General Smith, "Taking stock of the bigger picture, commanders can provide capability around the clock 'for a sustained period of time by taking advantage of all the strengths of all the weapon systems available and employing them accordingly.'"[49] To quote Mike Klausutis, a highly experienced special operations expert, "The AC-130 is arguably the single best CAS platform to support troops in contact in night engagements. It can find and attack targets at night when other assets like the A-10 and F-16 are not nearly as effective." Of course, all these aircraft have their strengths, and balancing these platforms against a given circumstance in order to provide around-the-clock coverage is the essential issue.[50]

During the second battle for Fallujah, the United States suffered 95 killed and 560 wounded, while the insurgents had 1,350 killed and 1,500 captured. Civilian deaths were put at 6,000. Just as bad, of a total population of 350,000, more than 200,000 civilians were displaced by the combat that totally destroyed nearly 40 percent of the city. Many of the casualties came in the earliest moments of the offensive, when in an effort not to cause collateral damage, Marines attempted to wind their way through the narrow streets that became perfect spots for ambushes and ideal killing zones. To stop the loss of life, commanders moved their forces at night, when the AC-130s could provide CAS. More important, they gave up on sparing homes and civilian lives, since the enemy was using them to shield their forces. Fallujah II proved the great virtues and vulnerabilities of the AC-130s and made it clear to keep this most effective weapon in the fight, somebody higher up needed to act to improve the gunships' survivability.[51]

Chapter Conclusion

During the last few years, US Marines have found the AC-130H/U gunship to be their favored aircraft for close air support. This was especially true during the insurgency phase of OIF, during which Marines faced most of their fighting in urban settings. They favored the gunships mainly because of their accurate and sustained firepower, time on station, and advanced optics. According to one Marine Corps report, the Marines on the ground liked the fact that the "AC-130s carried a lethal mix of firepower that varied slightly depending on whether it is an AC-130H Spectre, or AC-130U Spooky model." The report noted that "both models are equipped with a L60 40mm Bofors cannon capable of firing up to one hundred rounds per minute as well as a M102 105mm howitzer capable of shooting six to ten rounds per minute." In addition, they reported that the Spooky models are equipped with 25mm GAU-12 Equalizer Gatling-type guns capable of firing four or six thousand rounds per minute. The report went on to reiterate that: "The primary missions for the AC-130 are close air support, air interdiction, and armed reconnaissance. Other missions include perimeter and point defense, escort, landing, drop and extraction zone support, forward air control, limited command and control, and combat search and rescue." The report also focused on the fact that there was a proposal on the table to retrofit all the existing H models with 25mm guns to allow them to fly at higher altitudes to avoid shoulder-fired SAMs, which had begun to proliferate on the battlefield in OIF and after. The author not only recounted the virtues of the AC-130s, but also recommended that they be upgraded whenever possible to allow them to continue serving the Marines as they had in the past. This report is of interest, because in spite of the controversy mentioned above, AC-130s had, as they had in every other previous war, won the respect of those fighting on the ground. It was not so much the Air Force, albeit they believed in the gunships, who wanted more and better gunships, but those who served in the services for which the AC-130s worked so hard.[52]

The measure of any leader, especially a military leader, is his or her ability to embrace lessons learned from past experiences, most often mistakes. This does not suggest the leader should be tied to past circumstances, but should consider how not to make the same mistake and how to anticipate what the future will bring. No fact is truer than that military secrets are the most fleeting. This means that flexibility and constant concern for the men and women being asked to go in harm's way are the greatest talents these leaders can possess. In the case of the AC-130s, operational tempo was so high during the years from OAF to the end of the Iraqi surge that learning lessons seemed to take a back seat to committing assets as quickly and effectively as possible. However, in the last few years there have been efforts by some visionary Air Force leaders and some very innovative contractors and civil servants to upgrade not only the gunship's lethality but also its survivability. It was from OAF to OIF to OEF that the full flowering of the AC-130 took place. In the next chapter we will witness the repotting of the AC-130s and speculation on what airframe might be next in the long history of US fixed-wing gunship.

16 Recent Events, Modifications, and Policy Decisions

As America's role as occupier and rebuilder evolved in both Iraq and Afghanistan, the Spectre and the Spooky II, or "U-Boat," both faced new challenges on the battlefield, most notable increasingly sophisticated and mobile SAMs. This problem led the Air Force to initiate programs to upgrade not only the survival systems and tactics but also the armament of both variants. One of the primary changes was the replacement of the 20mm Gatling guns with a single 25mm GAU-12 Gatling gun capable of firing eighteen hundred rounds per minute. While the 40mm M2A1 Bofors cannon remained, its gun mount and other ancillary components were upgraded to provide an increased life cycle and improved firing rate. The M137A1 105mm cannon, originally derived from the Army's M1A1 howitzer, was also enhanced in the same manner to again improve its reliability and maintainability.[1]

The main reason for these changes, especially the replacement of the 20mm, came from the need to fly at higher altitudes in order to survive attacks by enemy antiaircraft weapons. At higher altitudes it was harder to hit the AC-130s. With their better sensors and weapons, they could still fire with relative accuracy and effectiveness. However, the 25mm rounds still have destructive power when they hit a target from high altitudes, whereas the 20mm round was often spent by the time it did. This was significant, since the 20mm guns had been removed from the AC-130Hs in the 1990s because from higher altitudes their rounds also tumbled, which affected proper aiming and detonation of the projectile. Of course, the U-Boats came with the 25mm already on them.[2]

According to the JCS's SOF reference manual, the AC-130

gunships still operate pretty much as they always have. Today, the U model is manned by thirteen crew members, including the pilot, copilot, navigator, fire control officer, EW officer, flight engineer, loadmaster, all light-level TV (ALLTV) sensor operator, IR detection sensor operator, and four gunners. The H model has the same crew except for an additional gunner. The H has a low-light-level TV (LLLTV) instead of the more modern ALLTV. The H has a range of thirteen hundred nautical miles, and the U, twenty-two hundred. Standard operating procedures call for the gunships to fly outside the target area or lethal envelope to reduce exposure to enemy ground antiaircraft weapons unless they are providing continuous surveillance. They become increasingly vulnerable the longer they spend over the target, since they lose the element of surprise and risk the chance that the enemy might accidentally gain target acquisition on them. The AC-130U, employing its APQ-180 radar, can reliably deliver its ordnance during adverse weather, while the AC-130H has a more limited adverse weather capability. Under ideal circumstances, if a ground controller is present, the crew can correct the AC-130U gunfire for target, range, and magnetic bearing, while a ground controller is almost always necessary to help the AC-130H during poor weather. Their visual sensors are most negatively affected by fog, haze, smoke, and clouds.[3]

During most standard operations, marking devices help identify friendly forces, improve fire support responsiveness, and limit the time the gunship is exposed to enemy acquisition. During instrument meteorological conditions, beacons become the only way for the AC-130H to locate friendly positions. On the other hand, radar-reflective items may be used with the AC-130U radar. These are line-of-sight methods and are generally employed when using offset firing modes. These beacon and reference point offsets extend 800–900 miles. Offset firing is not as accurate as direct firing, so it is usually used in poor weather conditions with the ground commander or team leader calling misses and corrections to the aircraft. Naturally, the shorter the offset distance, the more accurate the weapon. The AC-130U can track the PPN-19 and SST-181 beacons using the strike radar. The AC-130H can track the PPN-19 and SST-181 and also the PRD-7880 tactical electromagnetic impulse generator (TEMIG) and personal locator system beacons.[4]

The AC-130s remain the best low-threat, night CAS weapon system in the Air Force inventory. They provide surgically accurate fire support with minimal collateral damage and are capable of remaining on station for extended periods of time. Their visual sensors and radar provide real-time reconnaissance over the target area, and unlike other fixed-wing aircraft, the AC-130s provided their own FAC capabilities. The AC-130 fires its weapons during a pylon turn, so the target receives constant assault during the entire orbit. Its record of avoiding friendly fire casualties is by far the best of any aircraft in the US inventory and is one reason ground troops request it by name. Its other roles still include aerial interdiction against enemy supply and troop resupply efforts, so it cannot be brought to bear against friendly forces. It also operates during armed reconnaissance missions, supports ground troops at their landing zones, and flies in tandem with fighter aircraft, using them for top cover and providing them with FAC support so they can destroy targets such as radar and SAM sites. In recent years it has also begun flying reconnaissance, combat recovery, and limited airborne command and control missions.[5]

The AC-130U Plus 4

In late December 2001 a DOD program budget decision (PBD) called for purchasing at least eight additional AC-130U Spooky II gunships and initiating work on a possible replacement AC(X) gunship. Defense officials directed the Air Force to purchase and field four additional AC-130Us during FY2003 by converting four C-130H transport aircraft into the AC-130U configuration, which they believed would take less time to execute than building the other four from the ground up. This did not simply involve snapping one's fingers; it required a lot of work. It had taken more than six years to build the original thirteen U models. While no one expected the conversion to take that long, it would require acquisition of numerous gunship-unique parts and armament. It also necessitated pulling the four C-130Hs out of the military airlift inventory, leaving the Air Mobility Command four short. To replace the C-130Hs, Air Force leaders decided to purchase four additional C-130J cargo aircraft during FY03 from Lockheed Aerospace Corporation. The aircraft would be designated the AC-130U Plus 4. Experts estimated that the total cost of these new modified aircraft would range from $50 million to $80 million.[6]

Original plans called for Boeing to deliver the AC-130U Plus 4 gunships in June 2007. Officials directed the contractor to modify the C-130s to meet the same design as the thirteen existing AC-130Us, with one exception. Instead of 20mm or 25mm Gatling guns, they were to install the Bushmaster Mk44 30mm gun. The reason for this change was the increased number and lethality of SAMs. The notion was that if the 25mm would allow the AC-130s to fight at higher altitudes, the 30mm would allow them to go even higher. With the Bushmaster cannons protruding from the gun ports of the AC-130Us, the gunships truly looked more intimidating.[7]

Air Force contracting personnel awarded the contract for the AC-130U Plus 4 gunship program on January 23, 2003. No sooner had the program begun than the reality of how difficult the new ships would be to build became clear. In order to complete the program within budget, including paying for spares and training, and to integrate the new 30mm gun, development of enhanced survivability systems was delayed, since the original milestones for stage completions were delayed by the overall production schedule. The program was being managed under the Air Force's Integrated Weapons System Management Program. This management concept called for every aspect and phase of every weapon system to be competitively selected in an effort to cut costs. That was fine as long as the prime contractors were either the same for most of the components or at least familiar with them. In this case, the lowest bid did not come from the contractor with the best knowledge of the weapon system. As a result, each aspect of the AC-130U Plus Four project was comprised of individual acquisition strategies. In fairness this did save money, but the confusion it caused was often not worth the reduction in cost. The AC-130U was logistically supported at organizational, intermediate, and depot levels by personnel at the WR-ALC. In addition, the Air Force selected Lockheed-Martin's Gunship Multispectral Sensor System (GMS2) to replace ALLTV sensors on the new AC-130Us. Officials also considered installing them on all the gunships.[8]

On January 11, 2005, officials awarded the development contract worth $10.7 million. Ultimately, the program's total value reached $35 million, including production options. Planners determined they would integrate the GMS2 into the four new AC-130U aircraft. Boeing expected the delivery of the first of the four AFSOC AC-130Us during the second quarter of FY06. While there were minor delays, the aircraft were completed on time. The reason for the additional aircraft was to relieve operational pressure on the existing aircraft and crews. This was true for both combat rotations and daily functions such as pilot proficiency training, limited tactical training, and daily training flights. It also increased sortie and training rates at the 4th SOS and 16th SOS home stations (then both at Hurlburt Field), which allowed them to train new crew members to be formed into additional crews and better absorb the high operations tempo down range.[9]

Throughout this period, the integration of the two new 30mm guns seemed destined to improve the aircraft's firepower rate and accuracy and improve its sustainability. As the initial Plus 4 program wound down in late FY06, discussions were already underway to rotate the rest of the fleet through depot maintenance to have their armament replaced in FY07. Concurrently, experts considered adding PGM capabilities to the AC-130Us to give them the most accurate precision strike capability in the Air Force. The notion was that this upgrade would take the platform from being an accurate weapon system to being a precision system. Still, these changes would cost a great deal of time and money to implement and would affect the duties of the fire control officer as well as every other crew position on the aircraft. Experts all agreed it would require extensive training on how to execute these new missions.[10]

In FY07 engineers proposed the installation of a "fusion ball," which is a combination of an ALLTV and an infrared sensor. This combination sensor would allow the crew to take the best attributes of both systems and use them simultaneously as they examined the battle space below them. Like the changes mentioned above, this system, which had been proposed many years earlier, markedly improved the crew's ability for positive identification of targets and friendly forces. Finally, in FY07 the AC-130Us had their old VHS tape system replaced with a digital video recording system, which provided a clearer and faster transfer of information to those who needed it, whether on combat or training missions. The digitization also made it easier to store these recordings in the 4th SOS's library.[11]

As the U model Plus 4 modification program progressed during 2007, the reality that it was one of the most expensive and difficult gunship modification projects ever undertaken began to set in. The test program for the two 30mm Mk 44 Bushmaster II cannons had already begun in January 2007 before the first aircraft rolled off the assembly line, and the results were troubling, not only because of the cost, but also because of the 30mm's lack of performance. By the time the first U model Plus 4 was completed, Air Force leaders, particularly those in AFSOC, wanted to cancel plans to install the new cannons on all of the AC-130Us.[12]

Even so, at Boeing headquarters on April 27, 2007, company officials announced they had begun flight testing the initial AC-130U Plus 4 gunship with its new 30mm cannons at Hurlburt Field. With the other three aircraft due in late August 2007 and US forces in Iraq and Afghanistan needing more CAS, these tests proved crucial. The contractor and AFSOC believed the new cannons would increase the AC-130U's standoff range and improve its first-shot accuracy, and its new suite of countermeasures would significantly enhance its survivability.[13]

Testing lasted for nearly a year, and the results were not good. The hopes of all those involved were eventually dashed, and the Air Force decided to remove the guns and reinstall the original 40mm cannons and 25mm Gatling guns in order to get these vital aircraft into combat. On August 11, 2008, Brig. Gen. Bradley A. Heithold (now lieutenant general), then AFSOC's director of plans, programs, requirements, and assessments, announced the end of the program, explaining that it was because of problems with the Bushmaster's accuracy: "At the altitude we were employing it . . . [it] just did not do what we needed." He also pointed out that there were also schedule considerations that drove the decision, since other enhancements were being planned, and they simply could not keep that many planes in the shop for that long when they were so desperately needed in combat. During FY08, among the other modifications being considered was the possible replacement of the M102 105mm howitzer with a breech-loading 120mm mortar to afford the AC-130 a maximum standoff capability. To add to this standoff capability, experts were considering employing either the AGM-114 Hellfire missile, the Advanced Precision Kill Weapon System (based on the Hydra 70 rocket), or the GBU-44 Viper Strike glide bomb.[14]

In early 2009, with demand for AC-130s high, AFSOC officials continued to seek ways to increase the gunship force. One serious suggestion was the conversion of at least some of the MC-130W Combat Spears. This modification program proposed to combine the AC-130 and MC-130 missions in one aircraft. Roll-on, roll-off kits featuring a medium-caliber gun, sensors, communications systems, and even precision-guided standoff munitions were to be installed on the eight MC-130Ws. Funding for two of the eight kits was approved in early 2009, and installation immediately began. Officials believed these kits would allow them to convert their most modern special ops tankers into pinch-hitting gunships when the need arose. In May 2009 the SECAF announced plans to award a contract worth $31.6 million.[15]

Many in the SOF world were not convinced this was a long-term solution. Some Air Force technicians and many Army leaders suggested that the DOD should push for smaller and more numerous fixed-wing gunships. However, during the debates over the FY10 budget, service leaders decided to stick with the C-130 airframes and not move forward with plans to acquire sixteen C-27 Spartans for conversion. One poignant argument against using the two-engine, propeller-driven C-27s was that they would represent a "return to the days of the AC-47." While this was clearly an exaggeration, since the C-27 speed and airframe characteristics were much superior to those of the AC-47, it was a point that hit the mark with decision makers. No official explanation was provided on what weapons the new gunships would be armed with, but it was clear they would still be on a C-130 platform. On May 19, 2009, Air Force chief of staff Gen. Norton Schwartz stated that the new gunships would most likely feature a lighter armament package than that of the AC-130H/Us. He made it clear that the new gunships would probably look a little bit more like what they had been working on with the AC-27, but built on a C-130 airframe. Ultimately, problems with the C-27 airframe made the C-130 the logical choice once funding could be found.[16]

As this discussion has raised the issue of standoff weapons and missiles being put on the AC-130s, the examination of one specific kind of ordnance is important. Beginning in the middle of the decade, the AC-130U gunship underwent an advanced concept technology demonstration for standoff PGMs called Viper Strike. Designers made the Viper Strike to be a small PGM with guide and glide fins and a four-pound HEAT warhead. They provided it with a man-in-loop control unit capable of destroying mobile targets, such as armored vehicles, from standoff range.[17]

By June 2005, the Air Force had begun to test the Viper Strike in support of the global war on terrorism, since it was well suited for SOF missions in urban and mountainous areas during either day or night. At the time, three people from ASC's AC-130 Systems Squadron, working with counterparts at HQ AFSOC, advanced the program upgrade, preparing for potential future transition to the ASC. At the time, AFSOC had twenty-one gunships in its inventory. The 4th SOS flew thirteen AC-130U gunships, and the 16th SOS eight AC-130Hs—both out of Hurlburt Field at the time. The AC-130s had been some of the first air assets to deploy in preparation for operations in Afghanistan and Iraq, serving as a force multiplier by providing precision CAS with the ability to loiter over the battlefield for extended periods of time. With such a valuable asset in the inventory, leaders sought every means to upgrade and enhance its lethality. This was the primary reason for implementing Viper Strike.[18]

Original plans called for work to begin in the fall of 2005 at Northrop Grumman's Huntsville, Alabama, facility. The first phase of the contract was to demonstrate the use of Viper Strike from the gunship, and it was expected to be completed in December 2006. The contract's second phase was designed to test the military utility of the weapon system and address the possibility of incorporating a data link and additional communications.[19]

Sustainment at the Depot Level

From 2000 to 2009, the increase in operational tempo for the AC-130s and the increase in sophistication of enemy weapon systems made it imperative that depot-level support had to work feverishly to keep up with these ever-increasing demands for new components, modifications, and methods for standardizing sustainment work. Early in the decade, experts at the WR-ALC's SOF directorate began what became an ongoing process of constantly upgrading OFP software to keep the AC-130H and U automated systems always at the cutting edge of technology. Among these systems were programs for control panel display units, mission computers, and ground station computers as well as display generator units. Personnel worked not only to assure the function of each of these systems, but also to confirm that they worked well with all the other systems in an integrated computer package. By 2004 they had designed software that could predict subsystem failures, remind the maintainers that regular service was necessary, and anticipate the need for block cycle changes before the deficiency reports were generated.[20]

Other systems that received attention throughout the 2000s were electro-optical systems such as the FLIR, which today is one of the most accurate high-tech devices ever conceived, and the LLLTV on the H model and ALLTV on the U model. Improvements were also made to the AN/AJQ-24 stabilizing tracking set, the AN/AXQ-17 camera recorder system, and the AN/AAQ-7 laser illuminator. Not only did these modifications improve aircraft safety and lethality, but they also were performed in such as manner that they reduced the cost of operation and repair by replacing components that were vanishing vender items, or "old, scarce parts," with newer, more common parts. Perhaps one of the most significant modifications was upgrade of the remote operations video enhanced receiver on the AC-130Hs, which provided the gunships with real-time interfacing with other aircraft, especially unmanned aerial vehicles (UAVs). Contracted in 2001, it was completed in late 2002. From that time to this the little hatch-mounted-antenna receiver and flat-panel digital display and antenna coupler system have been constantly updated to be sure that even though the H models are late 1960s airframes, the guts that make them run are as modern as any in the Air Force inventory.[21]

Two very important contracted projects undertaken were the 2004 five-year indefinite delivery/indefinite quantity contracts with five separate small business firms for the SOF/CSAR Cross Platform Aircraft Modification Contract and the center wing box replacement on SOF aircraft. The companies in the first series of contracts included A1C Inc., Crestview, Florida; E. J. Mlynarczyk and Company, DeFuniak Springs, Florida; Cherokee Nation Distributors Inc., Stilwell, Oklahoma; Quality Networks Inc., Wetumpka, Alabama; and DoTec Inc., Saint Louis, Missouri. These contracts had the potential to total $97.7 million. The contractors were to support nonrecurring engineering, production, and installation of aircraft modifications that met the time and cost needs of the SOF/CSAR Systems Program Office, which included updating technical manuals within forty-five days and providing kit-proofing verification. The aircraft to be enhanced regularly were the AC-130s, EC-130s, HC-130s, and MC-130s.[22]

While Air Force officials had worried for some time about the stress and wear on the AC-130H and MC-130H center wing box, which holds the wings on the top of every C-130 airframe, it was not until April 11, 2005, that they approved and funded a three-phase program to execute these changes. Phase I involved completion of engineering and test plans as well as the acquisition of center wing box components in order to begin installation on October 1, 2006. Phase II began in March 2007, when the prime contractor, Lockheed-Martin

Aerospace Inc., and personnel of the 402nd Maintenance Wing at Robins AFB, Georgia, initiated the actual $74.4 million production program. Plans called for Phase III to begin as soon as Phase II ended. In addition, Phase III provisions called for a continuation of production and constant monitoring of the work with funding provided from FY07 to FY20. This important sustainment program guaranteed that the AC-130Hs would continue to fly cover for the ground forces in Iraq and Afghanistan or elsewhere for years to come.[23]

Gunships Unleashed

Throughout this period of "low-intensity conflict," especially between May 1, 2003, and the end of 2006, whether the AC-130s needed repairs or the crews could use some rest, if they were called to fly cover for their comrades on the ground, they answered that call.

On October 5, 2003, AC-130U Slayer 74 was vectored toward Fallujah by a joint terminal air controller (JTAC) from the 82nd Airborne Division to initiate a routine counter-mortar mission. Roughly five minutes from his orbit area over Fallujah, the pilot, employing his night-vision goggles, saw the launch of surface-to-surface fire through the small window by his left foot. He quickly rolled into a twenty-degree left bank and alerted his IR and ALLTV sensor operators to the tracers. Within thirty seconds they had identified stationary US military vehicles and several suspicious individuals fleeing the area in a vehicle. Already in contact with the JTAC, the gunship navigator notified him that there had been a probable insurgent attack and reported the exact coordinates of the attack and the fact that the gunship was tracking the fleeing individuals in an unpopulated area. Ground reconnaissance soon confirmed an attack on friendly forces and cleared Slayer 74 to engage the enemy. As the crew prepared to fire their 105mm gun at the fleeing insurgents, they observed them join more probable insurgents and requested further guidance from the JTAC. The Army ground commander requested that the gunships track the car while he assembled a helicopter and ground quick-reaction force.[24]

Over the next three hours the AC-130 followed the enemy force to a house where several of the insurgents got into a second vehicle and continued on to three more houses, picking up and dropping off personnel and on one occasion a suspicious coffin-sized box. With a flight of Army OH-58 Kiowa helicopters, two A-10s, and a JSTARS assisting, the AC-130 kept tabs on the four houses and the two vehicles while waiting for the quick-reaction force to be formed, briefed, and driven to the first two insurgent compounds. Wanting maximum time on station for the compound assaults, Slayer 74 executed an aerial refueling turn, leaving the A-10s and OH-58s on scene. When it returned thirty minutes later, it provided armed escort to the two quick-reaction forces and covered the armed assault of the four insurgent houses during the next three hours.[25]

The mission bagged fifteen insurgent prisoners, neutralized four enemy safe houses, and unearthed twelve rocket-propelled grenades and several dozen AK-47s from the suspicious box. The AC-130's infrared operator had such precise equipment that he literally "walked the troopers to the location of the box and told them where to start digging." It had been a typical night in the lives of the AC-130 crews during this period of occupation and counterinsurgency. While they had not captured a lot of enemy fighters or a large cache of arms, it was a consistent process that slowly but surely uncovered thousands of enemy troops and weapons. Perhaps as significant was the important psychological impact it had had. One of the prisoners later remarked that it seemed the United States had some "all-knowing" weapon capable of striking them without warning on a moment's notice, knowing exactly where they were and even where they had hidden things.[26]

One of the crew members on that mission was Robert Seifert, who later wrote an article entitled "Iraq and the AC-130s Unleashed." While his declared purpose was to, as he put it, "save American lives and improve the chances of a successful outcome in Iraq," the fact is that, having flown on forty-five other missions from March 21, 2003, to August 30, 2004, he provides a significant insight into the world of an AC-130 crew member during OIF. During those early days of insurgency, almost every night at least one AC-130 launched to carry out one or more air support requests (ASRs), which were arranged in priority order and approved by the Joint Special Operations Air Component (JSOAC), which worked for the Combined Forces Special Operations Component commander who exercised operational control of the AC-130. Generally, the units the gunships supported were individual SOF or conventional Army, Marine, and/or Coalition units. The SOF teams and the AC-130s worked together on a predetermined mission, while the conventional units usually requested an AC-130 to search for insurgents in their specific brigade or regiment area of responsibility. As Seifert recalls, "A typical mission has the AC-130 supporting a single brigade's ASRs followed by aerial refueling and another two hours with another brigade or SOF team." While this operational process had some success in both Iraq and Afghanistan, some, like Seifert, believe that such a "method of employment does not fully exploit the great potential of the AC-130 to hunt and kill insurgents, nor does it benefit from lessons learned in aerial conflict over the past 60 years."[27]

Looking back to World War II, the US Army, following its devastating defeat at Kasserine Pass in Tunisia in 1943, altered the use of air cover in Field Manual 100–20 *Command and Employment of Air Power.* Prior to this wakeup call, ground commanders possessed the power to demand that aircraft provide defensive umbrellas, known to airmen as "penny packets," in any ground battle they wished. The disaster at Kasserine had a great deal to do with a lack of coordination between ground and air assets. Under FM 100–20, Gen. George C. Marshall approved the notion that air and ground forces were coequal and that there should always be centralized command of all air assets. This has since that time been a generally accepted doctrine for all US military forces.[28]

According to critics of modern gunship deployment, Coalition forces have returned to the pre-1943 penny packets. In order for ground units to get support from AC-130s, they must submit an ASR that details the time, location, and reason for the requested support. Once approved, the designated gunship arrives at the appointed time and stays for the appointed time. This methodology is in stark contrast to the highly effective extemporaneous tactics used in the Slayer 74 mission. Ten months later, after the Mahdi Militia had begun a second uprising in southern Iraq, during a more standardized mission Seifert's gunship was sent on a five-hour sortie in support of a ground unit in Al Hayy. As the crew launched, they were optimistic that an opportunity to engage insurgents would present itself. Not long after they arrived over their station, this possibility evaporated. As soon as they could, the two visual sensor operators and the pilots, using their night-vision goggles "searched the town for activity, located the friendly positions, and received a situation report from the JTAC that revealed an absence of observed insurgent activity and no plans for friendly offensive operations."[29]

At that point in the sortie they had to take a mid-term break for aerial refueling, after which, as they began their return flight, they passed near the city of Najaf, a hotbed of the August uprising. For some reason there was no gunship on-site. In an instant, the copilot spotted small arms fire in the city, and the gunship swung around to support the Marines below. Since they had previously worked with the Marines, they contacted their JTAC on the radio and informed him that the gunship was nearby. The JTAC confirmed that he had troops in contact and asked for immediate support. In order to release the aircraft from their earlier assignment, this JTAC had to make a request to the Air Support Operations Center (ASOC). Unfortunately, the request crept from ASOC to the Combined Air Operations Center to the Special Operations Liaison Element to the JSOAC and then to the Air Force Special Operations Detachment. By the time the response came, it was no longer of use, and officials decided that the gunship should complete its mission to Al Hayy and then return to base. Instead of reassigning the gunship on-site to Najaf, JSOAC sent the gunship over Fallujah, thirty minutes away, to support the Marines since it had almost completed its current mission.[30]

Later that night, as the Al Hayy AC-130 departed the area, the crew heard radio communications from the Najaf JTAC calling for medical evacuation helicopters to airlift wounded Marines from Najaf. They had been victims of the firefight that the gunship over Al Hayy had witnessed and was prepared to support. Ultimately, the crew's frustration level would rise, since they would repeat this scenario for the next four nights in a row without spotting or contacting a single enemy fighter, even though August 2004 was one of the most violent months of the insurgency.[31]

One of the AC-130's most useful characteristics was its ability to work on the enemy's mind. As Frank Cooling writes in his seminal work on CAS, within a year after the AC-47s first arrived in Vietnam, they had flown cover for "500 outposts and in a single 90-day period broken up 166 enemy night attacks." The VC were so intimidated by these gunships that they were ordered not to fire at what they thought was a fire-breathing beast that might become enraged. As Seifert notes: "The gunships in 1966 did not accomplish this feat or earn this reputation by being tethered to a single ground unit and waiting for it to be attacked, but rather by being on call for whichever outpost needed them most. Every outpost was in contact with higher headquarters, and as soon as an outpost was attacked, an AC-47 was diverted to its position."[32]

One inadvertent drawback to providing CAS for every outpost, or for troops in Iraq rooting out insurgents, is that there are a limited number of gunships available. In Vietnam there were at first thirty to forty AC-47s and later as many as fifty on call. Not even that number was enough, so to guarantee that attacks on outposts were kept to a minimum, the AC-47s were sent to a centralized location and remained on call to respond to any unit experiencing an insurgent assault. Not only was this a discouraging situation to the enemy, but, as noted by Lt. Gen. Julian Ewell, commander, II Corps Field Force, Vietnam, between April 1969 and April 1970 the gunships provided every American infantryman with "a lot of assurance and security to know that if he got in a tight spot, a gunship would be there in fifteen or twenty minutes and start hosing off the countryside." Obviously, ground forces in Iraq did not operate under the same tactical policies because the AC-130s were tied to an individual ground unit for a prescribed period, which, in fact, was and is a basic violation of the doctrine of centralized control.[33]

Finding, Targeting, and Killing the Bastards

Another key aspect of AC-130 operations that seemed to be hindered by the employment policies in Iraq was their impact on targeting. One thing the interdiction campaigns along the Ho Chi Minh Trail proved was that gunships were the best vehicle and personnel killers because of their superior targeting capabilities. Because they were the most accurate aerial weapon, they were the deadliest and most efficient weapon system.[34]

The most successful air campaigns in US history took place during the first Gulf War and OAF. In both contingencies airmen were provided with a single air component commander who directed air assets to specific high-value and immediate-need targets with impunity. This resulted in two crushing victories accomplished almost entirely by airpower. They were the fulfillment of the theories of the fathers of airpower such as Gen. Henry H. Arnold, who said, "Offense is the essence of airpower."[35]

Today, things have changed, and frequently gunships are used more flexibly to attack targets of opportunity with their precise and accurate sensors and weapon systems. Often military leaders learn best from mistakes or disaster, and it frequently takes a while for these lessons to be embraced, since many policies are rooted in what at the time seemed like logical reasoning. The ability to adapt and be flexible is usually the best skill any battlefield commander can have. As these changes are implemented, the goal for all involved continues to be employing the AC-130s where they can do the most damage to those who would harm the men and women of the US military.

As the combat unfolded and debate over the employment of the AC-130s continued, many of the gunships had returned to be fitted with new armaments and communications systems. However, the need for their services was constant and urgent. Thus, as soon as they were refurbished they were sent back into action throughout the last years of the decade. In March 2006, during the US effort to root out the enemy once and for all, Air Force leaders ordered the AC-130s back into action. The first arrived in Iraq on March 23, 2006. They were placed under the command of the Combined Joint Special Operations Task Force. At first the deployment was shrouded in secrecy to keep the enemy in the dark as to their location and the purpose of their presence. Ultimately, they became a spearhead for upcoming joint operations to finally clear out enemy forces from key cities and towns throughout Iraq.[36]

With the gunships having been a key feature in the successful November 2004 US attacks that took the western city of Fallujah from insurgents, the news media speculated that another series of campaigns was on the verge of beginning. In an effort to cut down on deployment time for the AC-130s, they were based inside Iraq at an unnamed airfield. Their use had been a controversial choice, since in urban settings where insurgents may be among crowded populations of noncombatants, collateral damage was always possible and heavily criticized by human rights groups. However, most reports made it clear that they caused far less collateral damage than fast-moving jets. The slow-moving AC-130s also offered intelligence-gathering advantages with their sophisticated long-range video, infrared, and radar sensors, which allowed them to work at night when the enemy wanted to set up traps and ambushes. US commanders were particularly fond of the AC-130s, since they detected insurgents at night planting roadside bombs targeting US convoys.[37]

Since the AC-130 could be used in both high-intensity and low-intensity scenarios, Air Force senior tactical commander Brig. Gen. Frank Gorenc pointed out: "It's got tons of guns, and it's got all kinds of stuff on it that can be applied to the problems you have." As he noted, that "stuff" included "the ability to take these high-tech pods and to use them to find guys planting [bombs] and to find other nefarious activity."[38]

By June of 2007, regular air strikes against enemy fighters had increased on a monumental scale, and with the destruction of enemy targets and saving of American lives also came an increase in civilian casualties. As those who study combat know, more than 40 percent of all casualties are from friendly fire, and up to 20 percent of casualties during urban air strikes are civilian. As reporter Nick Turse wrote in a May 2007 article for *The Nation,* "In a two-day span in May, an airstrike in southern Afghanistan killed at least twenty-one civilians, while a US helicopter attack north of Baghdad killed five civilians, including two children." He argued that "little is known about the air war due to an apparent disregard by the mainstream media . . . ; the full story remains one of the best-kept secrets of the Iraq War."[39]

While this article was intended to expose excesses of US military power being used in Iraq and Afghanistan, what it inadvertently emphasized was the value of the AC-130s and their ability to place ordnance precisely into tight areas, avoiding not only civilian casualties but also friendly fire casualties as well. As for this being some kind of secret war, it was not. What had happened is that President Bush had, by his declaration "mission accomplished" on May 1, 2003, turned public attention and mainstream media attention away from the war in Iraq. With thousands of enemy insurgents planting booby traps and executing hit-and-run operations throughout Iraq, nothing had been settled, and that was why the war continued, why AC-130s were being deployed, and why civilian and military casualties were still happening. Marc Garlasco of Human Rights Watch reported that from April 2003 to April 2007 the United States had dropped nearly 60,000 pounds of cluster bombs alone in Iraq. Air Force officials announced that coalition aircraft had also dropped at least 111,000 pounds of other types of bombs in Iraq in 2006. This was during 10,519 CAS sorties. According to CENTAF, this did not include PGMs, unguided rockets or cannon rounds, or munitions used by some Marine Corps and other fixed-wing coalition aircraft or any Army or Marine helicopter gunships.[40]

To be sure, the AC-130 gunships added to this expenditure of ordnance in post–May 2003 missions. In one typical mission flown on January 28, 2007, a joint operation that included AC-130s, F-16s, and A-10s, CENTAF reported the expenditure of 3.5 tons PGMs, "1,200 rounds of 25mm and 1,100 rounds of 40mm cannon fire" in a five-square-mile area near the southern city of Najaf. The outcry of some pacifist organizations over the death of civilians was predictable. Depending on the source, estimates ran from 78,000 to 655,000 civilian deaths.[41]

The major problem with these types of reports is the lack of hard evidence regarding actual body counts and the identification and definition of civilian. As in most contingencies from the Roman assault on Masada to Filipino resistance during World War II to the American conflict with the VC tomodern-day combat in Fallujah, it is almost impossible to determine who the enemy is and who real noncombatants are. In the end, the object of any military commander is to achieve victory with the lowest number of casualties among his own forces as possible. Unless civilians make it easy to differentiate between themselves and the enemy, then civilians are going to die. That is a cruel fact of all wars: civilians die. In World War II, French workers compelled to labor for the Germans in French factories being bombed by US Army Air Force (USAAF) and RAF bombers died by the thousands. Did the Allies want to kill those people? No! But in order to shut down German war production, they had to bomb the plants. For that matter, no one really wanted to kill German, Italian, or Japanese civilians, either, but they did, and many more were killed than in Iraq. On August 6, 1945, when Col. Paul W. Tibbets's B-29 "Enola Gay" dropped Little Boy on Hiroshima, American POWs were being held there, and most of them died. It is not something combatants necessarily want to happen, but it does happen.

Iraq Isn't the Only Place

In January 2007 the United States launched an airstrike in Somalia against suspected terrorist targets. The primary attack weapons were AC-130 gunships, and according to DOD spokesperson Bryan Whitman, intelligence "showed that no high-value target was killed or captured" but that the United States planned on "going after al-Qaida in the global war on terrorism wherever it takes us." Earlier in the month, Ethiopian and US forces were hunting "three top al-Qaeda suspects but failed to capture or kill them in an AC-130 strike in the southern part of Somalia." Apparently one key target was "Fazul Abdullah Mohammed, one of the three senior al-Qaida members blamed for the 1998 bombings of the US embassies in Kenya and Tanzania."

According to US sources, "the latest operation came as Ethiopia began withdrawing troops that invaded Somalia last month to help Somalia's government drive out a radical Islamic militia officials say has been harboring al-Qaeda operatives." While no confirmation came on the deaths of terrorist leaders, the small camps that were attacked were obliterated, and Americans were satisfied that the AC-130s had destroyed these al-Qaeda safe havens.[42]

The radical, al-Qaeda-linked Somali al-Shabaab group, which had been nearly destroyed by earlier joint operations attacks by AC-130s and Ethiopian troops in December 2006 and January 2007, had reconstituted its fighting force and had developed insurgency tactics, causing a bloody, year-long fight in Mogadishu and other parts of the country against Ethiopian forces, the transitional government, and African Union peacekeepers.[43]

Al-Shabaab operated as the militant wing of the defunct Islamic Courts Union, whose top leaders had been captured and exiled in Eritrea. In February 2008, Shabaab broke ties with the union, declaring that its leadership "was not committed to establishing Islamic rule throughout the world through Jihad." Soon after, a skirmish between supporters of the union and Shabaab fighters reportedly killed several people in Dobley, near the Kenyan border, before the town was seized by forces loyal to Hassan Turki, a Shabaab leader in the Lower Juba area.

With violence on the rise, Allied forces initiated the March 2008 operation, which decimated not only radical Islamic forces but also several key sites used to train and hide al-Qaeda terrorists. In the operation the AC-130 played a vital role.[44] In one assault that gained some attention, several dozen residents of Dobley fled after an aerial strike on known terrorist nodes located in that area. Officials in Washington confirmed the launch of two cruise missiles that struck targets in Dobley. During these strikes against senior leaders of al-Shabaab, an AC-130 destroyed two houses known to be Islamic militant hideouts.

Time for More Repairs and Enhancements

While the gunships continued to have great success during all the missions they were involved in, the high mission tempo had begun to wear out not only the aircraft but the crews as well. This was a fact borne out during an interview by CBS news correspondent David Martin only nine days after the AC-130 attacks in Somalia.

In one of the main stories on the *CBS Evening News* for March 12, 2008, news anchor Katie Couric introduced David Martin, declaring: "There are new concerns tonight that America's aging AC-130s are falling apart." Martin opened his report by explaining that "the AC-130 gunship may well be the single most overworked piece of equipment in the American arsenal. . . .

Every time Special Operations Forces conduct a mission in Iraq and Afghanistan, an AC-130 covers them from the air." Lt. Col. Mark Clawson, an experienced AC-130 pilot, agreed, saying, "We are the number one aircraft for percentage of combat time, and total time over the course of the year." Martin noted that Clawson's aircraft was a seventeen-year-old airframe, making it a U model, since the H-models airframes were at that time thirty-nine to forty years old. To quote Martin: "The war is making the gunship old before its time." Clawson went on to point out: "We've been flying at a rate four times what they ever anticipated, so effectively this is a forty-year-old C-130 in the way it reacts."[45]

Most missions carried a maximum load in Iraq or Afghanistan. The aircraft carried thirteen or fourteen crew members, instruments, computers, guns, and ammo, forcing it to launch at its maximum gross weight. Clawson said, "That basically means I'm at max throttles, max gross weight, and it is max wear and tear on the aircraft on a daily basis." Since the main concern revolved around sustainment, Martin also interviewed Capt. James May, the squadron maintenance officer. May asserted, "We're flying the wings off them literally." He also said that cracks had already appeared in the wings, which "will have to be replaced five years ahead of schedule—and that's just the wings. For every hour of flying, a gunship needed fourteen hours of maintenance."[46]

On this particular training mission flown by the 4th SOS out of Hurlburt Field, Martin noted that it was "the guns that break down. First, the 40mm cannon jams, and then it's the big 105mm howitzer that refuses to fire on automatic. A few love taps with a wrench, but still no go." As one of the gunners exclaimed, "They're just old and tired. It's all right, old girl." The one thing that does work is for the guns to fire manually. As Martin put it, "Even firing manually, the AC-130 is a fearsome weapon. The one gun that does work flawlessly on this mission, the 25mm Gatling gun, firing at a rate of 1,800 rounds per minute." He concluded that the AC-130 was a vital component of US operations in Afghanistan and Iraq because "if Special Operations Forces ever get a chance to capture or kill Osama bin Laden, an AC-130 gunship will almost certainly be part of the operation; that is, if it's still flying by then."[47]

Gunship experts had known for some time that there was an urgent need to refurbish all the gunships. As early as May 2007, planning was underway to address the primary problems. When mulling over the future of the seventeen AC-130Us in the 4th SOS, then AFSOC vice commander Maj. Gen. Donald Wurster remarked that operational stress had placed a heavy burden on the center wing box that holds the wings to the fuselage. During the original assessment of the design in the late 1980s and early 1990s, Air Force engineers

4th Special Operations Squadron patch.

estimated that they would have to replace the boxes during 2013 or 2014. The high usage of the aircraft in Iraq, Afghanistan, and elsewhere left them to consider moving the date up to 2009. Wurster declared, "There's a chance we'll have most of the fleet grounded simultaneously. . . . We've got to find a way to prevent that." During a speech at the National Defense Industrial Association special operations conference, he argued that it was essential to find a way to keep all the AC-130s flying to protect our ground troops and still make sure the aircraft were airworthy and safe to fly.[48]

He believed: "We're flying three gunships in Iraq almost all night long. They make a tremendous difference on the battlefield—killing bad guys and doing over-the-shoulder watches." Of the seventeen AC-130U Spooky IIs and eight AC-130H Spectres in such demand in 2007, the typical aircraft was flying about 137 hours per month in-theater. Its peacetime tempo was 35 hours per month. The reputation of the gunships among ground forces made them a much desired battlefield partner in Iraq and Afghanistan. From their days in Vietnam, when AC-130As and Es were credited with destroying ten thousand North Vietnamese trucks, to their heroics in Operation Desert Storm to their 2007–2008 operations in Afghanistan, Iraq, and Somalia, ground troops saw them as watchdogs, always there to protect them from unseen danger and to destroy enemy targets. While some critics believed that the Air Force should build a new gunship that could survive in daylight, General Wurster noted that this was unlikely because there were, in 2007, plans to replace some of the aircraft with long-range bombers that could fly in the daytime and execute many of the gunship missions. However, most experts believed that it would not be until 2018 at the earliest that a new long-range bomber would come online. Besides, as of 2009 the program to develop a next-generation bomber remained in the conceptual phase.[49]

Professionals such as Richard Aboulafia, an aerospace analyst for the Teal Group, described the idea of using long-range strike aircraft to pick up the slack from the AC-130 as "unusual." He stated: "It's a notional concept and the idea of waiting to recapitalize an aging asset for some notional asset sounds impractical." Aboulafia said that the concept of such a long-range bomber was like a fifteenth-century ruler putting the words "'here there be dragons' on his map." As there had never been a single idea of what shape this new bomber would take, many Air Force leaders had attached new missions to the program. This evolved to the point that some critics predicted that the plane would end up being a jack of all trades resembling a multicolored quilt. Aboulafia said, "I'm surprised it hasn't become an air-to-air refueling tanker." This was all speculation, and the big issue in 2009 became what to do to provide CAS for ground forces while the gunships underwent maintenance and repair work. There were other weapons systems that could perform some of the AC-130's roles, but troops on the ground, especially Marines, had become very comfortable working with the AC-130s. No doubt an F-15 Strike Eagle or a Predator B has the capability to drop a bomb on a target, but over the past several years the crews of the AC-130s and their brothers on the ground have come to trust each other. As Wurster points out, the airmen will tell the ground commander, "Just around the corner there are four guys who look like they're coming to shoot you. Do you want us to kill them?" They respond, "Yeah, please do. . . . Our ground forces are extremely comfortable with the professionalism and the commitment of the AC-130 crews." He concluded: "That relationship between that [AC-130] platform and those people on the ground is a very strong bond."[50]

Fortunately, by FY09, when the AC-130s needed to be inducted through the US sustainment system, planners came up with more efficient methods of performing depot maintenance. Instead of being directed toward specific structural work, aircraft sent back for repairs went through as many aspects of servicing and sustainment as possible at the same time. Officials reinspected aircraft in the field to see which ones needed immediate attention and which ones could still fly, even if only limited missions. In short, they created a gunship triage process that sent only those AC-130s necessary back to the CONUS while keeping those in-theater on a strict schedule. Last but not least, those workers in the depots at WR-ALC and the contractor plants redoubled their efforts to push the gunships through the repair and sustainment procedures as quickly as possible, even if it meant working around the clock to get them back into combat. Considering what was at stake, no one could do less.[51]

The AC-130s Contracted F2AST

Not only is the AC-130s' armament important to their effectiveness, but it is vital to their ability to precisely target and destroy the enemy's vehicles, facilities, and forces, making it a particularly lethal killing machine. The Air Force never stops working to upgrade every aspect of the gunships' targeting sensors. On February 2, 2009, they awarded the Boeing Company a $19.1 million AFSOC contract, under the Air Force Future Flexible Acquisition and Sustainment Tool Program (F2AST), to upgrade AC-130U operational flight and simulation software sustainment and maintenance; field service representative support; configuration, data, and obsolescence management; and intermediate-level repairs. They also contracted for three annual options during the first quarter of the year. Each allowed the Air Force to activate the option every twelve months. Ken Hill, the director of SOF support for Boeing Integrated Defense Systems, Fort Walton Beach, Florida, told reporters: "Boeing is pleased to receive the first of what we believe will be many contract orders to support the F2AST program for the US Air Force. . . . We have assembled a world-class team to support our war fighters in this vital sustainment contract."[52]

In July 2008, Air Force contracting officials had selected Boeing as one of the companies to compete for the F2AST support program because of their vast experience supporting Air Force weapon systems and "their diverse network of large, small, and minority/women-owned suppliers to offer cost-effective and innovative sustainment solutions." In the case of the AC-130s, the F2AST program combined with the Integrated Weapons System Support Program to provide the gunships with a single indefinite delivery–indefinite quantity contract that will include development, modifications, depot maintenance, spares, and repairs on this vital Air Force platform as well as its key sensor support systems, subsystems, and components. Of course the primary items for upgrade in this program for the AC-130s were their sensors and targeting systems. Plans call for each contract to provide the latest hardware and software modifications to added to each gunship in the inventory as it returns through PDM.[53]

Where are the AC-130As Today?

Recent years have seen more combat and more enhancements for planes and crews of the 16th SOS and 4th SOS, and they also have seen some of the older A models honored by being displayed at various museums across the nation. The most famous is T/N 53-3129, *First Lady,* the first of the initial seven production AC-130A aircraft deployed to Vietnam. On March 25, 1971, while flying an interdiction mission over Laos, it was struck by a 37mm AAA shell that destroyed everything below the crew deck. In 1975, following the Vietnam War, the Air Force transferred it to the Air Force Reserve, where it and other A models served with the 711th SOS of the 919th SOW. In 1980 all the AC-130As received four-bladed propellers to replace the original three blades. In late 1995, the AFRC stopped flying gunships and retired them from the active inventory. The Air Force Armament Museum at Eglin AFB, Florida, received *First Lady* and placed it on display wearing its AFRC grey paint scheme and black markings and sporting its four-bladed Hamilton Standard propellers.[54]

The AC-130A, T/N 56–0509, *Ultimate End,* is today located at the AFSOC Heritage Air Park near the entrance to Hurlburt Field, Florida. The Air Force accepted its C-130 airframe on February 28, 1957, and modified it into a gunship on July 27, 1970. A stalwart in the Vietnam War, it played a key role in the rescue of the SS *Mayaguez.* Three times the aircraft was hit by AAA, surviving five 37mm hits, on December 12, 1970; extensive left wing leading edge damage on April 12, 1971; and a 57mm hit in its belly on March 4, 1972. Flying with the 711th SOS, it was retired from the active inventory on October 1, 1994, and relocated to its present location on October 20, 1994. It was dedicated on May 4, 1995.[55]

The AC-130A T/N 54–1630 is currently on display in the Cold War Gallery of the National Museum of the US Air Force, Wright-Patterson AFB, Ohio. It was named *Azrael,* after the angel of death in the Koran who severs the soul from the body. The name is no doubt appropriate, since the plane made major contributions in the final hours of Operation Desert Storm, when on February 26, 1991 it was sent to the Al Jahra Highway (Highway 80) near Basra, Iraq. It intercepted fleeing Iraqi convoys of tanks, trucks, buses, and cars and in spite of AAA and SAM threats cut the Iraqi columns to pieces, leaving smoldering hulks all along the line of retreat. It was retired to its current location in October 1995. Another AC-130A, T/N 54–1626, the original prototype AC-130 also known as Gunship II, is also on display at the outdoor Air Park at the National Museum at Wright-Patterson AFB. Last but not least, A/C 54–1623, the tenth production model C-130A, which was converted to an AC-130A in 1968, is currently located at Dobbins AFB, Georgia, sporting three-bladed props.[56]

While these are the only five on display, the others are not forgotten, especially by those who flew them. Like most aircraft built to fly in combat or in support of America's airborne warriors, most of the AC-130As wound up in the boneyard at Davis Monthan AFB, Arizona. Still, by preserving just these five, millions of Americans will be able to see up close some of the most important aircraft that have defended their freedom.

Rearranging the Gunship Squadrons

As of September 2009, the AC-130U aircraft and the crew personnel of the 4th SOS remain headquartered in magnificent facilities at Hurlburt Field in the panhandle of Florida, where they train and recoup from their numerous deployments to provide CAS and interdiction support for their brothers on the ground in Iraq and Afghanistan.[57]

While I was fortunate enough to visit the 16th SOS while I was at Hurlburt in 2008, that visit today would require a much longer trip, as the 16th has been transferred to Cannon AFB, New Mexico, as part of a realignment designed to provide more and better training facilities and easier access to more diverse locations from which to deploy. On October 1, 2007, the Air Force formally activated the 27th SOW and located it at Cannon. At first it had few assets, but that soon changed.

In May 2008, only five months after I flew with the 16th SOS (for a few minutes, anyway), members of the New Mexico congressional delegation received news in Washington that AFSOC planned to move the 16th SOS to Cannon. Specifically, Lt. Gen. Donald Wurster, AFSOC commander, told Senators Pete Domenici and Jeff Bingaman, as well as Representatives Heather Wilson, Tom Udall, and Steve Pearce, that the Air Force would be stationing the 16th's eight AC-130H aircraft, along with their crew members and support personnel, at the eastern New Mexico base. The aircraft began arriving in late October 2008, with the deployment eventually bringing more than six hundred military personnel and three hundred contractor and civilian individuals to Cannon AFB by the end of FY2009. The restationing of the squadron made the future survival of Cannon AFB more secure, and Tom Udall declared: "I welcome the squadron to New Mexico and to Cannon. I am confident they will enjoy the training benefits of all that Cannon has to offer, and the warm welcome they will receive from the community. Cannon has long played an important role in keeping America safe, and I am confident that the 16th Special Operations Squadron will help to continue the base's tradition of excellence." The delegation had worked very hard to provide FY08 funding in the omnibus appropriations bill, which included $10.7 million for military construction projects at Cannon AFB. The president's FY2009 budget request also recommended $18.1 million for a maintenance hangar at Cannon. The AC-130Hs were the fulfillment of this new Air Force footprint in New Mexico.[58]

On June 19, 2009, the 16th SOS held a squadron flag transfer ceremony to mark the formal move of the squadron from Hurlburt Field to Cannon AFB. Presiding over the ceremony was General Wurster, who declared: "The mighty Spectre has arrived! The 16th Special Operations Squadron, with a proven heritage of courage, precision and valor, has relocated to Cannon Air Force Base as of today, to the high desert of its New Mexico home."[59]

In his speech the general in a very real fashion not only recounted the remarkable history of the AC-130Hs and the 16th SOS, but also noted all the men and women who have flown all the fixed-wing gunships, from the first Spooky to the most modern U model. He recalled that even at that moment in Iraq and Afghanistan "this squadron has supported over 2,700 days of continuous combat and is directly responsible for over 4,500 enemy combatants killed or captured." And he concluded that we should also remember the constant sacrifice the gunship crews make and have made, saying, "Fully a quarter of the squadron is deployed, serving in combat, as we speak." Col. Stephen A. Clark, 27th SOW commander, echoed these sentiments, declaring: "The men and women of the 16th SOS have worked relentlessly to ensure that for them, the term 'impossible' is synonymous with the term 'normal.'"[60]

The actual deployment had gone without a major hitch. In July 2008, Detachment 1 of the 16th stood up at Cannon to prepare the way for the arrival of eight aircraft and nearly five hundred personnel of the 16th SOS and 16th Aircraft Maintenance Unit, and on May 19, 2009, the first two AC-130H Spectre gunships arrived. More than half of the crews and support personnel arrived by late June. Plans called for the final members of these units to be in place no later than November 30, 2009, under the command of Lt. Col. Sean M. Farrell.[61]

What's Next?

In many respects the redeployment of the 16th SOS was both a conclusion and a beginning. For the first time in thirty-four years only one gunship unit would be located along the Gulf Coast of Florida. The AC-130Hs that had spent nearly their entire existence in Florida were now in a new home. In this regard, it was the end of an era. At the same time, as one door closed a new one opened. With discussion on-going about the continuing upgrade of both the AC-130Hs and the AC-130Us and the construction of newer and better gunships based on newer, more powerful airframes, the future of these unique weapon systems seemed assured. One could say that as long as there are those who would destroy our nation and our way of life, there will be aircraft designed to root those enemies out and destroy their means to do us harm. In the case of the Afghan conflict, one of the most requested weapon system continued to be the AC-130 gunship.

Conclusion
Some Final Thoughts about the Night Hunters

In 1944, when asked how the Allies would defeat Hitler, Franklin D. Roosevelt declared, "Hitler built a fortress around Europe, but he forgot to put a roof on it." So it remains in the twenty-first century that the expenditure of manpower and treasure to provide America adequate airpower to defend its borders, its interests, and the peace of the planet has become essential in all that our foreign and defense policy seeks to accomplish.

Among the components of American airpower are many of the most modern fighter, bomber, cargo, and intelligence aircraft known to mankind. The technical advances made over just the last two decades are staggering, to be sure. However, in all this time one group of US airmen has continued to fly a low and slow weapon system that continues to link them with their comrades on the ground—the AC-130. Since the time the great gunships first launched, there have been those skeptics and naysayers who continually seek new systems to take their place. As of October 2009 they have not found such a replacement, and so to pay honor to those who have risked and continue to risk their existence for their fellow Americans, this work seeks to explain and analyze the history of the AC-130. To drive the message home, it is worth taking a look at one last example of what it is like to fly on an AC-130 in harm's way.

A Typical Mission

In the aftermath of the Persian Gulf War, the Air Force Studies and Analyses Agency put together a 1996 report on the Battle of Khafji. Since the AC-130 played such a vital role in that and other key engagements of that conflict, many of the interviews the author conducted were with members of the first gunship on site during the battle. While I have written throughout this book about various AC-130 missions that span the life of these gunships from Vietnam to current actions in Afghanistan and Iraq, the one described by the crew members of the first AC-130 at Khafji summarize a typical mission perhaps better than any other available and explain to the reader what it is like to fly the AC-130 into combat.

In late January 1991, Maj. Paul Havel was the command pilot of an AC-130H just before the first Persian Gulf War ground action. As noted in chapter 11, Al-Khafji is located on the border between Kuwait and Saudi Arabia. The Iraqis decided to send dozens of vehicles and thousands of troops to take the town. The only Coalition forces in the vicinity were a group of Marines in a long-range reconnaissance team. Havel and his crew were on alert when the call came from an ABCCC aircraft that there was trouble in Khafji. The Marines were trapped on the rooftop of a building inside the town, which was controlled by the Iraqis. As Havel put it: "So we took off headed to Khafji to that AO up there and as soon as we approached we contacted ABCCC who, in turn, passed us on to a Marine airborne FAC, who was flying an OV-10." The FAC reported minor threats from AAA and SAMs and directed them to "take out anything north of the town."[1]

As they arrived over the target, they saw the OV-10 dispensing decoy flares and random AAA fire from the north side of the town. The OV-10 requested that the AC-130 engage with its 105mm howitzer. The gunship turned and came in from over the nearby Persian Gulf at about nine thousand feet to avoid radar detection and to gain the element of surprise. They soon spotted eight personnel carriers, which were the lead elements of an armored reconnaissance unit. With AAA fire increasing, they decided to eliminate the AAA units first. Havel recalled: "I decided to use the number six gun, which is a 105mm howitzer, otherwise known as a 'crowd pleaser.'" The gun jammed, and as they were trying to fix it the loadmaster cried out, "Strela, Strela, Break right, break right!" During this delay the FAC called for artillery fire, so they had to pull back and wait for their turn to reengage.[2]

Once they returned, they hit the AAA sites with the 105mm but could only locate two of the eight vehicles. "Bad luck for these two." Havel's AC-130 "worked over the vehicles with the 40mm using four-round clips to fire about 100 rounds per minute." They got the two BRDMs (BTR-40Ps, Soviet–Eastern Bloc armed reconnaissance vehicles) and also "put down a whole bunch of extra rounds to suppress the area, in case there were any extra personnel." Low on fuel, they found an aerial refueling aircraft and headed home. Facing people, even when you do not see their faces, who are trying to kill you is a sobering event. Dodging 23mm, 37mm, and 57mm AAA and SAMs puts anyone on edge. Havel said, "I think the biggest thing that works for me is you're afraid to fail. You don't want to screw up. You're more afraid of failure than you are of the enemy. . . . I was really concentrating on doing my job. . . . I was really concerned about my crew. I wanted to make sure I made the right decisions for them. . . . You stay with your job, you stick to it, and you don't have time to really worry about it." Part of that job is knowing how long to stay in contact with the enemy. The most famous Gulf War incident is the downing of Spirit 03, which stayed too long and was caught in the daylight. Havel was an experienced gunship pilot and remembered the lessons he had learned from the veterans he had flown with a generation earlier. As he recalled: "A lot of the tactics that I know I learned from the Vietnam era pilots—three orbits, no more!" As he said, "As long as you keep mixing it up and doing different things, you're fine." Havel had some basic rules that nearly every pilot knew: never fly in daylight, do not fly more than three hours, and never "duel with AAA."[3]

Not only did Havel limit his attack runs to three orbits, but also when he attacked the enemy vehicles in Al-Khafji, his AC-130 flew in from over the Persian Gulf to confuse the Iraqi radar. In that case the tactics worked to perfection, and, as Havel said, "They didn't realize we were an airplane at first. And I think they thought we were part of the artillery barrage, because we were putting down 105mm, which is just like the artillery . . . and we didn't signature like a jet fighter. And we were the first gunship in the area, of all the gunships that did fly in the Battle of Khafji." Tactics and technology aside, Havel echoed the same sentiments all the other gunship pilots did concerning the quality of their crew members. The major declared: "I had an excellent crew, and I can't say enough about them. I had some of the most experienced sensor operators, load master, and gunners. And they knew when to shut up and they knew when to chime in. The best example of that was when we had to go back the second time." The second mission was in daylight, so he waited out over the Gulf and contacted the FAC to ask if any troops were in danger. When he discovered that they were safe and that there were only targets of opportunity, he asked the crew their opinion. Each provided a professional set of pros and cons. Havel decided not to attack, and it turned out to be "a good decision because the next day . . . , we lost one of our gunships, same area, same time of day, approximately, early in the morning."[4]

Major Havel was not the only crew member interviewed. Among the others queried was Capt. Charles Stoner, Havel's copilot and a three-year veteran of flying AC-130Hs. He had trained in Panama and was a combat veteran. While he reiterated Havel's memories of Khafji, he also emphasized that "we didn't have any serious threats when we were practicing for that or some of the other missions we were doing down there. Those were pretty much small arms or much lighter AAA." Indeed, Iraq and Kuwait were high-threat environments, and as Stoner recalled, he was most often too busy to be afraid. He said, "There are times when you do think about it, when it gets a little bit close and things like that. For me, I really didn't think about it too much at the time. It was more afterwards when you get back, and on the ground, and the adrenaline stops and you think that was kind of close at times." The crew was proud of their achievements on the mission, and after leadership back at base looked at the camera footage, they, too, were pleased with the support that the AC-130s had provided on that important first night.[5]

Major Clevenger interviewed five other crew members from various gunships, including gunners TSgt. William Alex and SSgt. Brad Sims, sensor operators TSgt. Ron Johnson and TSgt. Clay Watson, and loadmaster TSgt. Ken Taylor. One thing they mentioned was that they were headquartered at King Fahd International Airport. As Watson recalled, "I don't think I'll ever forget that night. When we launched out it was an alert launch. We had very little planning time. But it was basically an armed reconnaissance mission in the area of Khafji, over the coast." Watson's ship was Spirit 01, and it and most of the others, including Havel's gunship, had "already flown one mission out west, just to some spot in the desert where there was supposed to be some radar equipment, and we had already been to Wadi Al Kir."[6]

TSgt. Johnson noted that most of the targets were inside the Kuwaiti border just northwest of Al-Khafji. He recalled that "after we got launched, there was already another aircraft (Havel's) in the air over Khafji that was working targets there." Working together to maximize their efficiency, Johnson spoke to Havel's radio operator, who told him "that the forces were in Khafji and south of Khafji. They pointed out where some of the AAA pieces were that were brought down into Saudi, and so we decided work north of there, northwest. To Johnson the personnel carriers were "pretty easy targets. . . . There was more or less a free fire zone north of a certain latitude. There was a lot of stuff moving up there too. Pretty easy to find." Like most of the others interviewed, he was too busy to be afraid, but at one point he allowed himself to marvel at the night sky and all the activity underway. He remembered: "It was surreal up there—a lot of AAA. . . . From my perspective as a television operator, it looked like fireworks on a TV screen. . . . But you knew it was intense by the maneuvers of the aircraft, and actually smell the shells exploding around the airplane." These weren't fireworks; they were deadly projectiles designed to kill Johnson's aircraft, and he and his crew mates knew it all too well. But they had a job to do, and as he concluded, that job was "to kill as many of those guys as fast as possible, because like I said, we had been contemplating this massive army just rolling to the south and overrunning us. And so we were just up there giving them everything we had."[7]

The Battle of Ras Al-Khafji was not the first nor was it the last engagement that AC-130s were in. They began their missions over the jungles of Vietnam in 1967, flying test missions in the AC-130A prototype, and the H models and ultramodern U models are still flying missions. Al-Khafji was not the most lethal nor most ideal environment. It was not the largest battle or longest flight that AC-130s ever faced. However, what it does represent is the basic job that AC-130s perform. They fly to support ground troops, and often this is a very dangerous job that involves being very smart and very careful, but also one that makes the crew members recall that they have brothers on the ground who need them and that if risk is involved, then they must face that risk if it is necessary to protect the ground forces from harm.

Having had the honor of visiting the 16th SOS when it was still stationed at Hurlburt Field in January 2008, I can vouch for the stress and strain the crews and aircraft experience. Yet it is worth noting that the young men and women who crew and fly these gunships never seem to complain, nor do they expect great pay or cushy quarters or pats on the back. If they can physically make that old bird get airborne, they launch and fly their mission to preserve the lives of their comrades on the ground. In the training missions I experienced at Hurlburt, what struck me most was just how young most of the crew personnel are. The exceptions are the colonels and majors who are the commanders of each aircraft and are also usually the pilots. During training missions these longtime veterans are amazing teachers. As they go through the preflight briefings, they urge and encourage the younger officers, knowing that someday these twenty-somethings will take their place and have the lives of thirteen or fourteen people in their hands. The crews, the squadron, the commanders are all very close and see themselves as unique individuals playing a vital role in the defense of their nation. The truth is that they are unique and remarkable in their knowledge, talent, determination, and dedication to their aircraft, their unit, the Air Force, and the nation. They are able to make old and worn-out aircraft perform miracles.

The Legacy of the AC-130s

Of the nineteen AC-130As, eleven AC-130E/Hs, and seventeen AC-130Us built, a total of eight were lost during combat operations, including six over Southeast Asia, one during Desert Storm, and one over Somalia. Considering the nature of the combat environment that AC-130s usually fly in and the sophistication and number of enemy weapons arrayed against them, it is amazing that only seven have been lost to enemy fire. The seventy-five crew members who died during the Vietnam War and the twenty-one who perished in Desert Storm and in Somalia comprise the real tragedy and are the real heroes of this story. The first loss was T/N 54–1629, which was hit in 1969 over Laos and crashed during a landing attempt at Ubon RTAFB, Thailand. A second AC-130 was downed over Laos in April 1970. The third and fourth losses occurred within hours of each other in the spring of 1972, and a fifth was shot down a few weeks later while supporting friendly forces at the siege of An Loc in South Vietnam. A sixth gunship was shot down over Laos in December 1972. On January 31, 1991, the first AC-130H was lost in combat while supporting coalition forces engaged in ground combat during the Battle of Khafji in Operation Desert Storm. A second aircraft supporting operations in Somalia was lost on March 15, 1994, when the 105mm cannon exploded while the aircraft was airborne. The eight remaining AC-130H Spectre gunships are still flying with the 16th SOS.[8]

Three squadrons flew the AC-130s: the Air Force Reserve's 711th SOS, the 16th SOS, and most recently the 4th SOS. The 711th SOS was originally constituted as the 711th Heavy Bombardment Squadron on April 6, 1943, and it was not until July 1, 1975, that it became a special operations squadron. As the 711th SOS, its crews flew AC-130As until the A models were deactivated and the squadron converted to MC-130Es at the end of 1995. Their campaign streamers included World War II, Air Offensive, Europe; Normandy; Northern France; Rhineland; Ardennes-Alsace; Central Europe; Air Combat, EAME Theater and Southwest Asia; and Liberation and Defense of Kuwait. The unit also received an Armed Forces Expeditionary Streamer for combat operations in Panama from 1989 to 1990.[9]

The 16th SOS began as a ferrying squadron on February 18, 1942, and became a special operations squadron on October 30, 1968. It was the 16th SOS that flew the original nineteen AC-130As (including the prototype, *Surprise Package*), Pave Pronto, Plain Janes, and others. When the AC-130Es arrived, they were put into the 16th SOS as well, and it was not until they returned to Eglin AFB in 1975 that the Es were designated for assignment to the 16th SOS and the surviving A models were sent to the 711th SOS. The 16th SOS flew combat in Southeast Asia, Grenada, Panama, the Persian Gulf, OAF, OEF, and OIF. When the E models were converted to H models, the 16th SOS took charge of them, and they continue to fly these aircraft with great distinction today. .[10]

The 4th SOS, known as the "Ghost Riders," fly the most modern and sophisticated fixed-wing gunships ever built. Like the 16th SOS, they began as a ferrying squadron on February 18, 1942. They were activated as the 4th SOS on May 1, 1995. They, too, have served with great distinction in OAF, OEF, and OIF while flying the AC-130Us.[11]

Cutting Edge on Another Level

On February 20, 2009, the Ghost Riders became the first special operations squadron to be commanded by a woman when Lt. Col. Brenda Cartier took command. This appointment came almost exactly sixteen years after the Air Force first permitted women to fly in combat and only four and one-half years after Lt. Col. Martha McSally became the first female to command an Air Force combat flying squadron. Colonel Cartier graduated from undergraduate navigation training the same year women started flying combat missions. She was a navigator on an E-3 AWACS her first four years, which included deployments to Turkey and Saudi Arabia. In 1997 she transferred to AC-130Us, logging more than four thousand flying hours aboard the gunship. Moreover, she has deployed to Iraq and Afghanistan four times, flying on board one of the first AC-130Us into Iraq in order to provide CAS for special operations teams during the opening stages of OIF. Her most famous mission was flying cover as a fire control officer during the operation that rescued Army private Jessica Lynch in 2003.

Cartier assumed command of a unit that had just received significant recognition. In June 2008, three 4th SOS airmen received the Distinguished Flying Cross for a September 2007 mission in Iraq flying CAS for a Navy SEAL team under attack by insurgents. Cartier's combat experiences and the fact that she "grew up" a Ghost Rider moved Col. Dennis Pannell, 1st SOG commander, to remark: "There is no doubt Brenda Cartier is the perfect officer to lead the 4th SOS into the future. She has the skill, poise, and guts to take this squadron to the next level."[12]

What Does the Future Hold?

The late December 2001 Department of Defense PBD mentioned in the previous chapter called for the purchase of at least eight additional AC-130U Spooky gunships and initiated work on a possible replacement gunship. This remarkable budget directive added funding to accelerate and fully fund an advanced concept technology demonstration for the new AC(X) aircraft. Experts envisioned the AC(X) as either a further upgrade to the existing AC-130 or an entirely new follow-on system. At that time, a formal procurement program for the AC(X) was expected to begin in FY05. However, planning delays and political considerations meant that by the spring of 2008 it still had not taken place. Still, the fact that senior Air Force officers continued to have an interest in upgrading the fixed-wing gunship remains significant.[13]

Those who pushed for this new gunship were those in the special operations world, and they originally wanted the new gunship to be smaller than a

C-130 and to fly with fewer crew members. They wanted it to be stealthy, with the speed and maneuverability of a long-range jet fighter. They wanted it to be equipped with directed-energy weapons and nonlethal technologies and capable of engaging targets from any angle—above and below, front and back. Between 2003 and 2005, the USSOCOM Advanced Technology Development program experimented with many formats, expecting the initial budget request to total $55.5 million for the AC(X).[14]

Leading up to 2005, the US Marine Corps had also been working on the development of a Gunship Advanced Combined Arms Weapons Suite (GACAWS) able to operate in conjunction with any Marine Corps tactical weapon system or unit. Developers anticipated the GACAWS suite to provide an advanced combined-arms firepower capability that would integrate a variety of advanced nonkinetic and conventional kinetic weapons (DEW and KEW) capabilities for the flexible and effective application of force in support of all Marine ground units. This included plans to develop high-energy laser weapons designed to generate ultraviolet, optical, and infrared wavelengths in ultrashort- and short-pulse and continuous-wave (CW) coherent laser energy. Experts envisioned such weapons as being adaptable to different kinds of platforms, including tactical gunships. They anticipated that these weapons would have phase-locked fiber optic arrays for platform topological conformity and adaptive optics to optimize atmospheric propagation and maximize energy delivered to the target.[15] All this sounds like fixed-wing gunships on steroids and growth hormones, or perhaps something from *Star Trek: The Next Generation.*

The fact that the Air Force has spent so much time examining ways to upgrade the current gunships and find new platforms upon which to mount new cutting-edge weapons indicates the efficacy of the current gunship generation and the regard in which those on the ground hold it. However, it also echoes a need to make that next big step in this area of airpower. One can argue that we either are on the verge of making that next generational step in fixed-wing gunships, or we should be for the sake of those crews who fly them the young Americans on the ground who depend on them, and the defense of our nation.

However, as of this writing all the above plans and concepts remain just that—plans. While numerous studies on a next-generation gunship have been undertaken since 2001, as of October 2009 there is no gunship program in the works. As Otto Kreisher notes in his July 2009 article at Airforce-magazine.com: "America's long-running military struggles in Iraq and Afghanistan have reaffirmed a long-standing truth about airpower in irregular war: When you go into combat, never go without USAF's deadly side-firing gunships somewhere nearby."[16]

In today's never-ending brushfire wars, the AC-130s continue to uphold their history of excellence first forged in the days of the Vietnam War and continued through the end of the initial phases of OEF and OIF. Throughout these forty years of service, ground commanders have always asked, "Where are the gunships?" Indeed, one of the most knowledgeable gunship veterans, Maj. Gen. Clay T. McCutchan, reminded me that even today the gunships' roles are many and varied and that "the AC-130 Gunship is ideally suited to fight the War on Terrorism as either an ISR platform or as an ISR shooting platform."[17]

For the present the brave crews who fly the grand old ladies of the Air Force more than hold their own and still can rain down death and destruction upon the enemies of this nation, but for how long? So often in my past efforts to preserve historic buildings or sites, those who wish to bulldoze everything simply prolong the dispute with preservationists so long that in some cases the old building simply collapses. One has to wonder if that might not happen to our current gunship airframes. Although the U models are only fifteen to twenty years old, the wear and tear they have faced has caused stress damage much earlier than normal. Then again, what about the H models, whose airframes are roughly forty years old and need or will need major repairs and overhauls in the very near future? Even with these facts staring us in the face, as Lt. Col. Mike Nardo of the 1st SOW notes, "There's been no decision made to proceed with any other airframe."[18]

On the modern battlefield ground commanders and troops love the AC-130s, and if anyone would care to take a poll, I daresay they would ask to keep them coming no matter the numbers, no matter at what speed—keep making them and improving them and sending where we are fighting for our country. These sentiments have been echoed by President Barack Obama's national security advisor and former Marine Corps commandant Gen. James L. Jones, who witnessed firsthand the power of the AC-130 over Afghanistan in 2001. He commented in 2001 that he wanted more for the Marine Corps, and he says: "Frankly, I'm kicking myself that I waited so long." The current commandant, Gen. James T. Conway, admitted that "marines 'have lusted for years' for AC-130s of their own, but could not afford them."[19]

Ever since the Pentagon funded a technology demonstration project aimed at producing a new gunship in 2001, AFSOC officials have held out hope that they would be allowed to develop a new design that could overcome the AC-130's limitations. Still, there is no plan to exploit the original study and build a new generation gunship. Even as late as 2007, then AFSOC commander Lt.

Gen. Michael W. Wooley remarked that "the command was interested in developing a system of manned and unmanned platforms that would provide a 'technological leap' to replace the current gunships." He stressed the importance of stealth to reduce increasing battlefield threats, especially those that kept them from flying in the daylight. He even posited that a new gunship might be based on a newer generation of bomber that would be "a heavy, long-range aircraft intended to have the best of the current low observable technology and which was supposed to be fielded by 2018." In fact, it was a dream, since building bombers in the current economic climate is not a popular notion, even in the Air Force.[20]

In the late 2000s, feasibility studies have, as mentioned, focused on a smaller airframe with fewer crew members. Indeed, in 2008 one study determined that the best AC-X possibility was the C-27J twin-engine turboprop, which was to be funded by the Army/Air Force Joint Cargo Aircraft Program. It was to be a multimission weapon system able to transport special operations units covertly behind enemy lines and also provide CAS. Then CSAF, Gen. T. Michael Moseley, told Congress in 2008 that plans called for basing the AC-27J at Cannon along with the AC-130Hs. While it all seemed like a great plan, there were some problems. First of all, the economy went in the tank, and a new administration came to power with a public mandate to fix social and economic ills. This reduced the likelihood of funding for acquisition. Moreover, many observers and experts pointed out that while the sensors, electronics, and detection devices on the current and proposed gunships were all great, the smaller version could never carry or fire a 40mm Bofors or, for that matter, a 105mm howitzer, both of which provide the great killing power of the AC-130s. As a result, instead of pursuing acquisition funding, the Air Force continues to plan "for gunship upgrades, enhancements, and structural reinforcements to keep the AC-130s viable."[21]

With this situation in place, and having had extensive experience with the older transport versions of the C-130, the Air Force has already replaced the center wing box on the H models, and with the unusual usage of the U models, they are already in the initial phase of modification, which will be completed by late 2014. To this end, plans are to induct a few at a time and make sure that there are enough to support the ground forces overseas. At the same time, the entire C-130 fleet has been undergoing an avionics modernization program (AMP), in which AC-130s were originally to be included. However, in 2007 budget cuts and combat needs pushed their induction onto the AMP line to early 2010. At the same time, AC-130Us are to get the new GMS2, and the AC-130Hs are to get the much more reliable 241 weather radar systems.[22]

The sexiest aspects of the gunships have always been their armament. Air

Force leaders have been trying to find replacements for the hard-to-sustain old 40mm, 20mm, and 25mm guns. Flight tests scuttled the idea of using 30mm Bushmasters, but there are currently plans underway to replace some of the older weapons with energy weapons. A recent Air Force Scientific Advisory Board study advocated "a laser-armed gunship as a means to reduce collateral damage in an urban environment, but the study recommended maintaining a kinetic weapon as well because of the greater explosive power that a cannon can provide. A laser would need at least 100 kilowatts of power and a seven kilometer slant range to be effective, the science board said." While the Air Force admitted that this might be a far-off solution, in October 2007 it did award Boeing a "$30 million contract to continue developing and testing the Advanced Tactical Laser [ATL], following a ground test of the system in August 2008." In fact, on June 13, personnel from Boeing successfully fired the weapon in flight for the first time using a modified C-130H to carry the ATL. It launched from Kirtland AFB, New Mexico, "fired its laser, and hit a target on the ground at New Mexico's White Sands Missile Range." Boeing officials declared that "ATL's ultra-precision engagement capability will dramatically reduce collateral damage." The test was so successful that more demonstration tests have been scheduled to "support development of systems that will conduct missions on the battlefield and in urban operations."[23]

On May 7, 2009, Vice Adm. P. Stephen Stanley, the JCS's director of force structure, revealed that the Air Force planned on converting some of their MC-130W Combat Spears into gunships. The MC-130 already has an all-weather capability, wing tanks, and in-flight refueling capabilities. The desire and effort remain to keep a viable gunship fleet flying in the operational Air Force for the very reason they always have—to defend our troops on the ground. Fortunately, there are many in the Air Force who seem dedicated to learning from the past in order to keep from repeating the mistakes of the past, especially in the gunship world.

Center Wing Box (CWB)

Beginning in November 2006, officials at the WR-ALC at Robins AFB, Georgia, began a three-phase reconstruction program for all the C-130 variant airframes in the Air Force. The goal of the project was to replace the center wing box in all C-130 airframes to extend their life expectancy to 2030. Based the CWBs on the same design as those of the C-130J, the replacement program planned to include all the AC-130s at a cost of seven million dollars per airframe. In addition, since plans called for the vast majority of new AFSOC aircraft, such as the MC-130 and HC-130, to be based on the C-130J airframe, officials agreed that once funding became available, newly constructed gunship models would also follow this pattern in an effort to replace the older H models and realize the airframe and technological advantages provided by the C-130Js.[24]

By October 2009, WR-ALC employees had completed four MC-130H CWB replacements and planned to complete four more by the following summer. In January 2010 the workforce inducted two AC-130Us for CWB replacement, with the entire fleet scheduled for completion early in 2011.[25]

The joint SOF CWB Integrated Program Team (IPT) recommended several actions to the AFSOC commander to mitigate impacts of CWB replacement in critical out years. Based on these suggestions and direction from the AFSOC commander, Air Force moved Plus-4 AC-130Us into the area of responsibility to carry high equivalent baseline hours consumption loads, accelerated CWB delivery, and increased manufacturer delivery to reduce aircraft groundings. While the WR-ALC repair teams accelerated the first five aircraft (MC-130Hs), there was no more room to accelerate without decreasing availability. In turn, they had already sped up the entire AC-130U delivery schedule in the fall of 2007. The CWB IPT swapped two MC-130Hs with AC-130Us and pulled AC-130Us into CWB replacement in fiscal year 2009 by using scheduled MC-130H CWBs. At the same time, WR-ALC maintenance leadership implemented high-velocity maintenance initiatives to upgrade AC-130U fuel quantity in-tank harnesses and to implement new infrared tubs and tracks. They also developed a five-year plan to provide resources as needed in an effort to manage AC-130U flying by tail number management and field AMP upgrades across the fleet.[26]

Late the next year, many AC-130s were back on the line and still flying missions at a high tempo, continuing to face demanding conditions of high gross weights and austere environments.

The Latest Versions of the Fixed-Wing Gunship

At the end of 2012, two new gunship models were ready to be deployed. The first was a stopgap solution to meet the pressing need to augment the existing gunship fleets. This entailed adding a weapons package to the MC-130W special operations aircraft and renaming it the AC-130W Stinger II. The other was the creation of a new gunship, the AC-130J Ghost Rider, with the latest C-130 airframe, engines, sensors, and armaments.

As the operations tempo in the Afghan and Iraqi theaters of operations continued at a high level, especially for the existing fixed-wing gunships, it became increasingly difficult to maintain the AC-130Hs and Us. Beginning in fiscal year 2009 (FY09), a C-130H received modifications that included a precision strike package (PSP) of specific weapons that became known as

Dragon Spear. Project Dragon Spear was an urgent deployment acquisition to install and support the PSP for placement on twelve MC-130W Combat Spear aircraft. The workforce at WR-ALC began converting all MC-130W aircraft to Dragon Spears for AFSOC in order to relieve the relentless operational demands on its existing AC-130H and U gunships until the new AC-130Js began to enter the fleet. The WR-ALC leadership received approval of the acquisition plan on 28 July 2010 for all twelve aircraft. Under this program, the MC-130W went from concept to flying with a minimum capability in less than ninety days and to deployment in eighteen months. This original plan called for the aircraft to be deployed to Iraq and Afghanistan by January 2011.[27]

Since ground forces needed increased CAS, and H and U models had already flown twice as many hours as they had before 9/11, these new aircraft were essential. By 2010, SOF aircraft were dispersed over greater areas and on extended missions. Project Dragon Spear not only integrated a PSP on the MC-130Ws, but it also provided the gunships with new capabilities such as day-and-night, all-weather armed over-watch, precision fires, and close air support for troops in contact (CAS/TIC) with the enemy.[28]

The major components of the PSP were combat-proven systems that the secretary of defense could order quickly installed under his Resources Management Decision (RMD) 802. The PSP package included standoff precision guided munitions (SOPGM); medium-caliber weapons that provided CAS/TIC precision fire; intelligence, surveillance, and reconnaissance (ISR) full-motion video transmissions and data-link sensors; and a communications package that provided ISR and targeting capabilities. The new aircraft retained in-flight air refueling, air-land mobility, a forward air refueling point for helicopter ground operations, three pallet positions, and dual-stick container delivery system (CDS) bundles.[29]

There were two production phases. Phase 1, the proof of concept phase, included the Dragon 1 and Dragon 2 capability release (CR)1/CR2/CR2D configurations, which were accomplished at Eglin AFB, Florida, by personnel of the 2955th Combat Logistics Support Squadron, Robins AFB, Georgia. Dragons 1 and 2 were released in March and April 2010 at Cannon AFB for aircrew training and deployment. Phase 2, or CR3, production phase was also executed by a Robins AFB team through a contract with L-3 Telecommunications Systems, Inc. (L-3 TCS), in Waco, Texas. Company personnel at Warner Robins received the "undefinitized" contract action (UCA) worth $18 million. It called for the completion of eight aircraft under contract number FA8509-09-C-0037, which was amended to $45 million when it was "definitized" in August 2010. Over the fifteen months, eight aircraft were delivered.[30]

Dragon 3 and Dragon 4, the CR3-configured aircraft, were sent to Cannon AFB in May and July 2010. By December 2010, Dragons 5, 6, and 7 were undergoing CR3 installation on the modification line at Waco. Dragon 8 was inducted on 27 August 2010 and completed on 11 January 2011. Dragons 9 and 10 were inducted in December 2010 and put out in May 2011. The remaining four aircraft—the last two unmodified MC-130Ws plus the Dragon 1 and 2 prototype aircraft for CR3 installation—required a new contract, which was awarded on 30 September 2010.[31]

As noted earlier, beginning in July 2007, lessons learned from OEF and OIF led Air Force leaders to seek ways to expand the gunship fleet. The USSOC commander sought to augment the AC-130s rather than replace them. To this end, the Air Force modification contract with L-3 TCS eventually totaled $61 million. Under the initial program these new MC-130Ws were to be known as Dragon Spear, but in late 2011 management proposed to rename the MC-130W Dragon Spear the AC-130W Stinger II and to complete the project as a gunship modification.[32]

The proposal was approved on 4 May 2012, and the Air Force officially directed that the aircraft be redesignated the AC-130W Stinger II. The new gunships' mission focused on armed over-watch. In this case, the new birds had the same reconnaissance capabilities as the MC-130s with the added punch of a new array of gunship armaments. Thus, while capable of executing standard AC-130 missions, the Stinger IIs' main job was to keep a watchful eye over friendly forces and to attack enemy targets in support of those forces. In short, armed over-watch became on-station CAS. The purpose of this redefined mission was to prevent ambushes and to keep the enemy from reinforcing their units.[33]

Currently, the Stinger II can still perform CAS, strike coordination and reconnaissance, nontraditional ISR, and command and control missions. It can also deliver cargo or personnel in a limited-mobility role just as a standard C-130 cargo aircraft can. But in order to perform the armed over-watch role, all AC-130W aircraft are also modified with the PSP, which includes a mission management console, a communications suite, two electro-optical/infrared sensors, fire control equipment, a one-side-firing, trainable 30mm Mk-44 cannon with tracerless ammunition and an associated munitions storage system, and GPU-44 SOPGM anti-tank weapons designated Viper Strike or Griffin. The mission management system combines sensor, communication, environment, order of battle, and threat information in a common operating format. The Stinger II PSP affords ground forces a constant direct fire platform able to fire precision low-yield munitions ideally suited for urban operations.[34]

The AC-130Ws are powered by four Allison T56-A-15 turboprops and are capable of a maximum speed of 300 mph. They can take off with a maximum weight of 155,000 pounds and reach a ceiling of thirty-three thousand feet. They have a range of twenty-seven hundred nautical miles, and in-flight refueling extends that to unlimited range. The gunships carry a standard crew of two pilots, two navigators, a flight engineer, and two loadmasters. With the PSP package, the crew changes to two pilots, two combat system officers (CSOs), a flight engineer, and two loaders/gunners.[35]

Even as the Stinger II was being completed, Air Force officials initiated a program to construct sixteen new gunships that would have an airframe and combat package similar to that of the recently developed MC-130J Combat Shadow II special operations tankers. Plans called for them to have a PSP similar to that of the AC-130Ws. The Air Force asked for $1.6 billion for recapitalization from the FY11 through FY15 budgets. Leadership also determined to retire the existing AC-130Hs, which were well past their original intended retirement date. They anticipated buying the first J model in FY12, followed by two in FY13, five in FY14, and the final eight in FY15.[36]

The Air Force and DOD conclusion to continue to use C-130s airframes for gunship models evolved from a cut in FY10 funding for sixteen C-27s and the realization that the C-130s were still plentiful and capable. Planners expected to modify the AC-130Js much like their Dragon Spear cousins. However, budget disagreements in Congress and a refusal by members of the House leadership to vote on a standard defense budget, delayed the process. Even so, on 9 January 2013, using existing funds, the Air Force began converting the first MC-130J Combat Shadow II into the new AC-130J Ghost Rider. By the summer of 2013, experts anticipated that this first aircraft would be completed in late November 2013, with flight testing to begin in December 2013[37]

Clearly, DOD leaders as well as the troops on the ground appreciate the support they have received from the AC-130 gunships. With these new programs underway, they will be able to count on the best CAS possible for many years to come.

Night Hunters: Addendum

As if to remind us that the wars of our nation are never truly far away from our own current reality, on June 18, 2010, the American Forces Press Service issued the following report on the death of fourteen AC-130 crew members who died in Vietnam during 1972:

> Unidentified remains of 14 fallen Air Force AC-130 gunship crew members were laid to rest at Arlington National Cemetery here [June 17], nearly 40 years after their aircraft was shot down over southern Laos.

Lt. Col. Henry P. Brauner, Lt. Col. Richard Castillo, Lt. Col. Irving B. Ramsower II, Lt. Col. Howard D. Stephenson, Maj. Curtis D. Miller, Maj. Barclay B. Young, Capt. Richard C. Halpin, Capt. Charles J. Wanzel III, Chief Master Sgt. Edwin J. Pearce, Senior Master Sgt. James K. Caniford, Senior Master Sgt. Robert E. Simmons, Senior Master Sgt. Edward D. Smith Jr., Master Sgt. Merlyn L. Paulson and Master Sgt. William A. Todd were honored in a group burial with full military honors in the cemetery's Section 60.

The crew was killed in action March 29, 1972, in the midst of the Vietnam War.

Air Force Lt. Gen. Mark D. Shackelford presented an American flag to the families. Air Force Chaplain (Capt.) Anthony Wade and Rev. Martin McGill presided over the service.

Full military honors included a flag-draped casket and carrying team, a firing party, a band and bugler, a horse-drawn caisson and escorts from the Air Force Honor Guard. All 14 names will be included on the headstone.

Representatives from the families of 13 of the Airmen attended the ceremony. Several members of Rolling Thunder, an advocacy group for the return of all prisoners of war and those missing in action, also attended the service.

Remains for Captains Halpin and Wanzel, Chief Pearce, and Sergeants Caniford, Simmons, Smith and Todd were positively identified and returned to their families. Major Young and Sergeant Caniford were buried here individually in 2008, said Kaitlin Horst, a spokeswoman for the cemetery.

The remaining seven airmen could not be identified, but are accounted for, Larry Greer, a spokesman for the Pentagon's Joint Prisoners of War and Missing in Action Accounting Command, said in an interview with American Forces Press Service. Forensic anthropologists and scientists from the Defense Department are confident all 14 Airmen were involved in the crash, Mr. Greer said. The scientists used identification tools, circumstantial evidence and DNA tests to match the crew members' remains with their families, Mr. Greer said. Scientists also used dental comparisons to identify remains. "All of these men have been accounted for, and the families have accepted the identification," Mr. Greer said. "These final, full-honor services are to recognize the sacrifices that these men made and their families made, and all of us involved in this mission feel it an honor to bring closure to these families."

The crew's plane was shot down by a surface-to-air missile during an armed reconnaissance mission. Search and rescue efforts were hindered because of heavy enemy activity in the area and were stopped after only a few days, Mr. Greer said.

The first remains were recovered in 1986 by a joint US-Laos team, Mr. Greer said. Recovered items included two identification tags, life support equipment and aircraft wreckage, he added. Between 1986 and 1998, nine members of the aircrew were positively identified. Follow-on surveys and excavations in 2005 and 2006 found more remains, personal effects and other equipment, he said. The remains of more than 900 service members killed in the Vietnam War have been returned to their families since 1972. More than 1,700 remain unaccounted-for.

In the past year, the Joint Prisoners of War and Missing in Action Accounting Command has accounted for 98 service members missing from the Korean War, Vietnam War and World War II. More than 80,000 service members from the three wars remain unaccounted-for. Nearly 2,000 from the same wars have been accounted for and returned to their families.[38]

Notes

Introduction

1 For more on the history of the US Air Force, see Wesley Frank Craven and James Lea Cate, eds., *The United States Army Air Forces in World War II,* especially John Fagg, *Europe; Argument to VE Day: January 1944 to May 1945,* Vol. 3; William Head, *Every Inch a Soldier: Augustine Warner Robins and the Building of US Airpower;* Robert F. Futrell, *Ideas, Concepts, Doctrine: Basic Thinking in the United States Air Force,* Vol. 1, *1907–1960,* and Vol. 2, *1960–1984.*

2 For more on the Air Force during the early stages of Vietnam, see John Schlight, *The Air War in South Vietnam: The Years of the Offensive, 1965–1968;* Earl H. Tilford Jr., *Crosswinds: The Air Force's Setup in Vietnam;* Gen. William W. Momyer, *Air Power in Three Wars: World War II, Korea, and Vietnam;* John Morrocco, *Thunder from Above: Air War, 1941–1968,* Vol. 9 in *The Vietnam Experience,* ed. Robert Manning.

3 Tilford, *Crosswinds;* Schlight, *Air War In South Vietnam;* Morrocco, *Thunder from Above;* Morrocco, *Rain of Fire: Air War, 1969–1973,* Vol. 10 in *The Vietnam Experience,* ed. Robert Manning.

4 Tilford, *Crosswinds;* Morrocco, *Rain of Fire.*

Chapter 1

1 Walter J. Boyne, "The Awesome Power of the Air Force Gunships," *Air Force Magazine* 82, no. 4 (April 1999): 1.

2 Col. Michael E. Haas, "Air Commando! 1950–1975: 25 Years at the Tip of the Spear," Special Study, US Air Force, Washington, DC, n.d.

3 Marshall Michel, "The Birth of Spooky: How They Put the 'A' in AC-47," *Current Operations* 678 (3 June 2003): 24; See also, Haas, "Air Commando!"; Boyne, "Awesome Power."

4 Boyne, "Awesome Power"; Michel, "Birth of Spooky," 24.

5 Boyne, "Awesome Power."

6 Ibid.; Michel, "Birth of Spooky," 24.

7 *US Air Force Gunships,* Background Information, Pamphlet 68–13; WRAMA, IO, "Gooney Bird Becomes a Dragon in Mechanical Metamorphosis Process," news release 65-12-1777, 6 December 1965; Alvin M. Josephy Jr., *A History of Flight,* 267.

8 Boyne, "Awesome Power."

9 For more on gunships, see Lt. Col. David J. Dean, *The Air Force Role in Low-Intensity Conflict;* Stephen Blank et al., *Low-Intensity Conflict in the Third World;* Michel, "Birth of Spooky," 24.

10 Gen. William A. Kinney, "TACAIR Vietnam," *Airman* 12, no. 7 (July 1968): 40–41; Richard E. Maltais, "WRAMA's Role in Southeast Asia: AC-47 Gunship," Historical Study no. 17, WRAMA, Office of History, Robins AFB, Georgia, 1971, 141 (hereafter cited as Maltais, "AC-47 Gunship"); USAF, Institute of Technology, "Project Corona Harvest Logistics Background Digest," report, 1965, 184; Dixie Station, "The Air War in Vietnam," *Fly-*

ing Magazine, November 1966, 57–61; Harold Brown, "Supplement to Air Force Policy Letter for Commanders, No. 3-68," policy statement of the secretary of the Air Force, 1 March 1966.

11 Richard E. Maltais, "WRAMA's Role in Southeast Asia: AC-119G/K Gunship Program, 1967–1970," Project Combat Hornet, Historical Study no. 18, WRAMA Office of History, Robins AFB, Georgia, March 1971, 172 (hereafter cited as Maltais, "AC-119"); Lt. Col. Ross E. Hamlin, "Side-Firing Weapon Systems," *Air University Review* 21, no. 2 (January–February 1970): 77.

12 Boyne, "Awesome Power," 2; USAF, "'Gunships' and 'Dragonship' Credited to Reservist," *Air Force Times,* 16 April 1969; Donald J. Mrozek, "The Limits of Innovation: Aspects of Air Power in Vietnam," 25th Anniversary of Aviation website, Center for Aerospace Doctrine, Research, and Education (CADRE), Maxwell AFB, Alabama, 1985, http://www.airpower.au.af.mil/airchronicles/aureview/1985/jan-feb/mrozek.html; Michel, "Birth of Spooky," 24.

13 Hamlin, "Side-Firing Weapon Systems," 76–88; Mrozek, "Limits of Innovation," 2; Boyne, "Awesome Power," 2; Jack S. Ballard, *Development and Employment of Fixed-Wing Gunships, 1962–1972,* The United States Air Force in Southeast Asia, 1–34; Kenneth Sams, *First Test and Combat Use of the AC-47,* CHECO Project, December 1965.

14 Boyne, "Awesome Power," 2; Hamlin, "Side-Firing Weapon Systems," 76–88.

15 Hamlin, "Side-Firing Weapon Systems," 76–77.

16 Ibid.; Boyne, "Awesome Power," 2; USAF, "'Gunships' and 'Dragonship.'"

17 Michel, "Birth of Spooky," 25–26.

18 Boyne, "Awesome Power," 2–3; Hamlin, "Side-Firing Weapon Systems," 77–80; USAF, "'Gunships' and 'Dragonship'"; USAF, Aeronautical Systems Division (ASD), Annual History, 1965, 1A: 25–29 (unclassified pages used.).

19 Michel, "Birth of Spooky," 26.

20 Ibid., 26; Boyne, "Awesome Power," 2–3; Hamlin, "Side-Firing Weapon Systems," 78; USAF, "'Gunships' and 'Dragonship.'"

21 Michel, "Birth of Spooky," p. 26.

22 Ballard, *Fixed-Wing Gunships,* 70–73; Boyne, "Awesome Power," 2–3; USAF, ASD, Annual History, 1965, 27–29; Dixie Station, "Air War," 59–60; Mrozek, "Limits of Innovation," 2–4; Seventh Air Force, Office of History, Semiannual Chronology, July–December 1965, January–June 1966.

23 Larry Fletcher, "AC-119, Chapter 1," attachment to e-mail, Fletcher to William Head, "Chapters 1-6-7-8," 23 June 2004, 0753 hours.

24 Hamlin, "Side-Firing Weapon System," 77–79; Maltais, "AC-119," 173–74.

25 Hamlin, "Side-Firing Weapon System," 79–80; Maltais, "AC-119," 174–77.

26 Hamlin, "Side-Firing Weapon System," 80–88.

27 USAF, ASD, Annual History, 1965; Maltais, "AC-47 Gunship," 14; Pacific Air Forces, Maintenance Division, Aircraft Testing Unit, PACAF Capability Study (DPL/TSC-65-240), 12 March 1965; PACAF Commander to CSAF, "FC-47, Combat Testing (VC 30672)," message, 202030Z Mar 65; CSAF to AFLC/MA, AFRDQRA-2 71840, "C-47 Gunship Conversion," message, 120235Z May 65; AFLC Commander to WRAMA Commander/MCMTA 02385, message, 171235Z May 65; WRAMA/ NCTA to PACAF Commander,

"C-47 Modification," message, 270520Z May 65; WRNCT to AFSC, "C-47 Feasibility Study," message, 230630Z Jun 65; WRNCTA to WRNE, "Class V Modification, FS-1729, C-47 Aircraft," letter, 27 July 1965; WRNC to WRNE, "Class V Modification, T-1729, Installation of GAU-2B/A gun," letter with attachment, Staff Summary Sheet, WRNC, "WRNE first endorsement," 25 June 1965; WRNCTA to WRNCP, "Class V Modification, FS-1729, C-47 Aircraft," letter, 26 July 1965; AFSC Commander to CSAF, "SCS-6/28102," message, 140300Z Jul 65. The SUU-11 gun pod was used on the AC-47 and AC-119G/K. It is the housing or compartment that contains the six-barreled 7.62mm GAU-2B/A Gatling gun. The AC-47 had three pods, and the AC-119s four. The four C-47s equipped with M-2 .30-caliber machine guns were modified in-house at ASD facilities at Wright-Patterson AFB, Ohio, and should not be confused with those aircraft placed on contract with Air International Inc. for modification as part of an inspect and repair as necessary program (IRAN).

28 PACAF Commander to CSAF, DOP 31024, "Vietnam Gunship Requirements," message, 181235Z Jun 65; HQ USAF/AFRDQ-P to WRAMA Commander, "Modification Requirement no. 1445 (FS-1729/C-47)," letter, 17 July 1965.

29 WRAMA Information Office, "Col. Hahn Passes Praise to WRAMA Team," News Release 65-12-1778, 7 December 1965; AFLC to ALAFLC, MCOMO 082, message, 1 April 1966; WRNC to AFLC Commander, 00758, message, 230735Z Jul 65; HQ USAF/AFRDQ-A to WRAMA Commander, "M.R. No. 1445-1 (FS-1729/C-47)," letter, 12 August 1965.

30 HQ USAF/AFRDQ-P to WRAMA Commander, "M.R. No. 1445-2 (FS-1729/C-47), Amendment to a Modification Requirement," letter, 8 April 1966; AFLC/MCM to WRAMA Commander, "Camouflage Painting," letter, 9 July 1965; WRNC to AFLC/MCM, WRNC 00851, message, 151633Z Apr 66; HQ USAF/AFRDQ-P to WRAMA Commander, "M.R. 1445-3 (FS-1729/C-47)," letter, 15 July 1966; AFLC/MCMTA to WRNL, MCMP 04323, message, 050425Z Jul 66; CSAF to AFLC/MCM, AFSME 79276, message, 302055Z Jun 66; CSAF to PACAF/AFX-OPF 79501, "AC-47 Modification Agreement," message, 012250Z Jul 66; HQ USAF/AFRDQ-P to AFLC/MCM, "M.R. 1445-24 (FS-1729/C-47)," letter, 15 February 1967; WRNC to CSAF, "AC-47 Modification," message, 30235Z Feb 67; HQ USAF, "Modification Requirement for C-47 Aircraft," M.R. 1806 (FS-1729/C-47), report, 16 June 1967; CSAF to AFLC/MCM, AFSME 89995, message, 030830Z Jun 67; Sole Source Justification Document, WRAMA Director of Materiel Management (DMM), PR/MIPR no. WR 7-30501, 6 July 1967.

31 HQ USAF/AFRDQ-P, M.R. No. 1801 (FS-1729/C-47), report, 13 October 1967; CSAF to AFLC/MCM, AFSME 88769, "M.R. 7801 (FS-1729/C-47) Amendment," message, 090835Z Sep 67; WRNC to AFLC/MCM, WRNC 03584, "M.R. 1801 (FS-1729/C-47) Amendment," message, 201235Z Oct 67; Maj. Gen. Francis C. Gideon, WRAMA Commander, "Notebook on Vietnam," 31 January 1968 (located in WR-ALC Office of History Archives); USAF, "'Gunships' and 'Dragonship'"; USAF, *Releasable Data on USAF Aerospace Craft,* Air Force Publication (AFP) 190-2-1, 1 June 1960, 87; William Head, "AC-47 Gunship Development," *Air Power History* 37, no. 3 (Fall 1990): 40–42; Kinney, "TACAIR Vietnam."

32 Maltais, "AC-47 Gunship," 26–27; Head, "Gunship Development," 42–43; Ballard, *Fixed-Wing Gunships,* 40, 44.

33 Ballard, *Fixed-Wing Gunships,* 52–53, 57, 61–131; Maltais, "AC-47 Gunship," 113–24.

Chapter 2

1 Jack S. Ballard, *Development and Employment of Fixed-Wing Gunships, 1962–1972,* 176–78. For a history of the AC-119, see William P. Head, *Shadow and Stinger: The Development and Deployment of the AC-119G/K Gunships.*

2 William Head, "AC-47 Gunship Development," *Air Power History* 37, no. 3 (Fall 1990): 37–46; CINCPAC to CSAF, "Gunship Conversion," memo (Secret, since declassified), 20 March 1965; Richard E. Maltais, "WRAMA's Role in Southeast Asia: AC-119G/K Gunship Program, 1967–1970," Project Combat Hornet, Historical Study no. 18, WRAMA Office of History, Robins AFB, GA, March 1971(hereafter cited as Maltais, "AC-119"), 2.

3 USAF, "C-119 Boxcar," in *Releasable Data on USAF Aerospace Craft,* Air Force Publication (AFP) 190-2-1, 1 June 1960, 97; USAF, "Background Information: Gunships," Information Sheet no. 13, 1968.

4 Ballard, *Fixed-Wing Gunships,* 82, 176; Maltais, "AC-119," 2; Fairchild-Hiller, Inc., "Modification of the C-119," news release, 21 May 1968; Fairchild-Hiller, Inc., "AC-119 Gunship Program Supplemental Administrative Information," Letter Contract F09603-68-C-1633, 21 March 1969.

5 Ballard, *Fixed-Wing Gunships,* 93, 176–79; Maltais, "AC-119," 6–7; CSAF to CINCPACAF, "Follow On Aircraft for AC-47 and SEAOR 50/Hunter/Gunship," message, no time, 8 Jun 1967; SECAF to VCSAF, "C-119 G/K Gunship," memo, 8 June 1967.

6 Ballard, *Fixed-Wing Gunships,* 178–79.

7 Ibid., 93–95; Gen. William W. Momyer, 7AF Commander, to Gen. John D. Ryan, CINCPACAF, "Follow On Aircraft for AC-47," 30 Jun 1967; CSAF to AFSC/AFRDDH, "AC-130, AC-119K Gunships," message no. 81350, 1 Aug 67.

8 USAF, Directorate of Development, Semi-Annual History, July–December 1967, 182; CSAF to SECAF, "Additional Gunship II Aircraft for Night Operations," letter, 13 December 1967; Ballard, *Fixed-Wing Gunships,* 94; USAF, ASD, "Gunship II Flight Test and Combat Evaluations Interim Report," 11 December 1967.

9 Ballard, *Fixed-Wing Gunships,* 178–79; SECAF to CSAF, "Gunship Aircraft," memo, 20 December 1967; USAF, Directorate of Development, Semi-Annual History, January–June 1968, 168–70.

10 Gen. John P. McConnell, CSAF, to Dr. Brown, SECAF, "Gunship Aircraft," letter, 26 January 1968; USAF, Air Staff, "Gunship Aircraft," working paper, 5 January 1968; SECAF to CSAF, "Gunship Aircraft," memo, 20 December 1967; USAF, Directorate of Development, Semi-Annual History, January–June 1968, 168–70.

11 McConnell to Brown, "Gunship Aircraft," 26 January 1968; Ballard, *Fixed-Wing Gunships,* 179.

12 Maltais, "AC-119," 8; Col. John M. Christenson, Chief, AC-119 Program Office (WRNH-7), interview with Robert Barnwell, WRAMA/HO, published 30 October 1968.

13 USAF, MAE, Modification Program Management Directive (PMD) no. 1851-FS2150/C-119G (Secret, declassified 1984), 20 October 1967; Wade D. Carter, Deputy Chief, WRNH-7, interview with Robert W. Barnwell, WRAMA/HO, 3 December 1968.

14 USAF, MAE, Modification PMD no. 1851-FS2150/C-119G (Secret, declassified 1984), 20 October 1967; Carter interview with Barnwell, WRAMA/HO, 3 December 1968.

15 PDM no. 1851-FS2150/C-119G, 20 October 1967; "AFLC Lets Contract for 'Dragon Ship,'" *Robins RevUp,* 11 January 1968, 1.

16 7 AF to CINCPACAF, no subject, message, 180318Z Nov 67; HQ PACAF to 7 AF, "Gunship II CONOPS," message, 150030Z Dec 67; 7 AF to CINCPACAF, "Gunship II Requirements," message, 310810Z Dec 67; Seventh Air Force, Semi-Annual History, July–December 1967, Vol. 1, 143; 7 AF to CINCPACAF, DPL 3920, "Mixed Force of Gunships in SEA," message, 260800Z Dec 67; CINCPACAF to CSAF, "Gunship II Requirements," message, 122200Z Feb 68; Maj. Richard F. Kott, *The Role of United States Air Force Gunships in Southeast Asia (SEASIA),* 4–5; CSAF to SECAF, "Gunship Aircraft," letter, 5 January 1968, found in AFLC/HO, Historical Study no. 374, February 1971 (hereafter cited as AFLC, Study 374), Document 220.

17 Ballard, *Fixed-Wing Gunships,* 98, 182; SECAF to SECDEF, "AC-119 Gunship Force," memo, 8 February 1968; Maltais, "AC-119," 2; CSAF to AFLC Commander, no subject, message, 212007Z Feb 68; SECAF to Deputy SECDEF, "AC-130 Gunship II and C-130 BIAS/Hunter Aircraft," memo, 17 February 1968; Deputy SECDEF to SECAF, "AC-119 Gunship Force," memo, 24 February 1968.

18 Maltais, "AC-119," 37–38; "AC-119G Gunship Accepted," *Robins RevUp,* 30 May 1968, 1; Ballard, *Fixed-Wing Gunships,* 189.

19 Fairchild-Hiller, "First Production AC-119G Rolls Out," news release, 21 May 1968.

20 Tactical Air Command, History, 1 July 1969–30 June 1970, Vol. 1, Narrative, 340; USAF, Special Air Warfare Center, History, 1 January–30 June 1968, 33; AFLC, Study 374, 151–52; WRAMA (WRN) to AFLC, "AC-119K Rollout Ceremony," message 132355Z Sep 68; Wade D. Carter and Joseph A. Francavage, WRNH-7, interview with Robert W. Barnwell, WRAMA/HO, 20 May 1969.

21 "AC-119 Gunship Training," *Reservist Magazine,* May 1968; Ballard, *Fixed-Wing Gunships,* 190.

22 CSAF to AFLC Commander, "AC-119G Deployment," message, 092217Z May 68.

23 "AC-119 Gunship Training"; Maltais, "AC-119," 43–44; Continental Air Command (CAC) to OIP, no subject, message (Secret, since declassified), 04192Z Jun 68.

24 CSAF to CINCPACAF, "AC-119 Deployment," message, 161327Z Sep 68.

25 Ibid.; 7 AF/DPLG to CINCPACAF et al., "AC-119 Deployment," Staff Summary Sheet, 17 September 1968; 7 AF to CINCPACAF, "Gunship Force Adjustment," message, ca. 17 September 1968.

26 7 AF/DPLG to CINCPACAF, "'Combat Hornet' (AC-119G) Deployment," Staff Summary Sheet, 16 October 1968; Lt. Gen. Robert G. Ruegg, DCS for Systems & Logistics, "Staff Visit," notebook, 1 November 1968.

27 H. S. Sherrer, WRAMA (WRNH-7), interview with Robert W. Barnwell, WRAMA/HO, 21 November 68; WRAMA (WRN) to CSAF, no subject, message (Secret, since declassified), 261740Z Aug 68.

28 WRAMA (WRN) to AFLC, message on ferrying of AC-119G gunships (Confidential, since declassified), 152040Z Nov 68; TAC to WRAMA, "AC-119G Ferry," message, 122119Z Nov 68.

29 WRAMA (WRN) to AFLC, message, 152040Z Nov 68; WRAMA (WRN) to AFLC, message on ferrying of AC-119G gunships (Confidential, since declassified), 292050Z Nov 68;

Maltais, "AC-119," xxxi-xxxii; USAF, Tactical Air Command (TAC), "Report of Gunship G Deployment and Combat Evaluation—Combat Guard," Operations Plan (OPLAN) 118, 22 March 1969; TAC, "Final Report Combat Introduction Evaluation AC-119G Gunship III (Combat King), 1 August 1970," OPLAN 120.

30 TAC, OPLAN 118; TAC, OPLAN 120.

31 Ballard, *Fixed-Wing Gunships,* 192–93. Also see William P. Head, *Shadow and Stinger: The Development and Deployment of the AC-119G/K Gunships.*

32 TAC, OPLAN 118; TAC, OPLAN 120; Maltais, "AC-119," xxxiv; SSgt Robert J. Lessels, "Shadow," *Air Force Magazine,* November 1971, 38–40; William R. Casey, "AC-119, USAF's Flying Battleship," *Air Force/Space Digest,* February 1970, 48–50.

33 WRAMA (ARN) to AFLC, messages on deploying of AC-119K gunships (Secret, since declassified), 102050Z Jan 69 and 202050Z Dec 68.

34 WRAMA to AFLC, message on ferrying of AC-119K gunships (Confidential, since declassified), 212100Z Mar 69.

35 TAC, OPLAN 120, 36, 70.

36 Maltais, "AC-119," 68, 156.

37 Ibid., 196; Ballard, *Fixed-Wing Gunships,* 202; Senator William Proxmire, Chair, Subcommittee on Economy in Government, to Philip N. Whitaker, Assistant Secretary of the Air Force for Installations and Logistics, "AC-119 Program Cost Overruns," letter, 3 February 1970.

38 Whitaker to Proxmire, "Reply to Letter of 3 Feb 70," letter, 2 March 1970.

Chapter 3

1 For details on these aircraft, see Gordon Swanborough and Peter M. Bower, *United States Military Aircraft since 1909;* Al Adcock, *C-123 Provider in Action;* Larry Davis, *Gunships: A Pictorial History of Spooky.*

2 Swanborough and Bower, *Military Aircraft.*

3 Jack S. Ballard, *Development and Employment of Fixed Fixed-Wing Gunships, 1962–1972,* 77–110. One side note on using the C-47 in unique ways came from World War II. The Soviets loaded a C-47 with soldiers armed with submachine guns and other automatic weapons, then flew it over German lines to lure the enemy into launching a fighter to shoot it down. The plot worked, and when the fighter closed in for the kill, suddenly the Soviets stuck their weapons out of the open windows and riddled the fighter with holes. While it was a one-time success, it seems to have unintentionally foreshadowed the AC-47D.

4 Ibid., 110–22.

5 Ibid., 176–78. Also see William P. Head, *Shadow and Stinger: The Development and Deployment of the AC-119G/K Gunships.*

6 Ballard, *Fixed Wing Gunships,* 176–78.

7 TSgt. David P. Marks, "'First Lady' Retires, Era Ends," Air Force News Service article, original 11 September 1995; update, 18 September 2004, http://www.gunships.org/1stlady.htm, accessed 21 May 2009. The others are tail number (T/N) 54-1623, "Ghost Rider," at Dobbins AFB, Georgia; T/N 54-1626, "Vulcan Express," and T/N 54-1630, "Azrael/Angel of Death," at the Air Force Museum, Wright-Patterson AFB, Ohio; T/N

55-0014, "Jaws of Death," at the Museum of Aviation, Robins AFB, Georgia; and last, T/N 56-0509, "Ultimate End," on display at the Air Park at Hurlburt Field, Florida, with its original three-blade propellers and Vietnam paint scheme.

8 Director, Airlift Planning, Deputy Advanced Systems Planning, Aeronautical Systems Division (ASD), "Planning Document: Project 'Little Brother,'" Report, 1 July 1966.

9 Maj. Ronald W. Terry and Capt. Terry R. Jorris, "Gunship II: A Study of In House Response to Unique Operational Requirements," *Proceedings of 1968 Air Force Science and Engineering Symposium,* Vol. 4, Colorado Springs, US Air Force Academy, 30 October–1 November 1968.

10 Ballard, *Fixed-Wing Gunships,* 79.

11 V. V. McRae to Donald F. Hornig, "Case Study for the Vietnam Development Group: Night Vision for Aircraft Systems," memo, 13 December 1967.

12 Ibid.

13 Ibid.; Lee A. DuBridge, Special Assistant to the President on Science and Technology, to Robert C. Seamans Jr., SECAF, memo, 1 July 1969; Herman S. Wolk, *Air Force Plans, Policies, Research, and Design for South Asia, 1965–1967,* 59–62.

14 McRae to Hornig, memo, 13 December 1967.

15 Air Force DCS, Research and Development (AFRDD-S), to AFSC, TAC, AFLC, ATC, PACAF, "Shed Light Guidance," letter, 17 November 1966.

16 Ibid.; Ballard, *Fixed-Wing Gunships,* 80–83.

17 Terry and Jorris, "Gunship II," 118.

18 Richard P. Dougherty, *A Short History of the Development of the AC-130 Aircraft,* AFLC Historical Study no. 374, February 1971 (hereafter cited as AFLC, Study 374), 92–93; USAF, ASD, History, July 1968–June 1969, 1:132.

19 Director of Development, OSD, History, 1 January–30 June 1967, 81–82, 180–88; Military Assistance Command, Vietnam (MACV), History, 1967, 2:871–73.

20 Terry and Jorris, "Gunship II," U-26.

21 Maj. Richard F. Kott, *The Role of United States Air Force Gunships in Southeast Asia (SEASIA),* CHECO Project, 25; Seventh Air Force, History, 1 July–31 December 1967, 1:136.

22 Ballard, *Fixed-Wing Gunships,* 89.

23 Ibid.

24 Ibid., 90; USAF, ASD, History, July 1968–June 1969, 1:133.

25 14th Air Combat Wing, History, 1 January–31 March 1968, 23–25; USAF, ASD, History, 1 July–31 December 1968, 4; Kott *Role of Gunships,* 54.

26 USAF, Directorate of Operations, Requirements, and Development Plans, Semiannual History, 1 July–31 December 1968, 167.

27 Ballard, *Fixed-Wing Gunships,* 93–94; Momyer to Ryan, "Follow-on Aircraft for AC-47," message, 30 June 1967. Also see Head, *Shadow and Stinger.*

28 Head, *Shadow and Stinger;* Ballard, *Fixed-Wing Gunships,* 92–95.

29 "List of AC-130 Gunships: AC-130A," http:www.gunships.org/birds.html., accessed 24 September 2007.

30 WRAMA, History, 1 July 1969–30 June 1970, Part 5: "WRAMA's Weapon Systems, "The C-130 Hercules (Logistical Support), 1958–1969," Historical Study no. 20, WRAMA/HO,

Robins AFB, GA, October 1970, RCS HAF D-48, viii, 178–79, (hereafter cited as WRAMA History no. 20); WRAMA (WRN), "C-130A Gunship Modification," message, 022315Z 3 Nov 67; AFLC/MCMTA, message on gunship modification, 011701Z Dec 67; WRAMA/WRN, "C-130 Gunship II Mod T-2205," message, 141805Z Dec 67; CSAF/AFSME, "Logistics Support of AC-130A Gunship II Program," message, 032103Z May 68; Programming Checklist, AC-130A Aircraft, Contract No. F33657-68-C-0707, 9 January 1969; WRAMA/WRNE to WRAMA/WRNH, "AC-130 Gunship II, Modification Follow-on Procurement," letter, 17 October 1968 (follow-on procurement letter); WRAMA/WRNHTB to WRAMA/WRNH-4, "Comments on Gunship II Follow-on Program," memo, 17 October 1968.

31 WRAMA History no. 20; WRAMA Director of Materiel Management (WRAMA/WRNH), Operations Branch Cargo Aircraft SSM Division, WRAMA and Lockheed-Georgia Air Force Plant Representative and Master Scheduling Department, "Status of C-130," chart, 29 September 1967, rev. 12 June 1970.

32 WRAMA History no. 20, 180; SSM, "AC-130A Aircraft Modification Request (MR) 1885 FS2209 JC-130A," programming checklist (unclassified), 15 December 1967.

33 WRAMA History no. 20, 180–81; WRAMA/WRN, "Coordination of Follow-on Gunship II Program," message, 261451Z Sep 68; WRAMA/WRNNOB to WRAMA/WRNH, "AN/APQ-133 Radar," letter, 7 February 1969; WRAMA/WRNH-7 to WRAMA/WRNHP, "FY70 Repair AC-119/AC-130," letter, 30 January 1969.

34 WRAMA History no. 20, 181–82; USAF, ASD, "Gunship II CCB Membership," Special Order A-710, 20 June 1968. See Head, *Shadow and Stinger,* for more on the AC-119.

35 Gen. McConnell to Dr. Brown, "Additional Gunship II Aircraft for Night Operations," letter, 13 December 1967, with attached report, "Gunship II Flight Test and Combat Evaluation Interim Report," 11 December 1967.

36 Ballard, *Fixed-Wing Gunships,* 94–95. For the original source, see Brown to McConnell, "Gunship Aircraft," memo, 20 December 1967. See also USAF, Directorate of . . . Development, Semiannual History, 1 January–30 June 1968.

37 Kott, *Role of Gunships,* 4–5; 7 AF to CINCPACAF, "Mixed Forces of Gunships in SEA," message, no. 3290, 26 December 1967; 7 AF to CINCPACAF, no subject, message, 180318Z Nov 67; 7 AF, Semiannual History, 1 July–31 December 1967, 1:143; 7 AF to CINCPACAF, "Gunship II Requirements," message, 310815Z Dec 67; CINCPACAF to 7 AF, no subject, message, 150030Z Dec 67.

38 7 AF to CINCPACAF, "Gunship II Requirements," message, 31 December 1967.

39 Kott, *Role of Gunships,* 26; Gen. Ryan to CSAF, "Gunship II Requirements," message, 12 February 1968; Air Staff, "Gunship Aircraft," paper, 5 June 1968, in AFLC, Study 374, Document 220.

40 AFLC, Study 374, Document 220.

41 TAC to CINCPACAF, AFSC, ASD, AFLC, USAF/SAWC, "Gunship II Follow-on Aircraft," message, 200530Z Feb 68; CINCPACAF to TAC, "Gunship II Follow-on Aircraft," message, 200532Z Feb 68.

42 USAF, Directorate of . . . Development, Semiannual History, 1 January–30 June 1968, 168–69.

43 SAF to CSAF, "Increased Gunship Force," memo, 29 April 1968; Seventh Air Force, Personnel Office, "Gunship Force," Staff Summary Sheet, 15 April 1968.

44 Hugh E. Witt, Deputy Assistant Secretary of the Air Force for Support and Maintenance (Installation and Logistics), to Robert H. Charles, Assistant Secretary of the Air Force, Installation and Logistics, "Estimated Cost to Destroy/Damage a Truck in Laos," memo, 2 May 1968.

45 Bui Diem, "Reflections on the Vietnam War: The Views of a Vietnamese on Vietnamese-American Misconceptions," in *Looking Back on the Vietnam War: A 1990s Perspective on the Decisions, Combat, and Legacies,* ed. William P. Head, Lawrence E. Grinter, 245.

46 Bui Diem, "My Reflections of the Tet Offensive," in *The Tet Offensive,* ed. William P. Head and Marc Gilbert, 136.

47 Ballard, *Fixed-Wing Gunships,* 99; Kott, *Role of Gunships,* 7.

48 Air Force Systems Command, "Gunship Program Management: A Study of its Management Success," study, no date, 2; Director of Operational Requirements and Development Plans, "Installation of Gunship Equipment in JC-130 Aircraft," LTVE Contract with USAF, Modification Program Directive 1885 (FS-2209/JC-130A), 13 February 1968; WRAMA/WRNHT to PACAF/DMMB, "AC-130A Discrepancies," message, 121401Z Dec 68.

49 ATC, "Gunships," briefing, 19 April 1968; USAF, ASD, Special Order A-710; WRAMA History no. 20, 183.

50 WRAMA History no. 20, 183–84. TRW stands for Thompson, Ramo, and Wooldbridge. Charles E. Thompson founded Cleveland Cap Screws Inc. in 1901. In 1958 the company was merged with Ramo and Wooldbridge Corporation, founded by Simon Ramo and Dean Wooldbridge. It formally became TRW Inc. in 1965, expanding into the high-tech and space world in 1977. On 1 July 2002 it was bought out by Northrop Grumman, Inc.

51 WRAMA/WRN to AFLC/MCO, "C-130 Bias-Hunter I Support," message, 022118Z May 68; CSAF/AFSME to AFSC/SCS, "Logistics Support of AC-130A Gunship II Program," message, 032103Z May 68; WRAMA History no. 20, 184–85.

52 CSAF/AFSME to AFSC/SCS, "Logistics Support," message, 3 May 1968.

53 Ibid.; CSAF/AFSME to AFSC/SCG, "Gunship II and Combat Hornet Modification Programs," message, 032103Z May 68; PACAF/DM to CSAF/AFSME, "Logistics Support of AC-130A Gunship II Program," message, 090054Z May 68; WRAMA History no. 20, 185–86.

54 TAC/DML to CSAF/AFSME "Logistics Support of AC-130A Gunship II Program," message, 271740Z May 68; WRAMA History no. 20, 186–87; AFLC/MCM to PACAF/DM, message on AC-130A CLS, 171425Z Jun 68; WRAMA/ WRN to WRAMA/WRP, "Contractor Support, Gunship II and III," letter, 18 June 1968.

55 WRAMA/WRNH-4 to WRAMA/WRNH-7, "AC-119/AC-130 Gunship Contractor Support," letter, 14 May 1968; WRAMA History no. 20, 186–87.

56 AFLC/MCMTA to WRAMA/WRNH-7, "AC-119/AC-130 Gunship Contractor Support," message, 171717Z May 68; WRAMA History no. 20, 187–88.

57 WRAMA History no. 20, 188–89; CSAF/AFSME to AFSC/SCS, "Logistics Support of the AC-130A Gunship II Program," message, 172136Z May 68.

58 WRAMA History no. 20, 188–90; AFLC/MCM to AFSC/KGA, message on the AC-130, 231855Z May 68.

59 WRAMA History no. 20, 190–91; WRAMA/WRN to AFLC/MCMTA/ MCOOM/MCSC, message on the AC-130, 272022Z May 68.

60 WRAMA History no. 20, 190–92; WRAMA/WRN to WRAMA/WRP, "Contractor Support, Gunship II and III," letter, 18 June 1968.

61 WRAMA History no. 20, 191–93; CSAF/AFRDDH to AFSC/SCGA, "Support of the Gunship II Testbed Aircraft AC-130A AF S/N 54-1626," message, 271328Z Jun 68; WRAMA/WRN to AFLC/MCMA, "FY69 Contract Supply Support of AC-130 Gunship II and AC-119 Gunship III," message, 021341Z Jul 68.

62 ASD/ASZSG to CSAF/AFRDDH/AFSME/AFXOSLC, "First Article Configuration Inspection (FACI) Gunship II," message, 181814Z 19 Jul 68; ASD/ASZSG to CSAF/AFRDDH/AFSME/AFXOSLC, "Gunship II FACI," message, 071313Z Aug 68; ASD/ASZG to CSAF/AFRDDH, "First Article Configuration Inspection Review of Gunship II," message, 232054Z Apr 68.

63 HQ 317TAW/DM to WRAMA/WRN, LTVE Inc., Fairchild-Hiller, et al., "MOA for Gunship Supply," letter, 23 July 1968; WRAMA History no. 20, 194–95.

64 WRAMA/WRG to PACAF/DM, "Logistical Support for AC-130 and AC-119 Gunships," message, 262218Z Jul 68; PACAF/DM to WRAMA/WRG, "Logistical Support for AC-130 and AC-119 Gunships," message, 310250Z Jul 68.

65 PACAF/DM to AFLC/MCOOO/MCORO, "Logistics Support on AC-130/AC-119 Aircraft," message, 260101Z Sep 68; WRAMA/WRNH to PACAF/DML, "Combat Hornet RASS Team Theater Clearance," message, 291516Z Oct 68; Joseph F. Hall Jr., WRAMA/WRNHRM, "Visit to Pacific and Southeast Asia, AC-130 Program, TA-234," report, 9 January 1969; WRAMA/WRNH-4/WRNH-7 to AFLC/MCSC, "SRA and IM Status," message, 092030Z Jul 69; WRAMA/WRN to WRAMA/WRFM, "Request to Establish AC-130/AC-119 WSSLO at Ubon Airfield, Thailand," letter, 26 June 1969; "Gunship II, Southeast Asia, 1–30 November 1968," report, 13 December 1968; "Gunship II, Lockbourne AFB, Ohio, 1–31 December 1968," report, 2 January 1969; "Gunship II, Southeast Asia, 1–31 December 1968," report, 13 January 1969.

66 WRAMA/WRN to WRAMA/WRPW/WRP/WRPI, "Status of Extension to C-130 Gunship Support Contract with LTVE, F09603-68-C-0157," memo, 3 July 1969; WRAMA/WRNH-4/WRAMA/WRNH-7 to AFLC/MCSC, "SRA and IM Status and RASS Teams," message, 092030Z Jul 69; WRAMA History no. 20, 195–96.

67 AFLC, Study 374, 95; CSAF to AFSC, AFLC, "Gunship Program," message, 060135Z Jan 68.

68 AFLC, Study 374, , 98, 100.

69 Ibid., 102; ASD, "Gunship II Project," Semiannual History, 1 July–31 December 1968.

70 AFLC, Study 374, 102–3; Ballard, *Fixed-Wing Gunships,* 101; ASD, Semiannual History, 1 January 1969–June 1969, 1:137.

71 Directorate of Operational Requirements and Developmental Plans, "Install Gunship Equipment in JC-130 Aircraft," amendment to Modification Program Directive (MPD) 1885-2 (FS-2209/JC-130A), 5 March 1968; AFLC, Study 374, 106.

72 Directorate of Operational Requirements and Developmental Plans, "Install Gunship Equipment in JC-130 Aircraft," amendment to MPD 1885-2 (FS-2209/JC-130A), 5 March 1968; AFLC, Study 374, 106.

73 WRAMA/WRN to WRAMA/WRFM, "Request to Establish AC-130/AC-119 WSSLO," 26 June 1969; WRAMA/WRN to AFLC/MCOM, "Assignment of AC-130/AC-119 WSSLO," message, 17 June 1969; WRAMA/WRNH to WRAMA/WRNN/ WRNT/WRNQ, "AC-130 Aircraft, Gunship II," letter, 171740Z, 19 June 1969; WRAMA History no. 20, 196.

Chapter 4

1 Jack S. Ballard, *Development and Employment of Fixed Fixed-Wing Gunships, 1962–1972,* 106; Maj. Richard F. Kott, *The Role of United States Air Force Gunships in Southeast Asia (SEASIA),* CHECO Project, 27.

2 Kott, *Role of Gunships,* 29; 8th Tactical Fighter Wing, History, January–March 1969, 15.

3 For more on the Ho Chi Minh Trail and efforts to close it, see Eduard Mark, *Aerial Interdiction: Air Power and Land Battle in Three American Wars.*

4 Louis Seig, *Impact of Geography on Air Operations in Southeast Asia,* CHECO Project.

5 Ibid., 2–9; Ballard, *Fixed-Wing Gunships,* 110.

6 Ballard, *Fixed-Wing Gunships,* 110–11.

7 Mark, *Aerial Interdiction,* 329; Stanley Karnow, *Vietnam: A History,* 128–205; Larry Cable, *Unholy Grail: The United States and the Wars in Vietnam, 1965–1968.*

8 Mark, *Aerial Interdiction,* 330–31; Karnow, *Vietnam,* 319–48.

9 Mark, *Aerial Interdiction,* 331–32; MACV, History, January 1972–March 1973, vol. 1, Annex A, 35–36, 43–44.

10 Air University, *A Chronology of Important Airpower Events in Southeast Asia, 1950–1968,* Corona Harvest Study, 294.

11 Carl Berger, ed., *The United States Air Force in Southeast Asia, 1961–1973: An Illustrated Account,* 109–19; Earl H. Tilford, "Bombing Our Way Back Home: The Commando Hunt and Menu Campaigns of 1969–1973," in *Looking Back on the Vietnam War: A 1990s Perspective on the Decisions, Combat, and Legacies,* ed. William P. Head and Lawrence Grinter, 126–27. The term *Buff* or *BUFF* was how airmen at the time "lovingly" described the B-52. It stood for Big Ugly Fat Fellow or F——.

12 Mark, *Aerial Interdiction,* 336; Ballard, *Fixed-Wing Gunships,* 77–175.

13 Seventh Air Force, History, 1972, 67, 80–82; Mark, *Aerial Interdiction,* 353 (quote), original in Maj. Gen. Alton D. Slay, DCS Ops, Seventh Air Force, "End-of-Tour Report, August 1971–August 1972," 24 (hereafter cited as Slay, EOTR); Air University, *Chronology SEA,* 296; USAF, PACAF, "United States Air Force Operations in Laos, 1 Jan 70–30 Jun 71," Corona Harvest Project, 25; J. William Gibson, *The Perfect War: Technowar in Vietnam,* 396–97.

14 Tilford, "Bombing," 127–28.

15 Berger, *USAF in Southeast Asia,* 109–10.

16 Ibid., 110.

17 Ibid., 111.

18 Douglas Pike, *PAVN: People's Army of North Vietnam,* chap. 1, Conclusion; Douglas Pike, *Vietcong: The Organization and Techniques of the National Liberation Front of South Vietnam,* 85–105.

19 Berger, *USAF in Southeast Asia,* 111–12, 114; Earl H. Tilford Jr., *Crosswinds: The Air Force's Setup in Vietnam,* 114.

20 Berger, *USAF in Southeast Asia,* 114–18.

21 Ibid.

22 Ibid.

23 Slay, EOTR; Tilford, "Bombing," 132–33.

24 Mark, *Aerial Interdiction,* 332–33; Seventh Air Force, History, 1972, 20, 89.

25 Mark, *Aerial Interdiction,* 333–34; Seventh Air Force, History, 1972, 20. For an excellent study detailing the communist supply network, see Bernard C. Nalty, *Interdiction in Southern Laos,* 223–32.

26 Mark, *Aerial Interdiction,* 334–35; Nalty, *Interdiction,* 234–48.

27 Berger, *USAF in Southeast Asia,* 118; Mark, *Aerial Interdiction,* 344; 7 AF, History, 1972, 14–17. F-4s were not new to the Vietnam War itself in 1971. They were developed in the 1950s, mainly for the Navy, but in the 1960s the Air Force added later versions to their inventory. By the late 1960s they were being flown over the skies of Vietnam. Their original versions did not have cannon or machine guns for dogfights, but carried only missiles, which far too often did not properly function. In spite of some notable successes, such as that of Col. Robin Olds in his famous Operation Bolo ambush of MiG-21s over North Vietnam on 2 January 1967, the Phantoms did not do well until a gun pod was placed under the aircraft's belly. One of the main reasons for the creation of the Air Force's Red Flag and Navy's Top Gun schools was to improve US fighter pilots' dogfighter skills, which had plummeted in the period from the Korean War to the Vietnam War.

28 Berger, *USAF in Southeast Asia,* 118; Mark, *Aerial Interdiction,* 344; Seventh Air Force, History, 1972, 14.

29 Mark, *Aerial Interdiction,* 345–46; Seventh Air Force, History, 1972, 23–30.

30 Seventh Air Force, History,1972, 48–49 (quote), 118–27.

31 Berger, *USAF in Southeast Asia,* 118; Tilford, *Crosswinds,* 138; Mark, *Aerial Interdiction,* 344–45; Seventh Air Force, History, 1972, 14–17, 22–24.

32 Berger, *USAF in Southeast Asia,* 119; Mark, *Aerial Interdiction,* 345, 357–58; Seventh Air Force, History, 1972, 22–23. Original in Brig. Gen. Richard G. Cross, "End-of-Tour Report," 22 January 1973, File K740.131.2, Air Force Historic Research Agency (AFHRA).

33 Mark, *Aerial Interdiction,* 358; Berger, *USAF in Southeast Asia,* 119; Tilford, *Crosswinds,* 138–39, 140 (quote).

34 Tilford, "Bombing," 127–28; USAF, PACAF, "United States Air Force Operations in Laos," 76–79; Ballard, *Fixed-Wing Gunships,* 173.

35 Mark, *Aerial Interdiction,* 358–59; Nalty, *Southern Laos,* 250–51. For details on Commando Hunt V, see Seventh Air Force, Office of History, "Commando Hunt V, May 1971," 56–57.

36 Col. D. L. Evans, Director of Intelligence, "Task Force Alpha, End-of-Tour Report," 6 July 1972, 30, File 10015110, AFHRA (hereafter cited as Evans, EOTR); Mark, *Aerial Interdiction,* 360 (quotes).

37 Evans, EOTR, 16; Mark, *Aerial Interdiction,* 361–62.

38 Nalty, *Interdiction,* 148 (quote); Mark, *Aerial Interdiction,* 362–63; Slay, EOTR, 26.

39 Mark, *Aerial Interdiction,* 335, 347 (quotes); Berger, *USAF in Southeast Asia,* 119; Tilford, *Crosswinds,* 138–39; Evans, EOTR, 44, 59; Slay, EOTR, 26.

40 Mark, *Aerial Interdiction,* 335; Nalty, *Interdiction,* 228–30.

41 Mark, *Aerial Interdiction,* 348–50; Seventh Air Force, History, 1972, 66–67; Slay, EOTR, 23–24. For details on sensors, see Michael Horrocks, *The Air Force in Southeast Asia: The Sensor War, 1966–1971,* 17–19.

42 Mark, *Aerial Interdiction,* 350; Slay, EOTR, 28–29; Seventh Air Force, History, 1972, 47, 133.

43 Mark, *Aerial Interdiction,* 346–47, 355–56; Seventh Air Force, History, 1972, 33–40, 89–93, 140–41, 231; Evans, EOTR, 47–48.

44 Mark, *Aerial Interdiction,* 355–56; Seventh Air Force, History, 1972, 139–41.

45 Air Force Retiree Service to William P. Head, WR-ALC/HO, "Airmen MIA from the Vietnam War Are Identified," e-mail news release no. 05-07-08, 27 May 2008.

46 Mark, *Aerial Interdiction,* 356–57; Seventh Air Force, History, 1972, 21–22, 51–58, 132–42; Evans, EOTR, 48.

47 Berger, *USAF in Southeast Asia,* 119; Tilford, *Crosswinds,* 139.

48 Mark, *Aerial Interdiction,* 329–34; Berger, *USAF in Southeast Asia,* 109–19; Tilford, "Bombing," 126–33; Slay, EOTR; Seventh Air Force, History, 1972, 14, 20, 89; Nalty, *Interdiction,* 234–48.

49 Mark, *Aerial Interdiction,* 358–60; Berger, *USAF in Southeast Asia,* 119; Tilford, *Crosswinds,* 138–40; Seventh Air Force, History, 1972, 80; Nalty, *Interdiction,* 250–51; Tilford, "Bombing," 127–28; Ballard, *Fixed-Wing Gunships,* 173; Evans, EOTR.

50 Earl H. Tilford Jr., "Operation 'Commando Hunt': The Air War against the Ho Chi Minh Trail, 1969–1972," paper presented at Third Triennial Vietnam Symposium, Texas Tech University, 16 April 1999, 10.

51 Bruce Palmer, "US Intelligence and Vietnam," *Studies in Intelligence,* Special Spring Issue, 1984: 98–99.

52 Tilford, "Operation 'Commando Hunt,'" 10–11.

53 Ballard, *Fixed-Wing Gunships;* Joint Chiefs of Staff (JCS) to CINCPACAF, "The Use of Propeller and Jet Aircraft in Laos," message, 201740Z Dec 67. As anyone who has studied airpower doctrine knows, one of the basic principles of successful air operations is concentrated and coordinated efforts under a single air commander. For more on this, see Col. Philip S. Meilinger, *Ten Propositions Regarding Air Power.*

54 JCS to CINCPACAF, "Use of Propeller and Jet Aircraft in Laos," message, 20 December 1967; Scientific Advisory Group, "The Interdiction Campaign, 1 Apr–31 Oct 68," Working Paper no. 16-67, Report 69-5, 29; Aeronautical Science Institute, "Airpower in Southeast Asia, Aug 67–Jan 69," Report 69-3, July 69, 2, 22.

55 Meilinger, *Ten Propositions,* 20.

56 Ballard, *Fixed-Wing Gunships,* 112.

57 Aeronautical Science Institute (ASI), "Development of All-Weather and Night Truck Killing Capacities," Report 70-14, January 1970, 12–17.

58 Ibid.

59 COMUSMACV to 7 AF, "Anti-Truck Infiltration Campaign," message, 300238Z Jul 68; CSAF to CINCPACAF, message on Air Force anti-infiltration plan, 201492Z Jul 68; Aeronautical Science Institute (ASI), "Air Interdiction Campaign, 1 Nov 68–31 May 69," Report 69-7, December 1969 (hereafter cited as ASI, Report 69-7).

60 ASI, "Air Interdiction Campaign"; Ballard *Fixed-Wing Gunships,* 113.

61 Ballard, *Fixed-Wing Gunships,* 114. Original in 14th Air Combat Wing, 16th Special Operations Squadron, Det. 2, Crew of T/N 54-1629, "Mission 13/16/17," 30 December 1968 (hereafter cited as 16 SOS, Mission Report).

62 16 SOS, Mission Report.

63 Ibid.

64 ASI, "Development of All-Weather and Night Truck Killing Capacities," 14; 8th Tactical Fighter Wing (TFW), History, April–June 1969, 3:12.

65 8th TFW, History, April–June 1969, 3:16–18.

66 Ibid., 18–23; "List of AC-130 Gunships: AC-130A," http://www.gunships.org/birds.html, accessed 3 November 2009.

67 Ballard, *Fixed-Wing Gunships,* 116–19.

68 8th TFW, History, October–December 1968, 35–36.

69 Kott, *Role of Gunships,* 41–42; Evans, EOTR, 10 November 1969, 4.

70 Evans, EOTR, 3, 6; Ballard, *Fixed-Wing Gunships,* 121–22.

71 8th TFW, History, January–May 1969, 1:16; 16 SOS, Mission Report, 24 May 1969.

72 US Embassy, Laos, to Secretary of State, "Critique of Effectiveness of AC-130 Gunship against Enemy Trucks," letter, 6 May 1969; Warner Robins Air Materiel Area, History, 1 July 1970–30 June 1971, Part 4, "WRAMA's Weapon Systems: The AC-130E Aircraft Gunship Project PAVE SPECTRE, 1970-1971," vol. 1 (Secret, since declassified), Historical Study no. 25, January 1972, WRAMA HO RCS HAF D-48 (hereafter cited as WRAMA Study no. 25).

73 WRAMA Study no. 25, 5; Capt. James E. Knight and Howard Wright, WRAMA/MMHO-4, interview with Pat A. Finlayson, WRAMA/HO, 15 June 1971.

74 Maj. Gen. George S. Brown, 7 AF Commander, to 8 TFW, no subject, message, 090207Z Jun 69.

75 Ballard, *Fixed-Wing Gunships,* 124.

76 Kott, *Role of Gunships,* 33–34.

77 Ibid., 34.

78 8th TFW, History, April–June 1969, 30–31.

79 WRAMA Study no. 25, 5.

80 Ibid.

Chapter 5

1 Warner Robins Air Materiel Area, History, 1 July 1970–30 June 1971, Part 4, "WRAMA's Weapon Systems: The AC-130E Aircraft Gunship Project PAVE SPECTRE, 1970–1971," vol. 1 (Secret, since declassified), Historical Study no. 25, January 1972, WRAMA HO RCS HAF D-48 (hereafter cited as WRAMA Study No. 25), 5–6; US Air Force, Nomination Package, Harold Brown Award, General Technology Area: "Improvement for Combat Operations," January 1970 (hereafter cited as Brown Award); "Untold Story of the Ho Chi Minh Trail," *US News and World Report,* 15 June 1971, 23–24.

2 Brown Award; Seventh Air Force, "Combat Evaluation of 'Surprise Package,'" report, June 1970, 2.

3 CSAF to AFSC Commander, "Project Surprise Package," message, 022058Z Sep 69.

4 Brown Award.

5 Ibid.

6 Ibid.; Aeronautical Systems Division, Office of Public Information, "Presentation at Washington, DC," Press Release 70-244, 17 September 1970.

7 Brown Award; Tactical Air Command, "Final Report Combat Introduction/Evaluation (Cornet Surprise), August 1970," OPLAN 132, i-iii; 8th TFW, History, 1 October-31 December 1969, 32.

8 8th TFW, History, 1 October-31 December 1969, 32.

9 Seventh Air Force, "Combat Evaluation of 'Surprise Package,'" 7 June 1970, A-1.

10 Maj. James Wolverton, Richard E. Willes, and Lt. Col. Bradford W. Parkinson, "The Genesis and Development of Gunship II," ASD/USAFA, no date, 15-19.

11 Ibid.

12 James Lawrence Cole, "Fixed-Wing Gunships in Southeast Asia," PACAF, Directorate of Operations Analysis Division, CHECO Project, July 1969-June 1971, 11.

13 Ibid., 64, 75; 8th TFW, History, April-June 1969, 3:3, 38-39; 16th Special Operations Squadron, History, June-September 1970, Appendix A.

14 Ballard, *Fixed-Wing Gunships,* 135-37; USAF, Directorate of Operations, Requirements, and Development Plans," Semiannual History, 1 January-30 June 1969, 37.

15 Ballard, *Fixed-Wing Gunships,* 135-37; USAF, Directorate of Operations, Requirements, and Development Plans," Semiannual History, 1 January-30 June 1969, 37.

16 Cole, "Gunships in SEA," 68; 8th TFW, History, April-June 1969, 1:32; 3:3, 38-39.

17 USAF, Directorate of Operations, Requirements, and Development Plans," Semiannual History, 1 January-30 June 1969, 208-10.

18 Ballard, *Fixed-Wing Gunships,* 138-40.

19 Directorate of Operations, Requirements, and Development Plans, History, 1 January-30 June 1970, 207.

20 SECAF to SECDEF, "Trip Report: Far East Trip (10-21 Jan 70)," memo, 23 January 1970; 16th Special Operations Squadron, Chronology, 1 January-31 March 1970, in 8th TFW, History, 1 January-31 March 1970, 3:3; Directorate of Operations, Requirements, and Development Plans, Semiannual History, 1 January-30 June 1970, 204.

21 TAC, History, July 1969-June 1970, 1:354-58.

22 Dr. Lee A. DuBridge to SECDEF, no subject, letter, 26 June 1969.

23 VCSAF to SAF, "Status of Gunship Program," letter, 23 July 1969.

24 Ballard, *Fixed-Wing Gunships,* 144-45. For more on the Pentagon haggling, see Elizabeth H. Hartsook, *The Air Force in Southeast Asia: The Role of Air Power Grows,* 56.

25 Ballard, *Fixed-Wing Gunships,* 145-46.

26 WRAMA Study no. 25, 5-11; USAF, ASD, "Gunship Program Office," History, 1 January-31 December 1970, 5-8.

27 Directorate of Operations, Requirements, and Development Plans, Semiannual History, 1 January-30 June 1970, 206.

28 WRAMA Study no. 25, 12; Directorate of Operations, Requirements, and Developmental Plans, Semiannual History, 1 January-June 1970, 285.

29 WRAMA Study no. 25, 12; Directorate of Operations, Requirements, and Developmental Plans, Semiannual History, 1 January-June 1970, 285.

30 Hartsook, *Air Force in Southeast Asia,* 57; Ballard, *Fixed-Wing Gunships,* 148; Maj. Gen. Joseph J. Kruzel to Dr. DuBridge, Staff Summary Sheet on the gunship program, 11 May 1970.

31 Directorate of Operations, Requirements, and Development Plans, Semiannual History, 1 January–30 June 1970, 206.

32 Seventh Air Force, "Commando Hunt III," Report, May 1970; MACV, History, 1970, vol. 1, Annex A, 95–96.

33 Ballard, *Fixed-Wing Gunships,* 150.

34 Ibid., 150, 152; McLucas to Seamans, "PSAC and Surprise Package," memo, 12 June 1970; Department of Defense, Deputy Director of Operations, "Additional AC-130 Gunships for CY 70–71 Dry Season," Staff Summary Sheet, 2 July 1970.

35 WRAMA Director of Materiel Management (WRN) to AFLC Commander, "Additional AC-130 Gunships," message, 252220Z Jun 70.

36 SECAF to Deputy SECDEF, "Additional AC-130 Gunships for CY 70–71, Dry Season," memo, 2 July 1970.

37 Ballard, *Fixed-Wing Gunships,* 153; SECAF to Deputy SECDEF, "Acquisition of Additional Gunships," memo, 10 July 1970.

38 CSAF to AFSC, WRAMA, et al., "Additional AC-130A Gunships," message, 141731Z Jul 70.

39 ASD, "PAVE Pronto, Conference of 22–25 July 1970," memo for the record, 25 July 1970.

40 Deputy SECDEF to SECAF, SEC NAV, CJCS, memo on gunship tactics, 11 July 1970.

41 CSAF to SAF, Deputy SECDEF, letter on hunting season tactics, 29 July 1970; ASD, Gunship Program Office, History, 1 June–31 December 1970, 6; Directorate of Operational Research and Development, semiannual history, 1 January–30 June 1971, 294–96; ASD to SECAF, "Ninth Weekly Gunship Status Report," 1 October 1970.

42 SAF to Deputy SECDEF, "Requisition of Additional Gunships," memo, 1 October 1970.

Chapter 6

1 Warner Robins Air Materiel Area, History, 1 July 1970–30 June 1971, Part 4, "WRAMA's Weapon Systems: The AC-130E Aircraft Gunship Project PAVE SPECTRE, 1970–1971," vol. 1 (Secret, since declassified), Historical Study no. 25, January 1972, WRAMA HO RCS HAF D-48 (hereafter cited as WRAMA Study no. 25), 5–6.

2 Ibid., 72.

3 Ibid., 21–22.

4 Ibid.

5 Ibid.

6 Ibid., 72; Ted Lynch, ASD, Chief Engineer for Gunships, Program Office, Robins AFB, GA, interview with Pat A. Finlayson, WRAMA/HO, 16 November 1971 (hereafter cited as Lynch interview).

7 Lynch interview.

8 Ibid.; USAF, RDQPM, "Modification Requirement for C-130E Aircraft," paper (Secret, since declassified), MR no. 2272 (FS-2572/C-130E), 6 January 1971 (hereafter cited as USAF, Modification Requirement 2272); Capt. James E. Knight and Howard Wright, WRAMA/MMHO-4, interview with Pat A. Finlayson, WRAMA/HO, 15 June 1971 (hereafter cited as Knight/Wright interview).

9 USAF, Modification Requirement 2272; Knight/Wright interview; ASD, "Gunship II Surprise Package C-130 Aircraft Series Analysis and Program Costs," study (Secret, since declassified), 30 January 1970; WRAMA Study no. 25, 9–11.

10 WRAMA Study no. 25, 11–12, 72–74; WRAMA/MM to Col. Howard G. Beck, WRAMA Chief of Staff, "AC-130E Pave Spectre Program," memo (Confidential, since declassified), 20 October 1970; Lynch interview; MMHO, unclassified briefing on Pave Spectre Program, no date.

11 Lynch interview; WRAMA Study no. 25, 73–74.

12 Lynch interview, WRAMA Study no. 25, 75.

13 Lynch interview; AFLC to WRAMA/DMM/WRN, message on feasibility study (unclassified), 191959Z May 70; WRAMA to AFLC, message on feasibility study (unclassified) 201331Z May 70; Howard Wright, MMHO-4, "AC-130E Gunship Study for Organic Accomplishment," Staff Summary Sheet, 22 May 1970; WRAMA/WRN to AFLC/MCN, "AC-130E Gunship Prototype," message, 15 May 1970;WRAMA Study no. 25, 13, 75, 77.

14 Knight/Wright interview; WRAMA Study no. 25, 13.

15 WRAMA Study no. 25, 13–15.

16 Ibid., 14–15; WRAMA/CV for WRG-2 to AFLC/MCN, message on C-130E IRAN (unclassified), 281806Z May 70.

17 WRAMA Study no. 25, 15–16; WRAMA/CV for WRG-2 to AFLC/MCN, message on C-130E IRAN (unclassified), 281806Z May 70.

18 WRAMA Study no. 25, 16; WRAMA/CV for WRG-2 to AFLC/MCN, message on C-130E IRAN (unclassified), 281806Z May 70.

19 WRAMA Study no. 25, 17; H. H. Cotton, WRAMA/MM, to Col. Howard G. Beck, WRAMA/CS, "AC-130E Pave Spectre Program," memo (Confidential, since declassified), 20 October 1970 (hereafter cited as Cotton memo); AFSC to CSAF, "PAVE SPECTRE," message (unclassified), 161515Z Jun 70.

20 Cotton memo; WRAMA Study no. 25, 17–19.

21 Cotton memo; WRAMA Study no. 25, 17–19.

22 Cotton memo; WRAMA Study no. 25, 18–19.

23 WRAMA Study no. 25, 19–20.

24 Cotton memo.

25 Ibid.; WRAMA/MMHTB to ASD, "Re-designation of C-130E Gunship Aircraft to AC-130E Designation," message (unclassified), EFTO 161411Z Jul 70; WRAMA/MMH to WRAMA/MAP, "Modification of Two AC-130E Gunships, Project PAVE SPECTRE," letter (unclassified), 7 July 1970; WRAMA/MM to OOAMA/MM, OCAMA/MM, SMAMA/MM, SAAMA/MM, "AC-130E Gunship Priority," message (unclassified), 232134Z Dec 70; Bob Willingham, WRAMA Pave Spectre Office, interview with Pat A. Finlayson, WRAMA/HO, 6 October 1971.

26 WRAMA Study no. 25, 21–23; Ballard, *Fixed-Wing Gunships,* 158; ASD, "Gunship Program Office," History, 1 June–31 December 1971, 8.

27 WRAMA Study no. 25, 20–22; ASD to SECAF, "12th Weekly Gunship Status Report," 28 October 1970; 8th Tactical Fighter Wing, History, 1 July–30 September 1970.

28 WRAMA/MMHO-4 to CINCPACAF, "Pave Spectre," message (Confidential, since de-

classified), 261336Z Feb 71; Grover C. Combs Jr., WRAMA/MMH, to WRAMA/MMN, MMT, MMA, MMS, "AC-130E Pave Spectre Program," letter (Confidential, since declassified), 27 October 1970.

29 WRAMA Study no. 25, 23–25; CSAF to AFSC, "PAVE SPECTRE Program Funding," message (Unclassified), 241701Z Jul 70; CSAF to AFLC, "PAVE SPECTRE Funding," message (Unclassified), 061754Z Aug 70.

30 WRAMA Study no. 25, 25–29; "AC-130E Pave Spectre: Milestone Activities and Events," chart (Confidential, since declassified), no date; USAF, Modification Requirement 2272; Combs to WRAMA/MMN et al., letter, 27 October 1970.

31 Cotton memo; WRAMA Study no. 25, 29–30.

32 Col. Irving B. Schoenberg, WRAMA/MM, to Grover C. Combs Jr., Tactical Aircraft Division Chief in MM, MMH, memo routing slip, 29 September 1970; Cotton memo; WRAMA/MMHT to WRAMA/MMEW, "IRAN Cycle, C-130E Aircraft, Serial Numbers 69-6567 and 69-6568," letter, 9 November 1970.

33 WRAMA Study no. 25, 31–32; WRAMA/MAPACP to ASC et al., "Conference Project Pave Spectre," letter, 15 October 1970.

34 WRAMA MMH, "Technical Data Conference," minutes, 3–4 December 1970; WRAMA Study no. 25, 34–35; WRAMA/MM to ASD/SD, "Pave Spectre Group A Assemblies," message, 232107Z Dec 70; AFLC to WRAMA, message on Group A assemblies, 082035Z Feb 71; WRAMA to all other AMAs, "AC-130 Gunship Program," message (Secret, since declassified), 081830Z Apr 71.

35 CSAF to AFLC, "AC-130A Support," message (Secret, since declassified), 152100Z Jan 71; J. Howard Wright, WRAMA/MMHO-4, interview with Pat A. Finlayson, WRAMA/HO, 15 June 1971.

36 WRAMA Study no. 25, 37–39; ASD/SDY to WRAMA/ MA PACP, "Tooling for the AC-130E Prototypes," letter, 4 December 1970; WRAMA/MAP to WRAMA/ MMHO-4, "Pick Up of Gunship Templates and Tooling," letter, 26 January 1971.

37 WRAMA Study no. 25, 42–44; WRAMA/MMHO-4 to WRAMA/ACC, "Pave Spectre," letter, 29 March 1971.

38 AFLC to WRAMA/MM, "AC-130A Support," message, 192118Z Jan 71; Lynch interview; WRAMA Study no. 25, 45–50, 78

39 WRAMA Study no. 25, 49–50, 78–79; Lynch interview.

40 WRAMA Study no. 25, 50–51; WRAMA/MMH to WRAMA/MM, "Gunship Mod/ IRAN Update Program," memo (unclassified), 25 March 1971; WRAMA/MMHO-4 to WRAMA/ACC, "Pave Spectre," letter, 29 March 1971; WRAMA/MMHO-4 to WRAMA/ MMHR, "Initial Support Kits AC-130A/E," letter, 12 April 1971.

41 Lynch interview; WRAMA Study no. 25, 51–52; WRAMA/MMH to MMN, "Management Assignment Codes, Peculiar A-7 Fire Control System," letter, 29 April 1971; MMN to MMH, "Management Assignment Codes, Peculiar A-7 Fire Control System," letter, 30 April 1971.

42 WRAMA Study no. 25, 53–56; ASD to CINCPACAF DMMA, "Gunship Maintenance Support Concept," message (unclassified), 271640Z Apr 71.

43 ASD and WRAMA, "AC-130E Gunship Modification/ Development Program," joint agreement, no date (ca. 1 October 1970); WRAMA/MMHO-4 to WRAMA/ACC, "Pave

Spectre," letter, 29 March 1971, with attachment, AFLC to WRAMA/MM, message on Pave Spectre, 232229Z Mar 71; WRAMA Study no. 25, 57–60.

44 WRAMA Study no. 25, 59–60.

45 Maj. Ken B. Richardson, WRAMA Pave Spectre Management Office, "Pave Spectre Management Office," interview with Pat A. Finlayson, WRAMA/HO, 1 October 1971.

46 Ibid.; "WRAMA Pave Spectre Management Office," staffing list, ca. 1 October 1971, revised, 17 November 1971; WRAMA Study no. 25, 60–62.

47 Lynch interview; WRAMA Study no. 25, 62–63.

48 Lynch interview; WRAMA Study no. 25, 62–64; Capt. Gene Faggard WRAMA/MMHO, interview with Pat A. Finlayson, 17 January 1972.

49 Lynch interview; Robert F. "Bob" Willingham, WRAMA/MAB, interview with Pat A. Finlayson, WRAMA/OH, 6 October 1971; WRAMA Study no. 25, 64–67.

50 Willingham interview.

51 ASD to ADTC, "Pave Spectre Test Requirements," message (Confidential, since declassified), 281821Z Apr 71; Lynch interview; WRAMA Study no. 25, 79–86.

52 WRAMA Study no. 25, 87–89; Lynch interview; Faggard interview.

53 WRAMA Study no. 25, 90–93.

54 Ibid., 95–96; Capt. Faggard, WRAMA/MMHO-4, chart of AC-130E production program, 17 January 1972; Faggard interview.

55 Office of the Secretary of the Air Force to all AF Commanders, policy letter on AC-130E, 1 January 1972; Lynch interview; WRAMA Study no. 25, 104–5.

56 Office of the Secretary of the Air Force to all AF Commanders, policy letter on AC-130E, 1 January 1972; Lynch interview; WRAMA Study no. 25, 104–5.

Chapter 7

1 Jack S. Ballard, *Development and Employment of Fixed-Wing Gunships,* 1962–1972, 159; James Lawrence Cole, "Fixed-Wing Gunships in Southeast Asia," PACAF, Directorate of Operations Analysis, CHT Division, CHECO Project, July 1969–June 1971, 50–52.

2 ASD to SECAF, "12th Weekly Gunship Status Report," 28 October 1970; ASD to SECAF, "17th Weekly Gunship Status Report," 3 December 1970; ASD to SECAF, "20th Weekly Gunship Status Report," 28 December 1970.

3 Ballard, *Fixed-Wing Gunships,* 162–63.

4 CSAF to SECAF, "20th Weekly Gunship Status Report," 28 December 1970; SECAF to SECDEF, "AC-130 Gunship Program Status," memo, 4 January 1971.

5 Col. Bradford W. Parkinson, "Significant Concepts from the Air Force AC-130 Gunship Program," thesis, Naval War College, Newport, RI, 28 January 1972, 63.

6 Ballard, *Fixed-Wing Gunships,* 165–66; MACV, History, vol. 1, Annex A, sect. VI-94, 105. For more on Commando Hunt V, see chapters 5 and 6 in this book as well as Eduard Mark, *Aerial Interdiction: Air Power and Land Battle in Three American Wars,* and William P. Head, *War from Above the Clouds: B-52 Operations during the Second Indochina War and the Effects of the Air War on Theory and Doctrine.*

7 Mark, *Aerial Interdiction.*

8 Cole, "Gunships in Southeast Asia," 47. For details on this subject, see Head, *War from Above the Clouds,* and Mark, *Aerial Interdiction,* especially 320–412.

9 Ballard, *Fixed-Wing Gunships,* 167–68.
10 Cole, "Gunships in Southeast Asia," 47.
11 Ibid., 47; untitled article on Commando Hunt V, *Baltimore Sun,* 24 February 1971.
12 Cole, "Gunships in Southeast Asia," 50–55; Ballard, *Fixed-Wing Gunships,* 169.
13 "Air Force Management Summary in Southeast Asia," report, 18 August 1971, 23; Col. J. F. Loye Jr. et al., *Lom Son 719: The South Vietnamese Incursion into Laos, 30 January–24 March 1971,* CHECO Project, 24 March 1971, 15–20, 51–55.
14 Ballard, *Fixed-Wing Gunships,* 171.
15 WRAMA, "WRAMA's Weapon Systems, The AC-130E Aircraft Gunship Project PAVE SPECTRE, 1970–1971," 1 July 1970–30 June 1971 (Secret, since declassified), Part IV, Vol. 1, Historical Study no. 25, HO RCS HAF D-48, January 1972, 82–83; SECDEF to President Nixon, "Gunships in Southeast Asia," memo, 10 March 1971.
16 Air Force Directorate of Operations, History, 1 January–30 June 1971, 98–100.
17 CSAF to AFSC, ASD, "QRC-72-2 Chaff Cartridge," message, 091617Z Jul 71; CSAF to AFSC, ASD, "Improved ECM for Gunships (CROC6-71)," message, 20192Z Aug 71.
18 Ballard, *Fixed-Wing Gunships,* 172–73; Air Force Directorate of Operations, "Air Operations Review," January 1972, 1:I2–I4.
19 Cole, "Gunships in Southeast Asia," 45.
20 Ballard, *Fixed-Wing Gunships,* 221.
21 Ibid., 222–27.
22 Elizabeth H. Hartsook, *The United States Air Force in Southeast Asia: Shield for Vietnamization, 1971,* CHECO Project, May 1974, 5.
23 Ballard, *Fixed-Wing Gunships,* 229–30; Seventh Air Force, "Commando Hunt VII," CHECO Project, June 1972, 7, 14–20.
24 Seventh Air Force, "Commando Hunt VII," 18–20, 44, 59.
25 Ibid., 71–72, 201.
26 Lt. Col. Robert G. Zimmerman, interview with Lt. Col. Stephen J. Opitz, 18 July 1975, Air University, Historic Research Center, Maxwell AFB, Alabama, USAF Oral History Interview, IRIS Document 01016327, Document K239.0512-846, 6–8 (hereafter cited as Opitz interview).
27 Ibid.
28 Seventh Air Force, "Commando Hunt VII," 54–56, 201–22.
29 Opitz interview.
30 Seventh Air Force, "Commando Hunt VII," 222. For more on gunship losses, see Chris Hoban, *Vietnam Air Loses: United States Air Force, Navy, and Marine Corps Fixed-Wing Aircraft Losses in Southeast Asia, 1961–1973.*
31 Opitz interview, 43.
32 Ibid., 44–45.
33 Seventh Air Force, "Commando Hunt VII," 67.
34 8th Tactical Fighter Wing, History, 1 January–31 March 1972, 35.
35 Ibid., 35–36; Ballard, *Fixed-Wing Gunships,* 232–34.
36 Colonel Harry G. Graham, End-of-Tour Report, 31 January 1973, 15.
37 For details, see Head, *War from Above the Clouds;* Mark, *Aerial Interdiction.*
38 Opitz interview, 57–58.

39 Ibid., 59–60.

40 Ibid., 60.

41 Ibid., 61–62.

42 Ballard, *Fixed-Wing Gunships,* 234.

43 For more on intelligence on the Easter Offensive and Operation Proud Deep Alpha, see John Morrocco, *Rain of Fire: The Air War, 1969–1973;* Earl H. Tilford Jr., *Crosswinds: The Air Force's Setup in Vietnam.*

44 Morrocco, *Rain of Fire;* Tilford, *Crosswinds.*

45 Head, *War from Above the Clouds;* Tilford, *Crosswinds;* John Lake, *Stratofortress Units in Combat, 1955–1973;* Earl H. Tilford Jr., *Setup: What the Air Force Did in Vietnam and Why.*

46 Head, *War from Above the Clouds.*

47 Mark, *Aerial Interdiction;* Capt. Charles A. Nicholson, *The United States Air Force Response to the Spring 1972 North Vietnamese Offensive: Situation and Redeployment,* CHECO Project; Tilford, *Setup.*

Chapter 8

1 Earl H. Tilford Jr., *Crosswinds: The Air Force's Setup in Vietnam,* 143; Mark Clodfelter, *The Limits of Air Power: The American Bombing Campaign of North Vietnam,* 152–53; Eduard Mark, *Aerial Interdiction: Air Power and Land Battle in Three American Wars,* 365–66; Robert Frank Futrell, *Ideas, Concepts, Doctrine: Basic Thinking in the United States Air Force,* 267–68.

2 Truong Nhu Tang, *A Vietcong Memoir: An Inside Account of the Vietnam War and Its Aftermath,* 200–202, 210–13.

3 Henry Kissinger, *The White House Years,* 1109; Clodfelter, *Limits of Air Power,* 153.

4 Bruce Palmer, "US Intelligence and Vietnam," *Studies in Intelligence* (Special Spring Issue, 1984): 91; Mark, *Aerial Interdiction,* 368.

5 Capt. Charles A. Nicholson, *The United States Air Force Response to the Spring 1972 North Vietnamese Offensive: Situation and Redeployment,* CHECO Project, 21.

6 Capt. David Mann, *The 1972 Invasion of Military Region I: Fall of Quang Tri and Defense of Hue,* CHECO Project, 13–52; Capt. Peter A. W. Liebchen, *Kontum: Battle for the Central Highlands, 30 March–10 June 1972,* CHECO Project, 28–44; Maj. Pal T. Ringenbach and Capt. Peter J. Melly, *The Battle for An Loc, 5 April–26 June 1972,* CHECO Project, 1–16.

7 Gen. William W. Momyer, *Air Power in Three Wars,* 332; quote also found in Donald J. Mrozck, "The Limits of Innovation: Aspects of Air Power in Vietnam," 4, http://www.airpower.au.af.mil/airchronicles/aureview/1985/jan-feb/mrozek.

8 Jack S. Ballard, *Development and Employment of Fixed-Wing Gunships, 1962–1972;* 236–38; Tilford, *Crosswinds,* 146; Maj. Gen. Alton D. Slay, DCS Ops, 7 AF, "End-of-Tour Report, August 1971–August 1972," 51, 156; Futrell, *Ideas, Concepts, Doctrine,* 275; Maj. A. J. C. Lavalle, ed., *Air Power and the 1972 Spring Offensive,* USAF Monograph Series, 2:58, 98.

9 Nicholson, *United States Air Force Response,* 38, 67; Mark, *Aerial Interdiction,* 373; Seventh Air Force, History, 1 July 1971–30 June 1972, 273–77; Mark Clodfelter, "Nixon and

the Air Weapon," in *An American Dilemma: Vietnam, 1964–1973,* ed. Dennis E. Showalter and John G. Albert, 169; Brig. Gen. James R. McCarthy and Lt. Col. George B. Allison, *Linebacker II: A View from the Rock,* 11. The revised edition of the McCarthy and Allison book was published as Monograph 8, Vol. 6, of the USAF Southeast Asia Monograph Series.

10 All F-105s were known as Thunderchiefs except the F-105G, which was a SEAD aircraft. It was known as a Wild Weasel. In fact, the F-105Gs were modified F-105Fs upgraded into the SAM hunter role. Since that time, other kinds of fighters have been reconfigured into Wild Weasels to perform the SEAD (today DEAD) role. Among them was the F-4 airframe.

11 Clodfelter, *Limits of Air Power;* Morrocco, *Rain of Fire;* Nicholson, *United States Air Force Response.* Also see Ronald Frankum, *Like Rolling Thunder: The Air War in Vietnam, 1964–1975.*

12 Nicholson, *United States Air Force Response,* 67; Mark *Aerial Interdiction,* 373; Clodfelter, "Nixon and the Air Weapon," 169; Tilford, *Crosswinds,* 145; PACAF, History, 1 July 1971–30 June 1972, 1:121–22; Seventh Air Force, "History of Linebacker Operations," 10 May–23 October 1972, 3–5, File 740.04-24, Air Force Historic Research Agency.

13 Nicholson, *United States Air Force Response,* 123–24; Mark, *Aerial Interdiction,* 373; Clodfelter, "Nixon and the Air Weapon," 169.

14 Richard Nixon, *RN: The Memoirs of Richard Nixon,* 606.

15 Clodfelter, "Nixon and the Air Weapon," 172; Seymour M. Hersh, *The Price of Power: Kissinger in the Nixon White House,* 506; Melvin F. Porter, *Linebacker: Overview of the First 120 Days,* CHECO Project, 14–15.

16 Mark, *Air Interdiction,* 375; Clodfelter, "Nixon and the Air Weapon," 170, original in MACV, "Linebacker Study," unofficial/uncoordinated draft report, 20 January 1973, chap. 2, p. 2, File K712.041-19, AFHRA; Nixon, *RN,* 2:64–65; PACAF, *USAF Air Operations against NVN, 1 July–30 June 1972,* Corona Harvest Project, 52–61 (hereafter cited as PACAF, *Air Ops vs. NVN*).

17 Hersh, *Price of Power,* 568; Kissinger, *White House Years,* 1118, 1176; Clodfelter, "Nixon and the Air Weapon," 170–71; Mark, *Aerial Interdiction,* 375–76; Nixon, *RN,* 2:81.

18 PACAF, *Air Ops vs. NVN,* 90–91; Momyer, *Air Power in Three Wars,* 33; Tilford, *Crosswinds,* 149–50.

19 Porter, *Linebacker,* 16–17; Clodfelter, "Nixon and the Air Weapon," 171.

20 Nixon, *RN,* 2:79–80; Clodfelter, "Nixon and the Air Weapon," 171.

21 Mark, *Aerial Interdiction,* 378–79; PACAF, *Air Ops vs. NVN,* 65, 121–31. In more recent times the AGM-45 and AGM-78 have been replaced by the AGM-88 HARM to perform the Wild Weasel's SEAD or DEAD mission.

22 PACAF, *Air Ops vs. NVN,* 131.

23 Mark, *Aerial Interdiction,* 379.

24 PACAF, *Air Ops vs. NVN,* 132–36; Seventh Air Force, "History of Linebacker Operations," 51–52.

25 "North Vietnamese Current Assessment," vol. 7, "US Air Force Operations in Defense of RVN," CHECO Project, 1 June 1972, File K717.03-219, Document Collection, Air Force Historical Research Agency.

26 Mark, *Aerial Interdiction,* 132.

27 PACAF, *Air Ops vs. NVN,* 91–95; Momyer, *Air Power in Three Wars,* 174–75, 183–96.

28 PACAF, *Air Ops vs. NVN,* 98–103; Mark, *Aerial Interdiction,* 385–86; Clodfelter, "Nixon and the Air Weapon," 172.

29 PACAF, *Air Ops vs. NVN,* 103–4; Mark, *Aerial Interdiction,* 386–88. While the GBU-10 is the bomb, it is built using an Mk-84, which is a two-thousand-pound conventional warhead. When configured as an LGB, it became known as the GBU-10. It was based on the Paveway I system, which allowed a laser to guide the ordnance to the target. The Paveway II system began development in 1972, and its big improvement was the addition of folding wings.

30 Porter, *Linebacker,* 25; PACAF, *Air Ops vs. NVN,* 111–17.

31 PACAF, *Air Ops vs. NVN,* 109, 117.

32 Mark, *Aerial Interdiction,* 392–95; SAC, History, 1 July 1971–30 June 1972, 461–67.

33 Mark, *Aerial Interdiction,* 395–97.

34 Ibid.

35 Clodfelter, *Limits of Air Power,* 166, 173.

36 Palmer, "US Intelligence and Vietnam," 98–99.

37 MACV, History, January 1972–March 1973, 53, 74, 78–79.

38 Mark, *Aerial Interdiction,* 399, 408.

39 Ibid., 408.

40 For more on US airpower in Vietnam and since, see William P. Head and David R. Mets, *Plotting a True Course: Reflections on USAF Strategic Attack Theory and Doctrine: The Post World War II Experience,* especially chaps. 3–6; Tilford, *Crosswinds;* Clodfelter, *Limits of Air Power;* Head, *War from Above the Clouds;* John Morrocco, *Rain of Fire: Air War, 1968–1975,* vol. 10 in *The Vietnam Experience,* ed. Robert Manning; and Richard P. Hallion, *Storm over Iraq: Air Power and the Gulf War.*

Chapter 9

1 Jack S. Ballard, *Development and Employment of Fixed-Wing Gunships, 1962–1972,* 236–38; Capt. David K. Mann, *The 1972 Invasion of Military Region I: Fall of Quang Tri and Defense of Hue,* CHECO Project, 1–2, 14, 50–57, 69–70; Capt. Peter A. W. Liebchen, *Kontum: Battle for the Central Highlands, 30 Mar–10 Jun 72,* CHECO Project, 16–21.

2 Liebchen, *Kontum,* 43, 50, 67–70; John A. Poglione et al., *Air Power and the 1972 Spring Invasion,* 3:72–73.

3 Poglione, *Air Power,* 73–75; Maj. Paul T. Ringenbach and Capt. Peter J. Melly, *The Battle for An Loc, April 5–June 26, 1972,* CHECO Project, 5–25, 31–44.

4 Ringenbach and Melly, *An Loc,* 31–44.

5 Ibid., 19–25, 41–46; Gerald J. Till and James C. Thomas, *Pave Aegis Weapon System (AC-130E Gunship),* CHECO Project, 23–24.

6 Ballard, *Fixed-Wing Gunships,* 244–46.

7 8th Tactical Fighter Wing, History, 1 July–30 September 1972, 23–29.

8 Maj. Gen. Clay T. McCutchan, "USAF Gunship Overview," Air Force Special Operations Command Special Study, January 1994; 16th Special Operations Squadron, History (Secret, since declassified), 1973–93 (hereafter cited as 16 SOS History); 919th Special

Operations Group, History (unclassified), 1973–93 (hereafter cited as 919 SOG History); Air Force Special Operations Command, Public Affairs Office, Hurlburt Field, Florida, fact sheet (unclassified), October 2007 (hereafter cited as AFSOC Fact Sheet).

9 Chris Hobson, *Vietnam Air Losses: United States Air Force, Navy, and Marine Corps Fixed-Wing Aircraft Losses in Southeast Asia, 1961–1973,* 182, 202, 220, 228–29, 244.

10 Ibid., pp. 228–29.

11 McCutchan, "USAF Gunship Overview."

12 Ibid.

13 Ibid. Among the original sources for this information are 16 SOS History; 919 SOG History; 388th Tactical Fighter Wing, History (Secret, since declassified), 1 Jul–31 December 1974, 4 vols. (specifically vol. 2, "16 SOS leaves Vietnam"), IRIS Number 01005588. There are two excellent books on this era published by Air University: Herman L. Gilster, *The Air War in Southeast Asia,* specifically p. 36, and David R. Mets, *Land-Based Air Power in Third World Crises,* specifically pp. 40–41.

14 McCutchan, "USAF Gunship Overview"; AFSOC Fact Sheet, 18 May 1973; 16 SOS History, 15 August 1973, 17; 919 SOG History, n.d., 34.

15 McCutchan, "USAF Gunship Overview."

16 For details on the *Mayaguez,* see John L. Frisbee, "Mayaguez Incident," *Air Force Magazine* 74, no. 9 (September 1991); John P. Guilmartin, *A Very Short War: The Mayaguez and the Battle of Koh Tang,* 27–30.

17 Frisbee, "Mayaguez Incident"; Guilmartin, *Very Short War,* 32–52.

18 Frisbee, "Mayaguez Incident"; Guilmartin, *Very Short War,* 48–77; Ric Hunter, "The Last Battle of Vietnam," *Flight Journal* 5, no. 2 (April 2000); Ralph Wetterhahn, *The Last Battle: The Mayaguez Incident and the End of the Vietnam War.*

19 Hunter, "Last Battle of Vietnam"; Wetterhahn, *Last Battle;* Guilmartin, *Very Short War,* 53–81; Frisbee, "Mayaguez Incident."

20 Guilmartin, *Very Short War,* 82–104; Hunter, "Last Battle of Vietnam"; Wetterhahn, *Last Battle;* Frisbee, "Mayaguez Incident."

21 George M. Watson Jr., "The Mayaguez Rescue," *Air Force Magazine* 92, no. 7 (July 2009): 72.

22 Ibid.

23 Guilmartin, *Very Short War,* 77–102; Frisbee, "Mayaguez Incident."

24 Guilmartin, *Very Short War,* 100–121, 160; Hunter, "Last Battle of Vietnam"; Wetterhahn, *Last Battle;* Frisbee, "Mayaguez Incident."

25 Guilmartin, *Very Short War,* 100–121, 160; Hunter, "Last Battle of Vietnam"; Wetterhahn, *Last Battle;* Frisbee, "Mayaguez Incident."

26 Guilmartin, *Very Short War,* 128–60; Frisbee, "Mayaguez Incident"; Henry A. Kissinger, "Anatomy of a Crisis: The 'Mayaguez,'" in *Years of Renewal,* chap. 18.

27 Guilmartin, *Very Short War,* 128–60; Frisbee, "Mayaguez Incident"; Kissinger, "Anatomy of a Crisis."

28 McCutchan, "USAF Gunship Overview." For more details, see 16 SOS History.

29 Henry A. Kissinger, *Years of Renewal,* chap. 18.

30 George R. Dunham, *US Marines in Vietnam: The Bitter End, 1973–1975,* 239.

31 Ibid.

32 McCutchan, "USAF Gunship Overview." For more details, see 16 SOS History and 919 SOG History.

33 Ibid.

34 Ibid.

35 Ibid.

36 Maj. Gen. Clay T. McCutchan and Brig. Gen. Mike Wilson, interview with William Head, 30 January 2008, Eglin AFB, FL, 3 (hereafter cited as McCutchan/Wilson interview).

37 McCutchan/Wilson interview; Clay T. McCutchan, Maj. Gen., USAF, Ret., AAC/HO, to Dr. William P. Head, WR-ALC/HO, "AC-130 Chapters," e-mail, 8 December 2009.

38 McCutchan e-mail to Head.

39 Ibid.

40 McCutchan, "USAF Gunship Overview." For more details, see 16 SOS History and 919 SOG History.

41 For details on the Iranian Hostage Crisis, see David Patrick Houghton, *US Foreign Policy and the Iran Hostage Crisis.*

42 Ibid.

43 Ibid.

44 Ibid.

45 Ibid.

46 Ibid.

47 McCutchan, "USAF Gunship Overview." For more details, see 16 SOS History.

48 McCutchan, "USAF Gunship Overview"; Cara Best, *Nutmeg and Gunships: Operation "Urgent Fury" and the Invasion of Grenada,* USAF Monograph (Secret; all data used is unclassified or has since been declassified). For specific information about AFSOC and Urgent Fury, see Fred J. Pushies, *US Air Force Special Ops,* rev. ed., 27.

49 Best, *Nutmeg and Gunships.*

50 Ronald A. Cole, *Operation Urgent Fury: The Planning and Execution of Joint Operations in Grenada, 12 October–2 November 1983,* 6–7.

51 Ibid.

52 Ibid., 25–27.

53 Ibid., 1–6, 57–62.

54 Ibid.

55 McCutchan/Wilson interview, 5.

56 McCutchan, "Gunship Overview."

57 Ibid.

58 Bernard Nalty, "Post-Vietnam," in *Winged Shield, Winged Sword: A History of the United States Air Force,* vol. 2, *1950–1997,* 411–13.

59 McCutchan, "USAF Gunship Overview."

60 Nalty, "Post-Vietnam," 411.

61 Ibid., 413; Best, *Nutmeg and Gunships.*

62 Nalty, "Post-Vietnam," 414; Best, *Nutmeg and Gunships.*

63 Nalty, "Post-Vietnam," 416.

64 Ibid., 417.

65 Thomas Y'Blood, "Peace Is Not Always Peaceful," chap. 23 in *Winged Shield, Winged Sword,* vol. 2, *1950–1997,* ed. Bernard Nalty.

66 Cole, *Operation Urgent Fury,* 6, 62.

67 Ibid., 50; Ronald Reagan, *An American Life: The Autobiography,* 454; Margaret Thatcher, *The Downing Street Years,* 331.

68 Cole, *Operation Urgent Fury,* 60–62.

Chapter 10

1 Maj. Gen. Clay T. McCutchan, "USAF Gunship Overview," Air Force Special Operations Command Special Study, January 1994; Fred J. Pushies, *US Air Force Special Ops,* rev. ed., 33.

2 For details on Special Operations Command, see Gordon N. Lederman, *Reorganizing the Joint Chiefs of Staff: The Goldwater-Nichols Act of 1986.*

3 Ibid.

4 Ibid.

5 Ibid.

6 Ibid.

7 Ibid.; Steven L. Meyers and Thom Shanker, "A Nation Challenged: The Offensive; Special Operations Gunship Being Used against the Taliban," *New York Times,* 16 October 2001; Pushies, *US Air Force Special Ops,* 28. It should be noted that on 1 October 2007, AFSOC also added the 27th Special Operations Wing, which had previously been a fighter wing. It should also be noted that the 919th Special Operations Group of the Air Force Reserve and the 193rd Special Operations Group of the Air National Guard became the AFSOC Air Reserve components when they first stood up.

8 McCutchan, "USAF Gunship Overview"; Pushies, *US Air Force Special Ops,* 28, 31.

9 Pushies, *US Air Force Special Ops,* 25–33; McCutchan, "USAF Gunship Overview."

10 Bernard Nalty, "Post-Vietnam," in *Winged Shield, Winged Sword: A History of the United States Air Force,* vol. 2, *1950–1997,* 425. For a version of the history of Operation Just Cause, see Bruce W. Watson and Peter G. Tsouras, eds., *Operation Just Cause: The US Intervention in Panama.*

11 Timothy D. Bloechi, "Operation JUST CAUSE: An Application of Operational Art?" Monograph, School of Advanced Military Studies, Fort Leavenworth, KS, May 1993, 14.

12 Nalty, "Post-Vietnam," 426; Thomas Donnelly, Margaret Roth, and Cobb Baker, *Operation Just Cause: The Storming of Panama,* 99.

13 Nalty, "Post-Vietnam," 426; Susan G. Horowitz, "Indications and Warring Factors," in *Operation Just Cause: The US Intervention of Panama,* ed. Bruce W. Watson and Peter G. Tsouras, 53–54.

14 Donnelly, Roth, and Baker, *Operation Just Cause,* 18–20.

15 Howard Jones, *Crucible of Power: A History of US Foreign Policy since 1897,* 461–69; Frederick Kempe, *Divorcing the Dictator,* 26–30, 162–63; Bruce Curtis, "The Wimp Factor," *American Heritage* 40, no. 7 (November 1989), http://www.americanheritage.com/content/wimp-factor.

16 Nalty, "Post-Vietnam," 427.

17 Ibid., 428; Horowitz, "Warring Factors," 53.

18 Nalty, "Post-Vietnam," 428; Donnelly, Roth, and Baker, *Operation Just Cause,* 75.

19 Nalty, "Post-Vietnam," 429; Donnelly, Roth, and Baker, *Operation Just Cause,* 18; Bloechi, "Operation JUST CAUSE," 25. Also see Edward M. Flanagan Jr., *Battle for Panama: Inside Operation Just Cause.*

20 Donnelly, Roth, and Baker, *Operation Just Cause,* 94, 99.

21 Watson and Tsouras, eds., *Operation Just Cause,* 219; Nalty, "Post-Vietnam," 430–31.

22 Nalty, "Post-Vietnam," 433; "Residents Said That Many Wooden Houses Near the Headquarters Had Been Hit by Gunfire and Artillery Fire," *New York Times,* 21 December 1989, 1A.

23 USAF, "AC-130H/U Gunship," fact sheet, http://www.af.mil/information/factsheets/factsheet.asp?id=71; WR-ALC, History, FY02, 92–93 (unclassified pages used); Walter J. Boyne, "The Awesome Power of the Air Force Gunships,"*Air Force Magazine* 82, no. 4:7. There have been many accounts of this same story. Undoubtedly, the original, and most accurate, story comes from Brig. Gen. Carl A. Hagan, US Army Forces Command, who recounted it while speaking at an Air Force Association symposium in February 1990. The story was related to him by his son, then 82nd Airborne Division captain Steven Hagan. This author has heard this story over a dozen times. While based on Hagan's original account, the reader will forgive me if I have added the most vibrant and descriptive aspects of all the story versions.

24 Nalty, "Post-Vietnam," 433; "Combat in Panama, Operation Just Cause," *Los Angeles Times,* 21 December 1989, 1A.

25 Nalty, "Post-Vietnam," 434–35; Russell Baker, "Observer: Is This Justice Necessary?" *New York Times,* January 3, 1990. For details on the gunships and high-tech weapons used during Just Cause, see Malcolm McConnell, *The Real Story of America's High-Tech Invasion of Panama* (New York: St. Martin's Press, 1991).

26 Nalty, "Post-Vietnam," 434–35; Baker, "Observer," *New York Times,* January 3, 1990; McConnell, *Real Story.*

27 Nalty, "Post-Vietnam," 434–35; Baker, "Observer," *New York Times,* January 3, 1990; McConnell, *Real Story.*

28 Nalty, "Post-Vietnam," 436–37; William S. Ramshaw, "Operation Just Cause Command and Control: A Case Study," Defense Technical Information Center, March 1991, 100–104; David F. Chandler, Rear Adm., USN, ret., Joint Operations, Naval War College, Newport, RI, interview with Maj. David B. Haight, January 16, 1998.

29 Nalty, "Post-Vietnam," 437.

30 "50 Kilos of Cocaine Was Tamales," *Washington Post,* January 23, 1990.

31 Nalty, "Post-Vietnam," 438; Baker, "Observer."

32 Nalty, "Post-Vietnam," 438; "50 Kilos."

33 Maj. Gen. Clay T. McCutchan and Brig. Gen. Mike Wilson, interview, 30 January 2008, Eglin AFB, FL, 4.

34 McCutchan e-mail; John Lindsey-Poland, *Emperors in the Jungle: The Hidden History of the US in Panama,* 118. Also see Richard H. Schultz, *In the Aftermath of War: US*

Support for Reconstruction and Nation-Building in Panama Following Just Cause; US Congress, House Committee on Armed Services, "The Invasion of Panama: How Many Innocent Bystanders Perished?" Report, 102nd Cong., 2nd sess., vol. 4, p. 19.

35 Robert A. Pastor, *Exiting the Whirlpool: US Foreign Policy toward Latin America and the Caribbean,* 96.

36 McCutchan, "USAF Gunship Overview."

37 Ibid.

38 Ibid.; McCutchan/Wilson interview, 7–8; McCutchan e-mail.

39 McCutchan, "USAF Gunship Overview"; McCutchan/Wilson interview, 7–8; McCutchan e-mail.

40 McCutchan, "USAF Gunship Overview"; McCutchan/Wilson interview, 8–10.

Chapter 11

1 "Birth of the 'Spectre' Gunship," Spectre Association, Home of the AC-130 Spectre Gunships, http://www.spectre-association.org/historySpectre.htm.

2 Bernard Nalty, "Post-Vietnam," in *Winged Shield, Winged Sword: A History of the United States Air Force,* vol. 2, *1950–1997,* 441–42; Douglas A. Borer, "Inverse Engagement: Lessons from US-Iraqi Relations, 1982–1990," US Army Professional Writing Collection, Carlisle Barracks, PA, 2003. For details on the background of the first Gulf War, see William P. Head, "Introduction"; Daniel S. Papp, "The Gulf War Coalition: The Politics and Economics of a Most Unusual Alliance," chap. 2; and Sohail Hashmi, "But Was It Jihad? Islam and the Ethics of the Persian Gulf War," chap. 3, all in *The Eagle in the Desert: Looking Back on US Involvement in the Persian Gulf War,* ed. William P. Head and Earl H. Tilford Jr., 1–15.

3 Don Oberdorfer, "Missed Signals in the Middle East," *Washington Post Magazine,* 17 March 1991, 23.

4 William T. Y'Blood, "From the Desert to the Mountains," chap. 24 in *Winged Shield, Winged Sword: A History of the United States Air Force,* vol. 2, *1950–1997,* ed. Bernard Nalty, 442–43.

5 Y'Blood, "Desert to the Mountains," 441–42; "Confrontation in the Gulf: The Oilfield Lying Below the Iraq-Kuwait Dispute," *New York Times,* 23 September 1990.

6 Y'Blood, "Desert to the Mountains," 441–42; Nalty, "Post-Vietnam," 443–45; "The Gulf War: A Chronology," *Air Force Magazine* 84, no. 1 (January 2001) (hereafter cited as "Gulf War Chronology"). For more on the Gulf War and diplomacy, see Lawrence Friedman and Efraim Karsh, *The Gulf Conflict, 1990–1991: Diplomacy and War in the New World Order;* Rick Atkinson, *Crusade: The Untold Story of the Persian Gulf War;* Lance W. Bennett and David L. Paletz, eds., *Taken by Storm: The Media, Public Opinion, and US Foreign Policy in the Gulf War.*

7 Y'Blood, "Desert to the Mountains," 441–42; Nalty, "Post-Vietnam," 443–45; "Gulf War Chronology"; Friedman and Karsh, *Gulf Conflict;* Atkinson, *Crusade;* Bennett and Paletz, *Taken by Storm.*

8 Y'Blood, "Desert to the Mountains," 446–47; "Gulf War Chronology"; US Department of Defense, "The Operation Desert Shield/Desert Storm Timeline," American Forces Press

Service News Article, Defense Link, 8 August 2000, http://www.defenselink.mil/news/newsarticle.aspx?id=45404, (hereafter cited as DOD, "Timeline").

9 Hashmi, "But Was it Jihad?" 47–64; Y'Blood, "Desert to the Mountains," 445–47.

10 Y'Blood, "Desert to the Mountains," 445–47; WR-ALC, Office of History, *Time Capsule: A Chronology of the Role of the Warner Robins Air Logistics Center and Robins AFB, Georgia, in World History, 1937-1997.*

11 John W. Leland, "Air Mobility in Operations Desert Shield and Desert Storm: An Assessment," in *Eagle in the Desert: Looking Back on US Involvement in the Persian Gulf War,* ed. William P. Head and Earl H. Tilford Jr., 67–86; "Gulf War Chronology"; DOD, "Timeline."

12 David A. Deptula, "Parallel Warfare: What Is It? Where Did It Come From?" in *Eagle in the Desert,* ed. Head and Tilford, 127–56; "Gulf War Chronology."

13 "Gulf War Chronology"; James Titus, "The Battle of Khafji: An Overview and Preliminary Analysis," Paper, Airpower Research Institute, CADRE, Air University, September 1996. For more details on the air war, see Richard P. Hallion, *Storm over Iraq: Air Power and the Gulf War.*

14 McCutchan e-mail

15 Y'Blood, "Desert to the Mountains," 445–47; Papp, "Gulf War Coalition," 21–46; "Gulf War Chronology."

16 "Gulf War Chronology"; DOD, "Timeline."

17 "Gulf War Chronology"; DOD, "Timeline"; Y'Blood, "Desert to the Mountains," 462–70. For details on the air war, see Eliot Cohen et al., *Gulf War Airpower Survey,* vols. 1–5; US Air Force, *Reaching Globally, Reaching Powerfully: The United States Air Force in the Gulf War,* White Paper, 1991; Richard C. Davis, *Strategic Air Power in Desert Storm,* 43–45.

18 "Gulf War Chronology"; DOD, "Timeline"; Y'Blood, "Desert to the Mountains," 462–68. For more on the air war, see William Suit, "Sustaining the War Machine: US Air Force Logistics Support during the Gulf War," in *Eagle in the Desert,* ed. Head and Tilford, 87–105.

19 Y'Blood, "Desert to the Mountains," 462–68; "Gulf War Chronology"; Hallion, *Storm over Iraq;* Daniel T. Kuehl, "Thunder and Storm: Strategic Air Operations in the Gulf War," in *Eagle in the Desert,* ed. Head and Tilford, 111–26.

20 Y'Blood, "Desert to the Mountains," 470–72; "Gulf War Chronology."

21 Y'Blood, "Desert to the Mountains," 470–72; "Gulf War Chronology."

22 Y'Blood, "Desert to the Mountains," 473; "Gulf War Chronology."

23 Perhaps the most significant original document produced on the Battle of Khafji was the Air Force Study Report from 1996. See Maj. Daniel R. Clevenger, "The Battle of Khafji: Air Power Effectiveness in the Desert," vol. 1, Appendix A, "Historical Perspectives on Khafji: Air Power vs. Troops," Air Force Studies and Analyses Agency, Force Application Division, July 1996.

24 Clevenger, "Introduction and Executive Summary," in "Battle of Khafji," 1–36.

25 Ibid., Appendix B, "Interview with General (Ret) Charles Horner, USAF, CENTAF Commander during Operation Desert Storm," 26 February 1996.

26 Michael R. Gordon and Bernard E. Trainor, *The General's War: The Inside Story of the Conflict in the Gulf,* 284; Maj. Gen. Clay T. McCutchan and Brig. Gen. Mike Wilson, interview, 30 January 2008, Eglin AFB, FL, 11–14; Titus, "Battle of Khafji," 17–18; Atkinson, *Crusade,* 210–13; John T. Quinn and Jack Shulimson, "US Marine Operations in the Persian Gulf War, 1990–1991," in *Eagle in the Desert,* ed. Head and Tilford, 211–12.

27 McCutchan/Wilson interview, 14.

28 Y'Blood, "Desert to the Mountains," 474–78; "Gulf War Chronology." For more on Air Force Special Operations Command, see Fred J. Pushies, *US Air Force Special Ops,* 41–68.

29 Head, "Preface," in *Eagle in the Desert,* xi–x.

30 Ibid.

31 Larry Cable, "Playing in the Sandbox: Doctrine, Combat, and Outcome on the Ground," in *Eagle in the Desert,* ed. Head and Tilford, 175–200.

32 Ibid.; "Gulf War Chronology"; Y'Blood, "Desert to the Mountains," 479–80.

33 Y'Blood, "Desert to the Mountains," 480–82; Cable, "Playing in the Sandbox," 197–98.

34 Y'Blood, "Desert to the Mountains," 480–82; Cable, "Playing in the Sandbox," 197–98.

35 McCutchan/Wilson interview, 4. For more on the Highway of Death, see the same interview, 12.

36 Y'Blood, "Desert to the Mountains," 480–82; Gordon and Trainor, *General's War,* 268–75.

37 Y'Blood, "Desert to the Mountains," 482; Cable, "Playing in the Sandbox," 198–99; "Gulf War Chronology."

38 Y'Blood, "Desert to the Mountains," 482–83; Cable, "Playing in the Sandbox," 198–200; "Gulf War Chronology."

39 Y'Blood, "Desert to the Mountains," 484–85. The quote may be found in US Department of the Air Force, "Operations," in Eliot Cohen et al., *Gulf War Airpower Study,* vol. 2, *Operations and Effects and Effectiveness,* 358.

40 Clevenger, "Battle of Khafji," Appendix B.

41 Maj. Gen. Clay T. McCutchan, "USAF Gunship Overview," Air Force Special Operations Command Special Study, January 1994.

42 Ibid.

43 Ibid.

44 Ibid.

45 Ibid.

46 Ibid.

47 Clevenger, "Battle of Khafji," Appendix C, "Interview with Maj. Gen. (Ret) Thomas Olsen, USAF, CENTAF Deputy Commander during Operation Desert Storm," 13 May 1996.

48 Ibid.

49 Air Force Airlift Center, Quarterly Reports, 1 March–30 June 1991, Air Force Historical Records Agency, File K417.0734-10, IRIS no. 00888202.

50 Y'Blood, "Desert to the Mountains," 486–87.

51 Ibid., 488–89.

52 Ibid., 489.

53 Ibid., 491; Lt. Col. John L. Cirafici, *Airhead Operations: Where AMC Delivers,* 26–27; "Somalia: Relief and Hope," *World Air Power Journal* 14 (Fall 1993): 18–23.

54 Cirafici, *Airhead Operations;* Y'Blood, "Desert to the Mountains," 492.

55 Y'Blood, "Desert to the Mountains," 492; Robert Winship Stewart, *The United States Army in Somalia, 1992–1994,* CMH Publication 70-81-1, 1–8.

56 Y'Blood, "Desert to the Mountains," 492–93; Stewart, *US Army in Somalia,* 9–15.

57 Y'Blood, "Desert to the Mountains," 494; Stewart, *US Army in Somalia,* 15–19; McCutchan, "USAF Gunship Overview." Also see Pushies, *US Air Force Special Ops,* 41–68.

58 Y'Blood, "Desert to the Mountains," 494; Stewart, *US Army in Somalia,* 15–19; McCutchan, "USAF Gunship Overview"; Pushies, *US Air Force Special Ops,* 41–68.

59 Stewart, *US Army in Somalia,* 17–18.

60 Ibid., 18–19.

61 Ibid., 19–20; Y'Blood, "Desert to the Mountains," 494. For more on the Black Hawk Down incident, see Mark Bowden, *Black Hawk Down: A Story of Modern War.*

62 Y'Blood, "Desert to the Mountains," 495; Stewart, *US Army in Somalia,* 20–24.

63 Y'Blood, "Desert to the Mountains," 495–96; Stewart, *US Army in Somalia,* 24–26; Jonathan Gawne, "Spectre: America's Special Operation Gunships," *Raids,* no. 43 (June 1995): 42–44. For more details on the Somalia operation, see Kenneth Allard, *Somalia Operations: Lessons Learned.* The original account of the crash of the Predator is in 542nd Crew Training Wing, History (FOUO), 1 January–31 March 1994, 3 vols., ; specifically vol. 1; Ronald A. Carrillo, untitled report on AC-130 crash in Kenya (FOUO, since declassified), K-WG-542-HI, vol. 1, AFHRA, Maxwell AFB, AL, IRIS no. 01115307.

Chapter 12

1 Maj. Gen. Clay T. McCutchan, "USAF Gunship Overview," Air Force Special Operations Command Special Study, January 1994; Air Force Special Operations Command, Public Affairs Office, "AC-130U 'Spectre' Gunship," 1995; Air Force Special Operations Command, Office of History, *AC-130U Presentation Ceremony,* booklet, Hurlburt Field, Florida, 14 November 1994.

2 *AC-130U Presentation Ceremony.*

3 Ibid. The AC-130As never were refitted with universal aerial refueling receptacle slipway installation (UARRSI) modifications.

4 Warner Robins Air Logistics Center, History, FY82, 51–52; FY83, 185–87; USAF, Program Management Directive R-P9104 (1-12)/27423F-2483, 9 November 1979, and R-P9103 (1-5)/27423F-2482, 4 January 1980; "Have Quick," briefing, no date.

5 *AC-130U Presentation Ceremony.*

6 Ibid.

7 Ibid.; AFSOC/PA to AFSOC/HO, XP, DO, DS, CV, "AC-130U Name Change," Staff Summary Sheet, 17 August 1997.

8 *AC-130U Presentation Ceremony;* 6518 TESTS/DO to ASD/VXT, "AC-130U Test Program FY91 Status," memo, 15 October 1991; AFSOC/HO, "AC-130U," draft paper and final paper, 1992.

9 Mindy Taylor, "Rock Wins C-130 Gunship Conversion Pact," *Antelope Valley Press,* 5 July 1987, 1; Jim Skeen, untitled article on the AC-130, *Antelope Valley Press,* 9 September

1991, 1; Rockwell International Modification Division, "Rockwell's AC-130U Gunship," news report, no date.

10 Rockwell International Modification Division, "Rockwell's AC-130U Gunship"; "First Successful Test Flight of AC-130U," *Rockwell News, North American Edition* 19, no. 1 (18 January 1991): 1; Timothy McCune, "Dispute Looming over Rockwell Gunship," *Defense Week,* 22 June 1990, 6; Untitled article on the AC-130U, *Rockwell News, North American Edition* 20, no. 6 (March 1992): 1, and 20, no. 17 (June 1992): 1.

11 Lou Damiani, Rockwell International, North American Modification Division Director, "Rockwell Delivers AC-130U Gunship to Air Force Special Operations Command," news release, 1 July 1994; Lou Damiani, "Rockwell Delivers AC-130U Gunship to Air Force Special Operations Command," news report, 5 July 1994; USAFSOC, Public Affairs Office (PAO), "AC-130U Spectre Gunship," fact sheet, no date.

12 USAFSOC, PAO, "AC-130U Spectre Gunship"; *AC-130U Presentation Ceremony;* HQ AFSOC/TE to ASD/VXT, "Formal Coordination of the AC-130U Gunship Test and Evaluation Master Plan (TEMP)," memo, no date; Anton Roney, Rockwell Chief Program Engineer, "AC-130U History," interview with AFSOC/HO, no date; Maj. Gen. James L. Hobson Jr., "Our Journey Continues in '95," *Night Flyer* 3, no. 1 (June 1995): 2.

13 "The 'Forty' How 'Swede' It Is?" *Loader Jam* 97, no. 2 (April–June 1997): 2–3.

14 USAFSOC, PAO, "AC-130U Spectre Gunship"; *AC-130U Presentation Ceremony.*

15 HQ AFSOC/DOVF to Clay McCutchan, AFSOC, "AC-130H/U Facts for AF/HO Tasking," memo, 1 February 1994; ASC/LU to AFSOC AC-130U Office, "AC-130U Gunship Documentation," memo, 22 February 1996.

16 "AC-130U Adjustment Causes Slip in Rockwell Aerospace Earnings (Costs of AC-130U Gunship Program Affect First Quarter 1994 Earnings)," 19 January 1994, http://www.highbeam.com/doc/1G1-14737866.html.

17 HQ AFSOC/CC to USSOCOM/SOCC et al., "AC-130U Initial Operating Capability," message, 292100Z Mar 1996; ASC/CC to SAF/AQ, "AC-130U Gunship Status," memo, 6 June 1994.

18 ASC/CC to SAF/AQ, "AC-130U Gunship Status," memo.

19 James Kinsella, Department of Justice, to AFSOC/CC, "Rockwell International Corp. v. United States, Court of Federal Claims, No. 95-425C," faxed letter, 5 March 1996.

20 Boeing Company, "Boeing, Rockwell Aerospace and Defense Units to Merge," news release, 5 December 1996.

21 Marc Eichler, "AC-130 Spectre/Spooky," 20 May 2006, http://www.milavia.net/aircraft/ac-130/ac-130_ext.htm.

22 AFSOC/PA to AFSOC/CC, HO, 4 SOS, et al., "AC-130U Name Change," Staff Summary Sheet, 19 August 1997.

23 4th Special Operations Squadron, Public Affairs, "4th Special Operations Squadron," fact sheet, http://www2.hurlburt.af.mil/library/factsheets/factsheet.asp?id=3489.

24 Eichler, "Spectre/Spooky."

25 WR-ALC, History, FY89, 174–78. All data used is unclassified.

26 Ibid.

27 WR-ALC, History, FY90, 247. All data used is unclassified.

28 WR-ALC, History, FY91, 164–65. All data used is unclassified. The rainbow fitting is the

connection component between the center and outer wing boxes. It experiences a great deal of high cyclic loading (stress) and is prone to cracking. It is a constant issue of concern on all C-130 airframes.

29 Ibid., 20–25 (All data used is unclassified.); WR-ALC/LUKA with LASC, "Contract Number F09603-90-G-0060," 26 November 1990.

30 WR-ALC, History, FY92, 193–95; Support Systems Associates Inc., Warner Robins, Georgia, "Test Plan for Natural Resonant Frequency Test for Allied Signal IR Suppressor Prototype for AC-130H Gunship," report, 13 March 1993; Alan Lundsford, WR-ALC/LUFE, "AC-130H Gunship Infrared Radiation Suppressor Modification Program Flight Test Program," Flight Test Directive, 23 March 1992, 2; WR-ALC, History, FY93, 235, 253, 258. The AC-130 downed during the first Persian Gulf War was nicknamed Ghost Rider, a nickname it shared with A-model T/N 54-1623, which is today on display at Dobbins AFB, Georgia. During its fateful mission AC-130H Ghost Rider was flying under the call sign Spirit 03, and within the special operations community that is how it is remembered.

31 "Night Vision Imaging System (NVIS)," report, no date, WR-ALC History Office Archives, Robins AFB, GA.

32 WR-ALC, History, FY94, 170, 175; "Point Paper on C-130 Center Wing Box Replacement," 20 January 1995.

33 WR-ALC, History, FY95, 197–99; SECAF to WR-ALC/CC, "Program Management Direction for Additional Oxygen Supply on AC-130H Gunships," message, 051516Z Jan 95; 653 CLSS/DFT (Depot Field Team) to 653 CLSS/CC, LG, LGC and LGM, "653 CLSS DFT Status Report Number One," message, 231730Z Mar 95; 16 SOS/OM, OMGS, and 653 CLSS/DFT to 653 CLSS/CC, LG, LGM, and LGC and WR-ALC/LBPLC, "653 CLSS/DFT Status Report Number Four and Five," message, 132300Z Apr 95.

34 WR-ALC, History, FY97, 149–50; WR-ALC/LUG, "ALQ-172(v)3 Installation on AC-130H Gunship," point paper, no date.

35 WR-ALC, History, FY98, 188; Barbara A. Kirby, WR-ALC/LUG, "AC-130U Programmed Depot Maintenance (PDM) Working Group Meeting Minutes," report, no date.

Chapter 13

1 John Keegan, "Please Mr. Blair Never Take Such a Risk Again," *Daily Telegraph* (London), 6 June 1999.

2 For more on the military technical revolution (MTR) during the Gulf War, see Richard P. Hallion, *Storm over Iraq: Air Power and the Gulf War.*

3 Jim Garamone, "Behind the Crisis in Kosovo," *American Forces Information Service News Articles* (AFISNA), Defense Link, DOD, 17 June 1998, http://osd.dtic.mil/news/Ju11998/n07071998_9807074.html; United Kingdom, Ministry of Defense (MOD), "Kosovo—An Account of the Crisis: Historical Background," 14 December 1999, http://www.mod.uk.news/kosovo/account/historical.htm, accessed 17 December 1999. Two good works on the Operation Allied Freedom air war are Benjamin S. Lambeth's two books, *NATO's Air War for Kosovo: A Strategic and Operational Assessment,* and *The Transformation of American Air Power.*

4 Garamone, "Behind the Crisis"; UK, MOD, "Kosovo—Historical Background."

5 ABC News, "Newsmakers: Slobodan Milosevic," ABC.com, 15 December 1999, http://www.abcnews.go.com/reference/bios/Milosevic.htm, accessed 17 December 1999; North Atlantic Treaty Organization, "Kosovo Crisis, Historical Overview: NATO's Role in Relation to the Conflict in Kosovo," 15 July 1999, http://www.nato.int/kosovo/history.htm (hereafter cited as NATO, "NATO's Role"); "The Kosovo File: Who's Who," *Time*, 15 December 1999, http://www.pathfinder.com/time/daily/special/kosovo/who.html, accessed 17 December 1999.

6 ABC News, "Milosevic"; NATO, "NATO's Role"; Associated Press, "Crisis in Kosovo: Key Events in Kosovo Conflict," *USA Today*, 25 March 1999, http://www.usatoday.com/news/index/kosovo/kos0002.htm, accessed 17 December 1999; Reuters, "Kosovo: A Bitter Struggle in a Land of Strife: Chronology of the Crisis in Kosovo," *New York Times*, 24 March 1999, (hereafter cited as Reuters, "Land of Strife"); United Kingdom, Ministry of Defense, "Kosovo—An Account of the Crisis: The Crisis Unfolds," 14 December 1999, http://www.mod.uk/news/kosovo/account/crisis.htm.

7 AP, "Crisis in Kosovo"; Reuters, "Land of Strife"; NATO, "NATO's Role"; UK, MOD, "Kosovo—Crisis Unfolds."

8 NATO, "NATO's Role"; UK, MOD, "Kosovo—Crisis Unfolds"; Reuters, "Land of Strife"; United Kingdom, Ministry of Defense, "Kosovo—News, Background Resources," 7 October 1999, http://www.mod.uk/news/kosovo, accessed 17 December 1999.

9 NATO, "NATO's Role"; Reuters, "Land of Strife"; UK, MOD, "Kosovo—News."

10 William S. Cohen, "Lessons Learned from Kosovo," speech, International Institute for Strategic Studies, Coronado, CA, 9 September 1999, 10, available online at http://www.bu.edu/globalbeat/nato/Cohen091099.html.

11 Robert W. Apple Jr., "Conflict in the Balkans: News Analysis: With Decision to Attack, a Fresh Set of US Goals," *New York Times*, 25 March 1999.

12 Linda D. Kozaryn, "Clinton Says NATO Must Act in Kosovo," AFISNA, Defense Link, DOD, 22 March 1999, http://osd.dtic.mil/news/Mar1999/n03221999_9903222.html; Jim Garamone, "Clinton Makes Case for Kosovo Intervention," AFISNA, Defense Link, DOD, 24 March 1999, http://osd.dtic.mil/news/Mar1999/n03241999_9903243.html.

13 Central Intelligence Agency, *The World Fact Book, 1999*, Serbia and Montenegro, http://www.umsl.edu/services/govdocs/wofact99/265.htm; Linda D. Kozaryn, "US, NATO Pilots Face Air Defense Threat," AFISNA, Defense Link, DoD, 24 March 1999, http://www.defense.gov/News/NewsArticle.aspx?ID=41608.

14 Kozaryn, "US, NATO Pilots," 1; John A. Tirpak, "The First Six Weeks," and Guy Aceto, "Air Power in Allied Force," *Air Force Magazine* 82, no. 6 (June 1999): 27–29 and 39–46, respectively.

15 Kozaryn, "US, NATO Pilots," 1; Tirpak, "First Six Weeks"; Aceto, "Air Power in Allied Force," 27–29, 39–46.

16 Office of the Secretary of Defense, "Carrier Battle Groups in Support of NATO," News Release 144-99, 3 April 1999, http://www.defense.gov/releases/release.aspx?releaseid=2029. Also see, Lambeth, *NATO's Air War for Kosovo* and *Transformation of American Air Power*.

17 OSD, "Carrier Battle Groups."

18 Ibid.

19 Jim Garamone and Linda D. Kozaryn, "NATO Attacks Serbs to Stop Kosovo Killings," AFISNA, Defense Link, DoD, 24 March 1999, http://www.defense.gov/News/News Article.aspx?ID=41999.

20 Ibid. For similar remarks, see Apple, "Conflict in the Balkans . . . Fresh Set of US Goals."

21 Tirpak, "First Six Weeks," 27; Linda D. Kozaryn, "First NATO Strikes Aimed at Serb Air Defenses," AFISNA, Defense Link, DOD, 25 March 1999, http://osd.dtic.mil/news /Mar1999/n03251999_9903251.html.

22 Linda D. Kozaryn, "Allied Force Pilots Down Three Serb Fighters," AFISNA, Defense Link, DOD, 25 March 1999, http://www.defense.gov/News/NewsArticle.aspx?ID=41997.

23 Ibid., 1; "Verbatim Special: The Balkan War," *Air Force Magazine* 82, no. 6 (June 1999): 47.

24 ABC News, "B-2 Sees First Combat," ABC News.com, 24 March 1999, http://web .archive.org/web/19990508053951/http://abcnews.go.com/sections/world/Daily News/bomber990324.html; quotes from John A. Tirpak, "With Stealth in the Balkans," *Air Force Magazine* 82, no. 10 (October 1999), 23–28 (quotes on 23).

25 Linda D. Kozaryn, "Stealth Fighter Down in Yugoslavia, Pilot Rescued," AFISNA, Defense Link, DOD, 28 March 1999, http://osd.dtic.mil/news/Mar1999/n03281999_9903281 .html; Rowan Scarborough, "US Pilots Call NATO Targeting a 'Disgrace,'" *Washington Times,* 1 April 1999; "Serb Discusses 1999 Downing of Stealth," USATODAY.com, 26 October 2005, http://www.usatoday.com/news/world/2005-10-26-serb-stealth_x.htm.

26 Linda D. Kozaryn, "US Commits More Air Power to Allied Force," AFISNA, Defense Link, DOD, 30 March 1999, http://osd.dtic.mil/news/Mar1999/n03301999_9903301 .html.

27 Ibid.; United Kingdom, Ministry of Defence, "Kosovo—An Account of the Crisis: Responding to a Humanitarian Crisis," 15 December 1999, http://www.mod.uk.news /kosovo/account/response.htm.

28 MOD, UK, 'Kosovo—Humanitarian Crisis"; Linda D. Kozaryn, "Kosovo Matters Because Europe Matters, Cohen and Shelton Say," AFISNA, Defense Link, DOD, 30 March 1999, http://osd.dtic.mil/news/Mar1999/n03291999_9903291.html.

29 Linda D. Kozaryn, "Serb Forces Abduct Three US Soldiers," AFISNA, Defense Link, DOD, 1 April 1999, http://osd.dtic.mil/news/Apr1999/n04011999_9904012.html.

30 Linda D. Kozaryn, "More US Fighters Join NATO Air Campaign," AFISNA, Defense Link, DOD, 2 April 1999, http://www.defense.gov/News/NewsArticle.aspx?ID=42929.

31 Ibid.

32 Linda D. Kozaryn, "DOD Airlifts Rations to Balkans," AFISNA, Defense Link, DOD, 5 April 1999, http://osd.dtic.mil/news/Apr1999/n04051999_9904051.html.

33 Also see Eduard Mark, *Aerial Interdiction: Air Power and the Land Battle in Three American Wars;* Gen. William W. Momyer, *Air Power in Three Wars: World War II, Korea, and Vietnam.*

34 See again Mark, *Aerial Interdiction;* Momyer, *Air Power in Three Wars.* Also see Col. Phillip S. Meilinger, *Ten Propositions Regarding Air Power;* US Air Force, *Air Force Basic Doctrine Manual,* AFDD-1, September 1997.

35 "Verbatim Special," 47.

36 William M. Arkin, "Inside the Air Force, Officers Are Frustrated About the Air War," *Washington Post,* 25 April 1999.

37 Linda D. Kozaryn, "Pentagon Sends in Carrier Battle Group," AFISNA, Defense Link, DOD, 5 April 1999, http://osd.dtic.mil/news/Apr1999/n04051999_9904052.html; Jim Garamone, "Air Ops in Yugoslavia Pick Up; Apaches to Albania," AFISNA, Defense Link, DOD, 6 April 1999, http://www.defense.gov/News/NewsArticle.aspx?ID=42049.

38 Jim Garamone, "US Sending 82 More Aircraft to Join NATO Forces," AFISNA, Defense Link, DOD, 12 April 1999, http://osd.dtic.mil/news/Apr1999/n04121999_9904126.html.

39 Steven Lee Meyers, "Crisis in the Balkans: Pentagon Said to Be Adding 300 Planes to Fight Serbs," *New York Times,* 13 April 1999; Elaine M. Grossman, "Clark's Firepower Request for Kosovo Prompts Anxiety among Chiefs," *Inside the Pentagon,* 15 April 1999.

40 Bill Gertz and Rowan Scarborough, "No War," *Washington Times,* 16 April 1999.

41 Jim Garamone, "NATO Apologizes for Bombing Accident, Details Precautions," AFISNA, Defense Link, DOD, 16 April 99, http://osd.dtic.mil/news/Apr1999/n04161999_9904162.html.

42 "Verbatim Special," 46; Paul Richter, "Use of Ground Troops Not Fully Ruled Out," *Los Angeles Times,* 29 March 1999.

43 Richter, "Use of Ground Troops"; Dan Balz, "US Consensus Grows to Send in Ground Troops," *Washington Post,* 6 April 1999.

44 Jim Garamone, "Clinton Sets Kosovo Emergency Funding at $6 Billion," AFISNA, Defense Link, DOD, 21 April 1999, http://www.defense.gov/News/NewsArticle.aspx?ID=42033.

45 Eric Schmitt and Steven Lee Meyers, "Crisis in the Balkans: News Analysis: NATO Said to Focus Raids on Serb Elite's Property," *New York Times,* 19 April 1999; United Kingdom, Ministry of Defence, "Kosovo—An Account of the Crisis: The Politico-Military Interface," no date, http://www.mod.uk.news/kosovo/account/politico.htm (hereafter cited as UK, MOD, "Kosovo—Interface").

46 Schmitt and Meyers, "Raids on Serb Elite's Property."

47 Ibid.; Paul Richter, "Bunker-Busters Aimed at the Heart of Leadership," *Los Angeles Times,* 5 May 1999. The GBU-28 made its debut during Desert Storm and was dropped from an F-111 airframe. These unique bombs were originally constructed from salvaged eight-inch gun barrels.

48 UK, MOD, "Kosovo—Interface"; Robert W. Apple Jr., "Crisis in the Balkans: The Summit; Kosovo Overshadows Subdued NATO Event," *New York Times,* 24 April 1999.

49 Jim Garamone, "President Calls-up Reservists, AF Authorized Stop/Loss," AFISNA, Defense Link, DOD, 27 April 1999, http://osd.dtic.mil/news/Apr1999/n04271999_9904275.html.

50 Jim Garamone, "More B-52s Join Allied Force Mission," AFISNA, Defense Link, DOD, 30 April 1999, http://osd.dtic.mil/news/Apr1999/n04301999_9904302.html.

51 David Fulghum, "Electronic Bombs Darken Belgrade," *Aviation Week & Space Technology* 153 (10 May 1999): 34.

52 UK, MOD, "Kosovo—Interface"; United Nations, "Security Council Resolution 1244 (1999) on Situation Relating to Kosovo," 4011th meeting, 10 June 1999, http://www.un.org/ga/search/view_doc.asp?symbol=S/RES/1244(1999).

53 Robert Block, "In Belgrade, Hardship Grows under Sustained Air Assaults," *Wall Street*

Journal, 12 May 1999; Steven Erlanger, "Crisis in the Balkans: Economists Find Bombing Cuts Yugoslav's Production in Half," *New York Times,* 30 April 1999.

54 Michael Ignatieff, "The Virtual Commander: How NATO Invented a New Kind of War," *New Yorker,* 2 August 1999, 33–35; Lambeth, *NATO's Air War for Kosovo.*

55 Jim Garamone, "More Aircraft, Personnel Set for Allied Force," AFISNA, Defense Link, DOD, 11 May 1999, http://osd.dtic.mil/news/May1999/n05111999_9905111.html.

56 Tony Capaccio, "JSTARS Led to Most Lethal Attacks on Serbs, *Defense Weekly,* 6 July 1999, 12–13. For more on the E-8C Joint STARS, see WR-ALC, Histories, FY91, 114–20; FY92, 133–37; FY93, 77, 139, 157, 177–91, 182–89; FY94, 131–41; FY95, 124–39; FY96, 131–42; FY97, 153–63; FY98, 130–42. For more on the Highway of Death, see Michael T. Corgan, "Clausewitz's 'On War' and the Gulf War," in *The Eagle in the Desert: Looking Back on US Involvement in the Persian Gulf War,* ed. William P. Head and Earl H. Tilford Jr., 285–86.

57 For negative criticism of the numbers in Operation Allied Freedom, see John Barry and Evan Thomas, "The Kosovo Cover-Up," *Newsweek,* 15 May 2000, 23-27. Also see Gen. Wesley K. Clark, "Press Conference on the Kosovo Strike Assessment," NATO HQ, Brussels, http://www.nato.int/kosovo/press/p990916a.htm.

58 "Joint Statement by Secretary of Defense William S. Cohen and CIA Director George J. Tenet," press release, AFISNA, Defense Link, DOD, 8 May 1999, http://www.defense.gov/releases/release.aspx?releaseid=2083; Cable News Network, "Clinton Apologizes to China over Embassy Bombing," 10 May 1999, http://www.cnn.com/WORLD/europe/9905/10/kosovo.china.02/.

59 Tim Ripley, "Kosovo Crisis: Operations Allied Force/Allied Harbour/Joint Forge—Order of Battle/Basing/June 1999," *Jane's Defence Weekly,* 4 December 1999.

60 Linda D. Kozaryn, "Serbs Fold, US Hopeful for Peace Agreement, but Wary," AFISNA, Defense Link, DOD, 4 June 1999, http://osd.dtic.www.defenselink.mil/news/Jun1999/n06041999_9906041.html.

61 R. Jeffrey Smith and Molly Moore, "Plan for Kosovo, Pullout Signed," *Washington Post,* 10 June 1999; Jim Garamone, "Serb Withdrawal Begins, NATO Suspends Bombing," AFISNA, Defense Link, DoD, 10 June 1999, http://www.defense.gov/News/NewsArticle.aspx?ID=42086.

62 Smith and Moore, "Plan for Kosovo"; Garamone, "Serb Withdrawal Begins"; UN, "Security Council Resolution 1244."

63 UK, MOD, "Kosovo—Interface," 2; Tim Weiner, "Crisis in the Balkans: From President, Victory Speech and a Warning," *New York Times,* 11 June 1999; Robert W. Apple Jr., "Crisis in the Balkans: Washington Memo; Clinton Tailors Legacy but Kosovo Isn't Fabric," *New York Times,* 10 June 1999.

64 US European Command, "Operation Allied Force," 14 December 1999, http://www.eucom.mil/operations/af/; Cable News Network, "CNN In-Depth: Kosovo Crisis," 15 December 1999, http://www.cnn.com/news/kosovo/figures.html; and United Kingdom, Ministry of Defence, "NATO Air Strikes," 14 December 1999, http://www.mod.uk/news/kosovo/account/nato.htm, all accessed 17 December 1999.

65 CNN, "CNN In-Depth: Kosovo Crisis," 1.

66 US Department of Defense, "Operation Allied Force," Defense Link, DOD, 21 June 1999, http://www.defenselink.mil/specials/kosovo/.

67 "Verbatim Special," original in *New York Times,* 12 June 1999.

68 Ibid., original from Gen. Tony McPeak, *PBS News Hour,* 16 June 1999.

69 See Lambeth, *Transformation of American Air Power,* 126, 130, 135.

Chapter 14

1 Federation of American Scientists (FAS), untitled web page on modernization of the AC-130H/U fixed-wing gunship fleet, http://www.fas.org/programs/ssp/manuswpns/air/attack/ac-130.html, accessed 5 August 2009.

2 Ibid.

3 Ibid.

4 United Nations, "Security Council Condemns, 'In Strongest Terms,' Terror Attacks on United States," 12 September 2001, http://www.un.org/News/Press/docs/2001/SC7143.doc.htm; Canadian Broadcasting Company, "Bin Laden Claims Responsibility for 9/11," 29 October 2004, http://www.cbc.ca/world/story/2004/10/29/binladen_message041029.html.

5 Columbia Broadcasting System, "War Casualties Pass 9/11 Death Toll," 22 September 2006, http://www.cbsnews.com/2100-224_162-2035427.html; Cable News Network, "New York: 9/11 Toxins Caused Death," 24 May 2007,http://www.cnn.com/2007/US/05/24/wtc.dust/index.html, accessed 26 June 2009.

6 National Transportation Safety Board (NTSB), "Flight Path Study—American Airlines Flight 11," 19 February 2002, http://www.gwu.edu/~nsarchiv/NSAEBB/NSAEBB196/doc01.pdf; NTSB, "Flight Path Study—United Airlines Flight 175," 19 February 2002, http://www.gwu.edu/~nsarchiv/NSAEBB/NSAEBB196/doc03.pdf; NTSB, "Flight Path Study—American Airlines Flight 77," 19 February 2002, http://www.gwu.edu/~nsarchiv/NSAEBB/NSAEBB196/doc02.pdf; NTSB, "Flight Path Study—United Airlines Flight 93," 19 February 2002, http://www.ntsb.gov/doclib/foia/9_11/Flight_Path_Study_UA93.pdf; US, National Commission on Terrorist Attacks upon the United States, "The Attack Looms," *9/11 Commission Report,* 2004, http://govinfo.library.unt.edu/911/report/911Report_Ch7.htm, chaps. 1 and 7.

7 British Broadcasting Company, "The Hamburg Connection," 19 August 2005, http://news.bbc.co.uk/2/hi/europe/2349195.stm; Michael E. Rolince, "The Inspector General's Report and the September 11th Response," Federal Bureau of Investigation, US Department of Justice. http://www.fbi.gov/news/testimony/the-inspector-generals-report-and-the-september-11th-response; Lawrence Wright, *The Looming Tower: Al-Qaeda and the Road to 9/11,* 362–67.

8 Wright, *Looming Tower.*

9 Ibid., 302–15; Terry McDermott, *Perfect Soldiers: The 9/11 Hijackers,* 191–92; Rohan Gunarathna, *Inside Al Qaeda, Global Network of Terror,* 61–62.

10 Wright, *Looming Tower,* 298–305. For more on 9/11, see Richard A. Clarke, *Against All Enemies,* 10–15; Peter Bergen, *The Osama bin Laden I Know,* 276–83; McDermott, *Perfect Soldiers,* 180–92.

11 Wright, *Looming Tower,* 298–305.

12 Gunarathna, *Inside Al Qaeda,* 63–70; Jason Burke, *Al-Qaeda: The True Story of Radical Islam,* 23, 162–63.

13 Global Security.org, "Bush Announces Start of a 'War on Terror,'" 20 September 2001, http://www.globalsecurity.org/military/library/news/2001/09/mil-010920-usia01.htm;Global Security.org, "President Bush Announces Military Strikes in Afghanistan," 7 October 2001, http://www.globalsecurity.org/military/library/news/2001/10/mil-011007-usia01.htm; Global Security.org, "Operation Enduring Freedom—Afghanistan," no date, http://www.globalsecurity.org/military/ops/enduring-freedom.htm; BBC News, "Infinite Justice, Out—Enduring Freedom, In," 25 September 2001, http://news.bbc.co.uk/2/hi/americas/1563722.stm. See also, Clarke, *Against All Enemies.*

14 Global Security.org, "Bush Announces Start of a 'War on Terror'": Global Security.org, "President Bush Announces Military Strikes in Afghanistan"; Global Security.org, "Operation Enduring Freedom"; BBC News, "Infinite Justice, Out"; Clarke, *Against All Enemies.*

15 Global Security.org, "Bush Announces Start of a 'War on Terror'": Global Security.org, "President Bush Announces Military Strikes in Afghanistan"; Global Security.org, "Operation Enduring Freedom"; BBC News, "Infinite Justice, Out"; Clarke, *Against All Enemies.*

16 Don Chipman, "Air Power and the Battle for Mazare-e Sharif," *Air Power History* 50 (Spring 2003): 34–45.

17 Michael Scott Doran, *Understanding the War on Terror,* 72–75. See also Sean M. Maloney, *Enduring the Freedom: A Rogue Historian in Afghanistan.*

18 Doran, *Understanding the War on Terror,* 72–75.

19 Michael G. Schechter, *United Nations Global Conferences,* 177–82.

20 Ibid.

21 Ibid.

22 Doran, *Understanding the War on Terror;* Clarke, *Against All Enemies;* Maj. Denis P. Doty, "Command and Control of Special Operations Forces for 21st Century Contingency Operations," paper, Naval War College, Newport, RI, 3 February 2003. For more on the United States in the Afghan war, see Ahmed Rashid, *Descent into Chaos: The US and the Disaster in Pakistan, Afghanistan, and Central Asia.*

23 Doran, *Understanding the War on Terror;* Clarke, *Against All Enemies;* Doty, "Command and Control of SOF."

24 Doran, *Understanding the War on Terror;* Clarke, *Against All Enemies;* Doty, "Command and Control of SOF."

25 Doran, *Understanding the War on Terror;* Clarke, *Against All Enemies;* Doty, "Command and Control of SOF."

26 Carl Conetta, "Operation Enduring Freedom: Why a Higher Rate of Civilian Bombing Casualties," Project on Defense Alternatives Briefing Report no. 11, 31 March 2002, 1–3. Also see Anthony Davis, "How the Afghan War Was Won," *Jane's Intelligence Review* 14 (February 2002): 6–13; John Day, "After Afghanistan—The Role of Air Power," *Royal United Services Institute (RUSI) Journal* 147 (December 2002): 38–43; David Fulghum and Robert Wall, "Heavy Bomber Attacks Dominate Afghan War," *Aviation Week & Space Technology* 155 (3 December 2001): 22; David Fulghum and Robert Wall, "US

Stalks Taliban with New Air Scheme," *Aviation Week & Space Technology* 155 (15 October 2001): 32; Lt. Col. Eric E. Theisen, *Ground-Aided Precision Strike: Heavy Bomber Activity in Operation Enduring Freedom,* Air War College Maxwell Paper no. 31, 1–2. For more on SOF aircraft, see David Castellon, "Missions in Afghanistan Took EC-130Hs over Threat Areas," *Air Force Times* 62 (3 June 2002): 20.

27 Conetta, "Operation Enduring Freedom; Davis, "How the Afghan War Was Won," 6–13; Day, "After Afghanistan," 38–43; Fulghum and Wall, "Heavy Bomber Attacks," 22; Fulghum and Wall, "US Stalks Taliban," 32; Theisen, *Ground-Aided Precision Strike,* 1–2; Castellon, "Missions in Afghanistan," 20.

28 American Special Ops.com, photos by TSgt. Lee Schading, "AC-130 Spectre/Spooky II Gunship," 2009, http://www.americanspecialops.com/usaf-special-operations/aircraft/ac-130/ (hereafter cited as ASO, "Gunship"); US Air Force, "AC-130H/U Gunship," fact sheet, January 2009, http://www.af.mil/information/factsheets/factsheet.asp?id=71 (hereafter cited as AC-130H/U fact sheet); Glenn Goodman, "Close Air Support," *Armed Forces Journal International* 139 (January 2002): 54–55; Theisen, *Ground-Aided Precision Strike,* 2–4.

29 ASO, "Gunship"; AC-130H/U fact sheet; Goodman, "Close Air Support," 54; Theisen, *Ground-Aided Precision Strike,* 2–4.

30 ASO, "Gunship"; AC-130H/U fact sheet.

31 Day, "After Afghanistan"; Rebecca Grant, "An Air War Like No Other," *Air Force Magazine* 85 (November 2002): 30–37, http://www.airforcemag.com/MagazineArchive/Pages/2002/November%202002/1102airwar.aspx; Rebecca Grant, "The War Nobody Expected," *Air Force Magazine* 85 (April 2002): 34–40, http://www.airforcemag.com/MagazineArchive/Pages/2002/April%202002/0402airwar.aspx.

32 Conetta, "Operation Enduring Freedom," 3–7; Grant, "Air War Like No Other," 30–37; Grant, "War Nobody Expected," 34–40.

33 Grant, "Air War Like No Other," 30–37; Conetta, "Operation Enduring Freedom," 3–18; Rebecca Grant, "Reach-Forward," *Air Force Magazine* 85 (October 2002): 42–47; Theisen, *Ground-Aided Precision Strike,* 7–21. The CBU dispenses 202 BLU-97s, and when the CBU-87 is fitted with the wind corrected munitions dispenser (WCMD) kit it becomes a CBU-103.

34 Grant, "Reach-Forward," 42–47; Grant, "Air War Like No Other," 30–37; Day, "After Afghanistan," 38–43; Theisen, *Ground-Aided Precision Strike,* 4–7.

35 Grant, "Reach-Forward," 42–47; Grant, "Air War Like No Other," 30–37; Day, "After Afghanistan," 38–43; Theisen, *Ground-Aided Precision Strike,* 4–7.

36 Rebecca Grant, "The Airpower of Anaconda," *Air Force Magazine* 85 (September 2002): 60–63, http://www.airforcemag.com/MagazineArchive/Pages/2002/September%202002/0902anaconda.aspx. For details on joint operations and the Joint Force Air Component commander (JFACC), see Maj. Lawrence T. Brown, "You've Got to Be Kidding: Empowering the JFACC with Selected Ground Reconnaissance Forces," Joint Military Operations Department Paper, Naval War College, Newport, RI, 2 February 2003, 1–33; Doty, "Command and Control of SOF," 3–26.

37 ASO, "Gunship"; AC-130H/U fact sheet; Goodman, "Close Air Support," 54; Theisen, *Ground-Aided Precision Strike,* 2–4.

38 BBC News, "Transcript: Bin Laden Video Excerpts," 27 December 2001, http://news.bbc.co.uk/2/hi/middle_east/1729882.stm; Maggie Michael, "Bin Laden, in Statement to US People, Says He Ordered Sept 11 Attacks," Sign on San Diego.com, 29 October 2004, http://legacy.utsandiego.com/news/nation/terror/20041029-1423-binladentape.html; National Broadcasting Company (NBC), "Al-Jazeera: Bin Laden Tape Obtained in Pakistan," 30 October 2004, http://www.nbcnews.com/id/6363306/.

39 BBC News, "Transcript: Bin Laden Video Excerpts"; Michael, "Bin Laden, in Statement to US People."

40 JoAnne O'Bryant and Michael Waterhouse, "US Forces in Afghanistan," Congressional Research Service, CRS Report for Congress, Order Code RS22633, 15 July 2008, http://fas.org/sgp/crs/natsec/RS22633.pdf; David Rodhe, "Foreign Fighters of a Harsher Bent Bolster Taliban," *New York Times*, 30 October 2007; United for Justice and Peace, "Escalation: Bad for Them, Bad for Us," Afghanistan Fact Sheet no. 1, February 2009; Casualties.org, "Operation Enduring Freedom," 19 August 2009, http://icasualties.org/OEF/.

41. O'Bryant and Waterhouse, "US Forces in Afghanistan"; Rodhe, "Foreign Fighters"; United for Justice and Peace, "Escalation"; Casualties.org, "Operation Enduring Freedom."

42 O'Bryant and Waterhouse, "US Forces in Afghanistan"; Rodhe, "Foreign Fighters"; United for Justice and Peace, "Escalation"; Casualties.org, "Operation Enduring Freedom; Casualty numbers from CNN.com, "List: US and Coalition Casualties," 3 December 2012, http://www.cnn.com/SPECIALS/war.casualties/table.afghanistan.html.

43 ABC News, "Osama Bin Laden Operation Ended with Coded Message, 'Geronimo-E KIA,'" 2 May 2011, http://abcnews.go.com/Politics/osama-bin-laden-operation-code-geronimo/story?id=13507836#.UeVqQ6DD-lI.

Chapter 15

1 See Thomas E. Ricks, *Fiasco: The American Military Adventure in Iraq;* Thomas E. Ricks, *The Gamble: General David Petraeus and the American Adventure in Iraq, 2006–2008;* Robert K. Brigham, *Is Iraq Another Vietnam?;* John Keegan, *The Iraq War;* Williamson Murray and Robert H. Scales Jr., *The Iraq War: A Military History.*

2 CNN, "The Gulf War: A Nine-Year Timeline," 2001; revised, 21 October 2011, http://news.blogs.cnn.com/2011/10/21/the-iraq-war-a-nine-year-timeline/?iref=storysearch; CNN, "Coalition Planes Hit Iraq Sites in No-Fly Zone," 28 November 2002, http://archives.cnn.com/2002/WORLD/meast/11/28/sproject.irq.nofly.zone/. Also see James DeFronzio, *The Iraq War: Origins and Consequences,* and Christopher Cerf and Micah L. Sifry, eds., *The Iraq War Reader: History, Documents, Opinions.*

3 US Congress, "Iraq Liberation Act of 1998 (Enrolled as Agreed To or Passed by Both House and Senate)," June 1998; revised online 25 May 2006, http://thomas.loc.gov/cgi-bin/query/z?c105:H.R.4655.ENR:. Also see Ricks, *Fiasco.*

4 United Nations, "Security Council Resolution 687," 8 April 1991, http://www.fas.org/news/un/iraq/sres/sres0687.htm; William Arkin, "The Difference Was in the Details," *Washington Post,* 17 January 1999.

5 Republican Party Platform, 2000, no date, http://www.presidency.ucsb.edu/ws/?pid=25849; CNN, "O'Neill: 'Frenzy' Distorted War Plans Account," 14 January 2004, http://

edition.cnn.com/2004/ALLPOLITICS/01/13/oneill.bush/; Rebecca Leung, "Bush Sought 'Way' To Invade Iraq?" *CBS: 60 Minutes,* 11 January 2004, http://www.cbsnews.com/stories/2004/01/09/60minutes/main592330.shtml; Ricks, *Fiasco;* Joseph J. Collins, *Choosing War: The Decision to Invade Iraq and Its Aftermath.* Institute for National Strategic Studies Occasional Paper 5. For details on what Secretary O'Neill said, see Ron Suskind, *The Price of Loyalty: George W. Bush, the White House, and the Education of Paul O'Neill.*

6 Jeffrey R. Smith, "Hussein's Prewar Ties to Al Qaeda Discounted," *Washington Post,* 6 April 2007; George W. Bush, "President's Remarks at the United Nations General Assembly," White House Press Release, New York, 12 September 2002. Also see Rick Fawn and Raymond A. Hinnebusch, eds., *The Iraq War: Causes and Consequences.*

7 Hans Kochler, *The Iraq Crisis and the United Nations: Power Politics vs. the International Rule of Law,* Studies in International Relations 28.

8 International Atomic Energy Agency (IAEA), "The Status of Nuclear Inspections in Iraq: 14 February 2003 Update," http://www.iaea.org/newscenter/statements/2003/ebsp2003n005.shtml; updated 7 March 2003, http://www.iaea.org/NewsCenter/Statements/2003/ebsp2003n006.shtml.

9 Bootie Cosgrove-Mather, "Poll: Talk First, Fight Later," CBS.com, 24 January 2003, http://www.cbsnews.com/stories/2003/01/23/opinion/polls/main537739.shtml.

10 Kochler, *Iraq Crisis.*

11 CNN, "US has 100,000 Troops in Kuwait," 18 February 2003, http://www.cnn.com/2003/WORLD/meast/02/18/sprj.irq.deployment/index.html; "President Discusses Beginning of Operation Iraqi Freedom," White House Press Release, 17 March 2003, http://georgewbush-whitehouse.archives.gov/news/releases/2003/03/20030322.html. Also see James Fallows, *Blind into Baghdad: America's War in Iraq,* xxv, 228–30.

12 Ricks, *Fiasco;* Eric Lichtblau, "2002 Memo Doubted Uranium Sale Claim," *New York Times,* 18 January 2006.

13 CBS News, "Saddam's Last Line of Defense," 26 March 2003, http://www.cbsnews.com/2100-500257_162-546241.html; Mark Burgess, "Iraqi Military Effectiveness," Leatherneck.com, 12 November 2002, http://www.leatherneck.com/forums/showthread.php?3710-Iraqi-military-effectiveness; David Windle, "Military Muscle," *New Scientist,* 1 January 2003, http://www.newscientist.com/article.ns?id=dn3325; Scott Peterson, "The Rise and Fall of Ansar al-Islam," *Christian Science Monitor,* 16 October 2003, http://www.csmonitor.com/2003/1016/p12s01-woiq.html.

14 Evan Wright, *Generation Kill,* 249–50; David Zucchino, *Thunder Run: The Armored Strike to Capture Baghdad,* 189–91.

15 Peterson, "Rise and Fall of Ansar al-Islam."

16 Public Broadcasting System (PBS), "Operation Iraqi Freedom: A Chronology of the Six-Week Invasion of Iraq," 26 February 2004, http://www.pbs.org/wgbh/pages/frontline/shows/invasion/cron/ (hereafter cited as PBS Chronology); "The First Shot," *Airman Magazine,* July 2003; Michael R. Gordon and Gen. Bernard E. Trainor, "Iraqi Leader in Frantic Flight, Eluded US Strikes," *New York Times,* 12 March 2006. Also see Michael R. Gordon and Bernard E. Trainor, *Cobra II: The Inside Story of the Invasion and Occupation of Iraq.*

17 For details on the first day of Operation Iraqi Freedom, see Keegan, *Iraq War;* Zucchino, *Thunder Run;* Murray and Scales, *Iraq War;* Ricks, *Fiasco.*

18 Keegan, *Iraq War;* Zucchino, *Thunder Run;* Murray and Scales, *Iraq War;* Ricks, *Fiasco.*

19 Ali Balci and Murat Yesiltas, "Turkey's New Middle East Policy: The Case of the Meeting of the Foreign Ministers of Iraq's Neighboring Countries," *Journal of South Asian and Middle Eastern Studies* 29, no. 4 (Summer 2006): 18–38; Peter Ford, "A Weak Northern Front Could Lengthen Iraq War," *Christian Science Monitor,* 3 April 2003.

20 Gordon and Trainor, *Cobra II;* Col. Walter J. Boyne, *Operation Iraqi Freedom: What Went Right, What Went Wrong, and Why,* 20–35; Anthony H. Cordesman, *The Iraq War: Strategy, Tactics, and Military Lessons.*

21 Gordon and Trainor, *Cobra II;* Boyne, *Operation Iraqi Freedom,* 20–35; Cordesman, *Iraq War.*

22 Gordon and Trainor, *Cobra II;* Boyne, *Operation Iraqi Freedom,* 20–35; Cordesman, *Iraq War.*

23 Zucchino, *Thunder Run;* US Army, Official Records, "Attack on the 507th Maintenance Company," 17 July 2003, http://www.webcitation.org/5iSuYuP2L; Richard S. Lowry, *Marines in the Garden of Eden,* 88.

24 PBS Chronology.

25 Lowry, *Marines in the Garden of Eden,* 88, 131, 139.

26 Ibid., 139, 143, 146, 198–99, 308–18, 354–55, 395–99.

27 PBS Chronology.

28 Ibid.

29 Ibid.; Zucchino, *Thunder Run.*

30 PBS Chronology; Zucchino, *Thunder Run.*

31 Carl Conetta *The Wages of War: Iraqi Combatant and Noncombatant Fatalities in the 2003 Conflict,* Project on Defense Alternatives Special Monograph no. 8, 20 October 2003, http://www.comw.org/pda/fulltext/0310rm8.pdf; PBS Chronology; Zucchino, *Thunder Run;* Boyne, *Operation Iraqi Freedom;* Ricks, *Fiasco;* Thomas Donnelly, *Operation Iraqi Freedom: A Strategic Assessment;* Fallows, *Blind into Baghdad.*

32 Linwood B. Carter, "Iraq: Summary of US Forces," *CRS Report to Congress,* Order Code 31763, 28 November 2005, 1–10, http://www.fas.org/sgp/crs/mideast/RL31763.pdf.

33 Dana Bash, "White House Pressed on 'Mission Accomplished' Sign," *CNN News,* http://www.cnn.com/2003/ALLPOLITICS/10/28/mission.accomplished/; Associated Press, "Text of Bush Speech," news release, 1 May 2003, http://www.cbsnews.com/stories/2003/05/01/iraq/main551946.shtml. This event is also discussed in Ricks, *Fiasco;* Boyne, *Operation Iraqi Freedom;* Gordon and Trainor, *Cobra II;* and Keegan, *Iraq War.*

34 CNN, "US and Coalition Casualties," 14 May 2010, http://www.cnn.com/SPECIALS/2004/oef.casualties/index.html; Tina Susman, "Poll: Civilian Death Toll in Iraq May Top 1 Million," *Los Angeles Times,* 14 September 2007; Iraq Body Count Web Site, "A Dossier of Civilian Casualties in Iraq," 24 August 2009, http://www.iraqbodycount.org/; "Iraqi Health Minister Claims Insurgents Have Killed 150,000," Confederate Yankee.com, March 2007, http://confederateyankee.mu.nu/archives/204499.php; Icasulties.org, "Operation Iraqi Freedom," 2009, http://icasualties.org/Iraq/index.aspx.

35 BBC, "Iraq's Most Wanted," 11 November 2005, http://news.bbc.co.uk/2/hi/middle_east/2939125.stm.

36 CNN, "Pentagon: Saddam's Sons Killed in Raid," 22 July 2003, http://www.cnn.com/2003/WORLD/meast/07/22/sprj.irq.sons/.

37 FoxNews, "Saddam Captured 'Like a Rat' in Bind," 14 December 2003, http://www.foxnews.com/story/2003/12/14/saddam-captured-like-rat-in-raid/; NBC, "Saddam Hussein Executed, Ending Era in Iraq," 30 December 2006, http://www.msnbc.msn.com/id/16389128/.

38 "US Jets and Gunships Attack Iraqi Targets," Red Orbit.com, 24 December 2003, http://www.redorbit.com/news/general/37653/us_jets_gunships_attack_iraq_targets/, accessed 21 May 2009; American Special Ops.com, "Air Force Special Operations: Special Operations Aircraft," http://www.americanspecialops.com/aircraft/.

39 "US Jets and Gunships."

40 Elaine M. Grossman, "Services Spar over a Powerful but Vulnerable Aircraft: Troops in Fallujah Lost Bid for Daytime AC-130 Gunship Fire Support," *Inside the Pentagon,* 25 November 2004, http://www.dnipogo.org/grossman/troops_in_fallujah.htm, reprinted by permission of Inside Washington Publishers, http://defense.iwpnewsstand.com.

41 Ibid.; James Glanz "With Airpower and Armor, Troops Enter Rebel-Held City," *New York Times,* 8 November 2004, http://www.nytimes.com/2004/11/08/international/08CND_IRAQ.html. For books on the battles for Fallujah, see Bing West, *No True Glory: A Frontline Account of the Battle for Fallujah;* Patrick O'Donnell, *We Were One: Shoulder to Shoulder with the Marines Who Took Fallujah;* John R. Ballard, *Fighting for Fallujah: A New Dawn for Iraq;* Gary Livingston, *Fallujah With Honor: First Battalion, Eighth Marines' Role in Operation Phantom Fury;* Vincent L. Foulk, *Battle of Fallujah: Occupation, Resistance, and Stalemate in the War in Iraq;* Mike Tucker, *Among Warriors in Iraq: True Grit, Special Ops, and Raiding in Mosul and Fallujah.*

42 Grossman, "Services Spar."

43 Ibid.

44 Ibid.; Ballard, *Fighting for Fallujah,* 56–77.

45 Grossman, "Services Spar."

46 Ibid.

47 Ibid.

48 Ibid.; Ballard, *Fighting for Fallujah,* 56–77.

49 Grossman, "Services Spar."

50 Michael A. Klausutis, AAC/HO, to William P. Head, WR-ALC/HO, "Night Hunter Chapter 15," e-mail, 21 December 2009.

51 Ballard, *Fighting for Fallujah,* 56–77.

52 Robert Hornick, "AC-130 Employment," Marine Corps Command and Staff College, Quantico, VA, Accession no ADA492023, 2006, http://handle.dtic.mil/100.2/ ADA492023.

Chapter 16

1 Deagel, "C-130H Hercules," 3 July 2013, http://www.deagel.com/Military-Transport-Aircraft/C-130H-Hercules_a000526001.aspx.

2 Ibid.

3 US Department of Defense, Global Special Operations, Joint Chiefs of Staff (JCS), Special Operations Forces, Reference Manual," chap. 5, "US Air Force Special Operations Forces: Air Force Special Operations Command (AFSOC)," 2009, "http://www.fas.org/irp/agency/dod/socom/sof-ref-2-1/SOFREF_Ch5.htm.

4 Ibid.

5 Ibid.

6 Deagel, "C-130."

7 Ibid.; Deagel, "Spooky Gunship Armed with MK 44 Bushmaster Cannons," original released on 1 February 2007, by AFNEWS, Hurlburt Field, AFSOC/PA, as "Spooky Gunship Armed with New Cannons," http://www.deagel.com/news/Spooky-Gunship-Armed-with-MK-44-Bushmaster-Cannons_n000001418.aspx (hereafter cited as Deagel, "Bushmaster Cannons").

8 Deagel, "C-130."

9 Ibid.

10 Deagel, "Bushmaster Cannons."

11 Deagel, "C-130."

12 Deagel, "Bushmaster Cannons."

13 Deagel, "Boeing Starts AC-130U Gunship Flight Testing," 28 April 2007, http://www.deagel.com/news/Boeing-Starts-AC-130U-Gunship-Flight-esting_n000001901.aspx (hereafter cited as Deagel, "Boeing Flight Testing").

14 Ibid.

15 Sam LaGrone, "New Gunship Plan: 8 Modified MC-130Ws," *Air Force Times*, 4 June 2009, http://www.airforcetimes.com/news/2009/06/airforce_gunship_recap_060209w/.

16 Deagel, "Boeing Flight Testing."

17 Deagel, "Viper Strike Smart Munitions Tested on AC-130 Gunship," 31 October 2005, http://www.deagel.com/news/Viper-Strike-Smart-Munition-Tested-on-AC-130-Gunship_n000000565.aspx.

18 Ibid.

19 Ibid.

20 WR-ALC, History, FY00, 37–40; FY04, 204–5.

21 Ibid., FY01, 167–69; FY02, 92–96; FY04; FY08, chaps. 2 and 5.

22 Ibid., FY04, 266–68; FY05, 190–92.

23 Ibid., FY06, 194–96; FY08, chap. 5.

24 Robert J. Seifert, "Iraq and the AC-130: Gunships Unleashed," *Joint Forces Quarterly*, National Defense University, Second Quarter 2007, Issue 45, also published in Weapon System Technology Information Analysis Center, *WSTAIC Quarterly* 8, no. 3 (September 2007): 9–14, http://wstiac.alionscience.com/pdf/WQV8N3_ART03.pdf (hereafter cited as Seifert, "Gunships Unleashed"). Also see James S. Corum and Wray R. Johnson, *Airpower in Small Wars: Fighting Insurgents and Terrorists*, 274.

25 Seifert, "Gunships Unleashed."

26 Ibid.

27 Ibid.

28 Ibid.; Daniel R. Mortensen, *Airpower and Ground Armies*, 93–140.

29 Seifert, "Gunships Unleashed."
30 Ibid.
31 Ibid.
32 Ibid.; Benjamin Franklin Cooling, ed., *Case Studies in the Development of Close Air Support,* 444.
33 Seifert, "Gunships Unleashed;" Cooling, *Case Studies.*
34 Eduard Mark, *Aerial Interdiction: Air Power and Land Battle in Three American Wars,* 352.
35 Seifert, "Gunships Unleashed;" Charles M. Westenhoff, *Military Air Power: The Cadre Digest of Air Power Opinions and Thoughts,* 110.
36 Air-Attack.com, "Deadly AC-130 Gunships Returning to Iraq," 4 March 2006, http://air-attack.com/news/article/1204/03-04-2006-Deadly-AC-130-Gunships-Returning-to-Iraq.html.
37 Ibid.; "Lethal 'Flying Gunships' Returning to Iraq," MSNBC/Associated Press, 3 March 2006, http://www.nbcnews.com/id/11657894/ns/world_news_mideast_n_africa/t/lethal-flying-gunships-returning-iraq/; Tom N. Bowman, "Powerful Gunships Prowl Iraq, and Limits Show," NPR Website, 5 August 2009, http://www.npr.org/templates/story/story.php?storyId=7608428.
38 "Gunships Deploy"; Bowman, "Powerful Gunships."
39 Nick Turse, "The Secret Air War in Iraq," *The Nation,* 11 June 2007, http://www.thenation.com/doc/20070611/turse.
40 Ibid.
41 Ibid.
42 Robert Burns, "US Launches New Airstrike in Somalia," *Associated Press,* 24 January 2007, http://pantagraph.com/news/article_5ebbd73d-9ed6-5f12-85c6-777952462beb.html.
43 Air-Attack.com, "US Airstrike in Somalia Targets al-Qaida Suspect," Voice of America, 3 March 2008, http://www.air-attack.com/news/article/3063/03-03-2008-US-Airstrike-in-Somalia-Targets-al-Qaida-Suspect.html.
44 Ibid.
45 David Martin, "AC-130 Overworked in Iraq, Afghanistan," CBS News, 12 March 2008, Air Force Association transcript, http://eb.afa.org/2008/03/13/e20080313587303.html.
46 Ibid.
47 Ibid.
48 Stew Magnuson, "Air Force Gunships Could Be Grounded," *NDIA National Defense Magazine,* May 2007, http://www.nationaldefensemagazine.org/ARCHIVE/2007/MAY/Pages/AirForceGunships2638.aspx.
49 Ibid.
50 Ibid.
51 Ibid.
52 Deagel, "Boeing Receives F2AST Contract from US Air Force," 2 February 2009, http://www.deagel.com/news/Boeing-Receives-F2AST-Contract-From-US-Air-Force_n000005637.aspx.
53 Ibid.

54 Friends of the First Lady, "First Lady Tribute to First Production C-130," Spectre Association, http://www.spectre-association.org/First_Lady_129.htm.

55 "AC-130A Spectre," fact sheet, Hurlburt Field Aircraft Library, current as of 16 September 2009, http://www.hurlburt.af.mil/library/factsheets/factsheet.asp?id=3423.

56 National Museum of the United States Air Force, "Lockheed AC-130A Spectre," fact sheet, http://www.nationalmuseum.af.mil/factsheets/factsheet.asp?id=412; National Museum of the United States Air Force, "Lockheed AC-130A," fact sheet, http://www.nationalmuseum.af.mil/factsheets/factsheet.asp?id=3216.

57 In January 2008 the author visited the 16th Special Operations Squadron and the 4th Special Operations Squadron while both were still stationed at Hurlburt Field.

58 "New Mexico Delegation Welcomes News of Special Ops Squadron Deployment to Cannon Air Force Base," 14 May 2008, press release, http://targetednews.com/pr_disp.php?pr_id=1547328

59 Capt. Mae-Li Allison, "16 SOS Transfers Flag to Cannon," Air Force Special Operations Command, 25 June 2009, http://www.afsoc.af.mil/news/story.asp?id=123155363.

60 Ibid.

61 Ibid.

Conclusion

1 Maj. Daniel R. Clevenger, "The Battle of Khafji: Air Power Effectiveness in the Desert," Appendix G, "Interview with Major Paul Havel, USAF, Operation Desert Storm AC-130 Aircraft Commander," 90.

2 Ibid.

3 Ibid., 92–93.

4 Ibid., 93–94.

5 Ibid., Appendix H, "Interview with Capt. Charles Stoner, USAF, Operation Desert Storm AC-130 Combat Co-pilot," 100–102.

6 Ibid., Appendix I, "Interview with TSgt William Alex, USAF, Operation Desert Storm AC-130 Combat Gunner"; Appendix J, "Interview with TSgt Ron Johnson, USAF, Operation Desert Storm AC-130 Sensor Operator"; Appendix K, "Interview with TSgt Ken Taylor, USAF, Operation Desert Storm AC-130 Loadmaster"; Appendix L, "Interview with TSgt Clay Watson, USAF, Operation Desert Storm AC-130 Sensor Operator"; Appendix M, "Interview with SSgt Clay Sims, USAF, Operation Desert Storm AC-130 Sensor Operator," 102–26.

7 Ibid., Appendix J, "Interview with TSgt Ron Johnson," 107–8.

8 Daniel L. Haulman, *Air Force Manned Aircraft Combat Losses, 1990-2002.*

9 Global Security.org, "711th Special Operations Squadron (711th SOS)," 26 April 2005, http://www.globalsecurity.org/military/agency/usaf/711sos.htm.

10 Spectre Association, "16th SOS History," August 2009, http://www.spectre-association.org/history16SOS.htm.

11 1st Special Operations Wing, Public Affairs Office, "4th Special Operations Squadron," fact sheet, Hurlburt Field, FL, http://www2.hurlburt.af.mil/library/factsheets/factsheet.asp?id=3489.

12 1st Lt. Lauren Johnson, "AFSOC Welcomes First Female Flying Squadron Commander,"

23 February 2009, http://www2.hurlburt.af.mil/news/story.asp?id=123136801. Upon the conclusion of Cartier's tour she became a national security affairs fellow at the Hoover Institution, Stanford University.

13 Global Security.org. "AC-X Replacement Gunship," September 2008, http://www.globalsecurity.org/military/systems/aircraft/ac-x.htm.

14 Ibid.

15 Ibid.

16 Otto Kreisher, "Gunship Worries," *Air Force Magazine* 92, no. 7 (July 2009), http://www.airforce-magazine.com/MagazineArchive/Pages/2009/July%202009/0709gunship.aspx.

17 McCutchan/Wilson interview.

18 Kreisher, "Gunship Worries."

19 Ibid.

20 Ibid.

21 Ibid.

22 Ibid.

23 Ibid.

24 Damon Housman, WR-ALC Public Affairs, "Air Logistics Center Upgrades Center Wing Boxes on C-130s," *Air Force Print News,* 15 November 2006, http://www.afmc.af.mil/news/story_print.asp?id=123032021; "Keeping the C-130s Flying: Center Wing Box Replacements," *Defense Industry Daily,* 4 April 2007, http://www.defenseindustrydaily.com/keeping-the-c130s-flying-center-wing-box-replacements-03185/; Amanda Creel, "WR-ALC Completes First of Its Kind Center Wing Box Repair Two Months Ahead of Time," *Air Force Print News,* 15 June 2007, http://www.robins.af.mil/news/story_print.asp?id=123057299.

25 WR-ALC, History, FY09, chap. 5; SMSgt Bender, A4MYA, "Bullet Background Paper on MC-130H/J and AC-130U Center Wing Box Replacement," (unclassified) 29 September 2009.

26 WR-ALC, History, FY09, chap. 5; John Morrissette, HQ AFMC/A4U, "CSAF Weapon System Review (WRSR)," briefing, 21 May 2009.

27 Lt. Col. Bill Blauser, AFSOC Joint Acquisition Task Force–Dragon, "Project Dragon Spear,"briefing, 10 Mar 2011.

28 Ibid.

29 Blauser briefing. The Secretary of Defense comptroller in April 2009 issued Resource Management Decision 802, the goal of which was to reduce the proportion of contractor funding 13 percent for service contracts.

30 Blauser briefing. "Undefinitized contract action" means any contract action for which the contract terms, specifications, or price are not agreed upon before performance is begun under the action. Examples are letter contracts, orders under basic ordering agreements, and provisional item orders for which the price has not been agreed upon before performance has begun. "Definitized" usually includes a not-to-exceed price. DOD policy is that undefinitized contract actions shall be used only when (1) there was insufficient time for negotiation of a definitive contract action that met the government's needs, or (2) it is in the best interest of the government that the contractor

receive a binding commitment so that contract work can begin immediately. Such contracts shall be as complete and definite as feasible.

31 Francis S. Pirc, WR-ALC/GRUAB, "Bullet Background Paper On The Dragon Spear Program," 10 August 2010.

32 US Department of Defense, "Contracts: L-3 Dragon Spear," 21 September 2010; Michael Sirak, "The SOF Makeover," *Air Force Magazine* 93, no. 6 (June 2010), http://www.airforcemag.com/MagazineArchive/Pages/2010/June%202010/0610SOF.aspx; Ashley Wallace, "News: Stinger II," *Air International* 82, no. 5 (May 2012): 19.

33 Air Force Special Operations Command, Public Affairs Office, news release, Hurlburt Field, Florida, accessed 15 July 2013; US Air Force, "AC-130W Stinger II," fact sheet, 20 November 2012, http://www.af.mil/information/factsheets/factsheet.asp?id=4887.

34 US Air Force, "AC-130W Stinger II," fact sheet.

35 Ibid.

36 Sirak, "SOF Makeover."

37 Capt. Kristen D. Duncan, AFSOC/PA, "Benchmark 'Dragon Spear' Program Earns William J. Perry Award," *Air Force Special Operations Command Public Affairs,* 2 March 2011, http://www.afsoc.af.mil/news/story.asp?id=123244936; Raquel Sanchez, USAF/PA, "The Most Fearsome Weapon Is Evolving," Air Force.mil, posted 9 January 2013, http://www.af.mil/news/story.asp?id=123331866.

38 Sfc. Michael J. Carden, US Army, American Forces Press Service, "Fallen Airmen Laid to Rest after 38 Years," *Air Force Retiree News Service,* Release no. 06-07-10, 18 June 2010.

Glossary of Acronyms

AAA	antiaircraft artillery
AAC HO	Air Armament Center History Office
AB	air base
ABCCC	airborne command and control center *or* airborne command, control, and communications
AC	attack cargo
ACS	air commando squadron
ACW	air commando wing
AFAL	Air Force Avionics Laboratory
AFB	Air Force base
AFISNA	American Forces Information Service News Articles
AFLC	Air Force Logistics Command
AFM	Air Force manual
AFR	Air Force regulation
AFRC	Air Force Reserve Command
AFSC	Air Force Systems Command
AFSOC	Air Force Special Operations Command
AGE	aeronautical ground equipment *or* aerospace ground equipment
AH	attack helicopter
ALLTV	all-level light television
AMP	avionics modernization program
AOR	area of responsibility
APS	Armor Protection System
ARVN	Army of the Republic of Vietnam
ASD	Aeronautical Systems Division
ASOC	Air Support Operations Center
ATC	Air Training Command
AWACS	airborne warning and control system
BIU	blanking interface unit
BLU	bomb live unit
CAS	close air support
CBS	Columbia Broadcasting System
CBU	cluster bomb unit
CCTS	combat crew training squadron
CENTAF	Central Air Forces
CENTCOM	Central Command
CFE	Contractor Furnished Equipment
CH	Cargo Helicopter *or* Corona Harvest
CHECO	Contemporary Historical Examination of Current Operations

CIA	Central Intelligence Agency
CINCPACAF	Commander-in-Chief Pacific Air Forces
CLS	contractor logistics support
CMDS	countermeasures dispenser system
CONUS	continental United States
CSAF	Chief of Staff of the Air Force
CWB	center wing box
CY	calendar year
DCS	deputy chief of staff
DFC	Distinguished Flying Cross
DMM	Directorate of Materiel Management
DMZ	Demilitarized Zone
DOD	Department of Defense
ECM	electronic countermeasures
EF	electronic fighter
ETR	Eastern Test Range, *or* end of tour report
EW	electronic warfare
F	fighter
F2AST	Future Flexible Acquisition and Sustainment Tool Program
FA	fighter attack
FAC	forward air control
FACI	first article configuration inspection
FAD	force activity designator
FC	fighter cargo
FLIR	forward-looking infrared
FOL	forward operating location
FRY	Federal Republic of Yugoslavia
G8	Group of Eight industrialized nations
GACAWS	Gunship Advanced Combined Arms Weapons Suite
GBU	guided-bomb unit
GFE	government furnished equipment
GFP	government furnished parts
GMS2	Gunship Multispectral Sensor System
GPS	Global Positioning Satellite System
GWAPS	*Gulf War Air Power Survey*
HARM	high-speed antiradiation missile
HD/LD	high-demand/low-density
HH	heavy helicopter
HQ	headquarters
HUD	heads-up display
IADS	integrated air defense system
IDS	infrared detection set
IFF	identification friend or foe
ILS	instrument landing system

IM	item manager
INS	inertial navigation system *or* integrated navigation system
IO	illuminator operator
IOC	initial operational capability
IPT	integrated program team
IR	infrared
IRAN	inspect and repair as necessary
ISR	intelligence, surveillance, and reconnaissance
ITTAV	International Telephone and Telegraph Avionics
IWSM	integrated weapon system management
IWSSP	Integrated Weapon System Support Program
JC	joint cargo
JCS	Joint Chiefs of Staff
JDAM	joint direct attack munitions
JPO	Joint Program Office
JSOAC	Joint Special Operations Air Component
JSOTF	joint special operations task force
JSOW	joint standoff weapon
JSTARS *or* Joint STARS	Joint Surveillance Target Attack Radar System
JTAC	joint terminal air controller
JTF	joint task force
KIA	killed in action
KLA	Kosovar Liberation Army
LANTIRN	low-altitude navigation and targeting infrared for night
LASC	Lockheed Aircraft Service Company
LGB	laser-guided bomb
LLC	limited liability corporation
LLLTV	low-level light television
LORAN	long-range electronic navigation
LOX	liquid oxygen
LTVE	Ling-Temco-Vought Electrosystems
LWSG	Limited War Study Group
LZ	landing zone
M&R	manufacture and repair
M/R	modification requirement
MAC	Military Airlift Command
MACV	Military Assistance Command, Vietnam
MAG	Marine aircraft group
MAK	Maktab al-Khidamat
MANPAD	man-portable air defense
MAW	Marine air wing
MC	mission cargo
MEF	Marine expeditionary force

MFP	major force program
MH	mission helicopter
MOB	main operating base
MR	military region
MSB	main support base
NASA	National Aeronautical and Space Agency
NATO	North Atlantic Treaty Organization
NCO	noncommissioned officer
NJM	New Jewel Movement
NLF	National Liberation Front
NOD/NOS	night observation device/system
NOS	night observation sight
NSC	National Security Council
NVA	North Vietnamese Army
NVG	night vision goggles
NVIS	night vision imaging system
NVN	North Vietnam
OA	observation attack
OAF	Operation Allied Freedom
OECS	Organization of Eastern Caribbean States
OEF	Operation Enduring Freedom
OFP	operational flight program
OIF	Operation Iraqi Freedom
ONI	Oklahoma, Quality Networks Inc.
OPLAN	operations plan
OSD	Office of the Secretary of Defense
PACAF	Pacific Air Forces
PAVN	People's Army of Vietnam
PBD	program budget decision
PDF	Panamanian Defense Force
PDM	programmed depot maintenance
PGM	precision-guided munitions
PMD	program management directive
POL	petroleum, oil, and lubricants
PRC	People's Republic of China
R&D	research and development
RAF	Royal Air Force
RAP	rapid aerospace process
RASS	rapid area supply support
RATO	rocket-assist takeoff
RES-W	Raytheon E-Systems, Waco
Ro-Ro	roll-on, roll-off
RP	route package
RPG	rocket-propelled grenade

RTAB	Royal Thai air base
RTAFB	Royal Thai Air Force base
RTO	rocket takeoff
SO	special order
SAB	scientific advisory board
SAC	scientific advisory committee
SAC	Strategic Air Command
SAF/AQ	assistant secretary of the Air Force for acquisitions
SAIC	Science Applications International Company
SAMs	surface-to-air missiles
SAR	search and rescue
SBT	special boat team
SCNA	self-contained night attack
SEAD	suppression of enemy air defenses
SEALs	sea, air, and land teams
SECAF	secretary of the Air Force
SECDEF	secretary of defense
SIOP	single integrated operations plan
SIT	system integration test
SOAR	special operations airborne regiment
SOCOM	Special Operations Command
SOF	special operations forces
SOFI	special operations forces improvement *or* special operations forces instruction
SOG	special operations group
SOLLII	Special Operations Low Level II
SOS	special operations squadron
SOUTHCOM	Southern Command
SOW	special operations wing
SPO	system program office
SRA	specialized repair activity
SRL	systems research laboratories
SSM	single systems manager
STG	special tactical group
SVN	South Vietnam
TO	technical order
T/N	tail number
TAC	Tactical Air Command
TACAN	tactical air navigation
TAG	tactical airlift group
TAW	tactical airlift wing
TDY	temporary duty
TFS	tactical fighter squadron
TFW	tactical fighter wing

TLAM	Tomahawk land attack (cruise) missile
UAE	United Arab Emirates
UAV	unmanned aerial vehicle
UH	utility helicopter
UHF	ultra high frequency
UK	United Kingdom
UN	United Nations
UNSCR	United Nations Security Council resolution
USAF	United States Air Force
USCENTCOM	United States Central Command
USEUCOM	United States European Command
USSBS	United States Strategic Bombing Survey
USSOC	United States Special Operations Command
USSR	Union of Soviet Socialist Republics
UTF	united task force
VC	Viet Cong
VHF	very high frequency
VNAF	Vietnamese Air Force
VVI	vanishing vender item
WMD	weapons of mass destruction
WR-ALC	Warner Robins Air Logistics Center
WRAMA	Warner Robins Air Materiel Area
WRAMA/WRN	Warner Robins Air Materiel Area Directorate of Materiel Management
WSSLO	weapon systems support logistics office
ZI	zone of the interior

Bibliography

Archival and Library Sources

The majority of primary materials used in this work are located at the 78th Air Base Wing History Archives, Robins AFB, Georgia. Unless the provenance of an item is stated as otherwise, it is located there. The archives have a large number of Vietnam-era holdings, particularly Warner Robins Air Materiel Area (WRAMA) and Strategic Air Command (SAC) documents, histories, and studies. Among the other sources used were messages, letters, and memos among key political, military, and WRAMA players involved in the AC-130 story. They also include interviews; military situation reports; end-of-tour reports; site team reports; mission reports; background reports; command-, service-, and secretary-level briefings; and statements before Congress and other government agencies. Many of these primary sources were found in files of government agencies such as the US State Department and Defense Department; the US Senate and House of Representatives, including the Committees on Foreign Affairs and Armed Services; and the Departments of the Air Force, Army, and Navy as well as the Joint Chiefs of Staff. Other documents came from the National Archives in College Park, Maryland; the Kennedy, Johnson, Nixon, Ford, and Carter presidential libraries; the US Air Force archival holdings at the Air Force Historical Research Agency at Maxwell AFB, Alabama, and the Navy War College, Newport, Rhode Island. Specific documents may be found in the end notes.

Public Documents

The following are published and unpublished reports by government agencies or institutions and individuals contracted by government agencies to produce reports and analyses. Also included are official histories such as special studies, pamphlets, monographs, special publications, periodic histories, annual histories, CHECO reports, and Corona Harvest studies.

Aeronautical Science Institute. "Air Interdiction Campaign, 1 Nov 68–31 May 69." Report 69-7, December 1969.

———. "Airpower in Southeast Asia, Aug 67–Jan 69." Report 69-3, July 1969.

———. "Development of All-Weather and Night Truck Killing Capacities." Report 70-14, January 1970.

Allard, Kenneth. *Somalia Operations: Lessons Learned.* Washington, DC: National Defense University Press, 1995.

Ballard, Jack S. *Development and Employment of Fixed-Wing Gunships, 1962–1972.* The United States Air Force in Southeast Asia. Washington, DC: Office of Air Force History, 1982.

Belasco, Amy. *The Cost of Iraq, Afghanistan, and Other Global War on Terror Operations since 9/11.* Washington, DC: Congressional Research Service, 16 July 2007.

Berger, Carl, ed. *The United States Air Force in Southeast Asia, 1961–1973: An Illustrated Account.* Washington, DC: Office of Air Force History, 1984.

Best, Cara N. *Nutmeg and Gunships: Operation "Urgent Fury" and the Invasion of Grenada.* USAF Monograph (S). Robins AFB, GA: Warner Robins Air Logistics Center Office of History (WR-ALC/HO), 1985. (All data used is unclassified or has since been declassified.)

Blank, Stephen, et al. *Low-Intensity Conflict in the Third World.* Maxwell AFB, AL: Air University Press, 1988.

Bloechl, Timothy D. *Operation JUST CAUSE: An Application of Operational Art?* Fort Leavenworth, KS: School of Advanced Military Studies, May 1993.

Borer, Douglas A. "Inverse Engagement: Lessons from US-Iraqi Relations, 1982–1990." US Army Professional Writing Collection. Carlisle Barracks, PA, 2003.

Brown, Harold. "Supplement to Air Force Policy Letter for Commanders, No. 3-68." Policy Statement of the Secretary of the Air Force, 1 March 1966.

Brown, Maj. Lawrence T. "You've Got to Be Kidding: Empowering the JFACC with Selected Ground Reconnaissance Forces." Joint Military Operations Department Paper. Naval War College, Newport, RI, 2 February 2003.

Bush, George W. "President Discusses Beginning of Operation Iraqi Freedom." radio address, 20 March 2003. http://georgewbush-whitehouse.archives.gov/news/releases/2003/03/20030322.html.

———. "President's Remarks at the United Nations General Assembly." White House Press Release, New York, 12 September 2002.

Cirafici, Lt. Col. John L. *Airhead Operations: Where AMC Delivers.* Maxwell AFB, AL: Air University Press, 1995.

Clark, Gen. Wesley K., US Army. "Press Conference on the Kosovo Strike Assessment." NATO HQ, Brussels, 20 September 1999. http://www.nato.int/kosovo/press/p990916a.htm.

Clevenger, Maj. Daniel R. "The Battle of Khafji: Air Power Effectiveness in the Desert." Paper. Vol. 1, Appendixes A–M. US Air Force Studies and Analyses Agency, Force Application Division, July 1996.

Cohen, Eliot, et al. *Gulf War Airpower Survey.* Vols. 1–5. Washington, DC: Government Printing Office, 1993.

Cohen, William S. "Lessons Learned from Kosovo." Speech. International Institute for Strategic Studies, Coronado, CA, 9 September 1999. http://www.bu.edu/globalbeat/nato/Cohen091099.html.

Cole, James Lawrence. "Fixed-Wing Gunships in Southeast Asia." United States Air Force, Pacific Air Forces, Directorate of Operations Analysis, CHECO/CORONA Harvest Division, CHECO Project, July 1969–June 1971.

Cole, Marvin. *Fixed-Wing Gunships in SEA (July 1969–July 1971).* Hickam AFB, HI: Pacific Air Forces, Directorate of Operations Analysis, 1971.

Cole, Ronald A. *Operation Urgent Fury: The Planning and Execution of Joint Operations in Grenada, 12 October–2 November 1983.* Washington, DC: JCS History Office, 1997.

Collins, Joseph J. *Choosing War: The Decision to Invade Iraq and Its Aftermath.* Institute for National Strategic Studies Occasional Paper 5. Washington, DC: National Defense University Press, 2008.

Creel, Amanda. "WR-ALC Completes First of Its Kind Center Wing Box Repair Two Months Ahead of Time." *Air Force Print News,* 15 June 2007. http://www.robins.af.mil/news/story_print.asp?id=123057299.

Cross, Brig. Gen. Richard G. "End-of-Tour Report." 22 January 1973. File K740.131.2, Air Force Historical Research Agency, Maxwell AFB, AL.

Davis, Richard C. *Strategic Air Power in Desert Storm.* Washington, DC: Air Force History Support Office, 1995.

Dean, Lt. Col. David J. *The Air Force Role in Low-Intensity Conflict.* Maxwell AFB, AL: Air University Press, 1986.

Doty, Maj. Denis P. "Command and Control of Special Operations Forces for 21st Century Contingency Operations." Paper. Naval War College, Newport, RI, 3 February 2003.

Dougherty, Richard P. *A Short History of the Development of the AC-130 Aircraft.* AFLC Historical Study 374. Wright Patterson AFB, OH: Air Force Logistics Command, February 1971.

Dunham, George R. *US Marines in Vietnam: The Bitter End, 1973–1975.* Marine Corps Vietnam Operational Historical Series. Quantico, VA: Marine Corps Association, 1990.

8th Tactical Fighter Wing. History. 1 October–31 December 1968; 1 April–30 June 1969, Vol. 3; January–May 1969, Vol. 1; 1 October–31 December 1969.

Evans, Col. D. L., Director of Intelligence. "Task Force Alpha, End-of-Tour Report." 6 July 1972. File 10015110, Air Force Historical Research Agency.

Fagg, John. *Europe: Argument to VE Day: January 1944 to May 1945.* Vol. 3 in *The United States Army Air Forces in World War II.* Ed. Wesley Frank Craven and James Lea Cate. Washington DC: Government Printing Office, 1983.

Fairchild-Hiller, Inc. "AC-119 Gunship Program Supplemental Administrative Information." Letter Contract F09603-68-C-1633, 21 March 1969.

———. "Modification of the C-119." News Release, 21 May 1968.

1st Special Operations Wing, History Office. "AC-130A Spectre." Fact sheet, 8 July 2008, Hurlburt Field. http://www.hurlburt.af.mil/library/factsheets/factsheet.asp?id=3423.

542nd Crew Training Wing. History (FOUO declassified). 1 January–31 March 1994. 3 vols. File K-WG-542-HI. IRIS no. 01115307. Maxwell AFB, AL, Air Force Historical Research Agency, 17 October 1994.

14th Air Combat Wing. History. 1 January–31 March 1968.

4th Special Operations Squadron, Public Affairs. "4th Special Operations Squadron." Fact sheet, 30 September 2008, Hurlburt Field. http://www2.hurlburt.af.mil/library/factsheets/factsheet.asp?id=3489.

France, Armed Forces, Bureau of the Commander-in-Chief, Indo-China. *Notes on Combat in Indo-China.* 3 vols., 1954–56.

France, Armed Forces, Supreme Command, Far East. *Lessons from the Indo-China War.* 3 vols., 1954–56.

Futrell, Robert Frank. *Ideas, Concepts, Doctrine: Basic Thinking in the United States Air Force.* 2 vols. Maxwell AFB, AL: Air University Press, 1989.

Garamone, Jim. "Air Ops in Yugoslavia Pick Up; Apaches to Albania." AFISNA, Defense Link, DOD, 6 April 1999. http://www.defense.gov/News/NewsArticle.aspx?ID=42049.

———. "Behind the Crisis in Kosovo." AFISNA, Defense Link, DOD, 17 June 1998. http://osd.dtic.mil/news/Ju11998/n07071998_9807074.html.

———. "Clinton Makes Case for Kosovo Intervention." AFISNA, Defense Link, DOD, 24 March 1999. http://osd.dtic.mil/news/Mar1999/n03241999_9903243.html.

———. "Clinton Sets Kosovo Emergency Funding at $6 Billion." AFISNA, Defense Link, DOD, 21 April 1999. http://www.defense.gov/News/NewsArticle.aspx?ID=42033.

———. "More Aircraft, Personnel Set for Allied Force." AFISNA, Defense Link, DOD, 11 May 1999. http://osd.dtic.mil/news/May1999/n05111999_9905111.html.

———. "More B-52s Join Allied Force Mission." AFISNA, Defense Link, DOD, 30 April 1999. http://osd.dtic.mil/news/Apr1999/n04301999_9904302.html.

———. "NATO Apologizes for Bombing Accident, Details Precautions." AFISNA, Defense Link, DOD, 16 April 1999. http://osd.dtic.mil/news/Apr1999/n04161999_9904162.html.

———. "President Calls-up Reservists, AF Authorized Stop/Loss." AFISNA, Defense Link, DOD, 27 April 1999. http://osd.dtic.mil/news/Apr1999/n04271999_9904275.html.

———. "Serb Withdrawal Begins, NATO Suspends Bombing." AFISNA, Defense Link, DOD, 10 June 1999. http://www.defense.gov/News/NewsArticle.aspx?ID=42086.

———. "US Sending 82 More Aircraft to Join NATO Forces." AFISNA, Defense Link, DOD, 12 April 1999. http://osd.dtic.mil/news/Apr1999/n04121999_9904126.html.

———, and Linda D. Kozaryn. "NATO Attacks Serbs to Stop Kosovo Killings." AFISNA, Defense Link, DOD, 24 March 1999. http://www.defense.gov/News/NewsArticle.aspx?ID=41999.

Gideon, Maj. Gen. Francis C., WRAMA/CC. "Notebook on Vietnam." WR-ALC Office of History Archives, 31 January 1968.

Gilster, Herman L. *The Air War in Southeast Asia.* Maxwell AFB, AL: Air University Press, 1993.

Haas, Col. Michael E. "Air Commando! 1950–1975: 25 Years at the Tip of the Spear." Special Study. US Air Force, Washington, DC, no date.

Hartsook, Elizabeth H. *The Air Force in Southeast Asia: The Role of Air Power Grows.* Washington, DC: Office of Air Force History, 1972.

———. *The Air Force in Southeast Asia: Shield for Vietnamization, 1971.* CHECO Report, May 1974.

Haulman, Daniel L. *Air Force Manned Aircraft Combat Losses, 1990–2002.* Maxwell AFB, AL: Air Force Historical Research Agency, 9 December 2002.

Head, William, et al. *Annual History of the Warner Robins ALC.* Fiscal Years 1983–2009. History (FOUO/PV/DL). Robins AFB, GA: WR-ALC, History Office, 1984–2010. (Unclassified pages used.)

Hornick, Robert. "AC-130 Employment." Marine Corps Command and Staff College, Quantico, Virginia. Accession no. ADA492023, 2006. http://handle.dtic.mil/100.2/ADA492023.

Horrocks, Michael. *The Air Force in Southeast Asia: The Sensor War, 1966–1971.* Washington, DC: Air Force History Office, 1985.

International Atomic Energy Agency (IAEA). "The Status of Nuclear Inspections in Iraq: 14 February 2003 Update." http://www.iaea.org/newscenter/statements/2003/ebsp2003n005.shtml. Updated 7 March 2003. http://www.iaea.org/NewsCenter/Statements/2003/ebsp2003n006.shtml.

Johnson, Maj. Calvin R. *Linebacker Operations, September–December 1972.* CHECO Project. Washington, DC: Office of Air Force History, 1974.

"Joint Statement by Secretary of Defense William S. Cohen and CIA Director George J. Tenet." Press release. AFISNA, Defense Link, DOD, 10 May 1999. http://www.defense.gov/releases/release.aspx?releaseid=2083.

Kinney, Gen. William A. "TACAIR Vietnam." *Airman* 12, no. 7 (July 1968).

Kohn, Richard H., and Joseph P. Harahan, eds. *Strategic Air Warfare: An Interview with Generals Curtis E. LeMay, Leon W. Johnson, David A. Burchinal, and Jack J. Catton.* Washington, DC: Air Force Office of History, 1988.

Kott, Maj. Richard F. *The Role of United States Air Force Gunships in Southeast Asia (SEASIA).* CHECO Project. Hickam AFB, HI: HQ Pacific Air Forces, 30 August 1969.

Kozaryn, Linda D. "Air Chief's Kosovo Lesson: Go for Snake's Head First." AFISNA, Defense Link, DOD, 26 October 1990. http://osd.dtic.mil/news/Oct1999/n10261999_9910264.html.

———. "Allied Force Pilots Down Three Serb Fighters." AFISNA, Defense Link, DOD, 25 March 1999. http://www.defense.gov/News/NewsArticle.aspx?ID=41997.

———. "Clinton Says NATO Must Act in Kosovo." AFISNA, Defense Link, DOD, 22 March 1999. http://osd.dtic.mil/news/Mar1999/n03221999_9903222.html.

———. "DOD Airlifts Rations to Balkans." AFISNA, Defense Link, DOD, 5 April 1999. http://osd.dtic.mil/news/Apr1999/n04051999_9904051.html.

———. "First NATO Strikes Aimed at Serb Air Defenses." AFISNA, Defense Link, DOD, 25 March 1999. http://osd.dtic.mil/news/Mar1999/n03251999_9903251.html.

———. "Kosovo Matters Because Europe Matters, Cohen and Shelton Say." AFISNA, Defense Link, DOD, 30 March 1999. http://osd.dtic.mil/news/Mar1999/n03291999_9903291.html.

———. "More US Fighters Join NATO Air Campaign." AFISNA, Defense Link, DOD, 2 April 1999. http://www.defense.gov/News/NewsArticle.aspx?ID=42929.

———. "Pentagon Sends in Carrier Battle Group." AFISNA, Defense Link, DOD, 5 April 1999. http://osd.dtic.mil/news/Apr1999/n04051999_9904052.html.

———. "Serb Forces Abduct Three US Soldiers." AFISNA, Defense Link, DOD, 1 April 1999. http://osd.dtic.mil/news/Apr1999/n04011999_9904012.html.

———. "Serbs Fold, US Hopeful for Peace Agreement, but Wary." AFISNA, Defense Link, DOD, 4 June 1999. http://osd.dtic.mil/news/Jun1999/n06041999_9906041.html.

———. "Stealth Fighter Down in Yugoslavia, Pilot Rescued." AFISNA, Defense Link, DOD, 28 March 1999. http://osd.dtic.mil/news/Mar1999/n03281999_9903281.html.

———. "US Commits More Air Power to Allied Force." AFISNA, Defense Link, DOD, 30 March 1999. http://osd.dtic.mil/news/Mar1999/n03301999_9903301.html.

———. "US, NATO Pilots Face Air Defense Threat." AFISNA, Defense Link, DOD, 24 March 1999. http://www.defense.gov/News/NewsArticle.aspx?ID=41608.

———. "US, NATO Turn Thumbs Down on Milosevic Offer." AFISNA, Defense Link, DOD, 31 March 1999. http://osd.dtic.mil/news/Mar1999/n03311999_9903314.html.

Lavalle, Maj. A. J. C., ed. *Air Power and the 1972 Spring Offensive.* US Air Force Monograph Series, Vol. 2. Washington, DC: Government Printing Office, 1977.

Liebchen, Capt. Peter A. W. *Kontum: Battle for the Central Highlands, 30 March–10 June 1972.* CHECO Project. Hickam AFB, HI: HQ Pacific Air Forces, Seventh Air Force, 27 October 1972.

Loye, Col. J. F., Jr., et al. *Lom Son 719: The South Vietnamese Incursion into Laos, 30 January–24 March 1971.* CHECO Project. Hickam AFB, HI: HQ Pacific Air Forces, 24 March 1971.

Maltais, Richard E. "WRAMA's Role in Southeast Asia: AC-47 Gunship." Historical Study no. 17. Robins AFB, GA: WRAMA, Office of History, 1971.

———. "WRAMA's Role in Southeast Asia: AC-119G/K Gunship Program, 1967–1970." Project Combat Hornet, Historical Study no. 18. Robins AFB, GA: WRAMA Office of History, March 1971.

Mann, Capt. David K. *The 1972 Invasion of Military Region I: Fall of Quang Tri and Defense of Hue.* CHECO Project. Saigon, RVN: Seventh Air Force, 15 March 1973.

Mark, Eduard. *Aerial Interdiction: Air Power and Land Battle in Three American Wars.* Washington, DC: Center for Air Force History, 1994.

Marks, TSgt David P. "'First Lady' Retires, Era Ends." Air Force News Service article. Original, 11 September 1995; update, 18 September 2004. http://www.gunships.org/1stlady.htm. Accessed 21 May 2009.

McCarthy, Brig. Gen. James R., and Lt. Col. George B. Allison. *Linebacker II: A View from the Rock.* Maxwell AFB, AL: Air War College, Airpower Research Institute, 1979.

———. *Linebacker II: A View from the Rock.* US Air Force Southeast Asia Monograph Series, No. 8, Vol. 6. Washington, DC: Air Force History Office, 1985.

McCutchan, Maj. Gen. Clay T. "USAF Gunship Overview." Air Force Special Operations Command Special Study, January 1994. AFSOC Office of History, Hurlburt Field, FL.

Meilinger, Col. Phillip S. *Ten Propositions Regarding Air Power.* Washington, DC: Air Force History and Museum Program, 1995.

Mets, David R. *Land-Based Air Power in Third World Crises.* Maxwell AFB, AL: Air University Press, 1986.

Military Assistance Command, Vietnam (MACV). Annual Histories. 1967, Vol. 2; 1970, Vol. 1, Annex A; January 1972–March 1973, Vol. 1, Annex A. Declassified copies at Defense Technical Information Center, Fort Belvoir, VA, and Vietnam Archive, Texas Tech University, Lubbock.

———. "Linebacker Study." Unofficial/Uncoordinated Draft Report, 20 January 1973, Chap. 2, File K712.041-19, Air Force Historical Research Agency, Maxwell AFB, AL.

———, Office of History. Semiannual, Periodic, and Annual Histories of MACV. Narrative and Document Vols., 1965, January 1972–March 1973. Saigon, RVN, 15 July 1973. (Formerly Top Secret, now Unclassified.)

Momyer, Gen. William W. *Air Power in Three Wars.* Washington, DC: Office of Air Force History, 1978, 1983.

Mrozek, Donald J. "The Limits of Innovation: Aspects of Air Power in Vietnam." 25th Anniversary of Aviation Web Site. Original from Center for Aerospace Doctrine, Research, and Education. Maxwell AFB, AL, 1985. http://www.airpower.au.af.mil/airchronicles/aureview/1985/jan-feb/mrozek.

Murray, Williamson. "Air Power since World War II, Consistent with Doctrine?" In *The Future of Air Power in the Aftermath of the Gulf War.* Ed. Richard H. Shultz Jr. and Robert L. Pfaltzgraff Jr. Maxwell AFB, AL: Air University Press, 1992.

Nalty, Bernard C. *Interdiction in Southern Laos.* Washington, DC: Air Force History Office, 1988.

———. "Post-Vietnam." In *Winged Shield, Winged Sword: A History of the United States Air Force,* Vol. 2, *1950–1997.* Bolling AFB, DC: Air Force Museum and History Program, 1997.

National Commission on Terrorist Attacks upon the United States. "The Attack Looms." *9/11 Commission Report,* 2004. http://govinfo.library.unt.edu/911/report/911Report_Ch7.htm.

National Museum of the US Air Force. "Fairchild AC-119G." Fact sheet, 7 January 2009. http://www.nationalmuseum.af.mil/factsheets/factsheet.asp?id=3213.

———. "Fairchild AC-119K." Fact sheet, 7 January 2009. http://www.nationalmuseum.af.mil/factsheets/factsheet.asp?id=3214.

———. "Lockheed AC-130A." Fact sheet, 9 January 2009. http://www.nationalmuseum.af.mil/factsheets/factsheet.asp?id=3216.

———. "Lockheed AC-130A Spectre." Fact sheet, 27 July 2010. http://www.nationalmuseum.af.mil/factsheets/factsheet.asp?id=412.

National Transportation Safety Board. "Flight Path Study—American Airlines Flight 11." 19 February 2002. http://www.gwu.edu/~nsarchiv/NSAEBB/NSAEBB196/doc01.pdf.

———. "Flight Path Study—American Airlines Flight 77." 19 February 2002. http://www.gwu.edu/~nsarchiv/NSAEBB/NSAEBB196/doc02.pdf.

———. "Flight Path Study—United Airlines Flight 93." 19 February 2002. http://www.ntsb.gov/doclib/foia/9_11/Flight_Path_Study_UA93.pdf.

———. "Flight Path Study—United Airlines Flight 175." 19 February 2002. http://www.gwu.edu/~nsarchiv/NSAEBB/NSAEBB196/doc03.pdf.

"New Mexico Delegation Welcomes News of Special Ops Squadron Deployment to Cannon Air Force Base." Press release, 14 May 2008. http://targetednews.com/pr_disp.php?pr_id=1547328.

Nicholson, Capt. Charles A. *The United States Air Force Response to the Spring 1972 North Vietnamese Offensive: Situation and Redeployment.* CHECO Project. Saigon, RVN: Seventh Air Force, 1972.

North Atlantic Treaty Organization. "Kosovo Crisis, Historical Overview: NATO's Role in Relation to the Conflict in Kosovo." 15 July 1999. http://www.nato.int/kosovo/history.htm.

O'Bryant, JoAnne, and Michael Waterhouse. "US Forces in Afghanistan." CRS Report for Congress, Order Code RS22633. Washington, DC: Library of Congress, Congressional Research Service, 15 July 2008. http://fas.org/sgp/crs/natsec/RS22633.pdf.

Parkinson, Col. Bradford W. Thesis. "Significant Concepts from the Air Force AC-130 Gunship Program." Thesis, Naval War College, 28 January 1972.

Poglione, John A., et al. *Air Power and the 1972 Spring Invasion.* Air Force SEA Monograph Series, Vol. 3. Hickam AFB, HI: HQ PACAF, 1976.

Porter, Melvin F. *Linebacker: Overview of the First 120 Days.* CHECO Project. Saigon, RVN: Seventh Air Force, 1973.

Public Papers of the Presidents of the United States: John F. Kennedy, 1962. Washington, DC: Government Printing Office, 1963.

Pushies, Fred J. *US Air Force Special Ops.* London: MBI Publishing, 2000; rev. ed., 2007.

Ramshaw, William S. "Operation Just Cause Command and Control: A Case Study." Department of Defense, Defense Technical Information Center, March 1991.

Ringenbach, Maj. Paul T., and Capt. Peter J. Melly. *The Battle for An Loc, 5 April–26 June 1972.* CHECO Project. Hickam AFB, HI: HQ PACAF, 31 January 1973.

Rolince, Michael E. "The Inspector General's Report and the September 11th Response." US Department of Justice, Federal Bureau of Investigation. http://www.fbi.gov/news/testimony/the-inspector-generals-report-and-the-september-11th-response.

Roth, Bill. "News Release: Roth Floor Statement on Lessons Learned in Kosovo Conflict." Release 106-207, 16 September 1999. http://www.finance.senate.gov/newsroom/chairman/release/?id=585b488d-a7f0-4256-b3f3-1882bea89878.

Ryan, Gen. John, Chief of Staff of the Air Force, to Senator John C. Stennis, Chair, Senate Committee on the Armed Services. Memo, 26 July 1973. "Hearing before the Committee on Armed Services." 93rd Cong., 1st sess.

Sams, Kenneth. *First Test and Combat Use of the AC-47.* CHECO Project. Hickam AFB, HI: HQ PACAF, December 1965.

Schlight, John. *The War in South Vietnam: The Years of the Offensive, 1965–1968.* The United States Air Force in Southeast Asia. Washington, DC: Office of Air Force History, 1988.

Schultz, Richard H. *In the Aftermath of War: US Support for Reconstruction and Nation-Building in Panama Following Just Cause.* Maxwell AFB, AL: Air University Press, 1993.

Scientific Advisory Group. "The Interdiction Campaign, 1 Apr–31 Oct 68." Working Paper no. 16-67, Report 69-5. Air Force Historical Research Agency, Maxwell AFB, AL.

Seifert, Maj. Robert J. "Iraq and the AC-130: Gunships Unleashed." *Joint Forces Quarterly* 45 (Second Quarter 2007). National Defense University. Also published in Weapon System Technology Information Analysis Center, *WSTAIC Quarterly* 8, no. 3 (September 2007). http://wstiac.alionscience.com/pdf/WQV8N3_ART03.pdf.

Seig, Louis. *Impact of Geography on Air Operations in Southeast Asia.* CHECO Project. Hickam AFB, HI: HQ PACAF, 11 July 1970.

16th Special Operations Squadron. Chronology, 1 January–31 March 1970; 1 January–31 March 1970; 1 July–30 September 1970. Air Force Historical Research Agency, Maxwell AFB, AL.

———. History, June–September 1970, Appendix A. Air Force Historical Research Agency, Maxwell AFB, AL.

Slay, Maj. Gen. Alton D. "End-of-Tour Report, August 1971–August 1972." Seventh Air Force. 1973.

Stewart, Robert Winship. *The United States Army in Somalia, 1992–1994.* CMH Publication 70-81-1. Washington, DC: Center for Military History, 2003.

Summers, Col. Harry G., Jr. *On Strategy: The Vietnam War in Context.* Carlisle Barracks, PA: Army War College, 1981.

Terry, Maj. Ronald W., and Capt. Terry R. Jorris. "Gunship II: A Study of In House Response to Unique Operational Requirements." *Proceedings of 1968 Air Force Science and Engineering Symposium,* Vol. 4. Colorado Springs: US Air Force Academy, 30 October–1 November 1968.

Theisen, Lt. Col. Eric E. *Ground-Aided Precision Strike: Heavy Bomber Activity in Operation Enduring Freedom.* Air War College Maxwell Paper no. 31. Maxwell AFB, AL: Air University Press, July 2003.

Tilford, Earl H., Jr. *Setup: What the Air Force Did in Vietnam and Why.* Maxwell AFB, AL: Air University Press, 1991.

Till, Gerald J., and James C. Thomas. *Pave Aegis Weapon System (AC-130E Gunship).* CHECO Project. Hickam AFB, HI: HQ Pacific Air Forces, 30 July 1973.

Titus, James. "The Battle of Khafji: An Overview and Preliminary Analysis." Paper. Airpower Research Institute, College of Aerospace Doctrine, Research, and Education (CADRE), Air University, September 1996.

United Kingdom, Ministry of Defence. "Kosovo—An Account of the Crisis: The Crisis Unfolds." 14 December 1999. http://www.mod.uk/news/kosovo/account/crisis.htm. Accessed 17 December 1999.

———. "Kosovo—An Account of the Crisis: Historical Background.." 14 December 1999. Accessed 17 December 1999. http://www.mod.uk/news/kosovo/account/historical.htm.

———. "Kosovo—An Account of the Crisis: The Politico-Military Interface." No date. http://www.mod.uk.news/kosovo/account/politico.htm. Accessed 17 December 1999.

———. "Kosovo—An Account of the Crisis: Responding to A Humanitarian Crisis." 15 December 1999. http://www.mod.uk.news/kosovo/account/response.htm. Accessed 17 December 1999.

———. "Kosovo—News, Background Resources." 7 October 1999. http://www.mod.uk.news/kosovo/account/background.htm. Accessed 17 December 1999.

———. "NATO Air Strikes." 14 December 1999. http://www.mod.uk.news/kosovo/account/nato.htm. Accessed 17 December 1999.

United Nations. "Security Council Condemns, 'In Strongest Terms,' Terror Attacks on United States." 12 September 2001. http://www.un.org/News/Press/docs/2001/SC7143.doc.htm.

———. "Security Council Resolution 687." 8 April 1991. http://www.fas.org/news/un/iraq/sres/sres0687.htm.

———. "Security Council Resolution 1244 (1999) on Situation Relating to Kosovo." 4011th meeting. 10 June 1999. http://www.un.org/ga/search/view_doc.asp?symbol=S/RES/1244(1999).

US Air Force. "AC-130H/U." Fact sheet, 20 November 2012. http://www.af.mil/information/factsheets/factsheet.asp?id=71.

———. *Air Force Basic Doctrine Manual.* AFDD-1. September 1997.

———. "Background Information: Gunships." Information Sheet No. 13, 1968.
———. "Gunships." Pamphlet 68-14. In Aeronautical Systems Division, Annual History, 1965, Vol. 1A. (unclassified pages used.)
———. "'Gunships' and 'Dragonships' Credited to Reservist." *Air Force Times,* 16 April 1969.
———. "Modification Requirement for C-47 Aircraft, M.R. 1806 (FS-1729/C-47)." Report, 16 June 1967.
———. *Reaching Globally, Reaching Powerfully: The United States Air Force in the Gulf War.* Report, September 1991. http://www.globalsecurity.org/military/library/report/1991/desstorm.htm.
———. *Releasable Data on USAF Aerospace Craft.* Air Force Publication (AFP) 190-2-1, 1 June 1960.
———. *US Air Force Gunships.* Background Information, Pamphlet 68-13. Washington, DC: Government Printing Office, 1968.
———, Aeronautical Systems Division. Annual History, 1965, Vol. 1A (Unclassified pages used.).
———, Aeronautical Systems Division (ASD). "Gunship Program Office." History, 1 January-31 December 1970; 1 June-31 December 1971. Air Force Historical Research Agency, Maxwell AFB, AL.
———, ASD. "Gunship II Project." 1 July-31 December 1968; 1 January-June 1969, Vol. 1. Air Force Historical Research Agency, Maxwell AFB, AL.
———, ASD, Office of Public Information. "Presentation at Washington, DC." Press Release 70-244, 17 September 1970.
———, Airlift Center. Quarterly Reports, 1 March-30 June 1991. File K417.0734-10, IRIS no. 00888202. Air Force Historical Research Agency, Maxwell AFB, AL, 1992.
———, Air Staff. "Gunship Aircraft." Working Paper, 5 January 1968.
———, Air University. *A Chronology of Important Airpower Events in Southeast Asia, 1950-1968.* Corona Harvest Study. Maxwell AFB, Alabama: Air University, Aerospace Studies Institute, 1 May 1969.
———, Directorate of Operations, Requirements, and Development Plans. Semiannual Histories, 1 July-31 December 1967; 1 January-30 June 1968; 1 July-31 December 1968; 1 January-30 June 1969; 1 January-30 June 1970; 1 January-30 June 1971. Air Force Historical Research Agency, Maxwell AFB, AL.
———, Historic Research Agency, Research Division, Organizational History Branch. "14th Flying Training Wing." http:afhra.maxwell.af.mil/wwwroot/rso/wings_groups_pages/0014ftw.php. Accessed on 29 July 1999.
———, Institute of Technology. "Project Corona Harvest Logistics Background Digest." Report, 1965. Air Force Historical Research Agency, Maxwell AFB, AL.
———, News Service. "1970 Mackay Trophy Award citation." Press Release 7-6-71-447, 6 July 1971.
———, Pacific Air Forces. "Air Operations Summary, April, May, and June 1972." Southeast Asia Report, File K717.3063, Air Force Historical Research Agency.
———, Pacific Air Forces. Annual History, Vol. 1. 1 July 1971-30 June 1972. Air Force Historical Research Agency, Maxwell AFB, AL.

———, Pacific Air Forces. *Linebacker II Air Force Bombing Survey.* Hickam AFB, HI: HQ Pacific Air Forces, 1973.

———, Pacific Air Forces. "North Vietnamese Current Assessment." Vol. 7 in "US Air Force Operations in Defense of RVN." CHECO Project. HQ Pacific Air Forces, Hickam AFB, HI, 1 June 1972. File K717.03-219, Document Collection, Air Force Historical Research Agency.

———, Pacific Air Forces. *United States Air Force Operations in Laos: 1 Jan 70–30 Jun 71.* Corona Harvest Project. Maxwell AFB, AL: Air University, 1971.

———, Pacific Air Forces. *USAF Air Operations against NVN, 1 Jul 71–30 Jun 72.* Corona Harvest Project. Maxwell AFB, AL: Air University, 1973.

———, Pacific Air Forces. *US Air Operations against NVN, 1 July–30 June 1972.* CHECO Project. Hickam AFB, HI: HQ, Pacific Air Forces, 1973.

———, Pacific Air Forces, Maintenance Division, Aircraft Testing Unit. PACAF Capability Study (DPL/TSC 65-240), 12 March 1965.

———, Pacific Air Forces, Office of History. Annual Histories, Narrative and Document Vols., 1 July 1971–30 June 1972, Hickam AFB, HI.

———, Public Affairs and Office of History. "AC-130H/U Gunships." Fact sheet, January 2009. http://www.af.mil/information/factsheets/factsheet.asp?id=71.

———, RDQPM. "Modification Requirement for C-130E Aircraft," MR no. 2272 (FS-2572/C-130E). Paper (S, declassified), 6 January 1971.

———, Retiree Service. "Airmen MIA from the Vietnam War are Identified." News Release no. 05-07-08, 7 May 2008.

———, Seventh Air Force. "Commando Hunt VII, June 1972." Saigon, RVN.

———, Seventh Air Force. "Commando Hunt VII." CHECO Project. June 1972. Air Force Historical Research Agency, Maxwell AFB, AL.

———, Seventh Air Force, Office of History. Semi-Annual and Annual Histories and Chronology, Narrative and Document Vols., July–December 1965; January–June 1966; 1 July–31 December 1967; 1 January–30 June 1968; 1 July 1971–30 June 1972. Saigon, RVN. Air Force Historical Research Agency, Maxwell AFB, AL.

———, Seventh Air Force, Office of History. "7AF History of Linebacker Operations, 10 May–23 October 1972." File K740.04-24, Air Force Historical Research Agency, Maxwell AFB, Alabama, 1973.

———, Seventh Air Force, Office of History. "Commando Hunt V," Saigon, RVN, May 1971. Air Force Historical Research Agency, Maxwell AFB, Alabama.

———, Seventh Air Force, Office of History. "Commando Hunt VII," Saigon, RVN, June 1971. Air Force Historical Research Agency, Maxwell AFB, AL.

———, Special Air Warfare Center (SAWC). History, 1 January–30 June 1968.

———, Special Operations Command, Office of History. *AC-130U Presentation Ceremony.* Hurlburt Field, FL, 14 November 1994.

———, Special Operations Command, Public Affairs Office. "AC-130." Fact sheet, Hurlburt Field, FL, October 2007.

———, Special Operations Command, Public Affairs Office. "AC-130U Spectre Gunship." Fact sheet, 1995.

———, Strategic Air Command, Office of History. "Activity Input to Project Corona

Harvest, ARC LIGHT Operations, 1 January 1965–31 March 1968." 3 vols. Offutt AFB, NE: SAC/HO, 1970.

———, Strategic Air Command, Office of History. *Chronology of SAC Participation in Linebacker II.* Offutt AFB, NE: SAC/HO, 12 August 1973.

———, Strategic Air Command, Office of History. Semi-Annual and Annual Histories, Narrative Vols., January–June 1964; January–June 1965; July–December 1965 (Vol. 2); January–June 1966; January–June 1967; June–December 1967; 1 July 1971–30 June 1972. Offutt AFB, NE.

———, Systems Command. "Gunship II Program Management: A Study of Its Management Success." AFSC study, no date.

———, Tactical Air Command. History. July 1969–June 1970, Vol. 1, Narrative. Air Force Historical Research Agency, Maxwell AFB, AL, and Air Combat Command, History Office, Langley AFB, VA.

US Army, Official Records. "Attack on the 507th Maintenance Company." 17 July 2003. http://www.webcitation.org/5iSuYuP2L.

US Central Intelligence Agency. *The World Fact Book, 1999.* New York: Brassey's, 1999.

US Congress. "Iraq Liberation Act of 1998 (Enrolled as Agreed To or Passed by Both House and Senate)." June 1998, revised online 25 May 2006. http://thomas.loc.gov/cgi-bin/query/z?c105:H.R.4655.ENR:.

———, House, Committee on Armed Services. "The Invasion of Panama: How Many Innocent Bystanders Perished?" Report, 102nd Cong., 2nd sess, 4:19. Washington, DC: Government Printing Office, 1992.

US Department of Defense. "Operation Allied Force." Defense Link, DOD, 21 June 1999. http://www.defenselink.mil/specials/kosovo/.

———. "The Operation Desert Shield/Desert Storm Timeline." News, American Forces Press Service, 8 August 2000. http://www.defenselink.mil/news/newsarticle.aspx?id=45404.

———, Global Special Operations, Joint Chiefs of Staff, Special Operations Forces. "Reference Manual," chap. 5, "US Air Force Special Operations Forces: Air Force Special Operations Command (AFSOC)." 2009. http://www.fas.org/irp/agency/dod/socom/sof-ref-2-1/SOFREF_Ch5.htm.

———, Office of the Secretary of Defense. "Carrier Battle Group Deployments in Support of NATO." News release 144-99, 3 April 1999. http://www.defense.gov/releases/release.aspx?releaseid=2029.

US European Command. "Operation Allied Force." 14 December 1999. http://www.eucom.mil/operations/af/. Accessed 17 December 1999.

US Pacific Command, Office of History. "Command History, 1967," Vol. 2.

US Senate. *DOD Appropriations for FY75: Hearings before a Subcommittee of the Committee on Appropriations.* 93rd Cong., 2nd sess., 1974, Part 1.

Warner Robins Air Logistics Center, Office of History. *Time Capsule: A Chronology of the Role of the Warner Robins Air Logistics Center and Robins AFB, Georgia, in World History, 1937–1997.* Robins AFB, GA: WR-ALC, HO, 1998.

Warner Robins Air Materiel Area, Information Office. "Col. Hahn Passes Praise to WRAMA Team." News Release 65-12-1778, 7 December 1965.

———. “Gen. Gideon Accepts AC-119G Gunship Aircraft.” News release, 21 May 1968.

———. “Gooney Bird Becomes a Dragon in Mechanical Metamorphosis Process.” News Release 65-12-1777, 6 December 1965.

———. History, 1 July 1970–30 June 1971. Part IV, “WRAMA’s Weapon Systems: The AC-130E Aircraft Gunship Project PAVE SPECTRE, 1970–1971,” Vol. 1. Historical Study no. 25, HO RCS HAF D-48, January 1972. (S, declassified.)

———. History, 1 July 1969–30 June 1970. Part V, “WRAMA’s Weapon Systems: The C-130 Hercules (Logistical Support), 1958–1969.” Historical Study no. 20, RCS HAF D-48, October 1970.

———. “Modules for New Gunships Bought from General Electric.” News Release 68-5-524, 20 May 1968.

Westenhoff, Charles M. *Military Air Power: The Cadre Digest of Air Power Opinions and Thoughts.* Maxwell AFB, AL: Air University Press, 1990.

Wolk, Herman S. *Air Force Plans, Policies, Research, and Design for South Asia, 1965–1967.* Washington, DC: Office of Air Force History, June 1969.

Wolverton, Maj. James; Richard E. Willes; and Lt. Col. Bradford W. Parkinson. “The Genesis and Development of Gunship II.” Report. ASD/US Air Force Academy, no date.

Y’Blood, Thomas. “From the Deserts to the Mountains.” Chap. 24 in *Winged Shield, Winged Sword: A History of the United States Air Force,* vol. 2, *1950–1997.* Ed. Bernard Nalty. Bolling AFB, DC: Air Force Museum and History Program, 1997.

———. “Peace Is Not Always Peaceful.” Chap. 23 in *Winged Shield, Winged Sword: A History of the United States Air Force,* vol. 2, *1950–1997.* Ed. Bernard Nalty. Bolling AFB, DC: Air Force Museum and History Program, 1997.

Zimmerman, Lt. Col. Robert G. Oral history interview with Lt. Col. Stephen J. Opitz, 18 July 1975. IRIS Document 01016327, Document K239.0512-846. Air University, Historic Research Center, Maxwell AFB, AL.

Secondary Sources

BOOKS, THESES, AND DISSERTATIONS

Adcock, Al. *C-123 Provider in Action.* Carrollton, TX: Squadron Signals Publishers, 1985.

Atkinson, Rick. *Crusade: The Untold Story of the Persian Gulf War.* Boston: Houghton, Mifflin, 1993.

Ballard, John R. *Fighting for Fallujah: A New Dawn for Iraq.* Westport, CT: Praeger, 2006.

Bennett, Lance W., and David L. Paletz, eds. *Taken by Storm: The Media, Public Opinion, and US Foreign Policy in the Gulf War.* Chicago: University of Chicago Press, 1994.

Bergen, Peter. *The Osama bin Laden I Know.* New York: Free Press, 2006.

Boettcher, Thomas D. *Vietnam: The Valor and the Sorrow.* Boston: Little, Brown, 1985.

Bowden, Mark. *Black Hawk Down: A Story of Modern War.* New York: Atlantic Monthly Press, 1999.

Boyne, Col. Walter J. *Operation Iraqi Freedom: What Went Right, What Went Wrong, and Why.* New York: Forge Books, 2003.

Braestrup, Peter. *Big Story!* 2 vols. Boulder. CO: Westview Press, 1977, and New Haven, CT: Yale University Press, 1983.

Brigham, Robert K. *Is Iraq Another Vietnam?* New York: Public Affairs, 2008.

Bright, Charles D., ed. *Historical Dictionary of the US Air Force.* Westport, CT: Greenwood Publishing, 1992.

Brush, Peter. "The Battle of Khe Sanh." In *The Tet Offensive.* Ed. Marc Gilbert and William Head. Westport, CT: Praeger, 1996.

Bui Diem. "My Reflections of the Tet Offensive." In *The Tet Offensive.* Ed. William P. Head and Marc Gilbert. Westport, CT: Praeger, 1996.

———. "Reflections on the Vietnam War: The Views of a Vietnamese on Vietnamese-American Misconceptions." *Looking Back on the Vietnam War: A 1990s Perspective on the Decisions, Combat, and Legacies.* Ed. William Head and Lawrence E. Grinter. Westport, CT: Praeger Press, 1993.

——— and David Chanoff. *In the Jaws of History.* Boston: Houghton Mifflin, 1987.

Bui Tin. *Memoirs,* Vol. 1, *Hoa xuyen tuyet* [Snow Drops]. English ed. Irvine, CA: Nhan Quyen Editeur, 1991.

———. *Memoirs,* Vol. 2, *Mat that* [The Real Face]. Irvine, CA: Saigon Press, 1993.

Burke, Jason. *Al-Qaeda: The True Story of Radical Islam.* London and New York: I. B. Tauris, 2004.

Buzzanco, Robert. "The Myth of Tet: American Failure and the Politics of War." In *The Tet Offensive.* Ed. Marc Gilbert and William Head. Westport, CT: Praeger, 1996.

Cable, Larry. *Conflicts of Myths: The Development of American Counterinsurgency Doctrine and the Vietnam War.* New York: New York University Press, 1986.

———. "Don't Bother Me With the Facts; I've Made Up My Mind: The Tet Offensive in the Context of Intelligence and US Strategy." In *The Tet Offensive.* Ed. Marc Gilbert and William Head. Westport, CT: Praeger, 1996.

———. "Everything Is Perfect and Getting Better: The Myths and Measures of the American Ground War in Indochina, 1965–1968." In *Looking Back on the Vietnam War: A 1990s Perspective on the Decisions, Combat, and Legacies.* Ed. William Head and Lawrence E. Grinter. Westport, CT: Praeger, 1993.

———. "Playing in the Sandbox: Doctrine, Combat, and Outcome on the Ground." In *The Eagle in the Desert: Looking Back on US Involvement in the Persian Gulf War.* Ed. William P. Head and Earl H. Tilford Jr. Westport, CT: Praeger, 1996.

———. *Unholy Grail: The United States and the Wars in Vietnam, 1965–1968.* London: Routledge, 1991.

Cerf, Christopher, and Micah L. Sifry, eds. *The Iraq War Reader: History, Documents, Opinions.* New York: Touchstone Books, 2003.

Clarke, Richard A. *Against All Enemies.* New York: Simon and Schuster, 2004.

Clodfelter, Mark. *The Limits of Air Power: The American Bombing Campaign of North Vietnam.* New York: The Free Press, 1989.

———. "Nixon and the Air Weapon." In *An American Dilemma: Vietnam, 1964–1973.* Ed. Dennis E. Showalter and John G. Albert. Chicago: Imprint Publishers, 1993.

Conetta, Carl. *The Wages of War: Iraqi Combatant and Noncombatant Fatalities in the 2003 Conflict.* Project on Defense Alternatives Special Monograph no. 8. Cambridge, MA: Commonwealth Institute, 20 October 2003. http://www.comw.org/pda/fulltext/0310rm8.pdf.

Cooling, Benjamin Franklin, ed. *Case Studies in the Development of Close Air Support.* Washington, DC: Office of Air Force History, 1990.

Cordesman, Anthony H. *The Iraq War: Strategy, Tactics, and Military Lessons.* Westport, CT: Praeger, 2003.

Corgan, Michael T. "Clausewitz's 'On War' and the Gulf War." In *The Eagle in the Desert: Looking Back on US Involvement in the Persian Gulf War.* Ed. William P. Head and Earl H. Tilford Jr. Westport, CT: Praeger, 1996.

Corum, James S., and Wray R. Johnson. *Airpower in Small Wars: Fighting Insurgents and Terrorists.* Lawrence: University Press of Kansas, 2003.

Davidson, Phillip B. *Vietnam at War: The History, 1946–1975.* Novato, CA: Presidio Press, 1988.

Davis, Larry. *Gunships: A Pictorial History of Spooky.* Carrollton, TX: Squadron Signals Publishers, 1982.

DeFronzio, James. *The Iraq War: Origins and Consequences.* Boulder, CO: Westview Press, 2009.

Deptula, Lt. Gen. David A. "Parallel Warfare: What Is It? Where Did It Come From?" In *The Eagle in the Desert: Looking Back on US Involvement in the Persian Gulf War.* Ed. William P. Head and Earl H. Tilford Jr. Westport, CT: Praeger, 1996.

Donnelly, Thomas. *Operation Iraqi Freedom: A Strategic Assessment.* Washington, DC: AEI Press, 2004.

———; Margaret Roth; and Cobb Baker. *Operation Just Cause: The Storming of Panama.* New York: Lexington Books, 1991.

Doran, Michael Scott. *Understanding the War on Terror.* New York: Norton, 2005.

Douhet, Giulio. *The Command of the Air.* Trans. by Dino Ferrari. Maxwell AFB, AL: Air University Press, 1983.

Fallows, James. *Blind into Baghdad: America's War in Iraq.* New York: Vintage/Random House, 2006.

Fawn, Rick, and Raymond A. Hinnebusch, eds. *The Iraq War: Causes and Consequences.* Colorado Springs, CO: Lynne Rienner, 2006.

Flanagan, Edward M., Jr. *Battle for Panama: Inside Operation Just Cause.* Washington, DC: Brassey's US, 1993.

FitzGerald, Frances. *Fire in the Lake.* New York: Vintage Books, 1972.

Fletcher, Elton "Larry." *Shadows of Saigon: Air Commandos in Southeast Asia.* Philadelphia: Xlibris Corporation, 2001.

Foulk, Vincent L. *Battle of Fallujah: Occupation, Resistance, and Stalemate in the War in Iraq.* Jefferson, NC: McFarland & Company, 2006.

Frankum, Ronald. *Like Rolling Thunder: The Air War in Vietnam, 1964–1975.* Lanham, MD: Rowan & Littlefield Press, 2005.

Friedman, Lawrence, and Efraim Karsh. *The Gulf Conflict, 1990–1991: Diplomacy and War in the New World Order.* Princeton, NJ: Princeton University Press, 1993.

Gibson, J. William. *The Perfect War: Technowar in Vietnam.* Boston: Atlantic Monthly Press, 1986.

Gilbert, Marc Jason, and William Head, eds. *The Tet Offensive.* Westport, CT: Praeger, 1996.

Gordon, Michael R., and Bernard E. Trainor. *Cobra II: The Inside Story of the Invasion and Occupation of Iraq.* New York: Pantheon Press, 2006.

———. *The General's War: The Inside Story of the Conflict in the Gulf.* Boston: Little, Brown, 1995.

Guilmartin, John P. *A Very Short War: The Mayaguez and the Battle of Koh Tang.* College Station: Texas A&M University Press, 1995.

Gunarathna, Rohan. *Inside Al Qaeda, Global Network of Terror.* Berkeley, CA: Berkeley Books, 2002.

Haas, Col. Michael E. *Apollo's Warriors: US Air Force Special Operations during the Cold War.* Maxwell AFB, AL: Air University Press, 1987.

Hallion, Richard P. *Storm over Iraq: Air Power and the Gulf War.* Washington, DC: Smithsonian Institution Press, 1992.

Hamilton Merritt, Jane. *Tragic Mountains: The Hmong, the Americans, and the Secret Wars for Laos, 1942–1992.* Bloomington: Indiana University Press, 1993.

Hashmi, Sohail. "But Was It Jihad? Islam and the Ethics of the Persian Gulf War," In *The Eagle in the Desert: Looking Back on US Involvement in the Persian Gulf War.* Ed. William P. Head and Earl H. Tilford Jr. Westport, CT: Praeger, 1996.

Head, William P. *Every Inch A Soldier: Augustine Warner Robins and the Building of US Airpower.* College Station: Texas A&M University Press, 1995.

———. "Introduction." In *The Eagle in the Desert: Looking Back on US Involvement in the Persian Gulf War.* Ed. William P. Head and Earl H. Tilford Jr. Westport, CT: Praeger, 1996.

———. *Shadow and Stinger: The Development and Deployment of the AC-119G/K Gunships.* College Station: Texas A&M University Press, 2007.

———. "Vietnam and Its Wars: A Historical Overview of US Involvement." In *Looking Back on the Vietnam War: A 1990s Perspective on the Decisions, Combat, and Legacies.* Ed. William Head and Lawrence E. Grinter. Westport, CT: Praeger Press, 1993.

———. *War from Above the Clouds: B-52 Operations during the Second Indochina War and the Effects of the Air War on Theory and Doctrine.* Maxwell AFB, AL: Air University Press, 2002.

———, and Lawrence Grinter, eds. *Looking Back on the Vietnam War: A 1990s Perspective of Decisions, Combat, and Legacies.* Westport, CT: Greenwood, 1993.

———, and David R. Mets. *Plotting a True Course: Reflections on USAF Strategic Attack Theory and Doctrine: The Post World War II Experience.* Westport, CT: Praeger, 2003.

Herring, George C. *America's Longest War: The United States and Vietnam, 1950–1975.* New York: Wiley and Sons, 1979.

———. "The Johnson Administration's Conduct of Limited War in Vietnam." In *Looking Back on the Vietnam War: A 1990s Perspective on the Decisions, Combat, and Legacies.* Ed. William Head and Lawrence E. Grinter. Westport, CT: Praeger, 1993.

Hersh, Seymour M. *The Price of Power: Kissinger in the Nixon While House.* New York: Summit Books, 1983.

Hobson, Chris. *Vietnam Air Loses: United States Air Force, Navy, and Marine Corps Fixed-Wing Aircraft Losses in Southeast Asia, 1961–1973.* Hinckley, UK: Midland Publishing, 2001.

Horowitz, Susan G. "Indications and Warring Factors." In *Operation Just Cause: The US Intervention in Panama.* Ed. Bruce W. Watson and Peter G. Tsouras. Boulder, CO: Westview Press, 1991.

Houghton, David Patrick. *US Foreign Policy and the Iran Hostage Crisis.* Cambridge: Cambridge University Press, 2001.

"Jason Report." In *The Pentagon Papers: Department of Defense History of Decision Making in Vietnam.* Senator Mike Gravel Edition. Vol. 4. Boston: Beacon Press, 1971.

Jones, Howard. *Crucible of Power: A History of US Foreign Policy since 1897.* New York: Rowman and Littlefield, 2001.

Josephy, Alvin M., Jr. *A History of Flight.* New York: American Heritage Publishers, 1962.

Karnow, Stanley. *Vietnam: A History.* New York: Viking Press, 1983.

Keegan, John. *The Iraq War.* New York: Knopf, 2004.

Kempe, Frederick. *Divorcing the Dictator.* New York: Putnam, 1990.

Kinnard, Douglas. *The War Managers.* Hanover, NH: University of Vermont Press, 1977.

Kissinger, Henry A. *The White House Years.* Boston: Little, Brown, Inc., 1979.

———. *Years of Renewal.* Boston: Little, Brown, 1980.

Kochler, Hans. *The Iraq Crisis and the United Nations: Power Politics vs. the International Rule of Law.* Studies in International Relations 28. Vienna, Austria: International Progress Organization, 2004.

Kolko, Gabriel. *Anatomy of a War: Vietnam, the United States, and the Modern Historical Experience.* New York: Pantheon, 1985.

Korb, Lawrence J. *The Joint Chiefs of Staff: The First Twenty-Five Years.* Bloomington: Indiana University Press, 1976.

Kuehl, Daniel T. "Thunder and Storm: Strategic Air Operations in the Gulf War." In *The Eagle in the Desert: Looking Back on US Involvement in the Persian Gulf War.* Ed. William P. Head and Earl H. Tilford Jr. Westport, CT: Praeger, 1996.

Kutler, Stanley I., ed., *Encyclopedia of the Vietnam War.* New York: Charles Scribner's Sons, 1996.

Lake, John. *Stratofortress Units in Combat, 1955–1973.* Botley, Oxford, UK: Osprey Publishing, 2004.

Lambeth, Benjamin S. *NATO's Air War for Kosovo: A Strategic and Operational Assessment.* New York: Rand Corp, 2001.

———. *The Transformation of American Air Power.* Ithaca, NY: Cornell University Press, 2000.

Lederman, Gordon N. *Reorganizing the Joint Chiefs of Staff: The Goldwater-Nichols Act of 1986.* Westport, CT: Greenwood, 1999.

Leland, John W. "Air Mobility in Operations Desert Shield and Desert Storm: An Assessment." In *The Eagle in the Desert: Looking Back on US Involvement in the Persian Gulf War.* Ed. William P. Head and Earl H. Tilford Jr. Westport, CT: Praeger, 1996.

Lindsey-Poland, John. *Emperors in the Jungle:Tthe Hidden History of the US in Panama.* Durham, NC: Duke University Press, 2003.

Livingston, Gary. *Fallujah With Honor: First Battalion, Eighth Marines' Role in Operation Phantom Fury.* Snead's Ferry, NC: Caisson Press, 2006.

Lowry, Richard S. *Marines in the Garden of Eden.* New York: Berkley Caliber, 2006.

McDermott, Terry. *Perfect Soldiers: The 9/11 Hijackers.* New York: HarperCollins, 2005.

McDonnell, Malcolm. *The Real Story of America's High-Tech Invasion of Panama.* New York: St. Martin's Press, 1991.

Maloney, Sean M. *Enduring the Freedom: A Rogue Historian in Afghanistan.* Washington, DC: Potomac Books, 2005.

Moore, Lt. Gen. Hal, and Joe Galloway. *We Were Soldiers Once . . . and Young.* New York: Random House, 1992.

Morrocco, John. *Rain of Fire: Air War, 1968–1975.* Vol. 10 in *The Vietnam Experience.* Ed. Robert Manning. Boston: Boston Publishing, 1984.

———. *Thunder from Above: Air War, 1941–1968.* Vol. 9 in *The Vietnam Experience.* Ed. Robert Manning. Boston: Boston Publishing, 1984.

Mortensen, Daniel R. *Airpower and Ground Armies.* Maxwell AFB, AL: Air University Press, 1998.

Murray, Williamson, and Robert H. Scales Jr. *The Iraq War: A Military History.* Cambridge, MA: Belknap Press of Harvard University Press, 2005.

Nixon, Richard M. *In the Arena: A Memoir of Victory, Defeat, and Renewal.* New York: Simon & Schuster, 1990.

———. *RN: The Memoirs of Richard Nixon.* 2 vols. New York: Warner Books, 1978.

Ngo Vinh Long. "The Tet Offensive and Its Aftermath." In *The Tet Offensive.* Ed. Marc Gilbert and William Head. Westport, CT: Praeger, 1996.

Oberdorfer, Donald. *Tet!* Garden City, NJ: Doubleday, 1971, 1984.

O'Donnell, Patrick. *We Were One: Shoulder to Shoulder with the Marines Who Took Fallujah.* Cambridge, MA: Da Capo Press, 2006.

Palmer, Bruce, ed., *Grand Strategy for the 1980s.* Washington, DC: American Enterprises Institute for Public Policy Research, 1978.

Papp, Daniel S. "The Gulf War Coalition: The Politics and Economics of a Most Unusual Alliance." In *The Eagle in the Desert: Looking Back on US Involvement in the Persian Gulf War.* Ed. William P. Head and Earl H. Tilford Jr. Westport, CT: Praeger, 1996.

Pastor, Robert A. *Exiting the Whirlpool: US Foreign Policy toward Latin America and the Caribbean.* Boulder, CO: Westview Press, 2001.

Pentagon Papers: Department of Defense History of United States Decision Making in Vietnam. Senator Mike Gravel Edition. 4 vols. Boston: Beacon Press, 1971.

Pike, Douglas. *PAVN: People's Army of North Vietnam.* Novato, CA: Presidio Press, 1986.

———. *Vietcong: The Organization and Techniques of the National Liberation Front of South Vietnam.* Cambridge, MA: MIT Press, 1966, 1985.

Pisor, Robert. *The End of the Line: The Siege of Khe Sanh.* New York: Norton Press, 1982.

Quinn, John T., and Jack Shulimson. "US Marine Operations in the Persian Gulf War, 1990–1991." In *The Eagle in the Desert: Looking Back on US Involvement in the Persian Gulf War.* Ed. William P. Head and Earl H. Tilford Jr. Westport, CT: Praeger, 1996.

Rashid, Ahmed. *Descent into Chaos: The US and the Disaster in Pakistan, Afghanistan, and Central Asia.* Baltimore, MD: Penguin Press, 2009.

Reagan, Ronald. *An American Life: The Autobiography.* New York: Simon and Schuster, 1990.

Rice, Edward E. *Wars of the Third: Conflict in Underdeveloped Countries.* Berkeley, CA: University of California Press, 1988.

Ricks, Thomas E. *Fiasco: The American Military Adventure in Iraq.* Baltimore, MD: Penguin Press, 2006.

———. *The Gamble: General David Petraeus and the American Adventure in Iraq, 2006–2008.* Baltimore, MD: Penguin Press, 2009.

Schechter, Michael G. *United Nations Global Conferences.* London: Routledge, 2005.

Sharp, Adm. U. S. G. *Strategy for Defeat: Vietnam in Retrospect.* San Rafael, CA: Presidio Press, 1978; Reprint, 1986.

Sheehan, Neil; Hedrick Smith; E. W. Kenworthy; and Fox Butterworth. *The Pentagon Papers.* New York: Bantam Books, 1971.

Showalter, Dennis E., and John G. Albert, eds. *An American Dilemma: Vietnam, 1964–1973.* Chicago: Imprint Publishers, 1993.

Smith, R. Harris. *O.S.S.: The Secret History of America's First Central Intelligence Agency.* Berkeley, CA: University of California Press, 1972.

Stebbins, Richard P. *The United States in World Affairs, 1967.* New York: New York University Press, 1968.

Suit, William. "Sustaining the War Machine: US Air Force Logistics Support during the Gulf War." In *The Eagle in the Desert: Looking Back on US Involvement in the Persian Gulf War.* Ed. William P. Head and Earl H. Tilford Jr. Westport, CT: Praeger, 1996.

Summers, Harry G., Jr., *On Strategy: A Critical Analysis of the Vietnam War.* Novato, CA: Presidio Press, 1982; reprint, New York: Dell, 1984.

Suskind, Ron. *The Price of Loyalty: George W. Bush, the White House, and the Education of Paul O'Neill.* New York: Simon and Schuster, 2004.

Swanborough, Gordon, and Peter M. Bower. *United States Military Aircraft since 1909.* New York: Putnam, 1989.

Thatcher, Margaret. *The Downing Street Years.* London: HarperCollins, 1993.

Thayer, Thomas C. *War without Fronts: The American Experience in Vietnam.* Boulder, CO: Westview, 1985.

Tilford, Earl H., Jr. "Bombing Our Way Back Home: The Commando Hunt and Menu Campaigns of 1969–1973." In *Looking Back on the Vietnam War: A 1990s Perspective on the Decisions, Combat, and Legacies.* Ed. William P. Head and Lawrence Grinter. Westport, CT: Praeger, 1993.

———. *Crosswinds: The Air Force's Setup in Vietnam.* College Station: Texas A&M University Press, 1993.

Tran Van Tra. *Viet Nam: History Bulwark B-2 Theatre.* Vol. 5 in *Concluding the 30-Year War.* Ho Chi Minh City: Van Nghe Publishing House, 1983. English trans. reprinted Arlington, Virginia: Joint Publications Research Service, 1983.

Truong Nhu Tang. *A Vietcong Memoir: An Inside Account of the Vietnam War and Its Aftermath.* New York: Harcourt, Brace, Jovanovich, 1985.

Tucker, Mike. *Among Warriors in Iraq: True Grit, Special Ops, and Raiding in Mosul and Fallujah.* Greenwich, CT: Lyons Press, 2006.

Watson, Bruce W., and Peter G. Tsouras, eds. *Operation Just Cause: The US Intervention in Panama.* Boulder, CO: Westview Press, 1991.

West, Bing. *No True Glory: A Frontline Account of the Battle for Fallujah.* New York: Bantam Books, 2005.

Westmoreland, Gen. William C. *A Soldier Reports.* Garden City, NJ: Doubleday & Co., 1976.

Wetterhahn, Ralph. *The Last Battle: The Mayaguez Incident and the End of the Vietnam War.* New York: Plume Publishers (Penguin Group), 2002.

Wright, Evan. *Generation Kill.* New York: Berkley Publishing Group, 2004.

Wright, Lawrence. *The Looming Tower: Al-Qaeda and the Road to 9/11.* New York: Alfred P. Knopf, 2006.

Zucchino, David. *Thunder Run: The Armored Strike to Capture Baghdad.* New York: Atlantic Monthly Press, 2004.

ARTICLES AND OTHER SECONDARY DOCUMENTS

ABC News. "B-2 Sees First Combat." ABC News, 24 March 1999. http://web.archive.org/web/19990508053951/http://abcnews.go.com/sections/world/DailyNews/bomber990324.html. Accessed 17 December 1999.

———. "Newsmakers, Slobodan Milosevic." ABC News, 15 December 1999. http://www.abcnews.go.com/reference/bios/Milosevic.htm. Accessed 17 December 1999.

———. "Osama Bin Laden Operation Ended with Coded Message, 'Geronimo-E KIA.'" 2 May 2011. http://abcnews.go.com/Politics/osama-bin-laden-operation-code-geronimo/story?id=13507836#.UeVqQ6DD-lI.

AC-119 Association. "Welcome Page: Stories." 2 June 2004. http://www.ac-119gunships.com.

"AC-119 Gunship Training." *Reservist Magazine,* May 1968.

"AC-119G Gunship Accepted." *Robins RevUp,* 30 May 1968.

"AC-130U Adjustment Causes Slip in Rockwell Aerospace Earnings (Costs of AC-130U Gunship Program Affect First Quarter 1994 Earnings)." *Defense Daily,* 19 January 1994. http://www.highbeam.com/doc/1G1-14737866.html.

Aceto, Guy. "Air Power in Allied Force." *Air Force Magazine* 82, no. 6 (June 1999).

"AFLC Lets Contract for 'Dragon Ship.'" *Robins RevUp,* 11 January 1968.

Air-Attack.com. "US Airstrike in Somalia Targets al-Qaida Suspect." Voice of America, 3 March 2008. http://www.air-attack.com/news/article/3063/03-03-2008-US-Airstrike-in-Somalia-Targets-al-Qaida-Suspect.html.

Allison, Capt. Mae-Li. "16 SOS Transfers Flag to Cannon." Air Force Special Operations Command, 25 June 2009. http://www.afsoc.af.mil/news/story.asp?id=123155363.

American Special Ops.com. "Air Force Special Operations: Special Operations Aircraft." http://www.americanspecialops.com/aircraft/.

———. Photographs by TSgt. Lee Schading. "AC-130 Spectre/Spooky II Gunship." US Special Operations, 2009. http://www.americanspecialops.com/usaf-special-operations/aircraft/ac-130/.

Apple, Robert W., Jr. "Conflict in the Balkans: News Analysis; With Decision to Attack, a Fresh Set of US Goals." *New York Times,* 25 March 1999.

———. "Conflict In the Balkans: News Analysis; Bombs Fall, Goal Unmet." *New York Times,* 29 March 1999.

———. "Crisis in the Balkans: The Summit; Kosovo Overshadows Subdued NATO Event." *New York Times,* 24 April 1999.

———. "Crisis in the Balkans: Washington Memo; Clinton Tailors Legacy but Kosovo Isn't Fabric." *New York Times,* 10 June 1999.

Arkin, William M. "The Difference Was in the Details." *Washington Post,* 17 January 1999.

———. "Inside the Air Force, Officers Are Frustrated About the Air War." *Washington Post,* 25 April 1999.

Associated Press (AP). "Crisis in Kosovo: Key Events in Kosovo Conflict." *USA Today,* 25 March 1999. http://www.usatoday.com/news/index/kosovo/kos0002.htm.

———. "Text of Bush Speech." News release, 1 May 2003. http://www.cbsnews.com/stories/2003/05/01/iraq/main551946.shtml.

Borken, Maj. Bob. "The Last Flight of Shadow 78." AC-119 Gunship Association. http://www.ac-119gunships.com/stories/story10.htm. Accessed on 2 June 2004.

Baker, Russell. "Observer: Is This Justice Necessary?" *New York Times,* 3 January 1990.

Balci, Ali, and Murat Yesiltas. "Turkey's New Middle East Policy: The Case of the Meeting of the Foreign Ministers of Iraq's Neighboring Countries." *Journal of South Asian and Middle Eastern Studies* 29, no. 4 (Summer 2006).

Balz, Dan. "US Consensus Grows to Send in Ground Troops." *Washington Post,* 6 April 1999.

Barry, John, and Evan Thomas. "The Kosovo Cover-Up." *Newsweek,* 15 May 2000.

Bash, Dana. "White House Pressed on 'Mission Accomplished' Sign." CNN News. http://www.cnn.com/2003/ALLPOLITICS/10/28/mission.accomplished/.

"Birth of the 'Spectre' Gunship." Spectre Association, Home of the AC-130 Spectre Gunships. http://www.spectre-association.org/historySpectre.htm.

Block, Robert. "In Belgrade, Hardship Grows under Sustained Air Assaults." *Wall Street Journal,* 12 May 1999.

Boeing. "Boeing, Rockwell Aerospace and Defense Units to Merge." News release, 5 December 1996.

Bowman, Tom N. "Powerful Gunships Prowl Iraq, and Limits Show." NPR Website, 5 August 2009. http://www.npr.org/templates/story/story.php?storyId=7608428.

Boyne, Walter J. "The Awesome Power of the Air Force Gunships." *Air Force Magazine* 82, no. 4. April 1999.

———. "The Easter Halt." *Air Force Magazine* (online) 81, no. 9 (September 1998). http://www.afa.org/magazine/Sept1998/0998easter.asp.

———. "Linebacker II: A Look Back." *Air Force Magazine* 80, no. 11 (November 1997).

British Broadcasting Company (BBC) News. "The Hamburg Connection." 19 August 2005. http://news.bbc.co.uk/2/hi/europe/2349195.stm.

———. "Infinite Justice, Out—Enduring Freedom, In." 25 September 2001. http://news.bbc.co.uk/2/hi/americas/1563722.stm.

———. "Iraq's Most Wanted." 11 November 2005. http://news.bbc.co.uk/2/hi/middle_east/2939125.stm.

———. "Transcript: Bin Laden Video Excerpts." 27 December 2001. http://news.bbc.co.uk/2/hi/middle_east/1729882.stm.

Buchwald, Arthur. Editorial. *Washington Post,* 6 February 1968.

Burgess, Mark. "Iraqi Military Effectiveness." Leatherneck.com, 12 November 2002. http://www.leatherneck.com/forums/showthread.php?3710-Iraqi-military-effectiveness.

Burns, Robert. "US Launches New Airstrike in Somalia." Associated Press, 24 January 2007. http://pantagraph.com/news/article_5ebbd73d-9ed6-5f12-85c6-777952462beb.html.

Cable, Larry. "Reinventing the Round Wheel: Insurgency, Counterinsurgency, and Peacekeeping in the Post Cold War." *Small Wars and Insurgencies,* April 1990.

Cable News Network (CNN). "Clinton Apologizes to China over Embassy Bombing." 10 May 1999. http://www.cnn.com/WORLD/europe/9905/10/kosovo.china.02/.

———. "CNN In-depth; Kosovo Crisis." 15 December 1999. http://www.cnn.com/news/kosovo/figures.html. Accessed 17 December 1999.

———. "Coalition Planes Hit Iraq Sites in No-Fly Zone." 28 November 2002. http://archives.cnn.com/2002/WORLD/meast/11/28/sproject.irq.nofly.zone/.

———. "The Iraq War: A Nine-Year Timeline." 21 October 2011. http://news.blogs.cnn.com/2011/10/21/the-iraq-war-a-nine-year-timeline/?iref=storysearch.

———. "New York: 9/11 toxins caused death." 24 May 2007. http://www.cnn.com/2007/US/05/24/wtc.dust/index.html. Accessed 21 May 2009.

———. "O'Neill: 'Frenzy' Distorted War Plans Account." 14 January 2004. http://edition.cnn.com/2004/ALLPOLITICS/01/13/oneill.bush/.

———. "Pentagon: Saddam's Sons Killed in Raid." 22 July 2003. http://www.cnn.com/2003/WORLD/meast/07/22/sprj.irq.sons/.

———. "US and Coalition Casualties." 14 May 2010. http://www.cnn.com/SPECIALS/2004/oef.casualties/index.html.

———. "US has 100,000 Troops in Kuwait." 18 February 2003. http://www.cnn.com/2003/WORLD/meast/02/18/sprj.irq.deployment/index.html.

Canadian Broadcasting Company (CBC) News. "Bin Laden Claims Responsibility for 9/11." 29 October 2004. http://www.cbc.ca/world/story/2004/10/29/binladen_message041029.html.

Capaccio, Tony. "JSTARS Led to Most Lethal Attacks on Serbs." *Defense Weekly,* 6 July 1999.

Carter, Linwood B. "Iraq: Summary of US Forces." *CRS Report to Congress,* 28 November 2005. Order Code 31763. http://www.fas.org/sgp/crs/mideast/RL31763.pdf.

Carden, Sfc. Michael J. "Fallen Airmen Laid to Rest after 38 Years." Air Force Retiree News Service, Release no. 06-07-10, 18 June 2010.

Casey, William R. "AC-119, USAF's Flying Battleship." *Air Force/Space Digest,* February 1970.

Castellon, David. "Missions in Afghanistan Took EC-130Hs over Threat Areas." *Air Force Times* 62 (3 June 2002).

Icasualties.org. "Operation Iraqi Freedom." 2009. http://icasualties.org/Iraq/index.aspx.

———. "Operation Enduring Freedom." 19 August 2009. http://icasualties.org/OEF/.

Chain, Gen. John T., Jr., Commander-in-Chief, Pacific Air Force. "Strategic Bombers Conventional Warfare." *Strategic Review,* Spring 1988.

Chipman, Don. "Air Power and the Battle for Mazare-e Sharif." *Air Power History* 50 (Spring 2003).

Cohen, William S. "Secretary Cohen's Press Conference at NATO Headquarters." 7 April 1999. http://www.nyu.edu/globalbeat/balkan/Cohen04079999.html.

———, and Gen. Henry H. Shelton. "Joint Statement on the Kosovo After Action Review." Press release, 14 October 1999. http://www.nyu.edu/globalbeat/balkan/Cohen10149999.html.

Columbia Broadcasting System (CBS) News. "Saddam's Last Line of Defense." 11 February 2009. http://www.cbsnews.com/2100-500257_162-546241.html.

———. "War Casualties Pass 9/11 Death Toll." 22 September 2006. http://www.cbsnews.com/2100-224_162-2035427.html.

"Combat in Panama, Operation Just Cause." *Los Angeles Times*, 21 December 1989.

Comer, Maj. Gen. Richard. "AFSOC 2009–2010: A Steady Vision Guiding Many Changes." Defense Media Network, 3 August 2010. http://www.defensemedianetwork.com/stories/afsoc-2009-2010-a-steady-vision-guiding-many-changes/.

Conetta, Carl. "Operation Enduring Freedom: Why a Higher Rate of Civilian Bombing Casualties." Project on Defense Alternatives, Briefing Report no. 11, 31 March 2002. http://www.comw.org/pda/0201oef.html.

"Iraqi Health Minister Claims Insurgents Have Killed 150,000." Confederate Yankee.com, March 2007. http://confederateyankee.mu.nu/archives/204499.php.

"Confrontation in the Gulf: The Oilfield Lying Below the Iraq-Kuwait Dispute." *New York Times*, 23 September 1990.

Corbett, CMSgt. Craig. "The Shoot Down of Stinger 41: A Survivor's Story." AC-119 Gunships.com, 2 June 2004. http://www.ac-119gunships.com/stories/story3.htm.

Cosgrove-Mather, Bootie. "Poll: Talk First, Fight Later." CBS News, 24 January 2003. http://www.cbsnews.com/stories/2003/01/23/opinion/polls/main537739.shtml.

Curtis, Bruce. "The Wimp Factor." *American Heritage* 40, no. 7 (November 1989). http://www.americanheritage.com/content/wimp-factor.

Damiani, Lou. "Rockwell Delivers AC-130U Gunship to Air Force Special Operations Command." News release, Rockwell International, North American Modification Division Director, 1 July 1994.

———. "Rockwell Delivers AC-130U Gunship to Air Force Special Operations Command." News report, Rockwell International, North American Modification Division Director, 5 July 1994.

Davis, Anthony. "How the Afghan War was Won." *Jane's Intelligence Review* 14 (February 2002).

Day, John. "After Afghanistan: The Role of Air Power." *Royal United Services Institute Journal* 147 (December 2002).

"Deadly AC-130 Gunships Returning to Iraq." Air-Attack.com, 4 March 2006. http://air-attack.com/news/article/1204/03-04-2006-Deadly-AC-130-Gunships-Returning-to-Iraq.html.

Deagel. "Boeing Receives F2AST Contract from US Air Force." 2 February 2009. http://www.deagel.com/news/Boeing-Receives-F2AST-Contract-From-US-Air-Force_n000005637.aspx.

———. "Boeing Starts AC-130U Gunship Flight Testing." 28 April 2007. http://www.deagel.com/news/Boeing-Starts-AC-130U-Gunship-Flight-testing_n000001901.aspx.

———. "C-130H Hercules." 3 July 2013. http://www.deagel.com/Military-Transport-Aircraft/C-130H-Hercules_a000526001.aspx.

———. "Spooky Gunship Armed with MK 44 Bushmaster Cannons." Originally released on 1 February 2007 by AFNEWS, Hurlburt Field, AFSOC/PA, as "Spooky Gunship Armed with New Cannons." http://www.deagel.com/news/Spooky-Gunship-Armed-with-MK-44-Bushmaster-Cannons_n000001418.aspx.

———. "Viper Strike Smart Munitions Tested on AC-130 Gunship." 31 October 2005. http://www.deagel.com/news/Viper-Strike-Smart-Munition-Tested-on-AC-130-Gunship_n000000565.aspx.

Dixie Station. "The Air War In Vietnam." *Flying Magazine,* November 1966.

Doggett, Tom. "Cohen Fears 100,000 Kosovo Men Killed by Serbs." *Washington Post,* 16 May 1999.

Drozdiak, William. "Yugoslav Troops Devastated by Attack." *Washington Post,* 9 June 1999.

Eichler, Marc. "AC-130 Spectre/Spooky." Milavia, 20 May 2006. http://www.milavia.net/aircraft/ac-130/ac-130_ext.htm.

Erlanger, Steven. "Crisis in the Balkans: Economists Find Bombing Cuts Yugoslav's Production in Half." *New York Times,* 30 April 1999.

———. "Early Count Hints at Fewer Kosovo Deaths." *New York Times,* 11 November 1999.

Fairchild-Hiller. "First Production AC-119G Rolls Out." News release, 21 May 1968.

Federation of American Scientists. "AC-130H Spectre, AC-130U Spooky." http://www.fas.org/programs/ssp/man/uswpns/air/attack/ac130.html. 5 August 2009.

"50 Kilos of Cocaine Was Tamales." *Washington Post,* 23 January 1990.

"The First Shot." *Airman Magazine,* July 2003.

"First Successful Test Flight of AC-130U." *Rockwell News, North American Edition* 19, no. 1 (18 January 1991).

Fletcher, Larry. "Active Duty Chronology of 71SOS." Attachment to e-mail, Lee Kyser to William Head, "AC-119 History, 26 May 2004, 1202 hours.

———. "Chronology of the 17th Special Operations Squadron (17SOS), AC-119G Shadow Gunships." Attachment to e-mail, Lee Kyser to William Head, "AC-119 History," 26 May 2004, 1202 hours.

———. "18th Special Operations Squadron (18SOS) Chronology." Attachment to e-mail, Lee Kyser to William Head, "AC-119 History," 26 May 2004, 1202 hours.

Ford, Peter. "A Weak Northern Front Could Lengthen Iraq War." *Christian Science Monitor,* 3 April 2003.

"The 'Forty' How 'Swede' It Is?" *Loader Jam* 97, no. 2 (April–June 1997).

Fox News. "Saddam Captured 'Like a Rat' in Raid." 14 December 2003. http://www.foxnews.com/story/2003/12/14/saddam-captured-like-rat-in-raid/.

Friends of the First Lady. "First Lady Tribute to First Production C-130." Spectre Association. http://www.spectre-association.org/First_Lady_129.htm.

Frisbee, John L. "Mayaguez Incident." *Air Force Magazine* 74, no. 9 (September 1991).

Fulghum, David. "Electronic Bombs Darken Belgrade." *Aviation Week & Space Technology* 153 (10 May 1999).

———, and Robert Wall. "Heavy Bomber Attacks Dominate Afghan War." *Aviation Week & Space Technology* 155 (3 December 2001).

———, and Robert Wall. "US Stalks Taliban with New Air Scheme." *Aviation Week & Space Technology* 155 (15 October 2001).
Gawne, Jonathan. "Spectre: America's Special Operation Gunships." *Raids* 43 (June 1995).
Gertz, Bill, and Roman Scarborough. "No War." *Washington Times,* 16 April 1999.
Gilligan, Andrew. "Russia, Not Bombs, Brought End to War in Kosovo, Says Jackson." *London Telegraph* (Sunday), 1 August 1999.
Glanz, James. "With Airpower and Armor, Troops Enter Rebel-Held City." *New York Times,* 8 November 2004. http://www.nytimes.com/2004/11/08/international/08CND_IRAQ.html.
Global Security.org. "AC-X Replacement Gunship." September 2008. http://www.globalsecurity.org/military/systems/aircraft/ac-x.htm.
———. "Bush Announces Start of a 'War on Terror.'" 20 September 2001. http://www.globalsccurity.org/military/library/news/2001/09/mil-010920-usia01.htm.
———. "Operation Enduring Freedom—Afghanistan." No date. http://www.globalsecurity.org/military/ops/enduring-freedom.htm.
———. "President Bush Announces Military Strikes in Afghanistan." 7 October 2001. http://www.globalsecurity.org/military/library/news/2001/10/mil-011007-usia01.htm.
———. "711th Special Operations Squadron (711th SOS)." 26 April 2005. http://www.globalsecurity.org/military/agency/usaf/711sos.htm.
Goodman, Glenn. "Close Air Support." *Armed Forces Journal International* 139 (January 2002).
Gordon, Michael R., and Gen. Bernard E. Trainor. "Iraqi Leader in Frantic Flight, Eluded US Strikes." *New York Times,* 12 March 2006.
Grant, Rebecca. "The Airpower of Anaconda." *Air Force Magazine* 85 (September 2002). http://www.airforcemag.com/MagazineArchive/Pages/2002/September%202002/0902anaconda.aspx.
———. "An Air War Like No Other." *Air Force Magazine* 85 (November 2002). http://www.airforcemag.com/MagazineArchive/Pages/2002/November%202002/1102airwar.aspx.
———. "Reach-Forward." *Air Force Magazine* 85 (October 2002). http://www.afa.org/magazine/october2002/1002combo.asp.
———. "The War Nobody Expected." *Air Force Magazine* 85 (April 2002). http://www.airforcemag.com/MagazineArchive/Pages/2002/April%202002/0402airwar.aspx.
Grossman, Elaine M. "Clark's Firepower Request for Kosovo Prompts Anxiety among Chiefs." *Inside the Pentagon,* 15 April 1999.
———. "Services Spar over a Powerful but Vulnerable Aircraft: Troops in Fallujah Lost Bid for Daytime AC-130 Gunship Fire Support." *Inside the Pentagon,* 25 November 2004. http://www.dnipogo.org/grossman/troops_in_fallujah.htm. Reprinted by permission of Inside Washington Publishers, http://defense.iwpnewsstand.com.
"The Gulf War: A Chronology." *Air Force Magazine* 84, no. 1 (January 2001).
"Lethal 'Flying Gunships' Returning to Iraq." NBCNews.com/Associated Press. 3 March 2006. http://www.nbcnews.com/id/11657894/ns/world_news_mideast_n_africa/t/lethal-flying-gunships-returning-iraq/.

Hamlin, Lt. Col. Ross E. "Side-Firing Weapon Systems." *Air University Review* 21, no. 2 (January–February 1970).

Head, William. "AC-47 Gunship Development." *Air Power History* 37, no. 3 (Fall 1990).

———. "Playing Hide and Seek With the 'Trail': Operation *Command Hunt,* 1968–1972." *Journal of Third World Studies* 19, no. 1 (Spring 2003).

"To Help an Ally." *The Air Reservist,* June 1969.

Hobson, Maj. Gen. James L., Jr. "Our Journey Continues in '95." *Night Flyer* 3, no. 1 (June 1995).

Housman, Damon. WR-ALC Public Affairs. "Air Logistics Center Upgrades Center Wing Boxes on C-130s." *Air Force Print News,* 15 November 2006. http://www.afmc.af.mil/news/story_print.asp?id=123032021.

Human Rights Watch. "The Crisis in Kosovo." Civilian Deaths in the NATO Air Campaign. http://www/hrw.org/reports/2000/nato/Natbm200-01.htm.

Hunter, Ric. "The Last Battle of Vietnam." *Flight Journal* 5, no. 2 (April 2000).

Ignatieff, Michael. "The Virtual Commander: How NATO Invented a New Kind of War." *New Yorker,* 2 August 1999.

Iraq Body Count. "Iraq Body Count." http://www.iraqbodycount.org/.

"Jet-Augmented Gunship Aircraft." *Armed Forces Journal,* 5 October 1968.

Johnson, 1st Lt. Lauren. "AFSOC Welcomes First Female Flying Squadron Commander." 23 February 2009. http://www2.hurlburt.af.mil/news/story.asp?id=123136801.

Keegan, John. "Please, Mr. Blair, Never Take Such a Risk Again." *Daily Telegraph* (London), 6 June 1999.

"Keeping the C-130s Flying: Center Wing Box Replacements." *Defense Industry Daily,* 4 April 2007. http://www.defenseindustrydaily.com/keeping-the-c130s-flying-center-wing-box-replacements-03185/.

Kinney, Gen. William A. "TACAIR Vietnam." *Airman* 12, no. 7 (July 1968).

"The Kosovo File: Who's Who." *Time,* 15 December 1999. http://www.pathfinder.com/time/daily/special/kosovo/who.html. Accessed 17 December 1999.

Kreisher, Otto. "Gunship Worries." *Air Force Magazine.* 92, no. 7 (July 2009). http://www.airforce-magazine.com/MagazineArchive/Pages/2009/July%202009/0709gunship.aspx.

LaGrone, Sam. "New Gunship Plan: 8 Modified MC-130Ws." *Air Force Times,* 4 June 2009. http://www.airforcetimes.com/news/2009/06/airforce_gunship_recap_060209w/.

Lessels, SSgt. Robert J. "Shadow." *Air Force Magazine,* November 1971.

Leung, Rebecca. "Bush Sought 'Way' To Invade Iraq?" CBS, *60 Minutes,* 11 January 2004. http://www.cbsnews.com/stories/2004/01/09/60minutes/main592330.shtml.

Lichtblau, Eric. "2002 Memo Doubted Uranium Sale Claim." *New York Times,* 18 January 2006.

McCune, Timothy. "Dispute Looming over Rockwell Gunship." *Defense Week,* 22 June 1990.

McPeak, Gen. Tony. *PBS News Hour,* 16 June 1999.

Magnuson, Stew. "Air Force Gunships Could Be Grounded." *NDIA National Defense Magazine,* May 2007. http://www.nationaldefensemagazine.org/ARCHIVE/2007/MAY/Pages/AirForceGunships2638.aspx.

Martin, David. "AC-130 Overworked in Iraq, Afghanistan Info." CBS News, 12 March 2008. Air Force Association transcript. http://eb.afa.org/2008/03/13/e20080313587303.html.

Meilinger, Col. Phillip S. "The Problem with Our Air Power Doctrine." *Airpower Journal,* Spring 1992.

Meyers, Steven Lee. "Crisis in the Balkans: Pentagon Said to Be Adding 300 Planes to Fight Serbs." *New York Times,* 13 April 1999.

———, and Eric Schmitt. "Crisis in the Balkans: News Analysis; NATO Said to Focus Raids on Serb Elite's Property." *New York Times,* 19 April 1999.

Meyers, Steven L., and Thom Shanker. "A Nation Challenged: The Offensive; Special Operations Gunship Being Used against the Taliban." *New York Times,* 16 October 2001.

Michael, Maggie. "Bin Laden, in Statement to US people, Says He Ordered Sept 11 Attacks." Sign on San Diego.com, 29 October 2004. http://legacy.utsandiego.com/news/nation/terror/20041029-1423-binladentape.html.

Michel, Marshall. "The Birth of Spooky: How They Put the 'A' in the AC-47." *Current Operations* 678 (3 June 2003). http://www.airspacemag.com/military-aviation/birth-of-spooky.html.

Morrocco, John D.; David Fulgham; and Robert Wall. "Weather, Weapons, Death Slow NATO Strokes." *Aviation Week and Science Technology,* 5 April 1999.

National Broadcasting Company (NBC). "Al-Jazeera: Bin Laden Tape Obtained in Pakistan." 30 October 2004. http://www.nbcnews.com/id/6363306/?.

———. "Saddam Hussein Executed, Ending Era in Iraq." NBC News, 30 December 2006. http://www.msnbc.msn.com/id/16389128/.

Oberdorfer, Don. "Missed Signals in the Middle East." *Washington Post Magazine,* 17 March 1991.

Palmer, Bruce. "US Intelligence and Vietnam." *Studies in Intelligence,* Special Spring Issue, 1984.

Peterson, Scott. "The Rise and Fall of Ansar al-Islam." *Christian Science Monitor,* 16 October 2003. http://www.csmonitor.com/2003/1016/p12s01-woiq.html.

Petrie, CMSgt. Bill. "US Air Force AC-119 Gunships: A Gunship History." http://www.ac-119gunships.com/history/hist1.htm.

———. "US Air Force AC-119 Gunships: Vengeance by Night! Motto of the Famed Hunter/Killers of the Ho Chi Minh Trail." http://www.ac-119gunships.com/the119s/ac119k/gunshipk.htm.

———. "US Air Force AC-119 Gunships: Who Knows What Evil Lurks? The Shadow Knows: A History of the AC-119G Shadow Gunship." http://www.ac-119gunships.com/the119s/ac119g/gunshipg.htm.

Petrie, CMSgt. Bill, to William Head. "AC-119 Chapter Evaluation." Attachment to e-mail, 7 June 2004.

Public Broadcasting System (PBS). "Operation Iraqi Freedom: A Chronology of the Six-Week Invasion of Iraq." 26 February 2004. http://www.pbs.org/wgbh/pages/frontline/shows/invasion/cron/.

"Residents Said That Many Wooden Houses Near the Headquarters Had Been Hit by Gunfire and Artillery Fire." *New York Times,* 21 December 1989.

Reuters. "Kosovo: A Bitter Struggle in a Land of Strife, Chronology of the Crisis in Kosovo." *New York Times,* 24 March 1999. http://www.nytimes.com/learning/general/featured_articles/990324A.Wednesday.html. Accessed 17 December 1999.

Richter, Paul. "Bunker-Busters Aimed at the Heart of Leadership." *Los Angeles Times,* 5 May 1999.

———. "Use of Ground Troops Not Fully Ruled Out." *Los Angeles Times,* 29 March 1999.

Ripley, Tim. "Kosovo Crisis: Operations Allied Force/Allied Harbour/Joint Forge—Order of Battle/Basing/June 1999." *Jane's Defence Weekly,* 4 December 1999.

———. "Kosovo Crisis: 'Serbs Running Out of SAMs,' Says USA." 15 December1999. http://www.janes.com.defence/features/kosovo/. Accessed 17 December 1999.

Rockwell Modification Division. "Rockwell's AC-130U Gunship." News report, no date.

Rodhe. David. "Foreign Fighters of a Harsher Bent Bolster Taliban." *New York Times,* 30 October 2007.

Scarborough, Rowan. "US Pilots Call NATO Targeting a 'Disgrace.'" *Washington Times,* 1 April 1999.

"Serb Discusses 1999 Downing of Stealth." USA Today, 26 October 2005. http://www.usatoday.com/news/world/2005-10-26-serb-stealth_x.htm.

Simon, Lt. Col. Roy A. "Tony." "Bailout of Stinger #839." In e-mail, Lee Kyser to William Head, "Bailout of Stinger," 26 May 2004, 1556 hours.

Skeen. Jim. Untitled article on the AC-130. *Antelope Valley Press,* 9 September 1991.

Smith, Jeffrey R. "Hussein's Prewar Ties to Al Qaeda Discounted." *Washington Post,* 6 April 2007.

———, and Molly Moore. "Plan for Kosovo, Pullout Signed." *Washington Post,* 10 June 1999.

"Somalia: Relief and Hope." *World Air Power Journal* 14 (Fall 1993).

Spectre Association. "16th SOS History." August 2009. http://www.spectre-association.org/history16SOS.htm.

Susman, Tina. "Poll: Civilian Death Toll in Iraq May Top 1 Million." *Los Angeles Times,* 14 September 2007.

Taylor, Mindy. "Rock Wins C-130 Gunship Conversion Pact." *Antelope Valley Press,* 5 July 1987.

Nautilus Institute for Security and Sustainability. "Essentially Annihilated, Targeting the Ho Chi Minh Trail." http://nautilus.org/VietnamFOIA/background/HoChiMinhTrail.htm. Accessed on 9 October 2003.

Tilford, Earl H., Jr. "Operation 'Commando Hunt': The Air War against the Ho Chi Minh Trail, 1969–1972." Third Triennial Vietnam Symposium, Texas Tech University, 16 April 1999.

Tirpak, John A. "The First Six Weeks." *Air Force Magazine* 82, no. 6 (June 1999).

———. "With Stealth in the Balkans." *Air Force Magazine* 82, no. 10 (Oct. 1999).

Turse, Nick. "The Secret Air War in Iraq." *The Nation,* 11 June 2007. http://www.thenation.com/doc/20070611/turse.

United for Justice and Peace. "Escalation: Bad for Them, Bad for Us." Afghanistan Fact Sheet no. 1, February 2009. http://www.vfp143.0rg/lit/Afghanistan/UFPJ%20Escalation%20Fact%20Sheet.pdf.

"Untold Story of the Ho Chi Minh Trail." *US News and World Report,* 15 June 1971.

"US Jets and Gunships Attack Iraqi Targets." RedOrbit.com, 24 December 2003. http://www.redorbit.com/news/general/37653/us_jets_gunships_attack_iraq_targets/. Accessed 21 May 2009.

"Verbatim Special: The Balkan War." *Air Force Magazine* 82, no. 6 (June 1999).

Wall, Robert. "SEAD Concerns Raised in Kosovo." *Aviation Week & Space Technology,* 26 July 1999.

Watson, George M., "The Mayaguez Rescue." *Air Force Magazine* 92, no. 7 (July 2009).

Weapon System Technology Information Analysis Center. *WSTAIC Quarterly* 8, no. 3 (September 2007). http://wstiac.alionscience.com/pdf/WQV8N3_ART03.pdf.

Weiner, Tim. "Crisis in the Balkans: From President, Victory Speech and a Warning." *New York Times,* 11 June 1999.

Windle, David. "Military Muscle." *New Scientist,* 1 January 2003. http://www.newscientist.com/article.ns?id=dn3325.

"WRAMA Team Faces Gunship Challenge." *Robins RevUp,* 30 November 1967.

Zuckert, Eugene. "Keeping the Organizational Engine in Tune." *Air Force/Space Digest,* October 1964.

Index